D0761640

VEGETARIAN
& WHOLEFOODS BIBLE

VEGETARIAN & WHOLEFOODS BIBLE

A FABULOUS COLLECTION OF OVER 300 DELICIOUS RECIPES FROM AROUND THE WORLD, ALL SHOWN STEP BY STEP IN OVER 1600 EASY-TO-FOLLOW PHOTOGRAPHS

EDITED BY NICOLA GRAIMES

This edition is published by Southwater, an imprint of Anness Publishing Ltd,
Hermes House, 88–89 Blackfriars Road, London SE1 8HA; tel. 020 7401 2077; fax 020 7633 9499

www.southwaterbooks.com; www.annesspublishing.com

If you like the images in this book and would like to investigate using them for publishing, promotions or advertising, please visit our website www.practicalpictures.com for more information.

UK agent: The Manning Partnership Ltd; tel. 01225 478444; fax 01225 478440; sales@manning-partnership.co.uk
UK distributor: Book Trade Services; tel. 0116 2759086; fax 0116 2759090; uksales@booktradeservices.com; exportsales@booktradeservices.com
North American agent/distributor: National Book Network; tel. 301 459 3366; fax 301 429 5746; www.nbnbooks.com
Australian agent/distributor: Pan Macmillan Australia; tel. 1300 135 113; fax 1300 135 103; customer.service@macmillan.com.au
New Zealand agent/distributor: David Bateman Ltd; tel. (09) 415 7664; fax (09) 415 8892

Publisher: Joanna Lorenz
Project editor: Simona Hill
Production controller: Ben Worley
Designer: Jonathan Harley

© Anness Publishing Ltd 1999, 2009

ACKNOWLEDGEMENTS

The publishers would like to thank the following for their contributions to this book:
Recipe contributors: Alex Barker, Michelle Berridale-Johnson, Angela Boggiano, Carla Capalbo, Jacqueline Clark, Carole Clements, Roz Denny, Matthew Drennan, Sarah Edmonds, Joanna Farrow, Christine France, Silvana Franco, Sarah Gates, Shirley Gill, Shehzaid Husain, Christine Ingram, Peter Jordan, Manisha Kanani, Elizabeth Lambert Ortiz, Ruby Le Bois, Lesley Mackley, Norma MacMillan, Sue Maggs, Maggie Mayhew, Sallie Morris, Annie Nichols, Maggie Pannell, Anne Sheasby, Hilarie Walden, Laura Washburn, Steven Wheeler, Kate Whiteman, Elizabeth Wolf-Cohen, Jeni Wright
Photographers: William Adams-Lingwood, Karl Adamson, Steve Baxter, Edward Allwright, James Duncan, Christine France, Michelle Garrett, Amanda Heywood, Janine Hosegood, David Jordan, Don Last, Patrick McLeavey, Thomas Odulate, Peter Reilly, Bridget Sargeson
Stylists: Madeleine Brehaut, Michelle Garrett, Katherine Hawkins, Amanda Heywood, Clare Hunt, Marion McLornan, Blake Minton, Marian Price, Kirsty Rawlings, Judy Williams
Home economists: Hilary Guy, Jane Hartshorn, Wendy Lee, Lucy McKelvie, Jane Stevenson, Steven Wheeler

ETHICAL TRADING POLICY

Because of our ongoing ecological investment programme, you, as our customer, can have the pleasure and reassurance of knowing that a tree is being cultivated on your behalf to naturally replace the materials used to make the book you are holding.
For further information about this scheme, go to www.annesspublishing.com/trees

All rights reserved. No part of this publication may be reproduced, stored in a retrieval system, or transmitted in any way or by any means, electronic, mechanical, photocopying, recording or otherwise, without the prior written permission of the copyright holder.

Previously published as *Complete Vegetarian*

NOTES

For all recipes, quantities are given in both metric and imperial measures and, where appropriate, in standard cups and spoons.
Follow one set of measures, but not a mixture, because they are not interchangeable.
Standard spoon and cup measures are level. 1 tsp = 5ml, 1 tbsp = 15ml, 1 cup = 250ml/8fl oz.
Australian standard tablespoons are 20ml. Australian readers should use 3 tsp in place of 1 tbsp for measuring small quantities.
American pints are 16fl oz/2 cups. American readers should use 20fl oz/2.5 cups in place of 1 pint when measuring liquids.
Electric oven temperatures in this book are for conventional ovens. When using a fan oven, the temperature will probably need to be reduced by about 10–20°C/20–40°F. Since ovens vary, you should check with your manufacturer's instruction book for guidance.
The nutritional analysis given for each recipe is calculated per portion (i.e. serving or item), unless otherwise stated. If the recipe gives a range, such as Serves 4–6, then the nutritional analysis will be for the smaller portion size, i.e. 6 servings. Measurements for sodium do not include salt added to taste.
Medium (US large) eggs are used unless otherwise stated.

Main front cover image shows Wild Mushroom and Broccoli Tart – for recipe, see page 336.

PUBLISHER'S NOTE

Although the advice and information in this book are believed to be accurate and true at the time of going to press, neither the authors nor the publisher can accept any legal responsibility or liability for any errors or omissions that may be made nor for any inaccuracies nor for any harm or injury that comes about from following instructions or advice in this book.

CONTENTS

Introduction

Throughout history, every culture has used food to prevent and treat illness and disease, and promote good health. The Egyptians praised the lentil for its ability to enlighten the mind; the Ancient Greeks and Romans used honey to heal wounds; while in China, sprouted beans and grains were used to treat a wide range of illnesses, from constipation to dropsy.

However, around the time of the industrial revolution, people in Western countries came to disregard the medicinal and therapeutic properties of food, and it is only relatively recently that interest in the healing qualities of food has been revived. This renewed interest, owing to our growing concern about what we eat and drink, and our quest for good health, is spurred on by scientists who have undertaken extensive research into eating habits, and have also investigated the properties of individual foods.

Numerous studies have revealed the positive attributes of a diet that is rich in fruit and vegetables, whole grains, nuts and seeds, and beans, complemented by a moderate amount of dairy foods. Studies have shown that vegetarians suffer less from many diseases, such as obesity, cancer, heart disease, gallstones, diabetes and constipation, that plague modern Western cultures. In fact, every scientific study comparing vegetarians with people eating a typical Western diet has found the former to be healthier and less likely to suffer from illness. Yet, vegetarianism is not just about achieving optimum health, it should also be an enjoyable and delicious way of eating.

WHAT ARE WHOLE FOODS?

Whole foods are foods to which nothing has been added or taken away. They are foods that haven't been unnecessarily processed or subjected to chemical processing, or loaded with harmful additives, colourings, or flavourings. In the narrowest sense, whole foods are specifically unrefined dried ingredients, such as grains, pulses, beans and seeds, but in this book we have taken the liberty to expand the term to include all foods that should be included in a healthy diet. It is important to choose unrefined foods whenever you can, simply because they ensure the greatest intake of vitamins, minerals and fibre. When food is processed, precious nutrients are taken away as a result, although there are various degrees to which this occurs. However, some would argue that a diet consisting entirely of whole foods could be decidedly brown and boring. A healthy whole foods diet should include a wide range of other ingredients to add both

Right: A wide range of organic produce is available in health-food stores.

variety and essential nutrients. Plenty of fruit and vegetables, dairy products, fats and oils, and natural sweeteners are all needed to make whole foods palatable and appealing. And there's no reason why, if you are eating mainly whole foods, that you can't include a few refined foods. A little white flour added to a wholemeal cake or pastry, for instance, will give a much lighter end result and will only affect the nutritional value marginally. It is not such a sin to eat white rice instead of brown, or plain pasta rather than wholemeal occasionally, if the rest of the dish or meal is full of nutrient-packed, high-fibre foods.

Vegetarian Children

Children can thrive on a vegetarian diet as long as it is varied and balanced, and not based on foods such as chips and baked beans. Unlike adults, young children do not entirely benefit from a high-fibre, low-fat diet. They need plenty of calories and nutrients and, because they have small stomachs, require regular, small, nutritious meals.

A diet based on low-fat and high-fibre foods can leads to malnutrition in young children because it does not provide sufficient nutrients and calories for growth and development. Reduced fat foods, such as skimmed milk and low-fat cheeses, lack much-needed calories, and their full-fat equivalents should be given to children under 2 years of age. High-fibre foods, such as brown rice, and wholemeal bread and pasta, are too bulky for young children, and they become full before they have eaten enough nutrients. White bread and rice, and ordinary pasta are acceptable alternatives, provided they are eating plenty of fruit and vegetables, potatoes, cereals, beans and lentils.

Children should avoid fizzy, caffeine- and sugar-laden drinks, and drink only small amounts of juices and squashes that contain artificial sweeteners, which can cause diarrhoea if consumed in excess. Children should, instead, be encouraged to drink water, milk and diluted fruit juice.

Above: Try to eat at least five portions of fruits and vegetables a day.

It may be a cliché, but there is more than a grain of truth in the adage, "You are what you eat." Our bodies rely and thrive on a varied nutritious diet. Yet a healthy diet is not just about boosting physical welfare. Our mental and emotional well being is equally affected by what we put on our plates. The more appetizing and appealing, the better.

ORGANIC FOODS

As food scares continue, many people are increasingly concerned about the type of food that they eat. The growing use of antibiotics, artificial additives and chemicals, as well as the introduction of irradiation and genetically-modified foods, has added fuel to this concern. In 1995, 46 per cent of fruits and vegetables analyzed in a UK study contained pesticide residues. A group of pesticides known as organophosphates have been a particular problem in carrots, while the results for celery are also disturbing.

People are looking for healthier, less processed foods, and the demand for organic foods is growing at a rate of about 30 per cent every year. Organic foods were, until relatively recently, found only in health-food stores, but now there is an expanding range of fresh and packaged organic foods available from supermarkets. Reassuringly, every food that is labelled organic has to fulfil certain strict criteria. No artificial pesticides, fertilizers, or other chemicals can be used in the growing and/or production of organic food, and genetically-modified or irradiated ingredients are not permitted.

Traditional methods of agriculture, such as crop rotation, are used along with natural fertilizers. This preserves wildlife and minimizes pollution. Owing to their shorter shelf-life, organic fruits and vegetables are less likely to have travelled thousands of miles before reaching stores. This could mean that in the future there may be a return to locally produced, seasonal foods. Whether organic food tastes better or is higher in nutrients is open to debate, but the environment and our health will undoubtedly benefit in the long-run.

The Basic Vegetarian Whole Food Diet

We are often told to eat a balanced diet, but in the context of a vegetarian diet what does this mean? The key to good health is to eat a variety of foods that provide the right proportion of protein, carbohydrates, fibre, fat, vitamins and minerals as well as water. The ideal diet features enough calories to provide the body with vital energy, but not an excess, which leads to weight gain. Getting this balance right is crucial to health.

When people opt for a vegetarian diet, it is not simply a matter of swapping meat and fish for cheese and eggs. Vegetarians need to ensure they eat plenty of fruit and vegetables, legumes, nuts, seeds, rice, bread, pasta and potatoes, and some dairy foods. They should aim to eat nutrient-rich foods, rather than those that provide plenty of calories but few nutrients, such as cake and crisps. The following may be a useful guide:

Whole wheat bread (below), whole grain cereals (left), and potatoes in their skins (above) provide more nutrients in this form than if they were refined (or peeled).

Whole grains and potatoes

Aim for 6–11 servings a day

This group includes cereals, such as oats, wheat, corn, millet, barley, bread, rice,

Above: Butter and margarine provide few nutrients and are laden with calories.

pasta, as well as potatoes. They should form the main part of every meal. Wholemeal bread and pasta, brown rice, and potatoes with their skins on contain the most nutrients and provide starchy carbohydrates, fibre, protein, B complex vitamins, and minerals.

A serving equals: 1 slice of bread, ½ cup of cooked cereal, rice or pasta, or 1 medium potato.

Fruit and vegetables

Aim for at least 5 servings a day

Fruit and vegetables provide significant amounts of vitamins, minerals, and fibre and are low in fat and calories. Cruciferous vegetables, such as broccoli, cabbage, sprouts, cauliflower and chard, provide a powerful combination of antioxidants, which are believed to provide protection against certain cancers. Bright orange, yellow, and red fruit and vegetables are rich in the antioxidant beta carotene and vitamin C.

A serving equals: 1 medium apple, banana or orange, a handful of cherry tomatoes, a glass of fresh fruit juice, 2 or more heaped serving spoonfuls of cooked vegetables, or a bowl of salad.

Below: Peas, beans and corn provide fibre.

Legumes, nuts, and seeds

2–3 servings a day

Legumes, including beans, peas and lentils, tofu and tempeh, and nuts and seeds provide valuable protein, fibre, iron, calcium, zinc, and vitamins B and E. Legumes are low in fat and provide plenty of fibre. Nuts and seeds are very nutritious but are high in fat and should be eaten in moderation.

A serving equals: a small handful of nuts and seeds, ½ cup cooked beans or 115g/4oz tofu or tempeh.

Dairy foods and non-dairy alternatives

2–3 servings a day

This group includes milk, cheese, and yogurt and provides valuable amounts of protein, calcium, and vitamins B_{12}, A and D. These foods can be high in fat so should be eaten in moderation. Eggs are also included in this group; a maximum of 3–4 are recommended a week.

A serving equals: 1 egg, a small slice of cheese, a small glass of milk, or a small container of yogurt.

Fats, sweets and snacks

Eat sparingly

This diverse group includes chocolate, crisps, cakes and biscuits, as well as butter, margarine, and cooking oils. These foods provide few nutrients, but are laden with calories and, if eaten in excess, will lead to weight gain. Too many sugary foods can cause tooth decay.

Below: Tofu and bean curd

The Essentials for Good Health

Along with water, there are six essential components for good health, which if consumed in the correct proportions, will provide the body with both sustained energy and the correct balance of nutrients required.

Below: Soluble fibre found in oats helps reduce blood cholesterol.

Carbohydrates

At one time, carbohydrates, which are made up of starches, fibre and sugars, were considered to be fattening and less valuable than protein-rich foods. However, they are now recognized as the body's major source of energy and carbohydrate-rich foods supply a substantial amount of protein, vitamins, minerals and fibre, with very little fat. About half the food we eat should be unrefined complex carbohydrates, such as wholegrain cereals, wholemeal bread and pasta, and brown rice. These high-fibre foods are broken down slowly by the body and provide a steady supply of energy. They are preferable to sugars or simple carbohydrates because these foods are quickly absorbed into the bloodstream and give only a short-term energy boost. When feasible, opt for unrefined carbohydrates, as the refined versions, such as white flour, rice and sugar are stripped of nutrients, including vitamins, minerals, and fibre. It's important to remember that the more carbohydrates that you eat, the more you depend on them for supplying essential nutrients.

Below: Rice is a good source of insoluble fibre.

Fibre

Fruits, vegetables, grains, legumes, nuts and seeds are our main source of fibre, of which there are two types: insoluble and soluble. Insoluble fibre, which is found in whole wheat, brown rice, bran, and nuts, provides bulk to the diet and helps to combat constipation. Soluble fibre, found in legumes, vegetables and oats, binds with toxins in the gut and promotes their

Right: Carbohydrate-rich vegetables, such as plantains, yams and potatoes, provide a steady supply of energy.

excretion, and also helps to reduce blood cholesterol. Both types of fibre reduce the risk of bowel disorders, including diverticulitis, colon and rectal cancer, and irritable bowel syndrome (although bran has been found to aggravate symptoms of IBS). Few people get enough fibre. On average we eat about 12 grams of fibre a day, but we should be consuming about 18 grams. People who want to lose weight will find that a high-fibre diet is beneficial, as it provides bulk and naturally limits the amount of food eaten.

Protein

This macro-nutrient is essential for the maintenance and repair of every cell in the body, and also ensures that enzymes, hormones, and antibodies function properly. Protein is made up of amino acids, of which there are 20, and eight of these need to be supplied by diet. A food containing all eight amino acids is known as a "complete" or high-quality protein.

Above: Nuts contain fat as well as protein.

For vegetarians, these include eggs and dairy products, as well as soya beans. Protein from plant sources, such as nuts, pasta, potatoes, legumes, cereals and rice, does not usually contain all eight amino acids and is known as "incomplete" or low-quality protein. We should aim to get 10–15 per cent of calories from protein.

Vegetarians are often asked where they get their protein, and lack of this nutrient can be a concern for those cutting out meat and fish from their diet. Yet in reality most people eat too much protein and deficiency is virtually unheard of. In fact, an excess of protein can be detrimental, rather than beneficial to health. High-protein foods, such as dairy products and nuts, are a source of fat, and have been found to leach calcium from the body, which increases the risk of osteoporosis. It is also a common misconception that vegetarians have to meticulously combine protein foods in every meal to achieve the correct balance of amino acids. Nutritionists now believe that, provided a varied diet of grains, legumes, dairy produce, eggs and vegetables is eaten on a daily basis, intentionally combining proteins is unnecessary.

How to Increase Your Fibre Intake

- Base your diet on wholemeal bread and pasta, brown rice, and fruit and vegetables. Refined and processed foods contain less fibre and nutrients.
- Start the day with a wholegrain cereal, such as porridge or bran flakes.
- Eat plenty of dried fruit – add it to breakfast cereals, natural yogurt or use to make a compote.
- Add beans and lentils to salads and soups to boost their fibre content.
- Avoid peeling fruits and vegetables, if possible, as the skins contain valuable fibre.

Below: Buckwheat pasta is a "complete" protein.

Fats

A small amount of fat in the diet is essential for health. Fat not only provides vitamins A, D and E, and essential fatty acids that cannot be made in the body, but also contributes greatly to the taste, texture, and palatability of food. It contains a high number of calories, and should make up no more than 30 per cent of your diet. The type of fat is as crucial as the quantity.

Saturated fat (found mainly in dairy products in the vegetarian diet) has been associated with an increased risk of cancer and coronary heart disease. Eating too much saturated fat can raise blood cholesterol levels and lead to narrowed arteries, more so than eating foods, such as eggs, that are high in cholesterol.

Left: Rapeseed oil, which like olive and sesame oils is a monounsaturated fat and can help to reduce the levels of cholesterol in the body, also contains Omega-3 or linolenic acid, which is thought to reduce the risk of heart disease.

Unsaturated fats, both polyunsaturated and monounsaturated, can help reduce harmful "LDL" cholesterol (the type that clogs up arteries) and, importantly, increase the beneficial "HDL" cholesterol, which is thought to reduce cholesterol levels in the body. Monounsaturated fats, such as olive oil, sesame oil and rapeseed oil, are less vulnerable to oxidation than polyunsaturated fats. Polyunsaturated fats provide essential fatty acids, omega-3 and 6. Omega-3 (linolenic acid), which is found in walnuts, soya beans, wheatgerm and rapeseed oil, has been found to reduce the risk of heart disease, while omega-6 (linoleic acid), which is found in nuts, seeds and oils, is thought to reduce levels of blood cholesterol.

Below: Parmesan cheese is a high-fat cheese that should be eaten in moderation.

How to Reduce Dietary Fat

While a vegetarian diet is often lower in fat than one based on meat, it is very easy to eat too many dairy products, oil-laden salad dressings and sauces, and high-fat ready-meals. Here are a few simple ways to reduce fat in your diet:

- Use strong, aged cheese, such as Parmesan – only a small amount is needed to add flavour to a dish.
- Try making low-fat salad dressings using miso, orange juice, yogurt, herbs, spices or tomato juice instead of oils.
- Stir-fry foods using only a little oil. For best results make sure the wok/frying pan is very hot before adding the oil.
- Avoid blended oils, as they can contain coconut or palm oil, which are both saturated fats.
- Opt for low-fat cheeses, such as cottage, curd or mozzarella instead of high-fat cheeses, such as Cheddar.
- Use low-fat yogurt instead of cream in cooked recipes. Stir in a spoonful of cornflour (mixed to a paste with a little water) to prevent the yogurt from curdling when heated.
- Choose complex carbohydrates, including potatoes, pasta, brown rice and beans, instead of high-fat protein foods.

Above: Use naturally low-fat cheeses, such as cottage cheese, curd cheese, ricotta and quark.

Water

The importance of water is often taken for granted, yet although it is possible to survive for weeks without food, we can live for only a few days without water. Water plays a vital role in the body: it transports nutrients, regulates the body temperature, transports waste via the kidneys, and acts as a lubricating fluid. Most people do not drink enough water: it is thought that an adult requires around 2.5 litres/4 pints per day. A shortage of water can cause headaches and loss of concentration. Fizzy drinks, tea and coffee all act as diuretics and speed up the loss of water, which causes dehydration.

Above: Eggs contain all eight essential amino acids, and are a good source of vitamin B_{12}.

Vitamins and Minerals

These nutrients are vital for good health and the functioning of our bodies, and with a few exceptions must be supplied by diet. The levels our bodies require vary depending on health, lifestyle and age. Contrary to popular belief, vitamins and minerals do not provide energy, but assist in the release of energy provided by carbohydrates, fat and protein.

Below: Oranges are rich in vitamin C.

How to Preserve Nutrients

The nutrients in food, particularly fruits and vegetables, are unstable and are diminished by time, preparation methods and cooking. Leave a piece of cut fruit or a sliced potato exposed to air or soaking in water and its vitamin and mineral levels plummet. Old, wilted, or damaged produce also have reduced levels of vitamins and minerals. The following tips will ensure that you get the most from your fruit and vegetables:

- Buy fruits and vegetables that are as fresh as possible, and avoid those that have been stored under fluorescent light, as this can set off a chemical reaction that depletes nutrients.
- Buy loose fresh produce, which is much easier to check for quality than pre-packed foods.
- Buy fruit and vegetables in small quantities, do not keep them for too long, and remove them from plastic bags as soon as possible.
- Depending on the type of fruit or vegetable, store in a cool larder or in the bottom of the fridge.
- Avoid peeling fruits and vegetables, if possible, and do not prepare them too far in advance of cooking, as nutrients such as vitamin C will be destroyed.
- Eat fruits and vegetables raw, when they are at their most nutritious.
- Avoid boiling vegetables because this method of cooking destroys water-soluble vitamins, such as thiamine and vitamins B and C. If you must boil vegetables, use as little water as possible and do not overcook them. The cooking water can also be kept and used as stock for soup.

It is not just fruit and vegetables that benefit from careful storage and handling – nuts, seeds, legumes and grains will also be fresher and have a higher nutrient content if stored and cooked correctly.

Right: Miso contains a good amount of the water-soluble vitamin B_{12}.

Vitamins are either water-soluble or fat-soluble. Fat-soluble vitamins A, D, E and K are stored in the liver for some time. Water-soluble vitamins, B complex and C, cannot be stored and must be replaced on a daily basis. If you drink alcohol or smoke, increase your intake of vitamin B- and C-rich foods. Of the B-complex vitamins, vegetarians should make sure they get enough B_{12}, although this shouldn't be difficult as it is needed only in tiny amounts. It is found in dairy products, fortified breakfast cereals, yeast extract, miso and eggs.

There are 16 essential minerals; some, such as calcium, are needed in relatively large amounts, while trace elements, such as selenium and magnesium, are needed in tiny quantities. Minerals have various functions, but predominantly regulate and balance the body and maintain a healthy immune system. A deficiency of iron affects one-fifth of the world's population, and vegetarians need to make a point of eating iron-rich foods.

Essential Vitamins and Minerals

Vitamin	**Best Vegetarian Sources**	**Role in Health**	**Deficiency**
A (retinol in animal foods, beta carotene in plant foods)	*animal sources:* milk, butter, cheese, egg yolks and margarine *plant sources:* carrots, apricots, squash, red peppers, broccoli, green leafy vegetables, mango and sweet potatoes	Essential for vision, bone growth, and skin and tissue repair. Beta carotene acts as an antioxidant and protects the immune system	Deficiency is characterized by poor night vision, dry skin and lower resistance to infection, especially respiratory disorders
B_1 (thiamin)	Wholegrain cereals, brewer's yeast, potatoes, nuts, pulses and milk	Essential for energy production, the nervous system, muscles, and heart. Promotes growth and boosts mental ability	Deficiency is characterized by depression, irritability, nervous disorders, loss of memory. Common among alcoholics
B_2 (riboflavin)	Cheese, eggs, milk, yogurt, fortified breakfast cereals, yeast extract, almonds and pumpkin seeds	Essential for energy production and for the functioning of vitamin B6 and niacin, as well as tissue repair	Deficiency is characterized by lack of energy, dry cracked lips, numbness and itchy eyes
Niacin (part of B complex)	Pulses, potatoes, fortified breakfast cereals, wheatgerm, peanuts, milk, cheese, eggs, peas, mushrooms, green leafy vegetables, figs and prunes	Essential for healthy digestive system, skin and circulation. It is also needed for the release of energy	Deficiency is unusual, but characterized by lack of energy, depression and scaly skin
B_6 (piridoxine)	Eggs, wholemeal bread, breakfast cereals, nuts, bananas, and cruciferous vegetables, such as broccoli, cabbage and cauliflower	Essential for assimilating protein and fat, to make red blood cells, and a healthy immune system	Deficiency is characterized by anaemia, dermatitis and depression
B_{12} (cyanocobalamin)	Milk, eggs, fortified breakfast cereals, cheese and yeast extract	Essential for formation of red blood cells, maintaining a healthy nervous system and increasing energy levels	Deficiency is characterized by fatigue, increased risk of infection, and anaemia
Folate (folic acid)	Green leafy vegetables, fortified breakfast cereals, bread, nuts, pulses, bananas and yeast extract	Essential for cell division; makes genetic material (DNA) for every cell. Extra is needed pre-conception and during pregnancy to protect foetus against neural tube defects	Deficiency is characterized by anaemia and appetite loss. Linked with neural defects in babies
C (ascorbic acid)	Citrus fruit, melons, strawberries, tomatoes, broccoli, potatoes, peppers and green vegetables	Essential for the absorption of iron, healthy skin, teeth, and bones. An antioxidant that strengthens the immune system and helps fight infection	Deficiency is characterized by increased susceptibility to infection, fatigue, poor sleep and depression
D (calciferol)	Sunlight, margarine, vegetable oils, eggs, cereals and butter	Essential for bone and teeth formation; helps the body to absorb calcium and phosphorus	Deficiency is characterized by softening of the bones, muscle weakness and anaemia. Long-term shortage in children results in rickets
E (tocopherol)	Seeds, nuts, vegetable oils, eggs, wholemeal bread, green leafy vegetables, oats and cereals	Essential for healthy skin, circulation, and maintaining cells – an antioxidant	Deficiency is characterized by increased risk of heart attack, strokes and certain cancers

Mineral	Best Vegetarian Sources	Role in Health	Deficiency
Calcium	Milk, cheese, yogurt, green leafy vegetables, sesame seeds, broccoli, dried figs, pulses, almonds, spinach and watercress	Essential for building and maintaining bones and teeth, muscle function and the nervous system	Deficiency is characterized by soft and brittle bones, osteoporosis, fractures and muscle weakness
Iron	Egg yolks, fortified breakfast cereals, green leafy vegetables, dried apricots, prunes, pulses, whole grains and tofu	Essential for healthy blood and muscles	Deficiency is characterized by anaemia, fatigue and low resistance to infection
Zinc	Peanuts, cheese, whole grains, sunflower and pumpkin seeds, pulses, milk, hard cheese and yogurt	Essential for a healthy immune system, tissue formation, normal growth, wound healing and reproduction	Deficiency is characterized by impaired growth and development, slow wound healing, and loss of taste and smell
Sodium	Most salt we eat comes from processed foods, such as crisps, cheese and canned foods. It is also found naturally in most foods	Essential for nerve and muscle function and the regulation of body fluid	Deficiency is unlikely but can lead to dehydration, cramps and muscle weakness
Potassium	Bananas, milk, pulses, nuts, seeds, whole grains, potatoes, fruits and vegetables	Essential for water balance, normal blood pressure and nerve transmission	Deficiency is characterized by weakness, thirst, fatigue, mental confusion and raised blood pressure
Magnesium	Nuts, seeds, whole grains, pulses, tofu, dried figs and apricots, and green vegetables	Essential for healthy muscles, bones and teeth, normal growth, and nerves	Deficiency is characterized by lethargy, weak bones and muscles, depression and irritability
Phosphorus	Milk, cheese, yogurt, eggs, nuts, seeds, pulses and whole grains	Essential for healthy bones and teeth, energy production and the assimilation of nutrients, particularly calcium	Deficiency is rare
Selenium	Avocados, lentils, milk, cheese, butter, Brazil nuts and seaweed	Essential for protecting against free radical damage and may protect against cancer – an antioxidant	Deficiency is characterized by reduced antioxidant protection
Iodine	Seaweed and iodized salt	Aids the production of hormones released by the thyroid gland	Deficiency can lead to the formation of a goitre and a sluggish metabolism and apathy, as well as dry skin and hair
Chloride	Table salt and foods that contain table salt	Regulates and maintains the balance of fluids in the body	Deficiency is rare
Manganese	Nuts, whole grains, pulses, tofu and tea	Essential component of various enzymes that are involved in energy production	Deficiency is not characterized by any specific symptoms

The Vegetarian Kitchen

This fascinating guide includes every kind of natural food, from fruit and vegetables to grains, and from dairy foods to herbs and spices. It includes essential facts about key health benefits and traditional healing qualities, as well as information on buying and storing, preparing and cooking whole foods. It is an inspiration to anyone interested in finding out more about foods that can make you live, look and feel better.

Fruit

Perhaps the ultimate convenience food, most fruits can be simply washed and eaten and, because the nutrients are concentrated just below the skin, it is best to avoid peeling. Cooking fruit reduces valuable vitamins and minerals, so, if you can, eat it raw. Fruit is an excellent source of energy and provides valuable fibre and antioxidants, which are said to reduce the risk of heart disease and certain cancers. Thanks to modern farming methods and efficient transportation, most fruit is available all year round, although it is generally best when home-grown, organically produced and in season.

Orchard Fruits

These fruits have a long history, spanning thousands of years and offer an incredible range of colours and flavours. This group includes many favourites, from crisp, juicy apples, which are available all year round, to luscious, fragrant peaches – a popular summer fruit.

Apricots

APPLES

There are thousands of varieties of apple, although the choice in shops is often restricted to a mere few. Some of the most well-liked eating varieties are Cox's Orange Pippin, Granny Smith, Gala, Braeburn, and Golden and Red Delicious.

An Apple a Day

Numerous studies have shown that eating apples regularly could reduce harmful LDL cholesterol in the body. In France, 30 middle-aged men and women were asked to add 2–3 apples a day to their diet for a month. By the end of the month, 80 per cent of the group showed reduced cholesterol levels, and in half of the group the drop was more than 10 per cent. Additionally, the level of good HDL cholesterol went up. Pectin, a soluble fibre found particularly in apples, is believed to be the magic ingredient.

The Bramley Seedling, with its thick, shiny, green skin and tart flesh, is the most familiar cooking apple and is perfect for baking, or as the basis of apple sauce. Some less well-known varieties, many of which have a short season, are often available from farm shops. Home-grown apples bought out of season may have spent several months in cold storage, where ripening and maturation are artificially halted. When they are taken out of storage, the apples deteriorate quickly.

Apples are delicious when they are eaten raw with their skin on. However, this versatile fruit is often used in breakfast dishes, main meals, salads, desserts, pies and even soups. Large cooking apples are ideal puréed, stewed and baked, but their tartness means that sugar has to be added. Some varieties of eating apple are just as good cooked and don't need any added sugar.

To preserve the maximum amount of vitamins and minerals, cook apples over a low heat with little or no water. Most of the insecticides that are used on apples collect in the apple core and seeds, so, unless the apples are organic, these should be removed before cooking.

Buying and Storing: When buying apples, choose bright, firm fruits without any bruises. Organic apples are

Large cooking apples (left) and eating apples

Baked Apples

Baking is a simple and nutritious way of cooking this orchard fruit. Use cooking apples such as Bramley.

1 Preheat the oven to 180°C/350°F/Gas 4. Remove the core of the apples, then score the skin around the circumference to prevent the skin bursting. Place the apples in a baking dish with a little water.

2 Fill the cavity of the apples with a mixture of dark brown sugar, dried fruit and nuts. Top each with a knob of butter and bake for about 40 minutes or until the apples are soft.

more prone to blemishes than non-organic ones, and the fruits can look a little tatty but the taste will often be superior. Smaller apples tend to have a better flavour and texture than larger specimens. Store apples in a cool place, away from direct sunlight.

Glossy, red, sweet cherries

Health Benefits: The cleansing and blood-purifying qualities of apples are highly valued in natural medicine. Apples aid digestion and can remove impurities in the liver. They are a good source of vitamin C and fibre, if you eat the skin. Although low in calories, apples contain fructose, a simple sugar that is released slowly to supply the body with energy and balance blood sugar levels. Skin problems and arthritis are said to benefit from eating apples regularly.

APRICOTS

The best apricots are sunshine gold in colour and full of juice. They are delicious baked or used raw in salads.

Buying and Storing: An apricot is at its best when truly ripe. Immature fruits are hard and tasteless and never seem to attain the right level of sweetness.

Health Benefits: Extremely rich in beta carotene, minerals and vitamin A, apricots are a valuable source of fibre.

CHERRIES

There are two types: sweet and sour. Some are best eaten raw like the popular Bing, while others, such as Morello, are best cooked.

Buying and Storing: Choose firm, bright, glossy fruits that have fresh, green stems. Discard any that are soft, or have split or damaged skin.

Health Benefits: Cherries stimulate and cleanse the system, removing toxins from the kidneys. They are a remedy for gout and arthritis. Cherries also contain iron, potassium, vitamins C and B, as well as beta carotene.

Nectarines and peaches

NECTARINES

Like a peach without the fuzzy skin, this sweet juicy fruit is named after the drink of the gods – nectar – and is delicious baked or used raw in salads.

Buying and Storing: *see* Peaches.

Health Benefits: When eaten raw, nectarines are especially rich in vitamin C. They aid the digestion, effectively reduce high blood pressure and cleanse the body.

PEACHES

These summer fruits are prized for their perfume and luscious juiciness. Peaches range in colour from gold to deep red and the flesh can be orange or white.

Buying and Storing: Avoid overly soft fruit. Peaches and nectarines are extremely fragile and bruise easily, so buy when slightly under-ripe. To ripen them quickly, place in a brown paper bag with an already ripened fruit. Store ripe nectarines and peaches in the fridge but bring back to room temperature before eating.

Health Benefits: Much of the vitamin C content of a peach lies in and just under its delicate skin, so eat the fruit unpeeled. Peaches are an excellent source of the antioxidant beta carotene, which is said to lower the risk of heart disease and some forms of cancer.

PEARS

Pears have been popular for thousands of years and were extensively cultivated by both the Greeks and the Romans. Pears come into their own in the late summer and autumn with the arrival of the new season's crops. Particular favourites are green and brown-skinned Conference; Williams, with its thin, yellow skin and sweet, soft flesh; plump Comice, which has a pale yellow skin with a green tinge; and Packham, an excellent cooking pear.

Like certain apples, some types of pear are good for cooking, others are best eaten raw, and a few varieties fit happily into both camps.

Pears can be used in both sweet and savoury dishes; they are excellent in salads, and can be baked, poached in syrup, and used in pies and tarts. Pears are unlikely to cause any allergic reactions, so they make perfect weaning food when cooked and puréed.

Buying and Storing: Choose firm, plump fruit that are just slightly under-ripe. Pears can ripen in a day or so and then they pass their peak very quickly and become woolly or squashy. To tell if a pear is ripe, feel around the base of the stalk, where it should give slightly when gently pressed, but the pear itself should be firm.

Health Benefits: Despite their high water content, pears contain useful amounts of vitamin C, fibre and potassium. In natural medicine, they are used as a diuretic and laxative. Rich in pectin and soluble fibre, pears could also be valuable in lowering harmful cholesterol levels in the body. Eating pears regularly is said to result in a clear, healthy complexion and glossy hair.

From left, Conference, Comice and Williams pears

PLUMS

Ranging in colour from pale yellow to dark, rich purple, plums come in many different varieties, although only a few are available in shops. They can be sweet and juicy or slightly tart; the latter are best cooked in pies and cakes, or made into a delicious jam. Sweet plums can be eaten as they are, and are good in fruit salads, or they can be puréed and combined with custard or yogurt to make a fruit fool.

Plums

QUINCE

Fragrant, with a thin, yellow or green skin. These knobbly fruits, which can be either apple- or pear-shaped, are always cooked. Their high pectin content means that they are good for jellies and, in Spain and France, quinces are used to make a fruit paste that is served with soft cheeses.

Buying and Storing: Look for smooth ripe fruits that are not too soft. Quinces keep well and can be stored in a bowl in your kitchen or living room. They will fill the room with their delicious scent.

Health Benefits: Quinces are rich in soluble fibre and pectin. They also calm the stomach and allay sickness.

Plums should be just firm, and not too soft, with shiny, smooth skin that has a slight "bloom". Store ripe plums in the fridge. Unripe fruits can be kept at room temperature for a few days to ripen. Plums relieve constipation and are thought to stimulate the nerves.

Yellow, pear-shaped quince

Dried Fruit

A useful source of energy, dried fruit is higher in calories than fresh fruit, and packed with vitamins and minerals. The drying process boosts the levels of vitamin C, beta carotene, potassium and iron. Apricots and prunes are the most popular types, but dried apple rings, cherries and peaches are also available. Sulphur, often used as a preservative in dried fruits, is best avoided, especially by people who suffer from asthma. Look for unsulphured fruit.

Stoning Fruit

1 To remove the stone from peaches, apricots or plums, cut around the middle of the fruit down to the stone with a paring knife. Twist each half of the fruit in opposite directions.

2 Prize out the stone using the tip of the knife and discard. Rub the cut flesh with lemon juice.

Citrus Fruits

Juicy and brightly coloured, citrus fruits such as oranges, grapefruit, lemons and limes are best known for their sweet, slightly sour juice, which is rich in vitamin C. They are invaluable in the kitchen, adding an aromatic acidity to many dishes, from soups and sauces to puddings and pies. Buy organic fruit when you can, and eat within a week or two.

Oranges

ORANGES

Best eaten as soon as they are peeled, oranges start to lose vitamin C from the moment they are cut. Thin-skinned oranges tend to be the juiciest.

Popular varieties include the Navel (named after the belly button-type spot at the flower end), which contains no pips and so is good for slicing; sweet, juicy Jaffa and Valencia; and Seville, a sour orange used to make marmalade.

The outermost layer of the orange rind can be removed using a vegetable peeler or paring knife. This thin rind contains aromatic oils, which give a delightful perfumed flavour to both savoury and sweet dishes.

GRAPEFRUIT

The flesh of the grapefruit ranges in colour from vivid pink and ruby red to white; the pink and red varieties are sweeter. Heavier fruits are likely to be juicier. Served juiced, halved or cut into slices, grapefruit can provide a refreshing start to the day. The fruit also adds a refreshing tang to salads or a contrast to rich foods. Cooking or grilling mellows the tartness, but keep cooking times brief to preserve the nutrients. A glass of grapefruit juice before bed is said to promote sleep.

LEMONS

Both the juice and rind of this essential cooking ingredient can be used to enliven salad dressings, vegetables, marinades, sauces and biscuits. Lemon juice can also be used to prevent some fruits and vegetables from discolouring when cut. Lemons should be deep yellow in colour, firm and heavy for their size, with no hint of green in the skin as this is a sign of immaturity, while a thin, smooth skin is a sign of juicy flesh. A slice of lemon in hot water cleanses the system and invigorates the whole body.

Grapefruit

Citrus Nutrients

Eating an orange a day will generally supply an adult's requirement for vitamin C, but citrus fruits also contain phosphorus, potassium, calcium, beta carotene and fibre. Pectin, a soluble fibre that is found in the flesh and particularly in the membranes of citrus fruit, has been shown to reduce cholesterol levels. The membranes also contain bioflavonoids, which have powerful antioxidant properties. Drink fresh fruit juice when you can, as bottled, canned and concentrated citrus juices have reduced levels of vitamin C.

Lemons

With a spoonful of honey added, a hot lemon drink is an old and trusted remedy for alleviating colds and flu.

LIMES

Once considered to be rather exotic, limes are now widely available. Avoid fruits with a yellowing skin as this is a sign of deterioration. The juice has a sharper flavour than that of lemons and if you substitute limes for lemons in a recipe, you will need to use less juice. Limes are used a great deal in Asian cooking and the rind can be used to flavour curries, marinades and dips. Coriander, chillies, garlic and ginger are all natural partners.

The Powers of Vitamin C

Citrus fruit is best known for its generous vitamin C content, which is found predominantly in the flesh. An antioxidant, vitamin C has been found to thwart many forms of cancer (particularly cancer of the stomach and oesophagus) by defending body cells against harmful free radicals. Free radicals attack DNA – the cell's genetic material – causing them to mutate and possibly become cancerous.

Numerous population studies have also demonstrated that a high dietary intake of vitamin C significantly reduces the risk of death from the world's greatest killers: the heart attack and stroke. It has been found both to lower harmful LDL cholesterol in the body and to raise beneficial HDL cholesterol. It does this by converting LDL cholesterol into bile acids, which are normally excreted. If vitamin C is in short supply, LDL cholesterol accumulates in the body.

The ability of vitamin C to boost the immune system by helping to fight viruses is well documented. It can be particularly beneficial for infections of the urinary tract and the herpes simplex virus. Researchers are in two minds as to whether vitamin C actually prevents colds but they certainly agree that it can lessen the severity and length of colds and flu. It also boosts the body's ability to absorb iron from food.

Vitamin C is destroyed by heat as well as being water soluble, and is therefore easily lost in cooking. If fruits are cut some time before eating, much of their vitamin C content will also be lost.

Limes are a good source of vitamin C.

Grating Citrus Rind

1 To remove long, thin shreds of rind, use a zester. Scrape it along the surface of the fruit, applying firm pressure.

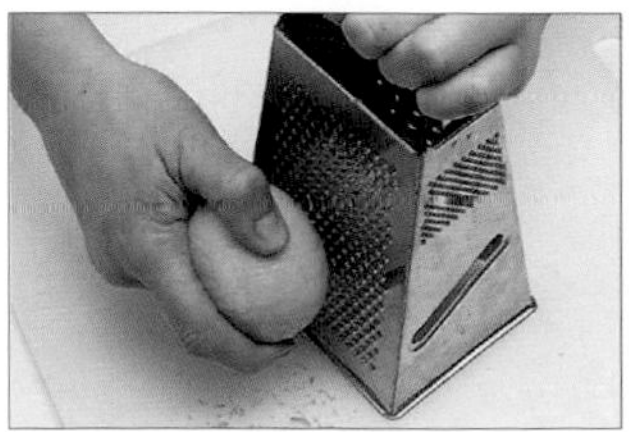

2 For finer shreds, use a grater. Rub the fruit over the fine cutters to remove the rind without any of the white pith.

Cutting Fine Strips or Julienne

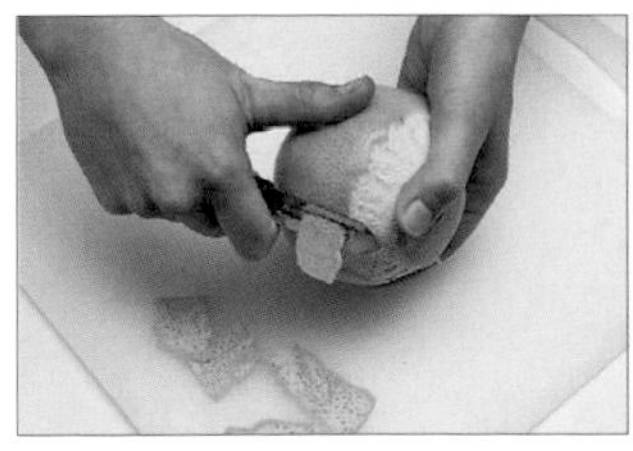

1 Using a vegetable peeler, remove strips of orange rind making sure the white pith is left behind on the fruit.

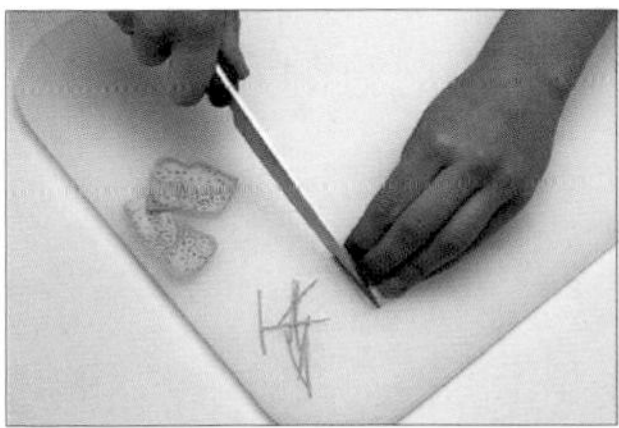

2 Stack several strips of citrus rind and, using a sharp knife, cut them into fine strips or julienne.

Buying and Storing: Look for plump, firm citrus fruit that feels heavy for its size, and has a smooth thin skin; this indicates that the flesh is juicy. Fruits with bruises, brown spots, green patches (or yellow patches on limes) and soft, squashy skin should be avoided, as should dry, wrinkled specimens. Citrus fruits can be kept at room temperature for a few days but if you want to keep them longer, they are best stored in the fridge and eaten within two weeks. Most citrus fruits are waxed or sprayed with fungicides so scrub them thoroughly to remove any residues. If you can, buy organic or unwaxed fruit.

Cook's Tips

- *Rolling citrus fruit firmly over a work surface or in the palms of your hands will help you extract the maximum amount of juice from the fruit.*
- *Limes and lemons will yield more juice if cut lengthways, rather than horizontally.*

Berries and Currants

These baubles of vivid red, purple and black are the epitome of summer and autumn, although they are now likely to be found all year round. Despite their distinctive appearance and flavour, berries and currants are interchangeable in their uses – jams, jellies, pies and tarts are the obvious choices. Interestingly, they also share health-giving qualities, including the ability to treat stomach problems and cleanse the blood, and therefore play a part in natural medicine.

STRAWBERRIES

These are the favourite summer fruits and do not need any embellishment. Serve ripe (avoid those with white or green tips) and raw, on their own, or with a little cream or some natural yogurt. Wash only if absolutely necessary and just before serving.

Strawberries

Health Benefits: Strawberries are rich in B complex vitamins and vitamin C. They contain significant amounts of potassium, and have good skin-cleansing properties.

RASPBERRIES

Soft and fragrant, raspberries are best served simply and unadulterated – maybe with a spoonful of natural yogurt. Those grown in Scotland are regarded as the best in the world. Raspberries are very fragile and require the minimum of handling, so wash only if really necessary. They are best eaten raw as cooking spoils their flavour and vitamin C content.

Raspberries

Health Benefits: Raspberries are a rich source of vitamin C. They are effective in treating menstrual cramps, as well as cleansing the body and removing toxins. Raspberry leaf tea is often drunk in the last few weeks of pregnancy, as it prepares the uterus for labour.

Cranberry Cure

A recent study reported in the Journal of the American Medical Research Association supports the long-held belief that cranberries combat cystitis and other infections of the urinary tract. It found that drinking cranberry juice reduces levels of bacteria not only in the urinary tract but also in the bladder and kidneys.

BLUEBERRIES

Dark purple in colour, blueberries are very popular in the USA. When ripe, the berries are plump and slightly firm, with a natural "bloom". Avoid any that are soft and dull-skinned, and wash and dry carefully to avoid bruising. Cultivated blueberries are larger than the wild variety. Both types are sweet enough to be eaten raw, but are also good cooked in pies and muffins, used for jellies and jams, or made into a sauce to serve with nut or vegetable roasts. Unwashed blueberries will keep for up to a week in the bottom of the fridge.

Health Benefits: Numerous studies show that eating blueberries regularly can improve night vision as well as protect against the onset of cataracts and glaucoma. Blueberries are also effective in treating urinary tract infections and can improve poor circulation.

BLACKBERRIES

These are a familiar sight in early autumn, growing wild in hedgerows. Cultivated blackberries have a slightly longer season and are generally much larger than the wild fruits. Juicy and plump, blackberries can vary in sweetness, which is why they are so often cooked. Wash them carefully to prevent bruising the fruits, then pat dry with kitchen paper. Use in pies and tarts, or make into jams and jellies. The berries can also be lightly cooked, then puréed and sieved to make a sauce to serve with other fruits or ice cream. Blackberries make an ideal partner to apples and pears.

Blackberries

Blueberries

Health Benefits: Blackberries are high in fibre and contain a wealth of minerals, including magnesium, iron and calcium. They are rich in vitamin C, and are one of the best low-fat sources of vitamin E. In natural medicine, blackberries are used to cleanse the blood and they have a tonic effect. They are also used to ease stomach complaints and to treat menstrual problems. Blackberries are rich in bioflavonoids, which act as antioxidants, inhibiting the growth of cancer cells and protecting against cell damage by carcinogens.

GOOSEBERRIES

A favourite fruit of Northern Europe, gooseberries are relatively rare in other parts of the world. They range from the hard and sour green type to the sweeter, softer purple variety. The skin can vary from smooth and silky to fuzzy and spiky. Slightly unripe, tart gooseberries make wonderful pies, crumbles, jams and jellies. Ripe, softer fruits can be puréed and mixed with cream, yogurt or custard, to make a delicious fruit fool.

Health Benefits: Rich in vitamin C, gooseberries also contain beta carotene, potassium and fibre.

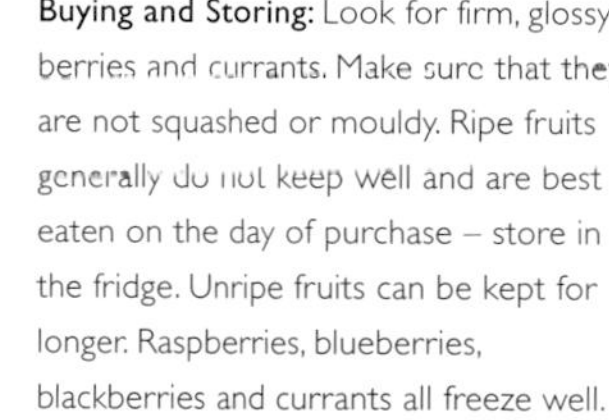

Blackcurrants

BLACKCURRANTS, REDCURRANTS AND WHITECURRANTS

These pretty, delicate fruits are usually sold in bunches on the stem. To remove the currants from the stalk, run the prongs of a fork down through the clusters, taking care not to damage the fruit. Wash the fruits carefully, then pat dry. Raw blackcurrants are quite tart, but this makes them ideal for cooking in sweet pies. They make delicious jams and jellies, and are especially good in summer pudding when they are partnered by other berries. Sweeter whitecurrants make a delightful addition to fruit salads.

Whitecurrants

Health Benefits: The nutritional value of currants has long been recognized. They are high in antioxidants, vitamins C and E, and carotenes. They also contain significant amounts of fibre, calcium, iron and magnesium. In natural medicine, blackcurrants are often used to settle stomach upsets.

Redcurrants

Buying and Storing: Look for firm, glossy berries and currants. Make sure that they are not squashed or mouldy. Ripe fruits generally do not keep well and are best eaten on the day of purchase – store in the fridge. Unripe fruits can be kept for longer. Raspberries, blueberries, blackberries and currants all freeze well.

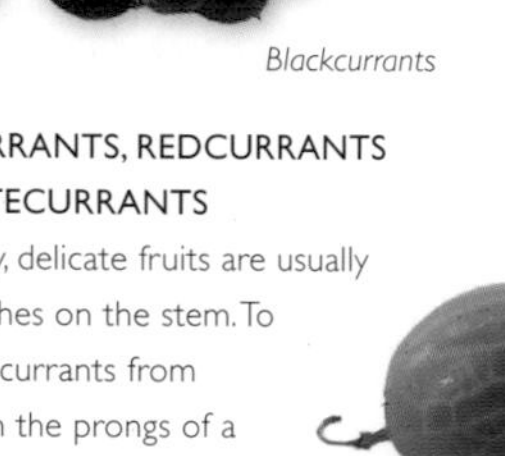

Gooseberries

Fruit Purée

Soft berries are perfect for making uncooked fruit purées or coulis. Sweeten if the fruit is tart and add a splash of lemon juice to bring out the flavour.

1 To make raspberry purée, place some raspberries, with lemon juice and icing sugar to taste, in a food processor or blender and process until smooth.

2 Press through a nylon sieve. Store in the fridge for up to two days.

Grapes, Melons, Dates and Figs

These fruits were some of the first ever to be cultivated and are therefore steeped in history. They are available in an immense variety of shapes, colours and sizes, and with the exception of melons, they can also be bought dried. As well as being a good source of nutrients, these fruits are high in soluble fibre.

GRAPES

There are many varieties of grape, each with its own particular flavour and character. Most are grown for wine production. Grapes for eating are less acidic and have a thinner skin than those used for wine-making. Seedless grapes are easier to eat and contain less tannin than the seeded fruit. Grapes range in colour from deep purple to pale red, and from bright green to almost white. The finest eating grapes are Muscat grapes, which have a wonderful, perfumed flavour. They may be pale green or golden, or black or red. Italia grapes, another popular eating variety, have a luscious musky flavour and may be green or black. Unless they are organic, grapes should be thoroughly washed before eating as they are routinely sprayed with pesticides and fungicides.

Serve grapes with cheese, in salads or as a topping for a tart. Before cooking them, remove the skin by blanching the grapes in boiling water for a few seconds, then peel with a small knife.

Red and green grapes

A Glass of Red Wine

According to a recent American study, phenolic is just one of the compounds found in red wine that may delay the onset of cancer. This news comes following research that wine – particularly red wine – may reduce the risk of heart disease. Nutritionally, wine is virtually worthless and should be drunk in moderation, although it may increase the absorption of iron if drunk with a meal.

Buying and Storing: Buy grapes that are plump, and fairly firm. They should be evenly coloured and firmly attached to the stalk. Unwashed fruit may be stored in the fridge for up to five days.

Health Benefits: Grapes contain iron, potassium and fibre. They are powerful detoxifiers and can improve the condition of the skin, and treat gout, liver and kidney disorders. Research has revealed that resveratrol, a natural substance produced by grapes, can help inhibit the formation

Galia melons (front left and back), Cantaloupe melons (centre), and Watermelon (right)

of tumours and that purple grape juice may be even more effective than aspirin in reducing the risk of heart attacks.

MELONS

Watermelons are very low in calories because of their high water content, which is around 90 per cent. They contain less vitamin C than the fragrant, orange-fleshed varieties, such as the Cantaloupe and Charentais. Avoid buying ready-cut melons, because most of the vitamins will have been lost.

Buying and Storing: Look for melons that feel heavy for their size and yield to gentle pressure at the stem end.

Health Benefits: When they are eaten on their own, melons are easy to digest, and pass quickly through the system. But, when they are consumed with other foods requiring a more complex digestive process, they may actually inhibit the absorption of nutrients.

Figs

FIGS

These delicate, thin-skinned fruits may be purple, brown or greenish-gold. Delicious raw, figs can also be poached or baked. Choose unbruised, ripe fruits that yield to gentle pressure and eat on the day of purchase. If they are not too ripe they can be kept in the fridge for a day or two. Figs are a well-known laxative and an excellent source of calcium.

DATES

Like figs, dates are one of the oldest cultivated fruits, possibly dating back as far as 50,000 BC. Fresh dates are sweet and soft and make a good natural sweetener: purée the cooked fruit, then add to cake or bread mixtures, or simply mix into natural yogurt to make a quick dessert. Dates should be plump and glossy. Medjool dates from Egypt and California have a wrinkly skin, but most other varieties are smooth. They can be stored in the fridge for up to a week. Dates are high in vitamin C and a good source of potassium and soluble fibre.

Fresh dates

Dried Vine Fruits

Currants, sultanas and raisins are the most popular dried fruits. Traditionally, these vine fruits are used for fruit cakes and breads, but currants and raisins are also good in savoury dishes. In Indian and North African cookery they are frequently used for their sweetness. Figs and dates are also popular – chopped or puréed – as an ingredient in cakes, tea breads and pastries.

It takes about 1.75–2.25kg/4–5lb fresh grapes to produce 450g/1lb sultanas, raisins or currants, while 1.5kg/3lb fresh figs and dates produces just 450g/1lb dried fruit. Although high in natural sugars, which can damage teeth if eaten to excess between meals, dried fruit is a concentrated source of nutrients, including iron, potassium, calcium, phosphorus, vitamin C, beta carotene and some B vitamins.

Tropical Fruit

This exotic collection of fruits ranges from the familiar bananas and pineapples to the more unusual papayas and passion fruit. The diversity in colours, shapes and flavours is sure to excite the tastebuds.

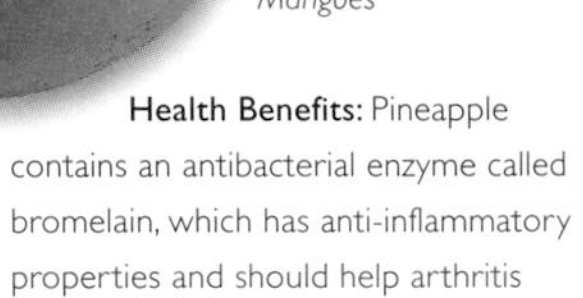

Mangoes

PINEAPPLES

These distinctive-looking fruits have a sweet, exceedingly juicy and golden flesh. Unlike most other fruits, pineapples do not ripen after picking, although leaving a slightly unripe fruit for a few days at room temperature may reduce its acidity.

Buying and Storing: Choose pineapples that have fresh green spiky leaves, are heavy for their size, and are slightly soft to the touch. Store in the fridge when ripe.

Health Benefits: Pineapple contains an antibacterial enzyme called bromelain, which has anti-inflammatory properties and should help arthritis sufferers. It also aids digestion.

Other Tropical Fruit

Kiwi fruit, which is also known as the Chinese gooseberry, has a brown, downy skin and vivid green flesh that is peppered with tiny black seeds. It is extremely rich in vitamin C.

Passion fruit is a dark purple, wrinkly, egg-shaped fruit, which hides a pulpy, golden flesh with edible black seeds. Cut in half and scoop out the inside with a spoon. Passion fruit is rich in vitamins A and C.

PAPAYA

Also known as pawpaw, these pear-shaped fruits come from South America. When ripe, the green skin turns a speckled yellow and the pulp is a glorious orange-pink colour. The numerous edible, small black seeds taste peppery when dried. Peel off the skin using a sharp knife or a vegetable peeler before enjoying the creamy flesh, which has a lovely perfumed aroma and sweet flavour. Ripe papaya is best eaten raw, while unripe green fruit can be used in cooking.

Health Benefits: Papaya contains an enzyme called papain, which aids the digestion, although levels of this enzyme diminish with ripening. Skin, hair and nails all benefit from the generous amounts of vitamin C and beta carotene found in papaya. Iron, potassium and calcium are also present.

MANGO

The skin of these luscious, fragrant fruits can range in colour from green to yellow, orange or red. Their shape varies tremendously, too. An entirely green skin is a sign of an unripe fruit, although in Asia, these are often used in salads. Ripe fruit should yield to gentle pressure and, when cut, it should reveal a juicy, orange flesh. Preparing a mango can be fiddly (see opposite). Serve sliced, or purée and use as a base for ice creams and sorbets.

Health Benefits: Rich in vitamin C and beta carotene, mangoes are also reputed to cleanse the blood.

Large and baby pineapples

Preparing Mango

Mangoes can be fiddly to prepare because they have a large, flat stone that is slightly off-centre. The method below produces cubed fruit. Alternatively, the mango can be peeled with a vegetable peeler and sliced around the central stone.

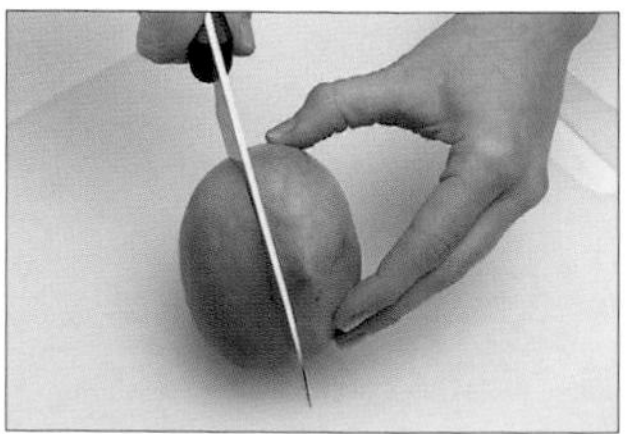

1 Hold the fruit with one hand and cut vertically down one side of the stone. Repeat on the opposite side. Cut away any remaining flesh around the stone.

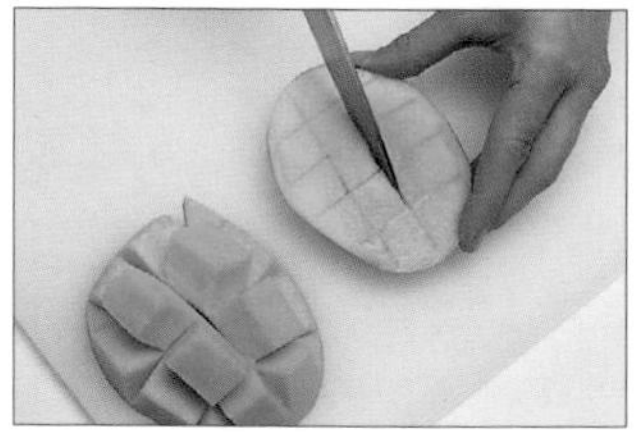

2 Taking the two large slices, and using a sharp knife, cut the flesh into a criss-cross pattern down to the skin. Holding the mango skin-side down, press it inside out, then cut the mango cubes away from the skin.

Cook's Tip

To ripen fruit, place it in a paper bag with an already ripened fruit and leave at room temperature or in a warm place.

Papaya

BANANAS

A concentrated bundle of energy, bananas are also full of valuable nutrients. The soft and creamy flesh can be blended into smooth, sweet drinks, mashed and mixed with yogurt, or the fruits can be baked and barbecued whole. Bananas also make an ideal weaning food for babies as they rarely cause an allergic reaction.

Health Benefits: Bananas are rich in dietary fibre, vitamins and minerals, especially potassium, which is important for the functioning of cells, nerves and muscles, and can relieve high blood pressure. Ripe bananas soothe the stomach and are believed to strengthen the stomach lining against acid and ulcers. Their high starch content makes them a good source of sustained energy, and they are also an effective laxative. Bananas are rich in the amino acid tryptophan, which is known to lift the spirits and aid sleep.

Buying and Storing: When buying, look for fruit that is heavy for its size. Mangoes and papayas should yield to gentle pressure. Avoid overly soft or bruised fruit, or those with any hard spots. Fully ripe mangoes and papayas are best kept in the fridge. If you wish to buy ripe bananas, choose yellow (or red) fruit that are patched with brown. Bananas with patches of green can be ripened at room temperature. Don't buy completely green bananas as these rarely ripen properly. Store bananas at cool room temperature.

Sweet, red-skinned bananas and the more familiar large and small yellow-skinned varieties

Vegetables

Vegetables offer an infinite number of culinary possibilities to the cook. The choice is immense and the growing demand for organic produce has meant that pesticide-free vegetables are now increasingly available. Vegetables are an essential component of a healthy diet and have countless nutritional benefits. They are at their best when freshly picked.

Roots and Tubers

Vegetables such as carrots, swedes, parsnips and potatoes, are a comforting and nourishing food, and it is not surprising that they should be popular in the winter. Their sweet, dense flesh provides sustained energy, valuable fibre, vitamins and minerals.

Fresh carrots with their green, feathery tops

CARROTS

The best carrots are not restricted to the cold winter months. Summer welcomes the slender sweet new crop, often sold with their green, feathery tops. (These are best removed after buying as they rob the root of moisture and nutrients.) Buy organic carrots if you can because high pesticide residues have been found in non-organic ones. As an added bonus, organic carrots do not need peeling.

Look for firm, smooth carrots – the smaller they are, the sweeter they are. Carrots should be prepared just before use to preserve their valuable nutrients. They are delicious raw, and can be steamed, stir-fried, roasted or puréed.

Health Benefits: A single carrot will supply enough vitamin A for an entire day and is reputed to cut the risk of lung cancer by half, even among ex-smokers. According to one American doctor, eating an extra carrot a day could prevent 20,000 lung cancer deaths each year in the USA. This may be due to the high level of the antioxidant beta carotene that carrots contain. Beta carotene may also reduce the risk of prostate cancer in men.

Brightly Coloured Vegetables

Ensure there is colour in your diet. Beta carotene is just one of the carotenoids found in green, yellow, orange and red vegetables (as well as fruit). Most carotenoids are antioxidants, which slow down or prevent cell damage from free radical oxidation in the body. Vitamins C and E are other carotenoids, along with bioflavonoids. These help to enhance the immune system, which protects us against viral and bacterial infections and boosts the body's ability to fight cancer and heart disease.

Beetroot

BEETROOT

Deep, ruby-red in colour, beetroot adds a vibrant hue and flavour to all sorts of dishes. It is often pickled in vinegar, but is much better roasted, as this emphasises its sweet earthy flavour. Raw beetroot can be grated into salads or used to make relishes. It can also be added to risottos or made into delicious soups. If cooking beetroot whole, wash carefully, taking care not to damage the skin or the nutrients and colour will leach out. Trim the stalks to about 2.5cm/1in above the root. Small beetroots are sweeter and more tender than larger ones.

Health Benefits: Beetroot has long been considered medicinally beneficial and is recommended as a general tonic. It can be used to help disorders of the blood, including anaemia, it is an effective detoxifier and, because of its high fibre content, is recommended to relieve constipation. Beetroot contains calcium, iron and vitamins A and C – all at their highest levels when it is eaten raw.

CELERIAC

This knobbly root is closely related to celery, which explains its flavour – a cross between aniseed, celery and parsley. Similar in size to a small swede, it has ivory flesh and is one of the few root vegetables that must be peeled before use. When grated and eaten raw in salads, celeriac has a crunchy texture. It can also be steamed, baked in gratins or combined with potatoes and mashed with butter or margarine and grainy mustard. Celeriac can also be used in soups and broths.

Health Benefits: Like celery, celeriac is a diuretic. It also contains vitamin C, calcium, iron, potassium and fibre.

Swede contains antioxidants and other compounds that may help to prevent cancer

Parsnips

Celeriac

SWEDE

The globe-shaped swede has pale orange flesh with a delicate sweet flavour. Trim off the thick peel, then treat in the same way as other root vegetables: grate raw into salads; dice and cook in casseroles and soups; or steam, then mash and serve as an accompaniment.

Health Benefits: Swedes are part of the cruciferous vegetable family, and contain compounds that are believed to have antioxidant and cancer-fighting properties. They also contain vitamins A and C.

PARSNIP

This vegetable has a sweet, creamy flavour and is delicious roasted, puréed or steamed. Parsnips are best purchased after the first frost of the year as the cold converts their starches into sugar, enhancing their sweetness. Scrub before use and only peel if tough. Avoid large roots, which can be woody.

Health Benefits: Parsnips are effective detoxifiers and are believed to fight some cancers. They contain vitamins C and E, iron, folic acid and potassium.

TURNIPS

This humble root vegetable has many health-giving qualities, and small turnips with their green tops intact are especially nutritious. Their crisp, ivory flesh, which is enclosed in white, green and pink-tinged skin, has a pleasant, slightly peppery flavour, the intensity of which depends on their size and the time of harvesting. Small turnips can be eaten raw. Alternatively, steam, bake or use in casseroles and soups.

Health Benefits: This cruciferous vegetable is said to halt the onset of certain cancers, particularly rectal cancer. It is also a digestive and maintains bowel regularity. The green tops are rich in beta carotene and vitamin C.

Baby turnips

POTATOES

There are thousands of potato varieties, and many lend themselves to particular cooking methods. Small potatoes, such as Pink Fir Apple and Charlotte, and new potatoes, such as Jersey Royals, are best steamed. They have a waxy texture, which retains its shape after cooking, making them ideal for salads. Main crop potatoes, such as Estima and Maris Piper, are more suited to roasting, baking or mashing, and can be used to make chips. Discard any potatoes with green patches as these indicate the presence of toxic alkaloids called solanines.

Vitamins and minerals are stored in, or just below, the skin, so it is best to use potatoes unpeeled. New potatoes and special salad potatoes need only be scrubbed.

Potatoes are not in themselves fattening – it is added ingredients such as cheese and the cooking method that can bump up the calories. Steam rather than boil, and bake instead of frying to retain valuable nutrients and to keep fat levels down.

Health Benefits: Potatoes are high in complex carbohydrates, and include both protein and fibre. They provide plenty of sustained energy, plus vitamins B and C, iron and potassium.

JERUSALEM ARTICHOKES

This small knobbly tuber has a sweet, nutty flavour. Peeling can be fiddly, although scrubbing and trimming is usually sufficient. Store in the fridge for up to one week. Use in the same way as potatoes – they make good creamy soups.

Health Benefits: Jerusalem artichokes contain vitamin C and fibre.

Cook's Tip

To prevent root vegetables and tubers discolouring after preparation, immerse them in a bowl of acidulated water – water containing 15ml/1 tbsp lemon juice. Don't soak them for long, because water-soluble vitamins will leach out into the water.

Potatoes

RADISHES

There are several types of this peppery-flavoured vegetable, which is a member of the cruciferous family. The round ruby red variety is most familiar; the longer, white-tipped type has a milder taste. Mooli or daikon radishes are white and very long; they can weigh up to several kilos or pounds. Radishes can be used to add flavour and a crunchy texture to salads and stir-fries. A renowned diuretic, radishes also contain vitamin C.

Jerusalem artichokes

Radishes

Mooli

HORSERADISH

This pungent root is never eaten as a vegetable. It is usually grated and mixed with cream or oil and vinegar, and served as a culinary accompaniment. It is effective in clearing blocked sinuses.

Buying and Storing: Seek out bright, firm, unwrinkled root vegetables and tubers, which do not have soft patches. When possible, choose organically grown produce, and buy in small quantities to ensure freshness. Store root vegetables in a cool, dark place.

Horseradish

Top Tuber

There are two types of this highly nutritious tuber; one has cream flesh, the other orange. The orange-fleshed variety has a higher nutritional content because it is richer in the antioxidant beta carotene, but both types contain potassium, fibre and vitamin C, as well as providing plenty of sustained energy. Sweet potatoes are thought to cleanse and detoxify the body and can boost poor circulation. When cooked, the cream-fleshed variety has a drier texture. Both are suited to mashing, baking and roasting.

Basic Vegetable Stock

Stock is easy to make at home and is a healthier option than shop-bought stock. It can be stored in the fridge for up to four days. Alternatively, it can be prepared in large quantities and frozen.

INGREDIENTS

15ml/1 tbsp olive oil
1 potato, chopped
1 carrot, chopped
1 onion, chopped
1 celery stick, chopped
2 garlic cloves, peeled
1 sprig of thyme
1 bay leaf
a few stalks of parsley
600ml/1 pint/2 1/2 cups water
salt and freshly ground black pepper

1 Heat the oil in a large saucepan. Add the vegetables and cook, covered, for 10 minutes or until softened, stirring occasionally. Stir in the garlic and herbs.

2 Pour the water into the pan and bring to the boil and simmer, partially covered, for 40 minutes. Strain, season and use as required.

Brassicas and Green Leafy Vegetables

This large group of vegetables boasts an extraordinary number of health-giving properties. Brassicas range from the crinkly-leafed Savoy cabbage to the small, walnut-sized Brussels sprout. Green, leafy vegetables include spinach, spring greens and Swiss chard.

Broccoli

BROCCOLI

This nutritious vegetable should be a regular part of everyone's diet. Two types are commonly available: purple-sprouting, which has fine, leafy stems and a delicate head, and calabrese, the more substantial variety with a tightly budded top and thick stalk. Choose broccoli that has bright, compact florets. Yellowing florets, a limp woody stalk and a pungent smell are an indication of overmaturity. Trim stalks before cooking, though young stems can be eaten, too. Serve raw in salads or with a dip. If you cook broccoli, steam or stir-fry it to preserve the nutrients and keep the cooking time brief to retain the vivid green colour and crisp texture.

Health Benefits: Broccoli is a member of the cruciferous family, which studies have shown to be particularly effective in fighting cancer of the lung, colon and breast. Sulphur compounds, found in broccoli, stimulate the production of anti-cancer enzymes, which prevent the growth of tumours and inhibit the spread of existing tumours. Raw broccoli contains almost as much calcium as milk and also provides plenty of B vitamins, vitamin C, iron, folate, zinc and potassium.

Cauliflower

CAULIFLOWER

The cream-coloured compact florets should be encased in large, bright green leaves. To get the most nutrients from a cauliflower, eat it raw, or bake or steam lightly. Cauliflower has a mild flavour and is delicious tossed in a vinaigrette dressing or combined with tomatoes and spices. Overcooked cauliflower is unpleasant and has a sulphurous taste.

Health Benefits: This creamy white cruciferous vegetable has many cancer-fighting qualities particularly against cancer of the lung and colon. Cauliflower also contains vitamin C, folate and potassium and is used in natural medicine as a blood purifier and laxative.

Preparing Broccoli

Trim the stalks from broccoli and divide it into florets before using. The stems of young broccoli can be sliced and eaten, too.

The Crucial Role of Phytochemicals

Cruciferous vegetables, such as broccoli, cabbages, kohlrabi, radishes, cauliflowers, Brussels sprouts, watercress, turnips, kale, pak choi, mustard greens, spring greens, chard and swede, are all packed with phytochemicals, which numerous studies have shown can fight off various forms of cancer. Phytochemicals are a group of compounds found in varying amounts in all fruit and vegetables, but particularly in cruciferous vegetables.

Phytochemicals are believed to provide an anticarcinogenic cocktail, which plays a crucial role in fighting disease by stimulating the body's enzyme defences against cancer-inducing substances. Eating cruciferous vegetables on a regular basis – at least three or four times a week – may halve the risk of lung, colon, breast, ovary, uterus or prostate cancer.

According to a senior British researcher, phytochemicals may be found to be as important as antioxidants in fighting disease. Phytochemicals include compounds such as carotenoids, selenium, fibre, isothiocyanates, indoles, phenols, tocopherols, bioflavonoids and protease inhibitors.

Kohlrabi (below left); Chinese cabbages and cavalo nero (below); and cauliflower, Savoy cabbage, Brussels sprouts, spinach leaves, broccoli and kale (right) are packed with phytochemicals

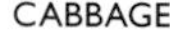

CABBAGE

Frequently overcooked, cabbage is best eaten raw, or cooked until only just tender. There are several different varieties: Savoy cabbage has substantial, crinkly leaves with a strong flavour and is perfect for stuffing; firm white and red cabbages can be shredded and used raw in salads (as can Chinese leaves); while pak choi is best cooked in stir-fries or with noodles.

Health Benefits: Studies show that eating cabbage more than once a week can reduce the likelihood of colon cancer in men by about 65 per cent. Raw or juiced cabbage is particularly potent and has antiviral and antibacterial qualities as well. Cabbage is thought to speed up the metabolism of oestrogen in women and this may provide protection against cancer of the breast and womb. It is a valuable source of vitamins C and E, beta carotene, folate, potassium, thiamine and fibre.

Cabbage

Mixed Cabbage Stir-fry

Stir-frying is a quick method of cooking that retains much of the vitamins and minerals that are lost during boiling. When cabbage is cooked in this way, it remains crisp and keeps its vivid colour.

INGREDIENTS

15ml/1 tbsp groundnut or sunflower oil
1 large garlic clove, chopped
2.5cm/1in piece fresh root ginger, chopped
450g/1lb/5 cups mixed cabbage leaves, such as Savoy, white, cavalo nero or pak choi, finely shredded
10ml/2 tsp soy sauce
5ml/1 tsp runny honey
5ml/1 tsp toasted sesame oil (optional)
15ml/1 tbsp sesame seeds, toasted

1 Heat the oil in a wok or large, deep frying pan, then sauté the garlic and ginger for about 30 seconds. Add the cabbage and stir-fry for 3–5 minutes until tender, tossing frequently.

2 Stir in the soy sauce, honey and sesame oil and cook for 1 minute. Sprinkle with sesame seeds and serve.

Health Benefits: Brussels sprouts contain significant amounts of vitamin C, folate, iron, potassium and some B vitamins. Because they are a cruciferous vegetable, sprouts can help prevent certain cancers.

Buying and Storing: Seek out bright, firm brassicas with no signs of discoloration or wilting. Avoid cauliflowers that have black spots or yellowing leaves. Ensure cabbages have a heavy heart. Chinese cabbages should be compact and heavy for their size with bright, undamaged leaves. Choose small Brussels sprouts with tightly packed leaves. Store cabbages and Brussels sprouts in a cool, dark place for up to a week. Broccoli and cauliflower should be stored in the fridge for only 2–3 days. Chinese leaves and pak choi don't keep well. Store them in the salad drawer of the fridge and use within 1–2 days.

Preparing Brussels Sprouts

1 Peel off any outer damaged leaves from the Brussels sprouts.

2 Before cooking, cut a cross in the base of each sprout, so that they cook quickly and evenly.

BRUSSELS SPROUTS

These are basically miniature cabbages that grow on a long tough stalk. They have a strong nutty flavour. The best are small with tightly packed leaves – avoid any that are very large or turning yellow or brown. Sprouts are sweeter when picked after the first frost. They are best cooked very lightly, so either steam or, better still, stir-fry to keep their green colour and crisp texture, as well as to retain the vitamins and minerals.

Brussels sprouts

GREEN LEAFY VEGETABLES

For years we have been told to eat up our greens and now we are beginning to learn why. Research into their health benefits has indicated that eating dark green leafy vegetables, such as spinach, spring greens, chard and kale, on a regular basis may protect us against certain forms of cancer.

Kale

Swiss chard

A member of the beet family, Swiss chard has large, dark leaves and thick, white, orange or red edible ribs. It can be used in the same way as spinach, or the stems may be cooked on their own. Swiss chard is rich in vitamins and minerals although, like spinach, it contains oxalic acid.

Spinach

This dark, green leaf is a superb source of cancer-fighting antioxidants. It contains about four times more beta carotene than broccoli. It is also rich in fibre, which can help to lower harmful levels of LDL cholesterol in the body, reducing the risk of heart disease and stroke. Spinach does contain iron but not in such rich supply as was once thought. Furthermore, spinach contains oxalic acid, which inhibits the absorption of iron and calcium in the body. However, eating spinach with a vitamin C-rich food will increase absorption. Spinach also contains vitamins C and B_6, calcium, potassium, folate, thiamine and zinc. Nutritionally, it is most beneficial when eaten raw in a salad, but it is also good lightly steamed, then chopped and added to omelettes.

Spinach

Spinach beet

Similar to Swiss chard, this form of the beetroot plant is grown only for its leaves and has a sweet, mild flavour. Use in the same way as spinach.

Spring greens

These leafy, dark green young cabbages are full of flavour. Rich in vitamin C and beta carotene, spring greens contain indoles, one of the phytochemicals that are thought to protect the body against breast and ovarian cancer.

Buying and Storing: Green, leafy vegetables do not keep well – up to 2 or 3 days at most. Eat soon after purchase to enjoy them at their best. Look for brightly coloured, undamaged leaves that are not showing any signs of yellowing or wilting. Wash the leaves thoroughly in cold water before use and eat them raw, or cook lightly, either by steaming or stir-frying to preserve their valuable nutrients.

Spinach beet

Mixed Swiss chard

Spring greens

Pumpkins and Squashes

Widely popular in the USA, Africa, Australia and the Caribbean, pumpkins and squashes come in a tremendous range of shapes, colours and sizes. Squashes are broadly divided into summer and winter types: cucumbers, courgettes and marrows fall into the summer category, while pumpkins, butternut and acorn squashes are winter varieties.

Pumpkins

WINTER SQUASHES

These have tough inedible skins, dense, fibrous flesh and large seeds. Most winter squashes can be used in both sweet and savoury dishes.

Acorn squash

This small to medium-size squash has an attractive, fluted shape and looks rather like a large acorn – hence its name. The orange flesh has a sweet flavour and slightly dry texture, and the skin colour ranges from golden to dark green. Its large seed cavity is perfect for stuffing.

Butternut squash

A large, pear-shaped squash with a golden brown skin and vibrant orange flesh. The skin is inedible and should be removed along with the seeds. Roast, bake, mash or use in soups or casseroles. The flesh has a rich, sweet, creamy flavour when cooked and makes a good substitute for pumpkin.

Pumpkins

These are native to America, where they are synonymous with Thanksgiving. Small pumpkins have sweeter, less fibrous flesh than the larger ones, which are perhaps best kept for making into lanterns. Deep orange in colour, pumpkin can be used in both sweet and savoury dishes, such as pies, soups, casseroles, soufflés and even ice cream. Avoid boiling pumpkin as it can become waterlogged and soggy. The seeds are edible and highly nutritious.

SUMMER SQUASHES

Picked when still young, summer squash have thin edible skins and tender, edible seeds. Their delicate flesh cooks quickly.

Pattypan squash

These pretty, baby squash resemble mini flying saucers. They are similar in taste to a courgette and are best steamed or roasted. They may be yellow or bright green, and although they can be expensive to buy, there is no waste. Pattypan squash will only keep for a few days in the fridge.

Courgettes

The most widely available summer squash, courgettes have the most flavour when they are small and young; the flavour diminishes when they are old and the seeds toughen. Young courgettes have a glossy, bright green skin and creamy coloured flesh. Extremely versatile, they can be steamed, grated raw into salads, stir-fried, griddled, puréed or used in soups and casseroles. Their deep yellow flowers are a delicacy and are perfect for stuffing.

Acorn, pattypan and butternut squashes

Courgettes

to use raw in salads or thinly sliced as a sandwich filling. However, they can also be pickled and cooked in other ways, such as steaming, baking or stir-frying.

Buying and Storing: Look for firm, bright, unblemished vegetables that are heavy for their size. Winter squash can be kept for several weeks if stored whole in a cool, dry place. Once cut, they should be kept in the fridge and eaten as soon as possible. Summer squash don't keep as well and should be stored in the fridge for only a few days.

Marrows

The grown-up equivalent of courgettes, marrows have a pleasant, mild flavour and are best baked either plain or with a stuffing. Spices, chillies and tomatoes are particularly good flavourings.

Marrows

Cucumbers

Probably cultivated as long ago as 10,000 BC, cucumbers were popular vegetables with the Greeks and the Romans. The long, thin, smooth-skinned variety is most familiar. Their refreshing, mild flavour makes cucumbers perfect

Health Benefits: Summer squash are effective diuretics and their potassium content means they are beneficial for those with high blood pressure. Pumpkins are also a diuretic, as well as a laxative, and like other winter squash contain high amounts of vitamin E, beta carotene and potassium. Beta carotene and vitamin E are antioxidants and are believed to reduce the risk of certain cancers. Summer squash contain smaller amounts of beta carotene. Because of their high water content, all squash are low in calories.

Peeling Pumpkin

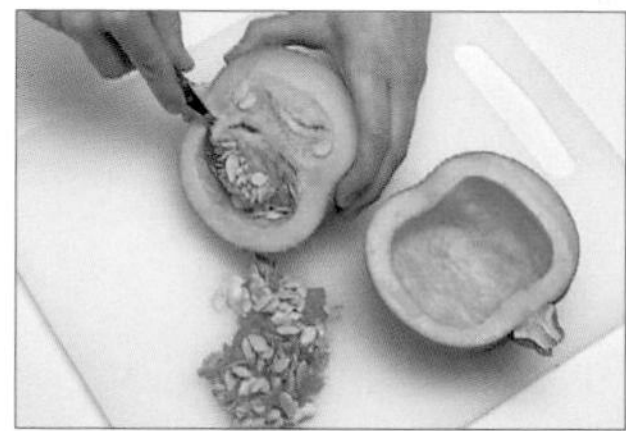

1 Cut the pumpkin in half using a large sharp knife and scoop out the seeds and fibrous parts with a spoon.

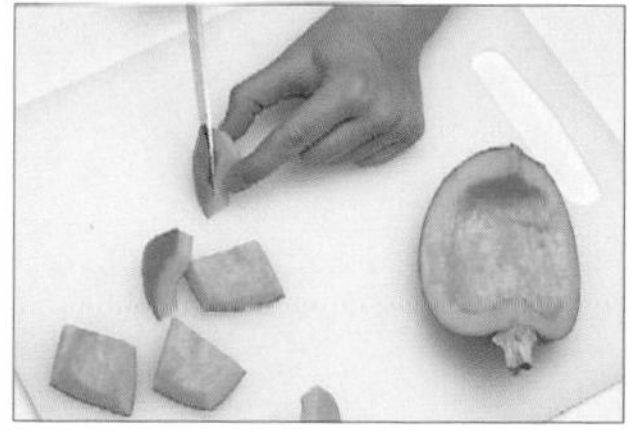

2 Cut the pumpkin into large chunks, then cut the skin using a sharp knife.

Roasting Squash

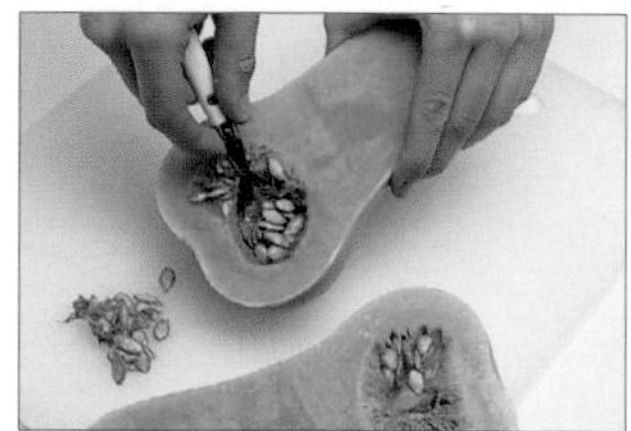

1 Preheat the oven to 200°C/400°F/ Gas 6. Cut the squash in half, scoop out the seeds and place the squash cut-side down on an oiled baking tray.

2 Bake for 30 minutes or until the flesh is soft. Serve in the skin, or remove the flesh and mash with butter.

Cucumber

Shoot Vegetables

This highly prized collection of vegetables, each honoured with a distinctive flavour and appearance, ranges from the aristocratic asparagus to the flowerbud-like globe artichoke.

FENNEL

Florence fennel is closely related to the herb and spice of the same name. The short, fat bulbs have a similar texture to celery and are topped with edible feathery fronds. Fennel has a mild aniseed flavour, which is most potent when eaten raw. Cooking tempers the flavour, giving it a delicious sweetness. When using fennel raw, slice it thinly or chop roughly and add to salads. Alternatively, slice or cut into wedges and steam, or brush with olive oil and roast or cook on a griddle. Fennel is at its best when it is fresh and should be eaten as soon as possible. It can, however, be stored in the fridge for a few days.

Fennel

Health Benefits: Fennel is a diuretic and also has a calming and toning effect on the stomach. It is low in calories and contains beta carotene and folate, which is known to reduce the risk of spina bifida in the unborn child. Fennel seeds are good for the digestion.

ASPARAGUS

Highly valued since Roman times, asparagus has been cultivated commercially since the 17th century. There are two main types: white asparagus is picked just before it sprouts above the surface of the soil; while green-tipped asparagus is cut above the ground and develops its colour when it comes into contact with sunlight. It takes three years to grow a crop from seed, which may account for its expense. Before use, scrape the lower half of the stalk with a vegetable peeler, then trim off the woody end.

Asparagus

Briefly poach whole spears in a frying pan containing a little boiling salted water, or tie the spears in a bundle and boil upright in an asparagus boiler or tall pan. Asparagus is delicious served with melted butter, or dipped into mayonnaise or vinaigrette. It can also be roasted in a little olive oil and served with a sprinkling of sea salt to bring out the flavour.

Health Benefits: Asparagus was used as a medicine long before it was eaten as a food. It is a rich source of vitamin C and also has diuretic and laxative properties. It contains the antioxidant glutathione, which has been found to prevent the formation of cataracts in the eyes.

Preparing Fennel

Cut the fennel bulb in half lengthways, then either cut into quarters or slice thinly.

White and red chicory

CHICORY

This shoot has long, tightly packed leaves. There are two kinds, white and red. Red chicory has a more pronounced flavour, while the white variety has crisper leaves. The crisp texture and slightly bitter flavour means that chicory is particularly good in salads. Chicory can also be steamed or braised, although in cooking, sadly, the red-

Health Benefits: Globe artichokes are a good source of vitamins A and C, fibre, iron, calcium and potassium. In natural medicine, they are used to treat high blood pressure.

Buying and Storing: When buying shoot vegetables, always choose the freshest-looking specimens. Asparagus spears should have firm stalks. Chicory should be neither withered nor brown at the edges – the best white chicory is sold wrapped in blue paper to keep out the sunlight and to stop it turning green and bitter. Fennel bulbs should be crisp and white, and have plenty of fresh fronds. Globe artichokes should have tightly closed, stiff leaves and still have the stalk attached.

Store all these vegetables in the salad drawer of the fridge. Asparagus, chicory and fennel should be eaten within 2–3 days; globe artichokes will keep for up to a week; and celery will keep for about 2 weeks if very fresh when purchased.

Left: Globe artichokes, celery, and chicory

leafed variety fades to brown. Before use, remove the outer leaves and wash thoroughly, then trim the base. In natural medicine, chicory is sometimes used to treat gout and rheumatism. It is also a digestive and liver stimulant, and good for a spring tonic.

CELERY

Like asparagus, celery was once grown primarily for medicinal reasons. Serve raw, steam or braise. Celery leaves have a tangy taste and are also useful for adding flavour to stocks. Low in calories, but rich in vitamin C and potassium, celery is a recognized diuretic and sedative.

GLOBE ARTICHOKES

Once cooked, the purple-tinged leaves of globe artichokes have an exquisite flavour. They are eaten with the fingers by dipping each leaf into garlic butter or vinaigrette dressing, then drawing each leaf through the teeth and eating the fleshy part. The heart is then dipped in the butter or dressing and eaten with a knife and fork.

Preparing Globe Artichokes

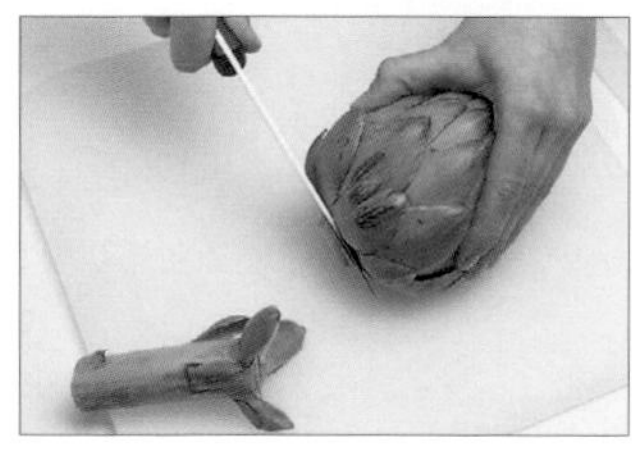

1 Hold the top of the artichoke firmly and using a sharp knife, remove the stalk and trim the base so that the artichoke sits flat.

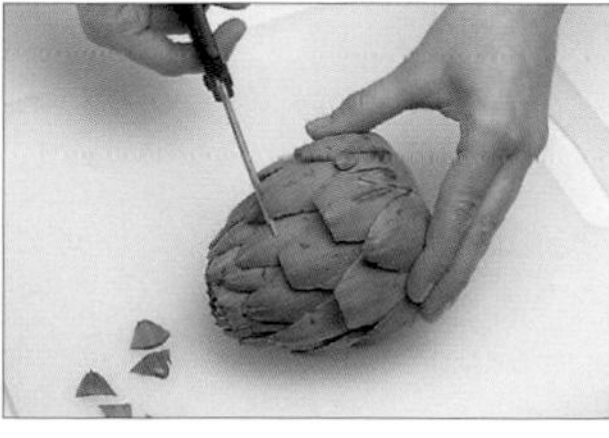

2 Using a sharp knife or scissors, trim off and discard the tops of the leaves and cut off the pointed top.

3 Cook the artichokes in a pan of boiling lightly salted water for 35–45 minutes until a leaf can be pulled out easily. Drain the artichokes upside down.

4 Pull out the central leaves then scoop out the hairy choke with a teaspoon and discard.

Vegetable Fruits

By cultivation and use, tomatoes, aubergines and peppers are all vegetables, but botanically they are classified as fruit. Part of the nightshade family, they have only relatively recently become appreciated for their health-giving qualities.

Tomatoes

TOMATOES

There are dozens of varieties to choose from, which vary in colour, shape and size. The egg-shaped plum tomato is perfect for cooking as it has a rich flavour and a high proportion of flesh to seeds – but it must be used when fully ripe. Too often, shop-bought tomatoes are bland and tasteless because they have been picked too young. Vine-ripened and cherry tomatoes are sweet and juicy and are good in salads or uncooked sauces. Large beefsteak tomatoes have a good flavour and are also excellent for salads. Sun-dried tomatoes add a rich intensity to sauces, soups and stews. Genetically engineered tomatoes are now sold in some countries, but at present they are only sold canned as a concentrated purée. Check the label before buying.

Buying and Storing: Look for deep-red fruit with a firm, yielding flesh. Tomatoes that are grown and sold locally will have the best flavour. To improve the flavour of a slightly hard tomato, leave it to ripen fully at room temperature. Avoid refrigeration because this stops the ripening process and adversely affects the taste and texture of the tomato.

Health Benefits: Vine-ripened tomatoes are higher in vitamin C than those picked when they are still green. They are also a good source of vitamin E, beta carotene, magnesium, calcium and phosphorus. Tomatoes contain the bioflavonoid lycopene, which is believed to prevent some forms of cancer by reducing the harmful effects of free radicals.

AUBERGINES

The dark-purple, glossy-skinned aubergine is the most familiar variety, although it is the small, ivory-white egg-shaped variety that has inspired the name "eggplant" in the USA. There is also the bright-green pea aubergine that is used in Asian cooking, and a pale-purple Chinese aubergine. Known in the Middle East as "poor man's caviar", aubergines give substance and flavour to spicy casseroles and tomato-based bakes and are delicious roasted, griddled and

Aubergines

Peeling and Seeding Tomatoes

Tomato seeds can give sauces a bitter flavour. Removing them and the tomato skins will also give a smoother end result.

1 Immerse the tomatoes in boiling water and leave for about 30 seconds – the base of each tomato can be slashed to make peeling easier.

2 Lift out the tomatoes with a slotted spoon, rinse in cold water to cool slightly, and peel off the skin.

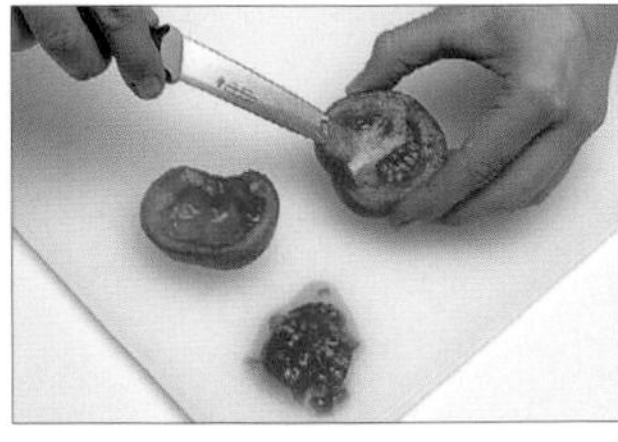

3 Cut the tomatoes in half, then scoop out the seeds and remove the hard core. Dice or roughly chop the flesh according to the recipe.

puréed into garlic-laden dips. It is not essential to salt aubergines to remove any bitterness; however, this method prevents the absorption of excessive amounts of oil during frying.

Buying and Storing: When buying, look for small to medium-size aubergines, which have sweet, tender flesh. Large specimens with a shrivelled skin are overmature and are likely to be bitter and tough. Store in the fridge for up to two weeks.

Health Benefits: An excellent source of vitamin C, aubergines also contain moderate amounts of iron and potassium, calcium and B vitamins. They also contain bioflavonoids, which help prevent strokes and reduce the risk of certain cancers.

Bird's eye chillies

Serrano chillies

Habanero chillies

Red and green chillies

Jalapeño chillies

CHILLIES

Native to America, this member of the capsicum family now forms an important part of many cuisines, including Indian, Thai, Mexican, South American and African. There are more than 200 different types of chilli, ranging from the long, narrow Anaheim to the lantern-shaped and incredibly hot Habanero. Red chillies are not necessarily hotter than green ones – but they will probably have ripened for longer in the sun. The heat in chillies comes from capsaicin, a compound found in the seeds, white membranes and, to a lesser extent, in the flesh. Chillies range in potency from the mild and flavourful to the blisteringly hot. Dried chillies tend to be hotter than fresh. Smaller chillies, such as Bird's eye chillies, contain proportionately more seeds and membrane, which makes them more potent than larger ones. It is very important to take care when using chillies and to wash your hands afterwards as they can irritate the skin and eyes.

Buying and Storing: Choose unwrinkled bright, firm chillies and store in the fridge.

Health Benefits: Chillies contain more vitamin C than an orange and are a good source of beta carotene, folate, potassium and vitamin E. They stimulate the release of endorphins, the body's "feel-good" chemicals and are a powerful decongestant, helping to open sinuses and air passages. Chillies stimulate the body and improve circulation, but if eaten to excess can irritate the stomach.

Chilli Boost

For an instant uplift, sprinkle some dried crushed chilli on your food. The chilli will stimulate the release of endorphins, which are the body's "feel-good" chemicals.

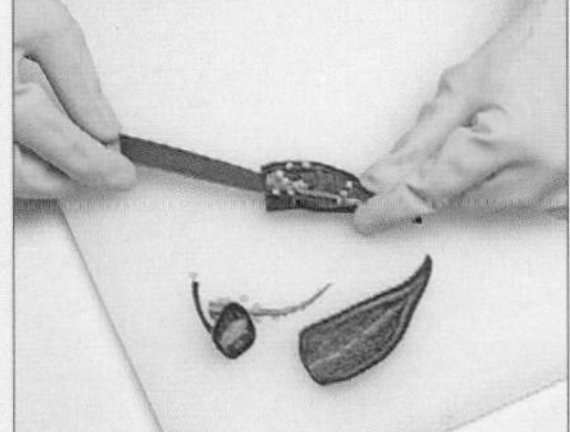

Handle chillies with care as they can irritate the skin and eyes. It is advisable to wear gloves when preparing chillies.

Avocados

Although avocados have a high fat content, the fat is monounsaturated, and is thought to lower blood cholesterol levels in the body. Avocados also contain valuable amounts of vitamins C and E, and iron, potassium and manganese. They are said to improve the condition of the skin and hair.

Once cut, avocados should be brushed with lemon or lime juice to prevent discoloration. They are usually eaten raw. Avocado halves can be dressed with a vinaigrette, or filled with soured cream sprinkled with cayenne pepper, or hummus. Slices or chunks of avocado are delicious in salads. In Mexico, where they grow in abundance, there are countless dishes based on avocados. Guacamole is the best known, but they are also used in soups and stews.

PEPPERS

Like chillies, sweet peppers are also members of the capsicum family. They range in colour from green through to orange, yellow, red and even purple. Green peppers are fully developed but not completely ripe, which can make them difficult to digest. They have refreshing, juicy flesh with a crisp texture. Other colours of peppers are more mature, have sweeter flesh, and are more digestible than less ripe green peppers. Roasting or chargrilling peppers will enhance their sweetness. They can also be stuffed, sliced into salads or steamed.

Buying and Storing: Choose peppers that are firm and glossy with an unblemished skin and store in the fridge for up to a week.

Health Benefits: Sweet peppers contain significant amounts of vitamin C, as well as beta carotene, some B complex vitamins, calcium, phosphorus and iron.

Peeling Peppers

1 Roast the peppers under a hot grill for 12–15 minutes, turning regularly until the skin is charred and blistered.

2 Alternatively, place on a baking tray and roast in an oven preheated to 200°C/400°F/Gas 6 for 20–30 minutes until blackened and blistered.

3 Put the peppers in a plastic bag and leave until cool – the steam will encourage the skin to peel away easily.

4 Peel off the skin, then slice in half. Remove the core and scrape out any remaining seeds. Slice or chop according to the recipe.

Peppers

Pods and Seeds

While most of these vegetables are delicious eaten fresh, many of them – peas, corn and broad and fresh beans, for example – can also be bought frozen. High in nutritional value, these popular vegetables can be enjoyed all year. Other types of pea include mangetouts and sugar snap peas, which can be eaten whole – pod and all.

Above: Clockwise from top left, runner beans, fine green beans, mangetouts, broad beans, peas and (centre) baby corn cobs.

PEAS

Peas are one of the few vegetables that taste just as good when frozen. Because freezing takes place soon after picking, frozen peas often have a higher nutritional value than fresh. Another advantage is that frozen peas are readily available all year round. Peas in the pod have a restricted availability and their taste diminishes if not absolutely fresh, because their sugars rapidly turn to starch. However, when they are at the peak of freshness, peas are delicious and have a delicate, sweet flavour. Pop them from the pod and serve raw in salads or steam lightly. Delicious cooked with fresh mint, peas also make satisfying purées and soups, and can be added to risottos and other rice dishes.

BROAD BEANS

When young and fresh these beans are a delight to eat. Tiny pods can be eaten whole; simply top and tail, and then slice. Usually, however, you will need to shell the beans as their skins can become tough. Elderly beans are often better skinned after they are cooked. Broad beans can be eaten raw or lightly cooked.

GREEN BEANS

French, runner and dwarf beans are eaten pod and all. They should be bright green and crisp-textured. Simply top and tail and lightly cook or steam them. Serve green beans hot, or leave to cool slightly and serve as a warm salad with a squeeze of fresh lemon juice or a vinaigrette dressing.

Buying and Storing: Look for bright-green, smooth, plump pods and keep in the fridge for no more than a day or two.

Health Benefits: Peas and beans are a good source of protein and fibre. They are rich in vitamin C, iron, thiamine, folate, phosphorous and potassium.

SWEETCORN

Corn cobs are best eaten soon after picking, before their natural sugars start to convert into starch when the flavour fades and the kernels toughen. Remove the green outer leaves and cook whole or slice off the kernels with a sharp knife. Baby corn cobs can be eaten raw, and are good in stir-fries.

Buying and Storing: Look out for very fresh, plump kernels that show no signs of discoloration, wrinkling or drying and eat soon after purchase. If you do not intend to eat them immediately, store in the coolest part of the fridge.

Health Benefits: Sweetcorn is a good carbohydrate food and is rich in vitamins A, B and C, and fibre. It contains useful amounts of iron, magnesium, phosphorus and potassium. Baby corn is high in folate, which is essential for maintaining the immune system.

Sweetcorn

The Onion Family

Onions and garlic are highly prized as two of the oldest remedies known to man. Both contain allicin, which has been found to stimulate the body's antioxidant mechanisms, raising levels of beneficial HDL cholesterol and combating the formation of clogged arteries. Additionally, these vegetables are indispensable in cooking. The wide variety of onions can be enjoyed raw or cooked and, with garlic, add flavour to a huge range of savoury dishes.

ONIONS

Every cuisine in the world includes onions in one form or another. They are an essential flavouring, offering a range of taste sensations, from the sweet and juicy red onion and powerfully pungent white onion to the light and fresh spring onion. Pearl onions and shallots are the babies of the family. Tiny pearl onions are generally pickled, while shallots are good roasted with their skins on, when they develop a caramel sweetness. Yellow onions are most common and are highly versatile.

Buying and Storing: When buying, choose onions that have dry, papery skins and are heavy for their size. They will keep for 1–2 months when stored in a cool, dark place.

Health Benefits: Numerous studies highlight the healing powers of the onion. It is a rich source of quercetin, a potent antioxidant that has been linked to preventing stomach cancer. Eating half a raw onion a day is said to thin the blood, lower the LDL cholesterol and raise beneficial HDL cholesterol by about 30 per cent. This means that cholesterol is transported away from the arteries, reducing the risk of heart disease and stroke. Whether raw or cooked, onions are antibacterial and antiviral, helping to fight off colds, relieve bronchial congestion, asthma and hay fever. They are also good for arthritis, rheumatism and gout.

GARLIC

For centuries, this wonder food has been the focus of much attention, and is praised for its medicinal powers, which range from curing toothache to warding off evil demons. The flavour of garlic is milder when whole or sliced; crushing or chopping releases the oils making the flavour stronger. Slow-cooking also tames the pungency of garlic, although it still affects the breath.

Onion and Garlic Cures

Onions have been used in all kinds of traditional remedies.

- In the past, babies would often be given a teaspoonful of onion infusion for colic: a slice of onion would be infused in hot water for a few minutes, and the water left to cool.
- Raw garlic can relieve symptoms of food poisoning. It has been shown to kill bacteria, even those that are resistant to antibiotics. Some people say that garlic keeps old age at bay.

Buying and Storing: Most garlic is semi-dried to prolong its shelf life, yet the cloves should still be moist and juicy. Young garlic, which is available in early summer, has a long green stem and soft white bulb. It has a fresher flavour than semi-dried garlic, but can be used in the same ways. Pungency varies, but the general rule when buying garlic is: the smaller the bulb, the more potent the flavour. If stored in a cool, dry place and not in

Above: Spring onions, red onions, shallots and white onions

Leeks

the fridge, garlic will keep for up to about eight weeks. If the air is damp garlic will sprout, and if it is too warm the cloves will eventually turn to grey powder.

Health Benefits: Garlic tops the American National Cancer Institute's list as a potential cancer-preventative food. Although the antiviral, antibacterial and antifungal qualities of garlic are most potent when eaten raw, cooking does not inhibit its anti-cancer, blood-thinning and decongestant capabilities. Studies show that eating 2–3 garlic cloves a day reduces by half the probability of a subsequent heart attack in previous heart patients. Garlic has also been found to lower blood cholesterol, reduce high blood pressure, boost the immune system, act as an anti-inflammatory, lift mood and have a calming effect. It should be eaten on a daily basis.

Below: Garlic bulbs and cloves

LEEKS

Like onions and garlic, leeks have a very long history. They grow in all sorts of climates and are known to have been eaten and enjoyed by the ancient Egyptians, Greeks and Romans. Leeks are very versatile, having their own distinct, subtle flavour. They are less pungent than onions but are still therapeutically beneficial. Excellent in soups and casseroles, leeks can also be used as a pie filling or in flans, or simply steamed and served hot with a light, creamy sauce, or cooled slightly and dressed with a vinaigrette. They are also delicious sliced or shredded and then stir-fried with a little garlic and ginger.

Commercially grown leeks are usually about 25cm/10in long, but you may occasionally see baby leeks, which are very tender and are best steamed.

Buying and Storing: Choose firm leeks with bright-green leaves. Avoid those without their roots as they deteriorate more quickly. Leeks will keep for up to a week in the salad drawer of the fridge.

Health Benefits: Leeks have the same active constituents as onions, but in smaller amounts. They also contain vitamins C and E, iron, folate and potassium.

Cleaning Leeks

Leeks need meticulous cleaning to remove any grit and earth that may hide between the layers of leaves. This method will ensure that the very last tiny piece of grit will be washed away.

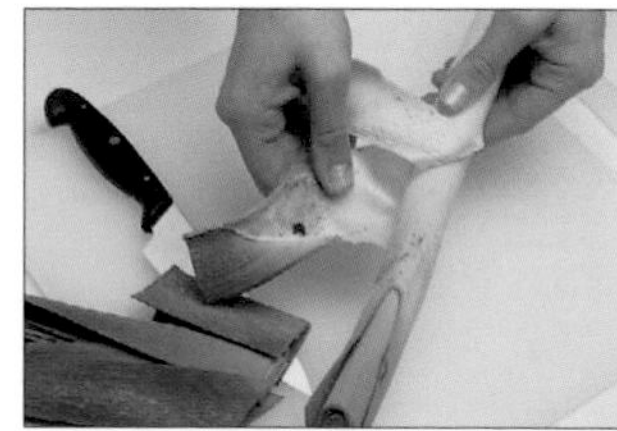

1 Trim off the root, then trim the top of the green part and discard. Remove any tough or damaged outer leaves.

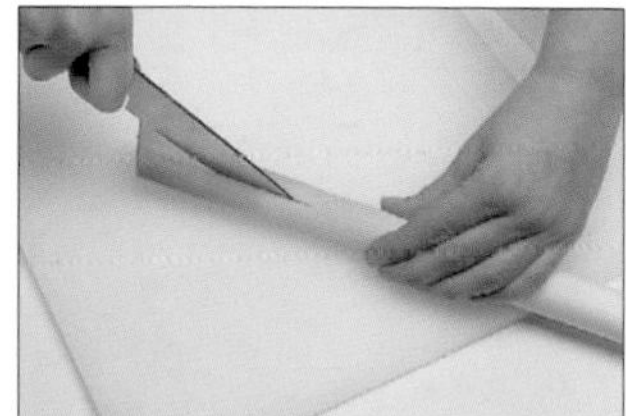

2 Slash the top green part of the leek into quarters and rinse the leek well under cold running water, separating the layers to remove any hidden dirt. Slice or leave whole, depending on the recipe.

Mushrooms

Thanks to their rich earthiness, mushrooms add substance and flavour to all sorts of dishes. There are more than 2,000 edible varieties but only a tiny proportion are readily available. These fall into three camps: common cultivated mushrooms, like the button; wild varieties that are now cultivated, such as the shiitake; and the truly wild types that have escaped cultivation, such as the morel.

Cultivated mushrooms come in a wide variety of sizes

BUTTON, CAP AND FLAT MUSHROOMS

The most common cultivated variety of mushrooms, these are actually one type in various stages of maturity. The button mushroom is the youngest and has, as its name suggests, a tight, white, button-like cap. It has a mild flavour and can be eaten raw in salads. Cap mushrooms are slightly more mature and larger in size, while the flat mushroom is the largest and has dark, open gills. Flat mushrooms have the most prominent flavour and are good grilled or baked on their own, or stuffed.

Chanterelles

Below: Field blewitts

Below: Chestnut (left) and portabello mushrooms

CHESTNUT MUSHROOMS

The brown-capped chestnut mushroom looks similar to the cultivated button but has a more assertive, nutty flavour.

PORTOBELLO MUSHROOMS

Similar in appearance to the cultivated flat mushroom, the portabello is simply a large chestnut mushroom. It has a rich flavour and a meaty texture and is good grilled.

FIELD MUSHROOMS

This wild mushroom has an intense, rich flavour. It is ideal for grilling and stuffing.

CHANTERELLES

This egg-yolk-coloured mushroom has a pretty, funnel shape and a fragrant but delicate flavour. Also known as the girolle, it is sold fresh in season and dried all year round. If buying fresh, eat as soon as possible and wipe rather than wash as the skin is very porous. Sauté, bake or add to sauces.

FIELD BLEWITTS

This wild mushroom is now widely cultivated in caves in Britain, Switzerland and France. It has a thick, lilac-blue stem,

Dried and fresh ceps

which is topped with a smooth, whitish cap. When cooked, field blewitts have a dense, meaty texture.

CEPS

This wild mushroom, which is also known by its Italian name, porcini, has a tender, meaty texture and woody flavour. Dried ceps are used for their rich flavour.

MORELS

Slightly sweet-flavoured mushrooms with a distinctive, pointed, honeycomb cap and a hollow stalk. They can be fiddly to clean. Morels are costly to buy fresh because they have a short season, but they can be bought dried.

Shiitake Mushrooms

In Asia, these mushrooms are recommended for a long and healthy life, and research has shown that they have antiviral properties that stimulate the immune system. Shiitake mushrooms may help lower blood cholesterol, even curtailing some of the side effects of saturated fat. They have also been found to halt the latter stages of certain cancers.

ENOKI MUSHROOMS

These Japanese mushrooms have a pretty, tiny cap on an elegant, long stalk. Sold in clusters, enoki have a slightly lemony flavour. Use in stir-fries or eat raw in salads.

Morels

OYSTER MUSHROOMS

Now cultivated and widely available, oyster mushrooms have an attractive shell-shaped cap and thick stalk. They are usually pale, grey-brown, although yellow and pink varieties are also available.

Buying and Storing: Buy mushrooms that smell and look fresh. Avoid ones with damp, slimy patches and any that are discoloured. Store in a paper bag in the fridge for up to 4 days.

Dried Mushrooms

These are a useful stand-by and have a rich, intense flavour. To reconstitute dried mushrooms, soak them in boiling water for 20–30 minutes, depending on the variety and size of mushroom, until tender. Drain and rinse well to remove any grit and dirt. Dried mushrooms often require longer cooking than fresh ones.

Health Benefits: Mushrooms do not contain a wealth of nutrients but they are a useful source of vitamins B_1 and B_2, potassium, iron and niacin.

Cleaning Mushrooms: Before use, wipe mushrooms with damp kitchen paper and trim the stem. Wild mushrooms often harbour grit and dirt and may need to be rinsed briefly under cold running water, but dry thoroughly. Never soak mushrooms or they will become soggy. Peeling is not usually necessary.

Oyster mushrooms

Salad Leaves

It is only a few years since the most exotic lettuce available was the crisp-textured iceberg. Today, salad leaves come in a huge variety of shapes, sizes, colours and flavours, from bitter-tasting endive to peppery rocket and red-leafed lollo rosso. Making a mixed leaf salad has never been so easy, or the result so delicious.

Left, clockwise from left: curly endive, oak leaf, cos, butterhead and iceberg lettuces

LETTUCES

Cultivated for thousands of years, lettuces were probably first eaten as a salad vegetable during Roman times. Nutritionally, lettuce is best eaten raw, but it can be braised, steamed or made into a soup. Large-leafed varieties can be used to wrap around a filling.

Butterhead lettuce

This soft-leafed lettuce has an unassuming flavour and is good as a sandwich-filler.

Cos lettuce

Known since Roman times, the cos lettuce has long, sturdy leaves and a strong flavour. Little Gem is a baby version of cos and has firm, densely packed leaves.

Iceberg lettuce

This lettuce has a round, firm head of pale-green leaves with a crisp texture. Like the butterhead, it has a mild, slightly bitter flavour and is best used as a garnish. It is reputed to be one of the most highly chemically treated crops, so choose organic iceberg lettuces if you can.

Oak leaf

This attractive lettuce has red-tinged, soft-textured leaves with a slightly bitter flavour. In salads, combine with green lettuces for a contrast of tastes and textures.

Lollo rosso

The pretty, frilly leaves of lollo rosso are green at the base and a deep, autumn-red around the edge. Its imposing shape means it is best mixed with other leaves if used in a salad or as a base for roasted vegetables. Lollo biondo is a pale-green version.

Curly endive

Also known as frisée, curly endive has spiky, ragged leaves that are dark green on the outside and fade to an attractive pale yellow-green towards its centre. It has a distinctive bitter flavour that is enhanced by a robust dressing.

Radicchio

Lamb's lettuce

Sorrel

Rocket

Watercress

Lamb's lettuce

This tiny lettuce has a cluster of small, rounded, velvety leaves with a delicate flavour. Serve on its own or mix with other leaves.

SALAD LEAVES

There is a great variety of different salad leaves that are now readily available.

Radicchio

A member of the chicory family, radicchio has deep-red, tightly packed leaves that have a bitter peppery flavour. It is good in salads and can be sautéed or roasted.

Rocket

Classified as a herb, rocket is a popular addition to salads, or it can be served as a starter with thin shavings of Parmesan cheese. It has a strong, peppery flavour, which is more robust when wild. Lightly steamed rocket has a milder flavour than the raw leaves but it is equally delicious.

Sorrel

The long pointed leaves of sorrel have a refreshing, sharp flavour that is best when mixed with milder tasting leaves. It contains oxalic acid which, when cooked, inhibits the absorption of iron. Sorrel is an effective diuretic.

Watercress

The hot, peppery flavour of watercress complements milder tasting leaves and is classically combined with fresh orange. It does not keep well and is best used within two days of purchase. Watercress is a member of the cruciferous family and shares its cancer-fighting properties.

Buying and Storing: Salad leaves are best when they are very fresh and do not keep well. Avoid leaves that are wilted, discoloured or shrivelled. Store in the fridge, unwashed, for between 2 days and 1 week, depending on the variety. As salad leaves are routinely sprayed with pesticides, they should be washed thoroughly, but gently, to avoid damaging the leaves, and then dried in a kitchen cloth. Better still, choose organically grown produce.

Health Benefits: Although all types of salad leaves are about 90 per cent water, they contain useful amounts of vitamins and minerals, particularly folate, iron and the antioxidants, vitamin C and beta carotene. The outer, darker leaves tend to be more nutritious than the paler leaves in the centre. More importantly, like other green, leafy vegetables, their antioxidant content has been found to guard against the risk of many cancers. Salad leaves are usually eaten raw when the nutrients are at their strongest. Lettuce is reputed to have a calming, sedative effect.

Herbs

Herbs have been highly prized by natural practitioners for centuries because, in spite of their low nutritional value, they possess many reputed healing qualities. In cooking, herbs can make a significant difference to the flavour and aroma of a dish and they have the ability to enliven the simplest of meals. Fresh herbs can easily be grown at home in the garden, or in a pot or window box.

Chives and bay leaves

BASIL

This delicate aromatic herb is widely used in Italian and Thai cooking. The leaves bruise easily, so are best used whole or torn, rather than cut with a knife. Basil is said to have a calming effect on the stomach, easing constipation, sickness and cramps, and aiding digestion.

BAY LEAVES

These dark-green, glossy leaves are best left to dry for a few days before use. They have a robust, spicy flavour and are an essential ingredient in bouquet garni. Studies show that bay has a restorative effect on the digestive system.

CHIVES

A member of the onion family, chives have a milder flavour and are best used as a garnish, snipped over egg or potato dishes, or added to salads or flans. Like onions, chives are an antiseptic and act as a digestive.

CORIANDER

Warm and spicy, coriander is popular in Indian and Thai curries, stir-fries and salads. It looks similar to flat leaf parsley but its taste is completely different. It is often sold with its root intact. The root has a more intense flavour than the leaves and can be used in curry pastes. Coriander is

Basil

Using Dried Herbs

Although fresh herbs have the best flavour and appearance, dried herbs can be a convenient and useful alternative, especially in the winter months when some fresh herbs are not available.

- A few dried herbs such as basil, dill, mint and parsley do not dry well, losing most of their flavour.
- Oregano, thyme, marjoram and bay retain their flavour when dried and are useful substitutes for fresh.
- Dried herbs have a more concentrated flavour than fresh, so much less is required – usually a third to a half as much as fresh.
- When using dried herbs in cooking, always allow sufficient time for them to rehydrate and soften.
- Dried herbs do little for uncooked dishes, but are useful for flavouring marinades, and are good in slow-cooked stews and soups.
- When buying dried herbs, they should look bright, not faded and, because light spoils their flavour and shortens shelf-life, store in sealed, airtight jars in a cool, dark place.

Coriander

marinades and is a good partner for mustard. An attractive herb with delicate, wispy leaves, add to dishes just prior to serving as its mild flavour diminishes with cooking. Dill is a popular herb for settling the stomach and is thought to reduce flatulence. It is also said to be mildly soporific and, in the form of gripe water, is sometimes given to babies to relieve wind and colic.

an effective digestive, easing indigestion and nausea. It is also said to act as a tonic for the heart.

DILL

The mild, yet distinctive, aniseed flavour of dill goes well with potatoes, courgettes and cucumber. It makes a good addition to creamy sauces and can be added to a wide variety of egg dishes. It can also be used as a flavouring for dressings and

Dill

Pesto

Freshly made pesto, spooned over warm pasta or spread over bread and topped with a round of goat's cheese, makes a perfect quick supper. It is usually made with basil, but other herbs, such as rocket, coriander or parsley, can be substituted. The pine nuts can also be replaced with walnuts, cashew nuts or pistachio nuts.

INGREDIENTS

50g/2oz/1 cup fresh basil leaves
2 garlic cloves, crushed
40g/1½oz/½ cups pine nuts
120ml/4fl oz/½ cup olive oil, plus extra for drizzling
60ml/4 tbsp freshly grated Parmesan cheese
salt and freshly ground black pepper

1 Place the basil, garlic and pine nuts in a food processor or blender and process until finely chopped.

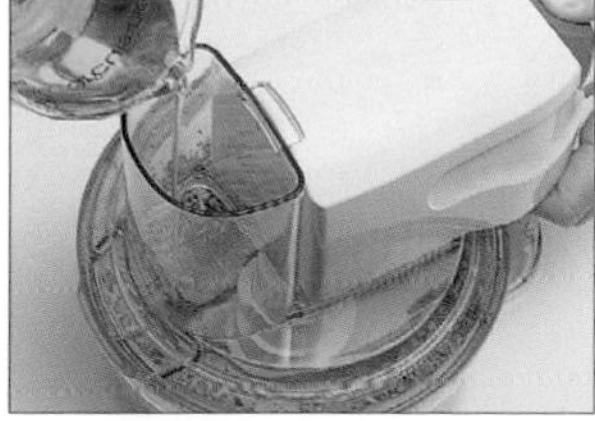

2 Gradually add the olive oil and then the Parmesan and blend to a coarse purée. Season to taste. Spoon into a lidded jar, then pour over the extra olive oil to cover. Use at once, or store in the fridge.

Freezing Herbs

This is an excellent method of preserving fresh delicate herbs such as basil, chives, dill, tarragon, coriander and parsley. The herbs will lose their fresh appearance and texture when frozen, but are still suitable for use in cooking. They will keep for up to 3 months in the freezer.

- Half-fill ice-cube trays with chopped herbs and top up with water. Freeze, then place the cubes in freezer-bags. The frozen cubes can be added to soups, stews and stocks, and heated until they melt.
- Place whole sprigs or leaves, or chopped herbs in freezer bags, expel any air and tightly seal.
- Freeze herb sprigs or leaves on trays. When the herbs are frozen, transfer them carefully to freezer-bags, expel any air, seal tightly and return to the freezer.
- Pack chopped fresh herbs in plastic pots and freeze. Scatter into soups and stews straight from the freezer.

Kaffir lime leaves

KAFFIR LIME LEAVES

These attractive glossy, green leaves are commonly used in Asian cuisines, lending a tantalizing citrus aroma and flavour to a wide variety of dishes. They are available fresh from Asian stores, or dried from large supermarkets. The fruit resembles a knobbly lime and its rind, which is rich in vitamin C, is used grated in Thai and Indonesian curries. The leaves can be used as a digestive.

LEMON BALM

This herb makes a refreshing tea and is good in any sweet or savoury dish that uses lemon juice. It has antibacterial, antiviral and antidepressant qualities. The calming and sedative attributes of lemon balm are beneficial for those suffering from stress or nervous exhaustion.

MARJORAM

Closely related to oregano, marjoram has a slightly sweeter flavour. It goes well in Mediterranean-style vegetable dishes, such as ratatouille, or in casseroles and tomato sauces, but should be added at the last minute as its flavour diminishes when heated. It also makes a good addition to a marinade. Majoram improves the circulation and relieves stomach pains.

MINT

The most familiar types are spearmint and peppermint, but there are other distinctly flavoured varieties, such as apple, lemon and pineapple mint, which are worth looking out for, and make a refreshing drink when infused in boiling water. Mint is used as a flavouring in a wide variety of dishes, from stuffings to fruit salads. It is a vital ingredient in the Middle Eastern salad, tabbouleh, and is also mixed with natural yogurt to make raita, a soothing accompaniment to hot curries. It is a traditional cure for nausea and indigestion and is also effective in stimulating and cleansing the system.

Lemon balm, marjoram, mint and oregano

OREGANO

This is a wild variety of marjoram but has a more robust flavour that goes well with tomato-based dishes. Oregano can relieve digestive problems.

PARSLEY

There are two types of parsley: flat leaf and curly. Both taste relatively similiar, but the flat leaf variety is preferable in cooked dishes. Parsley is an excellent source of vitamin C, iron and calcium. Chewing parsley after eating garlic or onions can neutralize the smell and freshen breath.

Parsley

Rosemary and sage

ROSEMARY

Wonderfully aromatic, rosemary is traditionally used in meat dishes, but it can also add a smoky flavour to hearty bean and vegetable dishes. Rosemary has a reputation for invigorating the circulation, and for relieving headaches and respiratory problems.

SAGE

The leaves of this herb, which may be silver-grey or purple, have a potent aroma and only a small amount is needed. Sage is commonly added to meat dishes but, if used discreetly, it is delicious with beans, cheese, lentils and in stuffings. Sage was used medicinally before it found its way into the kitchen and is regarded as a tonic for the stomach, kidneys and liver.

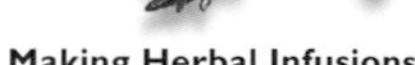

Thyme

THYME

This robustly flavoured aromatic herb is good in tomato-based recipes, and with roasted vegetables, lentils and beans. It is also an essential ingredient in a bouquet garni. Thyme aids the digestion of fatty foods and works as a powerful antiseptic.

TARRAGON

A popular herb in French cooking, tarragon has an affinity with all egg- and cheese-based dishes. The short slender-leafed French variety has a warm, aniseed flavour and is considered to be superior to Russian tarragon. Tarragon has diuretic properties and can relieve indigestion. Infused in a herbal tisane, it can soothe sore throats and promote restful sleep.

Tarragon

Buying and Storing: Fresh herbs are widely available, sold loose, in packets or growing in pots. The packets do not keep for as long and should be stored in the fridge. Place stems of fresh herbs in a half-filled jar of water and cover with a plastic bag. Sealed with an elastic band, the herbs should keep in the fridge for a week. Growing herbs should be kept on a sunny windowsill. If watered regularly, and not cut too often, they will keep for months.

Drying Herbs

Bay, rosemary, sage, thyme and marjoram all dry well. However, other more delicate herbs, such as basil, coriander and parsley, are better used fresh. Pick herbs before they flower, preferably on a sunny morning after the dew has dried. Avoid washing them – instead brush with a pastry brush or wipe with a dry cloth. Tie the herbs in bunches and hang them upside down in a warm, dark place. The leaves should be dry and crisp after a week. Leave the herbs in bundles or strip the leaves from the stems and store in airtight jars.

Making Herbal Infusions

Infusions, or tisanes, are made from steeping fresh herbs in boiling water. They can be used as a medicinal gargle or refreshing healthy drink. Peppermint tea is an excellent remedy for indigestion or irritable bowel syndrome and is best drunk after a meal.

To make peppermint tea: pour boiling water over fresh peppermint leaves. Cover the bowl and leave to stand for about 10 minutes, then strain the liquid into a cup and drink.

Sprouted Seeds, Pulses and Grains

Sprouts are quite remarkable in terms of nutritional content. Once the seed (or pulse or grain) has germinated, the nutritional value rises dramatically. There are almost 30 per cent more B vitamins and 60 per cent more vitamin C in the sprout than in the original seed, pulse or grain. Supermarkets and health food shops sell a variety of sprouts, but it is easy to grow them at home – all you need is a jar, some muslin and an elastic band.

MUNG BEANSPROUTS

The most commonly available beansprouts, these are popular in Chinese and Asian cooking, where they are used in soups, salads and stir-fries. They are fairly large, with a crunchy texture and a delicate flavour.

ALFALFA SPROUTS

These tiny, wispy white sprouts have a mild, nutty flavour. They are best eaten raw to retain their crunchy texture.

WHEAT BERRY SPROUTS

Sprouts grown from wheat berries have a crunchy texture and sweet flavour and are excellent in breads. If they are left to grow, the sprouts will become wheatgrass, a powerful detoxifier that is is usually made into a juice.

Alfalfa sprouts

Mung beansprouts

CHICK-PEA SPROUTS

Sprouts grown from chick-peas have a nutty flavour and add substance to dishes.

LENTIL SPROUTS

These sprouts have a slightly spicy, peppery flavour and thin, white shoots. Use only whole lentils: split ones won't sprout.

ADUKI BEANSPROUTS

These fine wispy sprouts have a sweet nutty taste. Use in salads and stir-fries.

Sprouting Seeds, Pulses and Grains

Larger pulses, such as chick-peas, take longer to sprout than small beans, but they are all easy to grow and are usually ready to eat in three or four days. Store sprouts in a covered container in the fridge for 2–3 days.

1 Wash 45ml/3 tbsp seeds, pulses or grains thoroughly in water, then place in a large jar. Fill the jar with lukewarm water, cover with a piece of muslin and fasten securely with an elastic band. Leave in a warm place to stand overnight.

2 The next day, pour off the water through the muslin and fill the jar again with water. Shake gently, then turn the jar upside down and drain thoroughly. Leave the jar on its side in a warm place, away from direct sunlight.

3 Rinse the seeds, pulses or grains three times a day, until they have grown to the desired size. Make sure they are drained thoroughly to prevent them turning rancid. Remove from the jar, rinse well and remove any ungerminated beans.

How to Use Beansprouts

- Sprouted pulses and beans have a denser more fibrous texture, while sprouts grown from seeds are lighter. Use a mixture of the three for a variety of tastes and textures.
- Mung beansprouts are often used in Oriental food, particularly stir-fries, and require little cooking.
- Alfalfa sprouts are good as part of a sandwich filling as well as in salads. They are not suited to cooking.
- Sprouted grains are good in breads, adding a pleasant crunchy texture. Knead them in after the first rising, before shaping the loaf.
- Use chick-pea and lentil sprouts in casseroles and bakes.

Wheat berry sprouts

Chick-pea sprouts

Lentil sprouts

Aduki beansprouts

Buying and Storing: If you can, choose fresh, crisp sprouts with the seed or bean still attached. Avoid any that are slimy or musty looking. Sprouts are best eaten on the day they are bought but, if fresh, they will keep, wrapped in a plastic bag, in the fridge for 2–3 days. Rinse and pat dry before use.

Health Benefits: Sprouted seeds, pulses and grains supply rich amounts of protein, B vitamins and vitamins C and E, potassium and phosphorus which, due to the sprouting process, are in an easily digestible form. In Chinese medicine, sprouts are highly valued for their ability to cleanse and rejuvenate the system.

Tips on Sprouting

- Use whole seeds and beans as split ones will not germinate.
- Regular rinsing with fresh water and draining is essential when sprouting to prevent the beans from turning rancid and mouldy.
- Cover the sprouting jar with muslin to allow air to circulate and water in and out.
- After two or three days, the jar can be placed in sunlight to encourage the green pigment chlorophyll and increase the sprout's magnesium and fibre content.
- Soya beans and chick-pea sprouts need to be rinsed four times a day.
- Keen sprouters may wish to invest in a special sprouting container that comes with draining trays.

Sprouting container

Sea Vegetables

The West has only relatively recently acknowledged the extraordinary variety and remarkable health benefits of sea vegetables, which have been an essential part of the Asian diet for centuries. Sea vegetables are highly versatile and can be used as the main component of a dish, to add texture and substance, or as a seasoning. Some sea vegetables, such as wakame, hijiki and kombu (or kelp) can be used in soups, stews and stir-fries, while others, such as agar-agar and carrageen, are used as a setting agent in jellies, mousses and cheesecakes.

Laver

NORI

This useful sea vegetable has a delicate texture and mild flavour. It is sold in thin purple-black sheets, which turn a pretty, translucent green when toasted or cooked. It is one of the few sea vegetables that does not require soaking. Nori is processed by being chopped, flattened and dried on frames, like paper. In Japanese cooking, the sheets are used to wrap delicate, small parcels of vinegared rice and vegetables that are eaten as sushi. Once toasted and crisp, nori is crumbled and used as a garnish.

LAVER

A relation of nori, which grows outside Japan, laver is commonly found around the shores of Britain. Unlike Japanese nori, it is not cultivated. Laver is used in traditional regional cooking – particularly in Wales, Scotland and Ireland. It is cooked into a thick dark purée, which can be spread on hot toast or mixed with oatmeal to make the Welsh delicacy, laverbread. It can also be added to sauces and stuffings. Available ready-cooked in cans from health food shops, laver has a stronger flavour than nori and a higher concentration of vitamins and minerals.

Nori sheets and flakes

Toasting Nori

Nori can be toasted, over either an electric hob plate or a gas burner until it is very crisp. The sheets can then be crumbled and used as a garnish for soups, salads or stir-fries. Take care when toasting the nori sheets that you do not scorch them – or your fingers.

1 Hold a sheet of nori with a pair of tongs about 5cm/2in above an electric hot plate or gas hob for about 1 minute, moving it around so it toasts evenly and turns bright green and crisp.

2 Leave the nori sheet to cool for a few moments, then crumble. Sprinkle over salad, or use to garnish soups or stir-fries.

Arame

ARAME

Sold in delicate, black strips, arame has a mild, slightly sweet flavour and, if you haven't tried sea vegetables before, it is a good one to try. It needs to be soaked before using in stir-fries or salads, but if using in moist or slow-cooked dishes, such as noodles and soups, it can be added straight from the packet. Arame has been used to treat female disorders and is recommended for high blood pressure. It is rich in iodine, calcium and iron.

Preparing Arame

Soaking and cooking times vary depending on how the arame is to be used.

1 Rinse the arame in a sieve under cold, running water, then place in a bowl and cover with cold water. Leave to soak for 5 minutes – it should double in volume. Drain and place in a saucepan.

2 Add fresh water and bring to the boil. Simmer for 20 minutes until tender.

WAKAME

This sea vegetable is often confused with its relative, kombu, because it looks very similar until it is soaked, when it changes colour from brown to a delicate green. Wakame has a mild flavour and is one of the most versatile sea vegetables. Soak briefly and use in salads and soups or toast, crumble and use as a condiment. It is rich in calcium and vitamins B and C.

KOMBU

Known as kelp in the West, kombu is now farmed in Britain. It is a brown sea vegetable and is usually sold dried in strips, although in Japan it is available in a multitude of forms. It has a very strong flavour and is used in slowly cooked dishes, soups and stocks – it is an essential ingredient in the Japanese stock, dashi. A small strip of kombu added to beans while they are cooking will soften them and increase their digestibility as well as their nutritional value. Kombu is richer in iodine than other sea vegetables, and also contains calcium, potassium and iron.

Kombu or kelp

Wakame

Hijiki

HIJIKI

This sea vegetable looks similar to arame but is thicker and has a slightly stronger flavour. Once soaked, hijiki can be sautéed or added to soups and salads, but it does require longer cooking than most sea vegetables. It expands considerably during soaking, so only a small amount is needed. It is particularly rich in calcium and iron.

Using Agar-agar to Make Jelly

Agar-agar can be used in place of gelatine; 10g/¼oz agar-agar flakes will set about 600ml/1 pint/2½ cups liquid.

1 Place 10g/¼oz agar-agar flakes in a saucepan with 300ml/½ pint/1¼ cups cold water; leave to soak for 15 minutes.

2 Bring to the boil, then simmer for a few minutes until the flakes dissolve. Stir in 300ml/½ pint/1¼ cups fresh orange juice. Pour into a jelly mould and leave to cool, then chill until set.

DULSE

A purple-red sea vegetable, dulse has flat fronds, which have a chewy texture and spicy flavour when cooked. For hundreds of years, dulse was popular in North America and northern Europe and was traded on both sides of the Atlantic. It needs to be soaked until soft before adding to salads, noodle dishes, soups and vegetable dishes. It can also be toasted and crumbled to make a nourishing garnish. Dulse is rich in several minerals – potassium, iodine, phosphorus, iron and manganese.

AGAR-AGAR

The vegetarian equivalent to the animal-derived gelatine, agar-agar can be used as a setting agent in both sweet and savoury dishes. Known as kanten in Japan, it can be bought as flakes or strands, both of which need to be dissolved in water before use. Agar-agar has a neutral taste and its gelling abilities vary according to the other ingredients in a dish, so you may need to experiment, if substituting it for gelatine in a recipe, to achieve the best results. It is more effective than gelatine, so only a small amount is needed. It is said to be an effective laxative.

Dulse

Carrageen (left) and agar-agar flakes

CARRAGEEN

This fern-like seaweed, also known as Irish moss, is found along the Atlantic coasts of America and Europe. Like agar-agar, it has gelling properties but produces a softer set, making it useful for jellies and mousses and as a thickener in soups and stews. It is used for treating colds and bronchial problems as well as digestive disorders.

Buying and Storing: Sea vegetables are usually sold dried and will keep for months. Once the packet is opened, transfer the sea vegetables to an airtight jar. Fresh sea vegetables may be stored in the fridge, but will only remain fresh for 1–2 days. Rinse well before use.

Health Benefits: The health benefits of sea vegetables have been recognized for centuries and range from improving the lustre of hair and clarity of the skin to reducing cholesterol levels in the body. Sea vegetables are particularly rich in the antioxidant beta carotene. They contain some of the B complex vitamins, and significant amounts of the major minerals, such as calcium, magnesium, potassium, phosphorus and iron, as well as useful amounts of trace elements, such as selenium, zinc and iodine.

The rich mineral content of sea vegetables benefits the nervous system, helping to reduce stress. It also boosts the immune system, aiding the metabolism, while the iodine content prevents goitre and helps thyroid function. Research shows that alginic acid found in some seaweeds, notably kombu, arame, hijiki and wakame, binds with heavy metals, such as cadmium, lead, mercury and radium, in our intestines and helps to eliminate them.

Cook's Tip

Some sea vegetables simply need washing and soaking for a few minutes before serving or adding to dishes; others require prolonged soaking and cooking before they are tender enough to eat. Most expand considerably after soaking, so only a small amount is required.

Rolled Sushi with Mixed Filling

INGREDIENTS

320g/11½ oz/1½ cups sushi rice
4 sheets nori seaweed, for rolling
soy sauce and gari (ginger pickles), to serve

For the mixed vinegar
40ml/8 tsp rice vinegar
22.5ml/4½ tsp sugar
3ml/⅔ tsp sea salt

For the filling
4 large dried shiitake mushrooms
37.5ml/7½ tsp soy sauce
15ml/1 tbsp each of mirin, sake or dry white wine and sugar
1 small carrot, quartered lengthways
½ cucumber, quartered lengthways, seeds removed

Makes 32 pieces

1 Cook the rice in salted boiling water, then drain. Meanwhile, heat the ingredients for the mixed vinegar. Leave the vinegar to cool, then add to the hot cooked rice. Stir well with a spatula, fanning the rice constantly – this gives the rice an attractive glaze. Cover with a damp cloth and leave to cool. Do not put in the fridge, as this will make the rice harden.

2 To make the filling, soak the shiitake mushrooms in 200ml/7fl oz/scant 1 cup water for 30 minutes; drain, reserving the soaking water, and remove their stems. Pour the reserved soaking water into a saucepan and add the remaining filling ingredients (except the cucumber), then simmer for 4–5 minutes. Remove the carrot and set aside. Continue cooking until all the liquid has evaporated, then thinly slice the shiitake mushrooms and set aside for the filling.

3 Place a bamboo mat (makisu) on a chopping board. Lay a sheet of nori, shiny side down on the mat.

4 Spread a quarter of the prepared, dressed rice over the nori, using your fingers to press it down evenly. Leave a 1cm/½ in space at the top and bottom. Place a quarter of each of the filling ingredients – the sliced mushrooms, carrot and cucumber – across the middle of the layer of rice.

5 Carefully hold the nearest edge of the nori and the mat, then roll up the nori using the mat as a guide to make a neat tube of rice with the filling ingredients in the middle. Roll the rice tightly to ensure that the grains stick together and to keep the filling in place. Roll the sushi off the mat and make three more rolls in the same way.

6 Using a wet knife, cut each roll into eight pieces and stand them upright on a platter. Wipe the blade and rinse it under cold water between cuts to prevent the rice from sticking. Serve soy sauce and gari with the sushi.

Cereal Grains

Grains have been cultivated throughout the world for centuries. The seeds of cereal grasses, they are packed with concentrated goodness and are an important source of complex carbohydrates, protein, vitamins and minerals. The most popular types of grain, such as wheat, rice, oats, barley and corn or maize, come in various forms, from whole grains to flours. Inexpensive and readily available, grains are incredibly versatile and should form a major part of our diet.

Wheat

Wheat is the largest and most important grain crop in the world and has been cultivated since 7,000 BC.

The wheat kernel comprises three parts: bran, germ and endosperm. Wheat bran is the outer husk, while wheat germ is the nutritious seed from which the plant grows. Sprouted wheat is an excellent food, highly recommended in cancer prevention diets. The endosperm, the inner part of the kernel, is full of starch and protein and forms the basis of wheat flour. In addition to flour, wheat comes in various other forms.

Wholewheat berries

Wheatgrass

WHEAT BERRIES

These are whole wheat grains with the husks removed and they can be bought in health food shops. Wheat berries may be used to add a sweet, nutty flavour and chewy texture to breads, soups and stews, or can be combined with rice or other grains. Wheat berries must be soaked overnight, then cooked in boiling salted water until tender. If they are left to germinate, the berries sprout into wheatgrass, a powerful detoxifier and cleanser (see below).

WHEAT BRAN

Wheat bran is the outer husk of the wheat kernel and is a by-product of white flour production. It is very high in soluble dietary fibre, which makes it nature's most effective laxative. Wheat bran makes a healthy addition to bread doughs, breakfast cereals, cakes, muffins and biscuits, and it can also be used to add substance to stews and bakes.

Wheatgrass – a Natural Healer

Grown from the wholewheat grain, wheatgrass has been recognized for centuries for its general healing qualities. When juiced, it is a powerful detoxifier and cleanser and is a rich source of B vitamins and vitamins A, C and E, as well as all the known minerals. Its vibrant green colour comes from chlorophyl (known as "nature's healer"), which works directly on the liver to eliminate harmful toxins. It is also reputed to have anti-ageing capabilities.

Once it is juiced, wheatgrass must be consumed within 15 minutes, preferably on an empty stomach. Some people may experience nausea or dizziness when drinking the juice for the first time, but this will soon disappear.

Wheat germ

Wheat flakes

Bulgur wheat

WHEAT FLAKES

Steamed and softened berries that have been rolled and pressed are known as wheat flakes or rolled wheat. They are best used on their own or mixed with other flaked grains in porridge, as a base for muesli, or to add nutrients and substance to breads and cakes.

WHEAT GERM

The nutritious heart of the whole wheat berry, wheat germ is a rich source of protein, vitamins B and E, and iron. It is used in much the same way as wheat bran and lends a pleasant, nutty flavour to breakfast cereals and porridge. It is available toasted or untoasted. Store wheat germ in an airtight container in the fridge as it can become rancid if kept at room temperature.

CRACKED WHEAT

This is made from crushed wheat berries and retains all the nutrients of wholewheat. Often confused with bulgur wheat, cracked wheat can be used in the same way as wheat berries (although it cooks in less time), or as an alternative to rice and other grains. When cooked, it has a slightly sticky texture and pleasant crunchiness. Serve it as an accompaniment, or use in salads and pilaffs.

BULGUR WHEAT

Unlike cracked wheat, this grain is made from cooked wheat berries, which have the bran removed, and are then dried and crushed. This light, nutty grain is simply soaked in water for 20 minutes, then drained – some manufacturers specify cold water but boiling water produces a softer grain. It can also be cooked in boiling water until tender. Bulgur wheat is the main ingredient in the Middle Eastern salad, tabbouleh, where it is combined with chopped parsley, mint, tomatoes, cucumber and onion, and dressed with lemon juice and olive oil.

Cooking Wheat Berries

Wheat berries make a delicious addition to salads, and they can also be used to add texture to breads and stews.

1 Place the wheat berries in a bowl and cover with cold water. Soak overnight, then rinse thoroughly and drain.

2 Place the wheat berries in a pan with water. Bring to the boil, then cover and simmer for 1–2 hours until tender, replenishing with water when necessary.

SEMOLINA

Made from the endosperm of durum wheat, semolina can be used to make a hot milk pudding or it can be added to cakes, biscuits and breads to give them a pleasant grainy texture.

COUSCOUS

Although this looks like a grain, couscous is a form of pasta made by steaming and drying cracked durum wheat. Couscous is popular in north Africa, where it forms the basis of a national dish of the same name. Individual grains are moistened by hand, passed through a sieve and then steamed in a couscousière, suspended over a bubbling vegetable stew, until light and fluffy. Nowadays, the couscous that is generally available is the quick-cooking variety, which simply needs soaking, although it can also be steamed or baked. Couscous has a fairly bland flavour, which makes it a good foil for spicy dishes.

Semolina

Cooking Couscous

Traditionally, the preparation of couscous is a time-consuming business, requiring lengthy steaming. The couscous found in most shops nowadays, however, is precooked, which cuts the preparation time drastically.

1 Place the couscous in a large bowl, add enough boiling water to cover and leave for 10 minutes or until all the water has been absorbed. Separate the grains, season and mix in a knob of butter.

2 Alternatively, moisten the grains and place in a muslin-lined steamer. Steam for 15 minutes or until the grains are tender and fluffy.

WHEAT FLOUR

This is ground from the whole grain and may be wholemeal or white, depending on the degree of processing. Hard, or strong flour is high in a protein called gluten, which makes it ideal for bread making, while soft flour is lower in gluten but higher in starch and is better for light cakes and pastries. Durum wheat flour comes from one of the hardest varieties of wheat and is used to make pasta. Most commercial white flour is a combination of soft and hard wheat, which produces an "all-purpose" flour.

Because the refining process robs many commercial flours of most of their nutrients, the lost vitamins and minerals are synthetically replaced. When buying flour, look for brands that are unbleached and organically produced as these have fewer chemical additives. Nutritionally, stoneground wholewheat flour is the best buy because it is largely unprocessed and

Couscous

Wheat flour (left) and malted brown flour, which contains flour from malted wheat grains. Stoneground versions are available

Coeliac Disease

This is caused by an allergy to gluten, a substance found in bread, cakes, pastries and cereals. It is estimated that millions of people suffer from the disease, many without diagnosis. Symptoms may include anaemia, weight loss, fatigue, depression and diarrhoea. Wheat, rye, barley and oats are the main culprits and sufferers are usually advised to remove these completely from their diet. Rice, soya, buckwheat, quinoa, millet and corn are gluten-free substitutes.

retains all the valuable nutrients. It produces slightly heavier breads, cakes and pastries than white flour, but can be combined with white flour to make lighter versions, although, of course, the nutritional value will not be as high.

SEITAN

Used as a meat replacement, seitan is made from wheat gluten and has a firm, chewy texture. It can be found in the chiller cabinet of health food shops. Seitan has a neutral flavour that benefits from marinating. Slice or cut into chunks and stir-fry, or add to stews and pasta sauces during the last few minutes of cooking time. Seitan does not need to be cooked for long, just heated through.

Buying and Storing: Buy wheat-based foods from shops with a high turnover of stock. Wheat berries can be kept for around 6 months, but wholewheat flour should be used within 3 months, as its oils turn rancid. Always decant grains into airtight containers and store in a cool, dark place. Wheat germ deteriorates very quickly at room temperature and should be stored in an airtight container in the fridge for no more than a month.

Health Benefits: Wheat is most nutritious when it is unprocessed and in its whole form. (When milled into white flour, wheat loses a staggering 80 per cent of its nutrients.) Wheat is an excellent source of dietary fibre, the B vitamins and vitamin E, as well as iron, selenium and zinc. Fibre is the most discussed virtue of whole wheat and most of this is concentrated in the bran. Eating one or more spoonfuls of bran a day is recommended to relieve constipation. Numerous studies show fibre to be effective in inhibiting colon and rectal cancer, varicose veins, haemorrhoids and obesity. Phytoestrogens found in wholegrains may also ward off breast cancer. On the negative side, wheat is also a well-known allergen and triggers coeliac disease, a gluten intolerance.

Seitan

Rice

Throughout Asia, a meal is considered incomplete without rice. It is a staple food for over half the world's population, and almost every culture has its own repertoire of rice dishes, ranging from risottos to pilaffs. What's more, this valuable food provides a good source of vitamins and minerals, as well as a steady supply of energy.

White and brown long grain rice

Jasmine fragrant rice

LONG GRAIN RICE

The most widely used type of rice is long grain rice, where the grain is five times as long as it is wide. Long grain brown rice has had its outer husk removed, leaving the bran and germ intact, which gives it a chewy nutty flavour. It takes longer to cook than white rice but contains more fibre, vitamins and minerals. Long grain white rice has had its husk, bran and germ removed, taking most of the nutrients with them and leaving a bland-flavoured rice that is light and fluffy when cooked. It is often whitened with chalk, talc or other preservatives, so rinsing is essential. Easy-cook long grain white rice, sometimes called parboiled or converted rice, has been steamed under pressure. This process hardens the grain and makes it difficult to overcook, and some nutrients are transferred from the bran and germ into the kernel during this process. Easy-cook brown rice cooks more quickly than normal brown rice.

JASMINE RICE

This rice has a soft, sticky texture and a delicious, mildly perfumed flavour – which accounts for its other name, fragrant rice. It is a long grain rice that is widely used in Thai cooking, where its delicate flavour tempers strongly spiced food.

Cooking Long Grain Brown Rice

There are many methods and opinions on how to cook rice. The absorption method is one of the simplest and retains valuable nutrients, which would otherwise be lost in cooking water that is drained away.

Different types of rice have different powers of absorption, however the general rule of thumb for long grain rice is to use double the quantity of water to rice. For example, use 1 cup of rice to 2 cups of water. 200g/7oz/1 cup long grain rice is sufficient for about four people as a side dish.

1 Rinse the rice in a sieve under cold, running water. Place in a heavy-based saucepan and add the measured cold water. Bring to the boil, uncovered, then reduce the heat and stir the rice. Add salt, to taste, if you wish.

2 Cover the pan with a tight-fitting lid. Simmer for 25–35 minutes, without removing the lid, until the water is absorbed and the rice tender. Remove from the heat and leave to stand, covered, for 5 minutes before serving.

Red rice

Wild rice

RED RICE

This rice comes from the Camargue in France and has a distinctive chewy texture and a nutty flavour. It is an unusually hard grain, which although it takes about an hour to cook, retains its shape. Cooking intensifies its red colour, making it a distinctive addition to salads and stuffings.

WILD RICE

This is not a true rice but an aquatic grass grown in North America. It has dramatic, long, slender brown-black grains that have a nutty flavour and chewy texture. It takes longer to cook than most types of rice – from 35–60 minutes, depending on whether you like it chewy or tender – but you can reduce the cooking time by soaking it in water overnight. Wild rice is extremely nutritious. It contains all eight essential amino acids and is particularly rich in lysine. It is a good source of fibre, low in calories and gluten free. Use in stuffings, serve plain or mix with other rices in pilaffs and rice salads.

BASMATI RICE

This is a slender, long grain rice, which is grown in the foothills of the Himalayas. It is aged for a year after harvest, giving it a characteristic light, fluffy texture and aromatic flavour. Its name means "fragrant".

Both white and brown types of basmati rice are available. Brown basmati contains more nutrients, and has a slightly nuttier flavour than the white variety. Widely used in Indian cooking, basmati rice has a cooling effect on hot and spicy curries. It is also excellent for biryanis and for rice salads, when you want very light, fluffy separate grains.

White and brown basmati rice

Quick Ways to Flavour Rice

• Cook brown rice in vegetable stock with sliced dried apricots. Sauté an onion in a little oil and add ground cumin, coriander and fresh chopped chilli, then mix in the cooked rice.

• Add raisins and toasted almonds to saffron-infused rice.

Valencia rice

Quick Ways to Flavour Risotto

• When making risotto, replace a quarter of the vegetable stock with red or white wine.

• Add a bay leaf, the juice and zest of a lemon, or a lemon grass stalk and cardamom pods to the cooking water.
• Saffron adds a yellow colour to risotto rice. Add a few strands to the vegetable stock.

VALENCIA RICE

Traditionally used for making Spanish paella, this short grain rice is not as sturdy as risotto rice and needs to be handled with care because it breaks down easily. The best way of cooking paella is to leave the rice unstirred once all the ingredients are in the pan.

RISOTTO RICE

To make Italian risotto, it is essential that you use a special, fat, short grain rice. Arborio rice, which originates from the Po Valley region in Italy, is the most widely sold variety of risotto rice, but you may also find varieties such as Carnaroli and Vialone Nano in specialist shops. When cooked, most rice absorbs around three times its weight in water, but risotto rice can absorb nearly five times its weight, and the result is a creamy grain that still retains a slight bite.

Above: Clockwise from left, arborio, carnaroli and vialone nano risotto rice

Making a Simple Risotto

A good risotto, which is creamy and moist with tender grains that retain a slight bite, is easy to make. The secrets are to use the correct type of rice (arborio, carnaroli, or vialone nano); to add the cooking liquid gradually – it should be completely absorbed by the rice before the next ladleful is added; and to stir the risotto frequently to prevent the grains sticking to the pan.

INGREDIENTS

15ml/1 tbsp olive oil
small knob of butter
1 onion, finely chopped
350g/12oz/1¾ cups risotto rice
1.2 litres/2 pints/5 cups hot vegetable stock
50g/2oz/⅔ cup freshly grated Parmesan cheese
salt and freshly ground black pepper

SERVES 4

Variations

- Add finely chopped cooked (not pickled) beetroot towards the end of the cooking time to give the rice a vibrant pink colour and slight sweetness.
- To make mushroom and broccoli risotto, sauté 175g/6oz/2 cups sliced or chopped flat mushrooms with the onion. Blanch 225g/8oz/2 cups broccoli florets for 3 minutes until tender, and add towards the end of cooking time.

1 Heat the oil and butter in a large, heavy-based pan, then cook the onion for 7 minutes until soft, stirring occasionally. Add the rice and stir to coat the grains in the hot oil and butter.

2 Add a quarter of the stock and cook over a low-medium heat, stirring frequently, until the liquid is absorbed. Add more stock, a little at a time, stirring, until all the liquid is added and absorbed.

3 After about 20 minutes, the grains will be creamy but still retain a bite. Turn off the heat, stir in the Parmesan and check the seasoning. Add salt and pepper to taste and serve immediately.

Japanese Rice Products

The Japanese are extremely resourceful when it comes to exploiting the vast potential of rice.

Sake This spirit is Japan's national drink, it can also be used in cooking.

Mirin Sweet rice wine that is delicious in marinades and savoury dishes, and is a key ingredient in teriyaki.

Rice vinegar Popular throughout Asia, this ranges in colour from white to brown. Japanese rice vinegar has a mild, mellow flavour. The Chinese version is much harsher.

Amasake A healthful rice drink made by adding enzymes from fermented rice to wholegrain pudding rice. It has a similar consistency to soya "milk" and can be flavoured. Amasake may be used for baking or to make creamy desserts. It is also an excellent and easily digestible weaning food.

Right, clockwise from top left: amasake, mirin, rice vinegar and sake.

PUDDING RICE

This rounded, short grain rice is suitable for milk puddings and rice desserts. The grains swell and absorb a great deal of milk during cooking, which gives the pudding a soft, creamy consistency. Brown pudding rice is also available.

GLUTINOUS RICE

This rice is almost round in shape and has a slightly sweet flavour. Despite its name, the rice is gluten-free. The grains stick together when cooked due to their high starch content, making the rice easier to eat with chopsticks.

Glutinous rice, which can be either white, black or purple, is used in many South-east Asian countries to make sticky, creamy puddings. In China, white glutinous rice is often wrapped in lotus leaves and steamed to make a popular dim sum dish.

Pudding rice

White and black glutinous rice

JAPANESE SUSHI RICE

Similar to glutinous rice, this is mixed with rice vinegar to make sushi. Most sushi rice eaten in the West is grown in California.

Sushi rice

Buying and Storing: To ensure freshness, always buy rice from shops that have a regular turnover of stock. Store in an airtight container in a cool, dry, dark place to keep out moisture and insects. Wash before use to remove any impurities. Cooked rice should be cooled quickly, then chilled and reheated thoroughly before serving.

Health Benefits: Rice is a valuable source of complex carbohydrates and fibre. In its whole form it is a good source of B vitamins. White rice is deprived of much of its nutrients because the bran and germ have been removed. The starch in rice is absorbed slowly, keeping blood sugar levels on an even keel and making it an important food for diabetics. Research shows that rice may benefit sufferers of psoriasis. It can also be used to treat digestive disorders, calm the nervous system, prevent kidney stones and reduce the risk of bowel cancer. However, the phytates found in brown rice can inhibit the absorption of iron and calcium.

Quick Ideas for Rice

Rice can be served plain, but it is also good in one-dish meals, marrying well with a host of exotic flavourings and simple store-cupboard ingredients.

- To make a Middle-Eastern inspired rice dish, cook long grain brown rice in vegetable stock, then stir in some toasted flaked almonds, pieces of dried date and fig, cooked chick-peas, and chopped fresh mint.
- For a simple pullao, gently fry a finely chopped onion in sunflower oil with cardamom pods, a cinnamon stick and cloves, then stir in basmati rice. Add water, infused with a pinch of saffron, and cook until tender. Towards the end of the cooking time, add sultanas and cashew nuts, then garnish with chopped fresh coriander.

Rice Products

Rice flakes These are made by steaming and rolling whole or white grains. They are light and quick-cooking, and can be added raw to muesli or used to make porridge, creamy puddings, bread, biscuits and cakes.

Rice bran Like wheat and oat bran, rice bran comes from the husk of the grain kernel. It is high in soluble dietary fibre and useful for adding texture and substance to bread, cakes and biscuits, and stews.

Rice flour Often used to make sticky Asian cakes and sweets, rice flour can also be used to thicken sauces. Because rice flour does not contain gluten, cakes made with it are rather flat. It can be combined with wheat flour to make cakes and bread, but produces a crumbly loaf. Rice powder is a very fine rice flour, found in Asian shops.

Right, clockwise from top left: rice bran, rice flour, rice powder and rice flakes.

Other Grains

Wheat and rice are undoubtedly the most widely used grains, yet there are others such as oats, rye, corn, barley, quinoa and spelt, that should not be ignored, because they provide variety in our diet and are packed with nutrients. Grains come in many forms, from whole grains to flour and are used for baking, breakfast cereals and cooked dishes.

OATS

Available rolled, flaked, as oatmeal or oatbran, oats are warming and sustaining when cooked. Like rye, oats are a popular grain in northern Europe, particularly Scotland, where they are commonly turned into porridge, oatcakes and pancakes.

Whole oats are unprocessed with the nutritious bran and germ remaining intact. Oat groats are the hulled, whole kernel, while rolled oats are made from groats that have been heated and pressed flat. Quick-cooking rolled oats have been pre-cooked in water and then dried, which diminishes their nutritional value. Medium oatmeal is best in cakes and breads, while fine is ideal in pancakes, and fruit and milk drinks. Oat-meal and oat flour contain very little gluten so should be mixed with wheat flour to make leavened bread. Oat bran can be sprinkled over breakfast cereals and mixed into plain or fruit yogurt.

Health Benefits: Oats are perhaps the most nutritious of.all the grains. Recent research has focused on the ability of oat bran to reduce blood cholesterol (sometimes with dramatic results), while beneficial HDL cholesterol levels increase. For best results, oat bran should be eaten daily at regular intervals.

High in fibre, oats are an effective laxative and also feature protease inhibitors, a combination that has been found to inhibit certain cancers. Oats also contain vitamin E and some B vitamins, as well as iron, calcium, magnesium, phosphorus and potassium.

Below, clockwise from top left: rolled oats, oatmeal, whole oats and oat bran

Rye: grain and flour

RYE

The most popular grain for bread-making in Eastern Europe, Scandinavia and Russia, rye flour produces a dark, dense and dry loaf that keeps well. It is a hardy grain, which grows where most others fail – hence its popularity in colder climates. Rye is low in gluten and so rye flour is often mixed with high-gluten wheat flours to create lighter textured breads; the colour of which is sometimes intensified using molasses.The whole grain can be soaked overnight, then cooked in boiling water until tender, but the flour, with its robust, full flavour and greyish colour, is the most commonly used form.The flour ranges from dark to light, depending on whether the bran and germ have been removed.

Health Benefits: Rye is a good source of vitamin E and some B vitamins, as well as protein, calcium, iron, phosphorus and potassium. It is also high in fibre, and is used in natural medicine to help to strengthen the digestive system.

CORN

Although we are most familiar with yellow corn or maize, blue, red, black and even multi-coloured varieties can also be found. Corn is an essential store-cupboard ingredient in the USA, the Caribbean and Italy, and comes in many forms.

Masa harina

Maize meal, or masa harina, is made from the cooked whole grain, which is ground into flour and commonly used to make the Mexican flat bread, tortilla.

Cornmeal

The main culinary uses for cornmeal are cornbread, a classic, southern American bread, and polenta, which confusingly is both the Italian name for cornmeal as well as a dish made with the grain. Polenta (the cooked dish) is a thick, golden porridge, which is often flavoured with butter and

Making Polenta

Polenta makes an excellent alternative to mashed potato. It needs plenty of seasoning and is even better with a knob of butter and cheese, such as Parmesan, Gorgonzola or Taleggio. Serve with stews or casseroles.

1 Pour 1 litre/1¾ pints/4 cups water into a heavy-based saucepan and bring to the boil. Remove from the heat.

2 In a steady stream, gradually add 185g/6½oz/1½ cups instant polenta and mix with a balloon whisk to avoid any lumps forming.

3 Return the pan to the heat and cook, stirring continuously with a wooden spoon, until the polenta is thick and creamy and starts to come away from the sides of the pan – this will only take a few minutes if you are using instant polenta.

4 Season to taste with salt and plenty of ground black pepper, then add a generous knob of butter and mix well. Remove from the heat and stir in the cheese, if using.

Clockwise from top left: Blue and yellow cornmeal, cornflour, popcorn masa harina and polenta

cheese or chopped herbs. Once cooked, polenta can also be left to cool, then cut into slabs and fried, barbecued or griddled until golden brown. It is delicious with roasted vegetables. Ready-to-slice polenta is available from some supermarkets.

Polenta grain comes in various grades, ranging from fine to coarse. You can buy polenta that takes 40–45 minutes to cook or an "instant" part-cooked version that can be cooked in less than 5 minutes.

In the Caribbean, cornmeal is used to make puddings and dumplings.

Cornflour

This fine white powder is a useful thickening agent for sauces, soups and casseroles. It can also be added to cakes.

Hominy

These are the husked whole grains of corn. They should be cooked in boiling water until softened, then used in stews and soups, or added to cakes and muffins.

Grits

Coarsely ground, dried yellow or white corn is known as grits. Use for porridge and pancakes or add to baked goods.

Popcorn

This is a separate strain of corn that is grown specifically to make the popular snack food. The kernel's hard outer casing explodes when heated.

Quinoa

Popcorn can easily be made at home and flavoured sweet or savoury according to taste. The shop-bought types are often high in salt or sugar.

Health Benefits: In American folk medicine, corn is considered a diuretic and a mild stimulant. Corn is said to prevent cancer of the colon, breast and prostate and to lower the risk of heart disease. It is believed to be the only grain that contains vitamin A as well as some of the B vitamins and iron.

BARLEY

Believed to be the oldest cultivated grain, barley is still a fundamental part of the everyday diet in Eastern Europe, the Middle East and Asia.

Pearl barley, the most usual form, is husked, steamed and then polished to give it its characteristic ivory-coloured appearance. It has a mild, sweet flavour and chewy texture, and can be added to soups, stews and bakes. It is also used to make old-fashioned barley water.

Pot barley is the whole grain with just the inedible outer husk removed. It takes much longer to cook than pearl barley. Barley flakes, which make a satisfying porridge, and barley flour are also available.

Health Benefits: Pot barley is more nutritious than pearl barley, because it contains extra fibre, calcium, phosphorus, iron, magnesium and B vitamins. Barley was once used to increase potency and boost physical strength. More recently, studies have shown that its fibre content may help to prevent constipation and other digestive problems, as well as heart disease and certain cancers. In addition, the protease inhibitors in barley have been found to suppress cancer of the intestines, and eating barley regularly may also reduce the amount of harmful cholesterol produced by the liver.

Clockwise from left, pot barley, barley flakes and pearl barley

Lemon Barley Water

INGREDIENTS

225g/8oz/1 cup pearl barley
1.75 litres/3 pints/7½ cups water
grated rind of 1 lemon
50g/2oz/¼ cup golden caster sugar
juice of 2 lemons

1 Rinse the barley, then place in a large saucepan and cover with the water. Bring to the boil, then reduce the heat and simmer gently for 20 minutes, skimming off any scum from time to time. Remove the pan from the heat.

2 Add the lemon rind and sugar to the pan, stir well and leave to cool. Strain, and add the lemon juice.

3 Taste the lemon barley water and add more sugar, if necessary. Serve chilled with ice and slices of lemon.

QUINOA

Hailed as the supergrain of the future, quinoa (pronounced "keen-wa") is a grain of the past. It was called "the mother grain" by the Incas, who cultivated it for hundreds of years, high in the Andes, solely for their own use.

Nowadays, quinoa is widely available. The tiny, bead-shaped grains have a mild, slightly bitter taste and firm texture. It is cooked in the same way as rice, but the grains quadruple in size, becoming translucent with an unusual white outer ring. Quinoa is useful for making stuffings, pilaffs, bakes and breakfast cereals.

Health Benefits: Quinoa's supergrain status hails from its rich nutritional value. Unlike other grains, quinoa is a complete protein because it contains all eight essential amino acids. It is an excellent source of calcium, potassium and zinc as well as iron, magnesium and B vitamins. It is particularly valuable for people with coeliac disease as it is gluten-free.

MILLET

Although millet is usually associated with bird food, it is a highly nutritious grain. It once rivalled barley as the main food of Europe and remains a staple ingredient in many parts of the world, including Africa, China and India. Its mild flavour makes it an ideal accompaniment to spicy stews and curries, and it can be used as a base for pilaffs or milk puddings. The tiny, firm grains can also be flaked or ground into flour. Millet is gluten-free, so it is a useful food for people with coeliac disease. The flour can be used for baking, but needs to be combined with high-gluten flours to make leavened bread.

Health Benefits: Millet is an easily digestible grain. It contains more iron than other grains and is a good source of zinc, calcium, manganese and B vitamins. It is believed to be beneficial to those suffering from candidiasis, a fungal infection caused by the yeast *Candida albicans*.

Millet

Amaranth

BUCKWHEAT

In spite of its name, buckwheat is not a type of wheat, but is actually related to the rhubarb family. Available plain or toasted, it has a nutty, earthy flavour. It is a staple food in Eastern Europe as well as Russia, where the triangular grain is milled into a speckled-grey flour and used to make blini. The flour is also used in Japan for soba noodles and in Italy for pasta. Buckwheat pancakes are popular in parts of the USA and France. The whole grain, which is also known as kasha, makes a fine porridge or a creamy pudding.

Health Benefits: Like quinoa, buckwheat is a complete protein. It contains all eight essential amino acids as well as rutin, which aids circulation and helps treat high blood pressure. It is an excellent, sustaining cereal, rich in both iron and some of the B complex vitamins. It is also reputed to be good for the lungs, the kidneys and the bladder. Buckwheat is gluten-free, and so is useful for people who suffer from coeliac disease.

LESSER-KNOWN GRAINS

There are several other grains that deserve a mention, as they are not only becoming more popular, but also are often far richer in nutrients than their better-known counterparts.

Amaranth

This plant, which is native to Mexico, is unusual in that it can be eaten as both a vegetable and a grain. Like quinoa, amaranth is considered a supergrain due to its excellent nutritional content. The tiny pale seed or "grain" has a strong and distinctive, peppery flavour. It is best used in stews and soups, or it can be ground into flour to make bread, pastries and biscuits. The flour is gluten-free and has to be mixed with wheat or another flour that contains gluten to make leavened bread. Amaranth leaves are similar to spinach and can be cooked or eaten raw in salads.

Health Benefits: Although its taste may take some getting used to, the nutritional qualities of amaranth more than make up for it. It has more protein than pulses and is rich in amino acids, particularly lysine. Amaranth is also high in iron and calcium.

Kamut

An ancient relative of wheat, this grain has long, slender, brown kernels with a creamy, nutty flavour. It is as versatile as wheat and, when ground into flour, can be used to make pasta, breads, cakes and pastry. Puffed kamut cereals and kamut crackers are available in health food shops.

Above, plain buckwheat, buckwheat flour and toasted buckwheat

Health Benefits: Kamut has a higher nutritional value than wheat and is easier to digest. Although it contains gluten, people suffering from coeliac disease have found that they can tolerate the grain if eaten in moderation.

Sorghum

This grain is best known for its thick sweet syrup, which is used in cakes and desserts. The grain is similar to millet and is an important, extremely nutritious staple food in Africa and India. It can be used much like rice, and when ground into flour is used to make unleavened bread.

Health Benefits: Sorghum is a useful source of calcium, iron and B vitamins.

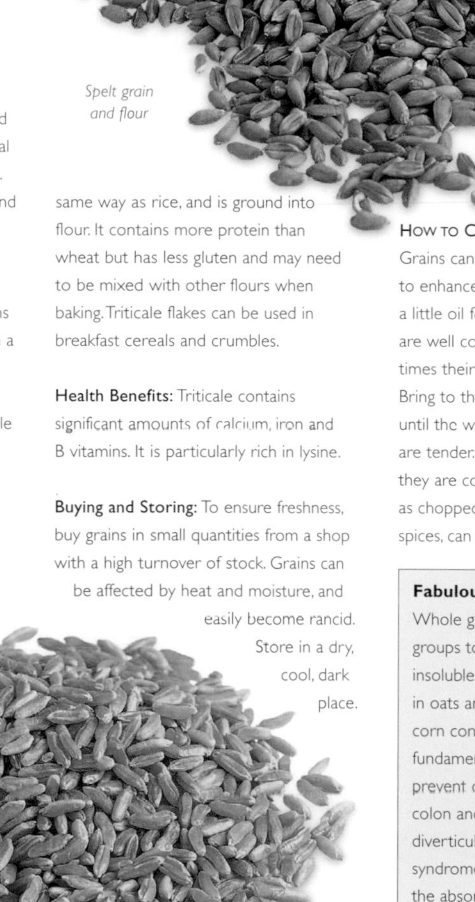

Spelt grain and flour

Spelt

This is one of the most ancient cultivated wheats and, because of its high nutritional value, is becoming more widely available. Spelt grain looks very similar to wheat and the flour can be substituted for wheat flour in bread.

Health Benefits: Spelt is richer in vitamins and minerals than wheat, and they are in a more readily digestible form. Although spelt contains gluten, it usually can be tolerated in moderate amounts by people suffering from coeliac disease.

Triticale

A hybrid of wheat and rye, triticale was created by Swedish researchers in 1875. It has a sweet, nutty taste and chewy texture and can be used in the same way as rice, and is ground into flour. It contains more protein than wheat but has less gluten and may need to be mixed with other flours when baking. Triticale flakes can be used in breakfast cereals and crumbles.

Health Benefits: Triticale contains significant amounts of calcium, iron and B vitamins. It is particularly rich in lysine.

Buying and Storing: To ensure freshness, buy grains in small quantities from a shop with a high turnover of stock. Grains can be affected by heat and moisture, and easily become rancid. Store in a dry, cool, dark place.

Kamut

How to Cook Grains

Grains can be simply boiled in water but, to enhance their flavour, first cook them in a little oil for a few minutes. When they are well coated in oil, add two or three times their volume of water or stock. Bring to the boil, then simmer, covered, until the water is absorbed and the grains are tender. Do not disturb the grains while they are cooking. Other flavourings, such as chopped herbs and whole or ground spices, can be added to the cooking liquid.

Fabulous Fibre

Whole grains are one of the few food groups to contain both soluble and insoluble fibre. The former is prevalent in oats and rye, while wheat, rice and corn contain insoluble fibre. Both are fundamental to good health and may prevent constipation, ulcers, colitis, colon and rectal cancer, heart disease, diverticulitis and irritable bowel syndrome. Soluble fibre slows down the absorption of energy from the gut, which means there are no sudden demands on insulin, making it especially important for diabetics.

Legumes

Lentils, peas and pulses provide the cook with a diverse range of flavours and textures. They have long been a staple food in the Middle East, South America, India and the Mediterranean, but there is hardly a country that does not have its own favourite legume-based dish, from Boston baked beans in the USA to lentil dahl in India. In Mexico, they are spiced and used to make refried beans, while in China they are fermented for black bean and yellow bean sauces. Low in fat and high in complex carbohydrates, vitamins and minerals, legumes are also an important source of protein for vegetarians and, when eaten with cereals, easily match animal-based sources.

Lentils and Peas

The humble lentil is one of our oldest foods. It originated in Asia and north Africa and continues to be cultivated in those regions, as well as in France and Italy. Lentils are hard even when fresh, so they are always sold dried. Unlike most other pulses, they do not need soaking.

Red lentils

Puy lentils

GREEN AND BROWN LENTILS

Sometimes referred to as continental lentils, these disc-shaped pulses retain their shape when cooked. They take longer to cook than split lentils – about 40–45 minutes – and are ideal for adding to warm salads, casseroles and stuffings. Alternatively green and brown lentils can be cooked and blended with herbs or spices to make a nutritious pâté.

PUY LENTILS

These tiny, dark, blue-green, marbled lentils grow in the Auvergne region in central France. They are considered to be far superior in taste and texture than other varieties, and they retain their bead-like shape during cooking, which takes around 25–30 minutes. Puy lentils are a delicious addition to simple dishes such as warm salads, and are also good braised in wine and flavoured with fresh herbs.

RED LENTILS

Orange-coloured red split lentils, sometimes known as Egyptian lentils, are the most familiar variety. They cook in just 20 minutes, eventually disintegrating into a thick purée. They are ideal for thickening soups and casseroles and, when cooked with spices, make a delicious dahl. In the Middle East, red or yellow lentils are cooked and mixed with spices and vegetables to form balls known as *kofte*.

YELLOW LENTILS

Less well-known yellow lentils taste very similar to the red variety and are used in much the same way.

PEAS

Dried peas come from the field pea not the garden pea, which is eaten fresh. Unlike lentils, peas are soft when young and require drying. They are available whole or split; the latter have a sweeter flavour and cook more quickly. Like split lentils, split peas do not hold their shape when cooked, making them perfect for dahls, purées, casseroles and

Green and brown lentils

Cooking Lentils

Lentils are easy to cook and don't need to be soaked. Split red and green lentils cook down to a soft consistency, while whole lentils hold their shape when cooked.

Green, Brown and Puy Lentils

1 Place 250g/9oz/generous 1 cup whole lentils in a sieve and rinse under cold running water. Tip into a saucepan.

2 Cover with water and bring to the boil. Simmer for 25–30 minutes until tender, replenishing the water if necessary. Drain and season with salt and freshly ground black pepper.

Split Red and Yellow Lentils

1 Place 250g/9oz/generous 1 cup split lentils in a sieve and rinse under cold running water. Tip into a saucepan.

2 Cover with 600ml/1 pint/2½ cups water and bring to the boil. Simmer for 20–25 minutes, stirring occasionally, until the water is absorbed and the lentils are tender. Season to taste.

soups. They take about 45 minutes to cook. Marrow fat peas are larger in size and are used to make the traditional British dish "mushy" peas. Like other whole peas, they require soaking overnight before use.

Buying and Storing: Although lentils and peas can be kept for up to a year, they toughen with time. Buy from shops with a fast turnover of stock and store in airtight containers in a cool, dark place. Look for bright, unwrinkled pulses that are not dusty. Rinse well before use.

Health Benefits: Lentils and peas share an impressive range of nutrients including iron, selenium, folate, manganese, zinc, phosphorus and some B vitamins. Extremely low in fat and richer in protein than most pulses, lentils and peas are reputed to be important in fighting heart disease by reducing harmful LDL cholesterol in the body. They are high in fibre, which aids the functioning of the bowels and colon. Fibre also slows down the rate at which sugar enters the bloodstream, providing a steady supply of energy, which can help control diabetes.

Marrow fat peas (above) and yellow and green split peas

Cook's Tip

Avoid adding salt to the water when cooking lentils and peas as this prevents them softening. Season when cooked.

Pulses

The edible seeds from plants belonging to the legume family, pulses, which include chick-peas and a vast range of beans, are packed with protein, vitamins, minerals and fibre, and are extremely low in fat. For the cook, their ability to absorb the flavours of other foods means that pulses can be used as the base for an infinite number of dishes. Most pulses require soaking overnight in cold water before use, so it is wise to plan ahead if using the dried type.

Aduki beans

BLACK BEANS

These shiny, black, kidney-shaped beans are often used in Caribbean cooking. They have a sweetish flavour, and their distinctive colour adds a dramatic touch to soups, mixed bean salads or casseroles.

ADUKI BEANS

Also known as adzuki beans, these tiny, deep-red beans have a sweet, nutty flavour and are popular in Oriental dishes. In Chinese cooking, they form the base of red bean paste. Known as the "king of beans" in Japan, the aduki bean is reputed to be good for the liver and kidneys. They cook quickly and can be used in casseroles and bakes. They are also ground into flour for use in cakes, breads and pastries.

BLACK-EYED BEANS

Known as black-eye peas or cow peas in the USA, black-eyed beans are an essential ingredient in Creole cooking and some spicy Indian curries. The small, creamy-coloured bean is characterized by the black spot on its side where it was once attached to the pod. Good in soups and salads, they can also be added to savoury bakes and casseroles, and can be used in place of haricot or cannellini beans in a wide variety of dishes.

Black beans (above), black-eyed beans (centre) and borlotti beans

Cannellini Bean Purée

Cooked cannellini beans make a delicious herb- and garlic-flavoured purée. Serve spread on toasted pitta bread or to use as a dip with chunky raw vegetable crudités.

INGREDIENTS

400g/14oz/2½ cups canned or 200g/7oz/1¼ cups dried cannellini beans
30ml/2 tbsp olive oil
1 large garlic clove, finely chopped
2 shallots, finely chopped
75ml/5 tbsp vegetable stock
30ml/2 tbsp chopped fresh flat leaf parsley
15ml/1 tbsp snipped fresh chives
salt and freshly ground black pepper

SERVES 4

1 If using dried beans, soak them overnight in cold water, then drain and rinse. Place in a saucepan and cover with cold water, then bring to the boil and boil rapidly for 10 minutes. Reduce the heat and simmer for about 1 hour, or until tender. If using canned beans, rinse and drain well.

2 Heat the oil in a saucepan and sauté the garlic and shallots for about 5 minutes, stirring occasionally, until soft. Add the beans, stock, parsley and seasoning, then cook for a few minutes until heated through.

3 To make a course purée, mash the beans with a potato masher. Alternatively, place in a food processor and blend until thick and smooth. Serve sprinkled with snipped chives.

Butter beans

> **The F Word**
>
> Many people are put off eating beans due to their unfortunate side effects. The propensity of beans to cause flatulence stems from the gases they produce in the gut. This can be reduced by following these guidelines:
>
> • Never cook pulses in their soaking water as it contains indigestible sugars.
>
> • Skim off any scum that forms on the surface of the water during cooking.
>
> • Add "digestive" spices, such as dill, asafoetida, ginger and caraway, to the cooking water.

BORLOTTI BEANS

These oval beans have red-streaked, pinkish-brown skin and a bitter-sweet flavour. When cooked, they have a tender, moist texture, which is good in Italian bean and pasta soups, as well as hearty vegetable stews. In most recipes, they are interchangeable with red kidney beans.

BROAD BEANS

These large beans were first cultivated by the ancient Egyptians. Usually eaten in their fresh form, broad beans change in colour from green to brown when dried, making them difficult to recognize in their dried state. The outer skin can be very tough and chewy, and some people prefer to remove it after cooking. They can also be bought ready-skinned.

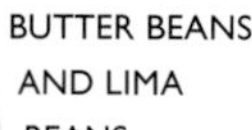

Cannellini beans

Broad beans

BUTTER BEANS AND LIMA BEANS

Similar in flavour and appearance, both butter beans and lima beans are characterized by their flattish, kidney shape and soft, floury texture. Cream-coloured butter beans are familiar in Britain and Greece, while lima beans are popular in the USA.

In Greek cooking, butter beans are oven-baked with tomato, garlic and olive oil until tender and creamy. The pale-green lima bean is the main ingredient in succotash, an American dish that also includes sweetcorn kernels. Butter and lima beans are also good with creamy herb sauces. Care should be taken not to overcook both butter and lima beans as they become pulpy and mushy in texture.

CANNELLINI BEANS

These small, white, kidney-shaped beans have a soft, creamy texture when cooked and are popular in Italian cooking. They can be used in place of haricot beans and, when dressed with olive oil, lemon juice, crushed garlic and fresh chopped parsley, make an excellent warm salad.

CHICK-PEAS

Also known as garbanzo beans, robust and hearty chick-peas resemble shelled hazelnuts and have a delicious nutty flavour and creamy texture. They need lengthy cooking and are much used in Mediterranean and Middle Eastern cooking. In India, they are known as gram and are ground into flour to make fritters and flat breads. Gram flour, also called besan, can be found in health food shops and Asian grocery stores.

Chick-peas

FLAGEOLET BEANS

These young haricot beans are removed from the pod before they are fully ripe, hence their fresh delicate flavour. A pretty, mint-green colour, they are the most expensive bean to buy and are best treated simply. Cook them until they are tender, then season and drizzle with a little olive oil and lemon juice.

HARICOT BEANS

Most commonly used for canned baked beans, these versatile, ivory-coloured beans are small and oval in shape. Called navy or Boston beans in the USA, they suit slow-cooked dishes, such as casseroles and bakes.

PINTO BEANS

A smaller, paler version of the borlotti bean, the savoury-tasting pinto has an attractive speckled skin – it is aptly called the painted bean. One of the many relatives of the kidney bean, pinto beans feature extensively in Mexican cooking, most familiarly in refried beans, when they are cooked until tender and fried with garlic, chilli and tomatoes. The beans are then mashed, resulting in a wonderful, spicy, rough purée that is usually served with warm tortillas. Soured cream and garlic-flavoured guacamole are good accompaniments.

RED KIDNEY BEANS

Glossy, mahogany-red kidney beans retain their colour and shape when cooked. They have a soft, "mealy" texture and are much used in South American cooking. An essential ingredient in spicy chillies, they can also be used to make refried beans (although this dish is traditionally made from pinto beans). Cooked kidney beans can be used to make a variety of salads, but they are especially good combined with red onion and chopped flat leaf parsley and mint, then tossed in an olive oil dressing.

It is essential to follow the cooking instructions when preparing kidney beans as they contain a substance that causes severe food poisoning if they are not boiled vigorously for 10–15 minutes.

Above, clockwise from left: haricot beans, red kidney beans, flageolet beans and pinto beans

Cooking Kidney Beans

Most types of beans, with the exception of aduki beans and mung beans, require soaking for 5–6 hours or overnight and then boiling rapidly for 10–15 minutes to remove any harmful toxins. This is particularly important for kidney beans, which can cause serious food poisoning if not treated in this way.

1 Wash the beans well, then place in a bowl that allows plenty of room for expansion. Cover with cold water and leave to soak overnight or for 8–12 hours, then drain and rinse.

2 Place the beans in a large saucepan and cover with fresh cold water. Bring to the boil and boil rapidly for 10–15 minutes, then reduce the heat and simmer for 1–1½ hours until tender. Drain and serve.

The Flatulence-free Bean

The American space programme NASA is involved in research into flatulence-free foods. One such food is the manteca bean, discovered by Dr Colin Leakey in Chile. This small, yellow bean is flatulence-free and easy to digest. It is now being grown both in Cambridgeshire, England and the Channel Islands, and should become more widely available, called either manteca beans or Jersey yellow beans.

FUL MEDAMES

A member of the broad bean family, these small Egyptian beans form the base of the national dish of the same name, in which they are flavoured with ground cumin and then baked with olive oil, garlic and lemon, and served topped with hard-boiled egg. They have a strong, nutty flavour and tough, light brown outer skin. Ful medames need to be soaked overnight in cold water, then cooked slowly for about 1 hour until soft.

Ful medames

SOYA BEANS

These small, oval beans vary in colour from creamy-yellow through brown to black. In China, they are known as "meat of the earth" and were once considered sacred. Soya beans contain all the nutritional properties of animal products but without the disadvantages. They are extremely dense and need to be soaked for 12 hours before cooking. They combine well with robust ingredients such as garlic, herbs and spices, and they make a healthy addition to soups, casseroles, bakes and salads.

Soya beans are also used to make tofu, tempeh, textured vegetable protein (TVP), flour and soy sauce.

White and black soya beans

How to Prepare and Cook Pulses

There is much debate as to whether soaking pulses before cooking is necessary, but it certainly reduces cooking times, and can enhance flavour by starting the germination process. First, wash pulses under cold running water, then place in a bowl of fresh cold water and leave to soak overnight. Discard any pulses that float to the surface, drain and rinse again. Put in a large saucepan and cover with fresh cold water. Boil rapidly for 10–15 minutes, then reduce the heat, cover and simmer until tender.

Cooking Times for Pulses

As cooking times can vary depending on the age of the pulses, this table should be used as a general guide.

Aduki beans	30–45 minutes
Black beans	1 hour
Black-eyed beans	1–1¼ hours
Borlotti beans	1–1½ hours
Broad beans	1½ hours
Butter/lima beans	1–1¼ hours
Cannellini beans	1 hour
Chick-peas	1½–2½ hours
Flageolet beans	1½ hours
Ful medames	1 hour
Haricot beans	1–1½ hours
Kidney beans	1–1½ hours
Mung beans	25–40 minutes
Pinto beans	1–1¼ hours
Soya beans	2 hours

MUNG BEANS

Instantly recognizable in their sprouted form as beansprouts, mung or moong beans are small, olive-coloured beans native to India. They are soft and sweet when cooked, and are used in the spicy curry, moong dahl. Soaking is not essential, but if they are soaked overnight this will reduce the usual 40 minutes cooking time by about half.

Mung beans

Using Canned Beans

Canned beans are convenient store-cupboard stand-bys, because they require no soaking or lengthy cooking. Choose canned beans that do not have added sugar or salt, and rinse well and drain before use. The canning process reduces the levels of vitamins and minerals, but canned beans still contain reputable amounts.

Canned beans tend to be softer than cooked, dried beans so they are easy to mash, which makes them good for pâtés, stuffings, croquettes and rissoles, but they can also be used to make quick salads. They can, in fact, be used for any dish that calls for cooked, dried beans: a drained 425g/15oz can is roughly the equivalent of 150g/5oz/¾ cup dried beans. Firmer canned beans such as kidney beans can be added to stews and re-cooked, but softer beans such as flageolet should be just heated through.

Buying and Storing: Look for plump, shiny beans with unbroken skin. Beans toughen with age so, although they will keep for up to a year in a cool, dry place, it is best to buy them in small quantities from shops with a regular turnover of stock. Avoid beans that look dusty or dirty and store them in an airtight container in a cool, dark, dry place.

Health Benefits: The health attributes of beans are plentiful. They are packed with protein, soluble and insoluble fibre, iron, potassium, phosphorous, manganese, magnesium, folate and most B vitamins.

Soya beans are the most nutritious of all beans. Rich in high-quality protein, this wonder-pulse contains all eight essential amino acids that cannot be synthesized by the body but are vital for the renewal of cells and tissues.

Insoluble fibre ensures regular bowel movements, while soluble fibre has been found to lower blood cholesterol, thereby reducing the risk of heart disease and stroke. Studies show that eating dried beans on a regular basis can lower cholesterol levels by almost 20 per cent. Beans contain a concentration of lignins, also known as phytoestrogens, which protect against cancer of the breast, prostate and colon. Lignins may also help to balance hormone levels in the body.

Cook's Tips

- If you are short of time, the long soaking process can be speeded up: first, cook the beans in boiling water for 2 minutes, then remove the pan from the heat. Cover and leave for about 2 hours. Drain, rinse and cover with plenty of fresh cold water before cooking.
- Cooking beans in a pressure cooker will reduce the cooking time by around three-quarters.
- Do not add salt to beans while they are cooking as this will cause them to toughen. Cook the beans first, then season with salt and pepper. Acid foods such as tomatoes or lemons, or vinegar will also toughen beans, so only add these ingredients once the beans are soft.

Quick Cooking and Serving Ideas for Pulses

- To flavour beans, add an onion, garlic, herbs or spices before cooking. Remove whole flavourings before serving.

- Spoon spicy, red lentil dahl and some crisp, fried onions on top of a warm tortilla, then roll up and eat.

- Dress cooked beans with extra virgin olive oil, lemon juice, crushed garlic, diced tomato and fresh basil.

- Mix cooked chick-peas with spring onions, olives and chopped parsley, then drizzle over olive oil and lemon juice.

- Mash cooked beans with olive oil, garlic and coriander and pile on to toasted bread. Top with a poached egg.

- Fry cooked red kidney beans in olive oil with chopped onion, chilli, garlic and fresh coriander leaves.

- Sauté a little chopped garlic in olive oil, add cooked or canned flageolet beans, canned tomatoes and chopped fresh chilli, then cook for a few minutes until the sauce has thickened slightly and the beans are heated through.

- Roast cooked chick-peas, which have been drizzled with olive oil and garlic, for 20 minutes at 200°C/400°F/Gas 6, then toss in a little ground cumin and sprinkle with chilli flakes. Serve with chunks of feta cheese and naan bread.

Soya Bean Products

Soya beans are incredibly versatile and are used to make an extensive array of by-products that can be used in cooking – tofu, tempeh, textured vegetable protein, flour, miso, and a variety of sauces. The soya bean is the most nutritious of all beans. Rich in high-quality protein, it is one of the few vegetarian foods that contains all eight essential amino acids that cannot be synthesized in the body and are vital for the renewal of cells and tissues.

TOFU

Also known as beancurd, tofu is made in a similar way to soft cheese. The beans are boiled, mashed and sieved to make soya "milk", and the "milk" is then curdled using a coagulant. The resulting curds are drained and pressed to make tofu, and there are several different types to choose from.

Firm tofu

This type of tofu is sold in blocks and can be cubed or sliced and used in vegetable stir-fries, kebabs, salads, soups and casseroles. Alternatively, firm tofu can be mashed and used in bakes and burgers. The bland flavour of firm tofu is improved by marinating, because its porous texture readily absorbs flavours and seasonings.

Silken tofu

Soft with a silky, smooth texture, this type of tofu is ideal for use in sauces, dressings, dips and soups. It is a useful dairy-free alternative to cream, soft cheese or yogurt, and can be used to make creamy desserts.

Other forms of tofu

Smoked, marinated and deep-fried tofu are all readily available in health food stores and Oriental shops as well as some supermarkets.

Deep-fried tofu is fairly tasteless, but it has an interesting texture. It puffs up during cooking and, underneath the golden, crisp coating the tofu is white and soft, and easily absorbs the flavour of other ingredients. It can be used in much the same way as firm tofu and, as it has been fried in vegetable oil, it is suitable for vegetarian cooking.

Buying and Storing: All types of fresh tofu can be kept in the fridge for up to 1 week. Firm tofu should be kept covered in water, which must be changed regularly. Freezing tofu is not recommended, because it alters the texture. Silken tofu is often available in long-life vacuum packs, which do not have to be kept in the fridge and have a much longer shelf life.

TEMPEH

This Indonesian speciality is made by fermenting cooked soya beans with a cultured starter. Tempeh is similar to tofu but has a nuttier, more savoury flavour. It can be used in the same way as firm tofu and also benefits from marinating. While some types of tofu are regarded as a dairy replacement, the firmer texture of tempeh means that it can be used instead of meat in pies and casseroles.

Buying and Storing: Tempeh is available chilled or frozen in health food stores and Oriental shops. Chilled tempeh can be stored in the fridge for up to a week. Frozen tempeh can be left in the freezer for 1 month; defrost before use.

BEANCURD SKINS AND STICKS

Made from soya "milk", dried beancurd skins and sticks, like fresh beancurd, have neither aroma nor flavour until they are cooked, when they will rapidly absorb the flavour of seasonings and other ingredients. Beancurd skins and sticks are used in Chinese cooking and need to be

Above, clockwise from left: Silken tofu, beancurd skins, firm tofu and deep-fried tofu

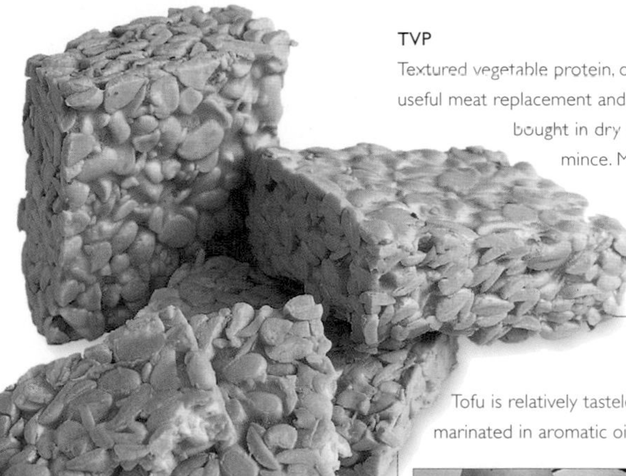

Tempeh

TVP

Textured vegetable protein, or TVP, is a useful meat replacement and is usually bought in dry chunks or as mince. Made from processed soya beans, TVP is very versatile and readily absorbs the strong flavours of ingredients such as herbs, spices and vegetable stock. It is inexpensive and is a convenient store-cupboard item. TVP needs to be rehydrated in boiling water or vegetable stock, and can be used in stews and curries, or as a filling for pies.

soaked until pliable before use. Beancurd skins should be soaked in cold water for an hour or two and can be used to wrap a variety of fillings.

Beancurd sticks need to be soaked for several hours or overnight. They can be chopped and added to soups, stir-fries and casseroles.

Tofu Fruit Fool

1 Place a packet of silken tofu in the bowl of a food processor. Add some soft fruit or berries – for example, strawberries, raspberries or blackberries.

2 Process the mixture to form a smooth purée, then sweeten to taste with a little honey, maple syrup or maize malt syrup.

Marinated Tofu Kebabs

Tofu is relatively tasteless but readily takes on other flavours. It is at its best when marinated in aromatic oils, soy sauce, spices and herbs.

1 Cut a block of tofu into 1cm/½in cubes and marinate in a mixture of groundnut oil, sesame oil, soy sauce, crushed garlic, grated fresh root ginger and honey for at least 1 hour.

2 Thread the cubes of tofu on to skewers with chunks of courgettes, onions and mushrooms. Brush with the marinade and grill or barbecue until golden, turning occasionally.

Soya flour

SOYA FLOUR

This is a finely ground, high-protein flour, which is also gluten-free. It is often mixed with other flours in bread and pastries, adding a pleasant nuttiness, or it can be used as a thickener in sauces.

Buying and Storing: Store TVP and soya flour in an airtight container in a cool, dry, dark place.

SOY SAUCE

This soya by-product originated over 2,000 years ago and the recipe has changed little since then. It is made by combining crushed soya beans with wheat, salt, water and a yeast-based culture called *koji*, and the mixture is left to ferment for between 6 months and 3 years.

There are two basic types of soy sauce: light and dark. Light soy sauce is slightly thinner in consistency and saltier. It is used in dressings and soups. Dark soy sauce is heavier and sweeter, with a more rounded flavour, and is used in marinades, stir-fries and sauces. Try to buy naturally brewed soy sauce as many other kinds are now chemically prepared to hasten the fermentation process, and may contain flavourings and colourings.

SHOYU

Made in Japan, shoyu is aged for 1–2 years to produce a full-flavoured sauce that can be used in the same way as dark soy sauce. You can buy it in health food stores and Oriental shops.

TAMARI

This form of soy sauce is a natural by-product of making miso, although it is often produced in the same way as soy sauce. Most tamari is made without wheat, which means that it is gluten-free. It has a rich, dark, robust flavour and is used in cooking or as a condiment.

Buying and Storing: Keep soy sauce, shoyu and tamari in a cool, dark place.

MISO

This thick paste is made from a mixture of cooked soya beans, rice, wheat or barley, salt and water. Miso is left to ferment for up to 3 years. It can be used to add a savoury flavour to soups, stocks, stir-fries and noodle dishes, and is a staple food in Asia. There are three main types: kome, or white miso, is the lightest and sweetest; medium-strength mugi miso, which has a mellow flavour and is preferred for everyday use; and hacho miso, which is a dark chocolate colour, and has a thick texture and a strong flavour.

Soya Bean Sauces

Black bean sauce Made from fermented black soya beans, this has a rich, thick consistency and a salty, full flavour. It should always be heated before use to bring out the flavour. Fermented black beans, which Chinese cooks use to make home-made black bean sauce, can be bought in vacuum-packs or cans from Oriental shops.

Yellow bean sauce Produced from fermented yellow soya beans, this sauce has an intense flavour.

Hoisin sauce A thick red-brown sauce made from soya beans, flour, garlic, chilli, sesame oil and vinegar. Mainly intended as a marinade, it can be used as a dipping sauce.

Kecap manis An Indonesian-style dark, sweet soy sauce, which can be found in Oriental shops.

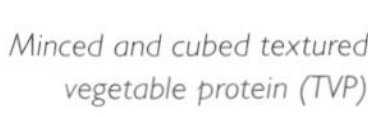
Minced and cubed textured vegetable protein (TVP)

Buying and Storing: Miso keeps well and can be stored for several months, but should be kept in the fridge once it has been opened.

Health Benefits: Soya is one of today's healthiest foods. Rich in minerals, particularly iron and calcium, it is also low in saturated fat and is cholesterol-free. It has the ability to help reduce osteoporosis, blood pressure and blood cholesterol, and there is evidence to suggest that it can help reduce the risk of cancer.

Japanese women (whose diets are rich in soya) have a lower incidence of breast cancer than women who consume a typical Western diet. Likewise, Japanese men have a lower incidence of prostate cancer than Western men. This is thought to be because soya contains hormone-like substances called phytoestrogens.

Studies have also shown that eating miso on a regular basis can increase the body's natural resistance to radiation. Additionally, miso is said to prevent cancer of the liver, and it can also help to expel toxins from the body.

Light soy sauce (below) and dark soy sauce

Watch Point

Although soya beans and products are nutritionally beneficial, they are also common allergens and can provoke reactions such as headaches and digestive problems. Avoid eating excessive amounts of soya, and always cook sprouted soya beans before use.

Mugi miso (left) and hacho miso

Tamari (left) and shoyu

Dairy Foods and Alternatives

Some people may question the inclusion of dairy products in a whole food cookbook, and while it would be foolish to advocate the consumption of vast quantities of high-fat milk, cream and cheese, a diet that includes moderate amounts of dairy products does provide valuable vitamins and minerals. There is little reason to reject dairy products as they can enrich vegetarian cooking. However, for those who choose to avoid dairy foods, there are plenty of alternatives.

Milk, Cream and Yogurt

This wide group of ingredients includes milk, cream and yogurt made from cow's, goat's and sheep's milk, as well as non-dairy products such as soya "milk" and "cream" and other non-dairy "milks", which are made from nuts and grains. They are used in a huge range of sweet and savoury dishes, from sauces and soups to drinks and desserts.

MILK

Often referred to as a complete food, milk is one of our most widely used ingredients. Cow's milk remains the most popular type although, with the growing concern about saturated fat and cholesterol, semi-skimmed and skimmed milks now outsell the full-fat version. Skimmed milk contains half the calories of full-fat milk and only a fraction of the fat, but nutritionally it is on a par, retaining its vitamins, calcium and other minerals.

Buy organic milk if you can, because it comes from cows that have been fed on a pesticide-free diet, and are not routinely treated with hormones, antibiotics, or BST (bovine somatotrophin), which is used in some countries to boost the milk yield from cows.

Soured cream and crème fraîche

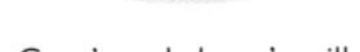

Goat's and sheep's milk

These milks make useful alternatives for people who are intolerant to cow's milk. The lactose in cow's milk can cause severe indigestion, and an intolerance to dairy products often manifests itself in eczema or sinus congestion. Goat's and sheep's milk are nutritionally similar to cow's milk, but are easier to digest.

Goat's milk has a distinctive, musky flavour, while sheep's milk is a little creamier and has a less assuming flavour.

CREAM

The high fat content of cream means that it is not an ingredient to be eaten lavishly on a daily basis. Used with discretion, however, cream lends a richness to soups, sauces, bakes and desserts.

The fat content of cream ranges enormously: half-cream contains about 12 per cent, single cream 18 per cent, double cream 48 per cent, and clotted cream, which is the highest contains about 55 per cent.

From left, goat's, cow's and sheep's milk, and soya "milk"

Smetana

SOURED CREAM

This thick-textured cream is treated with lactic acid, which gives it its characteristic tang. Full-fat soured cream contains about 20 per cent fat, although low- and non-fat versions are available. It can be used in the same way as cream. Care should be taken when cooking, as it can curdle if heated to too high a temperature.

CREME FRAICHE

This rich, cultured cream is similar to sour cream, but its high fat content, at around 35 per cent, means that it does not curdle when cooked. Crème fraîche is delicious served with fresh fruit such as ripe summer berries, puréed mangoes or sliced bananas.

BUTTERMILK

Traditionally made from the milky liquid left over after butter making, buttermilk is now more likely to be made from skimmed milk, mixed with milk solids and then cultured with lactic acid. It has a creamy, mild, sour taste and makes a tangy and distinctive addition to desserts. Used in baking, buttermilk gives cakes and soda bread a moist texture. It is low in fat, containing only 0.1 per cent.

SMETANA

Originally made in Russia, this rich version of buttermilk is made from skimmed milk and single cream with an added culture. It has a similar fat content to strained yogurt (about 10 per cent), and should be treated in the same way. Smetana can curdle if it is overheated.

Buying and Storing: When buying milk, cream and cream-related products, don't forget to check the label. Manufacturers and retailers are obliged to give a "best before" or "sell-by" date on the packet. The fat content, nutritional information and list of ingredients will also be detailed. Try to avoid products that contain unnecessary additives or flavourings. For instance, low-fat crème fraîche, yogurts and cream may contain animal-based gelatine, which acts as a thickener. Store dairy products in the fridge and consume within a few days of opening. Long-life cartons will keep indefinitely but once opened must be treated as fresh and kept in the fridge.

Buttermilk

Health Benefits: Milk is an important source of calcium and phosphorus, both of which are essential for healthy teeth and bones, and are said to prevent osteoporosis. Milk also contains significant amounts of zinc and the B vitamins, including B_{12}, along with a small amount of vitamin D. Numerous studies have revealed that, due to its high calcium content, milk fortified with vitamin D may have a role in preventing colon cancer. The antibodies found in milk may boost the immune system and help gastrointestinal problems, and skimmed milk may reduce the amount of cholesterol produced by the liver.

Above, clockwise from bottom left: whipping cream, single cream and whipped double cream

Other Non-dairy "Milks"

Apart from soya "milk", non-dairy "milks" or drinks are usually either nut- or grain-based. They can be used as a substitute for regular milk in a wide variety of sweet and savoury dishes such as milk puddings, custards, hot and cold milk drinks, sauces, but shouldn't be overheated or cooked for too long or they may curdle.

Oat "milk" Made from oat kernels and either vegetable or sunflower oil, this nutritious drink is high in fibre.

Rice "milk" With a similar consistency to soya "milk", rice "milk" is also non-mucous forming. Rice "milk" is easily digested and almost non-allergenic.

Nut "milk" Crushed and ground almonds or cashew nuts are mixed with water to form this mild-tasting non-dairy "milk".

Clockwise from left, "milks" made from rice, almonds and oats

Making Yogurt

It is easy to make yogurt at home – simply make sure that you use live yogurt as a starter and that it is as fresh as possible. Once you have made the first batch, you can reserve some of the yogurt as a starter for the next. Don't use too much starter or the yogurt may become sour and grainy. Yogurt can be flavoured with fresh or dried fruit, or honey, or to make a more substantial dish, stir in soaked oats, chopped nuts and toasted seeds.

1 Pour 600ml/1 pint/2½ cups whole, semi-skimmed or skimmed milk into a saucepan and bring to the boil. Remove the pan from the heat and leave the milk to cool to 45°C/113°F.

2 If you don't have a thermometer, you can use your finger – the milk should feel slightly hotter than is comfortable. Pour the warm milk into a medium-size, sterilized bowl.

3 Whisk in 15–30ml/1–2 tbsp live yogurt – this acts as a starter. Leave in the bowl or transfer it to a large jar.

4 Cover the bowl or jar with clear film, then insulate the bowl or jar with several layers of dish towels and place in a warm airing cupboard. Alternatively, the yogurt can be transferred to a vacuum flask to keep it warm. Leave for 10–12 hours until set. Transfer to the fridge.

SOYA SUBSTITUTES

Soya "milk"

This is the most widely used alternative to milk. Made from pulverized soya beans, it is suitable for both cooking and drinking and is used to make yogurt, cream and cheese. Soya "milk" is interchangeable with cow's milk, although it has a slightly thicker consistency and a nutty flavour. Fruit- and chocolate-flavoured soya "milk", and versions fortified with extra vitamins are widely available in health food shops and larger supermarkets.

Soya "cream"

This is made from a higher proportion of beans than that in soya "milk", which gives it a richer flavour and thicker texture. It has a similar consistency to single cream and can be used in the same ways.

Buying and Storing: Most soya "milks" and "creams" are sold in long-life cartons, which extends their shelf-life and means that they do not require refrigeration until opened. Buy soya "milk" that is fortified with extra vitamins and calcium and, depending on how you intend to use it, choose the sweetened or non-sweetened variety. Some retailers stock fresh soya "milk" and this should be treated in the same way as cow's milk.

Health Benefits: Soya "milk" and "cream" are a valuable source of protein, calcium, iron, magnesium, phosphorus and vitamin E. The "milk" is low in calories and contains no cholesterol. Numerous studies have shown that soya can reduce the risk of certain cancers, heart disease, kidney disease and osteoporosis.

YOGURT

Praised for its health-giving qualities, yogurt has earned a reputation as one of the most valuable health foods. The fat content ranges from 0.5g per 100g for very low-fat or virtually fat-free yogurts to 4g per 100g for wholemilk yogurt. The consistency may be thin or thick. Greek and Greek-style yogurt, which is made from cow's or sheep's milk, contains about 10g of fat per 100g – just enough to prevent it from curdling during cooking. However, although it is higher in fat than other types of yogurt, it contains less fat than cream and makes a healthier alternative. Lower fat yogurts can also be used instead of cream, but are best used in uncooked dishes. Strained yogurt has its watery whey removed to make it thicker and richer, and has a similar fat content to Greek and Greek-style yogurts. When buying yogurt, look for "live" on the label. This signifies that it has been fermented with a starter culture bacteria (usually *lactobacillus bulgaricus* or *streptococcus thermophilous*), which is beneficial to health. Bio yogurts, which contain extra bacteria (often *lactobacillus acidophilus* or *bifidobacterium bifidum*), have a milder, creamier flavour than other yogurts, and may have far wider healing benefits.

Buying and Storing: Yogurt has a limited shelf-life, so it is important to check the "best before" or "sell-by" date on the label. Although yogurt making is essentially a natural process, many manufacturers add unnecessary amounts of sugar, colourings, flavourings and other additives, such as thickeners and stabilizers. Some yogurts, especially low-fat varieties may contain gelatine, an animal by-product. Low-calorie yogurts usually contain artificial sweeteners. Fruit yogurts may contain a high amount of sugar as well as colourings and flavourings; check the label before buying, and choose varieties that have a high fruit content – those with the highest amount will mention fruit first in the list of ingredients. More expensive, specialist yogurts may be the least adulterated.

Health Benefits: Yogurt is rich in calcium, phosphorus and B vitamins. The bacteria present in live yogurt ensures that it is easily digestible; it may stimulate the friendly bacteria in the gut and suppress harmful bacteria, so aiding digestion and relieving gastrointestinal problems. Evidence suggests that yogurt can help protect against vaginal thrush and may be applied externally.

Live and bio yogurts have extra health benefits, although their levels of good bacteria can vary. The bacteria in bio yogurt may help boost natural resistance to food poisoning and tummy bugs and, if eaten after a course of antibiotics, may restore the internal flora of the intestines. There is also evidence to suggest that bio yogurt that contains the *acidophilus* culture could prevent cancer of the colon.

Cooking with Yogurt

Yogurt is a useful culinary ingredient, but does not respond well to heating. It is best added at the end of cooking, just before serving, to prevent it from curdling and to retain its vital bacteria. High-fat yogurts are more stable, but it is possible to stabilize and thicken low-fat yogurt by stirring in a little blended cornflour before cooking. Natural yogurt can be used in a wide range of sweet and savoury dishes, and it makes a calming addition to hot stews and curries.

Clockwise from top left: Thick cow's milk yogurt, thin cow's milk yogurt, Greek-style yogurt, soya yogurt, goat's milk yogurt and sheep's milk yogurt

Soft and Hard Cheeses

The selection of cheeses in this section is a mere fraction of the extensive range that is available in good cheese shops and supermarkets. Some, like mozzarella and feta, are more often cooked in pies or on pizzas, or used in salads, while others, like the soft, white, Camembert-type goat's cheeses, make a good addition to a cheese board.

Feta, which is packed in brine, can be bought as small rounds or larger blocks

MOZZARELLA

This delicate, silky-white cheese is usually made from cow's milk, although authentically it should be made from buffalo's milk. The sweet milky balls of cheese have excellent melting qualities, hence its use on pizzas and in bakes, but it is equally delicious served in salads. When combined with avocado and tomato it makes the classic Italian three-colour salad.

FETA

Believed to be one of the first cheeses, feta is curdled naturally without the addition of rennet. Although it was once made with goat's or sheep's milk, it is now more often made with milk from cows. It is preserved in brine, hence its saltiness, and has a firm, crumbly texture. It is used in the classic Greek salad with cucumber, tomatoes and olives. To reduce the salty taste of feta, rinse it in water, then leave to soak in cold water for 10 minutes.

GOAT'S CHEESE

Indispensable for those intolerant or allergic to cow's milk, goat's cheese varieties range from soft, mild and creamy through a Camembert-type, which has a soft centre and downy rind, to the firm Cheddar alternative. Similarly, the flavour of goat's cheese spans from fresh, creamy and mild to sharp and pungent.

HALLOUMI

This ancient cheese was first made by nomadic Bedouin tribes. It is commonly sold in small blocks, and is often sprinkled with mint. Halloumi has a firm, rubbery texture and retains its shape when grilled or fried. Some people consider it to be the vegetarian alternative to bacon.

CHEDDAR

Unfortunately, much of the Cheddar sold today is made in factories. Avoid these fairly tasteless, rubbery blocks and look for traditional farmhouse Cheddar, which is matured for between nine and 24 months, and has a rich, strong, savoury flavour.

Mozzarella

Goat's cheese comes in a multitude of different forms

Halloumi

Non-dairy Cheeses

Soya cheese is the most common non-dairy variety. It can lack the depth of flavour of cheese made from cow's, goat's or sheep's milk, but it is nevertheless a valuable alternative for people who prefer not to buy dairy products or who are lactose intolerant. Soya cheese is made from a blend of processed soya beans and vegetable fats and may be flavoured with herbs and spices. Other non-dairy cheeses include a Parmesan-type cheese made from rice and a spice-flavoured cheese produced from nuts.

PARMESAN

Allowed to mature for at least 18 months and up to four years, this richly flavoured cheese may be high in fat – though not as high as Cheddar – but a little goes a long way. Avoid ready-grated Parmesan and opt for a chunk freshly cut off the block. Parmesan keeps for a long time in the fridge and is excellent grated and added to pasta, risottos and bakes, or shaved over salads.

Buying and Storing: Hard cheeses are best stored in a cool larder but, if kept in the fridge, the cheese should be left at room temperature for at least an hour before eating. Cheese starts to dry out as soon as it is cut, so keep it loosely wrapped in foil or greaseproof paper.

Health Benefits: Semi-soft cheeses, such as mozzarella, and hard cheeses, such as Parmesan and Cheddar, contain valuable amounts of calcium, protein, vitamins and minerals. Hard cheeses are also high in saturated fat. When buying hard cheeses, choose a mature, good-quality type, as the strong flavour means that relatively small quantities are needed to add flavour to a dish. Saturated fat is known to increase blood cholesterol, which can lead to heart disease and stroke, so always eat cheese in moderation. On the plus side, research shows that cheese – particularly a waxy, hard cheese like Cheddar – eaten after a meal, may reduce the likelihood of tooth decay by as much as 50 per cent.

Parmesan

Fresh Unripened Cheeses

As their name suggests, fresh unripened cheeses are young and immature. They have a light, mild taste that readily accepts stronger flavoured ingredients, such as herbs and spices. They are lower in fat and are less likely to induce migraines than mature hard cheeses. Fresh cheeses can be used in both savoury dishes and desserts.

FROMAGE FRAIS

This smooth, fresh cheese has the same consistency as thick yogurt, but is less acidic. It can be used in the same way as yogurt; mixed with fruit purée to make fools, combined with dried fruit, nuts and grains, or in sweet and savoury flans. The fat content varies from almost nothing to about 8 per cent. Full-fat fromage frais is the best choice for cooking as it is less likely to separate.

RICOTTA

A soft, low-fat unsalted cheese, which can be made from sheep's, goat's or cow's milk, ricotta has a slightly granular texture and is widely used in Italian cooking. Its mild, clean flavour means that it is incredibly versatile. It makes a neutral base for pancake fillings, and can be used as a stuffing for pasta, when it is often combined with spinach. Ricotta is also good in tarts, cakes and cheesecakes, or it can be served simply on its own with fruit. Mixed with herbs and garlic, it makes a tasty sandwich filling.

Below, clockwise from left: Ricotta, fromage frais, quark, cream cheese and cottage cheese

QUARK

This low-fat curd cheese is usually made with semi-skimmed or skimmed milk. Its mild, slightly tangy flavour and light, creamy texture makes it perfect in cheesecakes and desserts, or it can be diluted with milk to make an alternative to cream. In northern European countries, it is used as a spread instead of butter.

COTTAGE CHEESE

Lower in fat than most other cheeses (between 2 and 5 per cent), cottage cheese is not usually used for cooking but is good in salads and dips. It makes a fine accompaniment to soft fruits and is best eaten as fresh as possible.

CREAM CHEESE

Commonly used in cheesecakes, dips and spreads, this cheese has a rich, velvety consistency, mild flavour and a high fat content – about 35 per cent – although it is possible to buy lower-fat alternatives made from skimmed milk.

NON-DAIRY SOFT CHEESES

A wide range of soft, soya-based cheeses is available from health food stores. They are a valuable alternative for people who prefer not to buy dairy products.

Buying and Storing: Fresh unripened cheeses do not keep for very long and are best bought in small quantities and eaten soon after purchase. Store in an airtight container in the fridge.

Health Benefits: Fresh unripened cheeses generally have a lower fat content than hard cheeses and are less likely to trigger migraines. They also provide plenty of protein, calcium and vitamin B_{12}.

Always Read the Label

Check the labels on low-fat yogurts and soft cheeses as these products sometimes contain animal-derived gelatine, which is used as a setting agent. Until relatively recently, the rennet use for cheese-making was obtained from animals. Nowadays, however, vegetarian rennet is more widely used, although this may not be mentioned on the pack. If in doubt, check with the manufacturer.

Making Fresh Soft Cheese

Fresh soft cheese can be made using soured milk (made from milk mixed with yogurt) or soured cream. Use plain or sweeten with honey, orange flower water or soft fruit. Alternatively, mix with fresh chopped herbs and garlic.

1 Place 1 litre/1¾ pints/4 cups semi-skimmed milk and 120ml/4fl oz/½ cup live yogurt or soured cream in a saucepan and mix well. Bring to the boil, then simmer for 5 minutes or until the milk curdles, stirring continuously.

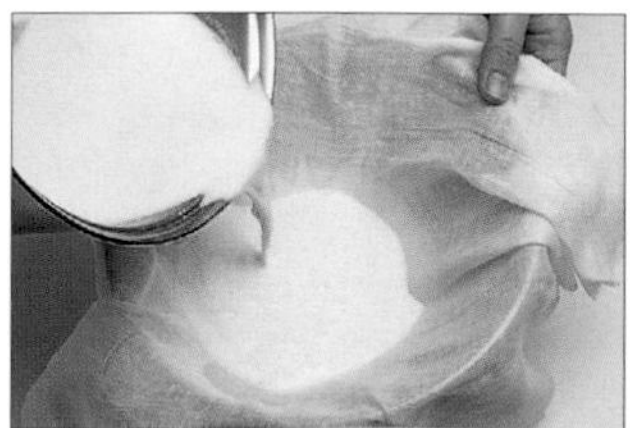

2 Line a metal sieve or colander with muslin and place over a large bowl. Pour the milk mixture into the sieve or colander and leave to drain for 1 hour or until it stops dripping. Alternatively, gather together the edges of the muslin, tie with string, and suspend over the bowl for about 1 hour until it stops dripping.

3 The residue in the muslin is the soft cheese. Store in a covered bowl in the fridge for 3–4 days.

Butter Versus Margarine

Whether butter is better than margarine has been the focus of much debate. The taste, especially of good-quality, farmhouse butter, is certainly superior to margarine. However, butter, which contains 80 per cent saturated fat, has the ability to raise cholesterol levels in the body.

Vegetable margarine contains the same amount of fat as butter, but the fat is polyunsaturated, which was once considered to give margarine greater health benefits. Unfortunately, margarine manufacturing processes change the fats into trans fats, or hydrogenated fats. Studies have shown that trans fats may be more likely than the saturated fat in butter to damage the heart and blood vessels. In addition, cooking removes many of the health benefits of polyunsaturated fats.

SPREADS

Lower fat margarines are known as spreads. They contain less than 80 per cent fat and those that are under 65 per cent fat can be classified as reduced-fat. When the fat content falls below 41 per cent, a spread can be called low-fat or half-fat. Very low-fat spreads may contain gelatine, and their high water content means they are not suitable for cooking. Olive-oil based spreads are rich in monounsaturated fats and are said to reduce cholesterol levels. They can be used for cooking.

Buying and Storing: When buying margarine and spreads always choose good-quality brands that contain no hydrogenated fats. Butter, margarines and spreads absorb other flavours, so they need to be kept well-wrapped. Always store these products in the fridge; unsalted butters will keep for up to 2 weeks, other butters for up to a month, and margarines and spreads will keep for about 2 months.

Below: There is a wide variety of different butters, margarines and spreads available. Whichever you choose to use, don't consume too much of these high-fat foods.

Eggs

An inexpensive, self-contained source of nourishment, hen's eggs offer the cook tremendous scope, whether served simply solo or as part of a dish. There are several different types, but the best are organic, free-range eggs from a small producer.

Organic free-range eggs

ORGANIC FREE-RANGE EGGS

These eggs are from hens that are fed on a natural pesticide-free diet, which has not had hormones or artificial colorants added. The hens are able to roam on land that has not been treated with chemical fertilizers and is certified organic. Free-range hens have the same indoor conditions as barn hens but also have daytime access to the open air – although the term "access" has sometimes been open to abuse.

Organic, free-range hens are said to have better conditions than normal free-range hens, and are not routinely debeaked.

BATTERY EGGS

Laid by hens that are kept in cages with a minimum amount of space in which to move. The hens are debeaked to prevent them pecking each other. These eggs are the cheapest to buy.

BARN OR PERCH EGGS

These eggs are produced by hens that are kept indoors. Each hen can roam around in the barn, but they have no access to the outside. Barn or perch eggs are more expensive than battery eggs, but cheaper than eggs from free-range hens.

FOURGRAIN EGGS

These eggs are produced by hens that are fed a diet based on barley, oats, wheat and rye. The hens have the same living conditions as barn or perch hens, in that they are kept indoors without access to the outside.

Cooking with Eggs: Eggs can be cooked in myriad ways. Simply boiled, fried or poached, they make a wonderful breakfast dish. Lightly cooked poached eggs are also delicious served as a lunch dish with high-fibre lentils or beans. Eggs are delicious baked, either on their own, with a drizzle of cream, or broken into a nest of lightly cooked peppers or leeks. They make delicious omelettes, whether cooked undisturbed until just softly set, combined with tomatoes and peppers to make an Italian frittata, or cooked with diced potato and onions to make the classic Spanish omelette. They are also often used as a filling for pies, savoury tarts and quiches.

Eggs are not, however, used only in savoury dishes. They are an essential ingredient in many sweet dishes, too. They are added to cake mixtures and batters for pancakes and popovers, are crucial to meringues, whisked sponges, mousses and hot and cold soufflés, and are used in all manner of desserts, from ice creams and custards to rice pudding.

When separated, egg yolks are used to thicken sauces and soups, giving them a rich, smooth consistency, while egg whites can be whisked into peaks to make meringues and soufflés. It is important to use eggs at room temperature, so remove them from the fridge about 30 minutes before cooking.

Misleading Labels

The labels on egg boxes often have phrases such as "farm fresh", "natural" or "country-fresh", which conjure up images of hens roaming around in the open, but they may well refer to eggs that are laid by birds reared in battery cages. It is advisable to avoid eggs that are labelled with such claims.

Battery eggs

Buying and Storing: Freshness is paramount when buying eggs. Buy from a shop that has a high turnover of stock. You should reject any eggs that have a broken, dirty or damaged shell. Most eggs are date stamped, but you can easily check if an egg is fresh, by placing it in a bowl of cold water: if the egg sinks and lays flat it is fresh. The older the egg, the more it will stand on its end. A really old egg will actually float and shouldn't be eaten. Store eggs in their box in the main part of the fridge and not in a rack in the door as this can expose them to odours and damage. The shells are extremely porous, so eggs can be tainted by strong smells. Eggs should be stored large-end up for no longer than 3 weeks.

Health Benefits: Eggs have received much adverse publicity due to their high cholesterol levels. However, attention has moved away from dietary cholesterol to cholesterol that is produced in the body from saturated fats. Saturated fats are now claimed to play a bigger role in raising cholesterol levels, and as eggs are low in saturated fat, they have been somewhat reprieved. They should, however, be eaten in moderation, and people with raised cholesterol levels should take particular care. Nutritionists recommend that we eat no more than four eggs a week. Eggs provide B vitamins, especially B_{12}, vitamins A and D, iron, choline and phosphorus, and cooking does not significantly alter their nutritional content.

Quick Ideas for Eggs

- Brush beaten egg on to pastries and bread before baking to give them a golden glaze.
- For a protein boost, top Thai- or Chinese-flavoured rice or noodle dishes with strips of thin omelette.
- Turn a mixed leaf salad into a light supper dish by adding a soft-boiled egg and some half-fat mayonnaise.
- For a simple dessert, make a soufflé omelette. Separate 2 eggs and whisk the whites and yolks separately. Fold together gently and add a little sugar. Cook in the same way as a savoury omelette and serve plain or fill with fruit conserve or lemon curd.

Herb Omelette

A simple, herb-flavoured omelette is quick to cook and, served with a salad and a chunk of crusty bread, makes a nutritious, light meal. Even if you are going to serve more than one, it is better to cook individual omelettes and eat them as soon as they are ready.

INGREDIENTS

2 eggs
15ml/1 tbsp chopped fresh herbs, such as tarragon, parsley or chives
5ml/1 tsp butter
salt and freshly ground black pepper

SERVES 1

1 Lightly beat the eggs in a bowl, add the fresh herbs and season to taste.

2 Melt the butter in a heavy-based, non-stick frying pan and swirl it around to coat the base evenly.

3 Pour in the egg mixture and, as the egg sets, push the edges towards the centre using a spoon, allowing the raw egg to run on to the hot pan.

4 Cook for about 2 minutes, without stirring, until the egg is just lightly set. Quickly fold over the omelette and serve immediately.

The Store Cupboard

The following section features a diverse range of foods that can enrich and add variety to a vegetarian diet. Some ingredients may be familiar, others less so, but all are useful to keep in the store cupboard. Each of the mentioned foods comes with notes on choosing, storage and preparation, when necessary, as well as nutritional or medicinal properties.

Nuts

With the exception of peanuts, nuts are the fruits of trees. The quality and availability of fresh nuts varies with the seasons, although most types are sold dried, either whole or prepared ready for use. Shelled nuts come in many forms: they may be whole, blanched, halved, sliced, shredded, chopped, ground or toasted.

Chestnuts

ALMONDS

There are two types of almond: sweet and bitter. The best sweet varieties are the flat and slender Jordan almonds from Spain. Heart-shaped Valencia almonds from Portugal and Spain, and the flatter Californian almonds are also widely available. For the best flavour, buy shelled almonds in their skins and blanch them yourself: cover with boiling water, leave for a few minutes, then drain and the skins will peel off easily. Almonds are available ready-blanched, flaked and ground. The latter adds a richness to cakes, tarts, pastry and sauces. Bitter almonds are much smaller and are used in almond oil and essence. They should not be eaten raw as they contain traces of the lethal prussic acid.

BRAZIL NUTS

These are, in fact, seeds, and are grown mainly in the Amazon regions of Brazil and other neighbouring countries. Between 12 and 20 Brazil nuts grow, packed snugly together, in a large brown husk, hence their three-cornered wedge shape. Brazil nuts have a sweet, milky taste and are used mainly as dessert nuts. They have a high fat content, so go rancid very quickly.

CASHEW NUTS

These are the seeds of the "cashew apple" – an evergreen tree with bright-orange fruit. Cashew nuts have a sweet flavour and crumbly texture. They make delicious nut butters, or can be sprinkled into stir-fries or over salads. They are never sold in the shell and undergo an extensive heating process that removes the seed from its outer casing.

CHESTNUTS

Raw chestnuts are not recommended as they are not only unpleasant to eat but also contain tannic acid, which inhibits the absorption of iron. Most chestnuts are imported from France and Spain and they are excellent after roasting, which complements their soft, floury texture. Unlike other nuts, they contain very little fat. Out of season, chestnuts can be bought dried, canned or puréed. Add

Blanched, whole and shelled almonds; shelled cashew nuts (in bowl); and shelled and whole Brazil nuts

whole chestnuts to winter stews, soups, stuffings or pies. The sweetened purée is delicious in desserts.

COCONUTS

This versatile nut grows all over the tropics. The white dense meat, or flesh, is made into desiccated coconut, blocks of creamed coconut and a thick and creamy milk. A popular ingredient in Asian, African and South American cuisines, coconut lends a sweet, creamy flavour to desserts, curries, soups and casseroles. Use coconut in moderation, as it is particularly high in fat

Hazelnuts

HAZELNUTS

Grown in the USA, Britain, Turkey, Italy and Spain, hazelnuts are usually sold dried, and can be bought whole, shelled and ground. They can be eaten raw, and the shelled nuts are especially good toasted. Hazelnuts can be grated or chopped for use in cakes and desserts, but they are also tasty in savoury dishes and can be added to salads, stir-fries and pasta.

Macadamia nuts

MACADAMIA NUTS

This round nut, about the size of a large hazelnut, is native to Australia, but is now grown in California and South America. Macadamia nuts are commonly sold shelled (the shell is extremely hard to crack). They have a crisp texture, a rich, buttery flavour and a high fat content.

Coconut Milk

Coconut milk or cream can be bought in cans or long-life cartons, but it is easy to make at home: tip 225g/8oz/2⅔ cups desiccated coconut into a food processor, add 450ml/¾ pint/scant 2 cups boiling water and process for 30 seconds. Leave to cool slightly, then tip into a muslin-lined sieve placed over a bowl and gather the ends of the cloth. Twist the cloth to extract the liquid, then discard the spent coconut. Store any unused coconut milk in the fridge for 1–2 days, or freeze.

Peeling Chestnuts

Peeling chestnuts can be fiddly and time-consuming but this is one of the simplest and quickest methods.

1 Place the chestnuts in a saucepan of boiling water, turn off the heat and leave to stand for 5 minutes.

2 Remove the nuts with a slotted spoon, then leave until cool enough to handle. Peel with a sharp knife.

Thick coconut cream, coconut milk and desiccated coconut

Pecan nuts

PEANUTS

Not strictly a nut but a member of the pulse family, peanuts bury themselves just below the earth after flowering – hence their alternative name, groundnuts. They are a staple food in many countries, and are widely used in South-east Asia, notably for satay sauce, and in African cuisines, where they are used as an ingredient in stews. In the West, peanuts are a popular snack food; the shelled nuts are frequently sold roasted and salted, and they are used to make peanut butter. Peanuts are particularly high in fat and should be eaten in moderation.

PECAN NUTS

A glossy, reddish-brown, oval-shaped shell encloses the pecan kernel, which looks like an elongated walnut but has a sweeter, milder flavour. This native American nut is a favourite in sweet pies, especially the classic pecan pie, but is also good eaten on its own, or added to salads. However, pecan nuts should be eaten only as an occasional treat, because they have the highest fat content of any nut, with a calorie content to match.

PINE NUTS

These tiny, cream-coloured nuts are the fruit of the Mediterranean stone pine tree. They have a rich, aromatic flavour, which lends itself to toasting. Buy in small quantities as their high oil content quickly turns them rancid. Pine nuts are a key ingredient in Italian pesto sauce, where they are pounded with garlic, olive oil and basil, and in the Middle Eastern sauce, tarator, in which toasted pine nuts are combined with bread, garlic, milk and olive oil to make a creamy paste that has a similar consistency to hummus.

PISTACHIO NUTS

Incredibly "moreish" when served as a snack, pistachio nuts have pale-green flesh and thin, reddish-purple skin. Sold shelled or in a split shell, these mild nuts are often used chopped as a colourful garnish, sprinkled over both sweet and savoury foods. Pistachio nuts have a wonderful flavour, they are good in all manner of desserts and can be made into

Peanuts

Pine nuts

Making Nut Butter

Shop-bought nut butters often contain unwanted hydrogenated oil and can be loaded with sugar. To avoid additives, make your own butter using a combination of peanuts, hazelnuts and cashew nuts.

1 Place 75g/3oz/½ cup shelled nuts in a food processor or blender and process until finely and evenly ground.

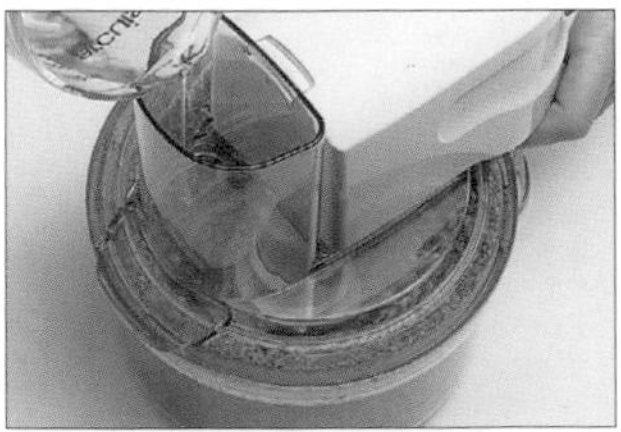

2 Pour 15–30ml/1–2 tbsp sunflower oil into the processor or blender and process to a coarse paste. Store in an airtight jar.

Walnuts

a delicious ice cream. They are widely used in Turkish and Arabic sweets, notably nougat and Turkish Delight. Check before buying pistachio nuts for cooking, as they are often sold salted.

WALNUTS

Most walnuts are imported from France, Italy and California, but they are also grown in the Middle East, Britain and China. This versatile nut has been around for hundreds of years. When picked young, walnuts are referred to as "wet" and have fresh, milky-white kernels, which can be eaten raw, but are often pickled.

Dried walnuts have a delicious bitter-sweet flavour and can be bought shelled, chopped or ground. They can be used to make excellent cakes and biscuits as well as rich pie fillings, but are also good added to savoury dishes such as stir-fries and salads – the classic Waldorf salad combines whole kernels with sliced celery and apples in a mayonnaise dressing.

Buying and Storing: Always buy nuts in small quantities from a shop with a high turnover of stock, because if kept for too long, they can turn rancid. Nuts in their shells should feel heavy for their size. Store nuts in airtight containers in a cool, dark place or in the fridge and they should keep fresh for at least 3 months. When buying a coconut, make sure that there is no sign of mould or a rancid smell. Give it a shake – it should be full of liquid. Keep coconut milk in the fridge or freezer once opened. Desiccated coconut can be stored in an airtight container, but don't keep it too long as its high fat content means that it is prone to rancidity.

Health Benefits: Rich in B complex vitamins, vitamin E, potassium, magnesium, calcium, phosphorus and iron, nuts offer the vegetarian an abundance of nutrients, although they contain a hefty number of calories. Most nuts are rich in monounsaturated and polyunsaturated fats, with the exception of Brazil nuts and coconuts, which are high in saturated fat, but do not contain cholesterol. Numerous studies highlight the substantial health benefits of walnuts. According to one study, the essential fatty acids found in walnuts can decrease cholesterol levels and may reduce the risk of heart disease by 50 per cent. Almonds and hazelnuts have similar properties.

Of all foods, Brazil nuts are the richest in selenium, which is a known mood enhancer. Apparently, a single Brazil nut each day will ensure that you are never deficient in this vital mineral.

Nuts are one of the richest vegetable sources of the antioxidant vitamin E, which has been associated with a lower risk of heart disease, stroke and certain cancers.

Pistachio nuts

Nut Allergy

Any food has the potential to cause an allergic reaction, but peanuts, as well as walnuts, Brazil nuts, hazelnuts and almonds are known to be common allergens. In cases of extreme allergy, nuts can trigger a life-threatening reaction known as anaphylaxis. Symptoms include facial swelling, shortness of breath, dizziness and loss of consciousness, so it is essential that sufferers take every precaution to avoid nuts.

Roasting and Skinning Nuts

The flavour of most nuts, particularly hazelnuts and peanuts, is improved by roasting. It also enables the thin outer skin to be removed more easily.

1 Place the nuts in a single layer on a baking sheet. Bake at 180°C/350°F/ Gas 4 for 10–20 minutes or until the skins begin to split and the nuts are golden.

2 Tip the nuts on to a dish towel and rub to loosen and remove the skins.

Seeds

They may look very small and unassuming, but seeds are nutritional powerhouses, packed with vitamins and minerals, as well as beneficial oils and protein. They can be used in a huge array of sweet and savoury dishes, and will add an instant, healthy boost, pleasant crunch and nutty flavour when added to rice and pasta dishes, salads, stir-fries, soups and yogurt.

Tahini (left) and black and white sesame seeds

Sunflower seeds

Black and white poppy seeds

SESAME SEEDS

These tiny, white or black seeds are a feature of Middle Eastern and Oriental cooking. In the Middle East they are ground into tahini, a thick paste that is a key component of hummus. Sesame seeds are also ground to make halvah, a sweet confection from Greece, Israel and Turkey. Gomassio, or gomashio, is the name of a crushed sesame seed condiment used in Japan. It can easily be made at home: toast the seeds, then crush with a little sea salt in a mortar using a pestle. Try a ratio of one part salt to five parts sesame seeds.

The flavour of sesame seeds is improved by roasting them in a dry frying pan; it gives them a distinctive nuttiness. The toasted seeds make a good addition to salads and noodle dishes. Unroasted seeds can be used as a topping for breads, buns, cakes and biscuits, and they can be added to pastry dough.

When buying sesame seeds, try to find seeds that have been mechanically rolled – the tell-tale sign is a matt appearance. Seeds that have been subjected to other methods of processing, such as salt-brining or a chemical bath, are usually glossy. Salt brining can affect the flavour of the seeds, as can chemical processing, which also damages their nutritional value.

SUNFLOWER SEEDS

These are the seeds of the sunflower, a symbol of summer and an important crop throughout the world. The impressive, golden-yellow flowers are grown for their seeds and oil; the leaves are used to treat malaria and the stalks are made into fertilizer. Rich in vitamin E, the pale-green, tear-drop-shaped seeds have a semi-crunchy texture and an oily taste that is much improved by dry-roasting. Sprinkle sunflower seeds over salads, rice pilaffs and couscous, or use in bread dough, muffins, casseroles and baked dishes.

POPPY SEEDS

These are the seeds of the opium poppy but without any of the habit-forming alkaloids. Poppy seeds can be blue (usually described as black) or white. The black variety looks good sprinkled over cakes and breads, adding a pleasant crunch.

Black poppy seeds can be used to make delicious seed cakes and teabreads, and they are used in German and Eastern European pastries, strudels and tarts. In India, the ground white seeds are used to thicken sauces, adding a nutty flavour.

PUMPKIN SEEDS

Richer in iron than any other seed and an excellent source of zinc, pumpkin seeds make a nutritious snack eaten on their own. They are also delicious lightly toasted, tossed in a little toasted sesame seed oil or soy sauce, and stirred into a mixed leaf or rice salad. Pumpkin seeds are widely used in South American cooking where they are generally roasted and ground to make into sauces.

Quick Ideas for Seeds

- Sprinkle over breads, cakes and biscuits just before baking.
- Combine with dried or fresh fruit, chopped nuts and natural yogurt to make a nutritious breakfast.
- Add to flapjacks, wholemeal scones and pastry to give them a nutty flavour.
- Add a spoonful of seeds to rissoles, vegetable burgers or casseroles.
- Mix with rolled oats, flour, butter or margarine, and sugar to make a sweet crumble topping. Omit the sugar to make a savoury topping and combine with chopped fresh or dried herbs.
- Use sunflower or pumpkin seeds in place of pine nuts to make pesto.
- Scatter over a mixed green salad.
- Add an instant nutritional boost to vegetable stir-fries or noodle dishes, by scattering a handful of seeds over the top before serving.

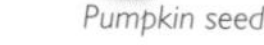

Pumpkin seeds

HEMP SEEDS

The cultivation of hemp has a long history but for various reasons it fell out of fashion. Today, hemp is making a comeback as a food. Hemp seeds are best roasted as this enhances their nutty flavour, and they can be used in a variety of sweet and savoury dishes.

LINSEEDS

Linseed oil has long been used to embellish wooden furniture. However, the golden seed, also known as flaxseed, is a rich source of polyunsaturated fat, including the essential fatty acid, linoleic acid. Linseeds can be added to muesli and other breakfast cereals, mixed into bread dough or sprinkled over salads.

Buying and Storing: Seeds are best bought in small quantities from shops with a high turnover of stock. Purchase whole seeds, rather than ground, and store them in a cool, dark place as they are prone to turning rancid. After opening the packet, decant the seeds into an airtight container.

Linseeds (left) and hemp seeds

Health Benefits: Seeds contain valuable amounts of the antioxidant vitamin E, which enhances the immune system and protects cells from oxidation. Vitamin E also improves blood circulation, and promotes healing and normal blood clotting as well as reducing infections associated with ageing. Numerous studies show that the vitamin works in tandem with beta carotene and vitamin C to fight off certain cancers and heart disease as well as slow the progression of Alzheimer's disease.

Seeds, particularly sunflower seeds, may help to reduce blood cholesterol levels in the body because they contain plentiful amounts of linoleic acid, which is also known as omega-6 fatty acid.

For their size, seeds contain a huge amount of iron. Sesame seeds are particularly rich – just 25g/1oz provides nearly half the daily requirement of iron, and 50g/2oz pumpkin seeds provide almost three-quarters of the iron we need each day. Sunflower seeds are often prescribed by natural medicine practitioners for their restorative qualities.

Roasting Seeds

The flavour of seeds is much improved by "roasting" them in a dry frying pan. Black poppy seeds won't turn golden brown, so watch them carefully to make sure that they don't scorch.

1 Spread out a spoonful or two of seeds in a thin layer in a large, non-stick frying pan and heat gently.

2 Cook over a medium heat for 2–3 minutes, tossing the seeds frequently, until they are golden brown.

Spices

Highly revered for thousands of years, spices – the seeds, fruit, pods, bark and buds of plants – have been the reason for wars and were sometimes traded as a currency. In addition to their ability to add flavour and interest to the most unassuming of ingredients, the evocative aroma of spices stimulates the appetite. Today, spices are still prized for their medicinal properties and culinary uses, and they play a vital role in healthy and appetizing vegetarian cooking.

Caraway seeds

Ground allspice

Cardamom pods

ALLSPICE

These small, dried berries of a tropical, South American tree have a sweet, warming flavour reminiscent of a blend of cloves, cinnamon and nutmeg. Although allspice is available ready-ground, it is best to buy the spice whole to retain its flavour, and grind just before use in cakes and biscuits. The whole berries can be added to marinades or mulled wine. Allspice is used to relieve digestive problems, including flatulence.

CARAWAY

An important flavouring in Eastern European, Austrian and German cooking, caraway seeds are sprinkled over rye bread, cakes and biscuits. They have a distinctive, sweet, aniseed flavour, which is also a welcome addition to potato- and cheese-based dishes, steamed carrots or cabbage. Caraway is recommended for colicky babies and has a similar effect in adults, relieving wind and aiding digestion. It can also be used to relieve menstrual pain.

CARDAMOM

Often used in Middle Eastern and Indian cooking, cardamom is best bought whole in its pod as it soon loses its aromatic flavour when ground. The pod can be used whole, slightly crushed, or for a more intense flavour, the seeds can be ground. Cardamom is superb in both sweet and savoury dishes. It can be infused in milk used to flavour rice pudding or ice cream, and is often added to curries and other Indian dishes. The seeds can be chewed whole to freshen the breath and calm indigestion. Colds and coughs are also said to be relieved by eating cardamom.

CAYENNE

This fiery, reddish-brown powder adds colour and heat, rather than flavour, to curries, soups and stews. It comes from the ground pod and seeds of a very pungent variety of chilli, *Capsicum frutescens*, and is sometimes referred to as red pepper. Cayenne possesses stimulant, antiseptic and digestive properties. It can improve blood circulation, but if eaten in large quantities may aggravate the stomach. A more unusual use of cayenne is to sprinkle it in your shoes to warm up cold feet!

Cayenne, celery seeds, chilli powder and chilli flakes.

Above, clockwise from left: cinnamon sticks, coriander seeds, cloves and ground cinnamon

CELERY SEEDS

These tiny brown seeds have a similar flavour to celery, but are more highly aromatic. It is important to grind or crush them before use to avoid any bitterness. Celery seeds can be used in almost any dish that calls for celery, and they add a pungent flavour to vegetarian bakes, stews, soups, sauces and egg dishes. Celery salt is a mixture of ground celery seeds, salt and other herbs. Celery seeds are carminative, relieving both flatulence and indigestion.

CHILLIES

Fresh chillies are covered in the vegetable section, but this versatile spice is also sold in dried, powdered and flaked form. Dried chillies tend to be hotter than fresh, and this is certainly true of chilli flakes, which contain both the seeds and the flesh. The best pure chilli powders do not contain added ingredients, such as onion and garlic. A powerful stimulant and expectorant, chilli also has a reputation as an aphrodisiac.

CINNAMON

This warm, comforting spice is available in sticks (quills) and ground. As the bark is difficult to grind, it is useful to keep both forms in the store cupboard. Cinnamon can enhance both sweet and savoury dishes. Use the sticks to flavour pilaffs, curries, couscous and dried fruit compotes, but remove before serving. Ground cinnamon adds a pleasing fragrance to cakes, biscuits and fruit. Cinnamon is an effective detoxifier and cleanser, containing substances that kill bacteria and other micro-organisms.

CLOVES

The unopened bud of an evergreen tree from South-east Asia, this spice is often used in combination with cinnamon to flavour puddings, cakes and biscuits. Cloves are often used to flavour the syrup when poaching oranges, but they are also delicious with cooked apples.

Clove oil has long been used as a cure for toothache, and both its antiseptic and anaesthetic qualities can relieve pain and discomfort throughout the body.

CORIANDER

Alongside cumin, ground coriander is a key ingredient in Indian curry powders and garam masala, and in northern Europe the ivory-coloured seeds are used as a pickling spice. Coriander seeds have a sweet, earthy, burnt-orange flavour that is more pronounced than the fresh leaves. The ready-ground powder rapidly loses its flavour and aroma, so it is best to buy whole seeds, which are easily ground in a mortar using a pestle, or in a coffee grinder. Before grinding, lightly dry-roast the seeds in a frying pan to enhance their flavour. Coriander has been prescribed as a digestive for thousands of years, relieving indigestion, diarrhoea and nausea. It also has antibacterial properties.

Cumin seeds, ground cumin and (front) fenugreek

CUMIN

Extensively used in Indian curries, cumin is also a familiar component of Mexican, North African and Middle Eastern cooking. The seeds have a robust aroma and slightly bitter taste, which is tempered by dry-roasting. Black cumin seeds, which are also known as nigella, are milder and sweeter. Ground cumin can be harsh, so it is best to buy the whole seeds and grind them just before use to ensure a fresh flavour. Cumin is good in tomato- or grain-based dishes, and its digestive properties mean that it is also ideal with beans.

Fresh root ginger

FENUGREEK

This spice is commonly used in commercial curry powders, along with cumin and coriander. On its own though, fenugreek should be used in moderation because its bitter-sweet flavour, which is mellowed by dry-frying, can be quite overpowering. The seeds have a hard shell and are difficult to grind, but they can be sprouted and make a good addition to mixed leaf and bean salads, as well as sandwich fillings. Fenugreek has long been prescribed to treat stomach and intestinal disorders, and its ability to cleanse the body may help in the release of toxins.

Preparing Fresh Ginger

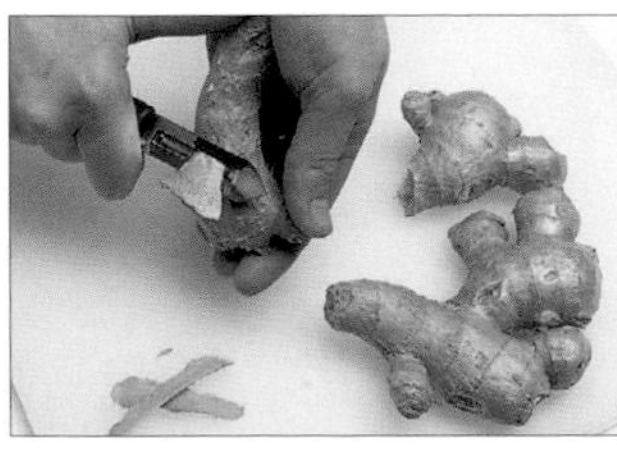

1 Fresh root ginger is most easily peeled using a vegetable peeler or a small, sharp paring knife.

2 Chop ginger using a sharp knife to the size specified in the recipe.

3 Grate ginger finely – special graters can be found in Asian shops, but a box grater will do the job equally well.

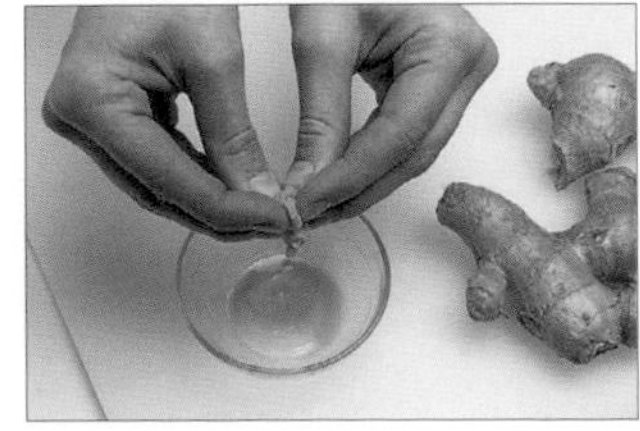

4 Freshly grated ginger can be squeezed to release the juice.

GINGER

This spice is probably one of the oldest and most popular herbal medicines. The fresh root, which is spicy, peppery and fragrant, is good in both sweet and savoury dishes, adding a hot, yet refreshing, flavour to marinades, stir-fries, soups, curries, grains and fresh vegetables. It also adds warmth to poached fruit, pastries and cakes.

Ground ginger is the usual choice for flavouring cakes, biscuits and other baked goods, but finely grated fresh ginger can also be used and is equally good.

Ground ginger

Ginger tea, made by steeping a few slices of fresh root ginger in hot water for a few minutes, can calm and soothe the stomach after a bout of food poisoning as well as ward off colds and flu.

Pink pickled ginger

This pretty, finely sliced ginger pickle is served as an accompaniment to Japanese food and is used to flavour sushi rice.

Stem ginger

Preserved in a thick sugar syrup and sold in jars, this sweet ginger can be chopped and used in desserts, or added to cake mixtures, steamed puddings, scones, shortbread and muffins.

Buying and Storing: Fresh root ginger should look firm, thin-skinned and unblemished. Avoid withered, woody looking roots as these are likely to be dry and fibrous. Store in the fridge. Ground ginger should smell aromatic; keep in a cool, dark place.

Pink pickled ginger

Health Benefits: The health benefits of ginger have been well documented for centuries. Recent studies confirm that ginger can successfully prevent nausea and may be more effective than prescribed drugs. Research also shows ginger to be effective in the treatment of pain and gastrointestinal disorders, and it may even halt certain cancers.

LEMON GRASS

This long fibrous stalk has a fragrant citrus aroma and flavour when cut and is a familiar part of South-east Asian and particularly Thai cooking, where it is used in coconut-flavoured curries. If you have difficulty finding lemon grass, lemon rind is a suitable alternative but it lacks the distinctive flavour of the fresh stalks. To use, remove the tough, woody outer layers, trim the root, then cut off the lower 5cm/2in and slice into thin rounds or pound in a mortar using a pestle. Bottled, chopped lemon grass and lemon grass purée are also available. Lemon grass is reputed to benefit rheumatism.

Lemon grass

GALANGAL

Closely related to ginger, fresh galangal looks similar but has a reddish-brown or cream-coloured skin. It was popular in England during the Middle Ages, but fell out of favour. With the increased interest in South-east Asian cooking, this knobbly root is again widely available and can be found in Oriental shops. Its fragrant, slightly peppery taste can be overpowering if used in excess. Avoid the powdered version as it is nothing like the fresh. Prepare the root in the same way as ginger: peel, then slice, grate or pound in a mortar using a pestle. Galangal has similar medicinal properties to ginger, relieving nausea and stomach problems.

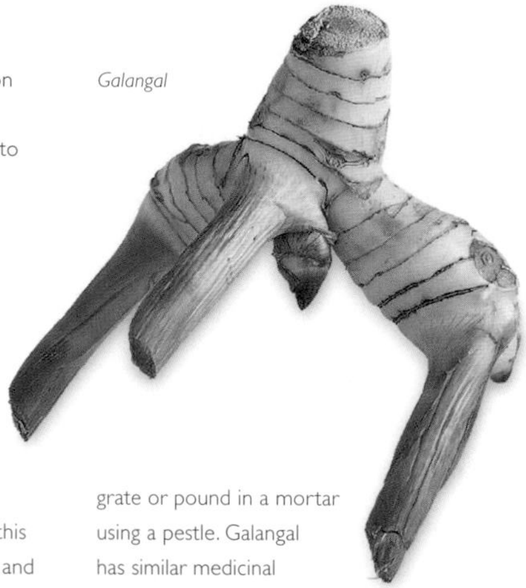

Galangal

MUSTARD

There are three different types of mustard seed, white, brown, and black, which is the most pungent. The flavour and aroma is only apparent when the seeds are crushed or mixed with liquid. If fried in a little oil before use, the flavour of the seeds is improved. As the intensity of mustard diminishes with both time and cooking; it is best added to dishes towards the end of cooking, or just before the dish is served.

Like many hot spices, mustard is traditionally used as a stimulant, cleansing the body of toxins and helping to ward off colds and flu.

Above: American mustard, Dijon mustard, wholegrain mustard, mustard powder and black and white mustard seeds

NUTMEG AND MACE

When it is picked, the nutmeg seed is surrounded by a lacy membrane called mace. Both are dried and used as spices. Nutmeg and mace taste similar, and their warm, sweet flavour enlivens white sauces, cheese-based dishes and vegetables, as well as custards, cakes and biscuits. Freshly grated nutmeg is far superior to the ready-ground variety, which loses its flavour and aroma with time. Although it is a hallucinogen if eaten in excess, when consumed in the small quantities that are needed in recipes, nutmeg improves both appetite and digestion.

White, black and pink peppercorns

Ground saffron and saffron threads

PEPPER

Undoubtedly the oldest, most widely used spice in the world, pepper was as precious as gold and silver in Medieval Europe. It is a very useful seasoning, because it not only adds flavour of its own to a dish, but also brings out the flavour of the other ingredients. Pepper is a digestive stimulant, as well as a decongestant and antioxidant.

Black peppercorns

These are the dried green berries of the vine pepper and they are relatively mild. Black peppercorns are best when freshly ground in a peppermill when you need them because they quickly lose their aroma.

White pepper

This has a less aromatic flavour than black pepper and is generally used in white sauces and other dishes to avoid dark specks of black pepper.

Green peppercorns

These unripened berries have a milder flavour than black or white peppercorns and may be dried or preserved in brine. They are sometimes used to make a spicy peppercorn sauce.

Pink peppercorns

These pretty, pink berries are not a true pepper. They are the processed berry of a type of poison ivy and should be used in small amounts as they are mildly toxic.

PAPRIKA

Paprika is a milder relative of cayenne and can be used more liberally, adding flavour as well as heat. Like cayenne, it is a digestive stimulant and has antiseptic properties. Paprika can also improve blood circulation but if eaten in large quantities may aggravate the stomach.

SAFFRON

The world's most expensive spice is made from the dried stigmas of *Crocus salivus*. Only a tiny amount of this bright-orange spice is needed to add a wonderful colour and delicate bitter-sweet flavour to rice, stews, soups and milky puddings. Saffron has the ability to calm and balance the body and is believed to be an aphrodisiac.

Right, clockwise from top left: mixed spice, ground and whole nutmegs, and paprika

Ground and fresh turmeric

Grinding Spices

Whole spices ground by hand provide the best flavour and aroma. Grind as you need them and do not be tempted to grind too much as they tend to lose their potency and flavour. Some spices such as mace, fenugreek, cloves, turmeric and cinnamon are difficult to grind at home and are better bought ready-ground.

Grind whole spices in a mortar using a pestle – or use an electric coffee grinder if you prefer.

Toasting Spices

This process enhances the flavour and aroma of spices and is thought to make them more digestible.

Put the spices in a dry frying pan and cook over a low heat, shaking the pan frequently, for 1 minute or until the spices release their aroma.

TURMERIC

Sometimes used as an alternative to saffron, turmeric delivers a similar yellow colour but has a very different flavour. It adds an earthy, peppery flavour to curries and stews. Turmeric is valued for its anti-bacterial and antifungal qualities. It can aid digestion and in Asia it is believed to be a remedy for liver problems.

VANILLA

These slender, chocolate-brown pods have a fragrant, exotic aroma and luscious, almost creamy flavour. They can be used more than once; simply rinse and dry before storing in an airtight jar. Buy natural vanilla essence or extract, which is made by infusing the pods in alcohol: artificial vanilla flavouring is nowhere near as good. Vanilla is considered to be an aphrodisiac and a tonic for the brain.

Buying and Storing: Buy spices in small quantities from a shop with a regular turnover of stock. Aroma is the best indication of freshness, as this diminishes when the spice is stale. Store in airtight jars in a cool place away from direct light.

Natural vanilla essence and vanilla pods

Salt

Moderate amounts of salt are needed by the body, but it is easy to consume too much, as salt is added to many processed foods. Too much salt can lead to high blood pressure, hypertension, water retention and may increase the risk of heart disease. Used in small amounts, salt can enhance the flavour of food. Use rock or sea salt rather than refined table salt.

Table salt (top), rock salt (right) and sea salt

Pasta

Once considered a fattening food, pasta is now recognized as an important part of a healthy diet. The variety of shapes is almost endless, from the myriad tiny soup pastas to huge shells used for stuffing. Pasta can be plain, made with egg or flavoured with ingredients such as tomato or spinach. Low in fat and high in complex carbohydrates, it provides plenty of long-term energy. Corn and buckwheat varieties are also available, as is wholewheat pasta, which is high in fibre.

Pasta is one of our most simple, yet most versatile foods. A combination of wheat flour and water produces the basic dough, which can then be formed into an infinite number of shape variations. Alter the type of flour, add fresh eggs or a vegetable purée, and the options are even greater. Although pasta is itself a low-fat food, it is important to take care when choosing the accompanying sauce, as overloading on cheese or cream can soon transform pasta into a high-fat food.

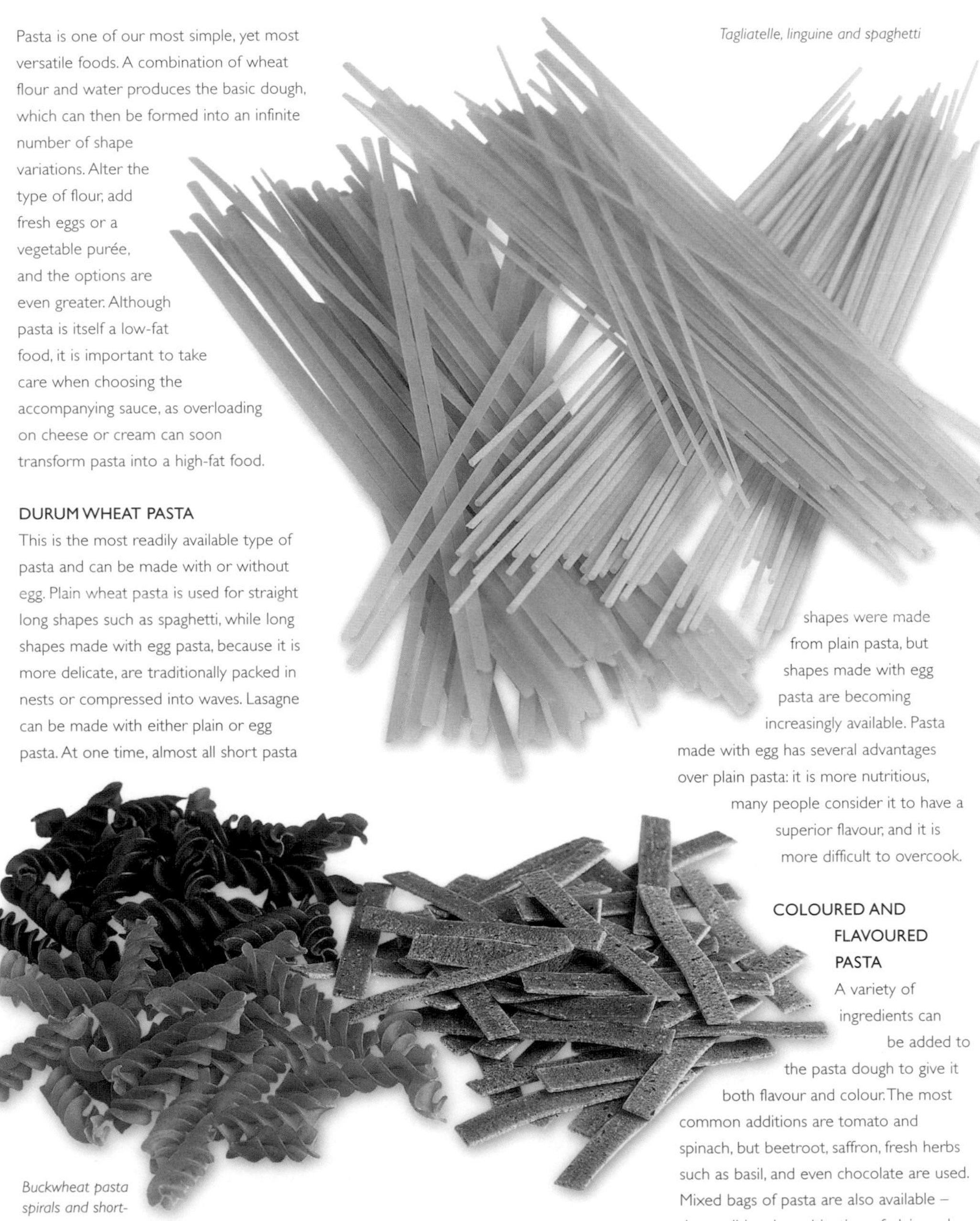

Tagliatelle, linguine and spaghetti

Buckwheat pasta spirals and short-cut pizzoccheri

DURUM WHEAT PASTA

This is the most readily available type of pasta and can be made with or without egg. Plain wheat pasta is used for straight long shapes such as spaghetti, while long shapes made with egg pasta, because it is more delicate, are traditionally packed in nests or compressed into waves. Lasagne can be made with either plain or egg pasta. At one time, almost all short pasta shapes were made from plain pasta, but shapes made with egg pasta are becoming increasingly available. Pasta made with egg has several advantages over plain pasta: it is more nutritious, many people consider it to have a superior flavour, and it is more difficult to overcook.

COLOURED AND FLAVOURED PASTA

A variety of ingredients can be added to the pasta dough to give it both flavour and colour. The most common additions are tomato and spinach, but beetroot, saffron, fresh herbs such as basil, and even chocolate are used. Mixed bags of pasta are also available – the traditional combination of plain and

Right: Corn or maize pasta can be bought in a wide variety of shapes, from simple elbow macaroni to fusilli and three-coloured radiatori

spinach-flavoured pasta is called paglia e fieno, which means straw and hay. But there are many other mixtures, some having as many as seven different flavours and colours of pasta.

WHOLEWHEAT PASTA

This substantial pasta is made using wholemeal flour and it contains more fibre than plain durum wheat pasta. It has a slightly chewy texture and nutty flavour and takes longer to cook. Wholewheat spaghetti (bigoli), a traditional Italian variety that comes from the area around Venice known as the Veneto, can be found in good Italian delicatessens, and in health food shops and supermarkets. There is an increasing range of wholewheat shapes, from tiny soup pastas to rotelle (wheels) and lasagne.

BUCKWHEAT PASTA

Pasta made from buckwheat flour has a nutty taste and is darker in colour than wholewheat pasta. Pizzoccheri from Lombardy is the classic shape. These thin, flat noodles are traditionally sold in nests like tagliatelle (although pizzoccheri are about half the length), but they are also available cut into short strips.

Other buckwheat pasta shapes are available in health food shops and supermarkets. Buckwheat pasta is gluten-free and suitable for people who are intolerant to gluten or wheat. It is also very nutritious, containing all eight amino acids, calcium, zinc and B vitamins.

Above: Pasta can be coloured and flavoured in a variety of ways, but plain, spinach and tomato varieties are the most popular

CORN PASTA

This pasta is made with corn or maize flour, is gluten-free and is a good alternative pasta for people who cannot tolerate gluten or wheat. It is made in a wide range of shapes, including spaghetti, fusilli (spirals) and conchiglie (shells), as well as more unusual varieties. Plain corn pasta is a sunshine-yellow colour, and may be flavoured with spinach or tomato. It is cooked and used in the same way as wheat pasta and is available from many health food stores and supermarkets.

PASTA SHAPES

Long pasta

Dried long pasta in the form of spaghetti is probably the best known, but there are many other varieties, from fine vermicelli to pappardelle – broad ribbon noodles. Tagliatelle, the most common form of ribbon noodles, is usually sold coiled into nests. Long pasta is best served with a thin sauce, made with olive oil, butter, cream, eggs, grated cheese or chopped fresh herbs. When vegetables are added to the sauce, they should be finely chopped.

Fresh spaghetti, tagliatelle and fettuccine are widely available.

Short pasta

There are hundreds of different short dried pasta shapes, which may be made with plain pasta dough or the more nutritious yellow, egg pasta. Short pasta isn't often sold fresh because most shapes are difficult to produce, but you may find one or two in some Italian delicatessens, and a few fresh shapes are also available from larger supermarkets.

Conchiglie (shells) are one of the most useful shapes because they are concave and trap virtually any sauce. Fusilli (spirals) are good with thick tomato-based sauces and farfalle (butterflies) can be served with creamy sauces, but are very versatile and work equally well with tomato- or olive oil-based sauces. Macaroni used to be the most common short shape, and being hollow, it is good for most sauces and baked dishes. However, penne (quills) have become more popular, perhaps because the hollow tubes with diagonally cut ends go well with virtually any sauce. They are particularly good with chunky vegetable sauces or baked with cheese sauce.

Spinach and whole wheat lasagne and plain cannelloni

Quick Ideas for Pasta

- To make a simple, but richly flavoured tomato sauce: place some plum or cherry tomatoes in a baking dish and drizzle with a little olive oil. Roast in a hot oven for 15 minutes, then add one or two peeled garlic cloves and continue roasting for about 15 minutes more. Transfer to a food processor and blend with basil leaves. Season and stir into cooked pasta.
- Toss cooked pasta in a little chilli oil, scatter over rocket leaves and pine nuts and serve with finely grated Parmesan cheese.
- Stir a spoonful of black olive tapenade into cooked pasta, then scatter a few lightly toasted walnuts on top before serving.
- Roast a head of garlic, then squeeze out the puréed cloves and mix with olive oil. Toss with cooked pasta and sprinkle over plenty of fresh, chopped flat leaf parsley.
- Olives, mushrooms, aubergines and artichokes bottled in olive oil make quick and delicious additions to pasta.
- Combine cooked pasta with small chunks of mozzarella cheese, sliced sun-dried tomatoes, chopped fresh mint and a splash of olive oil.

Flat pasta

Lasagne is designed to be baked between layers of sauce, or cooked in boiling water, then layered, or rolled around a filling to make cannelloni. Lasagne is made from plain or egg pasta and both fresh and dried versions are available. The pasta sheets may be flavoured with tomato or spinach, or made with wholewheat flour.

Stuffed pasta

The most common stuffed pasta shapes are ravioli, tortellini (little pies) and cappelletti (little hats), athough there are other less well-known shapes available from Italian delicatessens. Plain, spinach and tomato doughs are the most usual, and there is a wide range of vegetarian fillings.

Pasta for soup

These tiny shapes are mostly made from plain durum wheat pasta, though you may find them with egg. There are hundreds of different ones, from tiny risi, which look like grains of rice, to alfabeti (alphabet shapes), which are popular with children. Slightly larger shapes such as farfalline (little bows) and tubetti (little tubes) are used in thicker soups such as minestrone.

Buying and Storing: The quality of pasta varies tremendously – choose good-quality Italian brands of pasta made from 100 per cent durum wheat, and visit your local Italian delicatessen to buy fresh pasta, rather than buying pre-packed pasta from the supermarket. Dried pasta will keep almost indefinitely, but if you decant the pasta into a storage jar, it is a good idea to use up the remaining pasta before adding any from a new packet. Fresh pasta from a delicatessen is usually sold loose

Large and small conchiglie (shells)

Choosing the Right Shape

While it is unnecessary to stick rigidly to hard and fast rules, some pasta shapes definitely work better than others with particular sauces.

- Long pasta shapes such as spaghetti, linguine, tagliatelle and fettuccine suit smooth cream- or olive oil-based sauces, or vegetable sauces where the ingredients are very finely chopped.
- Hollow shapes such as penne (quills), fusilli (spirals) and macaroni all work well with more robust sauces, such as cheese, tomato and vegetable.
- Stuffed pasta shapes such as ravioli and cappelletti are good with simple sauces made with butter, extra virgin olive oil or tomatoes.
- In soups, the delicate small shapes, risi (rice), orzi (barley) and quadrucci (squares) suit lighter broths, while the more substantial conchigliette (little shells) and farfalline (little butterflies) go well in heartier vegetable soups.

and is best cooked the same day, but can be kept in the fridge for a day or two. Fresh pasta from a supermarket is likely to be packed in plastic packs and bags, and these will keep for 3–4 days in the fridge. Fresh pasta freezes well and should be cooked from frozen. Packs and bags of supermarket pasta have the advantage of being easy to store in the freezer.

Fresh tortellini

Health Benefits: Pasta provides the body with fuel for all kinds of physical activity, from running a marathon to walking to the bus stop. High in complex carbohydrates, pasta is broken down slowly, providing energy over a long period of time. Wholewheat pasta is the most nutritious, containing a richer concentration of vitamins, minerals and fibre. Nevertheless, all pasta is a useful source of protein, as well as being low in fat. Buckwheat is very nutritious; it contains all eight essential amino acids, making it a complete protein. It is also particularly high in fibre.

Cooking Pasta

Pasta should be cooked in a large pan of boiling salted water to allow the strands or shapes to expand, and stirred occasionally to prevent them from sticking together. Do not add oil to the cooking water as it makes the pasta slippery and prevents it from absorbing the sauce. Cooking instructions are given on the packaging but always taste just before the end of the given time to prevent overcooking. Dried pasta should be *al dente*, or firm to the bite, while fresh pasta should be just tender.

1 Bring a large pan of salted water to the boil. For shapes, tip in the pasta and cover the pan. Bring quickly back to the boil and remove the lid. Reduce the heat slightly, then stir the pasta and cook according to the packet instructions. For long straight pasta such as spaghetti, coil the pasta into the water as it softens.

Above: Tiny soup pasta is available in hundreds of different shapes

Noodles

The fast food of the East, noodles can be made from wheat flour, rice, buckwheat flour or mung bean flour. Both fresh and dried noodles are readily available in health food stores and Asian shops as well as supermarkets. Like pasta, noodles are low in fat and high in complex carbohydrates, so provide long-term energy.

Rice noodles

WHEAT NOODLES

There are two main types of noodle: plain and egg. Plain noodles are made from strong flour and water, they can be flat or round and come in various thicknesses.

Udon noodles

These thick Japanese noodles can be round or flat and are available fresh, pre-cooked or dried. Wholewheat udon noodles have a more robust flavour.

Somen noodles

Usually sold in bundles, held together by a paper band, these thin, white noodles are available from Oriental stores.

Egg noodles

Far more common than the plain wheat variety, egg noodles are sold both fresh and dried. The Chinese type come in various thicknesses. Very fine egg noodles, which resemble vermicelli, are usually sold in coils. Wholewheat egg noodles are widely available from larger supermarkets.

Ramen noodles

These Japanese egg noodles are also sold in coils and are often cooked and served with an accompanying broth.

RICE NOODLES

These fine, delicate noodles are made from rice and are opaque-white in colour. Like wheat noodles, they come in various widths, from the very thin strands known as rice vermicelli, which are popular in Thailand and southern China, to the thicker rice sticks, which are used more in Vietnam and Malaysia. A huge range of rice noodles is available dried in Oriental grocers and fresh ones are occasionally found in the chiller cabinets. Since all rice noodles are pre-cooked, they need only to be soaked in hot water for a few minutes to soften them before use in stir-fries and salads.

CELLOPHANE VERMICELLI AND NOODLES

Made from mung bean starch, these translucent noodles, also known as bean thread vermicelli and glass noodles, come in a variety of thicknesses and are only available dried. Although very fine, the strands are firm and fairly tough. Cellophane noodles don't need to be boiled, and are simply soaked in boiling water for 10–15 minutes. They have a fantastic texture, which they retain when cooked, never becoming soggy. Cellophane noodles are almost tasteless unless combined with other strongly flavoured foods and seasonings. They are

Udon noodles (above) and cellophane noodles

never eaten on their own, but used as an ingredient. They are good in vegetarian dishes, and as an ingredient in spring rolls.

BUCKWHEAT NOODLES

Soba are the best-known type of buckwheat noodles. They are a much darker colour than wheat noodles – almost brownish grey. In Japan, soba noodles are traditionally served in soups or stir-fries with a variety of sauces.

Dried and fresh egg noodles

Quick Ideas for Noodles

- To make a simple broth, dissolve mugi miso in hot water, add cooked soba noodles; sprinkle with chilli flakes and sliced spring onions.

- Cook ramen noodles in vegetable stock, then add a splash of dark soy sauce, shredded spinach and grated ginger (above). Serve sprinkled with sesame seeds and fresh coriander.

- Stir-fry sliced shiitake and oyster mushrooms in garlic and ginger, then toss with rice or egg noodles (above). Scatter with fresh chives and a little roasted sesame oil.
- In a food processor, blend together some lemon grass, chilli, garlic, ginger, kaffir lime leaves and fresh coriander. Fry the paste in a little sunflower oil and combine with cooked ribbon noodles. Sprinkle fresh basil and chopped spring onions on top before serving.

Buying and Storing: Packets of fresh noodles are found in the chiller cabinets of Asian shops. They usually carry a use-by date and must be stored in the fridge. Dried noodles will keep for many months if stored in an airtight container in a cool, dry place.

Health Benefits: Noodles are high in complex carbohydrates, which are broken down slowly, providing energy over a long period of time. Wholewheat noodles are the most nutritious, containing a richer concentration of vitamins, minerals and fibre. Nevertheless, all noodles are a useful source of protein, as well as being low in fat. Buckwheat noodles are made from buckwheat flour, which contains all eight essential amino acids, making it a complete protein. It is also particularly high in fibre. Cellophane noodles are made from mung bean starch, which is reputed to be one of the most powerful detoxifiers.

Cooking Wheat Noodles

Wheat noodles are very easy to cook. Both dried and fresh noodles are cooked in a large pan of boiling water; how long depends on the type of noodle and the thickness of the strips. Dried noodles need about 3 minutes cooking time, while fresh ones will often be ready in less than a minute. Fresh noodles may need to be rinsed quickly in cold water to prevent them from overcooking.

Wholewheat egg noodles

Oils

There is a wide variety of cooking oils and they are produced from a number of different sources: from cereals such as corn; from fruits such as olives; from nuts such as walnuts, almonds and hazelnuts; and from seeds such as rapeseed, safflower and sunflower. They can be extracted by simple mechanical means such as pressing or crushing, or by further processing, usually heating. Virgin oils, which are obtained from the first cold pressing of the olives, nuts or seeds, are sold unrefined, and have the most characteristic flavour. They are also the most expensive.

OLIVE OIL

Indisputably the king of oils, olive oil varies in flavour and colour, depending on how it is made and where it comes from. Climate, soil, harvesting and pressing all influence the end result – generally, the hotter the climate the more robust the oil. Thus oils from southern Italy, Greece and Spain have a stronger flavour and a darker colour than those from the rest of Italy and France. Olive oil is rich in monounsaturated fat, which has been found to reduce cholesterol, thereby reducing the risk of heart disease. There are different grades to choose from.

Extra virgin olive oil

This premium olive oil has a superior flavour. It comes from the first cold pressing of the olives and has a low acidity – less than 1 per cent. Extra virgin olive oil is not recommended for frying, as heat impairs its flavour, but it is good in salad dressings, especially when combined with lighter oils. It is delicious as a sauce on its own, stirred into pasta with chopped garlic and black pepper, or drizzled over steamed vegetables.

Virgin olive oil

Also a pure first-pressed oil, this has a slightly higher level of acidity than extra virgin olive oil, and can be used in much the same way.

Essential Fats

We all need some fat in our diet. It keeps us warm, adds flavour to our food, carries essential vitamins A, D, E and K around the body, and provides essential fatty acids, which cannot be produced in the body, but are vital for growth and development, and may reduce the risk of heart attacks.

What is more important is the type and amount of fat that we eat. Some fats are better for us than others, and we should adjust our intake accordingly. It is recommended that fat should make up no more than 35 per cent of our diet.

Extra virgin olive oil (left), sunflower oil (right) and safflower oil (far right)

Groundnut oil (left) and almond oil

Pure olive oil

Refined and blended to remove impurities, this type of olive oil has a much lighter flavour than virgin or extra virgin olive oil and is suitable for all types of cooking. It can be used for shallow frying.

OTHER OILS

There is a wide range of light, processed oils on the market, which are all relatively taste-free and have a variety of uses in the kitchen.

Corn oil

One of the most economical and widely used vegetable oils, corn oil has a deep golden colour and a fairly strong flavour. It is suitable for cooking and frying, but should not be used for salad dressings. Corn is rich in omega-6 (linoleic) fatty acids, which are believed to reduce harmful cholesterol in the body.

Safflower oil

This is a light, all-purpose oil, which comes from the seeds of the safflower. It can be used in place of sunflower and groundnut oils, but is a little thicker and has a slightly stronger flavour. It is suitable for deep frying, but is best used with other more strongly flavoured ingredients, and is ideal for cooking spicy foods. Safflower oil contains more polyunsaturated fat than any other type of oil and it is low in saturated fat.

Sunflower oil

Perhaps the best all-purpose oil, sunflower oil is very light and almost tasteless. It is very versatile, and can be used for frying and in cooking, or to make salad dressings, when it can be combined with a stronger flavoured oil such as olive oil or walnut oil. Sunflower oil is extracted from the seeds of the sunflower. It is very high in polyunsaturated fat and low in saturated fat.

Soya oil

This neutral flavoured, all-purpose oil, which is extracted from soya beans, is probably the most widely used oil in the world. It is useful for frying because it has a high smoking point, and remains stable at high temperatures. It is also widely used in margarines. It is rich in polyunsaturated and monounsaturated fats and low in saturates. Find a brand that is not made from genetically modified soya beans.

Groundnut oil

Also known as peanut oil, this relatively tasteless oil is useful for frying, cooking and dressing salads. Chinese peanut oil is darker in colour than groundnut oil and

Soya oil

Quick Ideas for Marinades

- Mix olive oil with chopped fresh herbs such as parsley, chives, oregano, chervil and basil. Add a splash or two of lemon juice and season with salt and pepper.
- Combine groundnut oil, toasted sesame oil, dark soy sauce, sweet sherry, rice vinegar and crushed garlic. Use as a marinade for tofu or tempeh.

- Mix together olive oil, lemon juice, sherry, honey and crushed garlic and and use as a marinade for vegetable and halloumi kebabs.

has a more distinctive nutty flavour. It is good in Oriental salads and stir-fries. Groundnut oil has a higher percentage of monounsaturated fat than soya oil but also contains polyunsaturated fat.

Rapeseed oil

This bland-tasting, all-purpose oil, also known as canola, can be used for frying, cooking and in salad dressings. It contains a higher percentage of monounsaturated fat than any other oil, with the exception of olive oil.

Grapeseed oil

A delicate, mild flavoured oil, which does not impose on other ingredients, grapeseed oil is pressed from grape seeds left over from wine-making. It is good in cooking and for frying, and can be used to make salad dressings, especially when combined with a stronger flavoured nut or olive oil. Grapeseed oil is high in polyunsaturated fat.

Rapeseed oil

SPECIALITY OILS

As well as the light, all-purpose oils that are used for everyday cooking, there are several richly flavoured oils that are used in small quantities, often as a flavouring ingredient in salad dressings and marinades, rather than for cooking.

Sesame oil

There are two types of sesame oil – the pale and light version that is pressed from untoasted seeds, and the rich, dark, toasted oil that is used in Oriental cuisines. The lighter oil, popular in India and the Middle East, has a mild flavour and a high smoking point and is useful for cooking. Dark sesame oil, which has a wonderfully nutty aroma and taste, is useful for flavouring marinades and stir-fries. It has a much stronger taste than either walnut oil or olive oil and is too overpowering to use in large quantities. However, it can be mixed with milder oils, such as groundnut or soya. Heating helps to intensify the aroma of toasted sesame oil, but it should never be heated for too long. Both types of sesame oil are high in polyunsaturated fat.

Walnut oil

This is an intensely flavoured oil that is delicious in salad dressings and marinades, but shouldn't be used for frying as heat diminishes its rich taste (it is also far too expensive to use in any great quantity). Instead, drizzle a little of the oil over roasted or steamed vegetables, use it to make a simple sauce for pasta, or stir into freshly cooked noodles just before serving. It can be used in small quantities, in place of some of the fat or oil in a recipe, to add flavour to cakes and biscuits, especially those that contain walnuts. Walnut oil does not keep for long and, after opening, should be kept in a cool, dark place to

Quick Ideas for Dressings and Salads

A good dressing should enhance rather than overpower the salad.

- To make a simple vinaigrette dressing, whisk together 60ml/4 tbsp extra virgin olive oil with 15ml/1 tbsp red or white wine vinegar or balsamic vinegar in a small jug. Add a pinch of sugar and 5ml/1 tsp Dijon mustard. Season to taste.
- To make a walnut oil dressing, whisk together 60ml/4 tbsp walnut oil with 15ml/1 tbsp sherry vinegar, then season to taste. This dressing is good with strong flavoured leaves, such as rocket, watercress or radicchio.

- Combine walnut oil and low-fat fromage frais or yogurt with chopped fresh flat leaf parsley. Season, then spoon the dressing over new potatoes and garnish with snipped chives and toasted chopped walnuts.
- Mix together grated fresh ginger, fresh coriander, lime juice and toasted sesame oil and pour over grated carrot. Sprinkle toasted sesame seeds over the carrot mixture.

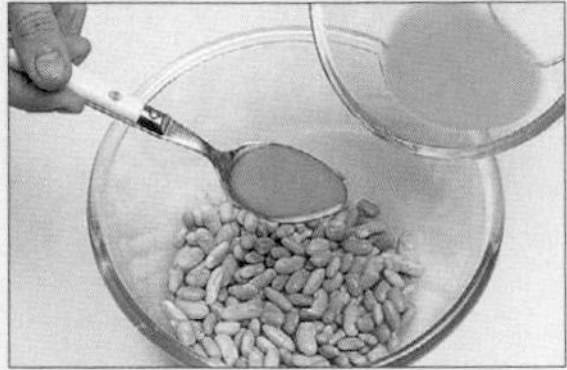

- Mix together extra virgin olive oil and lemon juice, and spoon over warm flageolet and cannellini beans. Add chopped tomatoes and chopped fresh flat leaf parsley.
- Toss steamed broccoli florets or sugar snap peas in a dressing made from hazelnut oil, olive oil, white wine vinegar and Dijon mustard.

prevent it from becoming rancid. It can be stored in the fridge, though this may cause the oil to solidify. Walnut oil is rich in polyunsaturated fats and contains vitamin E.

Hazelnut oil

This fine, fragrant oil is rich brown in colour and has a delicious, roasted hazelnut flavour. It is quite expensive to buy but, because it has such a strong flavour, only a little is needed. It is good, combined with less strongly flavoured oils, for salad dressings and sauces, and can be used to add a nutty flavour to teabreads, cakes, biscuits and pastry. Hazelnut oil is rich in monounsaturated fat.

Almond oil

This pale, delicate oil is mainly used in confectionery and desserts. It has a subtle, sweet flavour of almonds, though not enough to give an almond flavour to baked goods such as cakes and biscuits. Almond oil is rich in monounsaturated fat as well as vitamins A and E. It is reputed to be very good for the skin and is often used as a massage oil.

Buying and Storing: Cooking oils such as sunflower, soya and safflower are more stable than nut or seed oils, and have longer keeping properties. To keep them at their peak, store in a cool, dark place away from direct sunlight. Nut and seed oils are more volatile and turn rancid quickly and should be kept in the fridge after opening.

Health Benefits: Oils are undeniably high in calories and should always be used in moderation, but they also have a number of health benefits. Monounsaturated fats, found particularly in olive oil and rapeseed oil, stabilize or raise the level of the beneficial high density lipoproteins (HDLs), while lowering harmful low density lipoproteins (LDLs), thus keeping down cholesterol levels in the body. A high level of LDLs in the blood is usually an indication of increased cholesterol levels, as the LDLs carry the fatty substance (cholesterol) around the body; HDLs carry much less fat.

Olive oil also contains vitamin E, a natural antioxidant that can help fight off free radicals, which damage cells in the body and have the potential to cause cancer. Polyunsaturated fats provide essential fatty acids known as omega-3 (alpha-linolenic) and omega-6 (linolenic acid), which must be included in the diet. Omega-3, which is found in walnut, rapeseed and soya oil, has been found to reduce the likelihood of heart disease and blood clots; while omega 6, provided by safflower, sunflower and walnut oil, reduces harmful cholesterol levels. Polyunsaturated fats are more unstable than monounsaturated fats and are prone to oxidation, which can lead to the build-up of free radicals. Although polyunsaturates do contain vitamin E, it appears in varying amounts and so it is advisable to eat other foods that are rich in vitamin E to protect the fatty acids and the body from damage due to oxidation.

Walnut, sesame and hazelnut oils

Vinegars

One of our oldest condiments, vinegar is made by acetic fermentation, a process that occurs when a liquid containing less than 18 per cent alcohol is exposed to the air. Most countries produce their own type of vinegar, usually based on their most popular alcoholic drink – wine in France and Italy; sherry in Spain; rice wine in Asia; and beer and cider in Great Britain. Commonly used as a preservative in pickles and chutneys, it is also an ingredient in marinades and salad dressings. A spoonful or two of a good-quality vinegar can add flavour to cooked dishes and sauces.

WINE VINEGARS

These can be made from white, red or rosé wine, and the quality of the vinegar will depend on the quality of the original ingredient. The finest wine vinegars are made by the slow and costly Orleans method. Cheaper and faster methods of fermentation involve heating, which produces a harsher vinegar that lacks the complexities of the original wine. Use in dressings, mayonnaise, sauces or to add flavour to stews and soups.

BALSAMIC VINEGAR

This is a rich, dark, mellow vinegar, which has become hugely popular. Made in Modena in northern Italy, balsamic vinegar is made from grape juice (predominantly from Trebbiano grapes), which is fermented in vast wooden barrels for a minimum of four to five years and up to 40 or more years, resulting in an intensely rich vinegar with a concentrated flavour. Balsamic vinegar is delicious in dressings or sprinkled over roasted vegetables. It is even good with strawberries.

Balsamic vinegar

Sherry vinegar

SHERRY VINEGAR

This vinegar can be just as costly as balsamic vinegar and, if left to mature in wooden barrels, can be equally good. Sweet and mellow in flavour, sherry vinegar is caramel in colour and can be used in the same way as balsamic vinegar – in dressings, sprinkled over roasted vegetables or added to sauces and stews.

RASPBERRY VINEGAR

Any soft fruit can be used to enhance the flavour of white wine vinegar but raspberries are the most popular. Raspberry vinegar can be made at home by macerating fresh raspberries in good-quality wine vinegar for 2–3 weeks. Once the mixture is strained, the vinegar is delicious as part of a salad dressing, or in sauces. It can be mixed with sparkling mineral water to make a refreshing drink.

MALT VINEGAR

Made from soured beer, malt vinegar is used in Britain and other northern European countries for pickling onions and other vegetables, or for sprinkling over potato chips. It can be clear, but is often sold coloured with caramel. Malt vinegar has a robust, harsh flavour and it is not suitable for salad dressings.

Red and white wine vinegars

Raspberry vinegar

Above: Cider vinegar

RICE VINEGAR

There are two kinds of rice vinegar: the type from Japan is mellow and sweet and is most often used to flavour sushi rice, but it can also be added to dressings, stir-fries and sauces; Chinese rice vinegar is much sharper in taste. Rice vinegar is usually a clear, pale-brown colour, but it can also be inky-black, red or white.

CIDER VINEGAR

Made from cider and praised for its health-giving properties, cider vinegar is made in the same way as wine vinegar. It is a clear, pale-brown colour and has a slight apple flavour, but it is too strong and sharp to use in the same ways as wine vinegar. It can be used for salad dressings, but it is perhaps best kept for pickling fruits such as pears. Cider vinegar can be served as a soothing drink, mixed with honey, lemon juice and hot water, as a remedy for colds and flu.

Health Benefits: Hippocrates prescribed vinegar as a cure for respiratory problems, and it may also be beneficial in cases of food poisoning. Cider vinegar is said to have many therapeutic benefits, which were highlighted in a book written in the 1960s by Dr DeForest Clinton Jarvis, entitled *Folk Medicine*. He attributed cider as a cure for everything, from arthritis and headaches to obesity and hiccoughs.

Fragrant Spiced Vinegar

This aromatic vinegar is good in dressings and marinades. Any type of vinegar can be used as a base but, to achieve the best results, ensure that it is good quality. If the vinegar develops an unpleasant appearance or aroma, it should be discarded straight away.

Different flavourings including herb sprigs such as tarragon or rosemary, or whole spices such as cinnamon, star anise or black, white or green peppercorns can be used and will impart a distinctive flavour.

1 Place a few red chillies, 1–2 garlic cloves and some thick strips of lemon rind into a bottle of rice vinegar. Leave to infuse on a sunny window ledge or in a warm place for 3–4 weeks.

2 Strain the vinegar into a clean bottle and seal tightly with a cork. Store in a cool, dark place.

Rice vinegar (left) and brown malt vinegar

Teas & Tisanes

Tea has been a popular reviving drink for centuries and comes in many different forms, from traditional teas such as green tea, oolong tea and black tea to fragrant fruit infusions and healing herbal tisanes.

Black tea (left) and green tea

GREEN TEA

This tea is popular with the Chinese and Japanese who prefer its light, slightly bitter but nevertheless refreshing flavour. It is produced from leaves that are steamed and dried but not fermented, a process that retains their green colour.

OOLONG TEA

Partially fermented to produce a tea that falls between the green and black varieties in strength and colour. It is particularly fragrant.

BLACK TEA

This is the most widely available tea and is made by fermenting withered tea leaves, then drying them. It produces a dark brown brew that has a more assertive taste than green tea. Darjeeling and English breakfast tea are two examples.

Health Benefits: The latest research shows that drinking about five cups of tea a day may help to prevent heart disease, stroke and certain cancers. These benefits have been attributed to a group of antioxidants found in tea, which are called polyphenols or flavonoids. Flavonoids have antiviral, antibacterial and anti-inflamatory properties. Green tea contains the highest amount of flavonoids and black tea the lowest. Antioxidants help to mop up harmful free radicals, which cause damage to the body's cells and may cause cancer. Tea also contains fluoride, which can protect the teeth against decay. On the down side, tea can reduce the absorption of iron if drunk after a meal and it contains caffeine (although less than coffee), which is a well-known stimulant.

Oolong tea

FRUIT TEAS

These are made from a blend of fruit flavours, such as rosehip, strawberry, orange, raspberry and lemon, along with fruit pieces and sometimes herbs or real tea. It is a good idea to check the packaging to make sure the "tea" is naturally, rather than artificially, flavoured. Fruit teas make refreshing caffeine-free drinks, which are almost calorie-free. They are an ideal drink for pregnant women and, because of their low-sugar content, are suitable for diabetics.

Coffee

Although coffee is generally viewed as unhealthy, largely due to its high level of caffeine, studies have shown that it can enhance concentration and elevate mood. However, drinking more than six cups a day can increase the risk of heart disease and high blood pressure.

HERBAL TISANES

Below: *Naturally flavoured fruit teas are caffeine-free and contain hardly any calories*

Although herbal tisanes are of little nutritional value, herbalists have prescribed them for centuries for a multitude of ailments and diseases. These teas (made from the leaves, seeds and flowers of herbs) are a convenient and simple way of taking medicinal herbs. They do, however, vary in strength and effectiveness. Shop-bought teas are generally mild in their medicinal properties but are good, healthy, caffeine-free drinks. Even so, some varieties are not recommended for young children and pregnant women and so it is advisable to check the packaging. Teas that are prescribed by herbalists can be incredibly powerful and should be taken with care.

The most popular types of herbal teas are listed below.

Peppermint tea is recommended as a digestive to be drunk after a meal. It is also effective in settling other stomach problems and for treating colds. **Camomile tea** soothes and calms the nerves and can induce sleep. **Raspberry leaf tea** prepares the uterus for birth and is said to reduce labour pains, but it is not recommended in early pregnancy. It can also relieve period pains. **Rosehip tea** is high in Vitamin C and may help to ward off colds and flu. **Dandelion and lemon verbena** teas are effective diuretics. **Rosemary tea** can stimulate the brain and improve concentration. **Thyme tea** can boost the immune system and fight viral, bacterial and fungal infections. **Elderflower** tea can ease painful sinuses and bronchial conditions.

Elderflower and dandelion herbal tisanes

Flavoured Teas

These could not be easier to make: simply steep your chosen herb, spice or fruit in boiling water and leave to infuse before straining. Ginger tea is effective against nausea, colds and flu and stomach upsets.

1 To make ginger tea, roughly chop a 2.5cm/1in piece of fresh root ginger. Place in a cup and pour in boiling water.

2 Cover and leave for 7–10 minutes. Strain or drink as it is – the ginger will stay in the bottom of the cup.

Sweeteners

Nutritionists have wide-ranging – and often extreme – opinions on sugar and sugar alternatives. Some maintain that these products cause hyperactivity in children, while others believe that sugars can induce relaxation and sleep. Many recipes from breads and cakes to desserts and puddings contain different types of sugar and/or sugar substitutes such as molasses, honey, malt and grain syrups, as well as dried fruit, and wouldn't be palatable without them. So, provided that a diet is well balanced and varied, it is considered that moderate amounts of sugar are nutritionally acceptable.

Blackstrap molasses

MOLASSES

This rich, syrupy liquid is a by-product of sugar refining and ranges in quality and colour. The most nutritionally valuable type is thick and very dark blackstrap molasses, which contains less sugar than lighter alternatives and is richer in iron, calcium, copper, magnesium, phosphorus, potassium and zinc. However, it may be better to choose organically produced molasses, which doesn't contain the chemicals and additives that are used in the sugar-refining process.

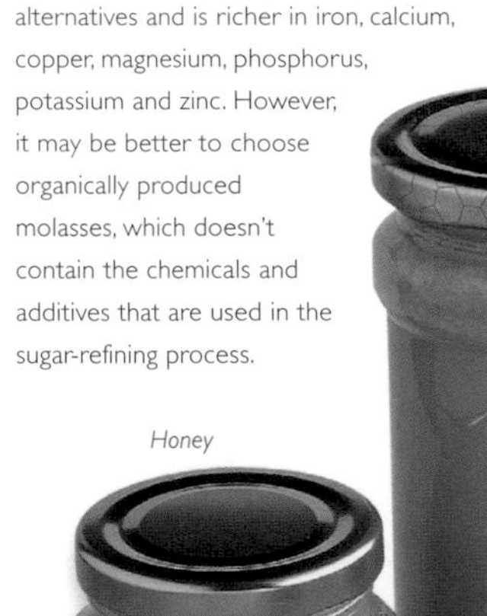

Honey

HONEY

One of the oldest sweeteners used by man, honey was highly valued by the ancient Egyptians for its medicinal and healing properties. The colour, flavour, consistency and quality of honey depends on the source of nectar as well as the method of production. In general the darker the colour, the stronger the flavour. Many commercial brands of honey are pasteurized and blended to give a uniform taste and texture, but from the point of view of both flavour and health, it is best to buy raw unfiltered honey from a single flower source.

Nutritionally, honey offers negligible benefits, but as it is much sweeter than sugar, less is needed; it is also lower in calories. Today, honey still retains its reputation as an antiseptic, and recent studies show that it is effective in healing and disinfecting wounds if applied externally. Mixed with lemon and hot water, it can relieve sore throats and is also thought to be helpful in treating diarrhoea and asthma.

Carob and carob powder

CAROB

This caffeine-free alternative to chocolate is made from the aromatic, fleshy bean pod of a Mediterranean tree. Carob

Malt extract

Dried fruit

powder (flour) looks and tastes similar to cocoa powder and can be used to replace it in hot drinks, confectionery and baked goods. It is naturally sweeter and lower in fat than cocoa powder, as well as being more nutritious, providing iron, calcium, vitamin B_6, riboflavin and potassium.

MAPLE SYRUP

This is made from the sap of the maple tree. Look for pure varieties rather than maple-flavoured syrup, which contains additives. Maple syrup has a rich, distinctive flavour and is sweeter than sugar, so less is required in cooking.

GRAIN SYRUPS

Corn, barley, wheat and rice can be transformed into syrups that are used in place of sugar in baked goods and sauces. Grain syrups tend to be easier to digest and enter the bloodstream more slowly than other forms of refined sugar, which cause swings in blood sugar levels. Grain syrups are not as sweet as sugar and have a mild, subtle flavour. Malt extract, a by-product of barley, has a more intense flavour and is good in breads and other baked goods.

FRUIT JUICE

Freshly squeezed fruit juice is a useful alternative to sugar in baked goods, sauces, pies and ice cream. Fruit juice concentrates such as apple, pear and grape, which have no added sugar or preservatives, are available from health food shops. They can be diluted or used in concentrated form in cakes, pies and puddings.

Clockwise from left: date syrup, barley malt syrup and brown rice syrup

DRIED FRUIT

Dates are made into a syrup that has a rich flavour and can be used to sweeten cakes. Puréed dried fruits such as prunes, figs, dates and apricots can also replace sugar in pies and cakes. Dried fruit can be added to both sweet and savoury foods.

Spiced Apricot Purée

This richly spiced purée is delicious stirred into thick natural yogurt or can be used to sweeten cakes, crumbles and pies.

1 Place 350g/12oz/1½ cups dried apricots in a saucepan with enough water to cover. Add 1 cinnamon stick, 2 cloves and 2.5ml/½ tsp freshly grated nutmeg. Bring to the boil, then simmer for 20 minutes until the apricots are plump.

2 Leave to cool, then purée in a food processor until smooth. Add more water if the mixture seems a little thick.

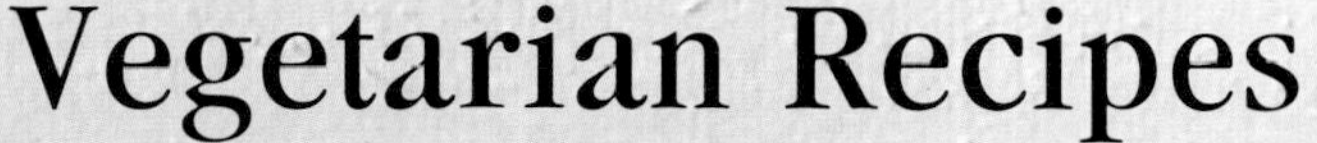

Vegetarian Recipes

If you've worked your way through the first section of this book, you'll be a mine of information about a wide range of whole foods. However, it's one thing to have a working knowledge of nutrition; quite another to put it into practice, so the pages that follow are packed with exciting and inspirational recipes. Each is designed to help you introduce more nutritious ingredients into your diet with minimum fuss but maximum flavour. Beginning with breakfast, the most important meal of the day, this section takes a lingering look at brunches, soups and light meals, main courses, recipes for special occasions, pastries, salads and side dishes, then moves on to delicious desserts and bakes. Many of the step-by-step recipes include information boxes that highlight the health benefits of key ingredients when used as part of a balanced diet, and there are also valuable variations and cook's tips.

BREAKFASTS and BRUNCHES

Start the day with a nutritious, low-fat meal. The selection presented here will boost your energy levels through the morning, keeping you alert and awake, ready to face the day. The delicious yogurts, juices and cereals , omelettes and brunches are all quick and easy to prepare.

Banana and Strawberry Smoothie

FULL OF ENERGY-GIVING OATS and fruits, this tasty drink makes a brilliant breakfast.

INGREDIENTS

2 bananas, quartered
250g/9oz/2 cups strawberries
30ml/2 tbsp oatmeal
500g/1¼lb/2½ cups natural live yogurt

Serves 2

COOK'S TIP

Prepare fruit drinks just before serving to gain maximum benefit from the nutrients.

1 Place the bananas, strawberries, oatmeal and yogurt in a food processor or blender and process for a few minutes until combined and creamy. Pour into tall glasses and serve.

Citrus Shake

PACKED WITH VITAMIN C, this refreshing juice is a great way to start the day.

INGREDIENTS

1 pineapple
6 oranges, peeled and chopped
juice of 1 lemon
1 pink grapefruit, peeled and chopped

Serves 4

1 To prepare the pineapple, cut the bottom and the spiky top off the fruit. Stand the pineapple upright and cut off the skin, removing all the spikes and as little of the flesh as possible. Lay the pineapple on its side and cut into bite-size chunks.

2 Place the pineapple, oranges, lemon juice and grapefruit in a food processor or blender and process for a few minutes until combined.

3 Press the juice through a sieve to remove any pith or membranes. Serve chilled.

Cranberry and Apple Juice

THIS GINGER-FLAVOURED, CLEANSING JUICE offers a fine balance of sweet and sour tastes.

INGREDIENTS

4 eating apples
600ml/1 pint/2½ cups cranberry juice
2.5cm/1in piece fresh root ginger, peeled and sliced

Serves 4

HEALTH BENEFITS

Brightly coloured fruits, such as cranberries, contain valuable amounts of antioxidant vitamins, which are believed to have cancer-fighting properties.

1 Peel the apples, if you wish, then core and chop.

2 Pour the cranberry juice into a food processor or blender. Add the chopped apples and sliced ginger and process for a few minutes until combined and fairly smooth. Serve chilled.

Zingy Vegetable Juice

GINGER PACKS A POWERFUL punch and certainly gets you going in the morning, even if you're feeling groggy.

INGREDIENTS

1 cooked beetroot in natural juice, sliced
1 large carrot, sliced
4cm/1½in piece fresh root ginger, peeled and finely grated
2 apples, peeled, if liked, chopped and cored
150g/5oz/1¼ cups seedless white grapes
300ml/½ pint/1¼ cups fresh orange juice

Serves 2

1 Place the beetroot, carrot, ginger, apples, grapes and orange juice in a food processor or blender and process for a few minutes until combined and fairly smooth. Serve immediately or chill until ready to serve.

Right: Clockwise from top right, Cranberry and Apple Juice, Citrus Shake, Banana and Strawberry Smoothie, Zingy Vegetable Juice.

Date, Banana and Walnut Yogurt

DATES AND bananas give a high fibre boost to this breakfast. Both fruits are also high in natural sugars.

INGREDIENTS

115g/4oz/⅔ cup dried dates, stoned and chopped

300ml/½ pint/1¼ cups low-fat natural yogurt

2 bananas

50g/2oz/½ cup chopped walnuts

Serves 4

COOK'S TIP

Use standard dried dates and not those which have been sugar-rolled. Bananas are probably the best and most convenient instant-energy food there is. If you haven't got time for breakfast, just unzip a banana!

1 Stir the dates into the yogurt in a mixing bowl. Cover and leave overnight in the fridge, to allow the fruit to soften.

2 Peel, then slice the bananas into the yogurt mixture. Spoon into dishes and top with the walnuts.

VARIATION

In place of walnuts you could use hazelnuts or toasted pecan nuts. Figs, mangoes or pawpaw can replace dates.

Mixed Berry Yogurt Shake

WHIZZ THIS in a blender or food processor for a quick, low-fat and high vitality breakfast in a glass. Rosewater adds an exotic touch. You could also experiment with other fruits to create your own flavour shake, such as banana with vanilla essence, or apricot with a few drops of almond essence.

INGREDIENTS

250ml/8fl oz/1 cup semi-skimmed milk, chilled

250ml/8fl oz/1 cup low-fat natural yogurt

115g/4oz mixed summer fruits

5ml/1 tsp rosewater

a little honey, to taste

Serves 2

1 Blend the milk, yogurt, fruits and rosewater in a food processor.

2 Add honey to taste if necessary, depending on the sweetness of the fruits. Pour into two glasses.

COOK'S TIP

Any combination of soft red fruits can be used such as strawberries, raspberries, bilberries, blackberries, morello cherries and/or redcurrants.

Melon, Pineapple and Grape Cocktail

A LIGHT fresh fruit salad, with no added sugar, makes a refreshing start to the day, and can easily be prepared the night before.

INGREDIENTS

1/2 melon
225g/8oz fresh pineapple, or 227g/8oz can pineapple chunks in own juice
225g/8oz seedless white grapes, halved
120ml/4fl oz/1/2 cup white grape juice
fresh mint leaves, to decorate (optional)
Serves 4

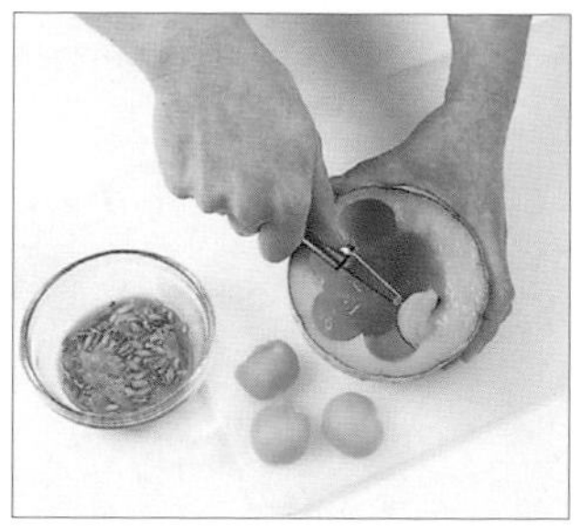

1 Remove the seeds from the melon half and use a melon baller to scoop out even-size balls.

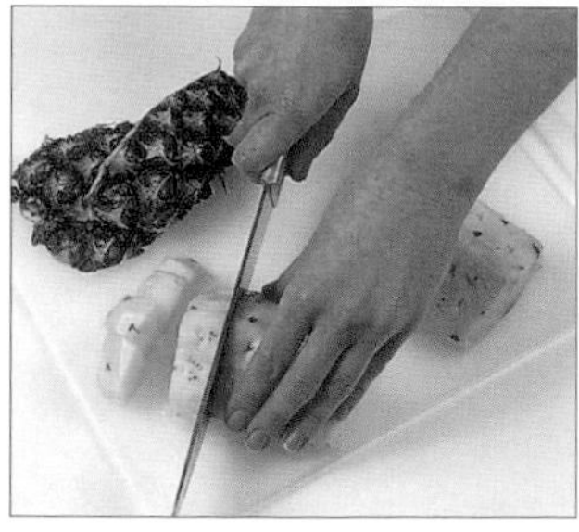

2 Using a sharp knife, cut the skin from the pineapple and discard. Cut the fruit into bite-size chunks.

3 Combine all the fruits in a glass serving dish and pour over the juice. If you are using canned pineapple, measure the drained juice and make it up to the required quantity with grape juice.

4 If not serving immediately, cover and chill. Serve decorated with mint leaves, if liked.

Three Fruit Compotes

INGREDIENTS

Orange and Prune Compote

1 juicy orange, peeled

50g/2oz/⅓ cup ready-to-eat prunes

75ml/5 tbsp orange juice

Pear and Kiwi Fruit Compote

1 ripe eating pear, cored

1 kiwi fruit

60ml/4 tbsp apple or pineapple juice

Grapefruit and Strawberry Compote

1 ruby grapefruit, peeled

115g/4oz/1 cup strawberries

60ml/4 tbsp orange juice

To serve

yogurt and toasted hazelnuts

Each compote serves 1

1 For the orange and prune compote, segment the orange and place in a bowl with the prunes.

2 For the pear and kiwi fruit compote, slice the pear. Peel and cut the kiwi fruit into wedges.

3 For the grapefruit and strawberry compote, segment the grapefruit and halve the strawberries.

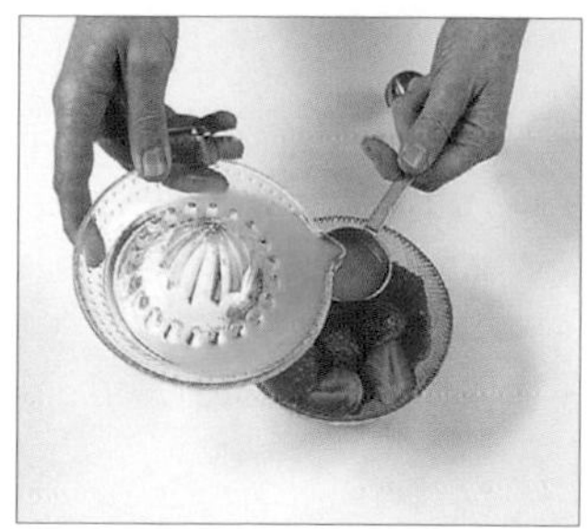

4 Place your selected fruits together in a bowl and pour over the juice. Choose "fresh-pressed" juices rather than those made from concentrates. Or, squeeze your own juice using a blender or food processor.

5 Serve the chosen compote topped with a spoonful of low-fat natural yogurt together with a sprinkling of chopped toasted hazelnuts.

VARIATION

This is particularly nice served with a Greek-style yogurt, made from ewes' or cows' milk. Its fat content will be higher than low-fat yogurt, but because of this it will taste slightly sweeter.

Fruity Sesame Porridge

PORRIDGE MADE with skimmed milk makes a wonderfully nourishing breakfast. Dried fruit and toasted sesame seeds make it even better, providing useful amounts of iron and magnesium. If you use so-called "old-fashioned" or "original" oats, the porridge will be quite thick and coarse textured. You could also use "jumbo" oats. If you prefer a smoother porridge, try ordinary rolled oats (sometimes called oatflakes).

INGREDIENTS

50g/2oz/½ cup porridge oats
475ml/16fl oz/2 cups skimmed milk
75g/3oz/½ cup ready-to-eat dried fruit salad, chopped
30ml/2 tbsp sesame seeds, toasted

Serves 2

1 Put the oats, milk and chopped dried fruit in a non-stick saucepan.

COOK'S TIP

To toast the sesame seeds, stir them in a pan over a high heat. When they are light brown, remove and let them cool before using.

2 Bring to the boil, then lower the heat and simmer gently for 3 minutes, stirring occasionally, until thickened. Serve in individual bowls, sprinkled with sesame seeds.

Trail Mix

EAT THIS nutritious snack on the run, or sprinkle it on top of yogurt or stewed fruit. It makes an excellent nibble between meals, but is quite high in calories, so don't get too carried away with it!

INGREDIENTS

Makes 250g/9oz/scant 2 cups

50g/2oz/⅓ cup ready-to-eat dried apricots or figs, quartered
50g/2oz/⅓ cup raisins or sultanas
50g/2oz/½ cup hazelnuts
50g/2oz/scant ½ cup sunflower seeds
50g/2oz/scant ½ cup pumpkin seeds

1 Cut the apricots or figs into quarters and place in a large bowl.

2 Add all the remaining ingredients and toss everything together. Store in an airtight container and use within 2–3 weeks.

COOK'S TIP

Other dried fruits or nuts may be added or substituted for those already present in the mix. Both nuts and seeds have a high oil content so will turn rancid quite quickly. Be sure to use them fresh.

Crunchy Fruit Layer

You can enjoy this all year round, choosing fresh fruit as it comes into season.

INGREDIENTS

1 peach or nectarine
75g/3oz/1 cup crunchy toasted oat cereal
150ml/¼ pint/⅔ cup low-fat natural yogurt
15ml/1 tbsp pure fruit jam
15ml/1 tbsp unsweetened fruit juice
Serves 2

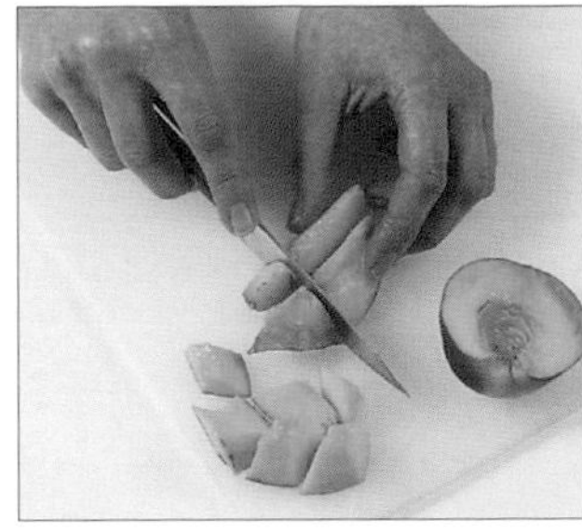

1 Remove the stone from the peach or nectarine and cut the fruit into bite-size pieces with a sharp knife. If you like to peel the fruit, immerse in boiling water for 30 seconds and remove the skin. Do this before taking out the stone.

2 Divide the chopped fruit between two tall glasses, reserving a few pieces for decoration.

3 Sprinkle the oat cereal over the fruit in an even layer, then top with the yogurt.

4 Stir the jam and fruit juice together in a jug, then drizzle the mixture over the yogurt. Decorate with the reserved peach or nectarine and serve at once.

Cook's Tip

If you prefer to use a flavoured toasted oat cereal (raisin and almond, perhaps, or tropical fruits) be sure to check the nutritional information on the label and choose the variety with the lowest amount of added sugar. Any fruit jam and juice which complement each other and the chosen fruit can be used.

Apricot and Almond Muesli

THIS CEREAL provides an excellent way of increasing the amount of fresh fruit in the diet. There is no added sugar in this wholewheat fruit and nut muesli, which is packed with fibre, vitamins and minerals.

INGREDIENTS

50g/2oz/½ cup whole blanched almonds
115g/4oz/⅔ cup ready-to-eat dried apricots
200g/7oz/2 cups whole rolled oats
75g/3oz/1 cup wheatflakes or oatbran flakes
50g/2oz/⅓ cup raisins or sultanas
40g/1½ oz/⅓ cup pumpkin seeds
40g/1½ oz/⅓ cup sunflower seeds
skimmed milk, low-fat natural yogurt or fresh fruit juice, and fresh fruit, to serve

Serves 8

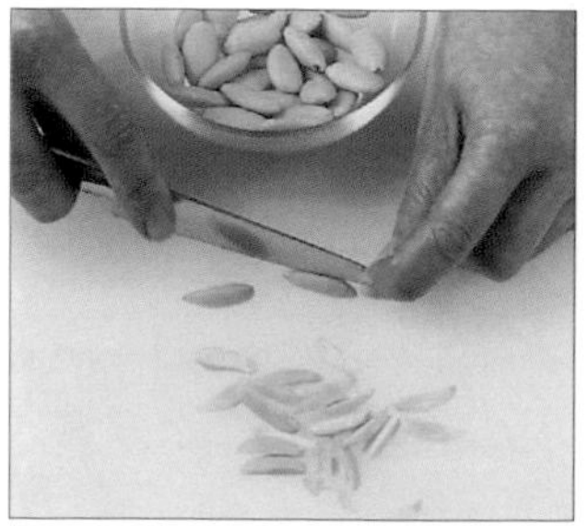

1 Using a sharp knife, carefully cut the almonds into slivers.

2 Cut the dried apricots into small even-size pieces.

3 Stir all the ingredients together in a large bowl. Store in an airtight container and use within 6 weeks.

4 Serve with skimmed milk, low-fat natural yogurt or fruit juice and top with fresh fruit, such as peach, banana or strawberry slices.

VARIATION

Ring the changes by adding other dried fruits, such as chopped dates, figs, peaches, pear, pineapple or apple chunks. Walnuts, brazil nuts or hazelnuts could be substituted for the almonds.

COOK'S TIP

To blanch shelled almonds, pour boiling water over the brown-skinned kernels and leave for a few minutes. Drain and rub off the skins. They are easier to cut when still warm.

Luxury Muesli

COMMERCIALLY MADE MUESLI really can't compete with this home-made version. This combination of seeds, grains, nuts and dried fruits works particularly well, but you can alter the balance of ingredients, or substitute others, if you like.

INGREDIENTS

50g/2oz/½ cup sunflower seeds
25g/1oz/¼ cup pumpkin seeds
115g/4oz/1 cup porridge oats
115g/4oz/heaped 1 cup wheat flakes
115g/4oz/heaped 1 cup barley flakes
115g/4oz/1 cup raisins
115g/4oz/1 cup chopped hazelnuts, roasted
115g/4oz/½ cup unsulphured dried apricots, chopped
50g/2oz/2 cups dried apple slices, halved
25g/1oz/⅓ cup desiccated coconut
Serves 4

1 Put the sunflower and pumpkin seeds in a dry frying pan and cook over a medium heat for 3 minutes until golden, tossing the seeds regularly to prevent them burning.

VARIATION

Serve the muesli in a long glass layered with fresh raspberries and fromage frais. Soak the muesli first in a little water or fruit juice in order to soften it slightly.

2 Mix the toasted seeds with the remaining ingredients and leave to cool. Store in an airtight container.

HEALTH BENEFITS

- *Sunflower seeds are rich in vitamin E, which is thought to reduce the risk of heart disease.*
- *Apricots are high on the list of fruits that are considered likely to help prevent certain cancers, notably that of the lung.*

Granola

HONEY-COATED NUTS, SEEDS AND oats, combined with sweet dried fruits, make an excellent and nutritious start to the day – without the additives often found in pre-packed cereals. Serve the granola with semi-skimmed milk or natural live yogurt and fresh fruit.

INGREDIENTS

115g/4oz/1 cup porridge oats
115g/4oz/1 cup jumbo oats
50g/2oz/½ cup sunflower seeds
25g/1oz/2 tbsp sesame seeds
50g/2oz/½ cup hazelnuts, roasted
25g/1oz/¼ cup almonds, roughly chopped
50ml/2fl oz/¼ cup sunflower oil
50ml/2fl oz/¼ cup clear honey
50g/2oz/½ cup raisins
50g/2oz/½ cup dried sweetened cranberries
Serves 4

1 Preheat the oven to 140°C/275°F/Gas 1. Mix together the oats, seeds and nuts in a bowl.

HEALTH BENEFITS

Oats have been the focus of much publicity in recent years; numerous studies have shown that their soluble fibre content can significantly lower blood cholesterol levels. They also supply vitamins B and E, and iron.

2 Heat the oil and honey in a large saucepan until melted, then remove the pan from the heat. Add the oat mixture and stir well. Spread out on one or two baking sheets.

3 Bake for about 50 minutes until crisp, stirring occasionally to prevent the mixture sticking. Remove from the oven and mix in the raisins and cranberries. Leave to cool, then store in an airtight container.

Porridge with Date Purée and Pistachio Nuts

FULL OF VALUABLE FIBRE and nutrients, dates give a natural sweet flavour to this warming winter breakfast dish.

INGREDIENTS

250g/9oz/scant 2 cups fresh dates
225g/8oz/2 cups porridge oats
475ml/16fl oz/2 cups semi-skimmed milk
pinch of salt
50g/2oz/½ cup shelled, unsalted pistachio nuts, roughly chopped

Serves 4

HEALTH BENEFITS

Oats have a reputation for being warming foods due to their fat and protein content, which is greater than that of most other grains. As well as providing energy and endurance, oats are one of the most nutritious cereals.

1 First make the date purée. Halve the dates and remove the stones and stems. Cover the dates with boiling water and leave to soak for about 30 minutes, until softened. Strain, reserving 90ml/6 tbsp of the soaking water.

2 Remove the skin from the dates and place them in a food processor with the reserved soaking water. Process to a smooth purée.

3 Place the oats in a saucepan with the milk, 300ml/½ pint/1¼ cups water and salt. Bring to the boil, then reduce the heat and simmer for 4–5 minutes until cooked and creamy, stirring frequently.

4 Serve the porridge in warm serving bowls, topped with a spoonful of the date purée and sprinkled with chopped pistachio nuts.

Apricot and Ginger Compote

FRESH GINGER ADDS WARMTH to this stimulating breakfast dish and complements the flavour of the plump, juicy apricots.

INGREDIENTS

350g/12oz/1½ cups dried unsulphured apricots
4cm/1½in piece fresh root ginger, finely chopped
200g/7oz/scant 1 cup natural live yogurt or low-fat fromage frais

Serves 4

COOK'S TIP

Fresh ginger freezes well. Peel the root and store it in a plastic bag in the freezer. You can grate it from frozen, then return the root to the freezer until the next time you need it for a recipe.

1 Cover the apricots with boiling water, then leave to soak overnight.

2 Place the apricots and their soaking water in a saucepan, add the ginger and bring to the boil. Reduce the heat and simmer for 10 minutes until the fruit is soft and plump and the water becomes syrupy. Strain the apricots, reserving the syrup, and discard the ginger.

3 Serve the apricots warm with the reserved syrup and a spoonful of yogurt or fromage frais.

HEALTH BENEFITS

- *In Chinese medicine, ginger is revered for its health-giving properties. It is antispasmodic, aids digestion and can help treat colds and flu.*
- *Of all the dried fruits, apricots are the richest source of iron. They also provide calcium, phosphorus and vitamins A and C.*
- *Live yogurt can relieve gastrointestinal disorders by replacing valuable bacteria in the gut. The lactic acids, which yogurt contains, can help to regulate bowel function and they have bacterial properties that can prevent infection. Yogurt also boosts our immune system.*

Griddled Pineapple and Mango on Toasted Panettone with Vanilla Yogurt

Griddling concentrates the sweetness of the pineapple and mango, giving a caramel flavour that is complemented by the vanilla yogurt.

INGREDIENTS

1 large pineapple
1 large mango
25g/1oz/2 tbsp unsalted butter, melted
4 thick slices panettone

For the vanilla yogurt
250g/9oz/generous 1 cup Greek yogurt
30ml/2 tbsp clear honey
2.5ml/½ tsp ground cinnamon
a few drops natural vanilla essence, to taste

Serves 4

1 To prepare the pineapple, cut the bottom and the spiky top off the fruit. Stand the pineapple upright and cut off the skin, removing all the spikes, but as little of the flesh as possible. Lay the pineapple on its side and cut into quarters; remove the core if it is hard. Cut the pineapple into thick wedges.

Health Benefits

Pineapple contains the powerful enzyme bromelain, which improves the digestion. It contains compounds that have an anti-inflammatory effect, so is good for people who suffer from arthritis. Pineapple has also been shown to reduce the incidence of blood clots and to ease bronchitis.

2 To prepare the mango, cut away the two thick sides of the mango as close to the stone as possible. Peel the mango, then cut the remaining flesh from the stone. Slice the fruit and discard the stone.

3 Heat a griddle pan over a medium heat. Add the pineapple and mango (you may need to do this in batches). Brush with melted butter, and cook for 8 minutes, turning once, until soft and slightly golden. Alternatively, heat the grill to high and line the rack with foil. Place the pineapple and mango on the foil and grill for 4 minutes on each side.

4 Meanwhile, make the vanilla yogurt. Place the yogurt in a bowl with the honey, cinnamon and vanilla and stir well.

5 Lightly toast the panettone, then serve, topped with the pineapple and mango and accompanied by the vanilla yogurt.

Oaty Pancakes with Caramel Bananas and Pecan Nuts

THESE PANCAKES ARE MORE LIKE drop scones than the classic thin French crêpes. Bananas and pecan nuts, cooked in maple syrup, make a sweet and delicious topping.

INGREDIENTS

75g/3oz/2/3 cup plain flour
50g/2oz/1/2 cup wholemeal flour
50g/2oz/1/2 cup porridge oats
5ml/1 tsp baking powder
pinch of salt
25g/1oz/2 tbsp golden caster sugar
1 egg
15ml/1 tbsp sunflower oil, plus extra for frying
250ml/8fl oz/1 cup semi-skimmed milk

For the caramel bananas and pecan nuts
50g/2oz/4 tbsp butter
15ml/1 tbsp maple syrup
3 bananas, halved and quartered lengthways
25g/1oz/1/4 cup pecan nuts

Makes 5

1 To make the pancakes, mix together the plain and wholemeal flours, oats, baking powder, salt and sugar in a bowl.

2 Make a well in the centre of the flour mixture and add the egg, oil and a quarter of the milk. Mix well, then gradually add the rest of the milk to make a thick batter. Leave to rest for 20 minutes in the fridge.

3 Heat a large, heavy-based, lightly oiled frying pan. Using 30ml/2 tbsp of batter for each pancake, cook 2–3 pancakes at a time. Cook for 3 minutes on each side or until golden. Keep warm while you cook the remaining 7–8 pancakes.

4 To make the caramel bananas and pecan nuts, wipe out the frying pan and add the butter. Heat gently until the butter melts, then add the maple syrup and stir well. Add the bananas and pecan nuts to the pan.

5 Cook for about 4 minutes, turning once, or until the bananas have softened and the sauce has caramelized. To serve, place two pancakes on each of five warm plates and top with the caramel bananas and pecan nuts. Serve immediately.

HEALTH BENEFITS

- *Pecan nuts are one of the richest sources of vitamin B_6, which can help relieve the symptoms of PMS (pre-menstrual syndrome), as well as giving our immune system a boost. However, they are high in fat, so eat in moderation.*
- *Bananas are a good source of energy, making them an excellent food to start the day. They also contain potassium, which is essential for the functioning of all the cells in our bodies.*
- *Porridge oats contain useful amounts of soluble fibre, which has been found to lower cholesterol levels in the body.*

Apple and Blackcurrant Pancakes

PANCAKES ARE easy to make and quick to cook. These use wholewheat batter and are filled with a delicious fruit mixture.

INGREDIENTS

115g/4oz/1 cup plain wholemeal flour
300ml/½ pint/1¼ cups skimmed milk
1 egg, beaten
15ml/1 tbsp sunflower oil, plus extra for greasing
half-fat crème fraîche, to serve (optional)
toasted nuts or sesame seeds, for sprinkling (optional)

For the filling
450g/1lb cooking apples
225g/8oz/2 cups blackcurrants
30–45ml/2–3 tbsp water
30ml/2 tbsp demerara sugar
Makes 8–10

1 Make the pancake batter. Place the flour in a mixing bowl and make a well in the centre.

2 Add a little of the milk with the egg and the oil. Whisk the flour into the liquid then gradually whisk in the rest of the milk, keeping the batter smooth and free from lumps. Cover the batter and place in the refrigerator to chill while you prepare the filling.

3 Quarter, peel and core the apples. Slice them into a pan and add the blackcurrants and water. Cook over a gentle heat for 10–15 minutes until the fruit is soft. Stir in enough demerara sugar to sweeten.

4 Lightly grease a pancake pan with just a smear of oil. Heat the pan, pour in about 30ml/2 tbsp batter, swirl it around and cook for about 1 minute. Flip the pancake over with a palette knife and cook the other side. Keep hot while cooking the remaining pancakes (unless cooking to order).

5 Fill the pancakes with the apple and blackcurrant mixture and roll them up. Serve with a dollop of crème fraîche, if using, and sprinkle with nuts or sesame seeds, if liked.

Warm Bagels with Poached Apricots

INGREDIENTS

a few strips of orange peel
225g/8oz/1 1/3 cups ready-to-eat dried apricots
250ml/8fl oz/1 cup fresh orange juice
2.5ml/1/2 tsp orange flower water
2 cinnamon and raisin bagels
20ml/4 tsp reduced-sugar orange marmalade
60ml/4 tbsp half-fat crème fraîche or soured cream
15g/1/2 oz/2 tbsp chopped pistachio nuts, to decorate

Serves 4

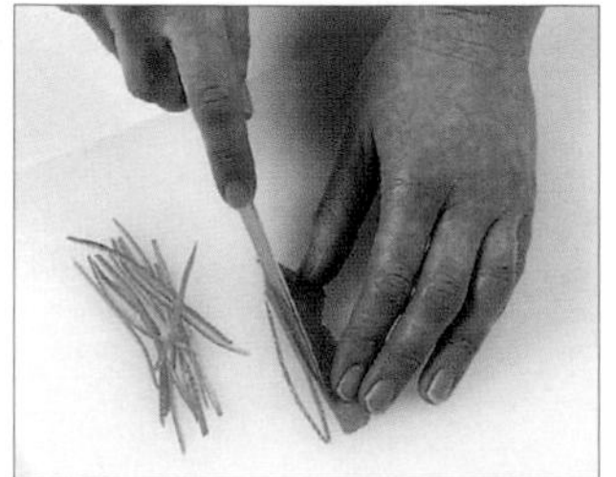

1 Cut the strips of orange peel into fine shreds. Place them in boiling water until softened, then drain and place in cold water.

2 Preheat the oven to 160°C/325°F/Gas 3. Combine the apricots and orange juice in a small saucepan. Heat gently for about 10 minutes until the juice has reduced and looks syrupy. Allow to cool, then stir in the orange flower water. Meanwhile, place the bagels on a baking sheet and warm in the oven for 5–10 minutes.

3 Split the bagels in half horizontally. Lay one half, crumb uppermost, on each serving plate. Spread 5ml/1 tsp orange marmalade on each bagel.

4 Spoon 15ml/1 tbsp crème fraîche or soured cream into the centre of each bagel and place a quarter of the apricot compôte at the side. Scatter orange peel and pistachio nuts over the top to decorate. Serve immediately.

COOK'S TIP

Pistachio nuts are a colourful addition to many dishes. If you find them in their natural tan shells, you will need to preserve their brilliant colour. Do this by shelling and boiling in water for a few minutes, then rub off their skins.

Kedgeree

THIS SPICY LENTIL and rice dish is a delicious variation of the original Indian version of kedgeree, *kitchiri*. You can serve it as it is, or topped with quartered hard-boiled eggs if you'd like to add more protein. It is also delicious served on grilled, large field mushrooms.

INGREDIENTS

50g/2oz/¼ cup dried red lentils, rinsed
1 bay leaf
225g/8oz/1 cup basmati rice, rinsed
4 cloves
50g/2oz/4 tbsp butter
5ml/1 tsp curry powder
2.5ml/½ tsp mild chilli powder
30ml/2 tbsp chopped flat leaf parsley
salt and freshly ground black pepper
4 hard-boiled eggs, quartered, to serve (optional)

Serves 4

1 Put the lentils in a saucepan, add the bay leaf and cover with cold water. Bring to the boil, skim off any foam, then reduce the heat. Cover and simmer for 25–30 minutes, until tender. Drain, then discard the bay leaf.

2 Meanwhile, place the rice in a saucepan and cover with 475ml/16fl oz/2 cups boiling water. Add the cloves and a generous pinch of salt. Cook, covered, for 10–15 minutes, until all the water is absorbed and the rice is tender. Discard the cloves.

3 Melt the butter over a gentle heat in a large frying pan, then add the curry and chilli powders and cook for 1 minute.

4 Stir in the lentils and rice and mix well until they are coated in the spiced butter. Season and cook for 1–2 minutes until heated through. Stir in the parsley and serve with the hard-boiled eggs, if using.

HEALTH BENEFITS

- *Lentils are especially good for the heart, because of their ability to lower cholesterol levels in the body. They also contain compounds that inhibit cancer and can regulate blood sugar levels.*
- *Rice is a high-carbohydrate food that provides sustained amounts of energy, making it a perfect food to start the day. Rice can also help to ease diarrhoea and stomach upsets.*

Griddled Tomatoes on Soda Bread

NOTHING COULD BE SIMPLER than this breakfast or brunch dish, yet a drizzle of olive oil and balsamic vinegar and shavings of Parmesan transform it into something really special.

INGREDIENTS

olive oil, for brushing and drizzling
6 tomatoes, thickly sliced
4 thick slices soda bread
balsamic vinegar, for drizzling
salt and freshly ground black pepper
shavings of Parmesan cheese, to serve

Serves 4

COOK'S TIP

Using a griddle pan reduces the amount of oil required for cooking the tomatoes and gives them a barbecued flavour.

1 Brush a griddle pan with olive oil and heat. Add the tomatoe slices and cook for 4–6 minutes, turning once, until softened and slightly blackened. Alternatively, heat a grill to high and line the rack with foil. Grill the tomatoe slices for 4–6 minutes, turning once, until softened.

2 Meanwhile, lightly toast the soda bread. Place the tomatoes on top of the toast and drizzle each portion with a little olive oil and vinegar. Season to taste and serve immediately with thin shavings of Parmesan.

HEALTH BENEFITS

Numerous studies have shown that tomatoes are effective in preventing many forms of cancer, including lung, stomach and prostate cancer. This is probably explained by their antioxidant content, notably beta carotene and vitamins C and E. Antioxidants are also believed to prevent appendicitis.

Cheese and Banana Toasties

WHOLEMEAL TOAST topped with reduced-fat soft cheese and sliced banana makes the perfect high-fibre breakfast and is especially delicious when drizzled with honey and grilled. It's easy to make, and provides a delicious start to any day.

INGREDIENTS

4 thick slices of wholemeal bread
115g/4oz/½ cup reduced-fat soft cheese
1.5ml/¼ tsp cardamom seeds, crushed (optional)
4 small bananas, peeled
20ml/4 tsp clear honey

Serves 4

1 Place the bread on a rack in a grill pan and toast on one side only.

2 Turn the bread over, and spread the untoasted side of each slice with soft cheese. Sprinkle over the crushed cardamom seeds, if using.

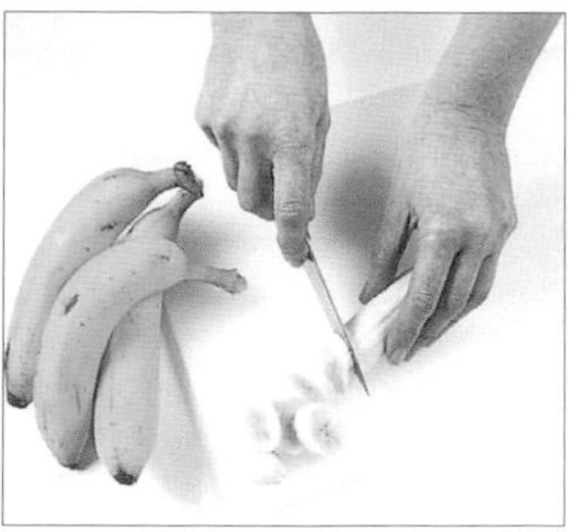

3 Slice the bananas and arrange the slices on top of the cheese, then drizzle each slice with 5ml/1 tsp of the clear honey. Slide the pan back under the moderately hot grill and leave for a few minutes until bubbling. Serve immediately.

COOK'S TIP

For a delicious variation, use fruited, sesame seed or caraway seed wholemeal bread. Omit the cardamom seeds and sprinkle ground cinnamon on the bananas before adding the honey.

Mixed Pepper Pipérade

INGREDIENTS

30ml/2 tbsp olive oil
1 onion, chopped
1 red pepper
1 green pepper
4 tomatoes, peeled and chopped
1 garlic clove, crushed
4 size large eggs, beaten with 15ml/1 tbsp water
freshly ground black pepper
4 large, thick slices of wholemeal toast, to serve

Serves 4

1 Heat the oil in a large frying pan and sauté the onion gently until it becomes softened.

2 Remove the seeds from the red and green peppers and slice them thinly. Stir the pepper slices into the onion and cook together gently for 5 minutes. Add the tomatoes and garlic, season with black pepper, and cook for a further 5 minutes.

3 Pour the egg mixture over the vegetables in the frying pan and cook for 2–3 minutes, stirring now and then, until the pipérade has thickened to the consistency of lightly scrambled eggs. Serve immediately with warm wholemeal toast.

COOK'S TIP

Choose eggs that have been date-stamped for freshness. Do not stir the pipérade too much or the eggs may become rubbery.

VARIATION

This recipe originates from the Basque region of France, where it is often served in the form of an omelette, or topped with fried eggs.

Chive Scrambled Eggs in Brioches

An indulgent, but delicious, breakfast that should be reserved for Sundays or special occasions.

INGREDIENTS

115g/4oz/½ cup unsalted butter
75g/3oz/generous 1 cup brown cap mushrooms, finely sliced
4 individual brioches
8 eggs
15ml/1 tbsp snipped fresh chives, plus extra to garnish
salt and freshly ground black pepper

Serves 4

1 Preheat the oven to 180°C/350°F/Gas 4. Place a quarter of the butter in a frying pan and heat until melted. Fry the mushrooms for 3 minutes or until soft, then set aside and keep warm.

Cook's Tip

Timing and temperature are crucial for perfect scrambled eggs. When cooked for too long over too high a heat, eggs become dry and crumbly; vice versa, and they are sloppy and unappealing.

Health Benefits

Eggs are a good source of protein, selenium (which is an efficient antioxidant), iron, zinc and the complete range of B vitamins. However, although they are low in saturated fat, they are high in cholesterol, so should be eaten only occasionally and in moderation.

2 Slice the tops off the brioches, then scoop out the centres and discard. Put the brioches and lids on a baking sheet and bake for 5 minutes until hot and slightly crisp.

3 Meanwhile, beat the eggs lightly and season to taste. Heat the remaining butter in a heavy-based saucepan over a gentle heat. When the butter has melted and is foaming slightly, add the eggs. Using a wooden spoon, stir constantly, to ensure the egg does not stick.

4 Continue to stir gently until about three-quarters of the egg is semi-solid and creamy – this should take 2–3 minutes. Remove the pan from the heat – the egg will continue to cook in the heat from the pan – then stir in the snipped chives.

5 To serve, spoon a little of the mushrooms into the bottom of each brioche and top with the scrambled eggs. Sprinkle with extra chives, balance the brioche lids on top and serve immediately.

Cannellini Bean and Rosemary Bruschetta

MORE BRUNCH THAN BREAKFAST, this dish is a sophisticated version of beans on toast.

INGREDIENTS

150g/5oz/⅔ cup dried cannellini beans
5 tomatoes
45ml/3 tbsp olive oil, plus extra for drizzling
2 sun-dried tomatoes in oil, drained and finely chopped
1 garlic clove, crushed
30ml/2 tbsp chopped fresh rosemary
salt and freshly ground black pepper
a handful of fresh basil leaves, to garnish

To serve

12 slices Italian-style bread, such as ciabatta
1 large garlic clove, halved

Serves 4

1 Place the beans in a large bowl and cover with water. Leave to soak overnight. Drain and rinse the beans, then place in a saucepan and cover with fresh water. Bring to the boil and boil rapidly for 10 minutes. Reduce the heat and simmer for 50–60 minutes or until tender. Drain and set aside.

2 Meanwhile, place the tomatoes in a bowl, cover with boiling water, leave for 30 seconds, then peel, seed and chop the flesh. Heat the oil in a frying pan, add the fresh and sun-dried tomatoes, garlic and rosemary. Cook for 2 minutes until the tomatoes begin to break down and soften.

3 Add the tomato mixture to the cannellini beans, season to taste and mix well.

HEALTH BENEFITS

- *Cannellini beans are high in protein and low in fat. They are also a valuable source of B vitamins and minerals.*
- *Rosemary is reputed to have many healing qualities. It is said to alleviate headaches, to improve the circulation and to ease rheumatism. Use fresh rosemary if possible, as dried will have lost most of its beneficial oils.*

4 Rub the cut sides of the bread slices with the garlic clove, then toast lightly. Spoon the cannellini bean mixture on top of the toast. Sprinkle with basil leaves and drizzle with a little extra olive oil before serving.

COOK'S TIP

Canned beans can be used instead of dried; use 275g/10oz/2 cups drained, canned beans and add to the tomato mixture in step 3. If the beans are canned in brine, then rinse and drain them well before use.

Courgette, Mushroom and Pesto Panino

GRILLED COURGETTES are layered with garlic mushrooms, creamy Italian Taleggio cheese and pesto in this very tasty picnic loaf. Use a round, crusty, country-style Italian or French loaf and chill overnight after filling, to allow the flavours to mingle together.

INGREDIENTS

1 medium country-style loaf
3 courgettes, sliced lengthways
45ml/3 tbsp olive oil
250g/9oz/3⅔ cups brown cap mushrooms, thickly sliced
1 garlic clove, chopped
5ml/1 tsp dried oregano
45ml/3 tbsp pesto
250g/9oz Taleggio cheese, rind removed and sliced
50g/2oz/2 cups green salad leaves
salt and freshly ground black pepper
Serves 6

1 Slice off the top third of the loaf and remove the inside of both the lid and base, leaving a thickness of about 1cm/½in around the edge. (Use the inside of the loaf to make breadcrumbs for another dish.)

2 Preheat the grill to high and line the grill rack with foil. Brush the courgettes with 15ml/1 tbsp of the olive oil and grill for 8–10 minutes, turning them occasionally, until tender and browned.

3 Meanwhile, heat the remaining oil in a frying pan. Add the mushrooms, garlic and oregano and fry for 3 minutes.

4 Arrange half of the courgettes in the base of the loaf, then spread with 25ml/1½ tbsp of the pesto. Top with half the cheese and salad leaves and all the mushroom mixture.

5 Add one more layer each of the remaining cheese, salad leaves and courgettes. Spread the remaining pesto over the inside of the bread lid and place it on top.

6 Press the lid down gently, wrap the loaf in clear film and leave to cool. Chill overnight or at least for a few hours. Serve cut into wedges.

HEALTH BENEFITS

- *Courgettes provide valuable amounts of vitamin C, beta carotene and folates.*
- *Garlic is highly valued, particularly for its ability to detoxify the body and strengthen the immune system.*

Mushroom Picker's Omelette

PERFECT FOR Sunday brunch, this omelette is simplicity itself to make.

INGREDIENTS

25g/1oz/2 tbsp unsalted butter, plus extra for cooking

115g/4oz/2 cups assorted wild and cultivated mushrooms such as young ceps, bay boletus, chanterelles, saffron milk-caps, closed field mushrooms, oyster mushrooms, hedgehog and St George's mushrooms, trimmed and sliced

3 eggs, at room temperature

salt and freshly ground black pepper

Serves 1

1 Melt the butter in a small omelette pan, add the mushrooms and cook gently over a low heat until the juices run. Season with salt and pepper, remove from pan and set aside. Wipe the pan.

2 Break the eggs into a bowl, season and beat with a fork. Heat the pan over high heat, add a knob of butter and let it begin to brown. Pour in the beaten egg and stir briskly with the back of a fork.

3 When the eggs are two-thirds set, add the mushrooms and let the omelette finish cooking for 10–15 seconds.

4 Tap the handle of the omelette pan sharply with your fist to loosen the omelette from the pan, then fold and turn on to a plate. Serve with warm crusty bread and a simple green salad.

SOUPS and STARTERS

Serve light flavoursome soups as starters or make a thick, nourishing soup as a meal in its own right for an ideal lunchtime choice. Many traditional favourites are included here as well as a selection of dips and pâtés to be served with seasonal vegetables.

Gazpacho with Avocado Salsa

Tomatoes, cucumber and peppers form the basis of this classic, chilled soup. Add a spoonful of chunky, fresh avocado salsa and a scattering of croutons, and serve for a light lunch on a warm summer's day.

INGREDIENTS

2 slices day-old bread
1kg/2¼lb tomatoes
1 cucumber
1 red pepper, seeded and chopped
1 green chilli, seeded and chopped
2 garlic cloves, chopped
30ml/2 tbsp extra virgin olive oil
juice of 1 lime and 1 lemon
a few drops Tabasco sauce
600ml/1 pint/2½ cups chilled water
salt and freshly ground black pepper
a handful of basil leaves, to garnish
8 ice cubes, to serve

For the croûtons
2 slices day-old bread, crusts removed
1 garlic clove, halved
15ml/1 tbsp olive oil

For the avocado salsa
1 ripe avocado
5ml/1 tsp lemon juice
2.5cm/1in piece cucumber, diced
½ red chilli, finely chopped
Serves 4

1 Soak the bread in 150ml/¼ pint/⅔ cup of water for 5 minutes.

2 Meanwhile, place the tomatoes in a bowl and cover with boiling water. Leave for 30 seconds, then peel, seed and chop the flesh.

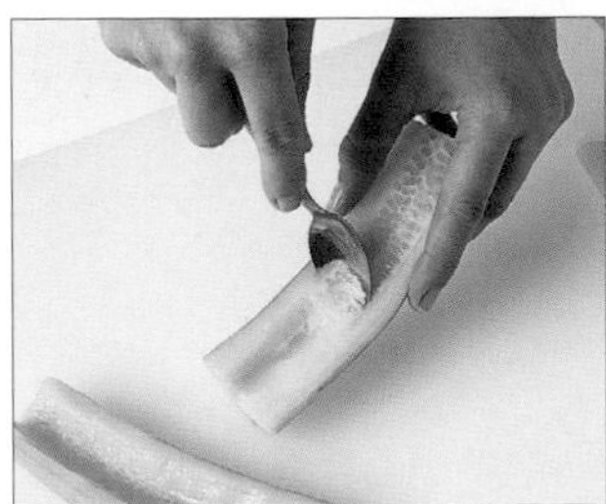

3 Peel the cucumber, cut it in half lengthways and scoop out the seeds with a teaspoon. Discard the seeds and chop the flesh.

4 Place the bread, tomatoes, cucumber, red pepper, chilli, garlic, olive oil, citrus juices and Tabasco in a food processor or blender with 450ml/¾ pint/scant 2 cups chilled water and blend until well combined but still chunky. Season to taste and chill for 2–3 hours.

5 To make the croûtons, rub the slices of bread with the garlic clove. Cut the bread into cubes and place in a plastic bag with the olive oil. Seal the bag and shake until the bread cubes are coated with the oil. Heat a large non-stick frying pan and fry the croûtons over a medium heat until crisp and golden.

6 Just before serving, make the avocado salsa. Halve the avocado, remove the stone, then peel and dice. Toss the avocado in the lemon juice to prevent it browning, then mix with the cucumber and chilli.

7 Ladle the soup into bowls, add the ice cubes, and top with a spoonful of avocado salsa. Garnish with the basil and hand round the croûtons separately.

HEALTH BENEFITS

The powerful combination of fresh raw vegetables, garlic, lemon and lime juice, olive oil and chilli boosts the immune system and the circulation, and helps to cleanse the body.

Borlotti Bean and Pasta Soup

A COMPLETE MEAL IN A BOWL, this is a version of a classic Italian soup. Traditionally, the person who finds the bay leaf is honoured with a kiss from the cook.

INGREDIENTS

1 onion, chopped
1 celery stick, chopped
2 carrots, chopped
75ml/5 tbsp olive oil
1 bay leaf
1 glass white wine (optional)
1.2 litres/2 pints/5 cups vegetable stock
400g/14oz/3 cups canned chopped tomatoes
175g/6oz/1 1/2 cups pasta shapes, such as farfalle or conchiglie
400g/14oz/3 cups canned borlotti beans, drained
250g/9oz spinach, washed and thick stalks removed
salt and freshly ground black pepper
50g/2oz/2/3 cup freshly grated Parmesan cheese, to serve

Serves 4

1 Place the chopped onion, celery and carrots in a large saucepan with the olive oil. Cook over a medium heat for 5 minutes or until the vegetables soften, stirring occasionally.

COOK'S TIP

Other pulses, such as cannellini beans, haricot beans or chick-peas, are equally good in this soup.

2 Add the bay leaf, wine, if using, stock and tomatoes and bring to the boil. Reduce the heat and simmer for 10 minutes until the vegetables are just tender.

3 Add the pasta and beans and bring the soup back to the boil, then simmer for 8 minutes until the pasta is *al dente*. Stir frequently to prevent the pasta sticking.

4 Season to taste, add the spinach and cook for a further 2 minutes. Serve, sprinkled with the Parmesan.

HEALTH BENEFITS

- *Spinach contains many valuable nutrients and is rich in folates, vitamin C, beta carotene, zinc, potassium and iron. Spinach, like rhubarb, contains oxalic acid, which limits the absorption of iron and calcium in the body. However, the vitamin C content found in spinach and other vegetables may temper the effects of the oxalic acid to some extent. In natural medicine, spinach is often prescribed to treat constipation, arthritis and high blood pressure.*
- *Onions are considered to have a powerful antibiotic effect and they are a strong diuretic.*

Wild Mushroom Soup

WILD MUSHROOMS are expensive, but dried porcini have an intense flavour, so only a small quantity is needed.

INGREDIENTS

25g/1oz/½ cup dried porcini mushrooms
30ml/2 tbsp olive oil
15g/½oz/1 tbsp butter
2 leeks, thinly sliced
2 shallots, roughly chopped
1 garlic clove, roughly chopped
225g/8oz/generous 3 cups fresh wild mushrooms
about 1.2 litres/2 pints/5 cups vegetable stock
2.5ml/½ tsp dried thyme
150ml/¼ pint/⅔ cup double cream
salt and freshly ground black pepper
sprigs of fresh thyme, to garnish

Serves 4

1 Put the dried porcini in a bowl, add 250ml/8fl oz/1 cup warm water and leave to soak for 20–30 minutes. Lift out of the liquid and squeeze over the bowl to remove as much of the soaking liquid as possible. Strain all the liquid and reserve to use later. Finely chop the porcini.

2 Heat the oil and butter in a large saucepan until foaming. Add the sliced leeks, chopped shallots and garlic and cook gently for about 5 minutes, stirring frequently, until softened but not coloured.

3 Finely chop or slice the fresh mushrooms and add to the pan. Stir over a medium heat for a few minutes until they begin to soften. Pour in the stock and bring to the boil. Add the porcini, soaking liquid, dried thyme and season. Bring to the boil again. Lower the heat, half cover the pan and leave the soup to simmer gently for 30 minutes, stirring occasionally.

4 Pour about three-quarters of the soup into a blender or food processor and process until smooth. Return the processed soup to the soup remaining in the pan, stir in the cream and heat through. Check the consistency and add more stock if necessary. Season with salt and pepper. Serve hot, garnished with thyme sprigs.

COOK'S TIP

Porcini are ceps. Italian cooks would make this soup with a combination of fresh and dried ceps, but if fresh ceps are difficult to obtain, you can use other wild mushrooms such as chanterelles.

Tomato and Fresh Basil Soup

A PUNGENT soup for late summer when fresh tomatoes are at their most flavoursome.

INGREDIENTS

15ml/1 tbsp olive oil
25g/1oz/2 tbsp butter
1 medium onion, finely chopped
900g/2lb ripe Italian plum tomatoes, roughly chopped
1 garlic clove, roughly chopped
about 750ml/1¼ pints/3 cups vegetable stock
120ml/4fl oz/½ cup dry white wine
30ml/2 tbsp sun-dried tomato paste
30ml/2 tbsp shredded fresh basil
150ml/¼ pint/⅔ cup double cream
salt and freshly ground black pepper
whole basil leaves, to garnish

Serves 4–6

1 Heat the oil and butter in a large saucepan until foaming. Add the onion and cook gently for about 5 minutes, stirring, until the onion is softened but not brown.

2 Stir in the chopped tomatoes and garlic, then add the stock, white wine and sun-dried tomato paste, with salt and pepper to taste. Bring to the boil, then lower the heat, half cover the pan and simmer gently for 20 minutes, stirring occasionally to stop the tomatoes sticking to the base of the pan.

3 Process the soup with the shredded basil in a blender or food processor, then press through a sieve into a clean pan.

4 Add the double cream and heat through, stirring. Do not allow the soup to approach boiling point. Check the consistency and add more stock if necessary and then season with salt and pepper. Pour into heated bowls and garnish with basil. Serve at once.

Asparagus Soup

HOME-MADE asparagus soup has a delicate flavour, quite unlike that from a can. This soup is best made with young asparagus, which are tender and blend well. Thin spokes of asparagus, known as sprue, can often be bargain buys. Serve the soup with wafer-thin slices of bread.

INGREDIENTS

450g/1lb young asparagus
40g/1½oz/3 tbsp butter
6 shallots, sliced
15g/½oz/2 tbsp plain flour
600ml/1 pint/2½ cups vegetable stock or water
15ml/1 tbsp lemon juice
250ml/8fl oz/1 cup milk
120ml/4fl oz/½ cup single cream
10ml/2 tsp chopped fresh chervil
salt and freshly ground black pepper

Serves 4

1 Cut 4 cm/1½ in off the tops of half the asparagus and set aside for a garnish. Cut the remaining asparagus into slices.

2 Melt 25 g/1oz/2 tbsp of the butter in a large saucepan and gently fry the sliced shallots for 2–3 minutes until soft, but not browned.

3 Add the asparagus and fry over a low heat for about 1 minute.

4 Stir in the flour and cook for 1 minute. Stir in the stock or water and lemon juice and season with salt and pepper. Bring to the boil, half cover the pan, then simmer for 15–20 minutes, until the asparagus is very tender.

5 Cool slightly and then process the soup in a food processor or blender until smooth. Pour the soup slowly through a sieve into a clean saucepan. Add the milk by pouring and stirring it through the sieve, with the asparagus, so as to extract the maximum amount of asparagus purée. Work the purée through with a wooden spoon.

6 Melt the remaining butter and fry the reserved asparagus tips gently for 3–4 minutes to soften.

7 Heat the soup gently for 3–4 minutes. Stir in the cream and the asparagus tips. Continue to heat gently and serve sprinkled with chopped fresh chervil.

Carrot and Coriander Soup

NEARLY ALL root vegetables make excellent soups as they purée well and have an earthy flavour, which complements the sharper flavours of herbs and spices. Carrots are particularly versatile, and this simple soup is elegant in both flavour and appearance.

INGREDIENTS

450g/1lb carrots, preferably young and tender
15ml/1 tbsp sunflower oil
40g/1½oz/3 tbsp butter
1 onion, chopped
1 stick celery, plus 2–3 pale leafy celery tops
2 small potatoes, peeled
1 litre/1¾ pints/4 cups vegetable stock
10–15ml/2–3 tsp ground coriander
15ml/1 tbsp chopped fresh coriander
200ml/7fl oz/⅞ cup milk
salt and freshly ground black pepper

Serves 4–6

1 Trim and peel the carrots and cut into chunks. Heat the oil and 25g/1oz/2 tbsp butter in a large flameproof casserole or heavy-based saucepan and fry the onion over a gentle heat for 3–4 minutes, until slightly softened. Do not allow it to brown.

2 Slice the celery and chop the potatoes. Add them to the onion in the pan, cook for a few minutes and then add the carrots. Continue to cook over a gentle heat for 3–4 minutes, stirring, and then cover.

3 Reduce the heat even further and sweat for about 10 minutes. Shake the pan or stir occasionally so the vegetables do not stick to the base.

4 Add the stock and bring the liquid to the boil. Half cover the pan and simmer for a further 8–10 minutes, until the carrots and potatoes are tender.

5 Remove 6–8 tiny celery leaves for garnish and finely chop the remaining celery tops (about 15ml/1 tbsp once chopped). Melt the remaining butter in a small saucepan and fry the ground coriander for about 1 minute, stirring constantly.

6 Reduce the heat and add the chopped celery tops and fresh coriander and fry for about 1 minute. Set aside.

7 Process the soup in a food processor or blender and pour into a clean saucepan. Stir in the milk and coriander mixture. Season, heat gently, taste and adjust seasoning. Serve the soup garnished with the reserved celery leaves.

COOK'S TIP

For a more piquant flavour, add a little lemon juice just before serving.

Fresh Pea Soup

THIS SOUP is known in France as Potage Saint-Germain, a name which comes from a suburb of Paris where peas used to be cultivated in market gardens. If fresh peas are not available, use frozen peas, but thaw and rinse them before use.

INGREDIENTS

25g/1oz/2 tbsp butter
2 or 3 shallots, finely chopped
400g/14oz/3 cups shelled fresh peas (from about 1.3 kg/3lb garden peas) or thawed frozen peas
45–60ml/3–4 tbsp whipping cream (optional)
salt and freshly ground black pepper
croûtons, to garnish

Serves 2–3

1 Melt the butter in a heavy saucepan or flameproof casserole. Add the shallots and cook gently for about 3 minutes, stirring occasionally. Do not allow them to brown.

2 Add 475ml/16fl oz/2 cups water and the peas, and season with salt and pepper.

3 Cover and simmer for 12 minutes for young or frozen peas and up to 18 minutes for large or older peas, stirring occasionally.

4 When the peas are tender, ladle them into a food processor or blender with a little of the cooking liquid and process until smooth.

5 Strain the soup into the saucepan or casserole, stir in the cream, if using, and heat through without boiling. Season with salt and pepper and serve hot, garnished with croûtons.

Pea, Leek and Broccoli Soup

A DELICIOUS and nutritious soup, ideal for warming those chilly winter evenings.

INGREDIENTS

1 onion, chopped
225g/8oz/2 cups leeks (trimmed weight), sliced
225g/8oz unpeeled potatoes, diced
900ml/1 ½ pints/3¾ cups vegetable stock
1 bay leaf
225g/8oz broccoli florets
175g/6oz/1 ½ cups frozen peas
30–45ml/2–3 tbsp chopped fresh parsley
salt and freshly ground black pepper
parsley leaves, to garnish

Serves 4–6

1 Put the onion, leeks, potatoes, stock and bay leaf in a large saucepan and mix together. Bring to the boil, cover, reduce the heat and simmer for 10 minutes, stirring occasionally.

2 Add the broccoli and peas, cover, return to the boil and then reduce the heat and simmer for a further 10 minutes, stirring occasionally.

3 Set aside to cool slightly and remove and discard the bay leaf. Purée in a blender or food processor until smooth.

4 Add the parsley, season with salt and pepper and process briefly. Return to the saucepan and reheat gently until piping hot. Ladle into soup bowls and garnish with parsley leaves.

Curried Celery Soup

THIS WARMING soup brings together an unusual combination of flavours. It is excellent served with warm wholemeal bread rolls or wholemeal pitta bread.

INGREDIENTS

10ml/2 tsp olive oil
1 onion, chopped
1 leek, washed and sliced
675g/1½lb/6 cups celery, chopped
15ml/1 tbsp medium or hot curry powder
225g/8oz unpeeled potatoes, washed and diced
900ml/1½ pints/3¾ cups vegetable stock
1 bouquet garni
30ml/2 tbsp chopped fresh mixed herbs
salt
celery seeds and leaves, to garnish

Serves 4–6

1 Heat the oil in a large saucepan. Add the onion, leek and celery, cover and cook gently for about 10 minutes, stirring occasionally.

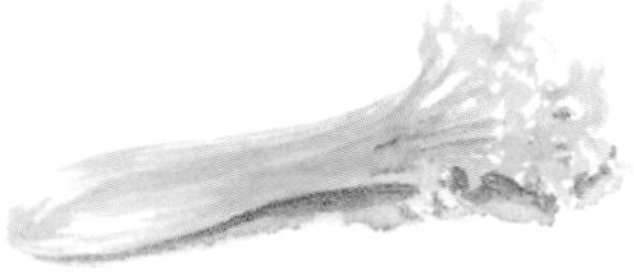

2 Add the curry powder and cook for a further 2 minutes, stirring occasionally.

3 Add the potatoes, stock and bouquet garni, cover and bring to the boil. Simmer for 20 minutes, until the vegetables are tender.

4 Remove and discard the bouquet garni and set the soup aside to cool slightly.

5 Purée the vegetables in a blender or food processor until smooth.

6 Add the mixed herbs, season to taste and process briefly. Return to the saucepan and reheat gently until piping hot. Ladle into soup bowls and garnish each with a sprinkling of celery seeds and some celery leaves.

VARIATION

For a tasty change, use celeriac and sweet potatoes in place of the celery and standard potatoes.

Minestrone with Pesto

MINESTRONE IS a thick, mixed vegetable soup using almost any combination of seasonal vegetables. Short pasta or rice may also be added. This version includes pesto sauce.

INGREDIENTS

45ml/3 tbsp olive oil
1 large onion, finely chopped
1 leek, sliced
2 carrots, finely chopped
1 stick celery, finely chopped
2 cloves garlic, finely chopped
2 potatoes, peeled and cut into small dice
1.5 litres/2½ pints/6¼ cups hot vegetable stock or water, or a combination of both
1 bay leaf
1 sprig of fresh thyme, or 1.5ml/¼ tsp dried thyme
115g/4oz/¾ cup peas, fresh or frozen
2–3 courgettes, finely chopped
3 medium tomatoes, peeled and finely chopped
425g/15oz/2 cups cooked or canned beans, such as cannellini
45ml/3 tbsp pesto sauce
salt and freshly ground black pepper
freshly grated Parmesan cheese, to serve

Serves 6

1 Heat the oil in a saucepan. Stir in the onion and leek, and cook for 5–6 minutes. Add the carrots, celery and garlic, and cook over moderate heat for 5 minutes. Add the potatoes and cook for 2–3 minutes more.

2 Pour in the hot stock or water, and stir well. Add the herbs and season with salt and pepper. Bring to the boil, reduce the heat and cook for 10–12 minutes.

3 Stir in the peas, if fresh, and the courgettes. Simmer for 5 minutes more. Add the frozen peas, if using, and the tomatoes. Cover the pan and boil for 5–8 minutes.

4 About 10 minutes before serving, uncover and stir in the beans. Simmer for 10 minutes. Stir in the pesto sauce. Simmer for another 5 minutes. Remove from heat and allow to stand for a few minutes. Serve with the grated Parmesan cheese.

Pumpkin Soup

THIS BEAUTIFULLY flavoured, golden-coloured soup would be perfect for an autumn dinner.

INGREDIENTS

450g/1lb piece of peeled pumpkin
50g/2oz/¼ cup butter
1 medium onion, finely chopped
750ml/1¼ pints/3 cups vegetable stock or water
475ml/16fl oz/2 cups milk
pinch of grated nutmeg
40 g/1½oz/7 tbsp spaghetti, broken into small pieces
90ml/6 tbsp freshly grated Parmesan cheese
salt and freshly ground black pepper

Serves 4

1 Chop the piece of pumpkin into 2.5cm/1in cubes.

2 Heat the butter in a saucepan. Add the onion and cook over moderate heat until it softens, 6–8 minutes. Stir in the pumpkin pieces and cook for about 2–3 minutes more.

3 Add the stock or water, bring to the boil, cover, reduce the heat and cook until the pumpkin is soft, about 15 minutes. Remove from the heat.

4 Process the soup in a blender or food processor. Return it to the pan. Stir in the milk and nutmeg. Season with salt and pepper. Bring the soup back to the boil.

5 Stir the broken spaghetti into the soup. Cook until the pasta is done. Stir in the Parmesan, sprinkle with nutmeg and serve at once.

Jerusalem Artichoke Soup with Gruyère Toasts

SMALL, KNOBBLY JERUSALEM artichokes have a delicious, mild, nutty flavour. They make a remarkably good, creamy soup, which is delicious served with crunchy, grilled Gruyère and French bread toasts.

INGREDIENTS

30ml/2 tbsp olive oil
1 large onion, chopped
1 garlic clove, chopped
1 celery stick, chopped
675g/1 1/2lb Jerusalem artichokes, peeled or scrubbed, and chopped
1.2 litres/2 pints/5 cups vegetable stock
300ml/1/2 pint/1 1/4 cups semi-skimmed milk
salt and freshly ground black pepper

To serve
8 slices French bread
115g/4oz/1 cup Gruyère cheese, grated
Serves 4–6

1 Heat the butter and oil in a large saucepan. Add the onion, garlic and celery, and cook over a medium heat for 5 minutes or until softened, stirring occasionally. Add the prepared Jerusalem artichokes and cook for a further 5 minutes.

2 Add the stock and seasoning, and bring the soup to the boil. Reduce the heat and simmer for 20–25 minutes, stirring occasionally, until the artichokes are tender.

3 Transfer the soup to a food processor or blender (or use a hand blender) and process for a few minutes until smooth. Return the soup to the pan, stir in the milk and heat through gently for 2 minutes.

4 To make the Gruyère toasts, heat the grill to high. Lightly grill the bread on one side, then sprinkle the untoasted side with the Gruyère. Grill until the cheese melts and is golden. Ladle the soup into bowls and top with the Gruyère toasts.

COOK'S TIP

To preserve soluble nutrients, scrub the jerusalem artichokes rather than peel them.

HEALTH BENEFITS

High in fibre and low in fat, jerusalem artichokes also contain valuable amounts of vitamin C.

Roasted Root Vegetable Soup

ROASTING THE VEGETABLES GIVES this winter soup a wonderful depth of flavour. You can use other vegetables, if you wish, or adapt the quantities depending on what's in season.

INGREDIENTS

50ml/2fl oz/¼ cup olive oil
1 small butternut squash, peeled, seeded and cubed
2 carrots, cut into thick rounds
1 large parsnip, cubed
1 small swede, cubed
2 leeks, thickly sliced
1 onion, quartered
3 bay leaves
4 thyme sprigs, plus extra to garnish
3 rosemary sprigs
1.2 litres/2 pints/5 cups vegetable stock
salt and freshly ground black pepper
soured cream, to serve

Serves 6

1 Preheat the oven to 200°C/400°F/Gas 6. Put the olive oil into a large bowl. Add the prepared vegetables and toss until coated in the oil.

2 Spread out the vegetables in a single layer on one large or two small baking sheets. Tuck the bay leaves and thyme and rosemary sprigs amongst the vegetables.

COOK'S TIP

Dried herbs can be used in place of fresh; sprinkle 2.5ml/½ tsp of each type over the vegetables in step 2.

3 Roast for 50 minutes until tender, turning the vegetables occasionally to make sure they brown evenly all over. Remove from the oven, discard the herbs and transfer the vegetables to a large saucepan.

HEALTH BENEFITS

This nutritious soup is packed with health-giving vegetables. Butternut squash is particularly high in beta carotene and potassium, which is essential for the functioning of the cells, nerves and muscles. Carrots also contain a high level of beta carotene and are effective detoxifiers.

4 Pour the stock into the pan and bring to the boil. Reduce the heat, season to taste, then simmer for 10 minutes. Transfer the soup to a food processor or blender (or use a hand blender) and process for a few minutes until thick and smooth.

5 Return the soup to the pan to heat through. Season and serve with a swirl of soured cream. Garnish each serving with a sprig of thyme.

Cream of Courgette Soup

THE BEAUTY of this soup is its delicate colour, rich and creamy texture and subtle taste. If you prefer a more pronounced cheese flavour, use Gorgonzola instead of dolcelatte.

INGREDIENTS

30ml/2 tbsp olive oil
15g/½oz/1 tbsp butter
1 medium onion, roughly chopped
900g/2lb courgettes, trimmed and sliced
5ml/1 tsp dried oregano
about 600ml/1 pint/2½ cups vegetable stock
115g/4oz/1 cup dolcelatte cheese, rind removed, diced
300ml/½ pint/1¼ cups single cream
salt and freshly ground black pepper
fresh oregano, extra dolcelatte and cream, to garnish

Serves 4–6

1 Heat the oil and butter in a large saucepan until foaming. Add the onion and cook gently for about 5 minutes, stirring frequently, until softened but not brown.

Cook's Tip

To save time, trim off and discard the ends of the courgettes, cut them into thirds, then chop in a food processor fitted with a metal blade.

2 Add the courgettes and oregano with salt and pepper to taste. Cook over a medium heat for 10 minutes, stirring frequently. Pour in the stock and bring to the boil, stirring.

3 Lower the heat, half cover the pan and simmer gently, stirring occasionally, for about 30 minutes. Stir in the diced dolcelatte until melted.

4 Process the soup in a blender or food processor until smooth, then press through a sieve into a clean pan.

5 Add two-thirds of the cream and stir over a low heat until hot, but not boiling. Add more stock or water if the soup is too thick. Season with salt and pepper.

6 Pour into heated bowls. Swirl in the remaining cream. Serve, garnished with oregano, extra cheese, cream and pepper.

Garlic, Chick-pea and Spinach Soup

THIS DELICIOUS, thick and creamy soup is richly flavoured and makes a great one-pot meal.

INGREDIENTS

30ml/2 tbsp olive oil
4 garlic cloves, crushed
1 onion, roughly chopped
10ml/2 tsp ground cumin
10ml/2 tsp ground coriander
1.2 litres/2 pints/5 cups vegetable stock
350g/12oz potatoes, peeled and finely chopped
425g/15oz can chick-peas, drained
15ml/1 tbsp cornflour
150ml/¼ pint/⅔ cup double cream
30ml/2 tbsp light tahini (sesame seed paste)
200g/7oz spinach, shredded
cayenne pepper
salt and freshly ground black pepper

Serves 4

1 Heat the oil in a large saucepan and cook the garlic and onion for 5 minutes, or until they are softened and golden brown.

2 Stir in the cumin and coriander and cook for a further minute.

3 Pour in the stock and add the chopped potatoes to the pan. Bring to the boil and simmer for 10 minutes. Add the chick-peas and simmer for a further 5 minutes, or until both the potatoes and chick-peas are just tender.

4 Blend together the cornflour, cream, tahini and plenty of seasoning. Stir into the soup with the spinach. Bring to the boil, stirring, and simmer for a further 2 minutes. Season with cayenne pepper, salt and black pepper. Serve immediately, sprinkled with a little cayenne pepper.

Classic French Onion Soup

When French onion soup is made slowly and carefully, the onions almost caramelize to a deep mahogany colour. It has a superb flavour and is a perfect winter supper dish.

INGREDIENTS

4 large onions
30ml/2 tbsp sunflower or olive oil, or 15ml/1 tbsp of each
25g/1oz/2 tbsp butter
900ml/1 ½ pints/3¾ cups vegetable stock
4 slices French bread
40–50g/1 ½–2oz/¼–½ cup Gruyère or Cheddar cheese, grated
salt and freshly ground black pepper
Serves 4

1 Peel and quarter the onions and slice or chop them into 5 mm/¼ in pieces. Heat the oil and butter in a deep saucepan, preferably with a medium-size base so that the onions form a thick layer.

2 Fry the onions briskly for a few minutes, stirring constantly.

3 Reduce the heat and cook gently for 45–60 minutes. At first, the onions need to be stirred only occasionally but as they begin to colour, stir frequently. The colour of the onions gradually turns golden and then more rapidly to brown, so take care to stir constantly as they reach this stage so that they do not burn on the base of the pan.

4 When the onions are a rich mahogany brown, add the vegetable stock and a little seasoning. Simmer, partially covered, for 30 minutes, then season again with salt and pepper.

5 Preheat the grill and toast the French bread. Spoon the soup into four ovenproof serving dishes and place a piece of bread in each. Sprinkle with the cheese and grill for a few minutes until golden. Season with plenty of freshly ground black pepper.

White Bean Soup

A THICK purée of cooked dried beans is at the heart of this substantial country soup from Tuscany. It makes a warming lunch or supper dish.

INGREDIENTS

350g/12oz/1 1/2 cups dried cannellini or other white beans
1 bay leaf
75ml/5 tbsp olive oil
1 medium onion, finely chopped
1 carrot, finely chopped
1 stick celery, finely chopped
3 medium tomatoes, peeled and finely chopped
2 cloves garlic, finely chopped
5ml/1 tsp fresh thyme leaves or 2.5ml/1/2 tsp dried thyme
750ml/1 1/4 pints/3 cups boiling water
salt and freshly ground black pepper
olive oil, to serve

Serves 6

1 Pick over the beans carefully, discarding any stones or other particles. Rinse thoroughly in cold water to ensure that they are clean. Soak in a large bowl of cold water overnight. Drain the beans and place them in a large saucepan of water, bring to the boil and cook for 20 minutes. Drain.

2 Return the drained beans to the pan, cover with cold water and bring to the boil again. Add the bay leaf and cook until the beans are tender, for approximately 1–2 hours. Drain again. Remove the bay leaf.

3 Purée about three-quarters of the beans in a food processor, or pass through a food mill, adding a little water if necessary, to create a smooth, creamy paste.

4 Heat the oil in a large pan. Stir in the onion and cook until it softens. Add the carrot and celery. Cook for 5 minutes, stirring frequently, until softened but not browned.

5 Stir in the tomatoes, garlic and thyme. Cook for 6–8 minutes more, stirring often.

6 Pour in the boiling water. Stir in the beans and the bean purée. Season with salt and pepper. Simmer for 10–15 minutes. Serve in individual soup bowls and sprinkle over a little olive oil.

COOK'S TIP

Other types of canned cooked beans, such as cannellini or borlotti, may be substituted in this recipe. Simply drain the beans and omit Steps 1 and 2.

Hot-and-sour Soup

THIS LIGHT AND INVIGORATING soup originates from Thailand. It is best served at the beginning of a Thai meal to stimulate the appetite.

INGREDIENTS

2 carrots
900ml/1 1/2 pints/3 3/4 cups vegetable stock
2 Thai chillies, seeded and finely sliced
2 lemon grass stalks, outer leaves removed and each stalk cut into 3 pieces
4 kaffir lime leaves
2 garlic cloves, finely chopped
4 spring onions, finely sliced
5ml/1 tsp sugar
juice of 1 lime
45ml/3 tbsp chopped fresh coriander
salt
130g/4 1/2oz/1 cup Japanese tofu, sliced
Serves 4

1 To make carrot flowers, cut each carrot in half crossways, then, using a sharp knife, cut four V-shaped channels lengthways. Slice the carrots into thin rounds and set aside.

COOK'S TIP

Kaffir lime leaves have a distinctive citrus flavour. The fresh leaves can be bought from Asian shops, and some supermarkets now sell them dried.

2 Pour the stock into a large saucepan. Reserve 2.5ml/1/2 tsp of the chillies and add the rest to the pan with the lemon grass, lime leaves, garlic and half the spring onions. Bring to the boil, then reduce the heat and simmer for 20 minutes. Strain the stock and discard the flavourings.

3 Return the stock to the pan, add the reserved chillies and spring onions, the sugar, lime juice, coriander and salt to taste.

4 Simmer for 5 minutes, then add the carrot flowers and tofu, and cook for a further 2 minutes until the carrot is just tender. Serve hot.

HEALTH BENEFITS

Hot spices, including chillies, are good for the respiratory system. They help to relieve congestion and may, as a result, soothe the symptoms of colds, flu and hayfever. Chillies encourage the brain to release endorphins, which increase the sensation of pleasure, and so they have been described as aphrodisiacs.

Japanese-style Noodle Soup

THIS DELICATE, FRAGRANT SOUP is flavoured with just a hint of chilli. It is best served as a light lunch or as a first course. According to Japanese etiquette, slurping while eating the soup is a sign of appreciation.

INGREDIENTS

45ml/3 tbsp mugi miso
200g/7oz/scant 2 cups udon noodles, soba noodles or Chinese noodles
30ml/2 tbsp sake or dry sherry
15ml/1 tbsp rice or wine vinegar
45ml/3 tbsp Japanese soy sauce
115g/4oz asparagus tips or mangetouts, thinly sliced diagonally
50g/2oz/scant 1 cup shiitake mushrooms, stalks removed and thinly sliced
1 carrot, sliced into julienne strips
3 spring onions, thinly sliced diagonally
salt and freshly ground black pepper
5ml/1 tsp dried chilli flakes, to serve

Serves 4

1 Bring 1 litre/1¾ pints/4 cups water to the boil in a saucepan. Pour 150ml/¼ pint/⅔ cup of the boiling water over the miso and stir until dissolved, then set aside.

2 Meanwhile, bring another large pan of lightly salted water to the boil, add the noodles and cook according to the packet instructions until just tender.

3 Drain the noodles in a colander. Rinse under cold running water, then drain again.

4 Add the sake or sherry, rice or wine vinegar and soy sauce to the pan of boiling water. Boil gently for 3 minutes or until the alcohol has evaporated, then reduce the heat and stir in the miso mixture.

5 Add the asparagus or mangetouts, mushrooms, carrot and spring onions, and simmer for about 2 minutes until the vegetables are just tender. Season to taste.

6 Divide the noodles among four warm bowls and pour the soup over the top. Serve immediately, sprinkled with the chilli flakes.

HEALTH BENEFITS

Miso shares many of the health qualities of soya. It has shown itself to be effective against stomach cancer, which no doubt stems from its antioxidant qualities.

Split Pea and Courgette Soup

RICH AND satisfying, this tasty and nutritious soup will warm a chilly winter's day.

INGREDIENTS

175g/6oz/1 7/8 cups yellow split peas
1 medium onion, finely chopped
5ml/1 tsp sunflower oil
2 medium courgettes, finely diced
900ml/1 1/2 pints/3 3/4 cups vegetable stock
2.5ml/1/2 tsp ground turmeric
salt and freshly ground black pepper
crusty bread, to serve

Serves 4

1 Place the split peas in a bowl, cover with cold water and leave to soak for several hours or overnight. Drain, rinse in cold water and drain again.

2 Cook the onion in the oil in a covered pan, shaking occasionally, until soft. Reserve a handful of diced courgettes to use later.

3 Add the remaining courgettes to the pan. Cook for 2–3 minutes. Add the stock, turmeric and drained split peas and bring to the boil. Reduce the heat, cover and simmer for 30–40 minutes. Season with salt and pepper.

4 When the soup is almost ready, bring a large saucepan of water to the boil, add the reserved diced courgettes and cook for 1 minute. Drain and add to the soup. Serve hot with warm crusty bread.

COOK'S TIP

For a quicker alternative, use red split lentils for this soup – they need no presoaking and cook very quickly. Adjust the amount of stock, if necessary.

Fresh Tomato, Lentil and Onion Soup

THIS DELICIOUS nourishing soup is ideal served with thick slices of wholemeal or granary bread.

INGREDIENTS

10ml/2 tsp sunflower oil
1 large onion, chopped
2 sticks celery, chopped
175g/6oz/¾ cup split red lentils
2 large tomatoes, skinned and roughly chopped
900ml/1½ pints/3¾ cups vegetable stock
10ml/2 tsp dried herbes de Provence
salt and freshly ground black pepper
chopped parsley, to garnish

Serves 4–6

1 Heat the oil in a large saucepan. Add the onion and celery and cook for 5 minutes, stirring occasionally. Add the red lentils and cook for a further minute.

2 Stir in the tomatoes, stock, dried herbs, salt and pepper. Cover, bring to the boil and simmer for about 20 minutes, stirring occasionally. Add a little more water if it seems necessary.

3 When the lentils are cooked and tender, remove the lid and set the soup aside to cool slightly.

4 Purée in a blender or food processor until smooth. Season with salt and pepper, return to the saucepan and reheat gently until piping hot. Ladle into soup bowls to serve and garnish each with chopped parsley.

Italian Pea and Basil Soup

PLENTY OF CRUSTY COUNTRY BREAD is a must with this fresh-tasting soup.

INGREDIENTS

75ml/5 tbsp olive oil
2 large onions, chopped
1 celery stick, chopped
1 carrot, chopped
1 garlic clove, finely chopped
400g/14oz/3 1/2 cups frozen petit pois
900ml/1 1/2 pints/3 3/4 cups vegetable stock
25g/1oz/1 cup fresh basil leaves, roughly torn, plus extra to garnish
salt and freshly ground black pepper
freshly grated Parmesan cheese, to serve

Serves 4

VARIATION

Use mint or a mixture of parsley, mint and chives in place of the basil.

1 Heat the oil in a large saucepan and add the onions, celery, carrot and garlic. Cover the pan and cook over a low heat for 45 minutes or until the vegetables are soft, stirring occasionally to prevent the vegetables sticking.

2 Add the peas and stock to the pan and bring to the boil. Reduce the heat, add the basil and seasoning, then simmer for 10 minutes.

3 Spoon the soup into a food processor or blender and process until the soup is smooth. Ladle into warm bowls, sprinkle with grated Parmesan and garnish with basil.

HEALTH BENEFITS

As freezing usually takes place soon after picking, frozen peas may have a higher vitamin C content than fresh.

Spiced Red Lentil and Coconut Soup

HOT, SPICY AND RICHLY FLAVOURED, this substantial soup is almost a meal in itself. If you are really hungry, serve with chunks of warmed naan bread or thick slices of toast.

INGREDIENTS

30ml/2 tbsp sunflower oil
2 red onions, finely chopped
1 bird's eye chilli, seeded and finely sliced
2 garlic cloves, chopped
2.5cm/1in piece fresh lemon grass, outer layers removed and inside finely sliced
200g/7oz/scant 1 cup red lentils, rinsed
5ml/1 tsp ground coriander
5ml/1 tsp paprika
400ml/14fl oz/1 2/3 cups coconut milk
juice of 1 lime
3 spring onions, chopped
20g/3/4oz/scant 1 cup fresh coriander, finely chopped
salt and freshly ground black pepper

Serves 4

1 Heat the oil in a large pan and add the onions, chilli, garlic and lemon grass. Cook for 5 minutes or until the onions have softened, stirring occasionally.

HEALTH BENEFITS

Lentils provide a rich supply of minerals, including iron and calcium, as well as folic acid. The latter is recommended for pregnant women as it can lower the risk of spina bifida in the unborn child.

2 Add the lentils and spices. Pour in the coconut milk and 900ml/1 1/2 pints/3 3/4 cups water, and stir. Bring to the boil, stir, then reduce the heat and simmer for 40–45 minutes or until the lentils are soft and mushy.

3 Pour in the lime juice and add the spring onions and fresh coriander, reserving a little of each for the garnish. Season, then ladle into bowls. Garnish with the reserved spring onions and coriander.

Guacamole

THIS IS quite a fiery version, although nowhere near as hot as you would be served in Mexico!

INGREDIENTS

2 ripe avocados, peeled and stoned
2 tomatoes, peeled, seeded and finely chopped
6 spring onions, finely chopped
1–2 fresh chillies, seeded and finely chopped
30ml/2 tbsp fresh lime or lemon juice
15ml/1 tbsp chopped fresh coriander
salt and freshly ground black pepper
coriander sprigs, to garnish

Serves 4

1 Put the avocado halves into a large bowl and mash them roughly with a large fork.

2 Add the remaining ingredients. Mix well and season. You can use a food processor, but combine briefly to keep some texture to the guacamole. Serve garnished with sprigs of fresh coriander.

Butter Bean, Watercress and Herb Dip

THIS IS a refreshing dip that is especially good served with fresh vegetable crudités and breadsticks.

INGREDIENTS

225g/8oz/1 cup plain cottage cheese
400g/14oz can butter beans, rinsed and drained
1 bunch spring onions, chopped
50g/2oz watercress, chopped
60ml/4 tbsp mayonnaise
45ml/3 tbsp chopped fresh mixed herbs
salt and freshly ground black pepper
watercress sprigs, to garnish
vegetable crudités and breadsticks, to serve

Serves 4–6

1 Put the cottage cheese, butter beans, spring onions, watercress, mayonnaise and herbs in a blender or food processor and blend them together until fairly smooth.

2 Season with salt and pepper and spoon the mixture into a dish.

3 Cover and chill for several hours before serving.

COOK'S TIP

Try using other canned beans such as cannellini beans or chick-peas in place of the butter beans.

4 Transfer to a serving dish (or individual dishes) and garnish with watercress sprigs. Serve with vegetable crudités and breadsticks.

Saffron Dip

SERVE THIS mild dip with fresh vegetable crudités – it is particularly good with florets of cauliflower. Saffron has a strong, slightly bitter flavour; the infusing brings out the deep yellow colour.

INGREDIENTS

small pinch of saffron strands
200g/7oz/scant 1 cup fromage frais
10 fresh chives
10 fresh basil leaves
salt and freshly ground black pepper
vegetable crudités, to serve

Serves 4

1 Pour 15ml/1 tbsp boiling water into a small heatproof bowl and add the saffron strands. Leave to infuse for about 3–4 minutes, stirring occasionally.

2 Beat the fromage frais until smooth, then stir in the infused saffron liquid.

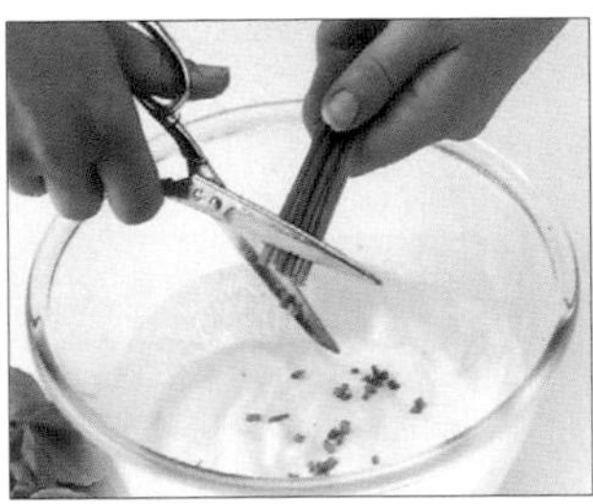

3 Use a pair of scissors to finely snip the chives into the dip. Tear the basil leaves into small pieces and stir them in.

4 Season with salt and pepper. Serve immediately with vegetable crudités to capture the enticing saffron fragrance.

VARIATION

Leave out the saffron and add a squeeze of lemon or lime juice instead. Alternatively, substitute the saffron strands with ready-ground saffron powder.

Spiced Carrot Dip

THIS IS a delicious dip with a sweet and spicy flavour. Serve wheat crackers or fiery tortilla chips as accompaniments for dipping.

INGREDIENTS

1 onion
3 carrots, plus extra to garnish
grated rind and juice of 2 oranges
15ml/1 tbsp hot curry paste
150ml/¼ pint/⅔ cup natural yogurt
handful of fresh basil leaves
15–30ml/1–2 tbsp fresh lemon juice, to taste
red Tabasco sauce, to taste
salt and freshly ground black pepper

Serves 4

1 Finely chop the onion. Peel and grate the carrots, then place the onion, carrots, orange rind and juice, together with the curry paste in a small saucepan. Bring to the boil, cover and simmer gently for 10 minutes, until tender.

2 Process the mixture in a blender or food processor until smooth. Leave to cool completely.

3 Stir in the yogurt. Then tear the basil leaves roughly into small pieces and stir them into the carrot mixture so that everything is well combined.

4 Add the lemon juice and Tabasco and season with salt and pepper. Serve within a few hours at room temperature. Garnish lightly with some grated carrot.

Aubergine Dip with Crispy Bread

THIS DELECTABLE Middle Eastern dish is flavoured with tahini (sesame seed paste), which gives it a subtle hint of spice.

INGREDIENTS

2 small aubergines
1 garlic clove, crushed
60ml/4 tbsp tahini (sesame seed paste)
25g/1oz/¼ cup ground almonds
juice of ½ lemon
2.5ml/½ tsp ground cumin
30ml/2 tbsp fresh mint leaves
30ml/2 tbsp olive oil
salt and freshly ground black pepper

Lebanese flatbread
4 pitta breads
45ml/3 tbsp toasted sesame seeds
45ml/3 tbsp chopped fresh thyme
45ml/3 tbsp poppy seeds
150ml/¼ pint/⅔ cup olive oil
Serves 6

1 Start by making the Lebanese flatbread. Split the pitta breads through the middle and carefully open them out. Mix the sesame seeds, chopped thyme and poppy seeds in a mortar. Crush them lightly with a pestle to release the flavour.

2 Stir in the olive oil. Spread the mixture lightly over the cut sides of the pitta bread. Grill until golden brown and crisp. When completely cool, break into pieces and set aside.

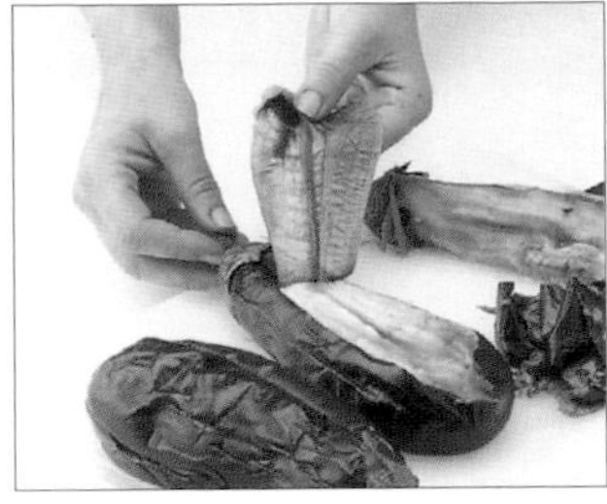

3 Grill the aubergines, turning them frequently, until the skin is blackened and blistered. Remove the skin, chop the flesh roughly and leave to drain in a colander. Wait for 30 minutes, then squeeze out as much liquid from the aubergines as possible.

4 Place the flesh in a blender or food processor. Add the garlic, tahini, almonds, lemon juice and cumin. Season, and process to a smooth paste. Chop half the mint and stir in.

5 Spoon into a bowl, scatter the remaining mint leaves on top and drizzle with olive oil. Serve with the Lebanese flatbread.

Chick-pea Falafel with Coriander Dip

LITTLE BALLS of spicy chick-pea purée, deep-fried until crisp, are served with a zesty coriander-flavoured mayonnaise.

INGREDIENTS

400g/14oz can chick-peas, drained
6 spring onions, finely chopped
1 egg
2.5ml/½ tsp ground turmeric
1 garlic clove, crushed
5ml/1 tsp ground cumin
60ml/4 tbsp chopped fresh coriander
oil for deep-frying
1 small fresh red chilli, seeded and finely chopped
45ml/3 tbsp mayonnaise
salt and freshly ground black pepper
sprig of fresh coriander, to garnish

Serves 4

1 Put the chick-peas into a food processor or blender. Add the spring onions and process to a smooth purée. Add the egg, ground turmeric, garlic, cumin and about 15ml/1 tbsp of the chopped coriander. Process briefly to mix, then season with salt and pepper.

2 Working with clean, wet hands, shape the chick-pea mixture into about 16 small balls.

3 Heat the oil for deep-frying. It should be sufficiently hot so that a cube of bread, when added to the oil, browns in 30–45 seconds. Deep-fry the falafel in batches for 2–3 minutes or until golden. Drain the falafel on kitchen paper. Place in a serving bowl and keep in a warm place.

4 Stir the remaining chopped coriander and the chilli into the mayonnaise. Garnish with the coriander sprig and serve alongside the bowl of falafel.

Crispy Spring Rolls with Sweet Chilli Dip

DAINTY MINIATURE spring rolls make delicious appetizers or perfect party finger food.

INGREDIENTS

25g/1oz/¼ cup rice vermicelli noodles
peanut oil
5ml/1 tsp fresh root ginger, finely grated
2 spring onions, finely shredded
50g/2oz carrot, finely shredded
50g/2oz mangetout, shredded
25g/1oz young spinach leaves
50g/2oz/¼ cup fresh beansprouts
15ml/1 tbsp fresh mint, finely chopped
15ml/1 tbsp fresh coriander, finely chopped
30ml/2 tbsp light soy sauce
20–24 spring roll wrappers, each 13cm/5in square
1 egg white, lightly beaten

For the dipping sauce
60ml/4 tbsp sugar
50ml/2fl oz/¼ cup rice vinegar
2 fresh red chillies, seeded and finely chopped

Makes 20–24

1 First make the dipping sauce. Place the sugar and vinegar in a small saucepan with 30ml/2 tbsp water. Heat gently, stirring until the sugar dissolves, then boil rapidly until it forms a light syrup. Stir in the chillies and leave to cool thoroughly.

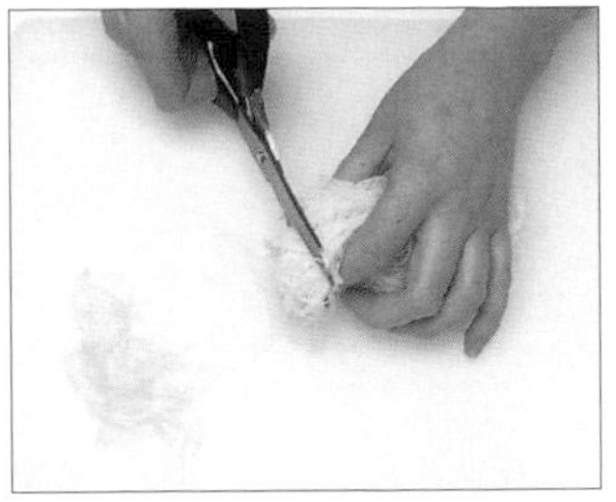

2 Soak the noodles according to the package instructions. Rinse and drain well. Using scissors, snip the noodles into short lengths.

3 Heat a wok until hot. Add 15ml/1 tbsp oil. Add the ginger and spring onions and stir-fry for 15 seconds. Add the carrot and mangetouts and stir-fry for 2–3 minutes. Add the spinach, beansprouts, mint, coriander, soy sauce and noodles and stir-fry for another minute. Set aside to cool.

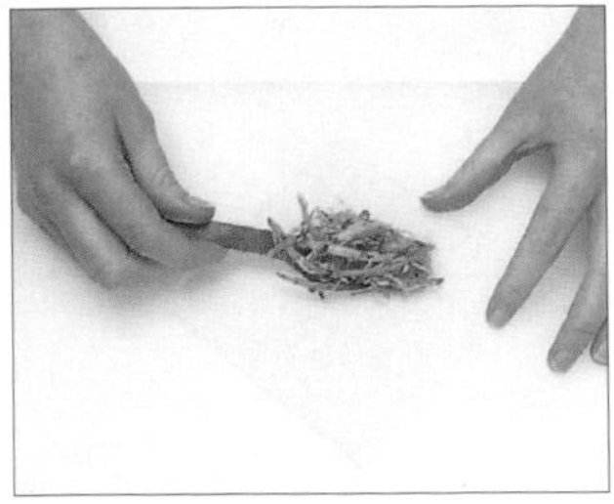

4 Place a spring roll wrapper on the work surface. Put a spoonful of filling in the middle. Fold over the wrapper to encase the filling completely.

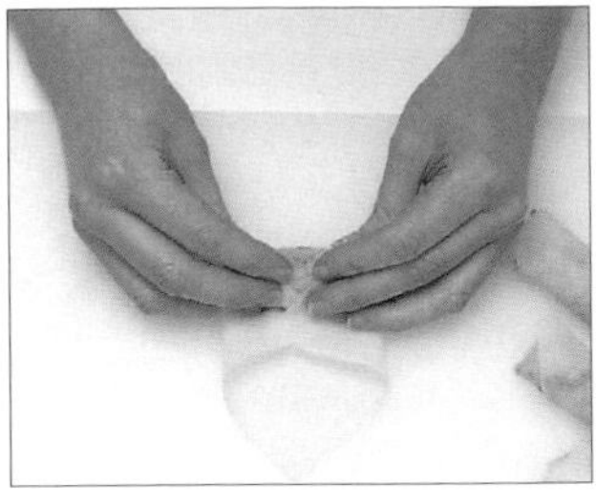

5 Fold in each side, then roll up tightly. Brush the end with beaten egg white to seal. Repeat until all the filling has been used.

6 Half-fill a wok with oil and heat to 180°C/350°F. Deep-fry the spring rolls in batches for 3–4 minutes, until golden and crisp. Drain on kitchen paper. Serve hot, with the sweet chilli dipping sauce.

COOK'S TIP

You can cook the spring rolls 2–3 hours in advance, then all you have to do is reheat them on a foil-lined baking sheet at 200°C/400°F/Gas 6 for about 10 minutes until they are ready to eat.

Marinated Vegetable Antipasto

THIS COLOURFUL selection of fresh vegetables and herbs makes a great starter when served with fresh crusty bread.

INGREDIENTS

For the peppers

3 red peppers
3 yellow peppers
4 garlic cloves, sliced
handful of fresh basil leaves
120ml/4fl oz/½ cup olive oil
salt and freshly ground black pepper

For the mushrooms

450g/1lb/6 cups open cap mushrooms, thickly sliced
60ml/4 tbsp olive oil
1 large garlic clove, crushed
15ml/1 tbsp chopped fresh rosemary
250ml/8fl oz/1 cup dry white wine
fresh rosemary sprigs, to garnish

For the olives

1 dried red chilli, crushed
grated rind of 1 lemon
120ml/4fl oz/½ cup olive oil
225g/8oz/1⅓ cups Italian black olives
30ml/2 tbsp chopped fresh flat leaf parsley
basil leaves, to garnish
1 lemon wedge, to serve

Serves 4

1 Place the peppers under a hot grill. Cook until they are black and blistered all over. Remove from the heat and place in a large plastic bag to cool.

2 When the peppers are cool, remove their skins, halve the flesh and remove the seeds. Cut into strips lengthways and place them in a bowl with the sliced garlic and basil leaves. Season and then cover with oil and marinate for 3–4 hours, tossing occasionally. Garnish with basil leaves.

3 Place the mushrooms in a large bowl. Heat the oil in a pan and add the garlic, rosemary and wine. Bring to the boil, then simmer for 3 minutes. Season. Pour over the mushrooms.

4 Mix well and leave to cool, stirring occasionally. Cover and marinate overnight. Serve at room temperature, garnished with rosemary sprigs.

5 Place the chilli and lemon rind in a small pan with the oil. Heat gently for about 3 minutes. Add the olives and heat for 1 minute more. Tip the olive mixture into a bowl and leave to cool. Cover and marinate overnight. Before serving, sprinkle with parsley and garnish with basil leaves. Serve with the lemon wedge.

Spicy Potato Wedges with Chilli Dip

THE SPICY crust on these potato wedges makes them irresistible, especially when served with a zesty chilli dip.

INGREDIENTS

2 baking potatoes, about 225g/8oz each
30ml/2 tbsp olive oil
2 garlic cloves, crushed
5ml/1 tsp ground allspice
5ml/1 tsp ground coriander
15ml/1 tbsp paprika
salt and freshly ground black pepper

For the dip

15ml/1 tbsp olive oil
1 small onion, finely chopped
1 garlic clove, crushed
200g/7oz can chopped tomatoes
1 fresh red chilli, seeded and finely chopped
15ml/1 tbsp balsamic vinegar
15ml/1 tbsp chopped fresh coriander, plus extra to garnish

Serves 2

1 Preheat the oven to 200°C/400°F/Gas 6. Wash the potatoes, leaving the skins on, cut each in half, and then into 8 wedges.

2 Place the potato wedges in a saucepan of cold water. Bring to the boil, then lower the heat and simmer gently for 8–10 minutes, or until the potatoes have softened slightly. Drain well and pat dry on kitchen paper.

3 Mix the oil, garlic, allspice, coriander and paprika in a roasting tin. Season with salt and pepper. Add the potatoes and shake to coat thoroughly. Roast for 20 minutes, turning occasionally.

4 Meanwhile, make the chilli dip. Heat the oil in a saucepan, add the onion and garlic and cook for 5–10 minutes until soft and golden. Add the tomatoes with their juice and stir in the chilli and vinegar.

5 Cook gently for 10 minutes, until the mixture has reduced and thickened. Season with salt and pepper. Stir in the fresh coriander and serve hot, with the potato wedges. Garnish with salt, freshly ground black pepper and fresh coriander.

Hummus with Pan-fried Courgettes

PAN-FRIED courgettes are perfect for dipping into home-made hummus, served with pitta bread and olives.

INGREDIENTS

225g/8oz can chick-peas
2 garlic cloves, coarsely crushed
90ml/6 tbsp lemon juice
60ml/4 tbsp tahini (sesame seed paste)
75ml/5 tbsp olive oil, plus extra to serve
5ml/1 tsp ground cumin
450g/1lb small courgettes
paprika
salt and freshly ground black pepper
pitta bread and black olives, to serve

Serves 4

1 Drain the chick-peas, reserving the liquid from the can, and put them into a blender or food processor. Blend to a smooth paste, adding a small amount of the reserved liquid, if necessary.

2 Mix the garlic, lemon juice and tahini together and add to the blender or food processor. Process until smooth. With the machine running, gradually add 45ml/3 tbsp of the olive oil through the feeder tube or lid.

3 Add the cumin. Season with salt and pepper. Process to mix. Scrape the hummus into a bowl. Cover and chill until required.

4 Remove the ends from the courgettes. Slice the courgettes lengthways into even-size pieces.

5 Heat the remaining oil in a large frying pan. Season the courgettes with salt and pepper and fry them for only 2–3 minutes on each side, until just tender.

6 Divide the courgettes among four individual plates. Spoon a portion of hummus on to each plate and sprinkle with paprika. Add two or three pieces of sliced pitta bread and serve with olives.

VARIATION

For a stronger nutty flavour, substitute the tahini paste with smooth peanut butter. This is also delicious when it is served with pan-fried or grilled aubergine slices or red peppers.

Potted Stilton with Herbs and Melba Toast

THIS STARTER is a great time saver, as the potted Stilton can be made the day before, and the Melba toast will keep in an airtight container for up to two days.

INGREDIENTS

225g/8oz blue Stilton or other blue cheese
115g/4oz/½ cup cream cheese
15ml/1 tbsp port
15ml/1 tbsp chopped fresh parsley
15ml/1 tbsp snipped fresh chives, plus extra to garnish
50g/2oz/½ cup finely chopped walnuts
salt and freshly ground black pepper

For the Melba toast
12 thin slices of white bread

Serves 8

1 Put the Stilton or blue cheese, cream cheese and port into a blender or food processor and process until smooth.

2 Stir in the remaining ingredients and then season with salt and black pepper.

3 Spoon the mixture into individual ramekin dishes and level the tops with the back of a spoon. Cover with clear plastic film and chill until firm. Sprinkle with snipped chives just before serving.

4 To make the Melba toast, preheat the oven to 180°C/350°F/Gas 4. Toast the bread on both sides.

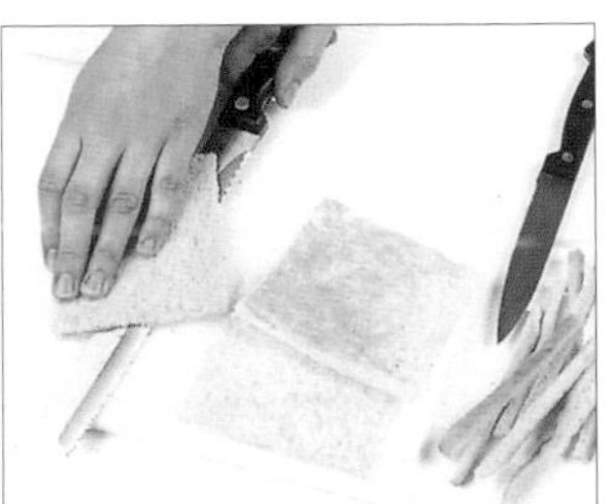

5 While the toast is still hot, cut off the crusts and cut each slice horizontally in two. While the bread is still warm, place it in a single layer on baking trays and bake for 10–15 minutes, until golden brown and crisp. Continue with the remaining slices in the same way. Serve warm with the potted Stilton.

Mushroom and Bean Pâté

A LIGHT and tasty pâté, delicious served on wholemeal bread or toast.

INGREDIENTS

450g/1lb/6 cups mushrooms, sliced
1 onion, chopped
2 garlic cloves, crushed
1 red pepper, seeded and diced
30ml/2 tbsp vegetable stock
30ml/2 tbsp dry white wine
400g/14oz can red kidney beans, rinsed and drained
1 egg, beaten
50g/2oz/1 cup fresh wholemeal breadcrumbs
15ml/1 tbsp chopped fresh thyme
15ml/1 tbsp chopped fresh rosemary
salt and freshly ground black pepper
lettuce and tomatoes, to garnish

Serves 12

1 Preheat the oven to 180°C/350°F/Gas 4. Lightly grease and line a non-stick 900g/2lb loaf tin. Put the mushrooms, onion, garlic, red pepper, stock and wine in a saucepan. Cover and cook for about 10 minutes, stirring occasionally.

2 Set aside to cool slightly, then purée the mixture with the kidney beans in a blender or food processor until smooth.

3 Transfer the mixture to a bowl, add the egg, breadcrumbs and herbs and mix thoroughly. Season with salt and pepper.

4 Spoon the mixture into the prepared tin and level the surface. Bake for 45–60 minutes, until lightly set and browned on top. Place on a wire rack and allow the pâté to cool completely in the tin. Once cool, cover and refrigerate for several hours. Turn out of the tin and serve in slices, garnished with lettuce and tomato.

Tomato Pesto Toasties

The flavour of pesto is so powerful that it can be used in very small amounts to good effect, as in these tasty snacks. Make your own pesto or use a ready-prepared version.

INGREDIENTS

2 thick slices crusty bread
45ml/3 tbsp cream cheese or fromage frais
10ml/2 tsp red or green pesto
1 beef tomato
1 red onion
salt and freshly ground black pepper
chopped basil, to garnish

Serves 2

1 Toast the slices of crusty bread until golden brown on both sides. Set aside to cool.

2 Mix together the cheese and pesto in a small bowl until well blended, then spread thickly on the toasted bread.

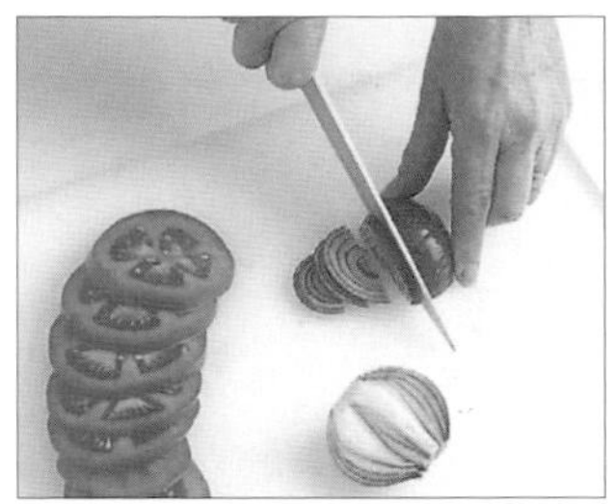

3 Using a large sharp knife, cut the beef tomato and red onion crossways into thin slices.

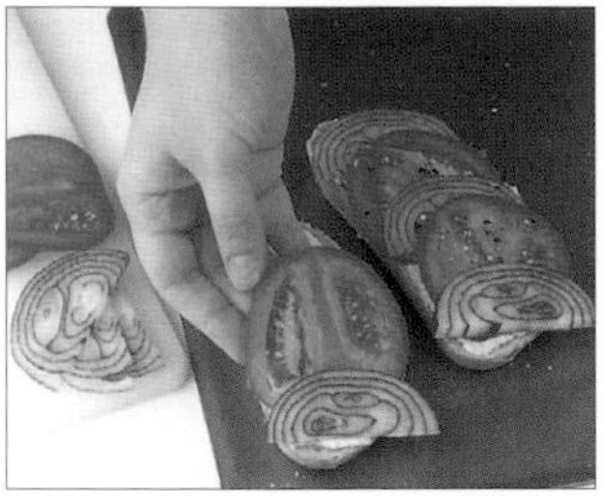

4 Arrange the tomato and onion slices, overlapping, on the toast and season with salt and pepper. Transfer to a grill rack and heat through under a hot grill. Serve, garnished with chopped basil.

Cook's Tip

Almost any type of crusty bread can be used for this recipe, but the texture and taste of Italian olive oil bread and French bread will give the best flavour.

Mushroom Croustades

THE RICH mushroom flavour of this filling is heightened by the addition of mushroom ketchup.

INGREDIENTS

1 short French stick, about 25cm/10in
10ml/2 tsp olive oil
250g/9oz/3½ cups open cup mushrooms, quartered
10ml/2 tsp mushroom ketchup
10ml/2 tsp lemon juice
30ml/2 tbsp skimmed milk
30ml/2 tbsp snipped fresh chives
salt and freshly ground black pepper
snipped fresh chives, to garnish

Serves 2–4

1 Preheat the oven to 200°C/400°F/Gas 6. Cut the French bread in half lengthways. Carefully cut a shallow scoop out of the soft middle of each half, leaving a thick border all the way round.

2 Brush the bread with oil, place on a baking sheet and bake for about 6–8 minutes, until golden and crisp.

3 Place the mushrooms in a small saucepan with the mushroom ketchup, lemon juice and milk. Simmer for about 5 minutes, or until most of the liquid is evaporated.

4 Remove from the heat, then add the chives and season with salt and pepper. Spoon into the bread croustades and serve hot, garnished with snipped chives.

Fried Mozzarella

THESE CRISPY cheese slices make an unusual and tasty starter. They must be cooked just before serving.

INGREDIENTS

300g/11oz mozzarella cheese
oil for deep frying
2 eggs
flour seasoned with salt and freshly ground black pepper
plain dry breadcrumbs
flat leaf parsley, to garnish

Serves 2–3

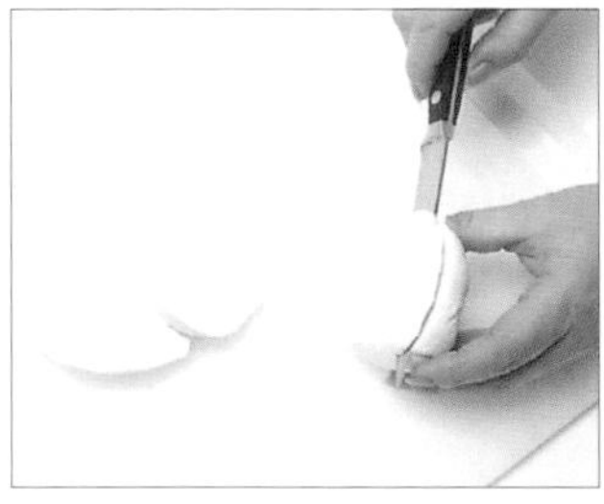

1 Cut the mozzarella cheese into slices, each about 1cm/½in thick. Gently pat off any excess moisture with kitchen paper.

2 Heat the oil to 185°C/360°F or until a small piece of bread sizzles as soon as it is dropped in. While the oil is heating, beat the eggs in a shallow bowl. Spread a layer of seasoned flour on one plate and some breadcrumbs on another.

3 Press the cheese slices into the flour, coating them evenly with a thin layer of flour. Shake off any excess. Dip them into the egg, then once into the breadcrumbs. Dip them once more into the egg, then again into the breadcrumbs.

4 Fry immediately in the hot oil until golden brown. (You may have to do this in two batches but do not let the breaded cheese wait for too long or the breadcrumb coating will separate from the cheese while it is being fried.) Drain on kitchen paper and serve hot, garnished with parsley.

Greek Cheese and Potato Patties

DELICIOUS LITTLE fried morsels of potato and feta cheese, flavoured with dill and lemon juice.

INGREDIENTS

500g/1 1/4lb potatoes
115g/4oz feta cheese
4 spring onions, chopped
45ml/3 tbsp chopped fresh dill
15ml/1 tbsp lemon juice
1 egg, beaten
flour for dredging
45ml/3 tbsp olive oil
salt and freshly ground black pepper

Serves 4

1 Boil the potatoes in their skins in lightly salted water until soft. Drain away the water, then peel the potatoes while they are still warm. Place in a bowl and mash. Crumble the feta cheese into the potatoes and add the spring onions, dill, lemon juice and egg. Season with salt and pepper (the cheese is salty, so taste before you add salt). Stir well.

2 Cover the mixture and chill until firm. Divide the mixture into walnut-size balls, then flatten them slightly. Dredge with the flour. Heat the oil in a frying pan and fry the patties until golden brown on each side. Drain on kitchen paper and serve at once.

Cheese-stuffed Pears

THESE PEARS, with their scrumptious creamy topping, make a sublime dish when served with a simple salad.

INGREDIENTS

50g/2oz/¼ cup ricotta cheese
50g/2oz/¼ cup dolcelatte cheese
15ml/1 tbsp honey
½ celery stick, finely sliced
8 green olives, pitted and roughly chopped
4 dates, stoned and cut into thin strips
pinch of paprika
4 ripe pears
150ml/¼ pint/⅔ cup apple juice

Serves 4

1 Preheat the oven to 200°C/400°F/Gas 6. Place the ricotta in a bowl and crumble in the dolcelatte. Add the rest of the ingredients except for the pears and apple juice and mix well.

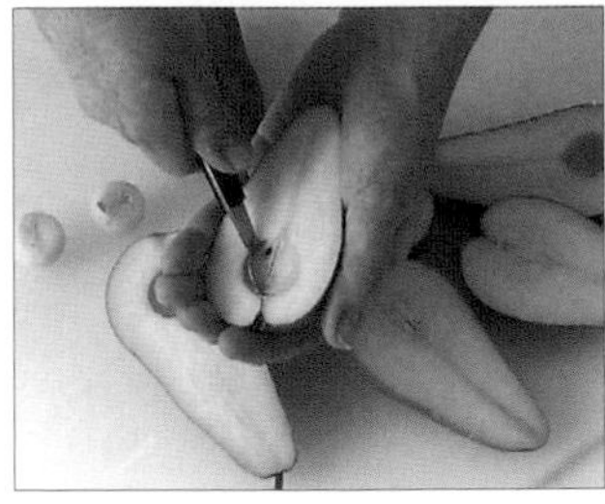

2 Halve the pears lengthways and use a melon baller to remove the cores. Place the pears in an ovenproof dish and divide the filling equally between them.

3 Pour in the apple juice and cover the dish with foil. Bake the pears for 20 minutes or until they are tender.

4 Remove the foil and place the dish under a hot grill for 3 minutes. Serve immediately.

COOK'S TIP

Choose ripe pears in season such as Conference, William or Comice.

Roquefort Tartlets

THESE CAN be made in shallow bun tins to serve hot as a first course. You could also make them in tiny cocktail tins, to serve warm as appetizing bite-size snacks with a drink before a meal.

INGREDIENTS

175g/6oz/1½ cups plain flour
large pinch of salt
115g/4oz/½ cup butter
1 egg yolk
30ml/2 tbsp cold water

For the filling

15g/½oz/1 tbsp butter
15g/½oz/2 tbsp flour
150ml/¼ pint/⅔ cup milk
115g/4oz/1 cup Roquefort cheese, crumbled
150ml/¼ pint/⅔ cup double cream
2.5ml/½ tsp dried mixed herbs
3 egg yolks
salt and freshly ground black pepper

Makes 12

1 To make the pastry, sift the flour and salt into a bowl and rub the butter into the flour until it resembles breadcrumbs. Mix the egg yolk with the water and stir into the flour to make a soft dough. Knead until smooth, wrap in clear film and chill for 30 minutes. (You can also make the dough in a food processor.)

2 In a saucepan, melt the butter, stir in the flour and then the milk. Boil to thicken, stirring continuously. Off the heat, beat in the cheese and season with salt and pepper. Cool. In another saucepan, bring the cream and herbs to the boil and cook until the liquid has reduced to 30ml/2 tbsp. Beat into the cheese sauce with the eggs.

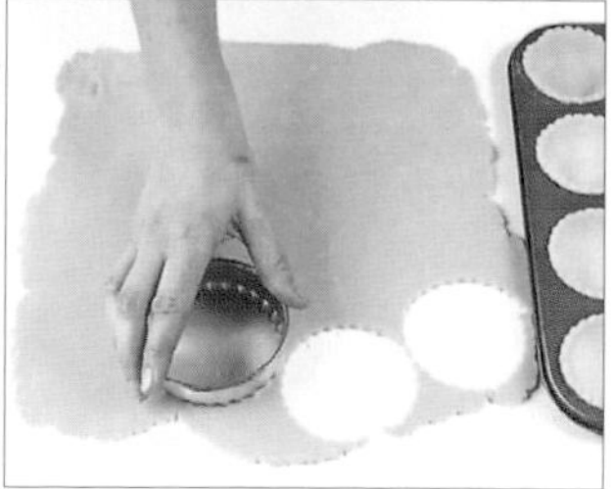

3 Preheat the oven to 190°C/375°F/Gas 5. On a lightly floured work surface, roll out the pastry to 3mm/⅛in thick. Stamp out rounds with a fluted cutter and use to line your chosen bun tins.

4 Divide the filling between the tartlets; they should be filled or two-thirds full. Stamp out smaller fluted rounds or star shapes for the tops and lay on top of each tartlet. Bake for 20–25 minutes, or until golden brown.

Buckwheat Blinis with Mushroom Caviar

THESE LITTLE Russian pancakes are traditionally served with fish roe caviar and soured cream. The term caviar is also given to fine vegetable mixtures called ikry. This wild mushroom ikry has a rich and silky texture.

INGREDIENTS

115g/4oz/1 cup strong white bread flour
50g/2oz/¼ cup buckwheat flour
2.5ml/½ tsp salt
300ml/½ pint/1¼ cups milk
5ml/1 tsp dried yeast
2 eggs, separated
oil for frying
200ml/7fl oz/⅞ cup soured cream or crème fraîche, to serve

For the caviar
350g/12oz/6 cups assorted wild mushrooms, such as field mushrooms, orange birch bolete, bay boletus, oyster and St George's mushrooms
5ml/1 tsp celery salt
30ml/2 tbsp walnut oil
15ml/1 tbsp lemon juice
45ml/3 tbsp chopped fresh parsley
freshly ground black pepper

Serves 4

1 To make the caviar, trim and chop the mushrooms and place them in a glass bowl. Toss with the celery salt and cover with a weighted plate.

2 Leave the mushrooms for 2 hours, until the juices have run out into the bottom of the bowl. Rinse them thoroughly to remove the salt.

3 Drain and press out as much liquid as you can with the back of a spoon. Return them to the bowl and toss with the walnut oil, lemon juice and parsley. Season with pepper and chill until ready to serve.

4 Sift the two flours together with the salt in a large mixing bowl. Warm the milk to approximately blood temperature. Add the yeast, stirring until dissolved, then pour into the flour. Add the egg yolks and stir to make a smooth batter. Cover with a damp cloth and leave in a warm place to rise, for about 30 minutes.

5 Whisk the egg whites in a clean bowl until stiff, then fold into the risen batter.

6 Heat an iron pan to moderate temperature. Moisten with oil, then drop spoonfuls of the batter on to the surface, turn them over and cook briefly on the other side. Spoon on the mushroom caviar and serve with the soured cream.

Broccoli Timbales

THIS ELEGANT but easy to make dish can be made with almost any puréed vegetable, such as carrot or celeriac. To avoid last-minute fuss, make the timbales a few hours ahead and cook while the first course is being eaten. Alternatively, serve them on their own as a starter with a little white wine butter sauce.

INGREDIENTS

15g/½oz/1 tbsp butter
350g/12oz broccoli florets
45ml/3 tbsp crème fraîche or whipping cream
1 egg, plus one egg yolk
15ml/1 tbsp chopped spring onion
pinch of freshly grated nutmeg
salt and freshly ground black pepper
white wine butter sauce, to serve (optional)
fresh chives, to garnish (optional)

Serves 4

1 Preheat the oven to 190°C/375°F/Gas 5. Lightly butter four 175ml/6fl oz/¾ cup ramekins. Line the bases with greaseproof paper and butter the paper.

2 Steam the broccoli in the top of a covered steamer over boiling water for 8–10 minutes, until very tender but still bright green.

3 Put the broccoli in a food processor fitted with the metal blade and process with the cream, egg and egg yolk until smooth.

4 Add the spring onion and season with salt, pepper and nutmeg. Pulse to mix.

5 Spoon the purée into the ramekins and place in a roasting tin. Add boiling water to the tin to come halfway up the sides of the ramekins. Bake for 25 minutes, until just set. Invert on to warmed plates and peel off the paper. If serving as a starter, pour sauce around each timbale and garnish with chives.

Garlic Mushrooms with a Parsley Crust

THESE GARLIC mushrooms are perfect for dinner parties, or you could serve them in larger portions as a light supper dish with a green salad.

INGREDIENTS

350g/12oz/6 cups large mushrooms, stems removed
3 garlic cloves, crushed
175g/6oz/¾ cup butter, softened
50g/2oz/1 cup fresh white breadcrumbs
50g/2oz/1 cup fresh parsley, chopped
1 egg, beaten
salt and cayenne pepper
8 cherry tomatoes, to garnish

Serves 4

1 Preheat the oven to 190°C/375°F/Gas 5. Arrange the mushrooms cup side uppermost on a baking tray. Mix together the garlic and butter in a small bowl and divide 115g/4oz/½ cup of the butter between all the mushrooms.

2 Heat the remaining butter in a frying pan and lightly fry the breadcrumbs until golden brown.

3 Place the parsley in a bowl, add the breadcrumbs, season with salt and cayenne pepper and mix well.

4 Stir in the egg and use the mixture to fill the mushroom caps. Bake for 10–15 minutes until the topping has browned and the mushrooms have softened. Garnish with quartered tomatoes.

COOK'S TIP

If you are planning ahead, stuffed mushrooms can be prepared up to 12 hours in advance and kept in the fridge before baking.

Asparagus Rolls with Herb Butter Sauce

FOR A taste sensation, try tender asparagus spears wrapped in crisp filo pastry. The buttery herb sauce makes the perfect accompaniment.

INGREDIENTS

4 sheets of filo pastry
50g/2oz/¼ cup butter, melted
16 young asparagus spears, trimmed

For the sauce

2 shallots, finely chopped
1 bay leaf
150ml/¼ pint/⅔ cup dry white wine
175g/6oz/¾ cup butter, softened
15ml/1 tbsp chopped fresh herbs
salt and freshly ground black pepper
chopped chives, to garnish

Serves 2

1 Preheat the oven to 200°C/400°F/Gas 6. Cut the filo sheets in half. Brush a half sheet with melted butter. Fold one corner of the sheet down to the bottom edge to give a wedge shape.

2 Place four asparagus spears in a bundle on top at the longest edge, and roll up toward the shortest edge. Using the remaining filo and asparagus spears, make three more rolls in the same way.

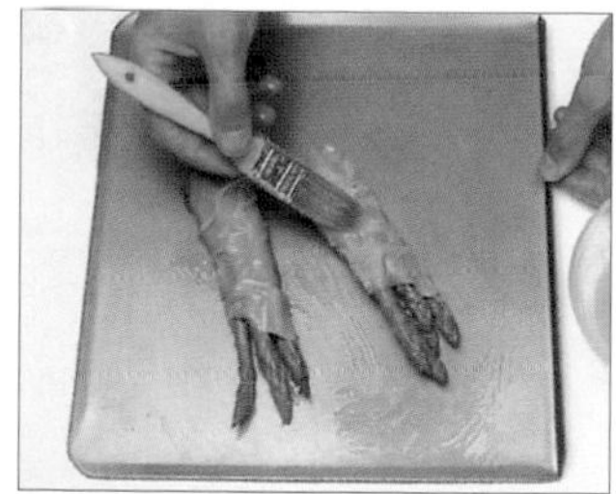

3 Lay the rolls on a greased baking sheet. Brush with the remaining melted butter. Bake in the oven for 8 minutes until golden brown.

4 Meanwhile, put the shallots, bay leaf and wine into a pan. Cover, and cook over a high heat until the wine is reduced to 45–60ml/3–4 tbsp.

5 Strain the wine mixture into a bowl. Whisk in the butter, a little at a time, until the sauce is smooth and glossy.

6 Stir in the herbs and add salt and pepper to taste. Return to the pan and keep the sauce warm. Serve the rolls on individual plates with a salad garnish, if desired. Serve the sauce separately, sprinkled with a scattering of chopped chives.

Curried Eggs

HARD-BOILED eggs are served on a bed of mild, creamy sauce with a hint of curry.

INGREDIENTS

4 eggs
15ml/1 tbsp sunflower oil
1 small onion, finely chopped
2.5cm/1in piece of fresh root ginger, peeled and grated
2.5ml/½ tsp ground cumin
2.5ml/½ tsp garam masala
7.5ml/1½ tsp tomato paste
10ml/2 tsp tandoori paste
10ml/2 tsp lemon juice
250ml/8fl oz/1 cup single cream
15ml/1 tbsp chopped fresh coriander
salt and freshly ground black pepper
coriander sprigs, to garnish

Serves 2

1 Put the eggs in a pan of water. Bring to the boil, lower the heat and simmer for 10 minutes.

2 Meanwhile, heat the oil in a frying pan. Cook the onion for 2–3 minutes. Add the ginger and cook for 1 minute more.

3 Stir in the ground cumin, garam masala, tomato paste, tandoori paste, lemon juice and single cream. Cook over a gentle heat for 1–2 minutes, then stir in the coriander. Season with salt and pepper.

4 Drain the eggs, remove the shells and cut each egg in half. Spoon the sauce into a serving bowl, top with the eggs and garnish with coriander sprigs. Serve at once.

Asparagus with Eggs

THE ADDITION of fried eggs and grated Parmesan turns asparagus into something special.

INGREDIENTS

450g/1lb fresh asparagus

65g/2½oz/5 tbsp butter

4 eggs

60ml/4 tbsp grated fresh Parmesan cheese

salt and freshly ground black pepper

Serves 4

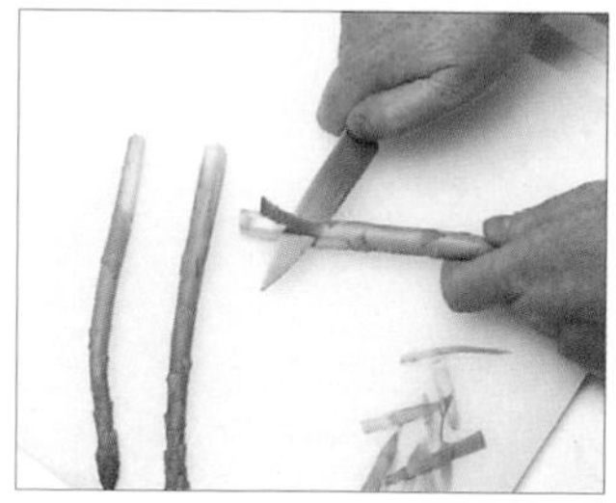

1 Cut off any woody ends from the asparagus. Peel the lower half of the spears by inserting a knife under the thick skin at the base and pulling up towards the tip. Wash the asparagus in cold water.

2 Bring a large pan of water to the boil. Add the asparagus and boil until just tender.

3 While the asparagus is cooking, melt a third of the butter in a frying pan. When bubbling, break in the eggs and cook them until the whites have set but the yolks are still soft.

4 As soon as the asparagus is cooked, remove it from the water with two slotted spoons. Place it on a wire rack covered with a clean dish towel to drain. Divide the spears between warm individual serving plates. Place a fried egg on each and sprinkle with the grated Parmesan.

5 Melt the remaining butter in the frying pan. As soon as it is bubbling, but before it browns, pour it over the cheese and eggs on the asparagus. Season with salt and pepper and serve at once.

Breaded Aubergine with Hot Vinaigrette

CRISP ON the outside, beautifully tender within, these aubergine slices taste wonderful with a spicy dressing flavoured with chillies and capers.

INGREDIENTS

1 large aubergine
50g/2oz/½ cup plain flour
2 eggs, beaten
115g/4oz/2 cups fresh white breadcrumbs
vegetable oil for frying
1 head radicchio
salt and freshly ground black pepper

For the dressing
30ml/2 tbsp olive oil
1 garlic clove, crushed
15ml/1 tbsp capers, drained
15ml/1 tbsp white wine vinegar
15ml/1 tbsp chilli oil
Serves 2

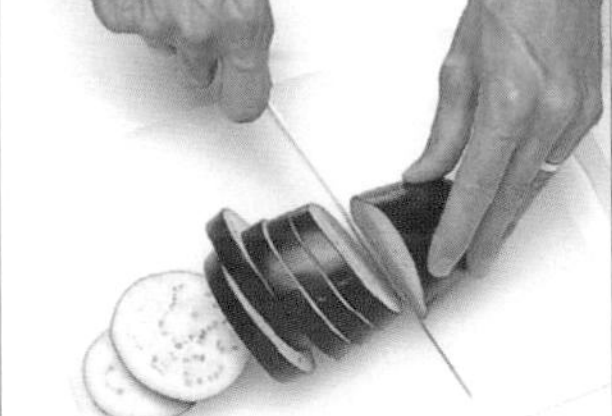

1 Remove the ends from the aubergine. Cut it into 1cm/½in slices. Set aside.

COOK'S TIP

It is a good idea to salt the aubergine slices before frying in order to draw out some of their moisture. This will also reduce the amount of oil they absorb.

2 Season the flour with a generous amount of salt and pepper. Place the sifted flour in a shallow dish. Pour the beaten eggs into a second dish, then spread out the breadcrumbs in a third.

3 Dip both sides of the aubergine slices in the flour, then in the beaten egg and finally in the breadcrumbs, patting them on top to make an even coating.

4 Pour oil into a large frying pan to a depth of about 5mm/¼in. Heat the oil, then fry the aubergine slices for 3–4 minutes, turning once. Drain well on kitchen paper.

5 To make the dressing, heat the olive oil in a small pan. Add the garlic and capers and cook over gentle heat for 1 minute. Increase the heat, add the vinegar and cook for 30 seconds. Stir in the chilli oil and remove the pan from the heat.

6 Arrange the radicchio leaves on two plates. Top with the hot aubergine slices. Drizzle over the vinaigrette and serve.

LIGHT MEALS

For suppers or lunches, meals that are easy to prepare and are tasty and nutritious are sure winners. This chapter contains a selection that will appeal to children and adults, suitable for entertaining or for family cooking.

Summer Tomato Pasta

THIS IS a deliciously light pasta dish, full of fresh flavours. Use buffalo-milk mozzarella if you can – the flavour is noticeably better.

INGREDIENTS

275g/10oz/2¼ cups dried penne
450g/1lb plum tomatoes
275g/10oz mozzarella, drained
60ml/4 tbsp olive oil
15ml/1 tbsp balsamic vinegar
grated rind and juice of 1 lemon
15 fresh basil leaves, shredded
salt and freshly ground black pepper
fresh basil leaves, to garnish

Serves 4

1 Cook the pasta in boiling salted water, according to the package instructions, until just tender.

2 Quarter the tomatoes and remove the seeds, then chop the flesh into small cubes. Slice up the mozzarella into similarly sized pieces.

3 Mix together the olive oil, balsamic vinegar, grated lemon rind, 15ml/1 tbsp of the lemon juice and the basil. Season with salt and pepper. Add the tomatoes and mozzarella and leave to stand until the pasta is cooked.

4 Drain the pasta thoroughly and toss with the tomato mixture. Serve immediately, garnished with a few fresh basil leaves.

Pappardelle and Provençal Sauce

A CLASSIC French sauce of tomatoes and fresh vegetables adds colour and robust flavour to pasta.

INGREDIENTS

2 small purple onions, peeled, root left intact
150ml/¼ pint/⅔ cup vegetable stock
1–2 garlic cloves, crushed
60ml/4 tbsp red wine
2 courgettes, cut into fingers
1 yellow pepper, seeded and sliced
400g/14oz can tomatoes
10ml/2 tsp chopped fresh thyme
5ml/1 tsp caster sugar
350g/12oz pappardelle
salt and freshly ground black pepper
fresh thyme and 6 black olives, stoned and roughly chopped, to garnish

Serves 4

1 Cut each onion into eight wedges through the root end, to hold them together during cooking. Put into a saucepan with the stock and garlic. Bring to the boil, cover and simmer for 5 minutes, until tender.

2 Add the red wine, courgettes, yellow pepper, tomatoes, thyme and sugar. Season with salt and pepper. Bring to the boil and cook gently for 5–7 minutes, shaking the pan occasionally to coat the vegetables with the sauce. (Do not overcook the vegetables as they are much nicer if they are slightly crunchy.)

3 Cook the pasta in a large pan of boiling salted water according to the instructions on the package, until tender. Drain the pasta thoroughly.

4 Transfer to a warmed serving dish and top with the vegetables. Garnish with fresh thyme and chopped black olives.

Fusilli with Peppers and Onions

GRILLING THE peppers for this simple pasta dish intensifies their natural sweetness and gives them a delicious smoky flavour. To save time you can prepare the peppers in advance. Put the strips into a bowl, cover with film and chill until needed.

INGREDIENTS

450g/1lb red and yellow peppers
90ml/6 tbsp olive oil
1 large red onion, thinly sliced
2 cloves garlic, crushed
400g/14oz/4 cups fusilli or other short pasta
45ml/3 tbsp finely chopped fresh parsley
salt and freshly ground black pepper
freshly grated Parmesan cheese, to serve

Serves 4

1 Place the peppers under a hot grill and turn occasionally until they are black and blistered on all sides. Remove, place in a paper bag and leave for 5 minutes.

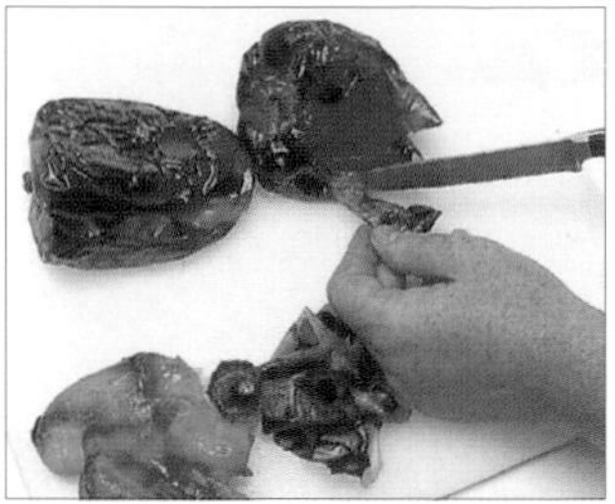

2 Peel the peppers. Cut them into quarters, remove the stems and seeds and slice the flesh into thin strips. Bring a large pan of water to the boil for the pasta.

3 Heat the olive oil in a large frying pan. Add the onion and cook over moderate heat until it is translucent, 5–8 minutes. Stir occasionally and do not let the onion brown. Stir in the garlic and cook for 2 minutes more.

4 Add salt and the pasta to the boiling water and cook until the pasta is tender.

5 Meanwhile, add the peppers to the onions and mix together gently. Stir in about 45ml/3 tbsp of the pasta cooking water. Season with salt and pepper, then stir in the chopped parsley.

6 Drain the pasta. Tip it into the pan with the vegetables and cook over moderate heat for 3–4 minutes, stirring constantly to mix the pasta into the sauce. Serve with the Parmesan passed separately.

COOK'S TIP

Peppers were brought to Europe by Christopher Columbus, who discovered them in Haiti. The large red, yellow and orange peppers are usually sweeter than the green varieties, and have a fuller, more intense flavour.

Pasta Primavera

THERE'S NO better way to use the best of the spring season's young vegetables than in this delightful pasta dish.

INGREDIENTS

225g/8oz thin asparagus spears, cut in half
115g/4oz mangetouts, topped and tailed
115g/4oz whole baby sweetcorn
225g/8oz/1 cup whole baby carrots
1 small red pepper, seeded and chopped
8 spring onions, sliced
225g/8oz/2 cups torchietti
150ml/¼ pint/⅔ cup cottage cheese
150ml/¼ pint/⅔ cup low-fat yogurt
15ml/1 tbsp lemon juice
15ml/1 tbsp chopped fresh parsley
milk (optional)
15ml/1 tbsp snipped chives
salt and freshly ground black pepper
sun-dried tomato bread, to serve

Serves 4

1 Cook the thin asparagus spears in a pan of boiling salted water for 3–4 minutes. Add the mangetouts halfway through the cooking time. Drain and rinse both under cold water.

2 Cook the baby sweetcorn, carrots, red pepper and spring onions in the same way until tender. Drain and rinse.

3 Cook the pasta in a large pan of boiling salted water until tender. Drain thoroughly.

4 Put the cottage cheese, yogurt, lemon juice and parsley into a food processor or blender. Season, then process until smooth. Thin the sauce with a little milk, if necessary.

5 Put the sauce into a large pan with the pasta and vegetables, heat through gently and toss the mixture carefully. Transfer to a warmed serving plate, scatter the snipped chives over the top and serve with sun-dried tomato bread.

Penne with Fennel, Tomato and Blue Cheese

THE ANISE flavour of the fennel makes it the perfect partner for tomato, especially when topped with blue cheese.

INGREDIENTS

1 fennel bulb
225g/8oz/2 cups penne or other dried pasta shapes
30ml/2 tbsp olive oil
1 shallot, finely chopped
300ml/½ pint/1¼ cups passata
pinch of sugar
5ml/1 tsp chopped fresh oregano
115g/4oz blue cheese
salt and freshly ground black pepper

Serves 2

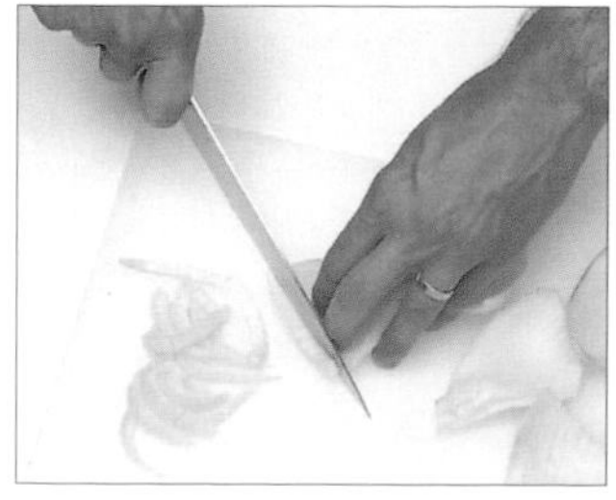

1 Cut the fennel bulb in half. Cut away the hard core and root. Slice the fennel thinly, then cut the slices into thin strips.

2 Bring a large pan of salted water to the boil. Stir in the pasta and cook for 10–12 minutes, until just tender.

3 Meanwhile, heat the oil in a small saucepan. Add the fennel and shallot and cook for 2–3 minutes over high heat, stirring occasionally. Do not let it brown.

4 Add the passata, sugar and oregano. Cover the pan and simmer gently for 10–12 minutes, until the fennel is tender. Season with salt and pepper. Drain the pasta and return it to the pan. Toss with the sauce. Serve with blue cheese crumbled over.

Peanut Noodles

ADD ANY of your favourite vegetables to this quick lunch recipe – and increase the quantity of chilli, if you can take the heat!

INGREDIENTS

200g/7oz/1¾ cups medium egg noodles
30ml/2 tbsp olive oil
2 garlic cloves, crushed
1 large onion, roughly chopped
1 red pepper, seeded and roughly chopped
1 yellow pepper, seeded and roughly chopped
350g/12oz courgettes, roughly chopped
150g/5oz/generous ¾ cup roasted unsalted peanuts, roughly chopped

For the dressing

50ml/2fl oz/¼ cup olive oil
grated rind and juice of 1 lemon
1 fresh red chilli, seeded and finely chopped
45ml/3 tbsp snipped fresh chives
15–30ml/1–2 tbsp balsamic vinegar
salt and freshly ground black pepper
snipped fresh chives, to garnish

Serves 4

1 Cook the noodles according to the package instructions and drain well.

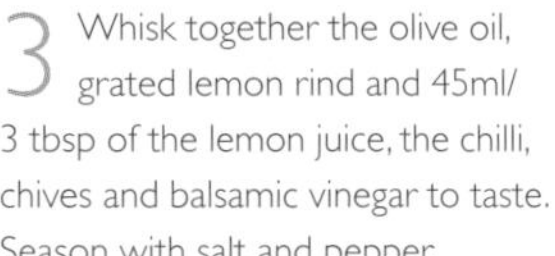

2 Meanwhile, heat the oil in a very large frying pan or wok and cook the garlic and onion for 3 minutes, or until beginning to soften. Add the peppers and courgettes and cook for a further 15 minutes over a medium heat until beginning to soften and brown. Add the peanuts and cook for a further 1 minute.

3 Whisk together the olive oil, grated lemon rind and 45ml/3 tbsp of the lemon juice, the chilli, chives and balsamic vinegar to taste. Season with salt and pepper.

4 Toss the noodles into the vegetables and stir-fry to heat through. Add the dressing, stir to coat and serve garnished with fresh chives.

Stir-fried Vegetables with Cashew Nuts

STIR-FRYING IS the perfect way to make a delicious, colourful and very speedy meal.

INGREDIENTS

900g/2lb mixed vegetables (see Cook's Tip)
30–60ml/2–4 tbsp sunflower or olive oil
2 garlic cloves, crushed
15ml/1 tbsp grated fresh root ginger
50g/2oz/½ cup cashew nuts or 60ml/4 tbsp sunflower, pumpkin or sesame seeds
soy sauce
salt and freshly ground black pepper

Serves 4

1 Prepare the vegetables according to type. Carrots and cucumber should be cut into very fine matchsticks.

2 Heat a frying pan, then trickle the oil around the rim so that it runs down to coat the surface. When the oil is hot, add the garlic and ginger and cook for 2–3 minutes, stirring. Add the harder vegetables and toss over the heat for 5 minutes, until they soften.

3 Add the softer vegetables and stir-fry all of them over a high heat for 3–4 minutes.

4 Stir in the cashew nuts or seeds. Season with soy sauce, salt and pepper. Serve at once.

COOK'S TIP

Use a pack of stir-fry vegetables or make up your own mixture. Choose from carrots, mangetouts, baby sweetcorn, pak choi, cucumber, beansprouts, mushrooms, peppers and spring onions. Drained canned bamboo shoots and water chestnuts are delicious additions.

Tofu Stir-fry with Egg Noodles

SWEET AND delicately flavoured, this is the perfect supper for lovers of Chinese food.

INGREDIENTS

225g/8oz firm smoked tofu
45ml/3 tbsp dark soy sauce
30ml/2 tbsp sherry or vermouth
3 leeks, thinly sliced
2.5cm/1in piece fresh root ginger, peeled and finely grated
1–2 fresh red chillies, seeded and sliced in rings
1 small red pepper, seeded and sliced thinly
150ml/¼ pint/⅔ cup vegetable stock
10ml/2 tsp runny honey
10ml/2 tsp cornflour
225g/8oz/2 cups medium egg noodles
salt and freshly ground black pepper

Serves 4

1 Cut the tofu into 2cm/¾in cubes. Put it into a bowl with the soy sauce and sherry or vermouth. Toss to coat each piece and then leave to marinate for about 30 minutes.

2 Put the leeks, ginger, chillies, red pepper and stock into a frying pan. Bring the ingredients to the boil and cook quickly over a high heat for 2–3 minutes, until all the ingredients are just soft.

3 Strain the tofu, reserving the marinade, and set the tofu aside. Mix the honey and cornflour into the marinade.

4 Put the egg noodles into a large pan of boiling water. Remove from the heat and leave to stand for about 6 minutes, until cooked (or follow the package instructions).

5 Heat a non-stick frying pan and quickly fry the tofu until lightly golden brown on all sides.

6 In a saucepan, add the vegetable mixture to the tofu with the marinade and stir well until the liquid is thick and glossy. Season. Spoon on to the egg noodles and serve at once.

VARIATION

Tofu absorbs flavours readily when marinated. If you are not a great fan of tofu, you could substitute it with a firm smoked cheese such as a smoked Bavarian variety, and omit step 5.

Sun-dried Tomato and Parmesan Carbonara

INGREDIENTS FOR this recipe can easily be doubled up to serve four. Why not try it with plenty of garlic bread and a big green salad?

INGREDIENTS

175g/6oz tagliatelle
50g/2oz/1 cup sun-dried tomatoes in olive oil, drained
2 eggs, beaten
150ml/¼ pint/⅔ cup double cream
15ml/1 tbsp wholegrain mustard
50g/2oz/⅔ cup freshly grated Parmesan cheese
12 fresh basil leaves, shredded
salt and freshly ground black pepper
crusty bread, to serve
fresh basil leaves, to garnish

Serves 2

1 Cook the pasta in boiling, salted water, following the instructions on the package, until it is just tender but still retains a little bite (*al dente*).

2 Meanwhile, cut the sun-dried tomatoes into small pieces.

3 Beat together the eggs, cream and mustard in a bowl. Add plenty of salt and pepper until they are well combined and smooth, but do not allow the mixture to become frothy.

4 Drain the pasta and immediately return to the hot saucepan with the cream mixture, sun-dried tomatoes, Parmesan cheese and shredded fresh basil. Return to a very low heat for 1 minute, stirring gently until the mixture thickens slightly. Adjust the seasoning and serve immediately, garnished with basil leaves. Serve with plenty of crusty bread.

Sliced Frittata with Tomato Sauce

THIS DISH – cold frittata with a tomato sauce – is ideal for a light summer lunch.

INGREDIENTS

6 eggs
30ml/2 tbsp finely chopped fresh mixed herbs, such as basil, parsley, thyme and tarragon
40g/1½oz/½ cup freshly grated Parmesan cheese
45ml/3 tbsp olive oil
salt and freshly ground black pepper

For the tomato sauce
30ml/2 tbsp olive oil
1 small onion, finely chopped
350g/12oz fresh tomatoes, chopped, or 400g/14oz can chopped tomatoes
1 garlic clove, chopped
salt and freshly ground black pepper

Serves 3–4

1 To make the frittata, break the eggs into a bowl and beat them lightly with a fork. Beat in the mixed herbs and Parmesan cheese. Season with salt and pepper. Heat the oil in a large non-stick or heavy frying pan until hot, but not smoking.

2 Pour in the seasoned egg mixture. Cook, without stirring, until the frittata is puffed and golden brown underneath.

3 Take a large plate, place it upside down over the pan and, holding it firmly with oven gloves, turn the pan and the frittata over on to it. Slide the frittata back into the pan and continue cooking for about 3–4 minutes more until it is golden brown on the second side. Remove from the heat and allow to cool completely.

4 To make the tomato sauce, heat the oil in a medium-heavy saucepan. Add the onion and cook slowly until it is soft. Add the tomatoes, garlic and 60ml/4 tbsp water and season with salt and pepper. Cover the pan and cook over moderate heat for about 15 minutes.

5 Remove from the heat and cool slightly before pressing the sauce through a food mill or sieve. Leave to cool completely.

6 To assemble, cut the frittata into thin slices. Place them in a serving bowl and toss lightly with the sauce. Serve at room temperature or chilled.

Spicy Bean and Lentil Loaf

An appetizing, high-fibre savoury loaf, ideal for packed lunches.

INGREDIENTS

10ml/2 tsp olive oil
1 onion, finely chopped
1 garlic clove, crushed
2 celery sticks, finely chopped
400g/14oz can red kidney beans
400g/14oz can lentils
1 egg
1 carrot, coarsely grated
50g/2oz/½ cup finely grated mature Cheddar cheese
50g/2oz/1 cup fresh wholemeal breadcrumbs
15ml/1 tbsp tomato purée
15ml/1 tbsp tomato ketchup
5ml/1 tsp each ground cumin, ground coriander and hot chilli powder
salt and freshly ground black pepper
salad, to serve

Serves 12

1 Preheat the oven to 180°C/350°F/Gas 4. Lightly grease a 900g/2lb loaf tin and set aside.

2 Heat the oil in a saucepan, add the onion, garlic and celery and cook gently for 5 minutes, stirring occasionally. Remove the pan from the heat and cool slightly.

3 Rinse and drain the beans and lentils. Put in a blender or food processor with the onion mixture and egg and process until smooth.

4 Transfer the mixture to a bowl, add all the remaining ingredients and mix. Season with salt and pepper.

5 Spoon the mixture into the prepared tin and level the surface. Bake for about 1 hour, then remove from the tin and serve hot or cold in slices, accompanied by a salad.

Savoury Nut Loaf

THIS DELICIOUS nut loaf makes perfect picnic food.

INGREDIENTS

15ml/1 tbsp olive oil, plus extra for greasing
1 onion, chopped
1 leek, chopped
2 celery sticks, finely chopped
225g/8oz/3 cups mushrooms, chopped
2 garlic cloves, crushed
425g/15oz can lentils, rinsed and drained
115g/4oz/1 cup mixed nuts, such as hazelnuts, cashew nuts and almonds, finely chopped
50g/2oz/½ cup flour
50g/2oz/½ cup grated mature Cheddar cheese
1 medium egg, beaten
45–60ml/3–4 tbsp chopped fresh mixed herbs
salt and freshly ground black pepper
chives and sprigs of fresh flat leaf parsley, to garnish

Serves 4

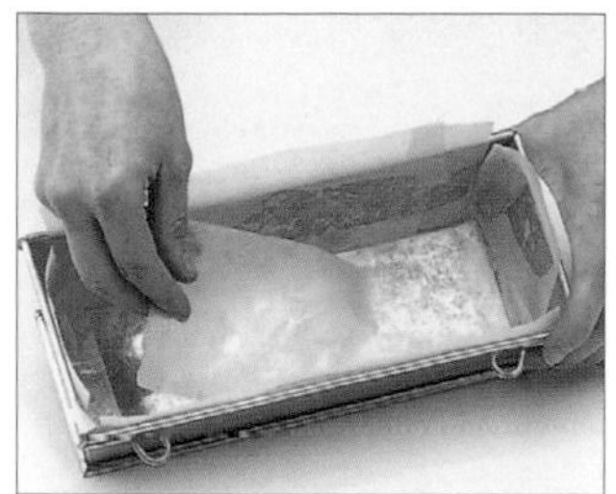

1 Preheat the oven to 190°C/375°F/Gas 5. Lightly grease the base and sides of a 900g/2lb loaf tin and line with greaseproof paper.

2 Heat the oil in a large saucepan, add the chopped onion, leek, celery sticks and mushrooms and the crushed garlic, then cook gently for 10 minutes, until the vegetables have softened, stirring occasionally. Do not let them brown.

3 Add the lentils, mixed nuts, flour, grated cheese, egg and herbs. Season and mix thoroughly.

4 Spoon the nut, vegetable and lentil mixture into the prepared loaf tin, ensuring that it is pressed into the corners, and level the surface. Bake, uncovered, for 50–60 minutes, or until the nut loaf is lightly browned on top and firm to the touch.

5 Cool the loaf slightly in the tin, then turn out on to a serving plate. Serve either hot or cold, cut into slices and garnished with chives and flat leaf parsley.

Omelette with Beans

EVERY GOOD cook should have a few omelettes in their repertoire. This version includes soft white beans and is finished with a layer of toasted sesame seeds.

INGREDIENTS

30ml/2 tbsp olive oil
5ml/1 tsp sesame oil
1 Spanish onion, chopped
1 small red pepper, seeded and diced
2 celery sticks, chopped
1 x 400g/14oz can soft white beans, drained
8 eggs
45ml/3 tbsp sesame seeds
salt and freshly ground black pepper
green salad, to serve

Serves 4

1 Heat the olive and sesame oils in a 30cm/12in flameproof frying pan. Add the onion, pepper and celery and cook to soften without colouring.

2 Add the beans and continue to cook over a gentle heat for several minutes to heat through.

VARIATION

You can also use sliced cooked potatoes, any seasonal vegetables, baby artichoke hearts and chick-peas in this omelette.

3 In a small bowl, beat the eggs with a fork, season with salt and pepper and pour over the ingredients in the pan.

4 Stir the egg mixture with a flat wooden spoon until it begins to stiffen, then allow to firm over a low heat for 6–8 minutes.

5 Preheat a moderate grill. Sprinkle the omelette with sesame seeds and brown evenly under the grill.

6 Cut the omelette into thick wedges and serve warm with a green salad.

Coriander Omelette Parcels with Oriental Vegetables

STIR-FRIED VEGETABLES in black bean sauce make a remarkably good omelette filling, which is quick and easy to prepare.

INGREDIENTS

130g/4½oz broccoli, cut into small florets
30ml/2 tbsp groundnut oil
1cm/½in piece fresh root ginger, finely grated
1 large garlic clove, crushed
2 red chillies, seeded and finely sliced
4 spring onions, sliced diagonally
175g/6oz/3 cups pak choi, shredded
50g/2oz/2 cups fresh coriander leaves, plus extra to garnish
115g/4oz/½ cup beansprouts
45ml/3 tbsp black bean sauce
4 eggs
salt and freshly ground black pepper

Serves 4

1 Blanch the broccoli in boiling salted water for 2 minutes, drain, then refresh under cold running water.

2 Meanwhile, heat 15ml/1 tbsp of the oil in a frying pan or wok. Add the ginger, garlic and half of the chilli and stir-fry for 1 minute. Add the spring onions, broccoli and pak choi, and stir-fry for 2 minutes more, tossing the vegetables continuously to prevent sticking and to cook them evenly.

3 Chop three-quarters of the coriander and add to the frying pan or wok. Add the beansprouts and stir-fry for 1 minute, then add the black bean sauce and heat through for 1 minute more. Remove the pan from the heat and keep warm.

HEALTH BENEFITS

Pak choi is a member of the brassica family. People who regularly eat this type of green leafy vegetable have a lower risk of developing certain cancers. These vegetables also assist in the treatment of asthma, gout and constipation.

4 Mix the eggs lightly with a fork and season well. Heat a little of the remaining oil in a small frying pan and add a quarter of the beaten egg. Swirl the egg until it covers the base of the pan, then scatter over a quarter of the reserved coriander leaves. Cook until set, then turn out the omelette on to a plate and keep warm while you make three more omelettes, adding more oil, when necessary.

5 Spoon the vegetable stir-fry on to the omelettes and roll up. Cut in half crossways and serve garnished with coriander leaves and chilli.

Spicy Jacket Potatoes

SIMPLE BAKED potatoes take on an exciting new character with the addition of a few herbs and spices.

INGREDIENTS

2 large baking potatoes
5ml/1 tsp sunflower oil
1 small onion, finely chopped
2.5cm/1in piece fresh root ginger, grated
5ml/1 tsp ground cumin
5ml/1 tsp ground coriander
2.5ml/½ tsp ground turmeric
garlic salt
natural yogurt and sprigs of fresh coriander, to serve

Serves 2–4

1 Preheat the oven to 190°C/375°F/Gas 5. Prick the potatoes with a fork. Bake for 1 hour, or until soft.

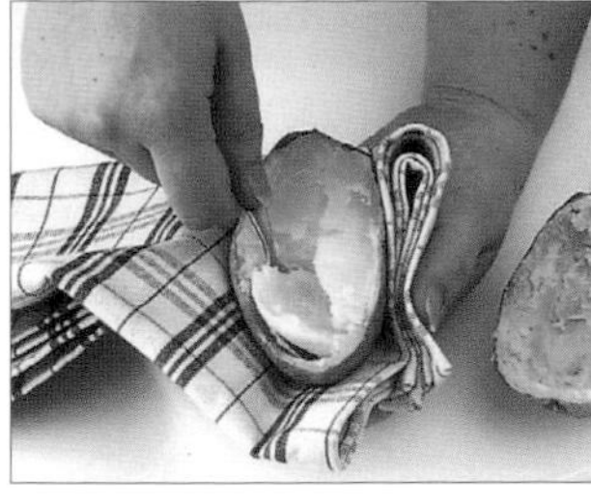

2 Cut the potatoes in half and scoop out the flesh. Heat the oil in a non-stick frying pan and fry the onion for a few minutes to soften. Stir in the ginger, cumin, coriander and turmeric.

3 Stir over a low heat for about 2 minutes, then add the potato flesh and garlic salt, to taste.

4 Cook the potato mixture for a further 2 minutes, stirring occasionally. Spoon the mixture back into the potato shells and top each with a spoonful of natural yogurt and a sprig or two of fresh coriander. Serve at once.

Baked Leeks with Cheese and Yogurt

LIKE ALL vegetables, the fresher leeks are, the better their flavour, and the freshest leeks available should be used for this dish. Small, young leeks are around at the beginning of the season and are perfect to use here.

INGREDIENTS

25g/1oz/2 tbsp butter
8 small leeks, about 675g/1 1/2lb
2 small eggs or 1 large one, beaten
150g/5oz/generous 1/2 cup fresh goat's cheese
85ml/3fl oz/1/3 cup natural yogurt
50g/2oz/2/3 cup Parmesan cheese, grated
25g/1oz/1/2 cup fresh white or brown breadcrumbs
salt and freshly ground black pepper

Serves 4

1 Preheat the oven to 180°C/350°F/Gas 4. Butter a shallow ovenproof dish. Trim the leeks, cut a slit from top to bottom and rinse well.

2 Place the leeks in a saucepan of water, bring to the boil and simmer gently for 6–8 minutes, until just tender. Remove and drain well using a slotted spoon. Arrange in the prepared dish.

3 Beat the eggs with the goat's cheese, yogurt and half the Parmesan cheese. Season well with salt and pepper.

4 Pour the cheese and yogurt mixture over the leeks. Mix the breadcrumbs and remaining Parmesan cheese together and sprinkle over the sauce. Bake for 35–40 minutes, until the top is crisp and golden brown.

Vegetable Fajitas

A COLOURFUL medley of mushrooms and peppers in a spicy sauce, wrapped in tortillas and served with creamy guacamole.

INGREDIENTS

I onion
I red pepper
I green pepper
I yellow pepper
I garlic clove, crushed
225g/8oz/3 cups mushrooms
90ml/6 tbsp vegetable oil
30ml/2 tbsp medium chilli powder
salt and freshly ground black pepper

For the guacamole
I ripe avocado
I shallot, coarsely chopped
I fresh green chilli, seeded and coarsely chopped
juice of I lime

To serve
4–6 flour tortillas, warmed
I lime, cut into wedges
sprigs of fresh coriander
Serves 2

I Slice the onion. Cut the peppers in half, remove the seeds and cut the flesh into strips. Combine the onion and peppers in a bowl. Add the crushed garlic and mix lightly.

2 Remove the mushroom stalks. Save for making stock, or discard. Slice the mushroom caps and add to the pepper mixture in the bowl. Mix the oil and chilli powder in a cup, pour over the vegetable mixture and stir well. Set aside.

3 Make the guacamole. Cut the avocado in half and remove the stone and the peel. Put the flesh into a food processor or blender with the shallot, green chilli and lime juice.

4 Process for I minute, until smooth. Scrape into a small bowl, cover tightly and put in the fridge to chill until required.

5 Heat a frying pan or wok until very hot. Add the marinated vegetables and stir-fry over high heat for 5–6 minutes, until the mushrooms and peppers are just tender. Season with salt and pepper. Spoon the filling on to each tortilla and roll up. Garnish with coriander and serve with the guacamole and lime wedges.

Baked Eggs with Creamy Leeks

THIS IS a traditional French way of enjoying eggs. You can vary the dish quite easily by experimenting with other vegetables, such as puréed spinach or ratatouille, as a base.

INGREDIENTS

15g/½oz/1 tbsp butter, plus extra for greasing
225g/8oz/2 cups small leeks, thinly sliced
65–85ml/4–6 tbsp whipping cream
freshly grated nutmeg
4 eggs
salt and freshly ground black pepper

Serves 4

1 Preheat the oven to 190°C/375°F/Gas 5.

2 Butter the base and sides of four ramekin dishes or individual soufflé dishes.

3 Melt the butter in a small frying pan and cook the leeks over medium heat, stirring frequently, until softened but not browned.

4 Add 45ml/3 tbsp of the cream and cook gently for about 5 minutes, until the leeks are very soft and the cream has thickened a little. Season with salt, pepper and nutmeg.

5 Arrange the ramekins or individual soufflé dishes in a small roasting tin and divide the leeks among them. Break an egg into each. Spoon 5–10ml/1–2 tsp of the remaining cream over each egg and season lightly with salt and pepper.

6 Pour boiling water into the roasting tin to come halfway up the side of the ramekins or soufflé dishes. Bake for about 10 minutes, until the whites are set and the yolks are still soft, or a little longer if you prefer them more well done.

VARIATION

Put 15ml/1 tbsp of cream in each dish with some chopped herbs. Break in the eggs, add 15ml/1 tbsp cream and a little grated cheese, then bake.

Baked Onions Stuffed with Feta

SERVE THESE cheesy, nutty onions with warm olive bread and a bowl of mixed leaf green salad for a fabulous lunch.

INGREDIENTS

4 large red onions
15ml/1 tbsp olive oil
25g/1oz/1/4 cup pine nuts
115g/4oz feta cheese, crumbled
25g/1oz/1/2 cup fresh white breadcrumbs
15ml/1 tbsp chopped fresh coriander
salt and freshly ground black pepper

Serves 4

1 Preheat the oven to 180°C/350°F/Gas 4. Lightly grease a shallow ovenproof dish. Peel the onions and cut a thin slice from the top and base of each. Place the onions in a large saucepan of boiling water and cook for 10–12 minutes.

2 Remove the onions with a slotted spoon. Lay them out to drain on a sheet of kitchen paper and leave to cool slightly.

3 Using a small knife or your fingers, remove the inner sections of the onions, leaving about two or three outer rings. Finely chop the inner sections and place the outer shells in an ovenproof dish.

4 Heat the oil in a medium-size frying pan and fry the chopped onions for 4–5 minutes, until golden, then add the pine nuts and stir-fry for a few minutes.

5 Place the feta cheese in a small bowl and stir in the onions, pine nuts, breadcrumbs and coriander. Season with a little salt and pepper.

6 Spoon the mixture into the onion shells. Cover loosely with foil and bake for about 30 minutes, removing the foil for the last 10 minutes to allow them to brown slightly. Serve hot.

Onion Tarts with Goat's Cheese

A VARIATION of a classic French dish, Tarte à l'Oignon, this recipe uses young goat's cheese as well as cream. The young goat's cheese is mild and creamy and complements the flavour of the onions.

INGREDIENTS

175g/6oz/1 1/2 cups plain flour
65g/2 1/2oz/5 tbsp butter
25g/1oz/1/4 cup goat's cheese or Cheddar cheese, grated

For the filling

15–25ml/1–1 1/2 tbsp olive or sunflower oil
3 onions, finely sliced
175g/6oz/3/4 cup young goat's cheese
2 eggs, beaten
15ml/1 tbsp single cream
50g/2oz/1/2 cup goat's cheddar, grated
15ml/1 tbsp chopped fresh tarragon
salt and freshly ground black pepper

Serves 8

1 To make the pastry, sift the flour into a bowl and rub in the butter until the mixture resembles fine breadcrumbs. Stir in the cheese and enough cold water to make a dough. Knead lightly, put in a polythene bag and chill. Preheat the oven to 190°C/375°F/Gas 5.

2 Roll out the dough on a lightly floured surface, then cut into eight rounds using a 12cm/4 1/2in pastry cutter, and line eight 10cm/4 in bun tins. Prick the bases with a fork and bake in the oven for 10–15 minutes. Reduce the heat to 180°C/350°F/Gas 4.

3 Heat the oil in a large frying pan and fry the onions over a low heat for 20–25 minutes, until they are a deep golden brown. Stir to prevent them from burning.

4 Beat the goat's cheese with the eggs, single cream, goat's cheddar and tarragon. Season with salt and pepper and then stir in the fried onions.

5 Pour the mixture into the part-baked pastry cases and bake in the oven for 20–25 minutes, until golden. Serve warm or cold with a green salad.

Aubergine, Smoked Mozzarella and Basil Rolls

SLICES OF GRILLED AUBERGINE are stuffed with smoked mozzarella, tomato and fresh basil to make an attractive hors-d'oeuvre, or a light lunch if served with a green salad. The rolls are also good barbecued.

INGREDIENTS

1 large aubergine
45ml/3 tbsp olive oil, plus extra for drizzling (optional)
165g/5½oz smoked mozzarella cheese, cut into 8 slices
2 plum tomatoes, each cut into 4 slices
8 large basil leaves
balsamic vinegar, for drizzling (optional)
salt and freshly ground black pepper
Serves 4

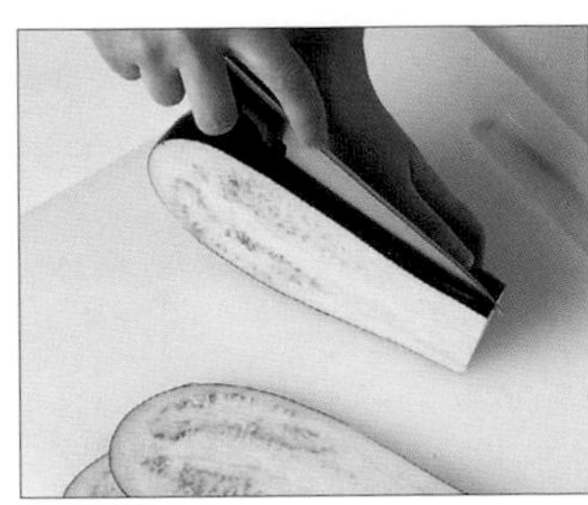

1 Cut the aubergine lengthways into 10 thin slices and discard the two outermost slices. Sprinkle the slices with salt and leave for 20 minutes. Rinse, then pat dry with kitchen paper.

2 Preheat the grill and line the rack with foil. Place the dried aubergine slices on the grill rack and brush liberally with oil. Grill for 8–10 minutes until tender and golden, turning once.

3 Remove the aubergine slices from the grill, then place a slice of mozzarella, a slice of tomato and a basil leaf in the centre of each and season to taste. Fold the aubergine over the filling and cook seam-side down under the grill until heated through and the mozzarella begins to melt. Serve drizzled with olive oil and a little balsamic vinegar, if using.

HEALTH BENEFITS

Aubergines are low in calories but frying will dramatically increase their calorific value. Salting the aubergine first not only draws out any bitter juices, it also makes the flesh denser, so that less fat is absorbed during cooking. Aubergines contain bioflavonoids, which help to prevent strokes and haemorrhages.

Creamy Lemon Puy Lentils

TINY, GREEN PUY LENTILS HAVE a very good flavour and, combined with lemon juice and crème fraîche, make a delicious, slightly tangy base for poached eggs.

INGREDIENTS

250g/9oz/generous 1 cup puy lentils
1 bay leaf
30ml/2 tbsp olive oil
4 spring onions, sliced
2 large garlic cloves, chopped
15ml/1 tbsp Dijon mustard
finely grated rind and juice of 1 large lemon
4 plum tomatoes, seeded and diced
4 eggs
60ml/4 tbsp crème fraîche
salt and freshly ground black pepper
30ml/2 tbsp chopped fresh flat leaf parsley, to garnish
Serves 4

1 Put the lentils and bay leaf in a saucepan, cover with cold water, and bring to the boil. Reduce the heat and simmer for 25 minutes or until tender. Drain. When the lentils are almost ready, poach the eggs in a saucepan of barely simmering, salted water.

2 Heat the oil and fry the spring onions and garlic for 1 minute or until softened.

3 Add the Dijon mustard, lemon rind and juice to the spring onion mixture, and mix well. Stir in the tomatoes and seasoning, then cook gently for 1–2 minutes until the tomatoes are heated through but still retain their shape. Add a little water if the mixture becomes too dry.

4 Stir in the lentils and crème fraîche, remove the bay leaf, and heat through for 1 minute. Top each portion with a poached egg, and sprinkle with parsley.

HEALTH BENEFITS

Studies have shown that lentils may help prevent heart disease and cancer, and lower cholesterol levels.

Ratatouille

A CLASSIC vegetable stew, packed full of fresh vegetables and herbs and absolutely bursting with wonderful, delicious flavour.

INGREDIENTS

2 large aubergines, roughly chopped
4 courgettes, roughly chopped
150ml/¼ pint/⅔ cup olive oil
2 onions, sliced
2 garlic cloves, chopped
1 large red pepper, seeded and roughly chopped
2 large yellow peppers, seeded and roughly chopped
sprig of fresh rosemary
sprig of fresh thyme
5ml/1 tsp coriander seeds, crushed
3 plum tomatoes, skinned, seeded and chopped
8 basil leaves, torn
salt and freshly ground black pepper
sprigs of fresh parsley or basil, to garnish
Serves 4

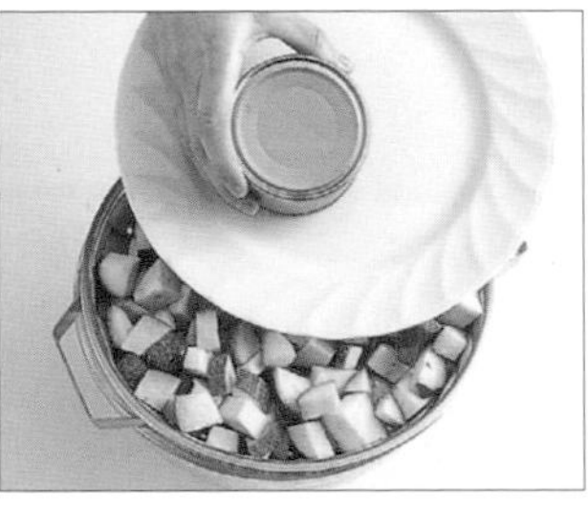

1 Sprinkle the aubergines and courgettes with salt, then put them in a colander with a plate and a weight on top to extract the bitter juices. Leave for about 30 minutes.

2 Heat the olive oil in a large saucepan. Add the onions and fry gently for 6–7 minutes, until just softened. Add the garlic and cook for another 2 minutes.

3 Rinse the aubergines and courgettes and pat dry with a clean dish towel. Add to the pan with the red and yellow peppers, increase the heat and sauté until the peppers are just turning brown.

4 Add the herbs and coriander seeds, then cover the pan and cook gently for about 40 minutes.

5 Add the tomatoes and season with salt and pepper. Cook gently for a further 10 minutes, until the vegetables are soft but not too mushy. Remove the sprigs of rosemary and thyme herbs. Stir in the torn basil leaves and check the seasoning. Leave to cool slightly and serve warm or cold, garnished with sprigs of parsley or basil.

Sweetcorn Cakes with Grilled Tomatoes

CRISP SWEETCORN fritters are simple to make and guaranteed to become a midday favourite.

INGREDIENTS

1 large cob sweetcorn
75g/3oz/2/3 cup plain flour
1 egg
a little milk
2 large firm tomatoes
1 garlic clove, crushed
5ml/1 tsp dried oregano
30–45ml/2–3 tbsp olive oil, plus extra for shallow-frying
salt and freshly ground black pepper
8 cupped leaves iceberg lettuce, to serve
shredded fresh basil leaves, to garnish

Serves 4

1 Pull the husks and silk away from the corn, then hold the cob upright on a board and cut downwards with a heavy knife to strip off the kernels. Put the kernels in a pan of boiling water and cook for 3 minutes after the water has returned to the boil. Drain the kernels and rinse under the cold tap to cool quickly.

2 Put the flour into a bowl and break the egg into a well in the middle. Start stirring with a fork, adding a little milk to make a soft dropping consistency. Stir in the drained sweetcorn and season with salt and black pepper.

3 Preheat the grill. Halve the tomatoes horizontally and make two or three criss-cross slashes across the cut side of each half. Rub in the crushed garlic and the oregano and season with salt and pepper. Trickle with oil and grill until lightly browned.

4 While the tomatoes grill, heat some oil in a wide frying pan and drop a tablespoon of batter into the centre. Cook, one at a time, over a low heat and turn as soon as the top is set. Drain on kitchen paper and keep warm while cooking the remaining fritters. The mixture should make at least 8 sweetcorn cakes.

5 For each serving, put 2 sweetcorn cakes on to lettuce leaves, garnish with basil and serve with a grilled tomato half.

Baked Mushrooms with Nutty Oat Stuffing

FLAT MUSHROOMS, rich in B-group vitamins, have a wonderful flavour and are perfect for this nutty stuffing.

INGREDIENTS

30ml/2 tbsp sunflower oil
8 large flat mushrooms, wiped
1 onion, chopped
1 garlic clove, crushed
25g/1oz/¼ cup porridge oats
225g/8oz can chopped tomatoes with herbs
2.5ml/½ tsp hot pepper sauce
25g/1oz/¼ cup pine nuts
25g/1oz/⅓ cup freshly grated Parmesan cheese
salt and freshly ground black pepper

Serves 4

1 Preheat the oven to 190°C/375°F/Gas 5. Use a little of the oil to grease a shallow ovenproof dish lightly. The dish should be large enough to hold the mushroom caps in a single layer. Remove the mushroom stalks, chop them roughly and set them aside. Reserve the whole caps.

2 Heat the oil in a small saucepan and sauté the onion, garlic and mushroom stalks until softened and lightly browned. Stir in the oats and cook for 1 minute more.

3 Stir in the tomatoes and hot pepper sauce and add salt and pepper to taste. Arrange the mushroom caps, gills uppermost, in the prepared dish. Divide the stuffing mixture between them.

4 Sprinkle the pine nuts and Parmesan cheese over the stuffed mushrooms. Bake for 25 minutes until the mushrooms are tender and the topping is golden brown.

COOK'S TIP

It is best to buy Parmesan in a block and grate it as required. Although this cheese may seem expensive, its fruity, fragrant flavour means you can use less to achieve a good taste.

Mushroom and Fennel Hotpot

MARVELLOUS flavours permeate this unusual vegetarian main course or accompaniment. Mushrooms provide useful amounts of vitamins, minerals and fibre. Dried mushrooms swell up a great deal after soaking, so a little goes a long way both in terms of flavour and quantity.

INGREDIENTS

25g/1oz dried shiitake mushrooms
1 small head of fennel or 4 celery sticks
30ml/2 tbsp olive oil
12 shallots, peeled
225g/8oz/2 cups button mushrooms, trimmed and halved
300ml/½ pint/1¼ cups dry cider
25g/1oz sun-dried tomatoes
30ml/2 tbsp/½ cup sun-dried tomato paste
1 bay leaf
chopped fresh parsley, to garnish

Serves 4

1 Place the dried mushrooms in a bowl. Pour over boiling water to cover and set aside for 10 minutes.

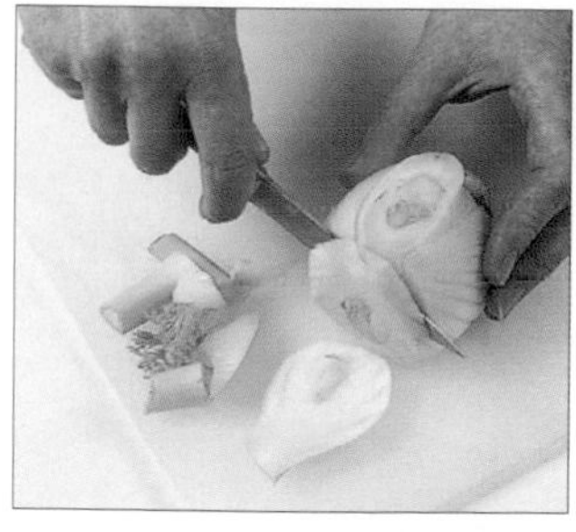

2 Roughly chop the fennel or celery sticks and heat the oil in a flameproof casserole. Add the shallots and fennel or celery and sauté for about 10 minutes over a moderate heat until the mixture is softened and lightly browned. Add the button mushrooms and fry for 2–3 minutes.

3 Drain the dried mushrooms, reserving the liquid. Cut up any large pieces and add to the pan.

COOK'S TIP

Fennel has many uses in the kitchen. Finely sliced it can be added to salads to give crispness and flavour. In small quantities it can be cooked with chicken or fish, or added to risotto.

4 Pour in the cider and stir in the sun-dried tomatoes and the paste. Add the bay leaf. Bring to the boil, then lower the heat, cover the casserole and simmer gently for about 30 minutes.

5 If the mixture seems dry, stir in the reserved liquid from the soaked mushrooms. Reheat briefly, then remove the bay leaf and serve, sprinkled with plenty of chopped parsley.

Rice Noodles with Vegetable Chilli Sauce

FRESH CHILLI and coriander combine to give this recipe quite a strong flavour kick.

INGREDIENTS

15ml/1 tbsp sunflower oil
1 onion, chopped
2 garlic cloves, crushed
1 fresh red chilli, seeded and finely chopped
1 red pepper, seeded and diced
2 carrots, finely chopped
175g/6oz baby sweetcorn, halved
225g/8oz can sliced bamboo shoots, rinsed and drained
400g/14oz can red kidney beans, rinsed and drained
300ml/½ pint/1¼ cups passata
15ml/1 tbsp soy sauce
5ml/1 tsp ground coriander
250g/9oz rice/2¼ cups noodles
30ml/2 tbsp chopped fresh coriander
salt and freshly ground black pepper
fresh parsley sprigs, to garnish

Serves 4

1 Heat the oil in a saucepan, add the onion, garlic, chilli and red pepper and cook gently for 5 minutes, stirring. Add the carrots, sweetcorn, bamboo shoots, kidney beans, passata, soy sauce and ground coriander and stir to mix.

2 Bring to the boil, then cover and simmer gently for 30 minutes, stirring occasionally, until the vegetables are tender. Season with salt and freshly ground pepper.

3 Meanwhile, place the noodles in a bowl and cover with boiling water. Stir with a fork and leave to stand for 3–4 minutes or according to the package instructions. Rinse and drain.

4 Stir the fresh coriander into the sauce. Spoon the noodles on to warmed serving plates, top with the vegetable chilli sauce, garnish with parsley and serve.

Frittata with Sun-dried Tomatoes

ADDING JUST a few sun-dried tomatoes gives this frittata a distinctly Mediterranean flavour.

INGREDIENTS

6 sun-dried tomatoes, dry or in oil and drained
60ml/4 tbsp olive oil
1 small onion, finely chopped
pinch of fresh thyme leaves
6 eggs
50g/2oz/⅔ cup freshly grated Parmesan cheese
salt and freshly ground black pepper

Serves 3–4

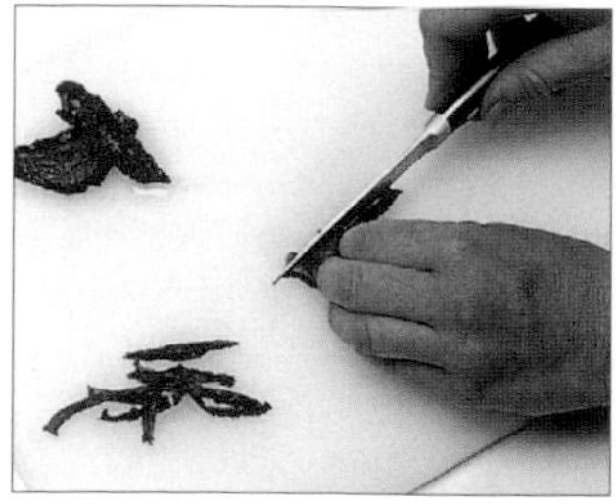

1 Place the tomatoes in a small bowl and pour on enough hot water to just cover them. Soak for about 15 minutes. Lift the tomatoes out of the water and slice them into thin strips. Reserve the soaking water.

2 Heat the oil in a large non-stick or heavy frying pan. Stir in the onion and cook for 5–6 minutes or until soft and golden. Add the tomatoes and thyme and continue to stir over moderate heat for 2–3 minutes. Season with salt and pepper.

3 Break the eggs into a bowl and beat lightly with a fork. Stir in 45–60ml/3–4 tbsp of the tomato soaking water and the grated Parmesan cheese.

4 Raise the heat under the pan. When the oil is sizzling, pour in the eggs. Mix them quickly into the other ingredients and stop stirring. Lower the heat to moderate and cook for 4–5 minutes on the first side, or until the frittata is puffed and golden brown underneath.

5 Take a large plate, place it upside down over the pan and, holding it firmly with oven gloves, turn the pan and the frittata over on to it. Slide the frittata back into the pan and continue cooking until golden brown on the second side, 3–4 minutes more. Remove from the heat. The frittata can be served hot, at room temperature or cold. Cut it into wedges to serve.

Thai Tempeh Cakes with Sweet Dipping Sauce

Made from soya beans, tempeh is similar to tofu but has a nuttier taste. Here, it is combined with a fragrant blend of lemon grass, coriander and ginger and formed into small patties.

INGREDIENTS

1 lemon grass stalk, outer leaves removed and inside finely chopped
2 garlic cloves, chopped
2 spring onions, finely chopped
2 shallots, finely chopped
2 chillies, seeded and finely chopped
2.5cm/1in piece fresh root ginger, finely chopped
60ml/4 tbsp chopped fresh coriander, plus extra to garnish
250g/9oz/2¼ cups tempeh, defrosted if frozen, sliced
15ml/1 tbsp lime juice
5ml/1 tsp caster sugar
45ml/3 tbsp plain flour
1 large egg, lightly beaten
vegetable oil, for frying
salt and freshly ground black pepper

For the dipping sauce
45ml/3 tbsp mirin
45ml/3 tbsp white wine vinegar
2 spring onions, finely sliced
15ml/1 tbsp sugar
2 chillies, finely chopped
30ml/2 tbsp chopped fresh coriander
large pinch of salt

Makes 8 Cakes

Health Benefits

Although tempeh does not contain quite the same levels of calcium, iron and B vitamins as tofu, in many ways it is healthier. It is made from fermented whole soya beans and the mould used in the fermentation process is said to boost the immune system and free the body of harmful toxins.

1 To make the dipping sauce, mix together the mirin, vinegar, spring onions, sugar, chillies, coriander and salt in a small bowl and set aside.

2 Place the lemon grass, garlic, spring onions, shallots, chillies, ginger and coriander in a food processor or blender, then process to a coarse paste. Add the tempeh, lime juice and sugar, then blend until combined. Add the seasoning, flour and egg. Process again until the mixture forms a coarse, sticky paste.

3 Take 1 heaped serving-spoonful of the tempeh mixture at a time and form into rounds with your hands – the mixture will be quite sticky.

4 Heat enough oil to cover the base of a large frying pan. Fry the tempeh cakes for 5–6 minutes, turning once, until golden. Drain on kitchen paper and serve warm with the dipping sauce, garnished with the reserved coriander.

Sesame Seed-coated Falafel with Tahini Yogurt Dip

SESAME SEEDS are used to give a crunchy coating to these spicy bean patties. Serve with the tahini yogurt dip and warm pitta bread as a light lunch or supper dish.

INGREDIENTS

250g/9oz/1 1/3 cups dried chick-peas
2 garlic cloves, crushed
1 red chilli, seeded and finely sliced
5ml/1 tsp ground coriander
5ml/1 tsp ground cumin
15ml/1 tbsp chopped fresh mint
15ml/1 tbsp chopped fresh parsley
2 spring onions, finely chopped
1 large egg, beaten
sesame seeds, for coating
sunflower oil, for frying
salt and freshly ground black pepper

For the tahini yogurt dip

30ml/2 tbsp light tahini
200g/7oz/scant 1 cup natural live yogurt
5ml/1 tsp cayenne pepper, plus extra for sprinkling
15ml/1 tbsp chopped fresh mint
1 spring onion, finely sliced

Serves 4

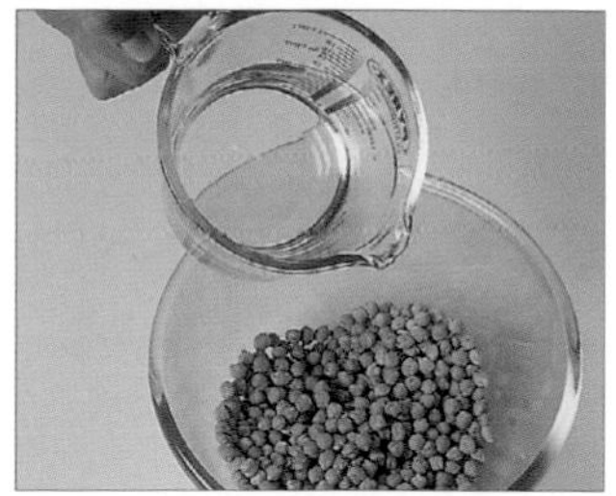

1 Place the chick-peas in a bowl, cover with cold water and leave to soak overnight. Drain and rinse the chick-peas, then place in a saucepan and cover with cold water. Bring to the boil and boil rapidly for 10 minutes, then reduce the heat and simmer for 1 1/2–2 hours until tender.

2 Meanwhile, make the tahini yogurt dip. Mix together the tahini, yogurt, cayenne pepper and mint in a small bowl. Sprinkle the spring onion and extra cayenne pepper and chopped mint on top and chill.

3 Combine the chick-peas with the garlic, chilli, ground spices, herbs, spring onions and seasoning, then mix in the egg. Place in a food processor and blend until the mixture forms a coarse paste. If the paste seems too soft, chill it for 30 minutes.

4 Form the chilled chick-pea paste into 12 patties with your hands, then roll each one in the sesame seeds to coat thoroughly.

5 Heat enough oil to cover the base of a large frying pan Fry the falafel, in batches if necessary, for 6 minutes, turning once.

HEALTH BENEFITS

Chick-peas are a good source of iron, manganese, folate, zinc and vitamin E.

Tortilla Wrap with Tabbouleh and Guacamole

To be successful this classic Middle Eastern salad needs spring onions, lemon juice, plenty of fresh herbs and lots of freshly ground black pepper. It is best served at room temperature and goes surprisingly well with the Mexican-style dip.

INGREDIENTS

175g/6oz/1 cup bulgur wheat
30ml/2 tbsp chopped fresh mint
30ml/2 tbsp chopped fresh flat leaf parsley
1 bunch spring onions (about 6), sliced
1/2 cucumber, diced
50ml/2fl oz/1/4 cup extra virgin olive oil
juice of 1 large lemon
salt and freshly ground black pepper
4 wheat tortillas, to serve
flat leaf parsley, to garnish (optional)

For the guacamole
1 ripe avocado, stoned, peeled and diced
juice of 1/2 lemon
1/2 red chilli, seeded and sliced
1 garlic clove, crushed
1/2 red pepper, seeded and finely diced

Serves 4–6

1 To make the tabbouleh, place the bulgur wheat in a large heatproof bowl and pour over enough boiling water to cover. Leave for 30 minutes until the grains are tender but still retain a little resistance to the bite. Drain thoroughly in a sieve, then tip back into the bowl.

2 Add the mint, parsley, spring onions and cucumber to the bulgur wheat and mix thoroughly. Blend together the olive oil and lemon juice and pour over the tabbouleh, season to taste and toss well to mix. Chill for 30 minutes to allow the flavours to mingle.

COOK'S TIP

The soaking time for bulgur wheat can vary. For the best results, follow the instructions on the packet and taste the grain every now and again to check whether it is tender enough.

3 To make the guacamole, place the avocado in a bowl and add the lemon juice, chilli and garlic. Season to taste and mash with a fork to form a smooth purée. Stir in the red pepper.

4 Warm the tortillas in a dry frying pan and serve either flat, folded or rolled up with the tabbouleh and guacamole. Garnish with parsley, if using.

HEALTH BENEFITS

- *Bulgur wheat is a useful source of dietary fibre and B complex vitamins.*
- *Parsley and mint are good digestives.*

Tomato and Lentil Dhal with Toasted Almonds

RICHLY FLAVOURED WITH spices, coconut milk and tomatoes, this lentil dish makes a filling supper. Warm naan bread and natural yogurt are all that are needed as accompaniments. Split red lentils give the dish a vibrant colour, but you could use larger yellow split peas instead, if you wish.

INGREDIENTS

30ml/2 tbsp vegetable oil
1 large onion, finely chopped
3 garlic cloves, chopped
1 carrot, diced
10ml/2 tsp cumin seeds
10ml/2 tsp yellow mustard seeds
2.5cm/1in piece fresh root ginger, grated
10ml/2 tsp ground turmeric
5ml/1 tsp mild chilli powder
5ml/1 tsp garam masala
225g/8oz/1 cup split red lentils
400ml/14fl oz/1⅔ cups water
400ml/14fl oz/1⅔ cups coconut milk
5 tomatoes, peeled, seeded and chopped
juice of 2 limes
60ml/4 tbsp chopped fresh coriander
salt and freshly ground black pepper
25g/1oz/¼ cup flaked almonds, toasted, to serve

Serves 4

HEALTH BENEFITS

• Spices have long been recognized for their medicinal qualities, from curing flatulence (useful when added to a pulse dish) to warding off colds and flu.

• Lentils are a useful source of low-fat protein. They contain good amounts of B vitamins and provide a rich source of zinc and iron.

• You need to eat foods rich in vitamin C at the same meal to improve absorption of iron. Limes are a good source, but you could also serve a fresh fruit dessert containing apples, kiwi fruit and oranges.

1 Heat the oil in a large heavy-based saucepan. Sauté the onion for 5 minutes until softened, stirring occasionally. Add the garlic, carrot, cumin and mustard seeds, and ginger. Cook for 5 minutes, stirring, until the seeds begin to pop and the carrot softens slightly.

2 Stir in the ground turmeric, chilli powder and garam masala, and cook for 1 minute or until the flavours begin to mingle, stirring to prevent the spices burning.

3 Add the lentils, water, coconut milk and tomatoes, and season well. Bring to the boil, then reduce the heat and simmer, covered for about 45 minutes, stirring occasionally to prevent the lentils sticking.

4 Stir in the lime juice and 45ml/3 tbsp of the fresh coriander, then check the seasoning. Cook for a further 15 minutes until the lentils soften and become tender. To serve, sprinkle with the remaining coriander and the flaked almonds.

MAIN COURSES

This enticing selection of weekday meals means you need never get stuck in a rut about what to serve the family. This year-round selection of substantial and inexpensive meals includes hotpots, casseroles, risottos, curries and many timeless classics, such as lasagne, moussaka and cannelloni.

Vegetable Hot-pot with Cheese Triangles

USE A selection of your favourite vegetables, so long as the overall weight remains the same. Firm vegetables may need a little longer cooking time.

INGREDIENTS

30ml/2 tbsp oil
2 garlic cloves, crushed
1 onion, roughly chopped
5ml/1 tsp mild chilli powder
450g/1lb potatoes, peeled and roughly chopped
450g/1lb celeriac, peeled and roughly chopped
350g/12oz/1¾ cups carrots, roughly chopped
350g/12oz trimmed leeks, roughly chopped
225g/8oz/3 cups brown-cap mushrooms, halved
20ml/4 tsp plain flour
600ml/1 pint/2½ cups vegetable stock
400g/14oz can chopped tomatoes
15ml/1 tbsp tomato purée
30ml/2 tbsp chopped fresh thyme
400g/14oz can kidney beans, drained and rinsed
salt and freshly ground black pepper
sprigs of fresh thyme, to garnish (optional)

For the topping

115g/4oz/8 tbsp butter
225g/8oz/2 cups self-raising flour
115g/4oz/1 cup Cheddar cheese, grated
30ml/2 tbsp snipped fresh chives
about 75ml/5 tbsp milk

Serves 6

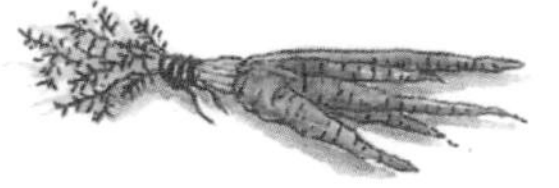

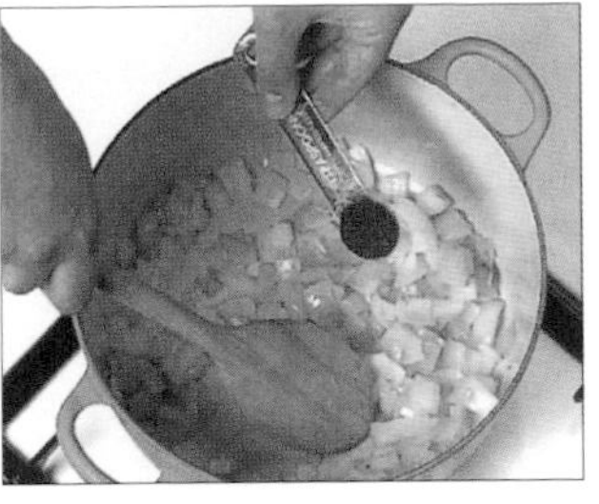

1 Preheat the oven to 180°C/350°F/Gas 4. Heat the oil in a large flameproof casserole and fry the garlic and onion for 5 minutes, or until beginning to brown. Stir in the chilli powder and cook for a further 1 minute.

2 Add the potatoes, celeriac, carrots, leeks and mushrooms. Cook for 3–4 minutes. Stir in the flour and cook for 1 minute.

3 Gradually stir in the stock with the tomatoes, tomato purée, thyme and seasoning. Bring to the boil, stirring. Cover and cook in the oven for 30 minutes.

4 Meanwhile, make the topping. Rub the butter into the flour, then stir in half the cheese with the chives and add plenty of salt and pepper. Add just enough milk to make a smooth dough.

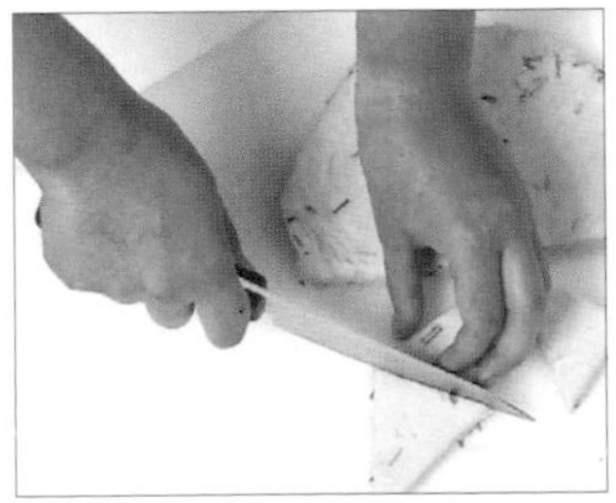

5 Roll out the dough until it is 2.5cm/1 in thick. Cut into 12 triangles and brush with milk.

6 Remove the casserole from the oven, add the beans and stir to combine. Place the triangles on top and sprinkle with the remaining cheese. Return to the oven, uncovered, for 20–25 minutes. Serve garnished with the fresh thyme sprigs, if using.

Baked Squash with Parmesan

SPAGHETTI SQUASH is an unusual vegetable – the flesh separates into long strands when baked. One squash makes an excellent supper dish for two.

INGREDIENTS

1 medium spaghetti squash
115g/4oz/½ cup butter
3 tbsp chopped mixed herbs such as parsley, chives and oregano
1 garlic clove, crushed
1 shallot, chopped
1 tsp lemon juice
40g/1½oz/½ cup freshly grated Parmesan cheese
salt and freshly ground black pepper

Serves 2

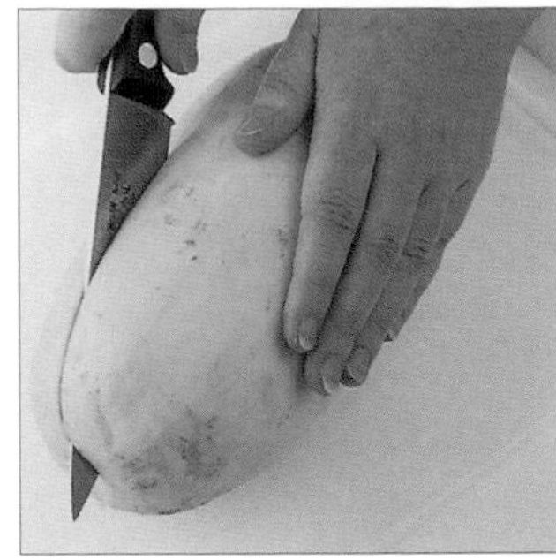

1 Preheat the oven to 180°C/350°F/ Gas 4. Cut the squash in half lengthwise. Place the halves, cut side down, in a roasting pan. Pour a little cold water around them, and then bake for about 40 minutes until just tender.

2 Meanwhile, put the butter, herbs, garlic, shallot and lemon juice in a food processor and process until thoroughly blended and creamy in consistency. Season to taste.

3 When the squash is tender, scrape out any seeds and cut a thin slice from the base of each half, so that they will sit level. Place the squash halves on warmed serving plates.

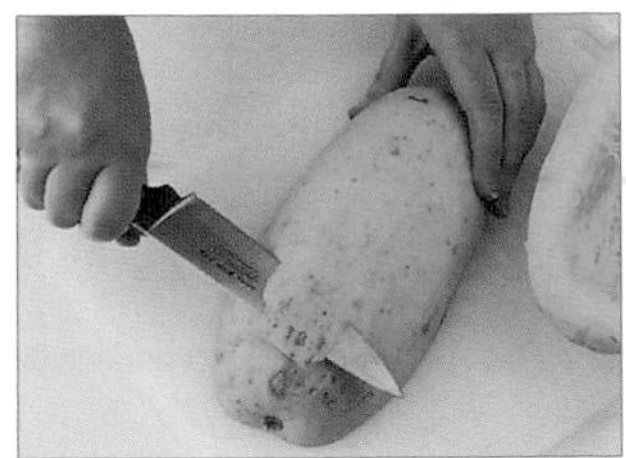

4 Using a fork, pull out a few of the spaghetti-like strands in the centre of each. Add a dollop of herb butter, then sprinkle with a little of the grated Parmesan. Serve the remaining herb butter and Parmesan separately, adding them as you pull out more of the strands.

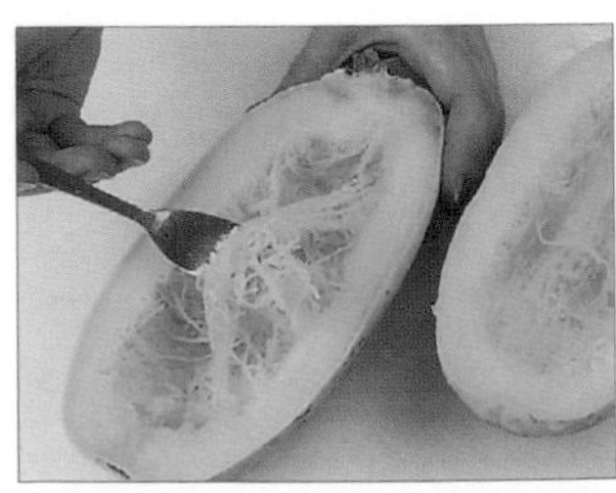

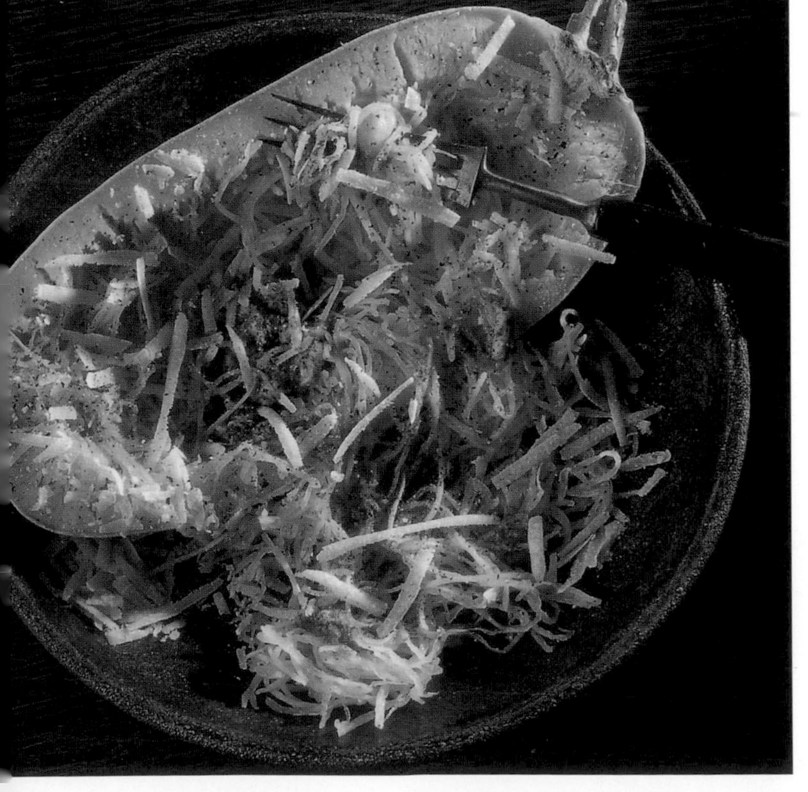

Beans with Mushrooms

WILD AND cultivated mushrooms give this dish a rich, nutty flavour.

INGREDIENTS

30ml/2 tbsp olive oil
50g/2oz/4 tbsp butter
2 shallots, chopped
2–3 garlic cloves, crushed
1 1/2lb/9 cups mixed mushrooms, thickly sliced
4 pieces sun-dried tomatoes in oil, drained and chopped
90ml/6 tbsp dry white wine
400g/14oz can red kidney, pinto or borlotti beans, drained
3 tbsp freshly grated Parmesan cheese
2 tbsp chopped fresh parsley
salt and freshly ground black pepper
freshly cooked pappardelle pasta, to serve

Serves 4

1 Heat the oil and butter in a frying pan and fry the shallots until soft.

2 Add the garlic and mushrooms to the pan and fry for 3–4 minutes. Stir in the sun-dried tomatoes, wine and seasoning to taste.

3 Stir in the beans and cook for about 5–6 minutes, until most of the liquid has evaporated and the beans are warmed through.

4 Stir in the grated Parmesan cheese. Sprinkle with parsley and serve immediately with pappardelle.

Beetroot, Wild Mushroom and Potato Gratin

THIS INEXPENSIVE dish captures the spirit of some of the traditional Polish autumn menus.

INGREDIENTS

30ml/2 tbsp vegetable oil
1 medium onion, chopped
20g/¾oz/3 tbsp plain flour
300ml/½ pint/1¼ cups vegetable stock
675g/1½lb cooked beetroot, peeled and chopped
75ml/5 tbsp single cream
30ml/2 tbsp creamed horseradish
5ml/1 tsp hot mustard
15ml/1 tbsp wine vinegar
5ml/1 tsp caraway seeds
25g/1oz/2 tbsp butter
1 shallot, chopped
225g/8oz/3 cups wild and cultivated mushrooms, trimmed and sliced
45ml/3 tbsp chopped fresh parsley

For the potato border
900g/2lb floury potatoes, peeled
150ml/¼ pint/⅔ cup milk
15ml/1 tbsp chopped fresh dill (optional)
salt and freshly ground black pepper

Serves 4

1 Preheat the oven to 190°C/375°F/Gas 5. Lightly oil a 23cm/9in round baking dish. Heat the oil in a large saucepan, add the onion and fry until soft, without colouring. Stir in the flour, remove from the heat and gradually add the stock, stirring until well blended.

2 Return to the heat, stir and simmer to thicken the stock, then add the beetroot, cream, creamed horseradish, mustard, vinegar and caraway seeds.

3 To make the potato border, bring the potatoes to the boil in salted water and cook for 20 minutes. Drain well and mash with the milk. Add the dill if using and season with salt and pepper.

4 Spoon the potatoes into the prepared dish and make a well in the centre. Spoon the beetroot mixture into the well and set aside.

5 Melt the butter in a large non-stick frying pan and fry the shallot until soft, without browning. Add the mushrooms and cook over a moderate heat until their juices begin to run. Increase the heat and boil off the moisture. When quite dry, season with salt and pepper and stir in most of the chopped parsley.

6 Spread the mushrooms over the beetroot mixture, cover and bake for about 30 minutes. Serve at once, garnished with the reserved parsley.

COOK'S TIP

If planning ahead, this entire dish can be made in advance and heated through when needed. Allow 50 minutes baking time from room temperature.

Potato Gnocchi

GNOCCHI ARE delicious little dumplings made either with mashed potato and flour, as here, or with semolina. They should be light in texture, and must not be overworked while being made.

INGREDIENTS

1 kg/2¼lb waxy potatoes, scrubbed
15ml/1 tbsp salt
250–300g/9–11oz/2–2½ cups flour
1 egg
pinch of grated nutmeg
25g/1oz/2 tbsp butter
freshly grated Parmesan cheese, to serve
Serves 4–6

1 Place the unpeeled potatoes in a large pan of salted water. Bring to the boil and cook until the potatoes are tender but not falling apart. Drain. Peel as soon as possible, while the potatoes are still hot but cool enough to handle.

VARIATION

Green gnocchi are made in exactly the same way as potato gnocchi, with the addition of fresh or frozen spinach. Use 675g/1½lb fresh spinach, or 400g/14oz frozen leaf spinach. Mix with the potato and the flour in Step 2. Almost any pasta sauce is suitable for serving with gnocchi; they are particularly good with a creamy Gorgonzola sauce, or simply drizzled with olive oil. Gnocchi can also be served in clear soup.

2 On a work surface, spread out a layer of flour. Mash the hot potatoes with a food mill, dropping them directly on to the flour. Sprinkle with about half of the remaining flour and mix very lightly into the potatoes.

3 Break the egg into the mixture, add the nutmeg and knead lightly, drawing in more flour as necessary. When the dough is light to the touch and no longer moist or sticky it is ready to be rolled. Do not overwork or the gnocchi will be heavy. At this point you can leave the dough to rest for about 20 minutes.

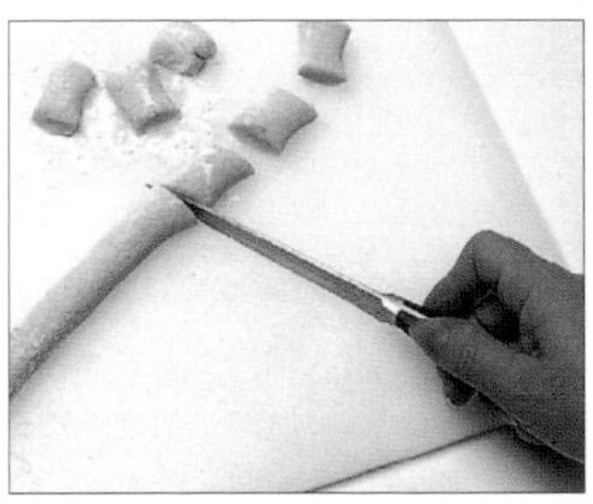

4 Divide the dough into 4 parts. On a lightly floured board form each part into a roll about 2cm/¾in in diameter, taking care not to overhandle the dough. Cut the rolls crosswise into pieces about 2cm/¾in long.

5 Hold an ordinary table fork with long tines sideways, leaning on the board. One by one, press and roll the gnocchi lightly along the tines of the fork towards the points, making ridges on one side and a depression from your thumb on the other.

6 Bring a large pan of water to a fast boil. Add salt and drop in the gnocchi in small batches so that they cook quickly.

7 When the gnocchi rise to the surface, after 3–4 minutes, the gnocchi are done. Scoop them out, allow to drain and place in a warmed serving bowl. Dot with butter. Keep warm while the remaining gnocchi are boiling. As soon as they are cooked, toss the gnocchi with the butter or a heated sauce, sprinkle with grated Parmesan and serve.

Red Cabbage and Apple Casserole

THE BRILLIANT colour and pungent flavour make this an excellent winter dish. Serve it with plenty of rye bread.

INGREDIENTS

675g/1½lb red cabbage
3 onions, chopped
2 fennel bulbs, roughly chopped
30ml/2 tbsp caraway seeds
3 large, tart eating apples or 1 large cooking apple
300ml/½ pint/1¼ cups natural yogurt
15ml/1 tbsp creamed horseradish sauce
salt and freshly ground black pepper
crusty rye bread, to serve
Serves 6

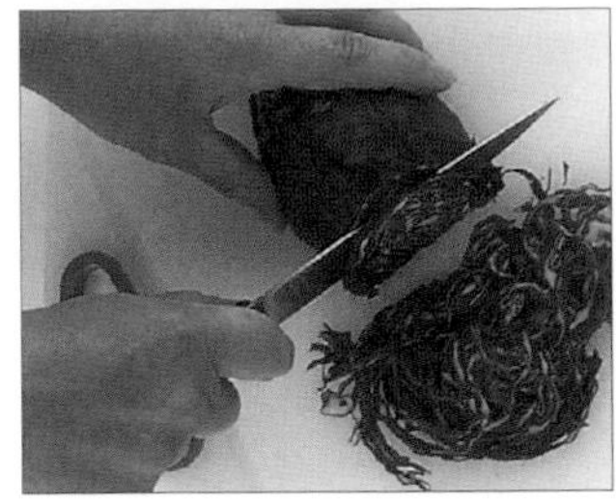

1 Preheat the oven to 150°C/300°F/ Gas 2. Cut the cabbage into quarters and shred finely, discarding any tough stalks. Mix with the onions, fennel and caraway seeds in a large bowl. Peel, core and chop the apples then stir them into the cabbage mixture. Transfer the ingredients to a casserole dish with a close fitting lid.

2 Mix the yogurt with the creamed horseradish sauce. Stir the yogurt and horseradish mixture into the casserole, season with salt and pepper and cover tightly.

3 Bake for 1½ hours, stirring once or twice during cooking. Serve hot, with crusty bread.

Mixed Vegetables with Artichokes

BAKING A vegetable medley in the oven is a wonderfully easy way of producing a quick and simple, wholesome mid-week meal.

INGREDIENTS

30ml/2 tbsp olive oil
675g/1½lb frozen broad beans
4 turnips, peeled and sliced
4 leeks, sliced
1 red pepper, seeded and sliced
200g/7oz fresh spinach leaves or 115g/4oz frozen spinach
2 x 400g/14oz cans artichoke hearts, drained
60ml/4 tbsp pumpkin seeds
soy sauce
salt and freshly ground black pepper
Serves 4

1 Preheat the oven to 180°C/350°F/ Gas 4. Pour the olive oil into a casserole. Cook the broad beans in a saucepan of boiling lightly salted water for about 10 minutes. Drain the broad beans and place them in the casserole with the turnips, leeks, red pepper, spinach and canned artichoke hearts. Stir the vegetables until they are well mixed.

2 Cover the casserole and bake the vegetables for 30–40 minutes, or until the turnips are slightly soft when you test them with a fork.

3 Stir in the pumpkin seeds and soy sauce to taste. Season with salt and pepper (you may not need very much) and serve immediately.

Sweet and Sour Mixed Bean Hot-pot

AN APPETIZING mixture of beans and vegetables topped with potato.

INGREDIENTS

450g/1lb unpeeled potatoes
15ml/1 tbsp olive oil
40g/1½oz/3 tbsp butter
40g/1½oz/⅓ cup plain wholemeal flour
300ml/½ pint/1¼ cups passata
150ml/¼ pint/⅔ cup unsweetened apple juice
60ml/4 tbsp each light soft brown sugar, tomato ketchup, dry sherry, cider vinegar and light soy sauce
400g/14oz can butter beans
400g/14oz can flageolet beans
400g/14oz can chick-peas
175g/6oz/1 cup green beans, chopped and blanched
225g/8oz/1 cup shallots, sliced and blanched
225g/8oz/3 cups mushrooms, sliced
15ml/1 tbsp each chopped fresh thyme and marjoram
salt and freshly ground black pepper
sprigs of fresh herbs, to garnish

Serves 6

1 Preheat the oven to 200°C/400°F/Gas 6. Thinly slice the potatoes and par-boil them for 4 minutes. Drain the potatoes thoroughly, toss them in the oil so they are lightly coated all over and set aside.

2 Place the butter, flour, passata, apple juice, sugar, tomato ketchup, sherry, vinegar and soy sauce in a saucepan. Heat gently, whisking continuously, until the sauce comes to the boil and thickens. Continue to simmer gently for 3 minutes, stirring all the time.

3 Rinse and drain the beans and chick-peas and add to the sauce with all the remaining ingredients, except the herb garnish. Stir well to mix them thoroughly.

4 Spoon the bean mixture into a casserole.

5 Arrange the potato slices over the top, overlapping them slightly so that they completely cover the bean mixture.

6 Cover the casserole with foil and bake for about 1 hour, until the potatoes are cooked and tender. Remove the foil for the last 20 minutes of the cooking time, to lightly brown the potatoes. Serve garnished with fresh herb sprigs.

COOK'S TIP

You can vary the proportions of beans used in this recipe, depending on what ingredients you have in your store cupboard.

Jamaican Black Bean Pot

MOLASSES IMPARTS A RICH treacly flavour to the spicy sauce, which incorporates a stunning mix of black beans, vibrant red and yellow peppers and orange butternut squash. This dish is delicious served with cornbread or plain rice.

INGREDIENTS

225g/8oz/1 1/4 cups dried black beans
1 bay leaf
30ml/2 tbsp vegetable oil
1 large onion, chopped
1 garlic clove, chopped
5ml/1 tsp English mustard powder
15ml/1 tbsp blackstrap molasses
30ml/2 tbsp soft dark brown sugar
5ml/1 tsp dried thyme
2.5ml/1/2 tsp dried chilli flakes
5ml/1 tsp vegetable bouillon powder
1 red pepper, seeded and diced
1 yellow pepper, seeded and diced
675g/1 1/2lb/5 1/4 cups butternut squash or pumpkin, seeded and cut into 1cm/1/2in dice
salt and freshly ground black pepper
sprigs of thyme, to garnish
Serves 4

1 Soak the beans overnight in plenty of water, then drain and rinse well. Place in a large saucepan, cover with fresh water and add the bay leaf. Bring to the boil, then boil rapidly for 10 minutes. Reduce the heat, cover, and simmer for 30 minutes until tender. Drain, reserving the cooking water. Preheat the oven to 180°C/350°F/Gas 4.

2 Heat the oil in the saucepan and sauté the onion and garlic for about 5 minutes until softened, stirring occasionally. Add the mustard powder, molasses, sugar, thyme and chilli and cook for 1 minute, stirring. Stir in the black beans and spoon the mixture into a flameproof casserole.

3 Add enough water to the reserved cooking liquid to make 400ml/14fl oz/1 2/3 cups, then mix in the bouillon powder and pour into the casserole. Bake for 25 minutes.

4 Add the peppers and squash or pumpkin and mix well. Cover, then bake for 45 minutes until the vegetables are tender. Serve garnished with thyme.

HEALTH BENEFITS

Blackstrap molasses is a by-product of sugar processing and contains less sugar than treacle. It is a good source of iron, calcium, zinc, copper and chromium. Eating molasses regularly is said to help acne, arthritis, angina, constipation and anaemia.

Aubergine and Chick-pea Tagine

Spiced with coriander, cumin, cinnamon, turmeric and a dash of chilli sauce, this Moroccan-style stew makes a filling supper dish.

INGREDIENTS

1 small aubergine, cut into 1cm/½in dice
2 courgettes, thickly sliced
60ml/4 tbsp olive oil
1 large onion, sliced
2 garlic cloves, chopped
150g/5oz/2 cups brown cap mushrooms, halved
15ml/1 tbsp ground coriander
10ml/2 tsp cumin seeds
15ml/1 tbsp ground cinnamon
10ml/2 tsp ground turmeric
225g/8oz new potatoes, quartered
600ml/1 pint/2½ cups passata
15ml/1 tbsp tomato purée
15ml/1 tbsp chilli sauce
75g/3oz/⅓ cup ready-to-eat unsulphured dried apricots
400g/14oz/3 cups canned chick-peas, drained and rinsed
salt and freshly ground black pepper
15ml/1 tbsp chopped fresh coriander, to garnish

Serves 4

1 Sprinkle salt over the aubergine and courgettes and leave for 30 minutes. Rinse and pat dry with a dish towel. Heat the grill to high. Arrange the courgettes and aubergine on a baking sheet and toss in 30ml/2 tbsp of the olive oil. Grill for 20 minutes, turning occasionally, until tender and golden.

2 Meanwhile, heat the remaining oil in a large heavy-based saucepan and cook the onion and garlic for 5 minutes until softened, stirring occasionally. Add the mushrooms and sauté for 3 minutes until tender. Add the spices and cook for 1 minute more, stirring, to allow the flavours to mingle.

3 Add the potatoes and cook for 3 minutes, stirring. Pour in the passata, tomato purée and 150ml/¼ pint/⅔ cup water, cover, and cook for 10 minutes or until the sauce begins to thicken.

4 Add the aubergine, courgettes, chilli sauce, apricots and chick-peas. Season and cook, partially covered, for 10–15 minutes until the potatoes are tender. Add a little extra water if the tagine becomes too dry. Sprinkle with chopped fresh coriander to serve.

HEALTH BENEFITS

High in fibre and low in fat, chick-peas, like other pulses, have the ability to reduce blood cholesterol, regulate blood sugar and prevent constipation.

Vegetable Kashmiri

THIS IS a delicious vegetable curry, in which a variety of fresh mixed vegetables are cooked in a spicy, aromatic yogurt sauce.

INGREDIENTS

10ml/2 tsp cumin seeds
8 black peppercorns
2 green cardamom pods, seeds only
5cm/2in cinnamon stick
2.5ml/½ tsp grated nutmeg
45ml/3 tbsp oil
1 fresh green chilli, chopped
2.5cm/1in piece of fresh root ginger, grated
5ml/1 tsp chilli powder
2.5ml/½ tsp salt
2 large potatoes, cut into 2.5cm/1in chunks
225g/8oz/2 cups cauliflower florets
225g/8oz okra, thickly sliced
150ml/¼ pint/⅔ cup natural yogurt
150ml/¼ pint/⅔ cup vegetable stock
toasted flaked almonds and sprigs of fresh coriander, to garnish

Serves 4

1 Grind the cumin seeds, peppercorns, cardamom seeds, cinnamon stick and nutmeg to a fine powder using a blender or a pestle and mortar.

2 Heat the oil in a large saucepan and fry the chilli and ginger for 2 minutes, stirring all the time.

3 Add the chilli powder, salt and ground spice mixture and fry for about 2–3 minutes, over a gentle heat, stirring all the time to prevent the spices from sticking.

4 Stir in the potatoes, cover and cook for 10 minutes over low heat, stirring occasionally.

5 Add the cauliflower and okra and cook for 5 minutes.

6 Add the yogurt and stock. Bring to the boil then reduce the heat. Cover and simmer for 20 minutes, or until all the vegetables are tender. Garnish with toasted almonds and coriander sprigs.

COOK'S TIP

This curry tastes good using most vegetables. Try to choose vegetables that have contrasting colours and textures.

Parsnip, Aubergine and Cashew Biryani

FULL OF the flavours of India, this hearty supper dish is great for chilly winter evenings.

INGREDIENTS

1 small aubergine, sliced
275g/10oz/1 1/2 cups basmati rice
3 parsnips
3 onions
2 garlic cloves
2.5cm/1in piece of fresh root ginger, peeled
about 60ml/4 tbsp vegetable oil
175g/6oz/1 cup unsalted cashew nuts
40g/1 1/2oz/1/4 cup sultanas
1 red pepper, seeded and sliced
5ml/1 tsp ground cumin
5ml/1 tsp ground coriander
2.5ml/1/2 tsp chilli powder
120ml/4fl oz/1/2 cup natural yogurt
300ml/1/2 pint/1 1/4 cups vegetable stock
25g/1oz/2 tbsp butter
salt and freshly ground black pepper
2 hard-boiled eggs, quartered, and sprigs of fresh coriander, to garnish

Serves 4–6

1 Sprinkle the aubergine with salt and leave for 30 minutes. Rinse, pat dry and cut into bite-size pieces.

2 Soak the rice in a bowl of cold water for 40 minutes. Peel and core the parsnips. Cut into 1cm/1/2in pieces. Process 1 onion, the garlic and ginger in a food processor. Add 30–45ml/2–3 tbsp water and process to a paste.

3 Finely slice the remaining onions. Heat 45ml/3 tbsp of the oil in a large flameproof casserole and fry the onions gently for 10–15 minutes until they are soft and deep golden brown. Remove and drain.

4 Add 40g/1 1/2oz/1/4 cup of the cashew nuts and stir-fry for 2 minutes, but do not burn them.

5 Add the sultanas and fry until they swell. Remove and drain on kitchen paper.

6 Add the aubergine and pepper to the pan and stir-fry for 4–5 minutes. Drain on kitchen paper. Fry the parsnips for 4–5 minutes. Stir in the remaining cashew nuts and fry for 1 minute. Transfer to the plate with the aubergine and set aside.

7 Add the remaining 15ml/1 tbsp of oil to the pan. Add the onion paste. Cook, stirring, over a moderate heat for 4–5 minutes, until the mixture turns golden. Stir in the cumin, coriander and chilli powder. Cook, stirring, for 1 minute, then reduce the heat and add the yogurt.

8 Bring the mixture slowly to the boil and stir in the stock, parsnips, aubergine and peppers. Season with salt and pepper, cover and simmer for 30–40 minutes, until the parsnips are tender and then transfer to an ovenproof casserole.

9 Preheat the oven to 150°C/300°F/Gas 2. Drain the rice and add to 300ml/1/2 pint/1 1/4 cups salted boiling water. Cook gently for 5–6 minutes, until the rice is tender but slightly undercooked.

10 Drain the rice and pile it in a mound on top of the vegetables. Make a hole from the top to the base using the handle of a wooden spoon. Scatter the reserved fried onions, cashew nuts and sultanas over the rice and dot with butter. Cover with a double layer of foil and then secure in place with a lid.

11 Cook in the oven for 35–40 minutes. To serve, spoon the mixture on to a warmed serving dish and garnish with quartered eggs and sprigs of fresh coriander.

Cheat's Lasagne with Mixed Mushrooms

THIS SIMPLE-TO-ASSEMBLE vegetarian version of lasagne requires neither baking nor the lengthy preparation of various sauces and fillings, but is no less delicious.

INGREDIENTS

40g/1½oz/⅔ cup dried porcini mushrooms
50ml/2fl oz/¼ cup olive oil
1 large garlic clove, chopped
375g/13oz/5 cups mixed mushrooms, including brown cap, field, shiitake and wild varieties, roughly sliced
175ml/6fl oz/¾ cup dry white wine
90ml/6 tbsp canned chopped tomatoes
2.5ml/½ tsp sugar
8 fresh lasagne sheets
40g/1½oz/½ cup freshly grated Parmesan cheese
salt and freshly ground black pepper
fresh basil leaves, to garnish

Serves 4

1 Place the porcini mushrooms in a bowl and cover with boiling water. Leave to soak for 15 minutes, then drain and rinse.

2 Heat the olive oil in a large heavy-based frying pan and sauté the soaked mushrooms over a high heat for 5 minutes until the edges are slightly crisp. Reduce the heat, then add the garlic and fresh mushrooms, and sauté for a further 5 minutes until tender, stirring occasionally.

3 Add the wine and cook for 5–7 minutes until reduced. Stir in the tomatoes, sugar and seasoning and cook over a medium heat for about 5 minutes until thickened.

4 Meanwhile, cook the lasagne according to the instructions on the packet until it is *al dente*. Drain lightly – the pasta should still be moist.

5 To serve, spoon a little of the sauce on to each of four warm serving plates. Place a sheet of lasagne on top and spoon a quarter of the remaining mushroom sauce over each serving. Sprinkle with some Parmesan and top with another pasta sheet. Sprinkle with black pepper and more Parmesan and garnish with basil leaves.

HEALTH BENEFITS

Shiitake mushrooms, a valuable source of zinc, iron and potassium, are reputed to help thin the blood and consequently reduce the risk of heart disease.

Courgette Fritters with Chilli Jam

CHILLI JAM IS HOT, sweet and sticky – rather like a thick chutney. It adds a piquancy to these light courgette fritters but is also delicious with pies or a chunk of cheese.

INGREDIENTS

450g/1lb/3½ cups coarsely grated courgettes
50g/2oz/⅔ cup freshly grated Parmesan cheese
2 eggs, beaten
60ml/4 tbsp unbleached plain flour
vegetable oil, for frying
salt and freshly ground black pepper

For the chilli jam
75ml/3fl oz/5 tbsp olive oil
4 large onions, diced
4 garlic cloves, chopped
1–2 Thai chillies, seeded and sliced
25g/1oz/2 tbsp dark brown soft sugar

Makes 12 Fritters

1 First make the chilli jam. Heat the oil in a frying pan until hot, then add the onions and garlic. Reduce the heat to low, then cook for 20 minutes, stirring frequently, until the onions are very soft.

HEALTH BENEFITS

• *Parmesan provides valuable amounts of vitamin B_{12}, protein and calcium but its high saturated fat content means it should be eaten in moderation.*

• *Vitamin C and beta carotene are both found in courgettes.*

2 Leave the onion mixture to cool, then transfer to a food processor or blender. Add the chillies and sugar and blend until smooth, then return the mixture to the saucepan. Cook for 10 minutes, stirring frequently, until the liquid evaporates and the mixture has the consistency of jam. Cool slightly.

3 To make the fritters, squeeze the courgettes in a dish towel to remove any excess water, then combine with the Parmesan, eggs, flour and salt and pepper.

4 Heat enough oil to cover the base of a large frying pan. Add 30ml/2 tbsp of the mixture for each fritter and cook three fritters at a time. Cook for 2–3 minutes on each side until golden, then keep warm while you cook the remaining fritters. Drain on kitchen paper and serve warm with a spoonful of the chilli jam.

COOK'S TIP

Stored in an airtight jar in the fridge, the chilli jam will keep for up to 1 week.

Vegetable Moussaka

THIS IS a really flavoursome main course dish. It can be served with warm fresh bread for a hearty, satisfying meal.

INGREDIENTS

450g/1lb aubergines, sliced
115g/4oz/½ cup whole green lentils
600ml/1 pint/2½ cups vegetable stock
1 bay leaf
45ml/3 tbsp olive oil
1 onion, sliced
1 garlic clove, crushed
225g/8oz/3 cups mushrooms, sliced
400g/14oz can chick-peas, rinsed and drained
400g/14oz can chopped tomatoes
30ml/2 tbsp tomato purée
10ml/2 tsp dried herbes de Provence
300ml/½ pint/1¼ cups natural yogurt
3 eggs
50g/2oz mature Cheddar cheese, grated
salt and freshly ground black pepper
sprigs of fresh flat leaf parsley, to garnish

Serves 6

1 Sprinkle the aubergine slices with salt and place in a colander. Cover and place a weight on top. Leave for at least 30 minutes, to allow the bitter juices to be extracted.

2 Meanwhile, place the lentils, stock and bay leaf in a saucepan, cover, bring to the boil and simmer for about 20 minutes, until the lentils are just tender but not mushy. Add a little extra water if necessary. Drain thoroughly and keep warm.

3 Heat 15ml/1 tbsp of the oil in a large saucepan, add the onion and garlic and cook for 5 minutes, stirring. Stir in the lentils, mushrooms, chick-peas, tomatoes, tomato purée, herbs and 45ml/3 tbsp water. Bring to the boil, cover and simmer gently for 10–15 minutes, stirring from time to time.

4 Preheat the oven to 180°C/350°F/Gas 4. Rinse the aubergine slices, drain and pat dry. Heat the remaining oil in a frying pan and fry the slices in batches for 3–4 minutes, turning once to brown both sides.

5 Season the lentil mixture with salt and pepper. Arrange a layer of aubergine slices in the bottom of a large, shallow, ovenproof dish or roasting tin, then spoon over a layer of the lentil mixture. Continue to build up the layers in this way until all the aubergine slices and lentil mixture are used up.

6 Beat the yogurt, eggs, salt and pepper together and pour the mixture over the dish. Sprinkle generously with the grated Cheddar cheese and bake for about 45 minutes, until the topping is golden brown and bubbling. Serve immediately, garnished with the flat leaf parsley.

VARIATION

Sliced and sautéed courgettes or potatoes can be used instead of the aubergines in this dish.

Broccoli and Ricotta Cannelloni

A FABULOUS pasta dish that looks very impressive but is actually quite quick and simple to prepare, and tastes wonderful.

INGREDIENTS

10ml/2 tsp olive oil
12 dried cannelloni tubes, 7.5cm/3in long
450g/1lb/4 cups broccoli florets
75g/3oz/1 1/2 cups fresh breadcrumbs
150ml/1/4 pint/2/3 cup milk
60ml/4 tbsp olive oil, plus extra for brushing
225g/8oz/1 cup ricotta cheese
pinch of grated nutmeg
90ml/6 tbsp freshly grated Parmesan or Pecorino cheese
30ml/2 tbsp pine nuts
salt and freshly ground black pepper

For the tomato sauce

30ml/2 tbsp olive oil
1 onion, finely chopped
1 garlic clove, crushed
2 x 400g/14oz cans chopped tomatoes
15ml/1 tbsp tomato purée
4 black olives, stoned and chopped
5ml/1 tsp dried thyme

Serves 4

1 Preheat the oven to 190°C/375°F/Gas 5. Lightly grease four small ovenproof dishes, or one large one, with olive oil.

2 Bring a large saucepan of water to the boil, add the olive oil to the water to prevent the pasta from sticking together and simmer the cannelloni, uncovered, for 6–7 minutes, or until it is nearly cooked.

3 Meanwhile, steam or boil the broccoli for 10 minutes, until tender. Drain the pasta, rinse under cold water, drain again and reserve. Drain the broccoli and leave to cool, then place in a food processor or blender and process until smooth. Set aside.

4 Place the breadcrumbs in a bowl, add the milk and oil and stir until softened. Add the ricotta, broccoli purée, nutmeg and 60ml/4 tbsp of the Parmesan or Pecorino cheese. Season with salt and pepper then set aside.

5 To make the sauce, heat the oil in a frying pan and add the onions and garlic. Fry for 5–6 minutes, until softened, then stir in the tomatoes, tomato purée, black olives and thyme. Season with salt and pepper. Boil rapidly for 2–3 minutes then pour into the four ovenproof dishes.

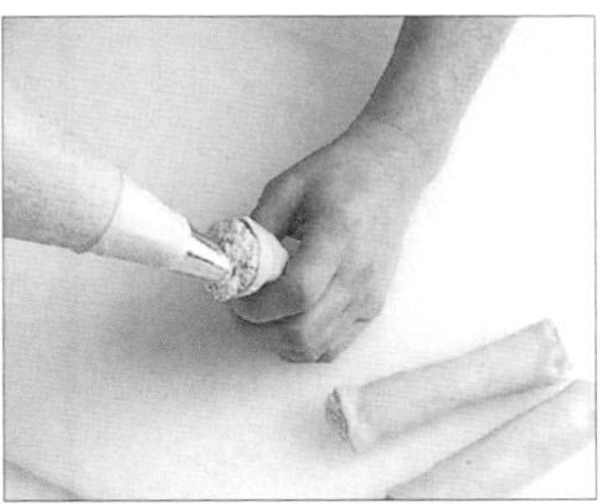

6 Spoon the cheese mixture into a piping bag fitted with a 1cm/1/2in nozzle. Carefully open the cannelloni tubes. Standing each one upright on a board, pipe the filling into each tube. If you do not have a piping bag, use a teaspoon for this. Divide the tubes equally between the four dishes and lay them in rows in the tomato sauce.

7 Brush the tops of the cannelloni with a little olive oil and sprinkle over the remaining Parmesan or Pecorino cheese and pine nuts. Bake in the oven for about 25–30 minutes, until golden.

COOK'S TIP

If you don't have cannelloni tubes, you can cook lasagne sheets until al dente, spoon the mixture along one short edge of the sheet and roll it up to completely enclose the filling.

Wholemeal Pasta with Caraway Cabbage

CRUNCHY CABBAGE and Brussels sprouts are the perfect partners for pasta in this healthy dish.

INGREDIENTS

90ml/6 tbsp olive oil or sunflower oil
3 onions, roughly chopped
350g/12oz round white cabbage, roughly chopped
350g/12oz Brussels sprouts, trimmed and halved
10ml/2 tsp caraway seeds
15ml/1 tbsp chopped fresh dill
400ml/14fl oz/1⅔ cups vegetable stock
200g/7oz/1¾ cups fresh or dried wholewheat pasta spirals
salt and freshly ground black pepper
fresh dill sprigs, to garnish

Serves 6

1 Heat the oil in a large saucepan and fry the onions over a low heat for 10 minutes, until softened.

2 Add the cabbage and Brussels sprouts and cook for 2–3 minutes, then stir in the caraway seeds and dill. Pour in the stock and season with salt and pepper. Cover and simmer for 5–10 minutes, until the cabbage and sprouts are crisp but tender.

3 Meanwhile, cook the pasta in a pan of lightly salted boiling water, following the package instructions, until just tender.

4 Drain the pasta, tip it into a warmed serving bowl and add the cabbage mixture. Toss lightly, adjust the seasoning to taste, garnish with dill and serve immediately.

Cauliflower and Broccoli with Tomato Sauce

A TASTY alternative to that old favourite, cauliflower cheese. The addition of broccoli to the cauliflower gives extra colour and texture to this recipe.

INGREDIENTS

1 onion, finely chopped
400g/14oz can chopped tomatoes
45ml/3 tbsp tomato purée
20g/¾oz/3 tbsp wholemeal flour
300ml/½ pint/1¼ cups skimmed milk
300ml/½ pint/1¼ cups water
1 kg/2¼lb/8 cups mixed cauliflower and broccoli florets
salt and freshly ground black pepper

Serves 6

1 Mix the onion, tomatoes and tomato purée in a small saucepan. Bring to the boil, lower the heat and simmer gently for 15–20 minutes until the sauce has reduced in quantity.

2 Mix the flour to a paste with a little of the milk. Stir the paste into the tomato mixture, then gradually add the remaining milk and water.

3 Stir the mixture constantly, until it boils and thickens. Season with salt and pepper. Cover with a lid to keep the sauce hot but do not let it continue to cook.

4 Steam the cauliflower and broccoli florets over boiling water for 5–7 minutes or until the florets are tender but still slightly crunchy. Tip into a dish, pour over the tomato sauce and serve with extra pepper sprinkled over the top, if liked.

Ravioli with Ricotta and Spinach

HOME-MADE RAVIOLI are fun to make, and can be stuffed with different delicious cheese or vegetable fillings. This filling is particularly quick and easy to make.

INGREDIENTS

400g/14oz fresh spinach or 175g/6oz frozen spinach
175g/6oz/¾ cup ricotta cheese
1 egg
50g/2oz/⅔ cup grated Parmesan cheese
pinch of grated nutmeg
salt and freshly ground black pepper

For the pasta
210g/7½oz/scant 2 cups flour
3 eggs

For the sauce
75g/3oz/6 tbsp butter
5–6 sprigs of fresh sage
Serves 4

1 Wash the fresh spinach well in several changes of water. Place in a saucepan, do not add any water, cover and cook until tender, about 5 minutes. The quantity of spinach will have reduced considerably. Drain. Cook frozen spinach according to the package instructions. When cool, squeeze out as much moisture as possible. Chop finely.

2 Combine the chopped spinach with the ricotta, egg, Parmesan and nutmeg. Season with salt and pepper. Cover and set aside.

3 To make the pasta, place the flour in the centre of a clean smooth work surface. Make a well in the middle. Break the eggs into the well. Add a pinch of salt.

4 Start beating the eggs with a fork, gradually drawing the flour from the inside walls of the well. As the paste thickens, continue mixing with your hands.

5 Incorporate as much flour as possible until the mixture forms a mass. It will still be lumpy. If it still sticks to your hands, add a little more flour. Set the dough aside. Scrape off the dough from the work surface until it is smooth.

6 Lightly flour the work surface. Knead the dough. Work for about 10 minutes, or until the dough is smooth and elastic.

7 Divide the dough in half. Flour the rolling pin and the work surface. Pat the dough into a disc and begin rolling out into a flat circle. Roll until it is about 3mm/⅛in thick. Cover with a clean cloth to prevent it drying out. Do the same for the second half of the dough.

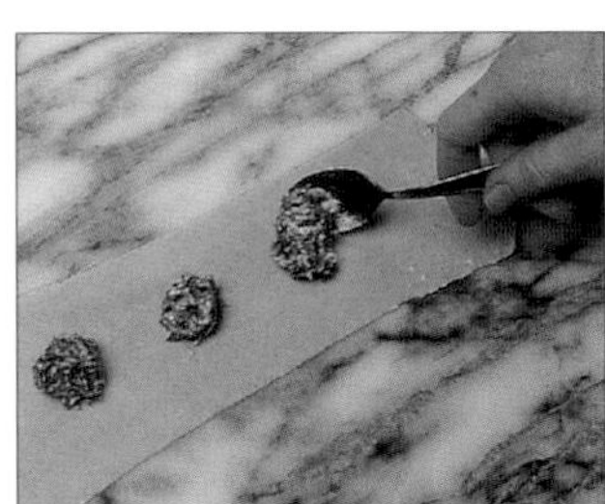

8 Cut the dough into sheets. Place small teaspoons of filling along the pasta in rows 5cm/2in apart. Cover with another sheet of pasta, pressing down gently to expel any air pockets.

9 Use a fluted pastry wheel to cut between the rows to form small squares with filling in the centre of each. If the edges do not stick well, moisten with milk or water and press together.

10 Place the ravioli on a lightly floured surface and allow to dry for at least 30 minutes. Turn occasionally so they are completely dry on both sides. Bring a large pan of salted water to the boil.

11 Heat the butter and sage together over very low heat, taking care that the butter melts but does not darken.

12 Drop the ravioli into the boiling water. Stir gently to prevent them from sticking together. They will be cooked as soon as they rise to the top. This will take very little time, about 4–5 minutes. Drain carefully and arrange in warmed individual serving dishes. Spoon on the sauce and serve at once.

Mushroom Bolognese

A QUICK – and exceedingly tasty – vegetarian version of the classic Italian dish. This dish is easy to prepare and makes a very satisfying meal.

INGREDIENTS

450g/1lb mushrooms
15ml/1 tbsp olive oil
1 onion, chopped
1 garlic clove, crushed
15ml/1 tbsp tomato purée
400g/14oz can chopped tomatoes
45ml/3 tbsp chopped fresh oregano
450g/1lb fresh pasta
salt and freshly ground black pepper
Parmesan cheese shavings, to serve

Serves 4

1 Trim the mushroom stems neatly. Then cut each mushroom into quarters.

COOK'S TIP

If you prefer to use dried pasta, make this the first thing that you cook. It will take 10–12 minutes, during which time you can make the mushroom mixture. Use 350g/12oz dried pasta.

2 Heat the oil in a large pan. Add the chopped onion and garlic and cook for 2–3 minutes.

3 Add the mushrooms to the pan and cook over a high heat for about 3–4 minutes, stirring occasionally to stop the ingredients sticking.

4 Stir in the tomato purée, chopped tomatoes and 15ml/1 tbsp of the oregano. Lower the heat, cover and then cook for about 5 minutes.

5 Meanwhile, bring a large pan of salted water to the boil. Cook the pasta until just tender, following the instructions on the package.

6 Season the Bolognese sauce with salt and pepper. Drain the pasta, turn it into a warmed bowl and add the mushroom mixture. Toss to mix well. Serve in individual bowls, topped with shavings of fresh Parmesan and the remaining chopped fresh oregano.

Spinach and Ricotta Conchiglie

LARGE PASTA shells are designed to hold a variety of delicious stuffings. Few are more pleasing than this mixture of chopped spinach and ricotta cheese.

INGREDIENTS

350g/12oz large conchiglie
450ml/¾ pint/scant 2 cups passata or tomato pulp
275g/10oz frozen chopped spinach, defrosted
50g/2oz crustless white bread, crumbled
120ml/4fl oz/½ cup milk
60ml/4 tbsp olive oil
250g/9oz/generous 1 cup ricotta cheese
pinch of grated nutmeg
1 garlic clove, crushed
2.5ml/½ tsp black olive paste (optional)
25g/1oz/⅓ cup freshly grated Parmesan cheese
25g/1oz/2 tbsp pine nuts
salt and freshly ground black pepper

Serves 4

1 Preheat the oven to 180°C/350°F/Gas 4. Bring a large saucepan of salted water to the boil. Toss in the pasta and cook according to the package instructions. Refresh under cold water, drain and reserve until needed.

2 Pour the passata or tomato pulp into a nylon sieve over a bowl and strain to thicken. (Keep the juice to add to a soup.) Place the spinach in another sieve and press out any excess liquid with the back of a spoon.

3 Place the bread, milk and 45ml/3 tbsp of the oil in a food processor and process. Add the spinach and ricotta and season with salt, pepper and nutmeg. Process briefly to combine.

4 Mix together the passata or tomato pulp, garlic, remaining oil and olive paste, if using. Spread the sauce evenly over the bottom of a flameproof dish.

5 Spoon the spinach mixture into a piping bag fitted with a large plain nozzle and fill the pasta shapes. (Alternatively, use a teaspoon to do this.) Arrange the pasta shapes over the sauce.

6 Heat the pasta through in the oven for 15 minutes. Preheat a moderate grill. Scatter with Parmesan cheese and pine nuts and finish under the grill to brown the cheese.

COOK'S TIP

Choose a large saucepan when cooking pasta and give an occasional stir to prevent the shapes from sticking together. If passata is not available, use a can of chopped tomatoes instead, sieved and puréed.

Risotto alla Milanese

THIS TRADITIONAL Italian risotto is rich and creamy, and deliciously flavoured with garlic, shavings of Parmesan and fresh parsley.

INGREDIENTS

2 garlic cloves, crushed
60ml/4 tbsp chopped fresh parsley
finely grated rind of 1 lemon

For the risotto

5ml/1 tsp (or 1 sachet) saffron strands
25g/1oz/2 tbsp butter
1 large onion, finely chopped
275g/10oz/1½ cups arborio rice
150ml/¼ pint/⅔ cup dry white wine
1 litre/1¾ pints/4 cups vegetable stock
salt and freshly ground black pepper
Parmesan cheese shavings, to serve

Serves 4

1 Mix together the garlic, parsley and lemon rind in a bowl. Reserve and set aside.

2 To make the risotto, put the saffron in a small bowl with 15ml/1 tbsp boiling water and leave to stand while the saffron is infused. Melt the butter in a heavy-based frying saucepan and gently fry the onion for 5 minutes, until softened and golden.

3 Stir in the rice and cook for about 2 minutes until it becomes translucent. Add the wine and saffron mixture and cook for several minutes until all the wine is absorbed.

4 Add 600ml/1 pint/2½ cups of the stock to the pan and simmer gently until the stock is absorbed, stirring frequently.

5 Gradually add more stock, a ladleful at a time, until the rice is tender. (The rice might be tender and creamy before you've added all the stock, so add it slowly towards the end of the cooking time.)

6 Season the risotto with salt and pepper and transfer to a serving dish. Scatter lavishly with shavings of Parmesan cheese and the garlic and parsley mixture.

Vegetable Chilli

THIS ALTERNATIVE to traditional chilli con carne is delicious served with brown rice.

INGREDIENTS

2 onions, chopped
1 garlic clove, crushed
3 sticks celery, chopped
1 green pepper, seeded and diced
225g/8oz/3 cups mushrooms, sliced
2 courgettes, sliced
400g/14oz can red kidney beans, rinsed and drained
400g/14oz can chopped tomatoes
150ml/¼ pint/⅔ cup passata
30ml/2 tbsp tomato purée
15ml/1 tbsp tomato ketchup
1 tsp each hot chilli powder, ground cumin and ground coriander
salt and freshly ground black pepper
natural yogurt and cayenne pepper, to serve
sprigs of fresh coriander, to garnish

Serves 4

1 Put the onions, garlic, celery, green pepper, mushrooms and courgettes in a large saucepan and mix together.

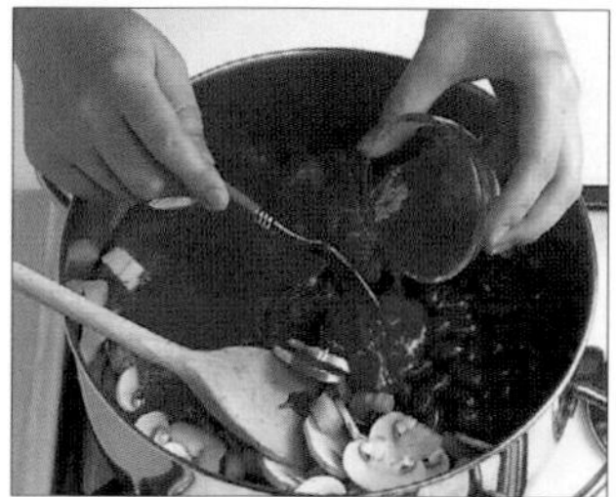

2 Add the kidney beans, tomatoes, passata, tomato purée and tomato ketchup.

3 Add the spices, season with salt and pepper and mix well.

4 Cover, and then bring to the boil. Simmer for 20–30 minutes, stirring occasionally, until the vegetables are just tender. Serve immediately with natural yogurt, sprinkled with cayenne pepper. Garnish with fresh coriander sprigs.

Leek, Mushroom and Lemon Risotto

A DELICIOUS risotto, packed full of flavour, this is a great recipe for an informal supper with friends.

INGREDIENTS

225g/8oz trimmed leeks
225g/8oz/3 generous cups brown-cap mushrooms
30ml/2 tbsp olive oil
3 garlic cloves, crushed
75g/3oz/6 tbsp butter
1 large onion, roughly chopped
350g/12oz/scant 1¾ cups arborio rice
1.2 litres/2 pints/5 cups hot vegetable stock
grated rind and juice of 1 lemon
50g/2oz/⅔ cup freshly grated Parmesan cheese
60ml/4 tbsp mixed chopped fresh chives and flat leaf parsley
salt and freshly ground black pepper
lemon wedges and flat leaf parsley, to serve

Serves 4

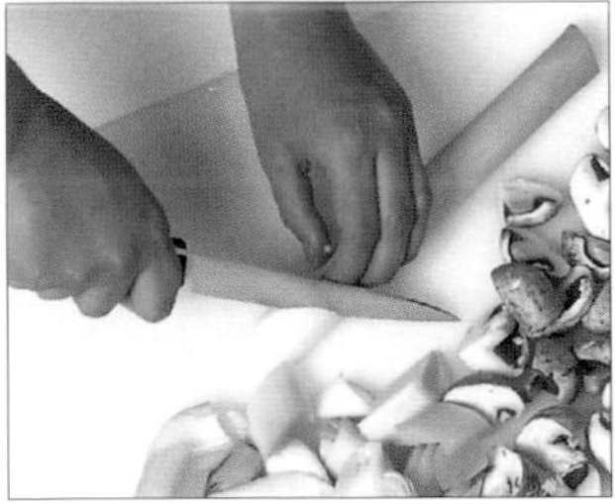

1 Wash the leeks well. Slice in half lengthways and roughly chop. Wipe the mushrooms with kitchen paper and roughly chop.

VARIATION

For a more zesty, tangy taste, you could substitute a lime for the lemon in this recipe.

2 Heat the oil in a large saucepan and cook the garlic for 1 minute. Add the leeks, mushrooms and plenty of seasoning and cook over a medium heat for about 10 minutes, or until softened and cooked through. Remove the ingredients from the pan and set aside.

3 Add 25g/1oz/2 tbsp of the butter to the pan and cook the onion over medium heat for about 5 minutes. Do not let it brown.

4 Stir in the rice and cook for 1 minute. Add a ladleful of stock to the pan and cook gently, stirring occasionally, until all the liquid is absorbed.

5 Stir in more liquid as each ladleful is absorbed – 20–25 minutes. Keep the stock over a gentle heat; it should be hot when you add it to the rice. The risotto will turn thick and creamy and the rice should be tender.

6 Just before serving, stir in the leeks, mushrooms, remaining butter, grated lemon rind and 45ml/3 tbsp of the juice, half the Parmesan and herbs. Adjust the seasoning to taste and sprinkle with the remaining Parmesan and herbs. Serve with lemon wedges and sprigs of flat leaf parsley.

Vegetable Pilau

A POPULAR vegetable rice dish that makes a tasty light supper. You can add baby broad beans instead of peas.

INGREDIENTS

225g/8oz/1 cup basmati rice
30ml/2 tbsp oil
2.5ml/½ tsp cumin seeds
2 bay leaves
4 green cardamom pods
4 cloves
1 onion, finely chopped
1 carrot, finely diced
50g/2oz/⅓ cup frozen peas, thawed
50g/2oz/⅓ cup frozen sweetcorn, thawed
25g/1oz/¼ cup cashew nuts, lightly fried
1.5ml/¼ tsp ground cumin
salt

Serves 4–6

1 Wash the basmati rice in several changes of cold water. Put into a bowl and cover with water. Leave to soak for about 30 minutes.

2 Heat the oil in a large frying pan and fry the cumin seeds for 2 minutes. Add the bay leaves, cardamoms and cloves and fry for a further 2 minutes.

3 Add the onion and fry for 5 minutes, until softened and lightly browned.

4 Stir in the carrot and cook for 3–4 minutes.

5 Drain the rice thoroughly and add to the pan together with the peas, sweetcorn and cashew nuts. Fry for 4–5 minutes.

6 Add 475ml/16fl oz/2 cups water, the ground cumin and salt to taste. Bring to the boil, cover and simmer for about 15 minutes over a low heat until all the water is absorbed. Leave to stand, covered, for 10 minutes, before serving.

Red Pepper Risotto

THE CHARACTER of this delicious risotto depends on the type of rice you use. With arborio rice, the risotto should be moist and creamy. If you use brown rice, reduce the amount of liquid for a drier dish with a nutty flavour.

INGREDIENTS

3 large red peppers
30ml/2 tbsp olive oil
3 large garlic cloves, thinly sliced
1½ x 400g/14oz cans chopped tomatoes
2 bay leaves
1.2–1.5 litres/2–2½ pints/5–6¼ cups vegetable stock
450g/1lb/2½ cups arborio rice or brown rice
6 fresh basil leaves, snipped
salt and freshly ground black pepper

Serves 6

1 Preheat the grill. Put the peppers in a grill pan and grill until the skins are blackened and blistered all over. Put the peppers in a bowl, cover with several layers of damp kitchen paper and leave for 10 minutes. Peel off the skins, then slice the peppers, discarding the cores and seeds.

2 Heat the oil in a wide, shallow pan. Add the garlic and tomatoes and cook over a gentle heat for 5 minutes, then add the pepper slices and bay leaves. Stir well and cook for about 15 minutes more, still over a gentle heat.

3 Pour the stock into a large, heavy-based saucepan and heat it to simmering point. Stir the rice into the vegetable mixture and cook for about 2 minutes, then add two or three ladlefuls of the hot stock. Cook, stirring occasionally, until all the stock has been absorbed into the rice.

4 Continue to add stock in this way, making sure each addition has been absorbed before pouring in the next. When the rice is tender, season with salt and pepper. Remove the pan from the heat, cover and leave to stand for 10 minutes before stirring in the basil and serving.

Risotto with Mushrooms

THE ADDITION of wild mushrooms gives this risotto a wonderfully authentic woody flavour.

INGREDIENTS

25g/1oz/⅓ cup dried wild mushrooms, preferably porcini
175g/6oz/2¼ cups fresh cultivated mushrooms
juice of ½ lemon
75g/3oz/6 tbsp butter
30ml/2 tbsp finely chopped parsley
900ml/1½ pints/3¾ cups vegetable stock
30ml/2 tbsp olive oil
1 small onion, finely chopped
275g/10oz/1½ cups medium grain risotto rice, such as arborio
120ml/4fl oz/½ cup dry white wine
45ml/3 tbsp grated Parmesan cheese
salt and freshly ground black pepper
sprig of flat leaf parsley, to garnish

Serves 3–4

1 Place the dried mushrooms in a small bowl with about 350ml/12fl oz/1½ cups warm water. Soak for at least 40 minutes. Rinse the mushrooms thoroughly. Filter the soaking water through a sieve lined with kitchen paper, and reserve.

2 Wipe the fresh mushrooms with a damp cloth and slice finely. Place in a bowl and toss thoroughly with the lemon juice.

3 In a large heavy-based frying pan or casserole melt a third of the butter. Stir in the freshly sliced mushrooms and cook over moderate heat until they give up their juices and begin to brown. Stir in the parsley, cook for 30 seconds more, and remove to a side dish.

4 Place the stock in a heavy-based saucepan. Add the mushroom water, bring it up to simmering point and simmer until needed.

5 Heat another third of the butter with the olive oil in the same pan the mushrooms were cooked in. Stir in the onion and cook until it is soft and golden. Add the rice, stirring for 1–2 minutes to coat it with the oils in the pan. Add the soaked and sautéed mushrooms and mix well.

6 Pour in the wine, raise the heat slightly, and cook over moderate heat until it evaporates.

7 Add one small ladleful of the hot stock. Over moderate heat cook until the stock is absorbed or evaporates, stirring the rice with a wooden spoon to prevent it sticking to the pan. Add a little more stock, and stir until the rice dries out again. Continue in this way, stirring and adding the liquid a little at a time. After abut 20 minutes taste the rice. Add salt and pepper.

8 Continue cooking, stirring and adding the liquid until the rice is *al dente*, or tender but still firm to the bite. The total cooking time of the risotto may be anything from 20–35 minutes. If you run out of stock you can use hot water.

9 Remove the risotto pan from the heat. Stir in the remaining butter and the Parmesan. Grind in a little black pepper and taste again for salt. Allow the risotto to rest for at least 3–4 minutes before serving from the pan, garnished with a sprig of flat leaf parsley.

Provençal Stuffed Peppers

STUFFED PEPPERS are easy to make for a light and healthy supper.

INGREDIENTS

15ml/1 tbsp olive oil
1 red onion, sliced
1 courgette, diced
115g/4oz/1¾ cups mushrooms, sliced
1 garlic clove, crushed
400g/14oz can chopped tomatoes
15ml/1 tbsp tomato purée
40g/1½oz/scant ⅓ cup pine nuts
30ml/2 tbsp chopped fresh basil
4 large yellow peppers
50g/2oz/½ cup finely grated red Leicester cheese
salt and freshly ground black pepper
fresh basil leaves, to garnish

Serves 4

1 Preheat the oven to 180°C/350°F/Gas 4. Heat the oil in a saucepan, add the onion, courgette, mushrooms and garlic and cook gently for 3 minutes, stirring occasionally.

VARIATION

Use the vegetable filling to stuff other vegetables, such as courgettes or aubergines, in place of the peppers.

2 Stir in the tomatoes and tomato purée, then bring to the boil and simmer, uncovered, for 10–15 minutes, stirring occasionally, until thickened slightly. Remove from the heat and stir in the pine nuts, basil and seasoning.

3 Cut the peppers in half lengthways and seed them. Blanch in a pan of boiling water for about 3 minutes. Drain.

4 Place the peppers in a shallow ovenproof dish and fill with the vegetable mixture.

5 Cover the dish with foil and bake for 20 minutes. Uncover, and then sprinkle each pepper with the finely grated cheese and bake for a further 5–10 minutes, until the cheese is melted and bubbling. Garnish with basil leaves and serve immediately.

Harvest Vegetable and Lentil Casserole

TAKE ADVANTAGE of root vegetables in season to make a hearty dish that is full of natural goodness.

INGREDIENTS

15ml/1 tbsp sunflower oil
2 leeks, sliced
1 garlic clove, crushed
4 celery sticks, chopped
2 carrots, sliced
2 parsnips, diced
1 sweet potato, diced
225g/8oz swede, diced
175g/6oz/¾ cup whole brown or green lentils
450g/1lb tomatoes, skinned, seeded and chopped
15ml/1 tbsp chopped fresh thyme
15ml/1 tbsp chopped fresh marjoram
900ml/1½ pints/3¾ cups vegetable stock
15ml/1 tbsp cornflour
salt and freshly ground black pepper
sprigs of fresh thyme, to garnish

Serves 6

1 Preheat the oven to 180°C/350°F/Gas 4. Heat the oil in a flameproof casserole over moderate heat. Add the leeks, garlic and celery and cook gently for 3 minutes.

2 Add the carrots, parsnips, sweet potato, swede, lentils, tomatoes, herbs, stock and seasoning. Stir well. Bring to the boil, stirring occasionally.

3 Cover and bake in the oven for about 50 minutes, until the vegetables and the lentils are cooked and tender. During the cooking period, remove the casserole from the oven and stir the vegetable mixture once or twice so that it is evenly cooked.

4 Remove the casserole from the oven. Blend the cornflour with 45ml/3 tbsp water in a bowl. Add to the casserole and heat, stirring, until the mixture boils and thickens. Simmer gently for 2 minutes. Spoon into bowls and garnish with thyme sprigs.

Roasted Vegetables with Salsa Verde

THERE ARE ENDLESS VARIATIONS of the Italian salsa verde, which means "green sauce". Usually a blend of fresh chopped herbs, garlic, olive oil, anchovies and capers, this is a simplified version. Here, it is served with roasted vegetables and a traditional rice and vermicelli dish from the island of Cyprus.

INGREDIENTS

3 courgettes, sliced lengthways
1 large fennel bulb, cut into wedges
450g/1lb butternut squash, cut into 2cm/¾in chunks
12 shallots
2 red peppers, seeded and cut lengthways into thick slices
4 plum tomatoes, halved and seeded
45ml/3 tbsp olive oil
2 garlic cloves, crushed
5ml/1 tsp balsamic vinegar
salt and freshly ground black pepper

For the salsa verde

45ml/3 tbsp chopped fresh mint
90ml/6 tbsp chopped fresh flat leaf parsley
15ml/1 tbsp Dijon mustard
juice of ½ lemon
30ml/2 tbsp olive oil

For the rice

15ml/1 tbsp vegetable or olive oil
75g/3oz/¾ cup vermicelli, broken into short lengths
225g/8oz/generous 1 cup long grain rice
900ml/1½ pints/3¾ cups vegetable stock

Serves 4

COOK'S TIP

The salsa verde will keep for up to 1 week if stored in an airtight container in the fridge.

1 Preheat the oven to 220°C/425°F/Gas 7. To make the salsa verde, place all the ingredients, with the exception of the olive oil, in a food processor or blender. Blend to a coarse paste, then add the oil, a little at a time, until the mixture forms a smooth purée. Season to taste.

2 To roast the vegetables, toss the courgettes, fennel, squash, shallots, peppers and tomatoes in the olive oil, garlic and balsamic vinegar. Leave for 10 minutes to allow the flavours to mingle.

3 Place all the vegetables – apart from the squash and tomatoes – on a baking sheet, brush with half the oil and vinegar mixture and season.

4 Roast for 25 minutes, then remove the tray from the oven. Turn the vegetables over and brush with the rest of the oil and vinegar mixture. Add the squash and tomatoes and cook for a further 20–25 minutes until all the vegetables are tender and lightly blackened around the edges.

5 Meanwhile, prepare the rice. Heat the oil in a heavy-based saucepan. Add the vermicelli and fry for about 3 minutes or until golden and crisp. Season to taste.

6 Rinse the rice under cold running water, drain well, and add it to the vermicelli. Cook for 1 minute, stirring to coat it in the oil.

7 Add the vegetable stock, then cover the pan and cook for about 12 minutes until the water is absorbed. Stir the rice, then cover and leave to stand for 10 minutes. Serve the warm rice with the roasted vegetables and salsa verde.

HEALTH BENEFITS

- *Brightly coloured vegetables, such as peppers, tomatoes and courgettes, are packed with the antioxidant vitamins C and E, and beta carotene, which are thought to reduce the risk of cancer.*
- *Mint aids the digestion and can help anyone who is suffering from irritable bowel syndrome.*

Spinach and Wild Mushroom Soufflé

WILD MUSHROOMS combine especially well with eggs and spinach in this sensational soufflé. Any combination of mushrooms can be used for this recipe, although the firmer varieties provide the best texture.

INGREDIENTS

225g/8oz fresh spinach, washed, or 115g/4oz frozen chopped spinach
50g/2oz/4 tbsp unsalted butter, plus extra for greasing
1 garlic clove, crushed
175g/6oz/2¼ cups assorted wild mushrooms such as ceps, bay boletus, saffron milk-caps, oyster, field and Caesar's mushrooms
200ml/7fl oz/⅞ cup milk
20g/¾oz/3 tbsp plain flour
6 eggs, separated
pinch of grated nutmeg
25g/1oz/⅓ cup grated Parmesan cheese
salt and freshly ground black pepper

Serves 4

1 Preheat the oven to 190°C/375°F/Gas 5. Steam the spinach over moderate heat for 3–4 minutes. Cool under running water, then drain. Press out as much liquid as you can with the back of a large spoon and chop finely. If using frozen spinach, defrost and prepare following the package instructions. Squeeze the spinach dry in the same way.

2 Melt the butter in a saucepan and cook the garlic and mushrooms over low heat until softened. Turn up the heat and evaporate the juices. When dry, add the spinach and transfer to a bowl. Cover and keep warm.

3 Measure 45ml/3 tbsp of the milk into a bowl. Bring the remainder to the boil. Stir the flour and egg yolks into the cold milk in the bowl and blend well. Stir the boiling milk into the egg and flour mixture, return to the pan and simmer to thicken. Add the spinach mixture to the pan. Season with salt, pepper and nutmeg to taste.

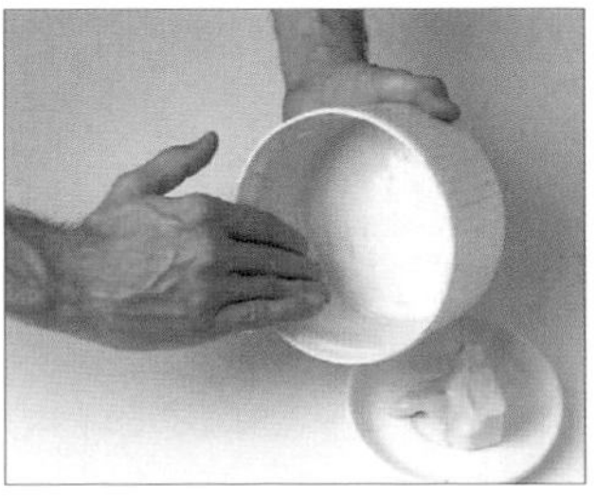

4 Butter a 900ml/1½ pint/3¾ cup soufflé dish, paying particular attention to the sides. Sprinkle with a little of the Parmesan. Set aside.

5 Whisk the egg whites until stiff. Bring the spinach mixture back to the boil. Stir in a spoonful of beaten egg white, then fold the mixture into the remaining egg white.

6 Turn the mixture into the soufflé dish, spread level, scatter with the remaining cheese and bake in the oven for about 25 minutes, until puffed and golden brown. Timing is critical with soufflés, so have everyone at the table and serve immediately, before the soufflé has a chance to deflate.

COOK'S TIP

The soufflé base can be prepared up to 12 hours in advance and reheated before the beaten egg whites are folded in.

Potato, Red Onion and Feta Frittata

THIS ITALIAN OMELETTE is cooked with vegetables and cheese, and is served flat, like a Spanish tortilla. Cut it into wedges and serve with crusty bread and a tomato salad for a light supper.

INGREDIENTS

25ml/1 1/2 tbsp olive oil
1 red onion, sliced
350g/12oz cooked new potatoes, halved or quartered, if large
6 eggs, lightly beaten
115g/4oz/1 cup feta cheese, diced
salt and freshly ground black pepper
Serves 2–4

1 Heat the oil in a large heavy-based, flameproof frying pan. Add the onion and sauté for 5 minutes until softened, stirring occasionally.

2 Add the potatoes and cook for a further 5 minutes until golden, stirring to prevent them sticking. Spread the mixture evenly over the base of the pan.

3 Preheat the grill to high. Season the beaten eggs, then pour the mixture over the onion and potatoes. Sprinkle the cheese on top and cook over a moderate heat for 5–6 minutes until the eggs are just set and the base of the frittata is lightly golden.

4 Place the pan under the grill and cook the top for 3 minutes until set and lightly golden. Serve the frittata warm or cold, cut into wedges.

HEALTH BENEFITS

Eggs are an important source of vitamin B_{12}, which is vital for the nervous system and the development of red blood cells. They also supply other B vitamins, zinc and selenium and a useful amount of iron. It is beneficial to eat a food rich in vitamin C at the same time in order to help the absorption of iron. Do not eat too many eggs, though – no more than a maximum of three per week.

Layered Polenta Bake

POLENTA, TOMATOES, SPINACH and beans make a tasty supper dish.

INGREDIENTS

5ml/1 tsp salt
375g/13oz/3 cups fine polenta
olive oil, for greasing and brushing
25g/1oz/⅓ cup freshly grated Parmesan cheese
salt and freshly ground black pepper

For the tomato sauce

15ml/1 tbsp olive oil
2 garlic cloves, chopped
400g/14oz/3 cups chopped tomatoes
15ml/1 tbsp chopped fresh sage
2.5ml/½ tsp soft brown sugar
200g/7oz/1½ cups canned cannellini beans, rinsed and drained

For the spinach sauce

250g/9oz spinach, tough stalks removed
150ml/¼ pint/⅔ cup single cream
115g/4oz/1 cup Gorgonzola cheese, cubed
large pinch of ground nutmeg

Serves 6

1 Make the polenta. Bring 2 litres/3½ pints/8 cups water to the boil in a large heavy-based saucepan and add the salt. Remove the pan from the heat. Gradually pour in the polenta, whisking continuously.

2 Return the pan to the heat and stir constantly for 15–20 minutes until the polenta is thick and comes away from the side of the pan. Remove the pan from the heat.

3 Season well with pepper, then spoon the polenta on to a wet work surface or piece of marble. Using a wet spatula, spread out the polenta until it is 1cm/½in thick. Leave to cool for about 1 hour.

4 Preheat the oven to 190°C/375°F/Gas 5. To make the tomato sauce, heat the oil in a saucepan, then fry the garlic for 1 minute. Add the tomatoes and sage and bring to the boil. Reduce the heat, add the sugar and seasoning, and simmer for 10 minutes until slightly reduced, stirring occasionally. Stir in the beans and cook for a further 2 minutes.

5 Meanwhile, wash the spinach thoroughly and place in a large pan with only the water that clings to the leaves. Cover the pan tightly and cook over a medium heat for about 3 minutes or until tender, stirring occasionally. Tip the spinach into a colander and drain, then squeeze out as much excess water as possible with the back of a wooden spoon.

6 Heat the cream, cheese and nutmeg in a small heavy-based saucepan. Bring to the boil, then reduce the heat. Stir in the spinach and seasoning, then cook gently until slightly thickened, stirring frequently.

7 Cut the polenta into triangles, then place a layer of polenta in an oiled deep baking dish. Spoon over the tomato sauce, then top with another layer of polenta. Top with the spinach sauce and cover with the remaining polenta triangles. Brush with olive oil, sprinkle with Parmesan and bake for 35–40 minutes. Heat the grill to high and grill until the top is golden before serving.

SPECIAL OCCASIONS

Colourful, nutritious and visually appealing, these vegetarian dishes from around the globe will impress your dinner guests.

Sweet Potato Roulade

SWEET POTATO works particularly well as the base for this roulade. Serve in thin slices for a truly impressive dinner party dish.

INGREDIENTS

225g/8oz/1 cup low-fat soft cheese
75ml/5 tbsp natural yogurt
6–8 spring onions, finely chopped
30ml/2 tbsp chopped Brazil nuts, roasted
450g/1lb sweet potatoes, peeled and cubed
12 allspice berries, crushed
4 eggs, separated
50g/2oz/½ cup finely grated Edam cheese
15ml/1 tbsp sesame seeds
salt and freshly ground black pepper
green salad, to serve

Serves 6

1 Preheat the oven to 200°C/400°F/ Gas 6. Grease and line a 33 x 25cm/ 13 x 10in Swiss roll tin with non-stick baking parchment, snipping the corners with scissors to fit.

COOK'S TIP

Choose the orange-fleshed variety of sweet potato for the most striking colour.

2 In a small bowl, mix together the soft cheese, yogurt, spring onions and Brazil nuts. Set aside.

3 Boil or steam the sweet potatoes until tender. Drain well. Place in a food processor with the allspice and blend until smooth. Spoon into a bowl and stir in the egg yolks and Edam. Season with salt and freshly ground black pepper.

4 Whisk the egg whites until stiff but not dry. Using a large metal spoon fold one third of the egg whites into the sweet potatoes to lighten the mixture before gently folding in the rest.

5 Pour into the prepared tin, tipping it to get the mixture right into the corners. Smooth the surface gently with a palette knife and bake for 10–15 minutes.

6 Meanwhile, lay a large sheet of greaseproof paper on a clean dish towel and sprinkle with the sesame seeds. When the roulade is cooked, tip it on to the paper, trim the edges and roll it up. Leave to cool. When cool, carefully unroll, spread with the cheese filling and roll up again. Cut into slices and serve with a green salad.

Goat's Cheese Soufflé

MAKE SURE everyone is seated before the soufflé comes out of the oven because it will begin to deflate almost immediately. The recipe works equally well with strong blue cheeses such as Roquefort.

INGREDIENTS

40g/1½oz/3 tbsp butter
25g/1oz/¼ cup plain flour
175ml/6fl oz/¾ cup milk
1 bay leaf
freshly grated nutmeg
grated Parmesan cheese, for sprinkling
40g/1½oz herb and garlic soft cheese
150g/5oz/1¼ cups goat's cheese, diced
6 egg whites, at room temperature
1.5ml/¼ tsp cream of tartar
salt and freshly ground black pepper

Serves 4–6

1 Melt 25g/1oz/2 tbsp butter in a heavy saucepan over medium heat. Add the flour and cook until golden, stirring occasionally.

2 Pour in half the milk, stirring vigorously until smooth. Stir in the remaining milk and add the bay leaf. Season with a pinch of salt and plenty of pepper and nutmeg. Reduce the heat to medium low, cover and simmer gently for about 5 minutes, stirring occasionally.

3 Preheat the oven to 190°C/375°F/Gas 5. Generously butter a 1.5 litre/2½ pint/6¼ cup soufflé dish and sprinkle with Parmesan cheese.

4 Remove the sauce from the heat and discard the bay leaf. Stir in both cheeses.

5 In a clean grease-free bowl, using an electric mixer or balloon whisk, beat the egg whites slowly until they become frothy.

6 Add the cream of tartar, increase the speed and beat until they form soft peaks, then stiffer peaks that just flop over a little at the top.

7 Stir a spoonful of beaten egg whites into the cheese sauce to lighten it, then pour the cheese sauce over the remaining whites. Using a large metal spoon, gently fold the sauce into the whites until the mixtures are just combined.

8 Pour the soufflé mixture into the prepared dish and bake for 25–30 minutes, until puffed and golden brown. Serve at once.

Celeriac and Blue Cheese Roulade

CELERIAC ADDS a delicate and subtle flavour to this attractive dish.

INGREDIENTS

15g/½oz/1 tbsp butter
225g/8oz cooked spinach, drained and chopped
150ml/¼ pint/⅔ cup single cream
4 large eggs, separated
15g/½oz/½ cup freshly grated Parmesan cheese
pinch of nutmeg
salt and freshly ground black pepper

For the filling
225g/8oz celeriac
lemon juice
75g/3oz St Agur cheese
115g/4oz/½ cup fromage frais

Serves 6

1 Preheat the oven to 200°C/400°F/Gas 6. Line a 33 x 23cm/13 x 9in Swiss roll tin with non-stick baking parchment.

2 Melt the butter in a saucepan and add the spinach. Cook until all the liquid has evaporated. Remove the pan from the heat. Stir in the cream, egg yolks, Parmesan and nutmeg. Season.

3 Whisk the egg whites until stiff, fold them gently into the spinach mixture and then spoon into the prepared tin. Spread the mixture evenly and use a palette knife to smooth the surface.

4 Bake for 10–15 minutes, until the roulade is firm to the touch. Turn out on to a sheet of greaseproof paper and peel away the lining paper. Roll up the roulade with the greaseproof paper inside and leave to cool slightly.

5 To make the filling, peel the celeriac and grate it into a bowl. Sprinkle with lemon juice to taste. Blend the St Agur cheese and fromage frais together and mix with the celeriac and a little black pepper.

6 Unroll the roulade, spread with the filling and roll up again, this time without the paper. Serve at once or wrap loosely and chill.

Purée of Lentils with Baked Eggs

THIS UNUSUAL dish makes an excellent supper. For a nutty flavour you could add a 400g/14oz can of unsweetened chestnut purée to the lentil mixture.

INGREDIENTS

450g/1lb/2 cups washed brown lentils
3 leeks, thinly sliced
10ml/2 tsp coriander seeds, crushed
15ml/1 tbsp chopped fresh coriander
30ml/2 tbsp chopped fresh mint
15ml/1 tbsp red wine vinegar
1 litre/1¾ pints/4 cups vegetable stock
4 eggs
salt and freshly ground black pepper
generous handful of fresh parsley, chopped, to garnish

Serves 4

1 Put the lentils in a deep saucepan. Add the leeks, coriander seeds, fresh coriander, mint, vinegar and stock. Bring to the boil, then lower the heat and simmer for 30–40 minutes, until the lentils are cooked and have absorbed all the liquid.

2 Preheat the oven to 180°C/350°F/Gas 4.

3 Season the lentils with salt and pepper and mix well. Spread the lentil mixture over the base of four lightly greased individual baking dishes.

4 Using the back of a spoon, make a hollow in the lentil mixture in each dish. Break an egg into each hollow.

5 Cover the dishes with foil and bake for 15–20 minutes, or until the egg whites are set and the yolks are still soft. Sprinkle with plenty of parsley and serve at once.

Leek Soufflé

SOUFFLÉS ARE a great way to impress guests at a dinner party. This one is simple to make but it looks very sophisticated.

INGREDIENTS

15ml/1 tbsp sunflower oil
40g/1 ½oz/3 tbsp butter plus extra for greasing
2 leeks, thinly sliced
about 300ml/½ pint/1 ¼ cups milk
25g/1oz/¼ cup plain flour
4 eggs, separated
75g/3oz/¾ cup Gruyère or Emmenthal cheese, grated
salt and freshly ground black pepper

Serves 2–3

1 Preheat the oven to 180°C/350°F/Gas 4. Butter a large soufflé dish.

2 Heat the sunflower oil and 15g/½oz/1 tbsp of the butter in a small saucepan or flameproof casserole and fry the leeks over gentle heat for 4–5 minutes, until soft but not brown.

3 Stir in the milk and bring to the boil. Cover and simmer for 4–5 minutes, until the leeks are tender. Strain the liquid through a sieve into a measuring jug.

4 Melt the remaining butter, stir in the flour and cook for 1 minute. Remove from the heat.

5 Make up the reserved liquid with milk to 300ml/½ pint/1 ¼ cups. Gradually stir the milk into the flour to make a smooth sauce. Return to the heat and bring to the boil, stirring. When thickened, remove from the heat. Cool slightly and beat in the egg yolks, cheese and leeks. Season to taste.

6 In a clean greasefree bowl whisk the egg whites until stiff. Using a large metal spoon, fold into the leek and egg mixture until just combined. Pour into the prepared soufflé dish and bake for about 30 minutes, until puffed and golden brown. Serve immediately.

Broccoli and Chestnut Terrine

SERVED HOT or cold, this versatile terrine is equally suitable for a dinner party or for a picnic. A light salad is an ideal accompaniment.

INGREDIENTS

450g/1 lb/4 cups broccoli, cut into small florets
225g/8oz/2 cups cooked chestnuts, roughly chopped
50g/2oz/1 cup fresh wholemeal breadcrumbs
60ml/4 tbsp natural yogurt
30ml/2 tbsp finely grated Parmesan cheese
2 eggs, beaten
pinch of grated nutmeg
salt and freshly ground black pepper
new potatoes, to serve

For the salad and dressing (optional)
60ml/4 tbsp olive oil
15ml/1 tbsp lemon juice
2.5ml/½ tsp caster sugar
salt and freshly ground black pepper
15ml/1 tbsp chopped fresh thyme or dill
250g/9oz mixed green salad leaves

Serves 4–6

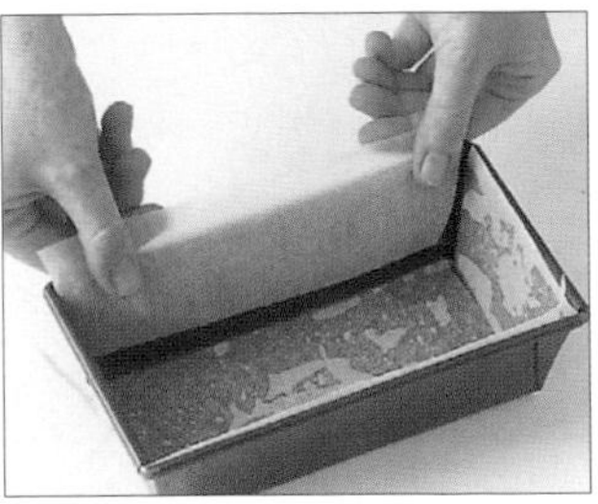

1 Preheat the oven to 180°C/350°F/Gas 4. Line a 900g/2lb loaf tin with non-stick baking parchment.

2 Blanch or steam the broccoli for 3–4 minutes, until just crunchy but tender. Drain thoroughly. Reserve ¼ of the smallest florets and chop the rest finely.

3 Mix together the chestnuts, breadcrumbs, yogurt and Parmesan. Season with salt, pepper and nutmeg.

4 Gradually fold in the chopped broccoli, reserved florets and the beaten eggs.

5 Spoon the broccoli mixture into the prepared tin.

6 Place in a roasting tin and pour in boiling water to come halfway up the sides of the loaf tin. Bake for 20–25 minutes.

7 Meanwhile, to make the salad dressing, if using, mix together the olive oil, lemon juice and sugar. Season with salt and pepper and stir in the chopped thyme or dill. Arrange the salad leaves on a plate. Pour the dressing over the salad.

8 Remove the roasting tin from the oven and tip out on to a plate or tray. Cut into even slices and serve with new potatoes.

Grilled Vegetable Terrine

IMPRESS YOUR guests with a colourful layered terrine using a mixture of Mediterranean vegetables.

INGREDIENTS

2 large red peppers, quartered, cored and seeded
2 large yellow peppers, quartered, cored and seeded
1 large aubergine, sliced lengthways
2 large courgettes, sliced lengthways
90ml/6 tbsp olive oil
1 large red onion, thinly sliced
75g/3oz/½ cup raisins
15ml/1 tbsp tomato purée
15ml/1 tbsp red wine vinegar
400ml/14fl oz/1⅔ cups tomato juice
15g/½oz/2 tbsp vegetarian gelatine
fresh basil leaves, to garnish

For the dressing
90ml/6 tbsp olive oil
30ml/2 tbsp red wine vinegar
salt and freshly ground black pepper

Serves 6

1 Place the peppers skin side up under a hot grill and cook until blackened. Put in a bowl. Cover.

2 Arrange the aubergine and courgette slices on separate baking sheets. Brush them with oil and cook under the grill.

3 Heat the remaining olive oil in a frying pan. Add the onion, raisins, tomato purée and red wine vinegar. Cook until soft.

4 Line a 1.75 litre/3 pint/7½ cup terrine with clear film.

5 Pour half the tomato juice into a saucepan. Sprinkle with the gelatine. Dissolve over a low heat.

6 Layer the red peppers in the terrine, and cover with some of the tomato juice and gelatine. Add the aubergine, courgettes, yellow peppers and onion mixture.

7 Pour tomato juice over each layer of vegetables. Finish the terrine with another layer of red peppers. Press them down firmly.

8 Add the remaining tomato juice to any juice and gelatine left in the pan and pour into the terrine. Give the terrine a sharp tap, to disperse the juice. Cover and chill in the refrigerator until set.

9 To make the dressing, whisk together the oil and vinegar. Season with salt and freshly ground black pepper.

10 Turn out the terrine and remove the clear film. Serve cut into thick slices, drizzled with the oil and wine vinegar dressing. Garnish with basil leaves.

Fonduta with Steamed Vegetables

FONDUTA IS a creamy cheese sauce from Italy. Traditionally it is garnished with slices of white truffles and eaten with toasted bread rounds.

INGREDIENTS

assorted vegetables, such as fennel, broccoli, carrots, cauliflower and courgettes
115g/4oz/8 tbsp butter
12–16 rounds of Italian or French baguette

For the fonduta

300g/11oz fontina cheese
15ml/1 tbsp flour
milk, as required
50g/2oz/4 tbsp butter
50g/2oz/⅔ cup freshly grated Parmesan cheese
pinch of grated nutmeg
2 egg yolks, at room temperature
a few slivers of white truffle (optional)
salt and freshly ground black pepper

Serves 4

1 About 6 hours before you want to serve the fonduta, cut the fontina into chunks and place in a bowl. Sprinkle with the flour. Pour in enough milk to barely cover the cheese and set aside in a cool place. The cheese should be at room temperature before being cooked.

2 Just before preparing the fonduta, steam the vegetables until tender. Cut into pieces. Place on a serving platter, dot with butter and keep warm.

3 Butter the bread and toast lightly in the oven or under the grill.

4 For the fonduta, melt the butter in a bowl set over a pan of simmering water, or in a double boiler. Strain the fontina and add it, with 45–60ml/3–4 tbsp of its soaking milk. Cook, stirring, until the cheese melts. When it is hot, and has formed a homogeneous mass, add the Parmesan and stir until melted. Season with nutmeg, salt and pepper.

5 Remove from the heat and immediately beat in the egg yolks, which have previously been passed through a sieve. Spoon into warmed individual serving bowls, garnish with white truffle, if using, and serve with the vegetables and toasted bread.

Spring Vegetable Boxes with Pernod Sauce

PERNOD IS the perfect companion for the tender taste of early vegetables in crisp cases. This is a very impressive dish for a dinner party and it tastes as good as it looks.

INGREDIENTS

225g/8oz puff pastry, defrosted if frozen
15ml/1 tbsp freshly grated Parmesan cheese
15ml/1 tbsp chopped fresh parsley
beaten egg to glaze
175g/6oz podded broad beans
115g/4oz/½ cup baby carrots, scraped
4 baby leeks, cleaned
75g/3oz/generous ½ cup peas, defrosted if frozen
50g/2oz mangetout, trimmed
salt and freshly ground black pepper
sprigs of fresh dill, to garnish

For the sauce
200g/7oz can chopped tomatoes
25g/1oz/2 tbsp butter
25g/1oz/¼ cup plain flour
pinch of sugar
45ml/3 tbsp chopped fresh dill
300ml/½ pint/1¼ cups water
15ml/1 tbsp Pernod

Serves 4

1 Preheat the oven to 220°C/425°F/Gas 7. Lightly grease a baking sheet.

2 Roll out the pastry very thinly. Sprinkle the grated cheese and parsley over the surface of the pastry sheets, fold and roll once more so that the cheese and parsley are mixed into the pastry. Cut into four 7.5 x 10cm/3 x 4in rectangles.

3 Lift the rectangles on to the baking sheet. With a sharp knife, cut an inner rectangle about 1cm/½in from the edge of the pastry, cutting halfway through. This will be removed once the boxes are cooked and the pastry has puffed up. Score criss-cross lines on top of the inner rectangle, brush with egg and bake for 12–15 minutes, until golden.

4 Meanwhile, make the sauce. Press the tomatoes through a sieve into a pan, add the remaining ingredients and bring to the boil, stirring all the time. Lower the heat and simmer until required. Season with salt and pepper.

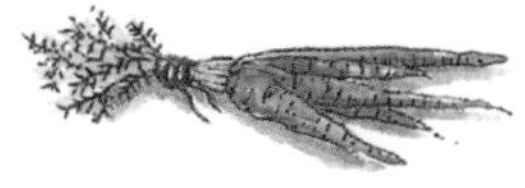

5 Cook the broad beans in a pan of lightly salted boiling water for about 8 minutes. Add the carrots, leeks and peas and cook for a further 5 minutes. Then add the mangetout and cook for 1 minute more. Drain all vegetables thoroughly, keeping them in a warm place till needed.

6 Using a knife, remove the notched squares from the pastry boxes. Set them aside to use as lids. Spoon the vegetables into the pastry cases, pour the sauce over, put the pastry lids on top and serve garnished with dill.

COOK'S TIP

If there is time, chill the pastry boxes for 20 minutes before baking.

Potato Rösti and Tofu with Fresh Tomato and Ginger Sauce

ALTHOUGH THIS DISH FEATURES various components, it is not difficult to make and the finished result is well worth the effort. Make sure you marinate the tofu for at least an hour to allow it to absorb the flavours of the ginger, garlic and tamari. Serve with a mixed leaf salad, dressed with a splash each of toasted sesame oil and lime juice.

INGREDIENTS

425g/15oz/3¾ cups tofu, cut into 1cm/½in cubes
4 large potatoes, about 900g/2lb total weight, peeled
sunflower oil, for frying
salt and freshly ground black pepper
30ml/2 tbsp sesame seeds, toasted

For the marinade

30ml/2 tbsp tamari or dark soy sauce
15ml/1 tbsp clear honey
2 garlic cloves, crushed
4 cm/1½ in piece fresh root ginger, grated
5ml/1 tsp toasted sesame oil

For the sauce

15ml/1 tbsp olive oil
8 tomatoes, halved, seeded and chopped

Serves 4

1 Mix together all the marinade ingredients in a shallow dish and add the tofu. Spoon the marinade over the tofu and leave to marinate in the fridge for at least 1 hour. Turn the tofu occasionally in the marinade to allow the flavours to infuse.

HEALTH BENEFITS

Made from processed soya beans, tofu is a highly nutritious protein food and is the richest non-dairy source of calcium. Tofu also contains valuable B vitamins and iron.

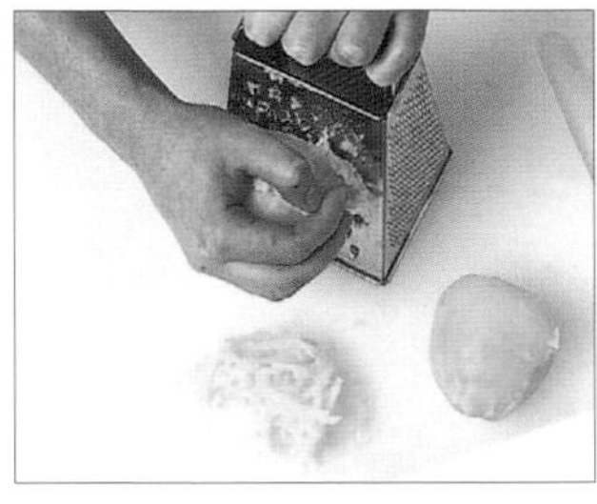

2 To make the rösti, par-boil the potatoes for 10–15 minutes until almost tender. Leave to cool, then grate coarsely. Season well. Preheat the oven to 200°C/400°F/Gas 6.

3 Using a slotted spoon, remove the tofu from the marinade and reserve the marinade. Spread out the tofu on a baking tray and bake for 20 minutes, turning occasionally, until golden and crisp on all sides.

4 Take a quarter of the potato mixture in your hands at a time and form into rough cakes.

5 Heat a frying pan with just enough oil to cover the base. Place the cakes in the frying pan and flatten the mixture, using your hands or a spatula to form rounds about 1cm/½in thick.

6 Cook for about 6 minutes until golden and crisp underneath. Carefully turn over the rösti and cook for a further 6 minutes until golden.

7 Meanwhile, make the sauce. Heat the oil in a saucepan, add the reserved marinade and the tomatoes and cook for 2 minutes, stirring. Reduce the heat and simmer, covered, for 10 minutes, stirring occasionally, until the tomatoes break down. Press through a sieve to make a thick, smooth sauce.

8 To serve, place a rösti on each of four warm serving plates. Scatter the tofu on top, spoon over the tomato sauce and sprinkle with sesame seeds.

COOK'S TIP

Tamari is a thick, mellow-flavoured Japanese soy sauce, which unlike conventional Chinese soy sauce is wheat-free, and so is suitable for people who are on wheat- or gluten-free diets. It is sold in Japanese food shops and some larger health food stores.

Cauliflower and Mushroom Gougère

THIS PUFFY, golden-brown, cheese-flavoured case filled with lovely fresh vegetables is a wonderful dinner party dish.

INGREDIENTS

115g/4oz/8 tbsp butter
150g/5oz/1 1/4 cups plain flour
4 eggs
115g/4oz/1 cup Gruyère or Cheddar cheese, finely diced
5ml/1 tsp Dijon mustard
salt and freshly ground black pepper

For the filling

1 small cauliflower
1 x 200g/7oz can tomatoes
15ml/1 tbsp sunflower oil
15g/1/2oz/1 tbsp butter
1 onion, chopped
115g/4oz/1 1/2 cup button mushrooms, halved if large
sprig of fresh thyme

Serves 4–6

1 Preheat the oven to 200°C/400°F/Gas 6. Butter a large ovenproof dish. Place 300ml/1/2 pint/1 1/4 cups water and butter together in a large saucepan and heat until the butter has melted. Remove from the heat and add all the flour at once. Beat well with a wooden spoon for about 30 seconds, until smooth. Allow to cool slightly.

2 Beat in the eggs, one at a time, and continue beating until the mixture is thick and glossy. Stir in the cheese and mustard and season with salt and pepper. Spread the mixture around the sides of the ovenproof dish, leaving a hollow in the centre to take the filling.

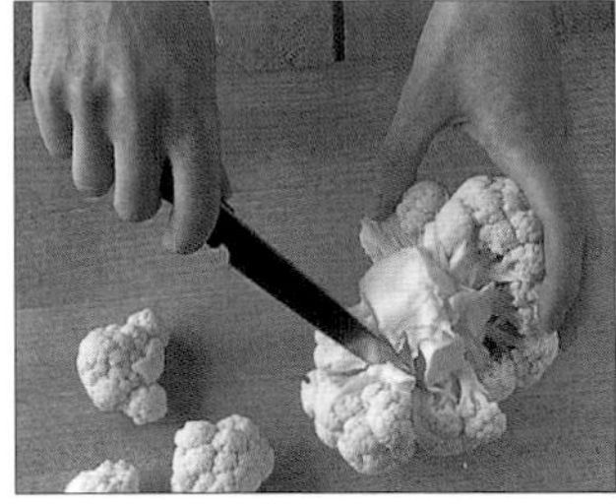

3 Cut the cauliflower into florets, discarding the woody, hard stalk in the centre.

4 To make the filling, purée the tomatoes in a blender or food processor, or push through a sieve with a spoon, and then pour into a measuring jug. Add enough water to make up to 300ml/1/2 pint/1 1/4 cups of liquid.

5 Heat the oil and butter in a flameproof casserole. Fry the onion for 3–4 minutes. Add the mushrooms and cook for 2–3 minutes. Add the cauliflower and stir-fry for 1 minute. Add the tomato liquid and thyme. Season. Cook over low heat for 5 minutes.

6 Spoon into the hollow in the ovenproof dish. Bake for 40 minutes, until the pastry is risen.

P… ch and Pine Nut Gratin

TARGET COUPON
EXPIRES 12/6/10
$1 off
4.3-oz. or larger Aquafresh toothpaste
Aquafresh EXTREME CLEAN WHITENING ACTION
Target accepts one manufacturer and one Target coupon per item. Void if copied, scanned, transferred, purchased, sold or prohibited by law. Item(s)

PI… thi… an… sau… and…

IN…

450g…
1 gar…
3 spri…
150m…
250m…
225g/…
defr…
115g/4…
40g/1…
salt and…
lettuce…

Serve…

1 Peel the potatoes and cut them carefully into wafer-thin slices. Spread them out in a large, heavy-bottomed, non-stick frying pan.

2 Sprinkle the crushed garlic and sliced spring onions evenly over the potatoes.

3 Pour the single cream and milk over the potatoes. Place the pan over a gentle heat, cover and cook for 8 minutes, or until the sliced potatoes are tender.

4 Using both hands, squeeze the spinach dry. Add the spinach to the potatoes, mixing lightly. Cover the pan and cook for 2 minutes more.

5 Season with salt and pepper, then spoon the mixture into a shallow, flameproof casserole. Preheat the grill.

6 Sprinkle the grated cheese and pine nuts over the spinach mixture. Heat under the grill for 2–3 minutes until the topping begins to turn golden. Serve with a lettuce and tomato salad.

Red Pepper and Watercress Filo Parcels

PEPPERY WATERCRESS combines well with sweet red pepper in these crisp little parcels.

INGREDIENTS

3 red peppers
175g/6oz watercress
225g/8oz/1 cup ricotta cheese
50g/2oz/¼ cup blanched almonds, toasted and chopped
8 sheets filo pastry
30ml/2 tbsp olive oil
salt and freshly ground black pepper
green salad, to serve
Makes 8

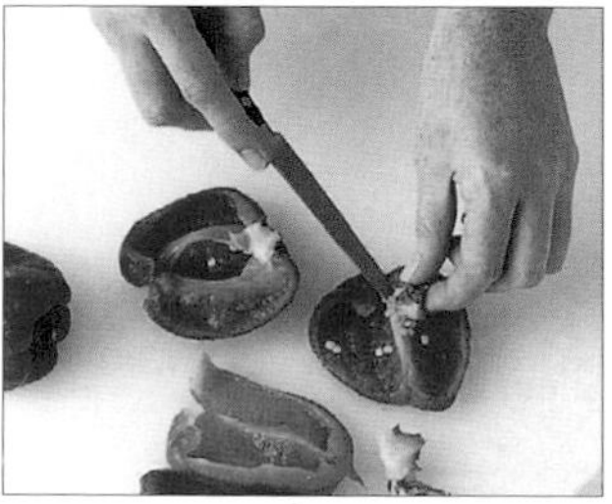

1 Preheat the oven to 190°C/375°F/Gas 5. Place the peppers under a hot grill until blistered and charred all over. Place in a paper bag. When the peppers are cool enough to handle, remove their skins, cut in half and seed and pat dry on kitchen paper.

2 Place the peppers and watercress in a food processor and pulse until coarsely chopped, or chop with a sharp knife. Spoon into a bowl.

3 Gradually mix the ricotta and almonds into the pepper and watercress mixture, and season.

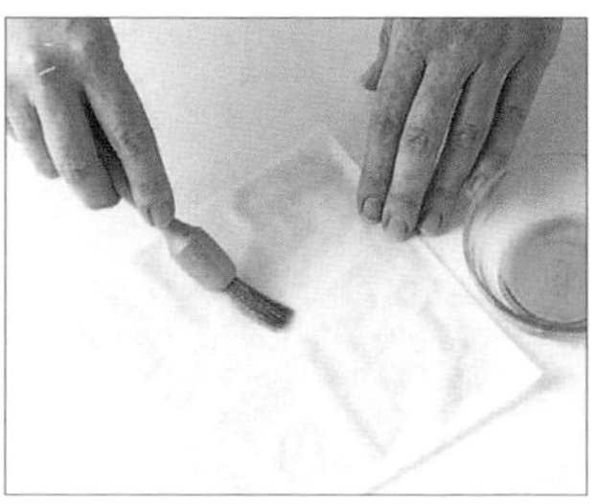

4 Working with 1 sheet of filo pastry at a time, cut out 2 × 18cm/7in and 2 × 5cm/2in squares from each sheet. Brush 1 of the large squares with a little olive oil and place the second large square at an angle of 90° to form a star shape.

COOK'S TIP

Keep filo pastry refrigerated until you need to use it. When working with the pastry, try to handle it as little as possible and keep the work area cool.

5 Carefully place 1 of the small squares in the centre of the star shape. Brush lightly with olive oil and top with the second small square. Brush lightly with oil.

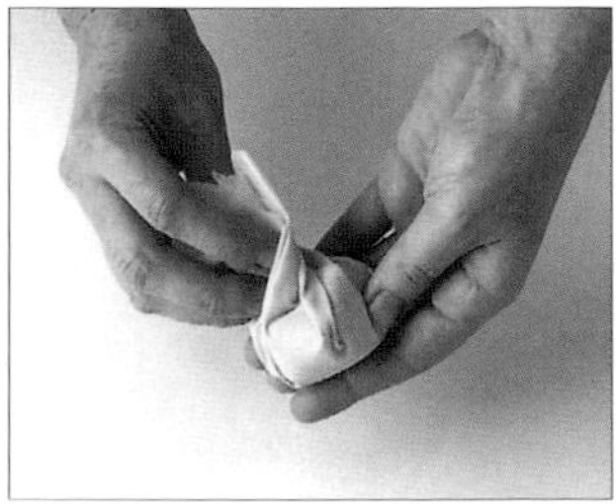

6 Top with ⅛ of the red pepper mixture. Bring the edges of the pastry together to form a purse shape and twist to seal. Place on a lightly greased baking sheet and cook for 25–30 minutes, until crisp and golden. Serve with green lettuce.

Asparagus Flan with Ricotta

A DELIGHTFUL flan filled with the delicate flavours of mixed cheeses and fresh asparagus.

INGREDIENTS

75g/3oz/6 tbsp butter
175g/6oz/1 1/2 cups plain flour
pinch of salt

For the filling

225g/8oz asparagus
2 eggs, beaten
225g/8oz/1 cup ricotta cheese
30ml/2 tbsp Greek yogurt
40g/1 1/2oz/1/2 cup grated Parmesan cheese
salt and freshly ground black pepper
Serves 4

1 Preheat the oven to 200°C/400°F/Gas 6. Rub the butter into the flour and salt. Stir in enough cold water to form a smooth dough and knead lightly on a floured surface.

2 Roll out the pastry and line a 23cm/9in flan ring. Press firmly into the tin and prick all over with a fork. Bake for about 10 minutes, until the pastry is firm but still pale. Remove from the oven and reduce the temperature to 180°C/350°F/Gas 4.

3 Trim the asparagus if necessary. Cut 5cm/2in from the tops and chop the remaining stalks into 2.5cm/1in pieces.

4 Add the stalks to boiling water and then the asparagus tips. Simmer for 4–5 minutes. Drain.

5 Beat together the eggs, ricotta, yogurt and Parmesan. Season, stir in the asparagus stalks and pour into the pastry case. Place the tips on top. Bake for 35–40 minutes, until golden. Serve warm or cold.

Asparagus with Tarragon Hollandaise

THIS IS the perfect starter for an early summer dinner party, when the new season's asparagus is just in and at its best. Making hollandaise sauce in a blender or food processor is incredibly easy and virtually foolproof!

INGREDIENTS

500g/1 1/4 lb fresh asparagus

For the hollandaise sauce

2 egg yolks
15ml/1 tbsp lemon juice
115g/4oz/8 tbsp butter
10ml/2 tsp finely chopped fresh tarragon
salt and freshly ground black pepper
Serves 4

1 Prepare the asparagus, lay it in a steamer or in an asparagus kettle and place over a saucepan of rapidly boiling water. Cover and steam for 6–10 minutes, until tender (the cooking time will depend on the thickness of the asparagus stems).

2 To make the hollandaise sauce, place the egg yolks and lemon juice in a blender or food processor. Season with salt and pepper and process briefly. Melt the butter in a small pan until foaming and then, with the blender or food processor running, pour it on to the egg mixture in a slow and steady stream.

3 Stir in the tarragon by hand or process it (for a sauce speckled with green or a pale green sauce).

4 Arrange the asparagus on small plates, pour over some of the hollandaise sauce and sprinkle with pepper. Serve the remainder in a jug.

Broccoli, Chilli and Artichoke Pasta

CHILLI FLAKES ADD A FIERY TOUCH to this simple southern Italian dish.

INGREDIENTS

350g/12oz/3 cups dried gnocchi pasta
300g/11oz broccoli florets
90ml/6 tbsp olive oil
1 large garlic clove, crushed
2.5–5ml/½–1 tsp dried chilli flakes
185g/6½oz/1½ cups artichoke hearts in oil, drained
salt and freshly ground black pepper
15ml/1 tbsp chopped fresh flat leaf parsley, to garnish
grated Pecorino, for sprinkling (optional)

Serves 6

1 Cook the pasta in a large saucepan of boiling salted water according to the instructions on the packet until it is *al dente*. Add the broccoli for the last 3 minutes of cooking time. Drain, reserving a little of the cooking water.

2 Meanwhile, heat the olive oil in a large heavy-based saucepan and sauté the garlic and chilli flakes for 1 minute.

HEALTH BENEFITS

The heart, blood and immune system will all benefit from the combination of garlic, chilli and broccoli in this dish.

3 Add the pasta, broccoli and artichoke hearts and cook for 2 minutes until hot. Add a little of the reserved pasta water if the mixture seems a little dry. Season and sprinkle with the parsley and Pecorino, if using.

Rustic Buckwheat Pasta and Fontina Cheese Bake

CHARACTERISTIC OF THE mountain regions of northern Italy, this bake is a spicy combination of nutty-flavoured buckwheat pasta, vegetables and Fontina cheese.

INGREDIENTS

2 potatoes, cubed
225g/8oz/2 cups buckwheat pasta shapes, such as spirals
275g/10oz/2½ cups Savoy cabbage, shredded
45ml/3 tbsp olive oil, plus extra for greasing
1 onion, chopped
2 leeks, sliced
2 garlic cloves, chopped
175g/6oz/2½ cups brown cap mushrooms, sliced
5ml/1 tsp caraway seeds
5ml/1 tsp cumin seeds
150ml/¼ pint/⅔ cup vegetable stock
150g/5oz/1¼ cups Fontina cheese, diced
25g/1oz/¼ cup walnuts, roughly chopped
salt and freshly ground black pepper

Serves 6

1 Preheat the oven to 200°C/400°F/Gas 6 and oil a deep baking dish. Cook the potatoes in boiling salted water for 8–10 minutes until tender, then drain and set aside.

2 Meanwhile, cook the pasta in boiling, salted water until it is only just cooked and is still very *al dente*. Add the cabbage in the last minute of cooking time. Drain, then rinse under cold running water.

3 Heat the olive oil in a large heavy-based saucepan and fry the onion and leeks for 5 minutes until softened. Add the garlic and mushrooms and cook for a further 3 minutes until tender, stirring occasionally. Stir in the spices and cook for 1 minute, stirring.

4 Add the cooked potatoes, pasta and cabbage and stir to combine, then season well. Spoon the mixture into the baking dish. Pour the stock over the vegetables, then sprinkle with the cheese and walnuts. Bake for 15 minutes or until the cheese is melted and bubbling.

HEALTH BENEFITS

Numerous studies have shown that, if eaten once a week, cabbage can reduce the risk of cancer and heart disease. Ideally, it should be raw or lightly cooked. It is also known to cleanse the blood and to treat kidney and bladder disorders.

Coriander Ravioli with Pumpkin Filling

A STUNNING pasta that combines fresh herbs with a superb creamy pumpkin and roast garlic filling.

INGREDIENTS

200g/7oz/scant 1 cup strong unbleached white flour
2 eggs
pinch of salt
45ml/3 tbsp chopped fresh coriander
sprigs of fresh coriander, to garnish

For the filling

4 garlic cloves in their skins
450g/1lb pumpkin, peeled and seeds removed
115g/4oz/½ cup ricotta cheese
4 halves sun-dried tomatoes in olive oil, drained and finely chopped (reserve 30ml/2 tbsp of the oil)
freshly ground black pepper

Serves 4–6

1 Place the flour, eggs, salt and coriander into a food processor. Pulse until combined.

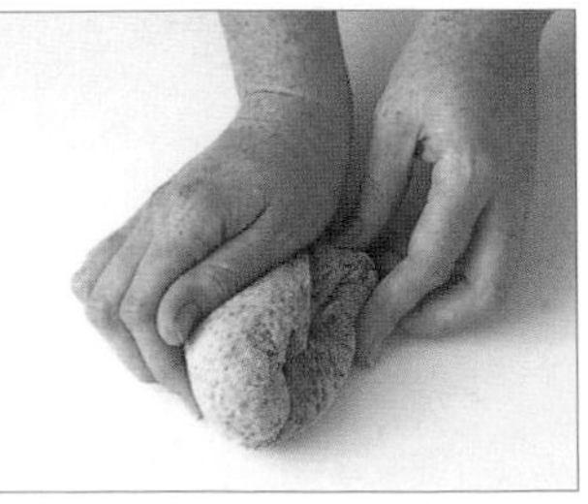

2 Knead the dough on a lightly floured board until smooth.

3 Wrap the dough in clear film and leave to rest in the fridge for 20–30 minutes.

4 Preheat the oven to 200°C/400°F/Gas 6.

5 Place the garlic cloves on a baking sheet and bake for 10 minutes, until softened. Steam the pumpkin for 5–8 minutes, until tender, and drain.

6 Peel the garlic cloves and mash into the pumpkin together with the ricotta and drained sun-dried tomatoes. Season with plenty of freshly ground black pepper.

7 Divide the pasta into 4 pieces and flatten slightly. Using a pasta machine, on its thinnest setting, roll out each piece. By hand, lightly flour the work surface and a rolling pin. Pat the dough into a disc and roll out into a sheet about 3mm/⅛in thick. Leave the sheets of pasta on a clean dish towel until slightly dried.

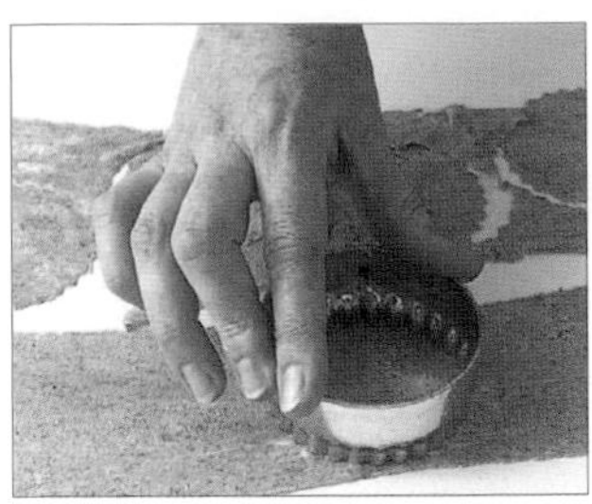

8 Using a 7.5cm/3in crinkle-edged round cutter, stamp out 36 rounds of pasta.

9 Top 18 of the rounds with a teaspoonful of the pumpkin mixture, brush the edges with water and place another round of pasta on top. Press firmly around the edges to seal. Bring a large pan of water to the boil, add the ravioli and cook for 3–4 minutes. Drain well and toss into the reserved tomato oil. Add pepper and serve garnished with coriander sprigs.

VARIATION

For an alternative filling substitute the ricotta cheese with 25g/1oz/⅓ cup grated Parmesan cheese mixed with 115g/4oz/½ cup cottage cheese. Serve with shavings of Parmesan.

Rice and Beans with Avocado Salsa

MEXICAN-STYLE RICE AND BEANS make a delicious supper dish. Spoon on to tortillas and serve with a tangy salsa. Alternatively, serve as an accompaniment to a spicy stew.

INGREDIENTS

40g/1½oz/¼ cup dried or 75g/3oz/½ cup canned kidney beans, rinsed and drained
4 tomatoes, halved and seeded
2 garlic cloves, chopped
1 onion, sliced
45ml/3 tbsp olive oil
225g/8oz/generous 1 cup long grain brown rice, rinsed
600ml/1 pint/2½ cups vegetable stock
2 carrots, diced
75g/3oz/¾ cup green beans
salt and freshly ground black pepper
4 wheat tortillas and soured cream, to serve

For the avocado salsa
1 avocado
juice of 1 lime
1 small red onion, diced
1 small red chilli, seeded and chopped
15ml/1 tbsp chopped fresh coriander

Serves 4

1 If using dried kidney beans, place in a bowl, cover with cold water and leave to soak overnight, then drain and rinse well. Place in a saucepan with enough water to cover and bring to the boil. Boil rapidly for 10 minutes, then reduce the heat and simmer for 40–50 minutes until tender. Drain and set aside.

2 Heat the grill to high. Place the tomatoes, garlic and onion on a baking tray. Pour over 15ml/1 tbsp of the olive oil and toss to coat. Grill for 10 minutes or until the tomatoes and onions are softened, turning once. Set aside to cool.

3 Heat the remaining oil in a saucepan, add the rice and cook for 2 minutes, stirring, until light golden.

HEALTH BENEFITS

Brown rice contains a good, healthy combination of valuable nutrients, including vitamin E, minerals and fibre.

4 Purée the cooled tomatoes and onion in a food processor or blender, then add the mixture to the rice and cook for a further 2 minutes, stirring frequently. Pour in the stock, then cover and cook gently, for 20 minutes, stirring occasionally.

5 Reserve 30ml/2 tbsp of the kidney beans for the salsa. Add the rest to the stock mixture with the carrots and green beans and cook for 10 minutes until the vegetables are tender. Season well. Remove the pan from the heat and leave to stand, covered, for 15 minutes.

6 To make the avocado salsa, cut the avocado in half and remove the stone. Peel and dice the flesh, then toss in the lime juice. Add the onion, chilli, coriander and reserved kidney beans, then season with salt.

7 To serve, spoon the hot rice and beans on to warm tortillas. Hand round the salsa and soured cream.

Teriyaki Soba Noodles with Tofu and Asparagus

YOU CAN, OF COURSE, BUY ready-made teriyaki sauce, but it is easy to prepare at home using ingredients that are now readily available in supermarkets and Asian shops. Japanese soba noodles are made from buckwheat flour, which gives them a unique texture and colour.

INGREDIENTS

350g/12oz soba noodles
30ml/2 tbsp toasted sesame oil
200g/7oz/½ bunch asparagus tips
30ml/2 tbsp groundnut or vegetable oil
225g/8oz block of tofu
2 spring onions, cut diagonally
1 carrot, cut into matchsticks
2.5ml/½ tsp chilli flakes
15ml/1 tbsp sesame seeds
salt and freshly ground black pepper

For the teriyaki sauce
60ml/4 tbsp dark soy sauce
60ml/4 tbsp Japanese sake or dry sherry
60ml/4 tbsp mirin
5ml/1 tsp caster sugar
Serves 4

1 Cook the noodles according to the instructions on the packet, then drain and rinse under cold running water. Set aside.

2 Heat the sesame oil in a griddle pan or in a baking tray placed under the grill until very hot. Turn down the heat to medium, then cook the asparagus for 8–10 minutes, turning frequently, until tender and browned. Set aside.

HEALTH BENEFITS

Sesame seeds are an excellent source of the antioxidant vitamin E, which acts as a natural preservative, preventing oxidation and strengthening the heart and nerves.

3 Meanwhile, heat the groundnut or vegetable oil in a wok or large frying pan until very hot. Add the tofu and fry for 8–10 minutes until golden, turning it occasionally to crisp all sides. Carefully remove from the wok or pan and leave to drain on kitchen paper. Cut the tofu into 1cm/½in slices.

VARIATION

Use dried egg or rice noodles instead of soba noodles, if you wish.

4 To prepare the teriyaki sauce, mix the soy sauce, sake or dry sherry, mirin and sugar together, then heat the mixture in the wok or frying pan.

5 Toss in the noodles and stir to coat them in the sauce. Heat through for 1–2 minutes, then spoon into warmed individual serving bowls with the tofu and asparagus. Scatter the spring onions and carrot on top and sprinkle with the chilli flakes and sesame seeds. Serve immediately.

Lemon, Thyme and Aduki Bean Stuffed Mushrooms with Pine Nut Tarator

PORTOBELLO MUSHROOMS have a rich flavour and a meaty texture that go well with this fragrant herb and lemon stuffing. The garlicky pine nut accompaniment is a traditional Middle Eastern dish with a smooth, creamy consistency similar to that of hummus. Green leafy vegetables, such as spinach or Swiss chard, and roast or baked potatoes are ideal side dishes.

INGREDIENTS

200g/7oz/1 cup dried or 400g/14oz/ 2 cups drained, canned aduki beans
45ml/3 tbsp olive oil, plus extra for brushing
1 onion, finely chopped
2 garlic cloves, crushed
30ml/2 tbsp fresh chopped or 5ml/1 tsp dried thyme
8 large field mushrooms, such as portobello mushrooms, stalks finely chopped
50g/2oz/1 cup fresh wholemeal breadcrumbs
juice of 1 lemon
185g/6½oz/¾ cup goat's cheese, crumbled
salt and freshly ground black pepper

For the pine nut tarator

50g/2oz/½ cup pine nuts toasted
50g/2oz/1 cup cubed white bread
2 garlic cloves, chopped
200ml/7fl oz/1 cup semi-skimmed milk
45ml/3 tbsp olive oil
15ml/1 tbsp chopped fresh parsley, to garnish (optional)

Serves 4–6

1 If using dried beans, soak them overnight, then drain and rinse well. Place in a saucepan, add enough water to cover and bring to the boil. Boil rapidly for 10 minutes, then reduce the heat, cook for 30 minutes until tender, then drain. If using canned beans, rinse, drain well, then set aside.

2 Preheat the oven to 200°C/400°F/Gas 6. Heat the oil in a large heavy-based frying pan, add the onion and garlic and sauté for 5 minutes until softened. Add the thyme and the mushroom stalks and cook for a further 3 minutes, stirring occasionally, until tender.

3 Stir in the beans, breadcrumbs and lemon juice, season well, then cook for 2 minutes until heated through. Mash two-thirds of the beans with a fork or potato masher, leaving the remaining beans whole.

4 Brush a baking dish and the base and sides of the mushrooms with oil, then top each one with a spoonful of the bean mixture. Place the mushrooms in the dish, cover with foil and bake for 20 minutes. Remove the foil. Top each mushroom with some of the goat's cheese and bake for a further 15 minutes, or until the cheese is melted and bubbly and the mushrooms are tender.

5 To make the pine nut tarator, place all the ingredients in a food processor or blender and blend until smooth and creamy. Add more milk if the mixture appears too thick. Sprinkle with parsley, if using, and serve with the stuffed mushrooms.

HEALTH BENEFITS

Aduki beans are high in protein and fibre and low in fat. They also contain some B vitamins and iron.

Spiced Couscous with Halloumi and Courgette Ribbons

A STAPLE FOOD IN North Africa, couscous is commonly served with meat or vegetable stews. Here, it forms the foundation of the dish and is topped with griddled sliced courgettes and halloumi, a mild cheese from Cyprus.

INGREDIENTS

275g/10oz/1⅔ cup couscous
1 bay leaf
1 cinnamon stick
30ml/2 tbsp olive oil, plus extra for brushing
1 large red onion, chopped
2 garlic cloves, chopped
5ml/1 tsp mild chilli powder
5ml/1 tsp ground cumin
5ml/1 tsp ground coriander
5 cardamom pods, bruised
50g/2oz/¼ cup whole almonds, toasted
1 peach, stoned and diced
25g/1oz/2 tbsp butter
3 courgettes, sliced lengthways into ribbons
225g/8oz halloumi cheese, sliced
salt and freshly ground black pepper
chopped fresh flat leaf parsley, to garnish

Serves 4

1 Place the couscous in a bowl and pour over 500ml/17fl oz/2¼ cups boiling water. Add the bay leaf and cinnamon stick and season with salt. Leave the couscous for 10 minutes until the water is absorbed, then fluff up the grains with a fork.

HEALTH BENEFITS

Almonds have long been regarded as having special protective properties. Although they have a high fat content, the fat is monounsaturated and can help lower cholesterol levels. Best eaten whole, almonds are also a useful source of calcium and vitamin E.

2 Meanwhile, heat the oil in a large heavy-based saucepan, add the onion and garlic and sauté for about 7 minutes until the onion has softened, stirring occasionally.

3 Stir in the chilli powder, cumin, coriander and cardamom pods, and cook for a further 3 minutes to allow the flavours to mingle. Add the couscous, almonds, diced peach and butter, and heat through for 2 minutes.

4 Brush a griddle pan with olive oil and heat until very hot. Turn down the heat to medium, then place the courgettes on the griddle and cook for 5 minutes until tender and slightly charred. Turn the courgettes over, add the halloumi and continue cooking for a further 5 minutes, turning the halloumi halfway through.

5 Remove the cinnamon stick, bay leaf and cardamom pods from the couscous, then arrange it on a plate and season well. Top with the halloumi and courgettes. Sprinkle the parsley over the top and serve.

COOK'S TIP

If you don't own a griddle pan, cook the courgettes under a hot grill, which will give them a similar smoky flavour.

Mushroom and Okra Curry

THIS SIMPLE but delicious curry with its fresh gingery mango relish is best served with plain basmati rice.

INGREDIENTS

4 garlic cloves, roughly chopped
2.5cm/1in piece of fresh root ginger, peeled and roughly chopped
1–2 fresh red chillies, seeded and chopped
175ml/6fl oz/¾ cup cold water
15ml/1 tbsp sunflower oil
5ml/1 tsp coriander seeds
5ml/1 tsp cumin seeds
5ml/1 tsp ground cumin
2 green cardamom pods, seeds removed and ground
pinch of ground turmeric
400g/14oz can chopped tomatoes
450g/1lb/6 cups mushrooms, quartered if large
225g/8oz okra, trimmed and cut into 1cm/½in slices
30ml/2 tbsp chopped fresh coriander

For the mango relish

1 large ripe mango, about 500g/1¼lb in weight
1 small garlic clove, crushed
1 onion, finely chopped
10ml/2 tsp grated fresh root ginger
1 fresh red chilli, seeded and finely chopped
pinch of salt and sugar

Serves 4

1 To make the relish, peel the mango and cut off the flesh from the stone.

COOK'S TIP

When buying okra, choose firm, brightly coloured pods that are less than 10cm/4in long.

2 In a bowl, mash the mango flesh with a fork or process in a food processor or blender. Mix in the rest of the relish ingredients. Cover and set to one side.

3 Place the garlic, ginger, chillies and 45ml/3 tbsp of the water into a blender or food processor and process until smooth.

4 Heat the sunflower oil in a large saucepan. Add the whole coriander and cumin seeds and allow them to sizzle for a few seconds. Add the ground cumin, ground cardamom and ground turmeric and cook for about 1 minute more.

5 Add the garlic paste, tomatoes and remaining water. Stir to mix well, then add the mushrooms and okra. Stir again, then bring to the boil. Reduce the heat, cover and simmer for 5 minutes.

6 Remove the cover, turn up the heat slightly and cook for another 5–10 minutes, until the okra is tender but not too soft.

7 Stir in the fresh coriander and serve with the mango relish and fragrant basmati rice.

Thai Vegetable Curry with Lemon Grass Rice

FRAGRANT JASMINE RICE, subtly flavoured with lemon grass and cardamom, is the perfect accompaniment to this richly spiced vegetable curry. Don't be put off by the long list of ingredients, this curry is very simple to make.

INGREDIENTS

10ml/2 tsp vegetable oil
400ml/14fl oz/1⅔ cups coconut milk
300ml/½ pint/1¼ cups vegetable stock
225g/8oz new potatoes, halved or quartered, if large
130g/4½oz baby corn cobs
5ml/1 tsp golden caster sugar
185g/6½oz broccoli florets
1 red pepper, seeded and sliced lengthways
115g/4oz spinach, tough stalks removed and shredded
30ml/2 tbsp chopped fresh coriander
salt and freshly ground black pepper

For the spice paste

1 red chilli, seeded and chopped
3 green chillies, seeded and chopped
1 lemon grass stalk, outer leaves removed and inside finely chopped
2 shallots, chopped
finely grated rind of 1 lime
2 garlic cloves, chopped
5ml/1 tsp ground coriander
2.5ml/½ tsp ground cumin
1cm/½in fresh galangal, finely chopped or 2.5ml/½ tsp dried (optional)
30ml/2 tbsp chopped fresh coriander
15ml/1 tbsp chopped fresh coriander roots and stems (optional)

For the rice

225g/8oz/generous 1 cup jasmine rice, rinsed
1 lemon grass stalk, outer leaves removed and cut into 3 pieces
6 cardamom pods, bruised

Serves 4

1 Make the spice paste. Place all the ingredients in a food processor or blender and blend to a coarse paste.

2 Heat the oil in a large heavy-based saucepan and fry the spice paste for 1–2 minutes, stirring constantly. Add the coconut milk and stock, and bring to the boil.

3 Reduce the heat, add the potatoes and simmer for 15 minutes. Add the baby corn and seasoning, then cook for 2 minutes. Stir in the sugar, broccoli and red pepper, and cook for 2 minutes more until the vegetables are tender. Stir in the shredded spinach and half the fresh coriander. Cook for 2 minutes.

HEALTH BENEFITS

Broccoli provides valuable amounts of calcium, vitamin C, folic acid, zinc and iron. The vitamin and mineral content of this dish is given a further boost by the addition of all the other vegetables.

4 Meanwhile, prepare the rice. Tip the rinsed rice into a saucepan and add the lemon grass and cardamom pods. Pour over 475ml/16fl oz/2 cups water.

5 Bring to the boil, then reduce the heat, cover, and cook for 10–15 minutes until the water is absorbed and the rice is tender and slightly sticky. Season with salt, leave to stand for 10 minutes, then fluff up the rice with a fork.

6 Remove the spices and serve the rice with the curry, sprinkled with the remaining fresh coriander.

Aubergine Curry

A SIMPLE and delicious way of cooking aubergines, which retains their full flavour.

INGREDIENTS

2 large aubergines, about 450g/1lb each
45ml/3 tbsp oil
2.5ml/½ tsp black mustard seeds
1 bunch spring onions, finely chopped
115g/4oz/1½ cups button mushrooms
2 garlic cloves, crushed
1 fresh red chilli, finely chopped
2.5ml/½ tsp chilli powder
1 tsp ground cumin
1 tsp ground coriander
1.5ml/¼ tsp ground turmeric
5ml/1 tsp salt
400g/14oz can chopped tomatoes
15ml/1 tbsp chopped fresh coriander
sprigs of fresh coriander, to garnish

Serves 4

1 Preheat the oven to 200°C/400°F/Gas 6. Brush both of the aubergines with 15ml/1 tbsp of the oil and prick with a fork. Bake in the oven for 30–35 minutes, until the aubergines are soft.

2 Meanwhile, heat the remaining oil in a saucepan and fry the mustard seeds for 2 minutes, until they begin to splutter.

3 Add the spring onions, halved mushrooms, garlic and chilli and fry for 5 minutes. Stir in the chilli powder, cumin, coriander, turmeric and salt and fry for 3–4 minutes. Add the chopped tomatoes and simmer for a further 5 minutes.

4 Cut each of the aubergines in half lengthways and scoop out the soft flesh into a bowl. Using a fork, mash the flesh briefly.

5 Add the mashed aubergine and fresh coriander to the saucepan. Bring to the boil and simmer for 5 minutes or until the sauce thickens. Serve garnished with coriander sprigs.

COOK'S TIP

If you want to omit some of the oil, wrap the aubergines in foil and bake in the oven for 1 hour.

Vegetable Korma

THE BLENDING of spices produces a subtle, aromatic curry.

INGREDIENTS

50g/2oz/4 tbsp butter
2 onions, sliced
2 garlic cloves, crushed
2.5cm/1in piece of fresh root ginger, grated
5ml/1 tsp ground cumin
15ml/1 tbsp ground coriander
6 cardamom pods
5cm/2in cinnamon stick
5ml/1 tsp ground turmeric
1 fresh red chilli, seeded and finely chopped
1 potato, peeled and cut into 2.5cm/1in cubes
1 small aubergine, chopped
115g/4oz/2½ cup mushrooms, sliced
115g/4oz French beans, cut into 2.5cm/1 in lengths
60ml/4 tbsp natural yogurt
150ml/¼ pint/⅔ cup double cream
5ml/1 tsp garam masala
salt and freshly ground black pepper
poppadums, to serve
sprigs of fresh coriander, to garnish

Serves 4

1 Melt the butter in a heavy based saucepan. Add the onions and cook for 5 minutes, until soft. Add the garlic and ginger and cook for 2 minutes, then stir in the cumin, coriander, cardamoms, cinnamon stick, turmeric and chilli. Cook, stirring over a gentle heat, for 30 seconds.

2 Add the potato, aubergine and mushrooms and about 175ml/6fl oz/¾ cup water. Cover the pan, bring to the boil, then lower the heat and simmer for 15 minutes. Add the beans and cook, uncovered, for 5 minutes.

VARIATION

Any combination of vegetables can be used for this korma, including carrots, cauliflower, broccoli, peas and chick-peas.

3 With a slotted spoon, remove the vegetables to a warmed serving dish and keep hot. Allow the cooking liquid to bubble up until it reduces a little. Season with salt and pepper, then stir in the yogurt, cream and garam masala. Pour the sauce over the vegetables and garnish with coriander. Serve with poppadums.

TARTS, PIES and PIZZAS

This indulgent selection of tarts, pies and pizzas are suitable for everyday cooking with ideas for warm and hearty winter meals to light and nourishing summer menu choices.

Wild Mushroom and Broccoli Flan

POTATO AND cheese pastry combines well with a mushroom and broccoli filling to ensure this savoury flan is a family favourite. Lightly cooked, sliced leeks can be used instead of broccoli florets, if preferred.

INGREDIENTS

115g/4oz/1 cup small broccoli florets
15ml/1 tbsp olive oil
3 shallots, finely chopped
175g/6oz/2 1/2 cups mixed wild mushrooms, such as ceps, shiitake mushrooms and oyster mushrooms, sliced or chopped
2 eggs
200ml/7fl oz/scant 1 cup semi-skimmed milk
15ml/1 tbsp chopped fresh tarragon
50g/2oz/1/2 cup grated Cheddar cheese
salt and ground black pepper
fresh herb sprigs, to garnish

For the pastry

75g/3oz/3/4 cup brown rice flour
75g/3oz/3/4 cup gluten-free cornmeal
pinch of salt
75g/3oz/6 tbsp soft margarine
115g/4oz cold mashed potatoes
50g/2oz/1/2 cup grated Cheddar cheese

Serves 8

1 First make the pastry. Place the rice flour, cornmeal and salt in a mixing bowl and stir to mix. Lightly rub in the margarine with your fingertips until the mixture resembles breadcrumbs.

2 Stir in the mashed potatoes and cheese and mix to form a smooth, soft dough. Wrap in a plastic bag and chill for 30 minutes.

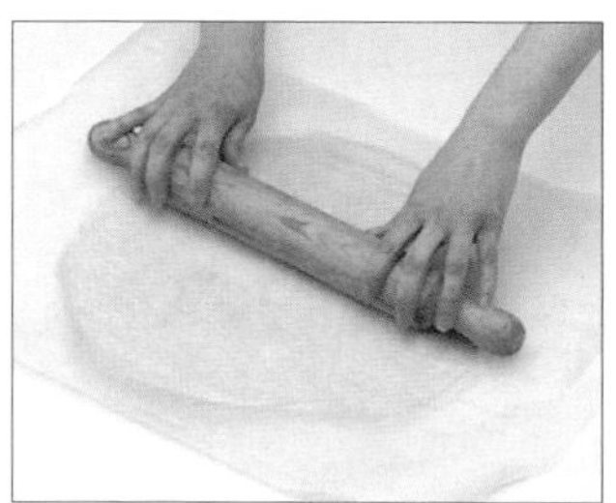

3 Roll out the pastry between two sheets of greaseproof paper and use to line a 24cm/9 1/2in loose-bottomed flan tin, gently pressing the pastry into the sides of the flan tin. Carefully trim around the top edge of the pastry case with a sharp knife. Cover the pastry, and chill while making the filling.

4 Preheat the oven to 200°C/400°F/ Gas 6. Cook the broccoli florets in a saucepan of lightly salted, boiling water for 3 minutes. Drain thoroughly and set aside.

5 Heat the oil in a frying pan, add the shallots and cook gently for 3 minutes, stirring. Add the mushrooms and cook gently for 2 minutes.

6 Spoon into the pastry case and top with broccoli. Beat the eggs, milk, tarragon and seasoning together and pour over the vegetables. Top with cheese. Bake for 10 minutes, reduce the oven temperature to 180°C/350°F/ Gas 4 and bake for about 30 minutes until lightly set. Serve warm or cold, garnished with fresh herbs.

Filo Vegetable Pie

THIS STUNNING pie makes a never-to-be-forgotten main course.

INGREDIENTS

225g/8oz leeks
165g/5½oz/11 tbsp butter
225g/8oz/1¼ cups carrots, cubed
225g/8oz/3 cups mushrooms, sliced
225g/8oz Brussels sprouts, quartered
2 garlic cloves, crushed
115g/4oz/½ cup cream cheese
115g/4oz Roquefort or Stilton cheese
150ml/¼ pint/⅔ cup double cream
2 eggs, beaten
225g/8oz cooking apples
225g/8oz/1 cup cashew nuts or pine nuts, toasted
350g/12oz frozen filo pastry, defrosted
salt and freshly ground black pepper

Serves 6–8

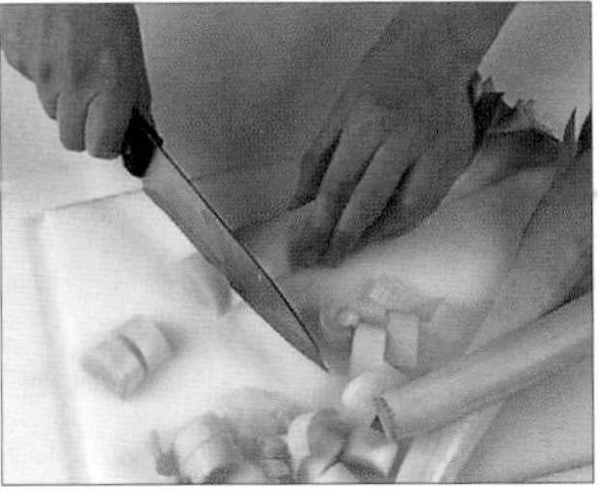

1 Preheat the oven to 180°C/350°F/ Gas 4. Cut the leeks in half through the root and wash them to remove any soil, separating the layers slightly to check they are clean. Slice into 1cm/½in pieces, drain and dry on kitchen paper.

2 Heat 40g/1½oz/3 tbsp of the butter in a large pan and cook the leeks and carrots over medium heat for 5 minutes. Add the mushrooms, sprouts and garlic and cook for another 2 minutes. Turn the vegetables into a bowl and let them cool.

3 Whisk the cream cheese and blue cheese, cream and eggs in a bowl. Season with salt and pepper. Pour over the vegetables.

4 Peel and core the apples and cut into 1cm/½in cubes. Add them to the vegetables with the toasted cashew or pine nuts.

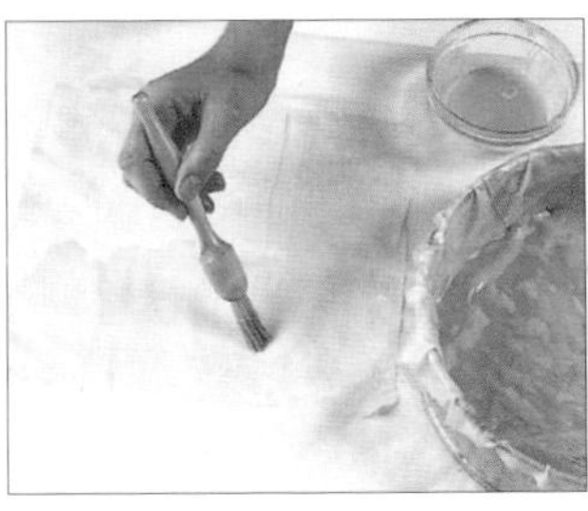

5 Melt the remaining butter in a pan. Brush the inside of a 23cm/ 9in loose-based springform cake tin with melted butter. Brush two-thirds of the filo pastry sheets with butter, one at a time, and use them to line the base and sides of the tin, overlapping the layers so that there are no gaps.

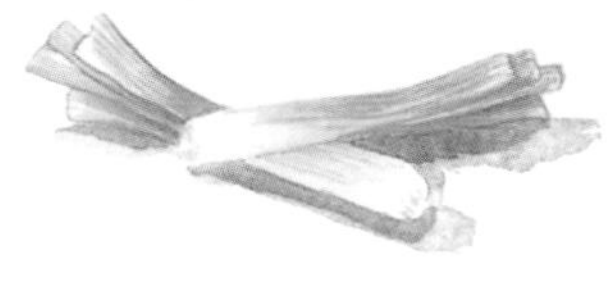

6 Spoon in the vegetable mixture and fold the excess filo pastry over towards the centre of the pie to cover the filling.

7 Brush the remaining filo sheets with butter and cut them into 2.5cm/1in strips. Cover the surface of the pie with the strips, arranging them decoratively in a rough mound.

8 Bake for 35–40 minutes, until golden brown and crispy all over. Allow to stand for 5 minutes to cool, then carefully remove the cake tin and transfer the pie to a serving plate.

COOK'S TIP

For a firmer crust on the pastry, brush the top of the pie with beaten egg just before baking.

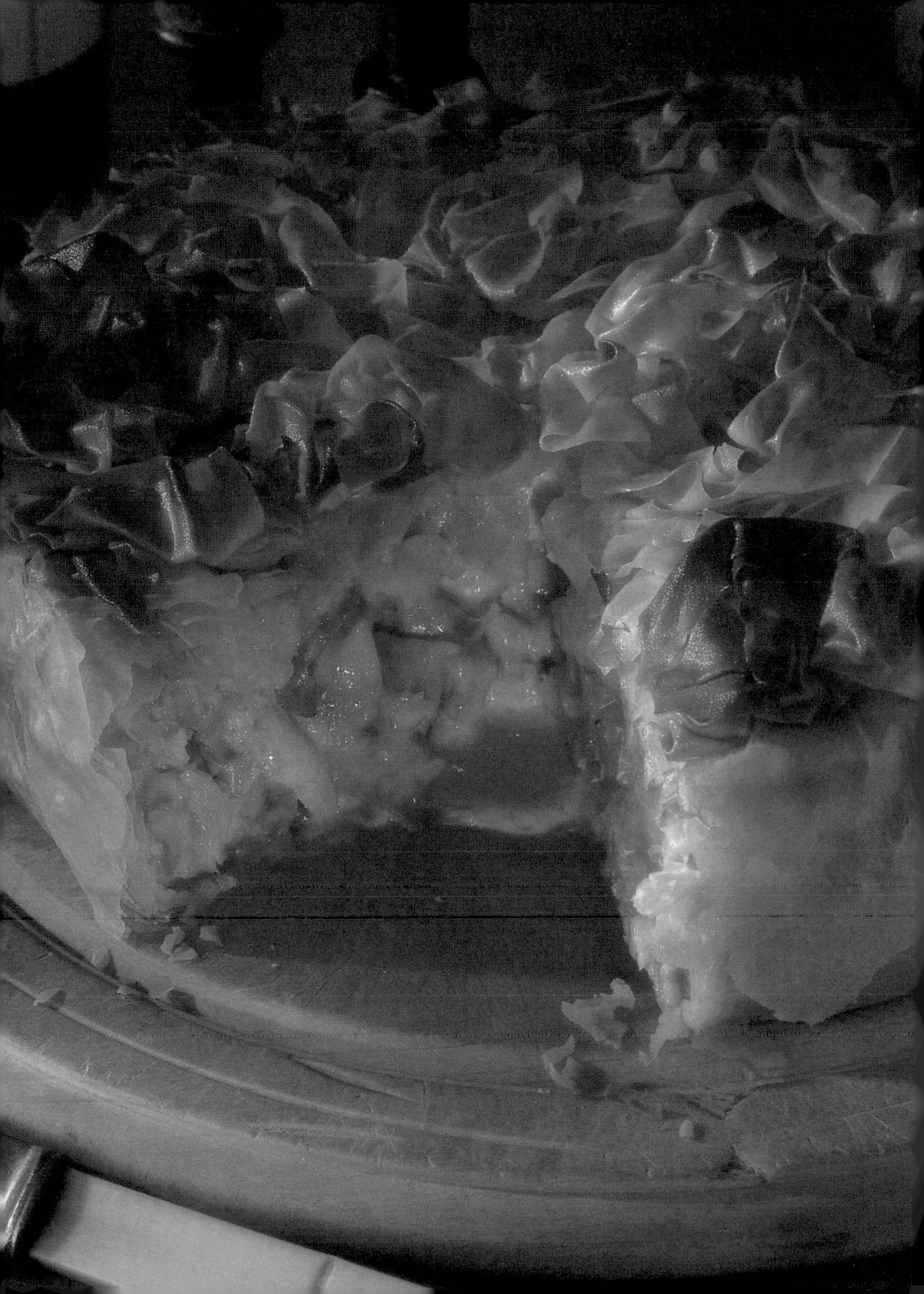

Sweetcorn and Bean Tamale Pie

INGREDIENTS

2 ears of fresh sweetcorn
30ml/2 tbsp vegetable oil
1 onion, chopped
2 garlic cloves, crushed
1 red bell pepper, seeded and chopped
2 green chillies, seeded and chopped
10ml/2 tsp ground cumin
450g/1lb ripe tomatoes, peeled, seeded and chopped
15ml/1 tbsp tomato paste
400g/14oz can red kidney beans, drained and rinsed
15ml/1 tbsp chopped fresh oregano
oregano leaves, to garnish

For the topping

115g/4oz/1 cup polenta
15ml/1 tbsp flour
pinch of salt
10ml/2 tsp baking powder
1 egg, lightly beaten
120ml/4fl oz/½ cup milk
15ml/1 tbsp butter, melted
50g/2oz/½ cup smoked Cheddar cheese, grated

Serves 4

1 Preheat the oven to 220°C/425°F/Gas 7. Remove the outer husks and silky threads from the ears of corn, then parboil in boiling, but not salted, water for 8 minutes. Drain and leave until cool enough to handle, then run a sharp knife down the ears of corn to remove the kernels.

2 Heat the oil in a large pan and fry the onion, garlic and pepper for 5 minutes, until softened. Add the chillies and cumin and fry for 1 minute.

3 Stir in the tomatoes, tomato paste, beans, sweetcorn and oregano. Season. Bring to a boil, then simmer, uncovered, for 10 minutes.

4 Meanwhile, make the topping. Mix together the polenta, flour, salt, baking powder, egg, milk and butter in a bowl to form a smooth, thick batter.

5 Transfer the sweetcorn mixture to an ovenproof dish, spoon the polenta mixture over the top and spread evenly. Bake for 30 minutes. Remove from the oven, sprinkle over the cheese, then return to the oven for a further 5–10 minutes, until golden.

Onion and Thyme Tart

INGREDIENTS

30ml/2 tbsp butter or olive oil
2 onions, thinly sliced
2.5ml/½ tsp fresh or dried thyme
1 egg
120ml/4fl oz/½ cup sour cream or plain yogurt
10ml/2 tsp poppy seeds
1.5ml/¼ tsp ground mace or nutmeg
salt and freshly ground black pepper

For the base
115g/4oz/1 cup flour
11.5ml/2 tsp baking powder
2.5ml/½ tsp salt
45ml/3 tbsp cold butter
90ml/6 tbsp milk

Serves 6

1 Heat the butter or oil in a medium-size frying pan. Add the onions and cook over low heat for 10–12 minutes, until soft and golden. Season with thyme, salt and pepper. Remove from the heat and let cool. Preheat the oven to 220°C/425°F/Gas 7.

2 For the base, sift the flour, baking powder, and salt into a bowl. Using a pastry blender or two knives, cut the butter into the dry ingredients until the mixture resembles bread crumbs. Add the milk and stir in lightly with a wooden spoon to make a dough.

3 Turn out the dough on to a floured surface and knead lightly.

4 Pat out the dough into a 20cm/8in round. Transfer to a deep 20cm/8in baking pan. Press the dough into an even layer then cover with the onions.

5 Beat together the egg and sour cream or yogurt. Spread evenly over the onions. Sprinkle with the poppy seeds and mace or nutmeg. Bake for about 35–30 minutes until the egg topping is puffed and golden.

6 Leave the tart to cool in the pan for 10 minutes. Slip a knife between the tart and the pan to loosen, then unmould on to a plate. Cut into wedges and serve warm.

Sweetcorn and Cheese Pasties

THESE TASTY pasties are really simple to make and extremely moreish. Why not make double – they'll go like hot cakes.

INGREDIENTS

250g/9oz sweetcorn
115g/4oz feta cheese
1 egg, beaten
30ml/2 tbsp whipping cream
15g/½oz freshly grated Parmesan cheese
3 spring onions, chopped
8–10 small sheets filo pastry
115g/4oz/8 tbsp butter, melted
freshly ground black pepper

Makes 16–20

1 Preheat the oven to 190°C/375°F/ Gas 5. Butter two bun tins.

2 If using fresh sweetcorn, strip the kernels from the cob using a large sharp knife, cutting downwards from top to bottom of the cob. Simmer in a little salted water for 3–5 minutes, until tender. For canned sweetcorn, drain and rinse well under cold running water then drain again.

3 Crumble the feta cheese into a bowl and stir in the sweetcorn. Add the egg, cream, Parmesan cheese, spring onions and plenty of freshly ground black pepper, and stir until well combined.

4 Take one sheet of pastry and cut it in half to make a square. (Keep the remaining pastry covered with a damp cloth to prevent it from drying out.) Brush with melted butter and then fold into four to make a smaller square (about 7.5cm/3in).

5 Place a heaped teaspoon of mixture in the centre of each pastry square and then squeeze the pastry around the filling to make a 'money bag' casing.

6 Continue making pasties until all the filling is used up. Brush the outside of each 'bag' with any remaining butter and then bake for about 15 minutes, or until golden brown. Serve hot.

Cheese and Spinach Flan

THIS FLAN freezes well and can be reheated. It makes an excellent addition to a festive buffet party.

INGREDIENTS

115g/4oz/8 tbsp butter
225g/8oz/2 cups plain flour
2.5ml/½ tsp English mustard powder
2.5ml/½ tsp paprika
large pinch of salt
115g/4oz/1 cup Cheddar cheese, grated
1 egg, beaten, to glaze

For the filling

450g/1lb frozen spinach
1 onion, chopped
pinch of grated nutmeg
225g/8oz/1 cup cottage cheese
2 large eggs, beaten
50g/2oz/⅔ cup grated Parmesan cheese
150ml/¼ pint/⅔ cup single cream
salt and freshly ground black pepper

Serves 8

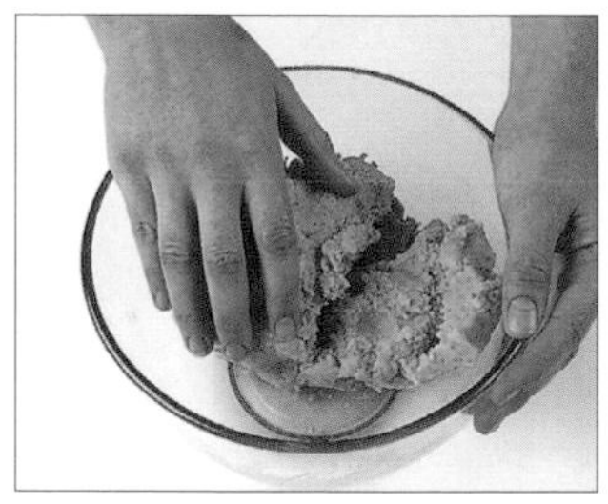

1 Rub the butter into the flour until it resembles fine breadcrumbs. Stir in the mustard powder, paprika, salt and cheese. Bind to a dough with 45–60ml/3–4 tbsp cold water. Knead until smooth, wrap and chill in the fridge for 30 minutes.

2 Put the spinach and onion in a pan, cover and cook slowly. Season with salt, pepper and nutmeg. Turn the spinach into a bowl and cool slightly. Add the remaining filling ingredients.

3 Roll out two-thirds of the pastry on a lightly floured surface and use it to line a 23cm/9in loose-based flan tin. Press it well into the edges, removing excess pastry. Spoon the filling into the flan case.

4 Preheat the oven to 200°C/400°F/Gas 6. Put a baking tray in the oven to preheat.

5 Roll out the remaining pastry and cut it with a lattice pastry cutter. With the help of a rolling pin, lay it over the flan. Brush the joins with egg glaze. Press the edges together and trim off the excess pastry. Brush the pastry lattice with egg glaze and bake on the hot baking tray for 35–40 minutes, or until golden brown. Serve hot or cold.

Caramelized Onion Tart

SERVED WARM WITH A MIXED leaf salad, this classic and elegant French tart makes a perfect light summer lunch.

INGREDIENTS

15ml/1 tbsp unsalted butter
15ml/1 tbsp olive oil
500g/1¼lb onions, sliced
large pinch of ground nutmeg
5ml/1 tsp soft dark brown sugar
2 eggs
150ml/¼ pint/⅔ cup single cream
50g/2oz/½ cup Gruyère cheese, grated
salt and freshly ground black pepper

For the pastry
75g/3oz/⅔ cup unbleached plain flour
75g/3oz/⅔ cup wholemeal flour
75g/3oz/6 tbsp unsalted butter
1 egg yolk

Serves 6

1 To make the pastry, rub together the plain and wholemeal flours and butter until the mixture resembles fine breadcrumbs. Mix in the egg yolk and enough cold water to form a dough.

2 Turn out the dough on to a lightly floured work surface and form into a smooth ball, then wrap in clear film and chill for about 30 minutes.

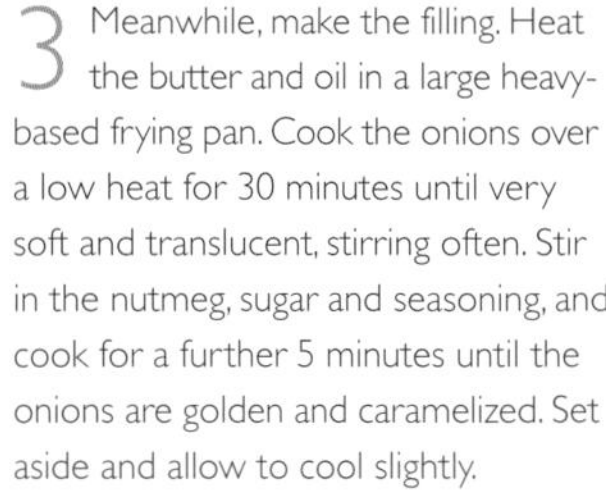

3 Meanwhile, make the filling. Heat the butter and oil in a large heavy-based frying pan. Cook the onions over a low heat for 30 minutes until very soft and translucent, stirring often. Stir in the nutmeg, sugar and seasoning, and cook for a further 5 minutes until the onions are golden and caramelized. Set aside and allow to cool slightly.

4 Preheat the oven to 220°C/425°F/Gas 7. Lightly grease a loose-based 35 x 12cm/14 x 4½in fluted baking tin. Roll out the pastry and use to line the prepared tin. Trim the top, then chill for 20 minutes.

5 Prick the pastry base with a fork, then line with greaseproof paper and baking beans and bake blind for 10 minutes until lightly golden. Remove the paper and beans, then spoon the onions into the pastry case.

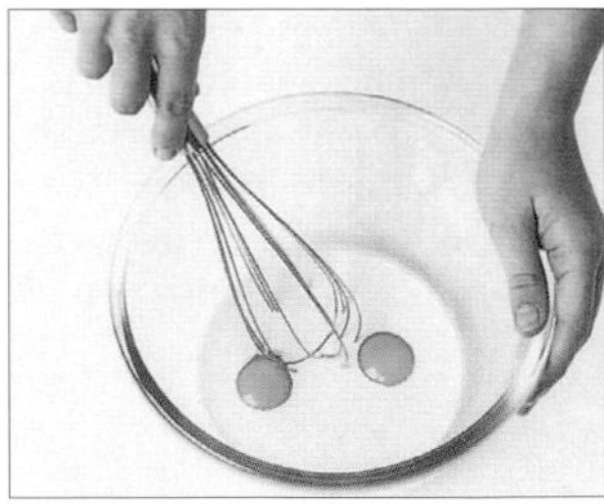

6 Beat the eggs with the cream, then add the cheese and season to taste. Pour the mixture over the onions and bake for 30 minutes until set and golden.

Mediterranean One-crust Pie

THIS FREE-FORM PIE ENCASES a rich tomato, aubergine and kidney bean filling. If your pastry cracks, just patch it up – it adds to the pie's rustic character.

INGREDIENTS

500g/1¼lb aubergine, cubed
1 red pepper
30ml/2 tbsp olive oil
1 large onion, finely chopped
1 courgette, sliced
2 garlic cloves, crushed
15ml/1 tbsp fresh oregano or 5ml/1 tsp dried, plus extra fresh oregano to garnish
200g/7oz/1½ cups canned red kidney beans, drained and rinsed
115g/4oz/1 cup pitted black olives, rinsed
375g/13oz/⅔ cup passata
1 egg, beaten, or a little milk
30ml/2 tbsp semolina
salt and freshly ground black pepper

For the pastry
75g/3oz/⅔ cup unbleached plain flour
75g/3oz/⅔ cup wholemeal flour
75g/3oz/6 tbsp vegetable margarine
50g/2oz/⅔ cup freshly grated Parmesan cheese

Serves 4

1 Preheat the oven to 220°C/425°F/Gas 7. To make the pastry, sift the the plain and wholemeal flours into a large bowl. Rub in the vegetable margarine until the mixture resembles fine breadcrumbs, then stir in the grated Parmesan. Mix in enough cold water to form a firm dough.

2 Turn out the dough on to a lightly floured work surface and form into a smooth ball. Wrap the dough in clear film or a plastic bag and chill for about 30 minutes.

3 To make the filling, place the aubergine in a colander and sprinkle with salt, then leave for 30 minutes. Rinse and pat dry with kitchen paper. Meanwhile, place the pepper on a baking tray and roast in the oven for 20 minutes. Put the pepper in a plastic bag and leave until cool enough to handle. Peel and seed the pepper, then dice the flesh. Set aside.

4 Heat the oil in a large heavy-based frying pan. Fry the onions for 5 minutes until softened, stirring occasionally. Add the aubergine and fry for 5 minutes until tender. Add the courgettes, garlic and oregano, and cook for a further 5 minutes, stirring frequently. Add the kidney beans and olives, stir, then add the passata and pepper. Cook until heated through, and set aside to cool.

5 Roll out the pastry on a lightly floured board or work surface to form a rough 30cm/12in round. Place on a lightly oiled baking sheet. Brush with a little of the beaten egg, sprinkle over the semolina, leaving a 4cm/1½in border, then spoon over the filling.

6 Gather up the edges of the pastry to partly cover the filling - it should be open in the middle. Brush with the remaining egg and bake for 30–35 minutes until golden.

Summer Herb Ricotta Flan

SIMPLE TO MAKE AND INFUSED with aromatic herbs, this delicate flan makes a delightful lunch dish.

INGREDIENTS

olive oil, for greasing and glazing
800g/1lb 11oz/3 1/2 cups ricotta cheese
75g/3oz/1 cup finely grated Parmesan cheese
3 eggs, separated
60ml/4 tbsp torn fresh basil leaves
60ml/4 tbsp snipped fresh chives
45ml/3 tbsp fresh oregano leaves
2.5ml/1/2 tsp salt
2.5ml/1/2 tsp paprika
freshly ground black pepper
chopped herbs, to garnish

For the tapenade

400g/14oz/3 1/2 cups pitted black olives, rinsed and halved, reserving a few whole to garnish (optional)
5 garlic cloves, crushed
75ml/5 tbsp/1/3 cup olive oil

Serves 4

1 Preheat the oven to 180°C/350°F/Gas 4 and lightly grease a 23cm/9in springform cake tin with oil. Mix together the ricotta, Parmesan and egg yolks in a food processor or blender. Add the herbs and seasoning, and blend until smooth and creamy.

2 Whisk the egg whites in a large bowl until they form soft peaks. Gently fold the egg whites into the ricotta mixture, taking care not to knock out too much air. Spoon the ricotta mixture into the tin and smooth the top.

3 Bake for 1 hour 20 minutes or until the flan is risen and the top golden. Remove from the oven and brush lightly with olive oil, then sprinkle with paprika. Leave the flan to cool before removing from the tin.

4 Make the tapenade. Place the olives and garlic in a food processor or blender and process until finely chopped. Gradually add the olive oil and blend to a coarse paste, then transfer to a serving bowl. Garnish the flan with the basil leaves and olives and serve with the tapenade.

Red Onion and Goat's Cheese Pastries

THESE ATTRACTIVE little pastries couldn't be easier to make. Ring the changes by spreading the pastry base with pesto or tapenade before you add the filling.

INGREDIENTS

15ml/1 tbsp olive oil
450g/1lb/1 1/2 cups red onions, sliced
30ml/2 tbsp fresh thyme or 10ml/2 tsp dried
15ml/1 tbsp balsamic vinegar
425g/15oz packet ready-rolled puff pastry
115g/4oz/1/2 cup goat's cheese, cubed
1 egg, beaten
salt and freshly ground black pepper
fresh thyme sprigs, to garnish (optional)
mixed green salad leaves, to serve

Serves 4

1 Heat the oil in a large heavy-based frying pan, add the onions and fry over a gentle heat for 10 minutes or until softened, stirring occasionally to prevent them browning. Add the thyme, seasoning and balsamic vinegar, and cook for a further 5 minutes. Remove the pan from the heat and leave to cool.

2 Preheat the oven to 220°C/425°F/Gas 7. Unroll the pastry and using a 15cm/6in plate as a guide, cut four rounds. Place the pastry rounds on a dampened baking sheet and, using the point of a knife, score a border, 2cm/3/4in inside the edge of each round.

3 Divide the onions among the pastry rounds and top with the goat's cheese. Brush the edge of each round with beaten egg and bake for 25–30 minutes until golden. Garnish with thyme, if using, before serving with salad leaves.

Wild Mushroom and Fontina Tarts

ITALIAN FONTINA CHEESE gives these tarts a creamy, nutty flavour. Serve them warm with rocket leaves.

INGREDIENTS

25g/1oz/½ cup dried wild mushrooms
30ml/2 tbsp olive oil
1 red onion, chopped
2 garlic cloves, chopped
30ml/2 tbsp medium-dry sherry
1 egg
120ml/4fl oz/½ cup single cream
25g/1oz Fontina cheese, thinly sliced
salt and freshly ground black pepper
rocket leaves, to serve

For the pastry
115g/4oz/1 cup wholemeal flour
50g/2oz/4 tbsp unsalted butter
25g/1oz/¼ cup walnuts, roasted and ground
1 egg, lightly beaten

Serves 4

1 To make the pastry, rub the flour and butter together until the mixture resembles fine breadcrumbs, then stir in the walnuts. Add the egg and mix to form a soft dough. Wrap the pastry in clear film and chill for about 30 minutes.

COOK'S TIP

You can prepare the pastry cases in advance, bake them blind for 10 minutes, then store in an airtight container for up to 2 days.

2 Meanwhile, soak the dried mushrooms in 300ml/½ pint/1¼ cups boiling water for 30 minutes. Drain and reserve the liquid. Heat the oil in a frying pan. Add the onion and fry for 5 minutes, then add the garlic and fry for 2 minutes, stirring.

3 Add the soaked mushrooms and cook for 7 minutes over a high heat until the edges become crisp. Add the sherry and the reserved liquid. Cook over a high heat for about 10 minutes until the liquid evaporates. Season and set aside to cool.

4 Preheat the oven to 200°C/400°F/Gas 6. Lightly grease four 10cm/4in tart tins. Roll out the pastry on a lightly floured work surface and use to line the tart tins.

5 Prick the pastry, line with greaseproof paper and baking beans and bake blind for 10 minutes. Remove the paper and beans.

6 Whisk the egg and cream to mix, add to the mushroom mixture, then season to taste. Spoon into the pastry cases, top with cheese slices and bake for 18 minutes until the filling is set. Serve warm with rocket.

Mushroom, Nut and Prune Jalousie

JALOUSIE, THE FRENCH WORD for shutter, refers to this pie's slatted top. The pie has a rich, nutty filling and, served with crisp roast potatoes and steamed vegetables, makes a great alternative to the Sunday joint.

INGREDIENTS

75g/3oz/⅓ cup green lentils, rinsed
5ml/1 tsp vegetable bouillon powder
15ml/1 tbsp sunflower oil
2 large leeks, sliced
2 garlic cloves, chopped
200g/7oz/3 cups field mushrooms, finely chopped
10ml/2 tsp dried mixed herbs
75g/3oz/¾ cup chopped mixed nuts
15ml/1 tbsp pine nuts (optional)
75g/3oz/⅓ cup ready-to-eat pitted prunes
25g/1oz/½ cup fresh breadcrumbs
2 eggs, beaten
2 sheets ready-rolled puff pastry, total weight about 425g/15oz
flour, for dusting
salt and freshly ground black pepper

Serves 6

1 Put the lentils in a saucepan and cover with cold water. Bring to the boil, then reduce the heat and add the vegetable bouillon powder. Partly cover the pan and simmer for 20 minutes or until the lentils are tender. Set aside.

2 Heat the oil in a large heavy-based frying pan, add the leeks and garlic and fry for 5 minutes or until softened. Add the mushrooms and herbs and cook for a further 5 minutes. Transfer the mushroom mixture to a bowl using a slotted spoon. Stir in the nuts, pine nuts, if using, prunes, breadcrumbs and lentils.

COOK'S TIP

Try other combinations of vegetables, nuts and dried fruit.

3 Preheat the oven to 220°C/425°F/Gas 7. Add two-thirds of the beaten egg to the mushroom mixture and season well. Set aside and leave to cool.

4 Meanwhile, unroll one of the pastry sheets. Cut off 2.5cm/1in from its width and length, then lay it on a dampened baking sheet. Unroll the second pastry sheet, dust lightly with flour, then fold in half lengthways. Make a series of cuts across the fold, 1cm/½in apart, leaving a 2.5cm/1in border around the edge of the pastry.

5 Spoon the mushroom mixture evenly over the pastry base, leaving a 2.5cm/1in border. Dampen the edges of the pastry with water. Open out the folded piece of pastry and carefully lay it over the top of the filling. Trim the edges, if necessary, then press the edges of the pastry together to seal and crimp the edges.

6 Brush the top of the pastry with the remaining beaten egg and bake for 25–30 minutes until golden. Leave to cool slightly before serving.

Apple, Onion and Gruyère Tart

INGREDIENTS

225g/8oz/2 cups flour
pinch of salt
1.5ml/¼ tsp dry mustard
75g/3oz/6 tbsp soft margarine
75g/3oz/6 tbsp/¾ cup finely grated Gruyère cheese

For the filling

30g/1oz/2 tbsp butter
1 large onion, finely chopped
1 large or 2 small eating apples, peeled and grated
2 eggs
150ml/¼ pint/⅔ cup heavy cream
1.5ml/¼ tsp dried mixed herbs
2.5ml/½ tsp dry mustard
115g/4oz Gruyère cheese
salt and freshly ground black pepper

Serves 4–6

1 To make the pastry, sift the flour, salt and dry mustard into a bowl. Rub in the margarine and cheese until the mixture forms soft breadcrumbs. Add 2 tbsp water and bring together into a ball. Chill, covered or wrapped for 30 minutes.

2 Meanwhile, make the filling. Melt the butter in a pan, add the onion and cook gently for 10 minutes, stirring occasionally, until softened but not browned. Stir in the apple and cook for 2–3 minutes. Leave to cool.

3 Roll out the pastry and use to line a lightly greased 20cm/8in fluted quiche pan. Chill for 20 minutes. Preheat the oven to 200°C/400°F/Gas 6.

4 Line the pastry with wax paper and fill with baking beans. Bake the pie shell for 20 minutes.

5 Beat together the eggs, cream, herbs, seasoning and mustard. Grate three-quarters of the cheese and stir into the egg mixture, then slice the remaining cheese and set aside. When the pastry is cooked, remove the paper and beans and pour in the egg mixture.

6 Arrange the sliced cheese over the top. Reduce the oven temperature to 190°C/375°F/Gas 5. Return the tart to the oven and cook for a further 20 minutes, until the filling is golden and just firm. Serve hot or warm.

Cook's Tip

You can substitute other hard cheeses, such as Cheddar, Provolone, Sage or Emmenthal for the Gruyère, if you prefer.

Chestnut, Stilton and Ale Pie

THIS HEARTY WINTER DISH has a rich Guinness gravy and a herb pastry top. The Stilton adds a delicious creaminess but can be left out to make a less rich version of the pie.

INGREDIENTS

30ml/2 tbsp sunflower oil
2 large onions, chopped
500g/1¼lb/8 cups button mushrooms, halved
3 carrots, sliced
1 parsnip, cut into thick slices
15ml/1 tbsp fresh thyme or 5ml/1 tsp dried
2 bay leaves
250ml/8fl oz/1 cup Guinness
120ml/4fl oz/½ cup vegetable stock
5ml/1 tsp vegetarian Worcestershire sauce
5ml/1 tsp soft dark brown sugar
350g/12oz/3 cups canned chestnuts, halved
30ml/2 tbsp unbleached plain flour
150g/5oz/1¼ cups Stilton cheese, cubed
1 egg, beaten, or milk, to glaze
salt and freshly ground black pepper

For the pastry
115g/4oz/1 cup wholemeal flour
a pinch of salt
50g/2oz/4 tbsp unsalted butter or vegetable margarine
15ml/1 tbsp fresh thyme or 5ml/1 tsp dried

Serves 4

1 To make the pastry, rub together the flour, salt and butter or margarine until the mixture resembles fine breadcrumbs. Add the thyme and enough water to form a soft dough.

HEALTH BENEFITS

Chestnuts contain useful amounts of B complex vitamins, potassium and calcium and, unlike other nuts, they are very low in fat.

2 Turn out the dough on to a floured board or work surface and gently knead for 1 minute until it forms a smooth dough. Wrap in clear film and chill for 30 minutes.

3 Meanwhile, to make the filling, heat the oil in a heavy-based saucepan and fry the onions for 5 minutes until softened, stirring occasionally. Add the mushrooms and cook for a further 3 minutes or until just tender. Add the carrots, parsnip and herbs, stir and cover the pan. Cook for 3 minutes until slightly softened.

4 Pour in the Guinness, vegetable stock and Worcestershire sauce, then add the sugar and seasoning. Simmer, covered, for 5 minutes, stirring occasionally. Add the chestnuts.

5 Mix the flour to a paste with 30ml/2 tbsp water. Add to the Guinness mixture and cook, uncovered, for 5 minutes until the sauce thickens, stirring. Stir in the cheese and heat until melted, stirring constantly.

6 Preheat the oven to 220°C/425°F/Gas 7. Roll out the pastry to fit the top of a 1.5 litre/2½ pint/6¼ cup deep pie dish. Spoon the chestnut mixture into the dish. Dampen the edges of the dish and cover with the pastry. Seal, trim and crimp the edges. Cut a small slit in the top of the pie and use any surplus pastry to make pastry leaves. Brush with egg or milk and bake for 30 minutes until the pastry is golden.

Butternut Squash and Sage Pizza

THE COMBINATION of sweet butternut squash, sage and sharp goat's cheese works wonderfully on this pizza.

INGREDIENTS

2.5ml/½ tsp active dried yeast
pinch of granulated sugar
450g/1lb/4 cups strong white flour
5ml/1 tsp salt
60ml/4 tbsp olive oil
15g/½oz/1 tbsp butter
2 shallots, finely chopped
1 butternut squash, peeled, seeded and cubed, about 450g/1lb prepared weight
16 sage leaves
2 x 400g/14oz cans fresh tomato sauce
115g/4oz mozzarella cheese, sliced
115g/4oz/½ cup firm goat's cheese
salt and freshly ground black pepper

Serves 4

1 Put 300ml/½ pint/1¼ cups warm water in a measuring jug. Add the yeast and sugar and leave for 5–10 minutes, until it is frothy.

2 Sift the flour and salt into a large bowl and make a well in the centre. Gradually pour in the yeast mixture and 30ml/2 tbsp olive oil. Mix to make a smooth dough. Knead on a lightly floured surface for about 10 minutes until smooth, springy and elastic. Place the dough in a floured bowl, cover and leave to rise in a warm place for 1½ hours.

3 Preheat the oven to 200°C/400°F/Gas 6. Oil four baking sheets. Put the butter and remaining olive oil in a roasting tin and heat in the oven for a few minutes. Add the shallots, squash and half the sage leaves. Toss to coat. Roast for 15–20 minutes, until tender. Raise the oven temperature to 220°C/425°F/Gas 7.

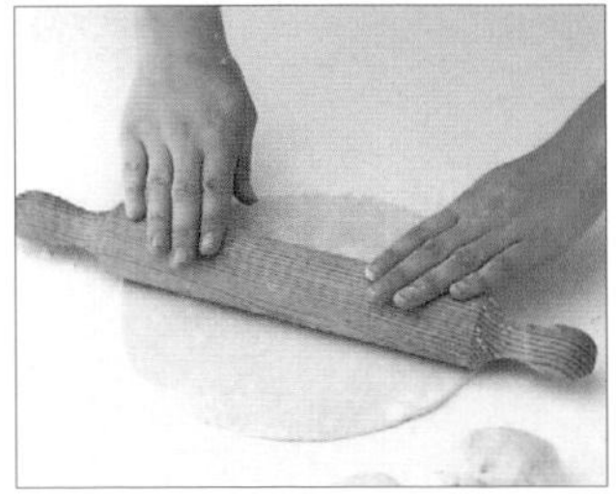

4 Divide the dough into four equal pieces and roll out each piece on a floured surface to a 25cm/10in round.

5 Transfer each round to a baking sheet and spread with tomato sauce, leaving a 1cm/½in border all around. Spoon the squash and shallot mixture over the top.

6 Arrange the mozzarella over the squash mixture and crumble the goat's cheese over. Scatter the remaining sage leaves over and season with plenty of salt and pepper. Bake for 15–20 minutes, until the cheese has melted and the crusts are golden.

Pizza with Fresh Vegetables

THIS PIZZA can be made with any combination of fresh vegetables. Most will benefit from being blanched or sautéed before being baked on the pizza.

INGREDIENTS

400g/14oz peeled plum tomatoes, fresh or canned, weighed whole, without extra juice
2 medium broccoli spears
225g/8oz fresh asparagus
2 small courgettes
75ml/5 tbsp olive oil
50g/2oz/⅓ cup shelled peas, fresh or frozen
4 spring onions, sliced
1 pizza base, 25–30cm/10–12in in diameter
75g/3oz mozzarella cheese, cut into small dice
10 leaves fresh basil, torn into pieces
2 cloves garlic, finely chopped
salt and freshly ground black pepper
Serves 4

1 Preheat the oven to 240°C/475°F/Gas 9 for at least 20 minutes before baking the pizza.

2 Strain the tomatoes through a food mill, scraping in all the pulp.

3 Peel the broccoli stems and asparagus, and blanch with the courgettes in a pan of boiling water for 4–5 minutes. Drain. Cut the vegetables into bite-size pieces and slice the courgettes lengthways.

4 Heat 30ml/2 tbsp of the olive oil in a small saucepan. Stir in the peas and spring onions and cook for 5–6 minutes, stirring often. Remove from the heat.

5 Spread the puréed tomatoes on to the pizza dough, leaving the rim uncovered. Add the other vegetables, spreading them evenly over the tomatoes.

6 Sprinkle with the mozzarella, basil, garlic, salt and pepper and remaining olive oil. Immediately place the pizza in the oven. Bake for about 20 minutes, or until the crust is golden brown and the cheese has melted.

Polenta Pan-pizza with Red Onions, Garlic Mushrooms and Mozzarella

THIS YEAST-FREE PIZZA IS COOKED in a frying pan rather than the oven. The slightly cakey texture of the base is complemented by the garlicky red onion and mushroom topping. Serve with a simple tomato and basil salad.

INGREDIENTS

30ml/2 tbsp olive oil
1 large red onion, sliced
3 garlic cloves, crushed
115g/4oz/1 1/2 cups brown cap mushrooms, sliced
5ml/1 tsp dried oregano
115g/4oz mozzarella cheese, crumbled
15ml/1 tbsp pine nuts (optional)

For the pizza base

50g/2oz/1/2 cup unbleached plain flour, sifted
2.5ml/1/2 tsp salt
115g/4oz/1 cup fine polenta
5ml/1 tsp baking powder
1 egg, beaten
150ml/1/4 pint/2/3 cup milk
25g/1oz/1/3 cup freshly grated Parmesan cheese
2.5ml/1/2 tsp dried chilli flakes
15ml/1 tbsp olive oil

Serves 2

1 To make the topping, heat half the olive oil in a heavy-based frying pan, add the onion and fry for 10 minutes until tender, stirring occasionally. Remove the onion from the pan and set aside.

2 Add the remaining oil to the pan and fry the garlic for 1 minute until slightly coloured. Add the sliced mushrooms and oregano and cook for 5 minutes more until the mushrooms are tender.

3 To make the pizza base, mix together the flour, salt, polenta and baking powder in a bowl. Make a well in the centre and add the egg. Gradually add the milk, and mix well with a fork to make into a thick, smooth batter. Stir in the Parmesan and chilli flakes.

4 Heat the olive oil in a 25cm/10in heavy-based flameproof frying pan until very hot. Spoon in the batter and spread evenly. Cook over a moderate heat for about 3 minutes or until the base is set. Remove the pan from the heat and run a knife around the edge of the pizza base.

5 Place a plate over the pan and, holding them tightly together, flip over. Slide the pizza base back into the pan on its uncooked side and cook for 2 minutes until golden.

6 Preheat the grill to high. Spoon the onions over the base, then top with the mushroom mixture. Scatter the mozzarella on top, then grill for about 6 minutes until the mozzarella has melted. Sprinkle over the pine nuts (if using) and grill until golden. Serve cut into wedges.

Rocket and Tomato Pizza

PEPPERY ROCKET and aromatic fresh basil add both colour and flavour to this crisp pizza.

INGREDIENTS

10ml/2 tsp olive oil, plus extra for drizzling
1 garlic clove, crushed
150g/5oz/1 cup canned chopped tomatoes
2.5ml/½ tsp sugar
30ml/2 tbsp torn fresh basil leaves
2 tomatoes, seeded and chopped
150g/5oz/⅔ cup mozzarella cheese, sliced
20g/¾oz/1 cup rocket leaves
rock salt and freshly ground black pepper

For the pizza base
225g/8oz/2 cups strong white flour, sifted
5ml/1 tsp salt
2.5ml/½ tsp easy-blend dried yeast
15ml/1 tbsp olive oil

Serves 2

1 To make the pizza base, place the flour, salt and yeast in a bowl. Make a well in the centre and add the oil and 150ml/¼ pint/⅔ cup warm water. Mix with a round-bladed knife to form a soft dough.

2 Turn out the dough on to a lightly floured work surface and knead for 5 minutes. Cover with the upturned bowl or a dish towel and leave to rest for about 5 minutes, then knead for a further 5 minutes until the dough is smooth and elastic. Place in a lightly oiled bowl and cover with clear film. Leave in a warm place for about 45 minutes until doubled in bulk.

3 Preheat the oven to 220°C/425°F/Gas 7. Make the topping. Heat the oil in a frying pan and fry the garlic for 1 minute. Add the tomatoes and sugar, and cook for 5–7 minutes until reduced and thickened. Stir in the basil and seasoning, then set aside.

VARIATION

To make a Roquefort and walnut pizza, replace half the strong white flour with wholemeal flour. Use 75g/3oz/¾ cup crumbled Roquefort cheese instead of the mozzarella. Omit the rocket and use 30ml/2 tbsp chopped walnuts.

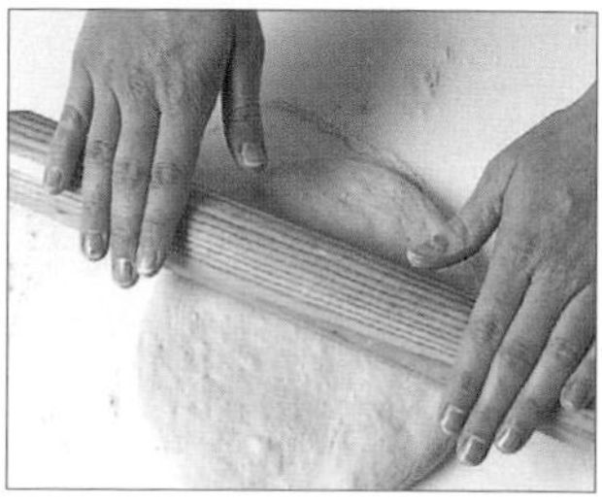

4 Knead the risen dough lightly, then roll out to form a rough 30cm/12in round. Place on a lightly oiled baking sheet and push up the edges of the dough to form a shallow, even rim.

5 Spoon the tomato mixture over the pizza base, then top with the chopped fresh tomatoes. Arrange the mozzarella on top. Season with rock salt and pepper and drizzle with a little olive oil. Bake in the top of the oven for 10–12 minutes until crisp and golden. Scatter the rocket over the pizza just before serving.

Ricotta and Fontina Pizza

THE EARTHY flavours of the mixed mushrooms perfectly complement the two creamy cheeses in this delectable recipe.

INGREDIENTS

2.5ml/½ tsp active dried yeast
pinch of granulated sugar
450g/1lb/4 cups strong white flour
5ml/1 tsp salt
30ml/2 tbsp olive oil

For the tomato sauce

400g/14oz can chopped tomatoes
150ml/¼ pint/⅔ cup passata
1 large garlic clove, finely chopped
5ml/1 tsp dried oregano
1 bay leaf
10ml/2 tsp malt vinegar
salt and freshly ground black pepper

For the topping

30ml/2 tbsp olive oil
1 garlic clove, finely chopped
350g/12oz/4½ cups mixed mushrooms (chestnut, flat or button), sliced
30ml/2 tbsp chopped fresh oregano, plus whole leaves, to garnish
250g/9oz/generous 1 cup ricotta cheese
225g/8oz Fontina cheese, sliced

Serves 4

1 To make the dough, put 300ml/½ pint/1½ cups warm water in a measuring jug. Add the yeast and sugar and leave for 5–10 minutes, until frothy.

2 Sift the flour and salt into a large bowl and make a well in the centre. Gradually pour in the yeast mixture and the olive oil. Mix to make a smooth dough. Knead on a lightly floured surface for about 10 minutes until smooth, springy and elastic. Place the dough in a floured bowl, cover and leave to rise in a warm place for 1½ hours.

3 Meanwhile, make the tomato sauce. Put all the ingredients in a saucepan, cover and bring to the boil. Lower the heat, then remove the lid and simmer for 20 minutes, stirring occasionally, until the liquid has reduced.

4 To make the topping, heat the oil in a frying pan. Add the garlic and mushrooms and season with salt and pepper. Cook, stirring, for about 5 minutes, or until the mushrooms are tender and golden. Set aside.

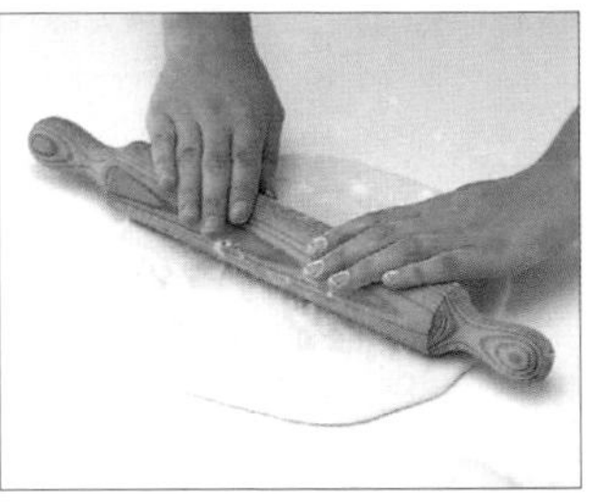

5 Preheat the oven to 220°C/425°F/Gas 7. Brush four baking sheets with oil. Knead the dough for 2 minutes, then divide into four equal pieces. Roll out each piece to a 25cm/10in round and place on a baking sheet.

6 Spoon the tomato sauce over each dough round. Brush the edge with a little olive oil. Add the mushrooms, oregano and cheeses. Season to taste. Bake for about 15 minutes, until golden brown and crisp. Garnish with oregano leaves.

COOK'S TIP

To freeze, allow to cool to room temperature after baking. Wrap in foil and freeze. Thaw completely and heat through in a warm oven before serving.

Chilli, Tomato and Spinach Pizza

THIS RICHLY flavoured topping makes a colourful and satisfying pizza.

INGREDIENTS

1–2 fresh red chillies
45ml/3 tbsp tomato oil (from jar of sun-dried tomatoes)
1 onion, chopped
2 garlic cloves, chopped
50g/2oz/1 cup (drained weight) sun-dried tomatoes in oil
400g/14oz can chopped tomatoes
15ml/1 tbsp tomato purée
175g/6oz fresh spinach
1 pizza base, 25–30cm/10–12in in diameter
75g/3oz/¾ cup smoked Bavarian cheese, grated
75g/3oz/¾ cup mature Cheddar, grated
salt and freshly ground black pepper

Serves 3

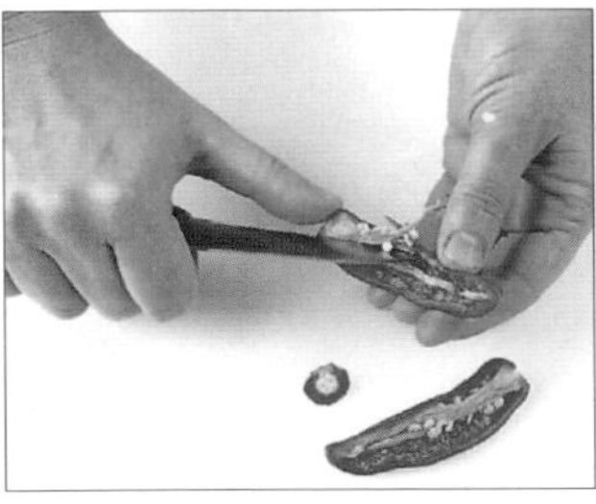

1 Seed and finely chop the chillies.

2 Heat 30ml/2 tbsp of the tomato oil in a saucepan, add the onion, garlic and chillies and fry over a gentle heat for about 5 minutes, until they are soft.

3 Roughly chop the sun-dried tomatoes. Add to the pan with the chopped tomatoes and tomato purée. Season with salt and pepper. Simmer, uncovered, stirring occasionally, for 15 minutes.

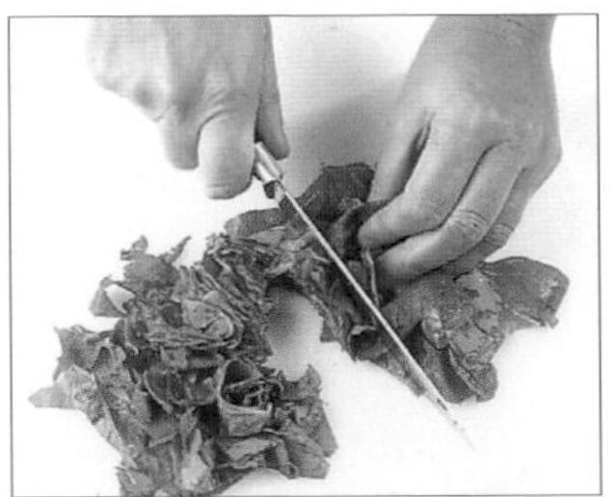

4 Remove the stalks from the spinach and wash the leaves in plenty of cold water. Drain well and pat dry with kitchen paper. Roughly chop the spinach.

5 Stir the spinach into the sauce. Cook, stirring, for a further 5–10 minutes until the spinach has wilted and no excess moisture remains. Leave to cool.

6 Meanwhile, preheat the oven to 220°C/425°F/Gas 7. Brush the pizza base with the remaining tomato oil, then spoon over the sauce. Sprinkle over the grated cheeses and bake in the oven for 15–20 minutes, until crisp and golden. Serve immediately.

COOK'S TIP

The smoked cheese used in this pizza topping creates an unusual rich flavour, which complements the hot, spicy chillies. If you want to heighten this taste, substitute the Cheddar with another 75g/3oz of the smoked Bavarian cheese.

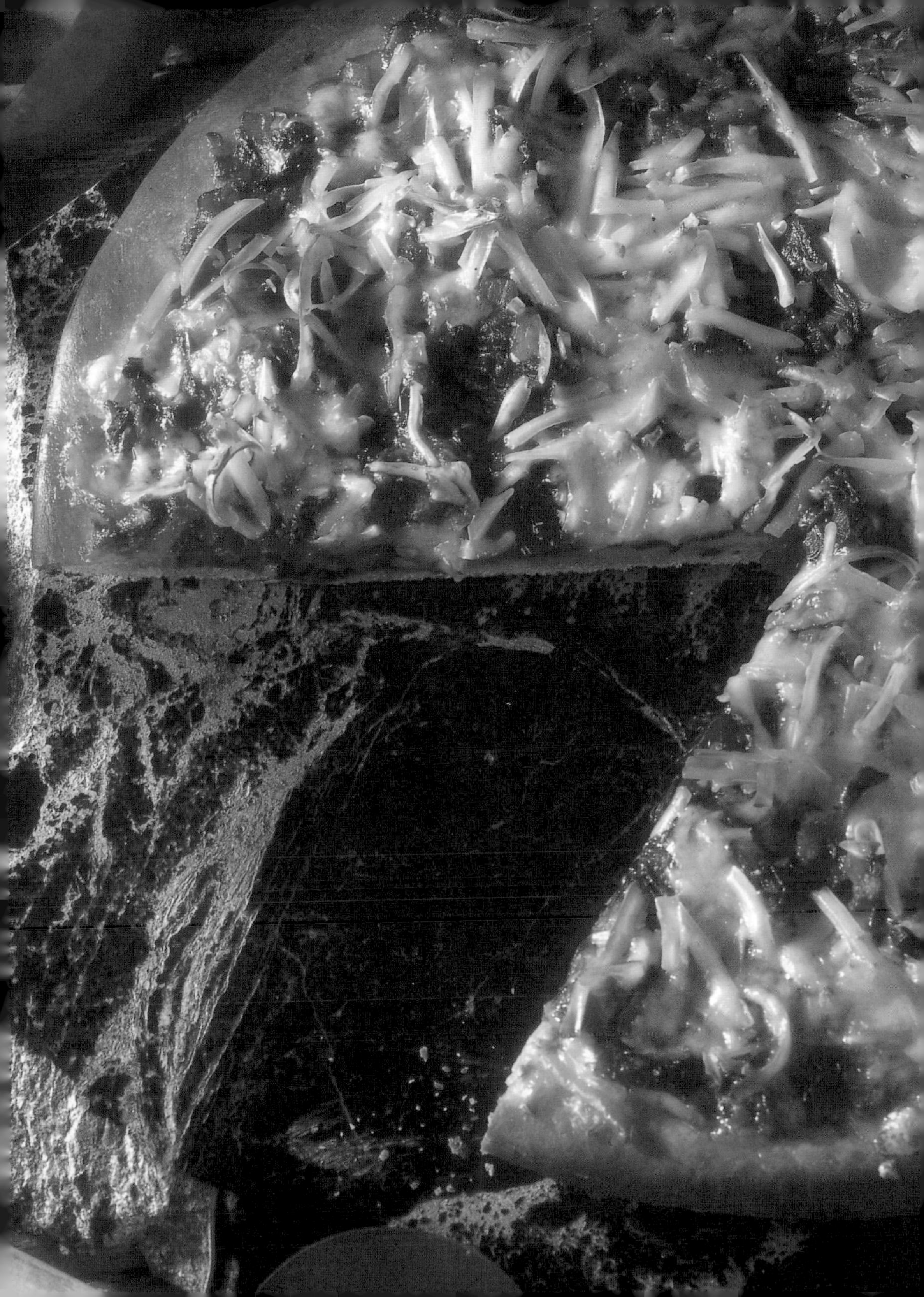

Aubergine, Shallot and Tomato Calzone

AUBERGINES, SHALLOTS and sun-dried tomatoes make an unusual filling for calzone. Add more or less red chilli flakes, depending on how fiery you like your food.

INGREDIENTS

1.5ml/¼ tsp active dried yeast
pinch of granulated sugar
225g/8oz/2 cups strong white flour
1 tsp salt
60ml/4 tbsp olive oil
4 baby aubergines
3 shallots, chopped
1 garlic clove, chopped
50g/2oz/1 cup (drained weight) sun-dried tomatoes in oil, chopped
1.5ml/¼ tsp dried red chilli flakes
10ml/2 tsp chopped fresh thyme
75g/3oz mozzarella cheese, cubed
salt and freshly ground black pepper
15–30ml/1–2 tbsp freshly grated Parmesan cheese, to serve

Serves 2

1 To make the dough, put 150ml/¼ pint/⅔ cup warm water in a measuring jug. Add the yeast and sugar and leave for 5–10 minutes, until frothy.

2 Sift the flour and salt into a large bowl and make a well in the centre. Gradually pour in the yeast mixture and 15ml/1 tbsp oil. Mix to make a smooth dough. Knead the dough on a lightly floured surface for 10 minutes until smooth. The dough should be springy and elastic.

3 Place the dough in a floured bowl, cover and leave to rise in a warm place for 1½ hours. Preheat the oven to 220°C/425°F/Gas 7. Trim the aubergines, then cut into small cubes.

4 Heat 15ml/1 tbsp of the oil in a frying pan and cook the shallots for 5 minutes until soft. Add the aubergines, garlic, sun-dried tomatoes, red chilli flakes, thyme and seasoning. Cook for about 4–5 minutes over medium heat, stirring frequently, until the aubergine flesh is beginning to soften.

5 Divide the pizza dough in half. Lightly flour a rolling pin and roll out each piece on a lightly floured surface to an 18cm/7in circle.

6 Spread the aubergine mixture over half of each round, leaving a 2.5cm/1in border, then scatter over the mozzarella.

7 Dampen the edges with water, then fold over the other half of the dough to enclose the filling. Press the edges firmly together to seal. Place the calzones on two lightly greased baking sheets.

8 Brush with half the remaining olive oil and make a small hole in the top of each to allow the steam to escape. Bake for about 15–20 minutes until golden. Remove from the oven and brush with the remaining oil. Sprinkle over the Parmesan cheese and serve immediately.

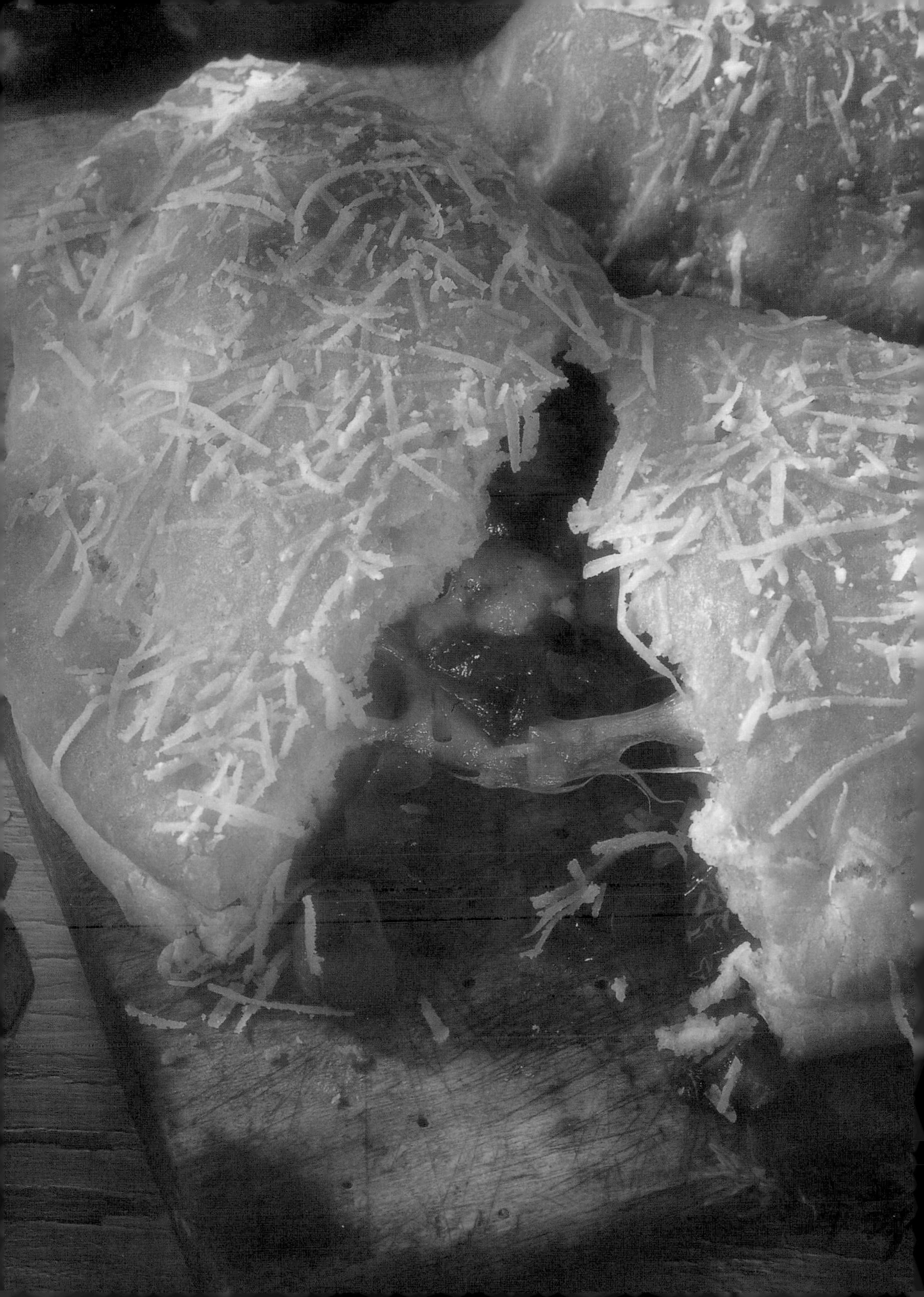

SALADS

Think of salads and you think of summer. The best salads are full of fresh tastes, textures and colours, appealing to the eye as well as your taste buds. Summer days make light eating, but plenty of these recipes have year-round appeal, with warm selections for spring and autumn.

Classic Greek Salad

IF YOU have ever visited Greece, you'll know that a Greek salad with a chunk of bread makes a delicious, filling meal.

INGREDIENTS

1 romaine lettuce
½ cucumber, halved lengthways
4 tomatoes
8 spring onions
50g/2oz/⅓ cup Greek black olives
115g/4oz feta cheese
90ml/6 tbsp white wine vinegar
120ml/4fl oz/½ cup olive oil
salt and freshly ground black pepper
olives and bread, to serve (optional)
Serves 4

1 Tear the lettuce into pieces, and place it in a large mixing bowl. Slice the cucumber and add to the bowl.

2 Cut the tomatoes into wedges and put them into the bowl.

3 Slice the spring onions. Add them to the bowl with the olives and toss well.

4 Cut the feta cheese into cubes and add to the salad.

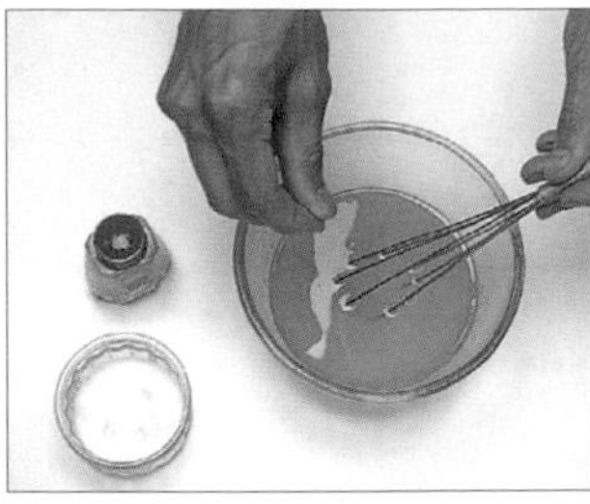

5 Put the vinegar, olive oil and salt and pepper into a small bowl and whisk well. Pour the dressing over the salad and toss to combine. Serve at once, with olives and chunks of bread, if desired.

COOK'S TIP

The salad can be assembled in advance and chilled, but add the lettuce and dressing just before serving. Keep the dressing at room temperature, as chilling deadens its flavour.

Fresh Spinach and Avocado Salad

YOUNG, TENDER spinach leaves make a change from lettuce and are delicious served with avocado, cherry tomatoes and radishes in a tofu sauce.

INGREDIENTS

1 large avocado
juice of 1 lime
225g/8oz fresh baby spinach leaves
115g/4oz cherry tomatoes
4 spring onions, sliced
½ cucumber
50g/2oz radishes, sliced

For the dressing
115g/4oz soft silken tofu
45ml/3 tbsp milk
10ml/2 tsp prepared mustard
2.5ml/½ tsp white wine vinegar
pinch of cayenne, plus extra to serve
salt and freshly ground black pepper

Serves 2–3

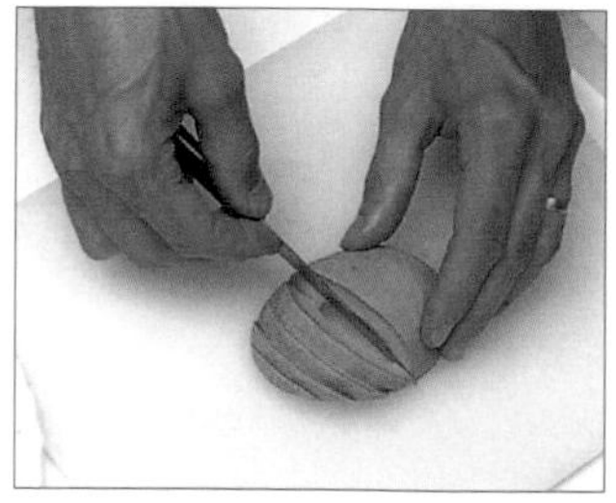

1 Cut the avocado in half, remove the stone, and strip off the skin. Cut the flesh into slices. Transfer to a plate, drizzle the lime juice over the avocado, and set aside.

2 Wash and dry the spinach leaves. Put them in a mixing bowl.

3 Cut the larger cherry tomatoes in half, and add all the tomatoes to the mixing bowl, with the sliced spring onions. Cut the cucumber into chunks, and add to the bowl with the sliced radishes.

4 Make the dressing. Put the tofu, milk, mustard, wine vinegar and cayenne in a food processor or blender. Add salt and pepper to taste. Process for 30 seconds until smooth. Scrape the dressing into a bowl, and add a little extra milk if you like a thinner dressing. Sprinkle with a little extra cayenne.

COOK'S TIP

Use soft, silken tofu rather than the firm block variety. It can be found in most supermarkets in long-life cartons.

Sweet and Sour Peppers with Pasta Bows

A ZESTY dressing makes this simple pasta salad really special.

INGREDIENTS

1 each red, yellow and orange pepper
1 garlic clove, crushed
30ml/2 tbsp capers
30ml/2 tbsp raisins
5ml/1 tsp wholegrain mustard
grated rind and juice of 1 lime
5ml/1 tsp runny honey
30ml/2 tbsp chopped fresh coriander
225g/8oz/2 cups pasta bows
salt and freshly ground black pepper
shavings of Parmesan cheese, to serve (optional)

Serves 4–6

1 Quarter the peppers and remove the stalks and seeds. Put into boiling water and cook for 10–15 minutes, until tender. Drain and rinse under cold water. Peel away the skins and seeds and cut the flesh lengthways into narrow strips.

2 Put the garlic, capers, raisins, mustard, lime rind and juice, honey and coriander into a bowl. Season well with salt and pepper and whisk together.

3 Cook the pasta in a large pan of boiling salted water for 10–12 minutes, until tender but still firm to the bite. Drain thoroughly.

4 Return the pasta to the pan, add the peppers and dressing. Heat gently and toss to mix. Transfer to a warm serving bowl. Serve with a few shavings of Parmesan cheese, if using.

Bulgur Wheat and Broad Bean Salad

THIS APPETIZING salad is ideal served with fresh crusty wholemeal bread and home-made chutney or pickle.

INGREDIENTS

350g/12oz/2 cups bulgur wheat
225g/8oz/1 1/3 cups frozen broad beans
115g/4oz/1 cup frozen petit pois
225g/8oz cherry tomatoes, halved
1 Spanish onion, chopped
1 red pepper, seeded and chopped
50g/2oz mangetout, chopped
50g/2oz watercress, chopped
15ml/1 tbsp chopped fresh parsley
15ml/1 tbsp chopped fresh basil
15ml/1 tbsp chopped fresh thyme
French dressing
salt and freshly ground black pepper

Serves 6

1 Soak and cook the bulgur wheat according to the package instructions. Drain thoroughly and put into a serving bowl.

2 Meanwhile, cook the broad beans and petit pois in boiling water for 3 minutes. Drain and add to the prepared bulgur wheat.

3 Add the cherry tomatoes, onion, pepper, mangetouts and watercress to the bulgur wheat, broad bean and petit pois mixture. Toss together in the serving bowl until all the ingredients are well combined.

4 Add the chopped fresh parsley, basil and thyme and French dressing to taste. Season with salt and pepper and toss the ingredients together. Serve immediately or cover and chill in the refrigerator before taking to the table.

COOK'S TIP

Use cooked couscous, boiled brown rice or wholewheat pasta in place of the bulgur wheat.

Sweet and Sour Artichoke Salad

AGRODOLCE IS a sweet and sour sauce which works perfectly in this salad.

INGREDIENTS

6 small globe artichokes
juice of 1 lemon
30ml/2 tbsp olive oil
2 medium onions, roughly chopped
175g/6oz/1 cup fresh or frozen broad beans (shelled weight)
175g/6oz/1 1/2 cups fresh or frozen peas (shelled weight)
salt and freshly ground black pepper
fresh mint leaves, to garnish

For the salsa agrodolce
120ml/4fl oz/1/2 cup white wine vinegar
15ml/1 tbsp caster sugar
handful fresh mint leaves, roughly torn

Serves 4

1 Peel the outer leaves from the artichokes and cut into quarters. Place them in a bowl of water with the lemon juice.

2 Heat the oil in a large saucepan and cook the onions until golden. Add the beans and stir.

3 Drain the artichokes and add them to the pan. Pour in about 300ml/1/2 pint/1 1/4 cups of water and cover. Simmer gently for 10–15 minutes.

4 Add the peas, season with salt and pepper and cook for a further 5 minutes, stirring from time to time, until the vegetables are tender but still slightly crunchy.

5 Strain the vegetables through a sieve and place them in a bowl. Leave to cool, then cover and chill in the refrigerator.

6 To make the salsa, mix all the ingredients in a pan. Heat gently until the sugar has dissolved. Simmer for 5 minutes, take off the heat and leave to cool. Drizzle over the salad. Garnish with mint leaves.

Spanish Asparagus and Orange Salad

SPANISH SALAD dressings simply rely on the wonderful flavour of a good quality olive oil.

INGREDIENTS

225g/8oz asparagus, trimmed and cut into 5 cm/2 in pieces
2 large oranges
2 tomatoes, cut into eighths
50g/2oz/1 cup romaine lettuce leaves, shredded
30ml/2 tbsp olive oil
2.5ml/½ tsp sherry vinegar
salt and freshly ground black pepper

Serves 4

1 Cook the asparagus in boiling salted water for 3–4 minutes, until just tender. Drain and refresh under cold water and drain again.

2 Grate the rind from half an orange and reserve. Peel both the oranges and cut into segments. Squeeze out the juice from the membrane and reserve the juice.

COOK'S TIP

Cos or Little Gem lettuce can be used in place of romaine.

3 Put the asparagus, orange segments, tomatoes and lettuce into a salad bowl. Mix together the oil and vinegar and add 15ml/1 tbsp of the reserved orange juice and 2.5ml/½ tsp of the rind. Season the dressing with salt and pepper. Just before serving, pour the dressing over the salad and mix gently to coat.

Grilled Goat's Cheese Salad

HERE IS the salad and cheese course on one plate – or serve it as a quick and satisfying starter or light lunch. The fresh tangy flavour of goat's cheese contrasts with the mild salad leaves.

INGREDIENTS

2 firm round whole goat's cheeses, such as Crottin de Chavignol (about 65–115g/2½–4oz each)
4 slices French bread
olive oil, for drizzling
175g/6oz mixed salad leaves, including soft and bitter varieties
snipped fresh chives, to garnish

For the dressing

½ clove garlic
5ml/1 tsp Dijon mustard
5ml/1 tsp white wine vinegar
5ml/1 tsp dry white wine
45ml/3 tbsp olive oil
salt and freshly ground black pepper

Serves 4

1 To make the dressing, rub a large salad bowl with the cut side of the garlic clove. Combine the mustard, vinegar, wine, salt and pepper in a bowl. Whisk in the oil, 15ml/1 tbsp at a time, to form a thick vinaigrette.

2 Cut the goat's cheeses in half crossways using a sharp knife.

3 Preheat the grill to hot. Arrange the bread slices on a baking sheet and toast on one side. Turn over and place a piece of cheese, cut side up, on each slice. Drizzle with oil and grill until the cheese is lightly browned.

4 Add the leaves and the dressing to the salad bowl and toss to coat the leaves thoroughly. Divide the salad among four plates, top each with a goat's cheese croûton and serve, garnished with chives.

Tomato and Feta Cheese Salad

SWEET SUN-RIPENED tomatoes are rarely more delicious than when served with feta cheese and olive oil. This salad, popular in Greece and Turkey, is enjoyed as a light meal with pieces of crispy bread.

INGREDIENTS

900g/2lb tomatoes
200g/7oz feta cheese
120ml/4fl oz/½ cup olive oil, preferably Greek
12 black olives
4 sprigs of fresh basil
freshly ground black pepper
Serves 4

1 Remove the tough cores from the tomatoes with a small sharp knife.

2 Slice the tomatoes thickly and arrange in a shallow dish.

3 Crumble the cheese over the tomatoes, sprinkle with olive oil, then strew with olives and fresh basil. Season with black pepper and serve at room temperature.

COOK'S TIP

Feta cheese is preserved in brine. It has a strong flavour and can be salty. The least salty variety is imported from Greece and Turkey and is available from specialist delicatessens. However, if you find feta too salty, it can be soaked in cold water for 1–2 hours to remove the brine.

Parmesan and Poached Egg Salad

SOFT POACHED eggs, hot garlic croûtons and cool, crisp salad leaves make an unforgettable combination.

INGREDIENTS

½ small loaf
75ml/5 tbsp olive oil
2 eggs
115g/4oz mixed salad leaves
2 garlic cloves, crushed
7ml/½ tbsp white wine vinegar
25g/1oz/⅓ cup Parmesan cheese
freshly ground black pepper (optional)

Serves 2

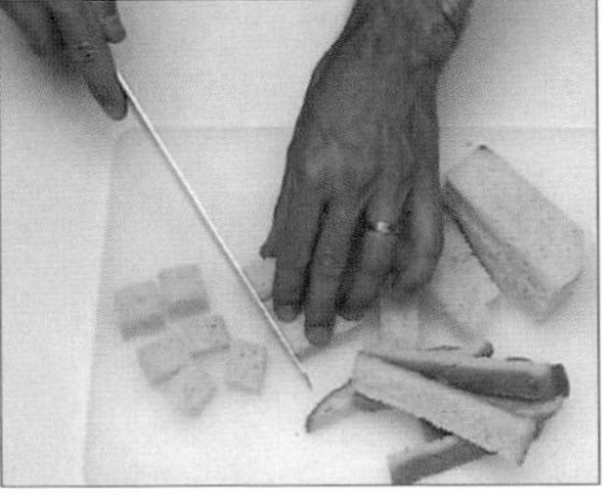

1 Remove the crusts from the bread. Cut the bread into 2.5 cm/1in cubes.

2 Heat 30ml/2 tbsp of the olive oil in a frying pan. Fry the bread cubes for about 5 minutes, tossing the cubes occasionally, until they are golden brown.

3 Meanwhile, bring a pan of water to the boil. Carefully slide in the shelled eggs, one at a time. Gently poach the eggs for 4 minutes, until lightly cooked.

4 Divide the salad leaves between two plates. Remove the croûtons from the pan, and arrange them over the leaves. Wipe the pan clean with kitchen paper.

5 Heat the remaining olive oil in the pan, add the garlic and vinegar, and cook over a high heat for 1 minute. Pour the warm dressing over each salad.

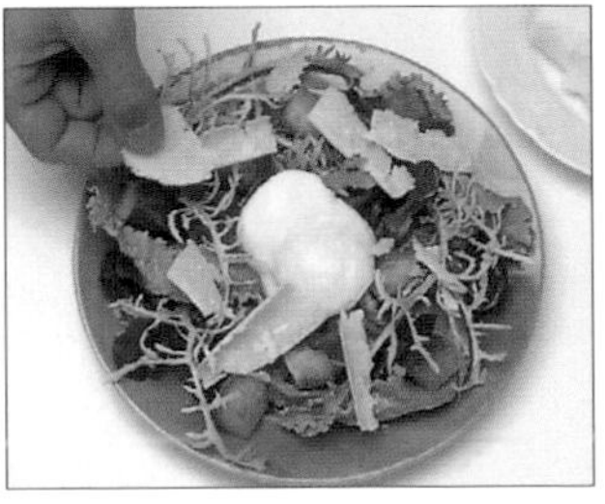

6 Place a poached egg on each salad. Sprinkle with shavings of Parmesan and freshly ground black pepper, if using.

VARIATION

As an alternative to the poached eggs, you could add 40g/1½oz/¾ cup of Greek black olives.

COOK'S TIP

Add a dash of vinegar to the water before poaching the eggs. This helps to keep the whites together. To make sure that a poached egg has a good shape, swirl the water with a spoon, whirlpool-fashion, before sliding in the egg.

Roasted Tomato and Mozzarella Salad with Basil Dressing

ROASTING THE TOMATOES adds a new dimension to this salad. Make the basil oil just before serving to retain its fresh flavour and vivid colour.

INGREDIENTS

6 large plum tomatoes
olive oil, for brushing
2 balls fresh mozzarella cheese, cut into 8–12 slices
salt and freshly ground black pepper
basil leaves, to garnish

For the basil oil
25 basil leaves
60ml/4 tbsp extra virgin olive oil
1 garlic clove, crushed
Serves 4

1 Preheat the oven to 200°C/400°F/ Gas 6 and oil a baking tray. Cut the tomatoes in half lengthways and remove the seeds. Place skin-side down on the baking tray and roast for 20 minutes or until the tomatoes are tender but still retain their shape.

2 Meanwhile, make the basil oil. Place the basil leaves, olive oil and garlic in a food processor or blender and process until smooth. Transfer to a bowl and chill until required.

3 For each serving, place the tomato halves on top of 2 or 3 slices of mozzarella and drizzle over the oil. Season well. Garnish with basil leaves and serve at once.

HEALTH BENEFITS

Basil is a natural tranquillizer and calms the nervous system. It can also stimulate the appetite and is good for the digestion, easing cramps and nausea.

Mixed Herb Salad with Toasted Mixed Seeds

THIS SIMPLE SALAD is the perfect antidote to a rich, heavy meal as it contains fresh herbs that can ease the digestion. Balsamic vinegar adds a rich, sweet taste to the dressing, but red or white wine vinegar could be used instead.

INGREDIENTS

90g/3½oz/4 cups mixed salad leaves
50g/2oz/2 cups mixed salad herbs, such as coriander, parsley, basil and rocket
25g/1oz/3 tbsp pumpkin seeds
25g/1oz/3 tbsp sunflower seeds

For the dressing
60ml/4 tbsp extra virgin olive oil
15ml/1 tbsp balsamic vinegar
2.5 ml/½ tsp Dijon mustard
salt and freshly ground black pepper
Serves 4

1 To make the dressing, combine the ingredients in a bowl or screw-top jar, shake or mix with a small whisk or fork until combined.

HEALTH BENEFITS

- *Parsley contains useful amounts of vitamin C and iron.*
- *Pumpkin and sunflower seeds, although high in calories, are full of useful vitamins, minerals and fibre, including iron, vitamin E and zinc.*

2 Put the salad and herb leaves in a large bowl.

3 Toast the pumpkin and sunflower seeds in a dry frying pan over a medium heat for 2 minutes until golden, tossing frequently to prevent them burning. Allow the seeds to cool slightly before sprinkling them over the salad.

4 Pour the dressing over the salad and toss with your hands until the leaves are well coated, then serve.

Pear and Pecan Salad with Blue Cheese

TOASTED PECAN nuts have a special union with crisp white pears. Their robust flavours combine especially well with a rich blue cheese dressing and make this a salad to remember.

INGREDIENTS

75g/3oz/½ cup shelled pecan nuts, roughly chopped
3 crisp pears
175g/6oz young spinach, stems removed
1 escarole or butterhead lettuce
1 radicchio
30ml/2 tbsp ready-made blue cheese dressing
salt and freshly ground black pepper
crusty bread, to serve

Serves 4

1 Toast the pecan nuts under a moderate grill, to bring out their sweet, rich flavour.

2 Cut the pears into even slices, leaving the skin intact and discarding the cores.

3 Wash the salad leaves and spin dry. Add the pears together with the toasted pecans, then toss with the dressing. Distribute between 4 large plates and season with salt and pepper. Serve with warm crusty bread.

VARIATION

If you want a lighter non-cheese dressing, combine 5ml/1 tsp of wholegrain mustard, 2.5ml/½ tsp of granulated sugar, 1.5ml/¼ tsp of dried tarragon, 10ml/2 tsp of lemon juice and 60ml/4 tbsp of olive oil in a jar and shake vigorously.

New Spring Vegetable Salad

THIS CHUNKY salad makes a satisfying meal. Use other spring vegetables, if you like.

INGREDIENTS

675g/1½lb small new potatoes, halved
400g/14oz can broad beans, drained
115g/4oz cherry tomatoes
75g/3oz/½ cup walnut halves
30ml/2 tbsp white wine vinegar
15ml/1 tbsp wholegrain mustard
60ml/4 tbsp olive oil
pinch of sugar
225g/8oz young asparagus spears, trimmed
6 spring onions, trimmed
salt and freshly ground black pepper
baby spinach leaves, to serve

Serves 4

1 Put the potatoes in a saucepan. Cover with cold water and bring to the boil. Cook for 10–12 minutes, until tender. Meanwhile, put the broad beans in a bowl. Cut the tomatoes in half and add them to the bowl with the walnuts and mix.

2 Put the white wine vinegar, mustard, olive oil and sugar into a jar. Season with salt and pepper. Close the jar tightly and shake well.

3 Add the asparagus to the potatoes and cook for 3 minutes more. Drain the cooked vegetables well. Cool under cold running water and drain. Thickly slice the potatoes and cut the spring onions in half.

4 Add the asparagus, potatoes and spring onions to the bowl containing the broad bean mixture. Pour the dressing over the salad and toss well. Serve on a bed of baby spinach leaves.

Couscous Salad

THIS IS a spicy variation on a classic lemon-flavoured tabbouleh, which is traditionally made with bulgur wheat, rather than couscous.

INGREDIENTS

45ml/3 tbsp olive oil
5 spring onions, chopped
1 garlic clove, crushed
1 tsp ground cumin
350ml/12fl oz/1½ cups vegetable stock
175g/6oz/1 cup couscous
2 tomatoes, peeled and chopped
60ml/4 tbsp chopped fresh parsley
60ml/4 tbsp chopped fresh mint
1 fresh green chilli, seeded and finely chopped
30ml/2 tbsp lemon juice
salt and freshly ground black pepper
crisp lettuce leaves, to serve
toasted pine nuts and grated lemon rind, to garnish

Serves 4

1 Heat the oil in a saucepan. Add the spring onions and garlic. Stir in the cumin and cook for 1 minute. Add the stock and bring to the boil.

2 Remove the pan from the heat, stir in the couscous, cover the pan and leave it to stand for 10 minutes, until the couscous has swelled and all the liquid has been absorbed. If you are using instant couscous, follow the package instructions.

3 Tip the couscous into a bowl. Stir in the tomatoes, parsley, mint, chilli and lemon juice. Season with salt and pepper. If possible, leave to stand for up to an hour, to allow the flavours to develop fully.

4 To serve, line a bowl with lettuce leaves and spoon the couscous salad over the top. Scatter the toasted pine nuts and grated lemon rind over the top, to garnish.

Brown Bean Salad

BROWN BEANS, sometimes called 'ful medames', are widely used in Egyptian cooking, and are occasionally seen in health food shops here. Dried broad beans, black or kidney beans make a good substitute.

INGREDIENTS

350g/12oz/1½ cups dried brown beans
2 sprigs of fresh thyme
2 bay leaves
1 onion, halved
4 garlic cloves, crushed
2.5ml/½ tsp cumin seeds, crushed
3 spring onions, finely chopped
90ml/6 tbsp chopped fresh parsley
20ml/4 tsp lemon juice
90ml/6 tbsp olive oil
3 hard-boiled eggs, shelled and roughly chopped
1 pickled cucumber, roughly chopped
salt and freshly ground black pepper

Serves 6

1 Put the beans in a bowl with plenty of cold water and leave to soak overnight. Drain, transfer to a saucepan and cover with fresh water. Bring to the boil and boil rapidly for 10 minutes.

2 Reduce the heat and add the thyme, bay leaves and onion. Simmer very gently for about 1 hour, until tender, adding more water if necessary. Drain and discard the herbs and onion.

3 Mix together the garlic, cumin, spring onions, parsley, lemon juice and oil. Season with salt and pepper. Pour over the beans and toss lightly together. Gently stir in the eggs and cucumber and serve at once.

COOK'S TIP

The cooking time for dried beans can vary considerably. They may need only 45 minutes, or a lot longer.

Pepper and Wild Mushroom Pasta Salad

A COMBINATION of grilled red, green and yellow peppers with wild mushrooms makes this pasta salad colourful as well as nutritious.

INGREDIENTS

1 red pepper, halved
1 yellow pepper, halved
1 green pepper, halved
350g/12oz/3 cups wholewheat pasta shells or twists
30ml/2 tbsp olive oil
45ml/3 tbsp balsamic vinegar
75ml/5 tbsp tomato juice
30ml/2 tbsp chopped fresh basil
15ml/1 tbsp chopped fresh thyme
175g/6oz/2 cups shiitake mushrooms
175g/6oz/2 cups oyster mushrooms
400g/14oz can black-eyed beans, rinsed and drained
115g/4oz/$^2/_3$ cup sultanas
2 bunches spring onions, finely chopped
salt and freshly ground black pepper

Serves 6

1 Preheat the grill. Put the peppers cut-side down on a grill pan rack and place under the hot grill for 10–15 minutes, until the skins are charred. Cover the peppers with a clean, damp dish towel and set aside to cool.

2 Meanwhile, cook the pasta in lightly salted boiling water for 10–12 minutes, until tender, then drain thoroughly.

3 Mix together the oil, vinegar, tomato juice, fresh basil and thyme. Add to the warm pasta and toss together.

4 Remove and discard the skins from the peppers. Seed and slice the peppers and add to the pasta with the sliced raw mushrooms, canned beans, sultanas and spring onions. Season with salt and freshly ground pepper. Toss the ingredients to mix and serve immediately, or cover and chill in the fridge before serving.

Wholewheat Pasta Salad

THIS SUBSTANTIAL salad is easily assembled from any combination of seasonal vegetables.

INGREDIENTS

450g/1lb/4 cups short wholewheat pasta, such as fusilli or penne
45ml/3 tbsp olive oil
2 medium carrots
1 small head broccoli
175g/6oz/1 cup shelled peas, fresh or frozen
1 red or yellow pepper, seeded
2 sticks celery
4 spring onions
1 large tomato
75g/3oz/½ cup stoned olives

For the dressing

45ml/3 tbsp wine or balsamic vinegar
60ml/4 tbsp olive oil
15ml/1 tbsp Dijon mustard
15ml/1 tbsp sesame seeds
10ml/2 tsp chopped mixed fresh herbs such as parsley, thyme and basil
115g/4oz/1 cup diced Cheddar or mozzarella, or a combination of both
salt and freshly ground black pepper
coriander, to garnish

Serves 8

1 Cook the pasta in a large pan of rapidly boiling salted water until it is tender. Drain and rinse under cold water to stop the cooking.

2 Drain the pasta well and turn into a large bowl. Toss with the olive oil and set aside. Allow to cool completely before mixing with the other ingredients.

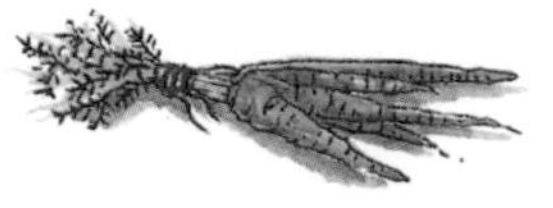

3 Lightly blanch the carrots, broccoli and shelled peas in a large pan of boiling water. Refresh under cold water. Drain well.

4 Chop the carrots and broccoli into bite-size pieces and add to the pasta with the peas. Slice the pepper, celery, spring onions and tomato into small pieces. Add them to the salad with the olives.

5 Make the dressing in a small bowl by whisking the vinegar with the oil and mustard to make a thick dressing. Stir in the sesame seeds and herbs. Mix the dressing into the salad so that the leaves are well coated. Taste for seasoning, add salt and pepper or more oil and vinegar as necessary. Stir in the cheese. Allow the salad to stand for 15 minutes before serving. Garnish with coriander.

Rocket, Pear and Parmesan Salad

FOR A sophisticated start to an elaborate meal, try this simple salad of honey-rich pears, fresh Parmesan and the aromatic leaves of rocket.

INGREDIENTS

3 ripe pears, Williams or Packhams
10ml/2 tsp lemon juice
45ml/3 tbsp hazelnut or walnut oil
115g/4oz rocket
75g/3oz Parmesan cheese
freshly ground black pepper
open-textured bread, to serve

Serves 4

1 Peel and core the pears and slice thickly. Moisten with lemon juice to keep the flesh white.

2 Combine the nut oil with the pears. Add the rocket leaves and toss the ingredients to mix.

3 Turn the salad out on to 4 small plates and top with shavings of Parmesan cheese. Season with freshly ground black pepper and serve with open-textured bread.

COOK'S TIP

If you are unable to buy rocket easily, you can grow your own from early spring to late summer.

Tomato, Spring Onion and Coriander Salad

KNOWN AS Cachumbar, this salad relish is most commonly served with Indian curries. There are many versions, and this one will leave your mouth feeling cool and fresh after a spicy meal.

INGREDIENTS

3 ripe tomatoes
2 spring onions, chopped
1.5ml/¼ tsp caster sugar
45ml/3 tbsp chopped fresh coriander
salt

Serves 4

2 Halve the tomatoes and remove the seeds. Place the tomatoes upside down in a sieve and leave to drain. Cut the flesh into small dice.

3 Combine the tomatoes with the spring onions, sugar, chopped coriander and salt. Serve at room temperature.

1 Remove the tough cores from the tomatoes with a small sharp knife.

COOK'S TIP

This refreshing salad also makes a fine filler for pitta bread with hummus.

Fresh Ceps with a Parsley Dressing

To capture the just-picked flavour of mushrooms, try this delicious salad enriched with an egg yolk and walnut oil dressing. Choose small ceps or bay boletus for a firm texture and a fine flavour.

INGREDIENTS

350g/12oz/5 cups fresh ceps or bay boletus
175g/6oz mixed salad leaves such as batavia, young spinach and frisée
50g/2oz/½ cup broken walnut pieces, toasted
50g/2oz Parmesan cheese
salt and freshly ground black pepper

For the dressing
2 egg yolks
2.5ml/½ tsp French mustard
75ml/5 tbsp groundnut oil
45ml/3 tbsp walnut oil
30ml/2 tbsp lemon juice
30ml/2 tbsp chopped fresh parsley
pinch of caster sugar
Serves 4

1 For the dressing, place the egg yolks in a screw-top jar with the mustard, oils, lemon juice, parsley and sugar. Shake well.

Cook's Tip

The dressing for this salad uses raw egg yolks. Be sure to use only the freshest eggs from a reputable supplier. Pregnant women, young children and the elderly are not advised to eat raw egg yolks. If this presents a problem, the dressing can be made without the egg yolks.

2 Slice the mushrooms thinly using a sharp knife.

3 Place the mushrooms in a large salad bowl and pour over the dressing and mix together well. Leave to stand for 10–15 minutes for the flavours to mingle.

4 Wash and spin the salad leaves, then toss with the mushrooms.

5 Arrange the salad on four large plates, season with salt and freshly ground pepper then scatter with toasted walnut pieces and shavings of Parmesan cheese.

Gado Gado

THE PEANUT sauce on this traditional Indonesian vegetable dish owes its flavour to galangal, an aromatic rhizome that resembles ginger.

INGREDIENTS

250g/9oz/2¼ cups white cabbage, shredded
4 carrots, cut into matchsticks
4 celery sticks, cut into matchsticks
250g/9oz/generous 1 cup beansprouts
½ cucumber, cut into matchsticks
fried onion, salted peanuts and sliced fresh chilli, to garnish

For the peanut sauce
15ml/1 tbsp oil
1 small onion, finely chopped
1 garlic clove, crushed
1 small piece galangal, peeled and grated
5ml/1 tsp ground cumin
1.5ml/¼ tsp ground chilli powder
5ml/1 tsp tamarind paste or lime juice
60ml/4 tbsp crunchy peanut butter
5ml/1 tsp soft light brown sugar

Serves 4

1 Steam the cabbage, carrots and celery for about 3–4 minutes, until just tender. Leave to cool. Spread out the beansprouts on a large serving dish. Arrange the cabbage, carrots, celery and cucumber on top.

2 To make the sauce, heat the oil in a saucepan, add the onion and garlic and cook gently for 5 minutes, until soft.

3 Stir in the spices and cook for 1 minute more. Add the tamarind paste or lime juice, peanut butter and sugar. Mix well.

4 Heat the sauce gently, stirring occasionally and adding a little hot water if necessary, to make the sauce runny enough to coat the vegetables when poured.

5 Spoon a little of the sauce over the vegetables and toss lightly together. Garnish with fried onions, peanuts and sliced chilli. Serve the rest of the sauce in a bowl separately.

COOK'S TIP

As long as the sauce remains the same, the vegetables can be altered at the whim of the cook and to reflect the contents of the vegetable rack or chiller.

Fruity Rice Salad

An appetizing and colourful rice salad combining many different flavours, ideal for a packed lunch.

INGREDIENTS

225g/8oz/1 cup mixed brown and wild rice
1 yellow pepper, seeded and diced
1 bunch spring onions, chopped
3 sticks celery, chopped
1 large beefsteak tomato, chopped
2 green-skinned eating apples, chopped
175g/6oz/¾ cup ready-to-eat dried apricots, chopped
115g/4oz/⅔ cup raisins
30ml/2 tbsp unsweetened apple juice
30ml/2 tbsp dry sherry
30ml/2 tbsp light soy sauce
dash of Tabasco sauce
30ml/2 tbsp chopped fresh parsley
15ml/1 tbsp chopped fresh rosemary
salt and freshly ground black pepper

Serves 4–6

1 Cook the rice in a large saucepan of lightly salted boiling water for about 30 minutes (or according to the package instructions) until tender. Rinse the cooked rice under cold running water to cool quickly, and then drain thoroughly.

2 Place the pepper, spring onions, celery, tomato, apples, apricots, raisins and the cooked rice in a serving bowl and mix well.

3 In a small bowl, mix together the apple juice, sherry, soy sauce, Tabasco sauce and herbs. Season with salt and pepper.

4 Pour the dressing over the rice mixture and toss the ingredients together to mix thoroughly. Serve immediately or cover and chill in the fridge before serving.

COOK'S TIP

You can substitute fennel for celery, and it will give a sweet aniseed flavour. Drop the chopped pieces into acidulated water to preserve their whiteness.

Marinated Cucumber Salad

SPRINKLING THE cucumber with salt draws out some of the water and makes it crisper.

INGREDIENTS

2 medium cucumbers
15ml/1 tbsp salt
90g/3½oz/½ cup granulated sugar
175ml/6fl oz/¾ cup dry cider
15ml/1 tbsp cider vinegar
45ml/3 tbsp chopped fresh dill
pinch of freshly ground black pepper
sprig of dill, to garnish

Serves 4–6

1 Slice the cucumbers thinly and place them in a colander, sprinkling salt between each layer. Put the colander over a bowl and leave to drain for 1 hour.

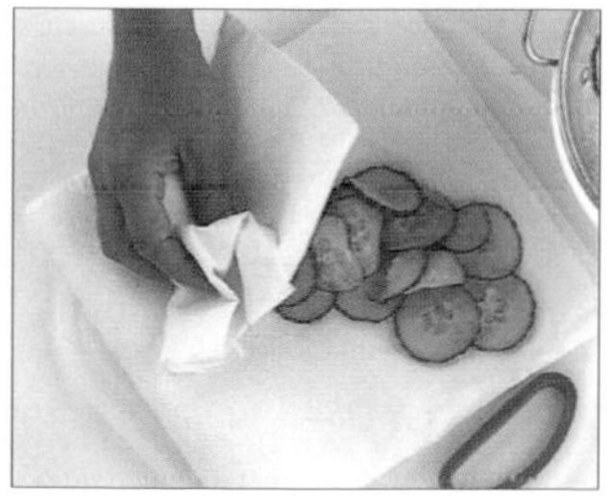

2 Thoroughly rinse the cucumber slices under cold running water to remove excess salt, then pat dry on absorbent kitchen paper.

3 Gently heat the sugar, cider and vinegar in a saucepan, until the sugar has dissolved. Remove from the heat and leave to cool. Put the cucumber slices in a bowl, pour over the cider mixture and leave to marinate for 2 hours.

4 Drain the cucumber and sprinkle with the dill and pepper to taste. Mix well and transfer to a serving dish. Garnish with a sprig of dill. Chill in the fridge until ready to serve.

Fennel, Orange and Rocket Salad

THIS LIGHT and refreshing salad is the ideal companion for spicy or rich foods.

INGREDIENTS

2 oranges
1 fennel bulb
115g/4oz rocket leaves
50g/2oz/⅓ cup black olives

For the dressing
30ml/2 tbsp olive oil
15ml/1 tbsp balsamic vinegar
1 small garlic clove, crushed
salt and freshly ground black pepper
Serves 4

1 With a vegetable peeler, cut strips of rind from the oranges, leaving the pith behind.

2 Cut the strips into thin julienne strips. Cook in boiling water for a few minutes. Drain.

3 Peel the oranges, removing all the white pith. Cut the orange flesh crossways into thin rounds and discard any pips.

4 Cut the fennel bulb in half lengthways and slice across the bulb as thinly as possible. It is easier to do this with a food processor fitted with a slicing disk or using a mandoline.

5 Combine the oranges and fennel in a serving bowl and toss with the rocket leaves.

6 Blend oil, vinegar, garlic, salt and pepper, and pour over the salad. Toss and leave to stand for 5 minutes. Sprinkle with olives and orange peel.

Aubergine, Lemon and Caper Salad

THIS COOKED vegetable relish is delicious served with pasta or simply on its own with crusty bread.

INGREDIENTS

1 large aubergine, about 675g/1½lb
5ml/1 tsp salt
60ml/4 tbsp olive oil
grated rind and juice of 1 lemon
30ml/2 tbsp capers, rinsed
12 stoned green olives
1 small garlic clove, chopped
30ml/2 tbsp chopped fresh flat leaf parsley
salt and freshly ground black pepper
Serves 4

1 Cut the aubergine into 2.5cm/1in cubes. Place the cubes in a colander and sprinkle over the salt. Set aside for 30 minutes, then rinse thoroughly under cold running water. Pat dry with kitchen paper.

2 Heat the olive oil in a large frying pan. Cook the aubergine cubes over medium heat for about 10 minutes, tossing regularly, until golden and softened. You may need to do this in two batches to ensure that all the aubergine cubes brown well. Drain on kitchen paper and season with a little salt.

COOK'S TIP

This will taste even better when made the day before. It will keep, covered in the fridge, for up to 4 days. To enrich this dish to serve on its own as a main course, add toasted pine nuts and shavings of Parmesan cheese. Serve with warmed crusty bread.

3 Place the aubergine cubes in a large serving bowl, toss with the lemon rind and juice, capers, olives, garlic and chopped parsley.

4 Season with salt and pepper. Serve at room temperature.

Warm Vegetable Salad with Peanut Sauce

BASED ON THE CLASSIC Indonesian salad, gado-gado, this salad features raw red pepper and sprouted beans, which make a crunchy contrast to the warm steamed broccoli, green beans and carrots. Topped with slices of hard-boiled egg. this salad is substantial enough to serve as a main course.

INGREDIENTS

8 new potatoes
225g/8oz broccoli, cut into small florets
200g/7oz/1 ½ cups fine green beans
2 carrots, cut into thin ribbons with a vegetable peeler
1 red pepper, seeded and cut into strips
50g/2oz/½ cup sprouted beans
sprigs of watercress, to garnish

For the peanut sauce

15ml/1 tbsp sunflower oil
1 bird's eye chilli, seeded and sliced
1 garlic clove, crushed
5ml/1 tsp ground coriander
5ml/1 tsp ground cumin
60ml/4 tbsp crunchy peanut butter
75ml/5 tbsp water
15ml/1 tbsp dark soy sauce
1cm/½in piece fresh root ginger, finely grated
5ml/1 tsp soft dark brown sugar
15ml/1 tbsp lime juice
60ml/4 tbsp coconut milk

Serves 2–4

HEALTH BENEFITS

Sprouted beans, which are available from health food shops and some supermarkets, are easily digestible and packed with concentrated goodness. When fresh, their vitamin and enzyme content is at its peak and they are believed to stimulate the body's ability to cleanse itself. They provide valuable amounts of vitamin E, which is said to improve fertility.

1 First make the peanut sauce. Heat the oil in a saucepan, add the chilli and garlic, and cook for 1 minute or until softened. Add the spices and cook for 1 minute. Stir in the peanut butter and water, then cook for 2 minutes until combined, stirring constantly.

2 Add the soy sauce, ginger, sugar, lime juice and coconut milk, then cook over a low heat until smooth and heated through, stirring frequently. Transfer to a bowl.

3 Bring a saucepan of lightly salted water to the boil, add the potatoes and cook for 10–15 minutes, until tender. Drain, then halve or thickly slice the potatoes, depending on their size.

4 Meanwhile, steam the broccoli and green beans for 4–5 minutes until tender but still crisp. Add the carrots 2 minutes before the end of the cooking time.

5 Arrange the cooked vegetables on a serving platter with the red pepper and sprouted beans. Garnish with watercress and serve with the peanut sauce.

Avocado, Red Onion and Spinach Salad with Polenta Croûtons

THE SIMPLE LEMON DRESSING gives a sharp tang to the creamy avocado, sweet red onions and crisp spinach. Golden polenta croûtons, with their crunchy golden exterior and soft centre, add a delicious contrast.

INGREDIENTS

1 large red onion, cut into wedges
300g/11oz ready-made polenta, cut into 1cm/½in cubes
olive oil, for brushing
225g/8oz baby spinach leaves
1 avocado, peeled, stoned and sliced
5ml/1 tsp lemon juice

For the dressing
60ml/4 tbsp extra virgin olive oil
juice of ½ lemon
salt and freshly ground black pepper

Serves 4

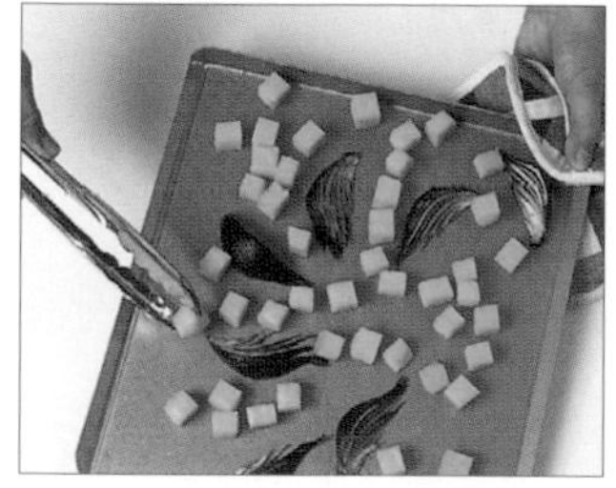

1 Preheat the oven to 200°C/400°F/Gas 6. Place the onion wedges and polenta cubes on a lightly oiled baking sheet and bake for 25 minutes or until the onion is tender and the polenta is crisp and golden, turning them regularly to prevent them sticking. Leave to cool slightly.

2 Meanwhile, make the dressing. Place the olive oil, lemon juice and seasoning to taste in a bowl or screw-top jar. Stir or shake thoroughly to combine.

3 Place the spinach leaves in a serving bowl. Toss the avocado in the lemon juice to prevent it browning, then add to the spinach with the roasted onions.

4 Pour the dressing over the salad and toss gently to combine. Sprinkle the polenta croûtons on top or hand them round separately and serve immediately.

HEALTH BENEFITS

Avocados have been traditionally regarded as a high fat food that should be avoided. However, although they do contain high amounts of fat, it is beneficial monounsaturated fat, and new research has revealed that regularly eating avocados can actually decrease the level of cholesterol in the body. Avocados also have a valuable mineral content and eating them can improve the condition of your skin and hair.

COOK'S TIP

If you can't find ready-made polenta, you can make your own using instant polenta grains. Simply cook according to the packet instructions, then pour into a tray and leave to cool and set.

Feta and Mint Potato Salad

FETA CHEESE, YOGURT AND fresh mint combine perfectly with warm new potatoes in this salad.

INGREDIENTS

500g/1 1/4lb pink fir apple potatoes
90g/3 1/2oz feta cheese, crumbled

For the dressing

225g/8oz/1 cup natural live yogurt
15g/1/2oz/1/2 cup fresh mint leaves
30ml/2 tbsp mayonnaise
salt and freshly ground black pepper
Serves 4

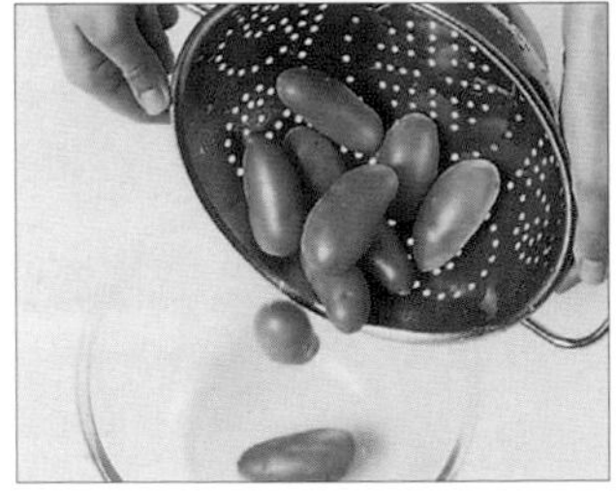

1 Steam the potatoes over a saucepan of boiling water for about 20 minutes until tender, then drain well and tip into a large bowl.

2 Meanwhile, make the dressing. Place the yogurt and mint in a food processor for a few minutes until the mint leaves are finely chopped. Transfer the dressing to a small bowl.

3 Stir in the mayonnaise and season to taste. Spoon the dressing over the warm potatoes and scatter with the feta cheese. Serve immediately.

COOK'S TIPS

Pink fir apple potatoes have a smooth waxy texture and retain their shape when cooked, making them ideal for salads. Charlotte and other special salad potatoes could be used instead.

HEALTH BENEFITS

Potatoes are often considered to be fattening, but it is usually the method of preparation that is to be blamed. Steaming adds no calories and preserves the vitamin C content.

Apple and Beetroot Salad with Red Leaves

BITTER LEAVES ARE COMPLEMENTED by sweet-flavoured apples and beetroot in this summer salad.

INGREDIENTS

50g/2oz/1/3 cup whole unblanched almonds
2 red apples, cored and diced
juice of 1/2 lemon
115g/4oz/4 cups red salad leaves, such as lollo rosso, oak leaf and radicchio
200g/7oz cooked beetroot in natural juice, sliced

For the dressing

30ml/2 tbsp olive oil
15ml/1 tbsp walnut oil
15ml/1 tbsp red or white wine vinegar
salt and freshly ground black pepper
Serves 4

1 Toast the almonds in a dry frying pan for 2–3 minutes until golden brown, tossing frequently to prevent them burning.

2 Meanwhile, make the dressing. Put the olive and walnut oils, vinegar and seasoning in a bowl or screw-top jar. Stir or shake thoroughly to combine.

3 Toss the apples in lemon juice to prevent them browning, then place in a large bowl and add the salad leaves, beetroot and almonds. Pour over the dressing and toss gently.

HEALTH BENEFITS

Red fruits and vegetables have high levels of vitamins C and E and beta carotene.

Sesame Noodle Salad

TOASTED SESAME OIL ADDS a nutty flavour to this Asian-style salad. Best served warm, it is substantial enough to serve as a main meal.

INGREDIENTS

250g/9oz medium egg noodles
200g/7oz/1 cup sugar snap peas or mangetouts, sliced diagonally
2 carrots, cut into julienne
2 tomatoes, seeded and diced
30ml/2 tbsp chopped fresh coriander
15ml/1 tbsp sesame seeds
3 spring onions, shredded
fresh coriander, to garnish

For the dressing
10ml/2 tsp light soy sauce
30ml/2 tbsp toasted sesame seed oil
15ml/1 tbsp sunflower oil
4cm/1 1/2in piece fresh root ginger, finely grated
1 garlic clove, crushed

Serves 2–4

1 Place the noodles in a saucepan of lightly salted boiling water and bring back to the boil. Cook for 2 minutes, then add the sugar snap peas or mangetouts and cook for a further 2 minutes. Drain and rinse under cold running water.

HEALTH BENEFITS

Garlic is highly antiseptic, particularly in its raw form, and, like ginger, can help to ward off colds and flu and stimulate circulation.

2 Meanwhile, make the dressing. Combine the soy sauce, sesame and sunflower oils, ginger and garlic in a screw-top jar or bowl. Shake or mix to combine thoroughly.

3 Place the noodles and the peas or mangetouts in a bowl and add the carrots, tomatoes and coriander. Pour the dressing over the top, and toss with your hands to combine. Sprinkle with the sesame seeds and top with the spring onions and coriander.

Japanese Salad

HIJIKI IS A MILD-TASTING seaweed, and combined with radishes, cucumber and beansprouts, it makes a delicate, refreshing salad.

INGREDIENTS

15g/1/2oz/1/2 cup hijiki
250g/9oz/1 1/4 cups radishes, sliced into very thin rounds
1 small cucumber, cut into thin sticks
75g/3oz/1/2 cup beansprouts

For the dressing
15ml/1 tbsp sunflower oil
15ml/1 tbsp toasted sesame oil
5ml/1 tsp light soy sauce
30ml/2 tbsp rice vinegar or 15ml/1 tbsp wine vinegar
15ml/1 tbsp mirin

Serves 4

1 Soak the hijiki in a bowl of cold water for 10–15 minutes until rehydrated, drain, rinse under cold running water and drain again. It should almost triple in volume.

2 Place the hijiki in a saucepan of water. Bring to the boil, then reduce the heat and simmer for about 30 minutes or until tender. Drain.

3 Meanwhile, make the dressing. Place the sunflower and sesame oils, soy sauce, vinegar and mirin in a bowl or screw-top jar. Stir or shake thoroughly to combine.

4 Arrange the hijiki in a shallow bowl or platter with the radishes, cucumber and beansprouts. Pour over the dressing and toss lightly.

HEALTH BENEFITS

Hijiki is treasured as one of nature's richest sources of minerals, the balance of which is said to counteract high blood pressure. The seaweed has a distinguished reputation in Japan for enhancing beauty and adding lustre to hair.

Watercress, Pear, Walnut and Roquefort Salad

SHARP-TASTING BLUE ROQUEFORT and peppery watercress leaves are complemented in this salad by sweet pears and crunchy walnuts.

INGREDIENTS

75g/3oz/½ cup shelled walnuts, halved
2 red Williams pears, cored and sliced
15ml/1 tbsp lemon juice
150g/5oz/1 large bunch watercress, tough stalks removed
200g/7oz/scant 2 cups Roquefort cheese, cut into chunks

For the dressing

45ml/3 tbsp extra virgin olive oil
30ml/2 tbsp lemon juice
2.5ml/½ tsp clear honey
5ml/1 tsp Dijon mustard
salt and freshly ground black pepper
Serves 4

1 Toast the walnuts in a dry frying pan for 2 minutes until golden, tossing frequently to prevent them burning.

HEALTH BENEFITS

Watercress is reputed to energize the liver, kidney and bladder. It provides vitamins A and C, thought to play a role in combating cancer. It also contains natural antibiotic compounds.

2 Meanwhile, make the dressing. Place the olive oil, lemon juice, honey, mustard and seasoning in a bowl or screw-top jar. Stir or shake thoroughly to combine.

3 Toss the pear slices in the lemon juice, then place them in a bowl and add the watercress, walnuts and Roquefort. Pour the dressing over the salad, toss well and serve immediately.

Panzanella

OPEN-TEXTURED, ITALIAN-STYLE bread is essential for this colourful, classic Tuscan salad.

INGREDIENTS

275g/10oz/10 slices day-old Italian-style bread, thickly sliced
1 cucumber, peeled and cut into chunks
5 tomatoes, seeded and diced
1 large red onion, chopped
200g/7oz/1⅓ cups good quality olives
20 basil leaves, torn

For the dressing

60ml/4 tbsp extra virgin olive oil
15ml/1 tbsp red or white wine vinegar
salt and freshly ground black pepper
Serves 6

1 Soak the bread in water for about 2 minutes, then lift out and squeeze gently, first with your hands and then in a dish towel to remove any excess water. Chill for 1 hour.

HEALTH BENEFITS

Rich in healthy monounsaturated fat, olives act as a gentle laxative and have a soothing effect on the digestive system.

2 Meanwhile, to make the dressing, place the oil, vinegar and seasoning in a bowl or screw-top jar. Shake or mix thoroughly to combine. Place the cucumber, tomatoes, onion and olives in a bowl.

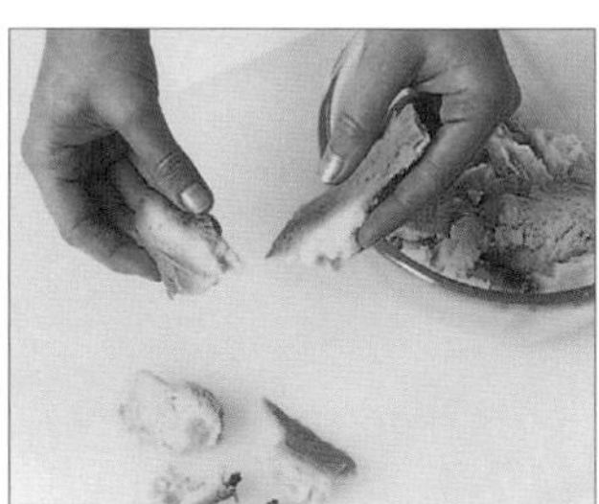

3 Break the bread into chunks and add to the bowl with the basil. Pour the dressing over the salad, and toss before serving.

White Bean Salad with Roasted Red Pepper Dressing

The speckled herb and red pepper dressing adds a wonderful colour contrast to this salad, which is best served warm. Canned beans are used for convenience – substitute cooked, dried beans, if you prefer.

INGREDIENTS

1 large red pepper
60ml/4 tbsp olive oil
1 large garlic clove, crushed
25g/1oz/1 cup fresh oregano leaves or flat leaf parsley
15ml/1 tbsp balsamic vinegar
400g/14oz/3 cups canned flageolet beans, drained and rinsed
200g/7oz/1 1/2 cups canned cannellini beans, drained and rinsed
salt and freshly ground black pepper
Serves 4

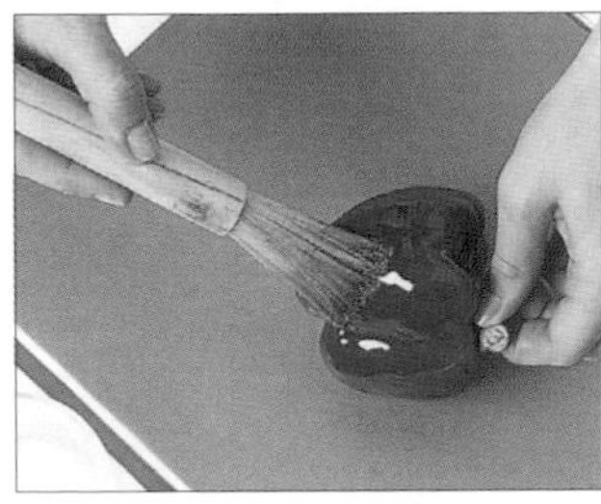

1 Preheat the oven to 200°C/400°F/Gas 6. Place the red pepper on a baking sheet, brush with oil and roast for 30 minutes or until the skin wrinkles and the flesh is soft.

2 Remove the pepper from the oven and place in a plastic bag. Seal and leave to cool. (This makes the skin easier to remove.)

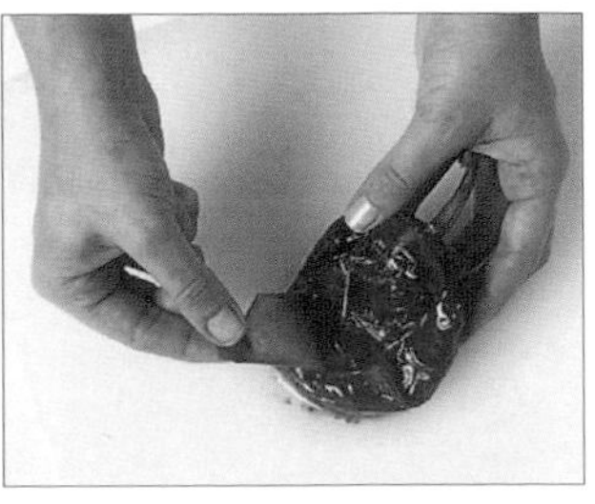

3 When the pepper is cool enough to handle, remove it from the bag and peel off the skin. Rinse under cold running water. Slice the pepper in half, remove the seeds and dice. Set aside.

4 Heat the remaining oil in a saucepan and cook the garlic for 1 minute until softened. Remove from the heat, then add the oregano or parsley, the red pepper and any juices, and the balsamic vinegar.

5 Put the beans in a large bowl and pour over the dressing. Season to taste, then stir gently until combined. Serve warm.

Health Benefits

Low in fat and high in fibre and protein, pulses such as cannellini beans should be a regular part of a healthy balanced diet. They are also a good source of many minerals, including iron, potassium, phosphorus and magnesium, as well as B complex vitamins.

Roasted Beetroot with Horseradish Dressing

FRESH BEETROOT IS ENJOYING a well-deserved renaissance. Roasting gives it a delicious sweet flavour, which contrasts wonderfully with this sharp, tangy dressing.

INGREDIENTS

450g/1lb baby beetroot, preferably with leaves
15ml/1 tbsp olive oil

For the dressing

30ml/2 tbsp lemon juice
30ml/2 tbsp mirin
120ml/8 tbsp olive oil
30ml/2 tbsp creamed horseradish
salt and freshly ground black pepper

Serves 4

1 Cook the beetroot in boiling salted water for 30 minutes. Drain, add the olive oil and toss gently. Preheat the oven to 200°C/400°F/Gas 6.

2 Place the beetroot on a baking sheet and roast for 40 minutes or until tender when pierced with a knife.

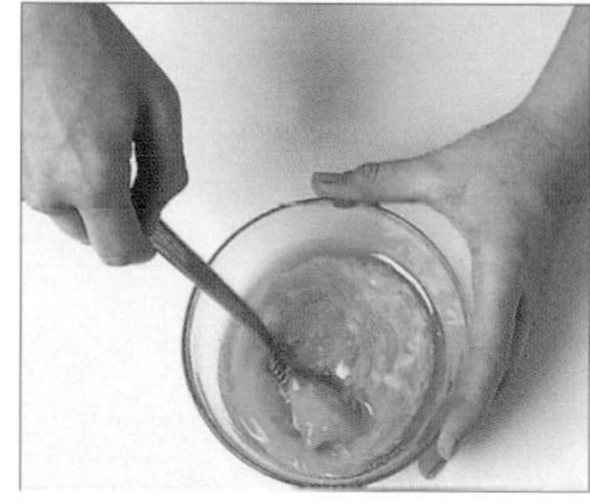

3 Meanwhile, make the dressing. Whisk together the lemon juice, mirin, olive oil and horseradish until smooth and creamy. Season.

4 Cut the beetroot in half, place in a bowl and add the dressing. Toss gently and serve immediately.

HEALTH BENEFITS

Beetroot has a reputation for containing cancer-fighting compounds and is thought to enhance the immune system. It is a powerful blood-purifier and is rich in iron, vitamins C and A, and folates, which are essential for healthy cells.

COOK'S TIP

This salad is probably at its best served warm, but you can make it in advance, if you wish, and serve it at room temperature. Add the dressing to the beetroot just before serving.

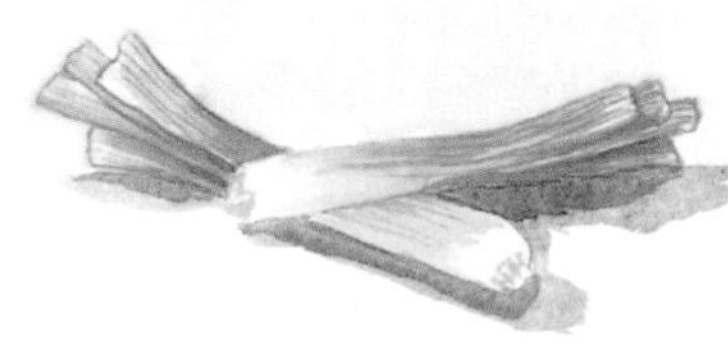

SIDE DISHES

These delicious dishes make enticing and interesting accompaniments to all sorts of main courses.

Sautéed Potatoes

THESE ROSEMARY-SCENTED, crisp golden potatoes are a favourite in French households.

INGREDIENTS

1.3kg/3lb baking potatoes

60–90ml/4–6 tbsp oil or clarified butter

2 or 3 sprigs of fresh rosemary, leaves removed and chopped

salt and freshly ground black pepper

Serves 6

1 Peel the potatoes and cut into 2.5cm/1in pieces. Place them in a bowl, cover with cold water and leave to soak for 10–15 minutes. Drain, rinse and drain again, then dry thoroughly in a dish towel.

2 Heat about 60ml/4 tbsp of the oil or butter over a medium-high heat, until very hot but not smoking. Add the potatoes and cook for 2 minutes without stirring, to seal completely and brown on one side.

3 Shake the pan and toss the potatoes to brown on another side. Season with salt and pepper.

4 Add a little more oil or butter and continue cooking the potatoes over medium-low to low heat for 20–25 minutes, until tender when pierced with a knife, stirring and shaking the pan frequently. About 5 minutes before the end of cooking, sprinkle the potatoes with the chopped rosemary and add further seasoning if wished.

Straw Potato Cake

THESE FRIED, grated potatoes resemble straw, hence the name of the recipe. You could make several small cakes instead of a large one, if you prefer – simply adjust the cooking time accordingly.

INGREDIENTS

450g/1lb baking potatoes

25ml/1½ tbsp melted butter

15ml/1 tbsp vegetable oil, plus more if needed

salt and freshly ground black pepper

Serves 4

1 Peel the potatoes and grate them coarsely, then immediately toss them with melted butter and season with salt and pepper.

2 Heat the oil in a large frying pan. Add the potato mixture and press down to form an even layer covering the pan. Cook over a medium heat for 7–10 minutes to brown the base.

3 Loosen the potato cake by shaking the pan or running a thin palette knife under it.

4 To turn the potato cake over, invert a large baking tray over the frying pan and, holding it tightly against the pan, turn them both over together. Lift off the frying pan, return it to the heat and add a little oil if it looks dry. Slide the potato cake into the frying pan and continue cooking until crisp and browned on both sides. Serve hot.

Salines de Guérande
LE SEL DE LA VIE

Puffy Creamed Potatoes

THIS DELICIOUS accompaniment consists of creamed potatoes incorporated into mini Yorkshire puddings. Serve them with a vegetable casserole or, for a meal on its own, serve two or three per person and accompany with salads.

INGREDIENTS

275g/10oz potatoes
creamy milk and butter for mashing
5ml/1 tsp chopped fresh parsley
5ml/1 tsp chopped fresh tarragon
75g/3oz/⅔ cup plain flour
1 egg
about 120ml/4fl oz/½ cup milk
oil or sunflower margarine, for baking
salt and freshly ground black pepper
Makes 6

1 Boil the potatoes until tender and mash with a little milk and butter. Stir in the chopped parsley and tarragon and season with salt and pepper. Preheat the oven to 200°C/400°F/Gas 6.

2 Process the flour, egg, milk and a pinch of salt in a food processor or blender to make a smooth batter, or whisk together by hand in a bowl.

3 Place about 2.5ml/½ tsp oil or a small knob of sunflower margarine in each of six ramekin dishes and place in the oven on a baking tray for 2–3 minutes, until the oil or fat is very hot.

4 Working quickly, pour a small amount of batter (about 20ml/4 tsp) into each ramekin dish. Add a heaped tablespoon of mashed potatoes and then pour an equal amount of the remaining batter in each dish. Return the baking tray with the ramekins to the oven and bake for 15–20 minutes, until the puddings are puffy and golden brown.

5 Using a palette knife, carefully ease the puddings out of the ramekin dishes and arrange on a large, warm serving dish. Serve at once.

Potatoes Dauphinois

RICH, CREAMY and satisfying, this is a really comforting dish to serve when it's cold outside.

INGREDIENTS

675g/1½lb potatoes, peeled and thinly sliced
1 garlic clove
25g/1oz/2 tbsp butter
300ml/½ pint/1¼ cups single cream
50ml/2fl oz/¼ cup milk
salt and freshly ground white pepper

Serves 4

1 Preheat the oven to 150°C/300°F/Gas 2. Place the potato slices in a bowl of cold water to remove the excess starch. Drain and pat dry with kitchen paper.

2 Cut the garlic in half and rub the cut side around the inside of a wide shallow ovenproof dish. Butter the dish generously. Blend the cream and milk in a jug.

3 Cover the base of the ovenproof dish with a layer of potatoes. Dot a little butter over the potato layer, then season with salt and pepper. Pour a little of the cream and milk mixture over the potatoes.

4 Continue making layers, until all the ingredients have been used up, ending with a layer of cream. Bake in the oven for about 1¼ hours. If the dish begins to brown too quickly, cover with a lid or with a piece of foil. The potatoes are ready when they are very soft and the top has a golden brown crust.

Spicy Potatoes and Cauliflower

THIS DISH is simplicity itself to make and can be eaten as a main meal with Indian breads or rice, a raita such as cucumber and yogurt, and a fresh mint relish.

INGREDIENTS

225g/8oz potatoes
75ml/5 tbsp peanut oil
5ml/1 tsp ground cumin
5ml/1 tsp ground coriander
1.5ml/¼ tsp ground turmeric
1.5ml/¼ tsp cayenne pepper
1 fresh green chilli, seeded and finely chopped
1 medium cauliflower, broken up into small florets
5ml/1 tsp cumin seeds
2 garlic cloves, cut into shreds
15–30ml/1–2 tbsp fresh coriander, finely chopped
salt

Serves 2

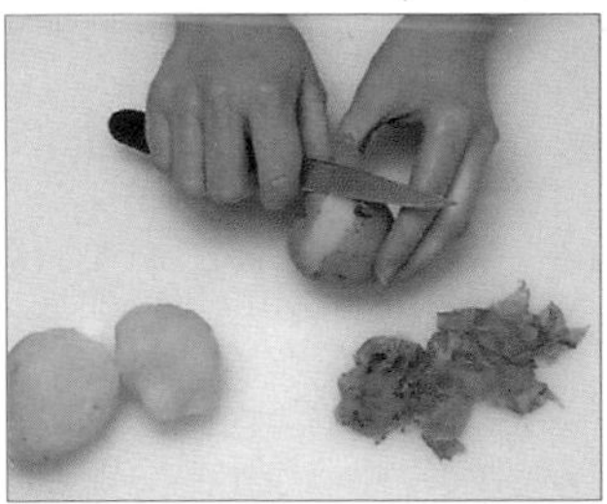

1 Cook the potatoes in their skins in boiling salted water for about 20 minutes, until just tender. Drain and let cool. When cool enough to handle, peel and cut into 2.5cm/1in cubes.

2 Heat 45ml/3 tbsp of the oil in a frying pan or wok. When hot, add the ground cumin, coriander, turmeric, cayenne pepper and chilli. Let the spices sizzle for a few seconds.

3 Add the cauliflower and about 60ml/4 tbsp water. Cook over medium heat, stirring continuously, for 6–8 minutes. Add the potatoes and stir-fry for 2–3 minutes. Season with salt, then remove from the heat.

4 Heat the remaining oil in a small frying pan. When hot, add the cumin seeds and garlic and cook until lightly browned. Pour the mixture over the vegetables. Sprinkle with the chopped coriander and serve at once.

Garlic Mashed Potatoes

THESE CREAMY mashed potatoes have a wonderful aroma. Although two bulbs seems like a lot of garlic, the flavour is sweet and subtle when cooked in this way.

INGREDIENTS

2 garlic bulbs, separated into cloves, unpeeled
115g/4oz/½ cup unsalted butter
1.3kg/3lb baking potatoes
120–175ml/4–6fl oz/½–¾ cup milk
salt and freshly ground white pepper
Serves 6–8

1 Bring a small saucepan of water to the boil over high heat. Add the garlic cloves and boil for 2 minutes, then drain and peel.

2 In a heavy frying pan, melt half of the butter over a low heat. Add the blanched garlic cloves, then cover and cook gently for 20–25 minutes, until very tender and just golden, shaking the pan and stirring occasionally. Do not allow the garlic to scorch or brown.

3 Remove the pan from the heat and cool slightly. Spoon the garlic and any butter from the pan into a blender or food processor fitted with a metal blade and process until smooth. Tip into a small bowl, press clear film on to the surface to prevent a skin forming and set aside.

4 Peel and quarter the potatoes, place in a large saucepan and add enough cold water to just cover them. Salt the water generously and bring to the boil over a high heat.

5 Cook the potatoes until tender, then drain and work through a food mill or press through a sieve back into the saucepan. Return the pan to a medium heat and, using a wooden spoon, stir the potatoes for 1–2 minutes to dry them out completely. Remove from the heat.

6 Warm the milk gently until bubbles form around the edge. Gradually beat the milk, remaining butter and garlic purée into the potatoes, then season as needed.

Roasted Potatoes, Peppers and Shallots

THIS POPULAR dish from America's Deep South is often served in elegant New Orleans restaurants.

INGREDIENTS

500g/1¼lb waxy potatoes
12 shallots
2 sweet yellow peppers
olive oil
2 sprigs of fresh rosemary
salt and freshly ground black pepper
Serves 4

1 Preheat the oven to 200°C/400°F/Gas 6. Wash the potatoes and then blanch them for 5 minutes in boiling water. Drain.

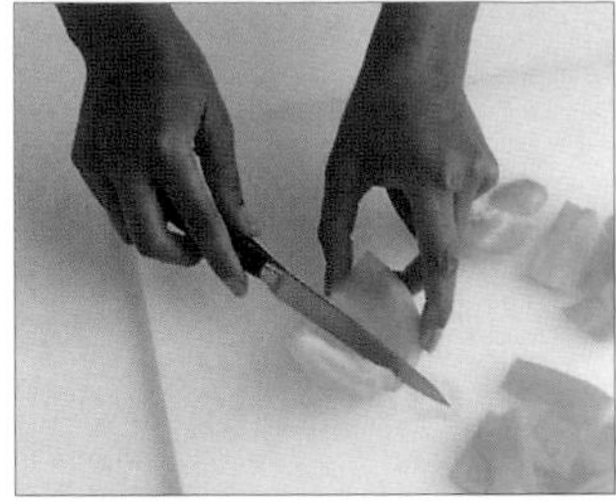

2 When the potatoes are cool enough to handle, skin them and halve lengthways. Peel the shallots, allowing them to fall into their natural segments.

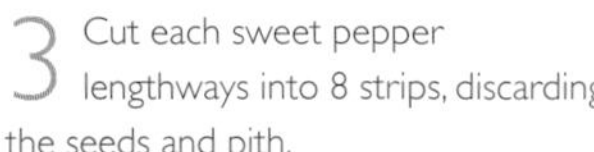

3 Cut each sweet pepper lengthways into 8 strips, discarding the seeds and pith.

4 Oil a shallow ovenproof dish thoroughly with olive oil.

5 Arrange the potatoes and peppers in alternating rows and stud with the shallots.

6 Cut the rosemary sprigs into 5cm/2in lengths and tuck among the vegetables. Season the dish generously with olive oil, salt and pepper and bake in the oven, uncovered, for 30–40 minutes, until all the vegetables are tender.

Baked Sweet Potatoes

GIVE SWEET potatoes a Cajun flavour with salt, three different kinds of pepper and lavish quantities of butter. Serve half a potato per person as an accompaniment, or a whole one as a supper dish with a green watercress salad.

INGREDIENTS

3 pink-skinned sweet potatoes, about 450g/1lb each
75g/3oz/6 tbsp butter, sliced
black, white and cayenne peppers
salt

Serves 3–6

1 Wash the potatoes and leave the skins wet. Rub salt into the skins, prick them all over with a fork and place on the middle shelf of the oven. Turn on the oven to 200°C/400°F/Gas 6 and bake for about an hour, until the potato flesh yields and feels soft when pressed.

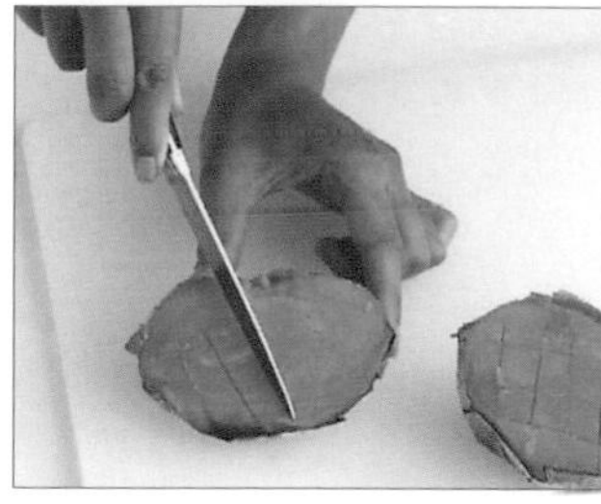

2 The potatoes can either be served in halves or whole. For halves, split each one lengthways and make close criss-cross cuts in the flesh of each half. Then spread with slices of butter, and work the butter and seasonings roughly into the cuts with a knife point.

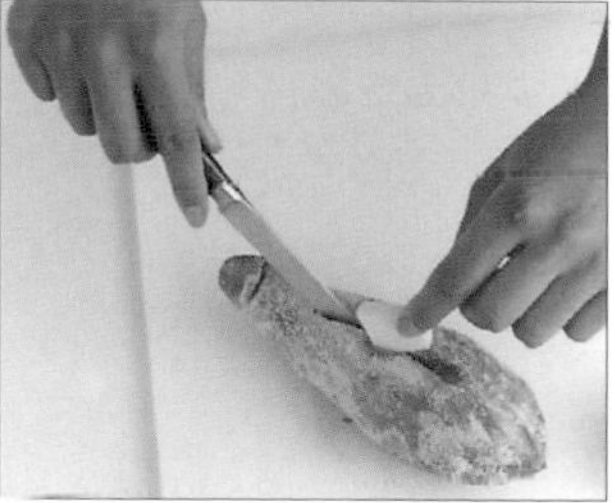

3 Alternatively, make an incision along the length of each potato if they are to be served whole. Open them slightly and put in butter slices along the length, seasoning to taste with the three peppers and a pinch of salt.

COOK'S TIP

Sweet potatoes cook more quickly than ordinary ones, and there is no need to preheat the oven.

Thai Fragrant Rice

THIS LOVELY, soft, fluffy rice dish, perfumed with fresh lemon grass, is a classic Thai accompaniment to red and green curries.

INGREDIENTS

1 stalk of lemon grass
2 limes
225g/8oz/1 cup brown basmati rice
15ml/1 tbsp olive oil
1 onion, chopped
2.5cm/1in piece of fresh root ginger, peeled and finely chopped
7.5ml/1 ½ tsp coriander seeds
7.5ml/1 ½ tsp cumin seeds
750ml/1 ¼ pints/3 cups vegetable stock
60ml/4 tbsp chopped fresh coriander
lime wedges, to serve

Serves 4

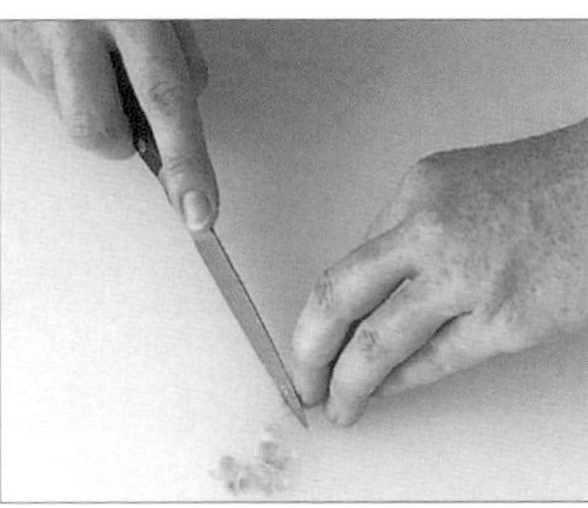

1 Finely chop the lemon grass using a sharp knife.

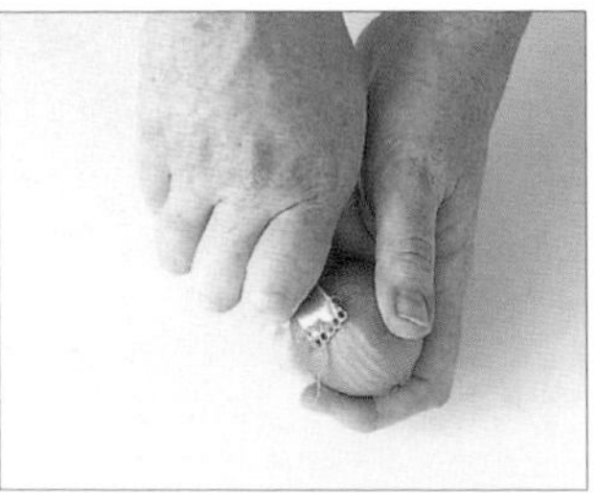

2 Remove the zest from the limes using a zester or fine grater. Avoid removing the pith with the zest.

3 Rinse the rice in plenty of cold water until the water runs clear. Drain through a sieve.

4 Heat the oil in a large pan and add the onion, spices, lemon grass and lime zest and cook gently for 2–3 minutes.

COOK'S TIP

Other varieties of rice, such as white basmati or long grain, can be used for this dish, but you will need to adjust the cooking times accordingly.

5 Add the rice and cook for another minute, then add the stock and bring to the boil. Reduce the heat to very low and cover the pan. Cook gently for 30 minutes then check the rice. If it is still crunchy, cover the pan again and leave for a further 3–5 minutes over gentle heat. Remove from the heat.

6 Stir in the chopped fresh coriander, fluff up the grains with a fork, cover and leave for 10 minutes. Serve with lime wedges.

Rice with Seeds and Spices

A CHANGE from plain boiled rice, and a colourful accompaniment to serve with spicy curries. Basmati rice gives the best texture and flavour, but you can use ordinary long grain rice instead, if you prefer.

INGREDIENTS

5ml/1 tsp sunflower oil
2.5ml/½ tsp ground turmeric
6 cardamom pods, lightly crushed
5ml/1 tsp coriander seeds, lightly crushed
1 garlic clove, crushed
200g/7oz/scant 1 cup basmati rice
400ml/14fl oz/1⅔ cups vegetable stock
115g/4oz/½ cup natural yogurt
15ml/1 tbsp toasted sunflower seeds
15ml/1 tbsp toasted sesame seeds
salt and freshly ground black pepper
coriander leaves, to garnish

Serves 4

1 Heat the oil in a non-stick frying pan and fry the spices and garlic for about 1 minute, stirring all the time.

2 Add the rice and stock, bring to the boil, then cover, reduce the heat and simmer for 10–12 minutes, or until just tender.

3 Stir in the yogurt and the toasted sunflower and sesame seeds. Season with salt and pepper and serve hot, garnished with coriander leaves.

COOK'S TIP

Seeds are particularly rich in minerals, so they are a good addition to all kinds of dishes. Light toasting will improve their flavour.

Red Fried Rice

THIS VIBRANT rice dish owes its appeal as much to the bright colours of red onion, red pepper and tomatoes as it does to their flavours.

INGREDIENTS

145g/4½oz/¾ cup basmati rice
30ml/2 tbsp peanut oil
1 small red onion, chopped
1 red pepper, seeded and chopped
225g/8oz cherry tomatoes, halved
2 eggs, beaten
salt and freshly ground black pepper

Serves 2

1 Wash the rice several times under cold running water. Drain well. Bring a large pan of water to the boil. Add the rice and cook for 10–12 minutes or until tender.

2 Meanwhile, heat the oil in a wok until very hot. Add the onion and red pepper and stir-fry for 2–3 minutes. Add the cherry tomatoes and continue stir-frying for 2 minutes more.

3 Pour in the beaten eggs all at once. Cook for 30 seconds without stirring, then stir to break up the egg as it sets. Do not let the egg overcook and become leathery.

4 Drain the cooked rice thoroughly. Add to the wok and toss it over the heat with the vegetables and egg mixture for 3 minutes. Season with salt and pepper and serve immediately.

Herby Rice Pilaf

A QUICK and easy recipe to make, this simple pilaf is delicious to eat. Serve with a selection of fresh seasonal vegetables such as broccoli florets, baby sweetcorn and carrots.

INGREDIENTS

225g/8oz/1 cup mixed brown basmati and wild rice
15ml/1 tbsp olive oil
1 onion, chopped
1 garlic clove, crushed
5ml/1 tsp ground cumin
5ml/1 tsp ground turmeric
50g/2oz/½ cup sultanas
750ml/1¼ pints/3 cups vegetable stock
30–45ml/2–3 tbsp chopped fresh mixed herbs
salt and freshly ground black pepper
sprigs of fresh herbs and 25g/1oz/¼ cup pistachio nuts, chopped, to garnish

Serves 4

1 Wash the rice under cold running water, then drain well. Heat the oil, add the onion and garlic and cook gently for 5 minutes, stirring occasionally.

2 Add the spices and rice and cook gently for 1 minute, stirring. Stir in the sultanas and stock, bring to the boil, cover and simmer gently for 20–25 minutes, stirring occasionally.

3 Stir in the chopped mixed herbs and season with salt and pepper. Spoon the pilaf into a warmed serving dish and garnish with fresh herb sprigs and a scattering of chopped pistachio nuts. Serve immediately.

Cheese-topped Roast Baby Vegetables

THIS IS a simple way to bring out the real flavour of baby vegetables.

INGREDIENTS

1kg/2¼lb mixed baby vegetables, such as aubergines, onions or shallots, courgettes, sweetcorn, button mushrooms
1 red pepper, seeded and cut into large chunks
1–2 garlic cloves, finely chopped
15–30ml/1–2 tbsp olive oil
30ml/2 tbsp chopped fresh mixed herbs
225g/8oz cherry tomatoes
115g/4oz/1 cup mozzarella cheese, coarsely grated
salt and freshly ground black pepper
black olives, to garnish (optional)

Serves 6

1 Preheat the oven to 220°C/425°F/Gas 7. Cut the aubergines and onions or shallots in half lengthways. Leave other vegetables whole.

2 Place the baby vegetables, red pepper and garlic in a shallow ovenproof dish. Season with salt and pepper, drizzle over the oil and toss the vegetables to coat. Bake for 20 minutes, until tinged brown at the edges, stirring once.

3 Stir in the herbs, scatter over the tomatoes and top with the mozzarella cheese. Bake for a further 5–10 minutes, until the cheese has melted and is bubbling. Serve at once, garnished with black olives, if using.

Chinese Brussels Sprouts

IF YOU are bored with plain boiled Brussels sprouts, try pepping them up Chinese-style with this unusual stir-fried method.

INGREDIENTS

450g/1lb Brussels sprouts
5ml/1 tsp sesame or sunflower oil
2 spring onions, sliced
2.5ml/½ tsp Chinese five-spice powder
15ml/1 tbsp light soy sauce

Serves 4

1 Trim the Brussels sprouts, then shred them finely using a large sharp knife or a food processor.

2 Heat the oil and add the sprouts and spring onions. Stir-fry for about 2 minutes, without allowing the mixture to brown.

3 Stir in the five-spice powder and soy sauce, then cook, stirring, for a further 2–3 minutes, until just tender. Serve hot with other Chinese dishes.

Festive Brussels Sprouts

THIS RECIPE originated in France, where it is a popular side dish at Christmas time.

INGREDIENTS

225g/8oz chestnuts
120ml/4fl oz/½ cup milk
500g/1¼lb small tender Brussels sprouts
25g/1oz/2 tbsp butter
1 shallot, finely chopped
30–45ml/2–3 tbsp dry white wine or water

Serves 4–6

1 Using a small, sharp knife, score a cross in the base of each chestnut.

2 Bring a saucepan of water to the boil over a medium-high heat, then drop in the chestnuts and boil for a further 6–8 minutes. Remove the pan from the heat.

3 Using a slotted spoon, remove a few chestnuts from the pan, leaving the others immersed in the water until ready to peel. Before the chestnuts cool, remove the outer shell with a knife and peel off the inner skin.

4 Rinse the pan, return the peeled chestnuts to it and add the milk. Top up with enough water to completely cover the chestnuts. Simmer over medium heat for 12–15 minutes until the chestnuts are just tender. Drain and set aside.

5 Remove any wilted or yellow leaves from the Brussels sprouts. Trim the root ends but leave intact or the leaves will separate. Using a small knife, score a cross in the base of each sprout so they cook evenly.

6 In a large, heavy frying pan, melt the butter over medium heat. Stir in the chopped shallot and cook for 1–2 minutes until just softened, then add the Brussels sprouts and wine or water. Cook, covered, over medium heat for 6–8 minutes, shaking the pan and stirring occasionally, adding a little more water if necessary.

7 Add the poached chestnuts and toss gently to combine, then cover and cook for 3–5 minutes more, until the chestnuts and Brussels sprouts are tender.

Szechuan Aubergine

THIS MEDIUM-HOT dish is also known as fish-fragrant aubergine in China, because the aubergine is cooked with flavourings that are often used with fish.

INGREDIENTS

2 small aubergines
5ml/1 tsp salt
3 dried red chillies
peanut oil, for deep frying
3–4 garlic cloves, finely chopped
1 cm/½ in piece of fresh root ginger, finely chopped
4 spring onions, cut into 2.5cm/1in lengths (white and green parts separated)
15ml/1 tbsp Chinese rice wine or medium-dry sherry
15ml/1 tbsp light soy sauce
5ml/1 tsp sugar
1.5ml/¼ tsp ground roasted Szechuan peppercorns
15ml/1 tbsp Chinese rice vinegar
5ml/1 tsp sesame oil

Serves 4

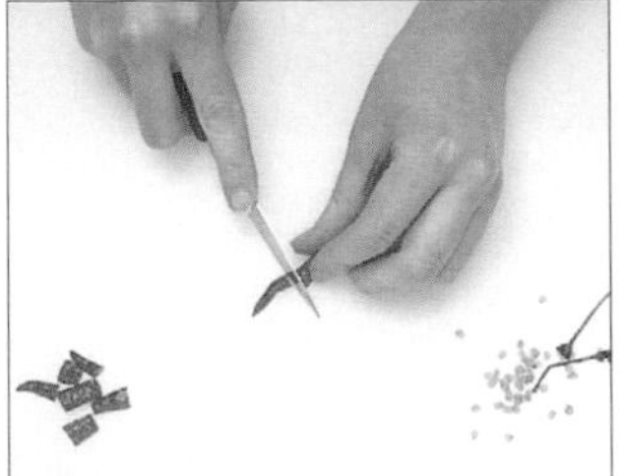

1 Trim the aubergines and cut into strips about 4cm/1½in wide and 7.5cm/3in long. Place the aubergine strips in a colander and sprinkle over the salt. Set aside for 30 minutes, then rinse thoroughly under cold running water. Pat dry with kitchen paper.

2 Meanwhile, soak the chillies in warm water for 15 minutes. Drain, then cut each chilli into four pieces, discarding the seeds.

3 Half-fill a wok with oil and heat to 180°C/350°F. Deep fry the aubergine until golden brown. Drain on kitchen paper. Pour off most of the oil from the wok. Reheat the oil and add garlic, ginger and white spring onion.

4 Stir-fry for 30 seconds. Add the aubergine and toss, then add the chillies, rice wine or sherry, soy sauce, sugar, ground peppercorns and rice vinegar. Stir-fry for 1–2 minutes. Sprinkle over the sesame oil and green spring onion and serve immediately.

Chinese Greens with Plum Sauce

IN THIS recipe, Chinese greens are prepared in a very simple way – stir-fried and served with plum sauce. The combination makes a very simple, quickly prepared, tasty accompaniment.

INGREDIENTS

450g/1lb Chinese greens
30ml/2 tbsp peanut oil
15–30ml/1–2 tbsp plum sauce
Serves 3–4

1 Trim the Chinese greens, removing any discoloured leaves and damaged stems. Tear into manageable pieces.

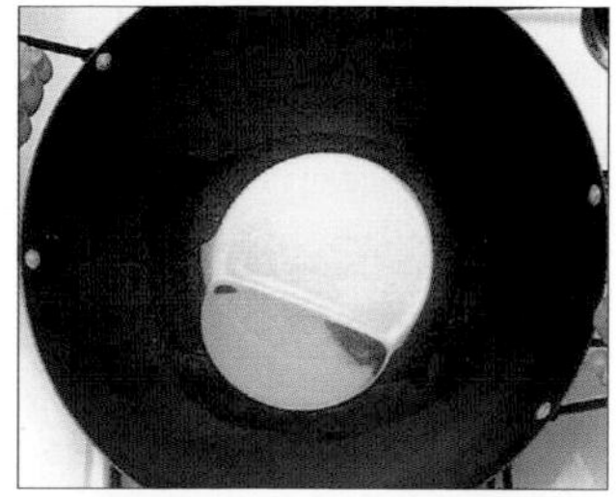

2 Heat a wok until hot, add the oil and swirl it around.

3 Add the Chinese greens and stir-fry for 2–3 minutes, until the greens have wilted a little.

4 Add the plum sauce and continue to stir-fry for a few seconds more, until the greens are cooked but still slightly crisp. Serve immediately.

VARIATION

You can replace the Chinese greens with Chinese flowering cabbage or Chinese broccoli, which is also known by its Cantonese name, choi sam. It has green leaves and tiny yellow flowers, which are eaten along with the leaves and stalks. It is available at Asian markets.

Spring Vegetable Stir-fry

FAST, FRESH AND PACKED with healthy vegetables, this stir-fry is delicious served with marinated tofu and rice or noodles.

INGREDIENTS

15ml/1 tbsp groundnut or vegetable oil
5ml/1 tsp toasted sesame oil
1 garlic clove, chopped
2.5cm/1in piece fresh root ginger, finely chopped
225g/8oz baby carrots
350g/12oz/3 cups broccoli florets
175g/6oz/1⁄3 cup asparagus tips
2 spring onions, cut on the diagonal
175g/6oz/1 1⁄2 cups spring greens, finely shredded
30ml/2 tbsp light soy sauce
15ml/1 tbsp apple juice
15ml/1 tbsp sesame seeds, toasted

Serves 4

1 Heat a frying pan or wok over a high heat. Add the groundnut or vegetable oil and the sesame oil, and reduce the heat. Add the garlic and sauté for 2 minutes.

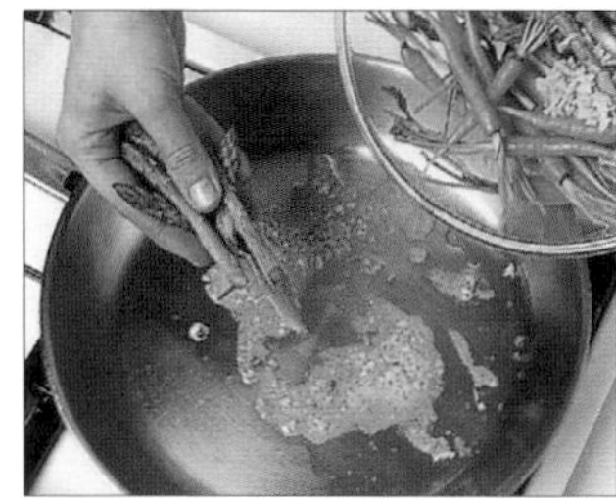

2 Add the chopped ginger, carrots, broccoli and asparagus tips to the pan and stir-fry for 4 minutes. Add the spring onions and spring greens and stir-fry for a further 2 minutes.

3 Add the soy sauce and apple juice and cook for 1–2 minutes until the vegetables are tender; add a little water if they appear dry. Sprinkle the sesame seeds on top and serve.

HEALTH BENEFITS

Green and orange vegetables are an excellent source of beta carotene, as well as vitamins C and E.

Oriental Green Beans

THIS IS A SIMPLE and delicious way of enlivening green beans. The dish can be served hot or cold and, accompanied by an omelette and some crusty bread, makes a perfect light lunch or supper.

INGREDIENTS

450g/1lb/3 cups green beans
15ml/1 tbsp olive oil
5ml/1 tsp sesame oil
2 garlic cloves, crushed
2.5cm/1in piece fresh root ginger, finely chopped
30ml/2 tbsp dark soy sauce

Serves 4

VARIATION

Substitute other green beans, if you wish. Runner beans and other flat varieties should be cut diagonally into thick slices before steaming.

1 Steam the beans over a saucepan of boiling salted water for 4 minutes or until just tender.

HEALTH BENEFITS

- *This dish contains good amounts of garlic and fresh root ginger, both of which are said to give the immune system a significant boost.*
- *Recent studies confirm that ginger may be more effective in preventing nausea than prescribed drugs.*

2 Meanwhile, heat the olive and sesame oils in a heavy-based saucepan, add the garlic and sauté for 2 minutes.

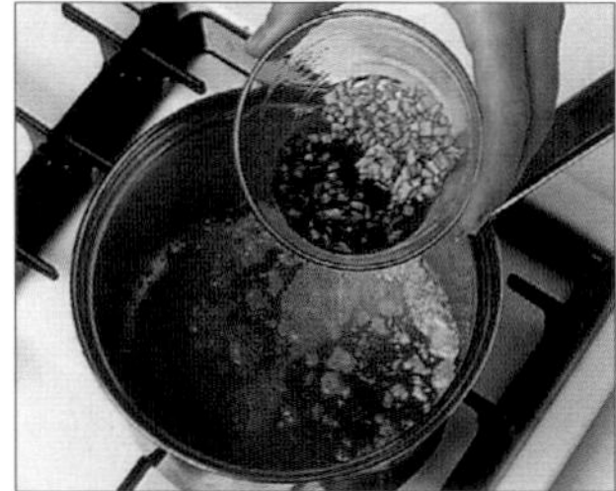

3 Stir in the ginger and soy sauce and cook, stirring constantly, for a further 2–3 minutes until the liquid has reduced, then pour this mixture over the warm beans. Leave for a few minutes to allow all the flavours to mingle before serving.

Sweet and Sour Onions

COOKED IN this way, sweet baby onions make an unusual yet tasty side dish. This recipe originated in the Provence region of France.

INGREDIENTS

450g/1lb baby onions, peeled
50ml/2fl oz/1/4 cup wine vinegar
45ml/3 tbsp olive oil
40g/1 1/2oz/3 tbsp caster sugar
45ml/3 tbsp tomato purée
1 bay leaf
2 sprigs of fresh parsley
65g/2 1/2oz/1/2 cup raisins
salt and freshly ground black pepper

Serves 6

1 Put all the ingredients in a saucepan with 300ml/1/2 pint/1 1/4 cups water.

2 Bring to the boil and simmer gently, uncovered, for 45 minutes or until the onions are tender and most of the liquid has evaporated.

3 Remove the bay leaf and parsley, check the seasoning and transfer to a serving dish. Serve at room temperature.

Spinach with Raisins and Pine Nuts

RAISINS AND pine nuts are perfect partners. Here, tossed with wilted spinach and croûtons their contrasting textures make a delicious main meal accompaniment.

INGREDIENTS

50g/2oz/⅓ cup raisins
1 thick slice crusty white bread
45ml/3 tbsp olive oil
25g/1oz/⅓ cup pine nuts
500g/1¼lb young spinach, stalks removed
2 garlic cloves, crushed
salt and freshly ground black pepper
Serves 4

1 Put the raisins in a small bowl with boiling water and leave to soak for 10 minutes. Drain.

2 Cut the bread into cubes and discard the crusts. Heat 30ml/2 tbsp of the oil and fry the bread until golden. Drain.

3 Heat the remaining oil in the pan. Fry the pine nuts until they are beginning to colour. Add the spinach and garlic and cook quickly, turning the spinach until it has just wilted.

4 Toss in the raisins and season with salt and pepper. Transfer to a warmed serving dish. Scatter with croûtons and serve hot.

VARIATION

You can use Swiss chard or spinach beet instead of the spinach, but you will need to cook them a little longer.

Hot Parsnip Fritters on Baby Spinach

DEEP FRYING BRINGS out the luscious sweetness of parsnips, and their flavour is perfectly complemented by walnut-dressed baby spinach leaves.

INGREDIENTS

2 large parsnips
115g/4oz/1 cup plain flour
1 egg, separated
120ml/4fl oz/½ cup milk
115g/4oz baby spinach leaves, washed and dried
30ml/2 tbsp olive oil
15ml/1 tbsp walnut oil
15ml/1 tbsp sherry vinegar
oil for deep frying
15ml/1 tbsp coarsely chopped walnuts
salt, freshly ground black pepper and cayenne pepper

Serves 4

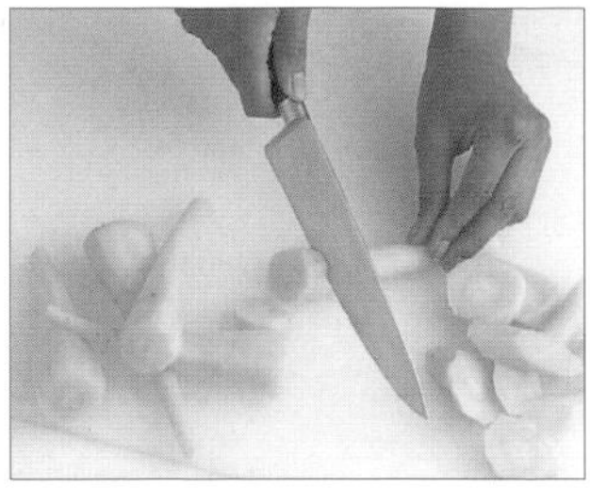

1 Peel the parsnips, bring to the boil in a pan of salted water and simmer for 10–15 minutes, until tender but not in the least mushy. Drain, cool and cut diagonally into slices about 5cm/2in long x 5mm–1cm/¼–½in thick.

2 Put the flour in a bowl and make a well in the centre. Put the egg yolk in the well and mix into the flour with a fork. Add the milk, while continuing to mix in the flour. Season with salt and black and cayenne peppers, and beat with a whisk until the batter is smooth.

3 Put the spinach leaves in a bowl. Mix the oils and vinegar. Season with salt and pepper.

4 When you are ready to serve, whisk the egg white to soft peaks, fold in a little of the yolk batter, then fold the white into the batter. Heat the oil for frying.

5 Shake the dressing vigorously, then toss the salad in the dressing. Arrange the leaves on 4 plates and scatter with walnuts.

6 Dip the parsnip slices in batter and fry until puffy and golden. Drain on kitchen paper and keep warm. Arrange the fritters on top of the salad leaves.

Parsnip and Chestnut Croquettes

THE DISTINCTIVE, sweet nutty taste of chestnuts blends perfectly with the similarly sweet but earthy flavour of parsnips. Fresh chestnuts need to be peeled, but frozen chestnuts are easy to use and are nearly as good as fresh for this recipe.

INGREDIENTS

450g/1lb parsnips, cut roughly into small pieces
115g/4oz frozen chestnuts
25g/1oz/2 tbsp butter
1 garlic clove, crushed
15ml/1 tbsp chopped fresh coriander
1 egg, beaten
40–50g/1½–2oz fresh white breadcrumbs
vegetable oil, for frying
salt and freshly ground black pepper
sprigs of fresh coriander, to garnish

Makes 10–12

1 Place the parsnips in a saucepan with enough water to cover. Bring to the boil, cover and allow to simmer for 15–20 minutes.

2 Place the frozen chestnuts in a pan of water, bring to the boil and simmer for 8–10 minutes. Drain well, place in a bowl and mash roughly into a pulp.

3 Melt the butter in a saucepan and cook the garlic for 30 seconds. Drain the parsnips and mash with the garlic butter. Stir in the chestnuts and coriander. Season with salt and pepper.

4 Take about 15ml/1 tbsp of the mixture at a time and form into small croquettes, about 7.5cm/3in long. Dip each croquette into the beaten egg and then roll in the breadcrumbs.

5 Heat a little oil in a frying pan and fry each of the croquettes for 3–4 minutes until crisp and golden, turning frequently so they brown evenly.

6 Drain the croquettes on sheets of kitchen paper, wiping away any excess oil, and serve at once, garnished with sprigs of fresh coriander.

Balti Baby Vegetables

THERE IS a wide and wonderful selection of baby vegetables available in supermarkets these days, and this simple recipe does full justice to their delicate flavour and attractive appearance. Serve as part of a main meal or even as a light appetizer.

INGREDIENTS

10 new potatoes, halved
12–14 baby carrots
12–14 baby courgettes
30ml/2 tbsp corn oil
15 baby onions
30ml/2 tbsp chilli sauce
5ml/1 tsp garlic pulp
5ml/1 tsp ginger pulp
5ml/1 tsp salt
400g/14oz can chick-peas, drained
10 cherry tomatoes
5ml/1 tsp crushed dried red chillies and 30ml/2 tbsp sesame seeds, to garnish

Serves 4–6

1 Bring a medium pan of salted water to the boil and add the new potatoes and baby carrots. After about 12–15 minutes, add the courgettes and boil for a further 5 minutes, or until all the vegetables are just tender.

2 Drain the vegetables well and set to one side.

3 Heat the oil in a deep round-bottomed frying pan or wok and add the baby onions. Fry until the onions turn golden brown. Lower the heat and add the chilli sauce, garlic, ginger and salt, taking care not to burn the mixture.

4 Add the chick-peas and stir-fry over medium heat until the moisture has been absorbed.

5 Add the cooked vegetables and cherry tomatoes and continue frying over medium heat, stirring with a slotted spoon for about 2 minutes.

6 Garnish with crushed red chillies and sesame seeds, and serve.

VARIATION

By varying the vegetables chosen and experimenting with different combinations, this recipe can form the basis for a variety of delicious vegetable accompaniments. Try different vegetables, such as baby sweetcorn, French beans, mangetouts, okra, sugar snap peas and cauliflower florets, too.

Fried Noodles, Beansprouts and Asparagus

SOFT FRIED noodles contrast beautifully with crisp beansprouts and asparagus in this super-quick recipe.

INGREDIENTS

115g/4oz/1 cup dried egg noodles
60ml/4 tbsp vegetable oil
1 small onion, chopped
2.5cm/1in piece of fresh root ginger, peeled and grated
2 garlic cloves, crushed
175g/6oz young asparagus spears, trimmed
115g/4oz beansprouts
4 spring onions, sliced
45ml/3 tbsp soy sauce
salt and freshly ground black pepper

Serves 2

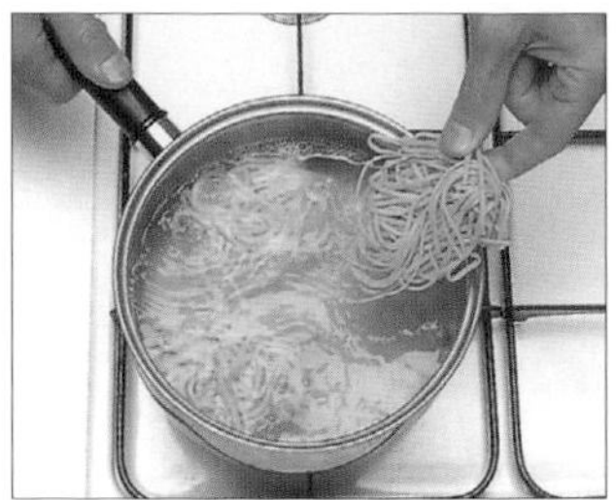

1 Bring a pan of salted water to the boil. Add the noodles and cook for 2–3 minutes, until just tender. Drain thoroughly and toss in 30ml/2 tbsp of the oil.

2 Heat the remaining 2 tbsp of oil in a wok or frying pan until it is very hot. Add the onion, ginger and garlic and stir-fry for 2–3 minutes. Add the asparagus and stir-fry for 2–3 minutes more.

3 Add the egg noodles and beansprouts and stir-fry for 2 minutes.

4 Stir in the spring onions and soy sauce. Season with salt and pepper, adding salt sparingly as the soy sauce will probably supply enough salt in itself. Stir-fry for 1 minute then serve at once.

Deep-fried Root Vegetables with Spiced Salt

ALL KINDS of root vegetables may be finely sliced and deep fried to make "chips". Serve as an accompaniment to an oriental-style meal or simply by themselves as a nibble.

INGREDIENTS

1 carrot
2 parsnips
2 raw beetroot
1 sweet potato
peanut oil, for deep frying
1.5ml/¼ tsp cayenne pepper
1 tsp sea salt flakes

Serves 4–6

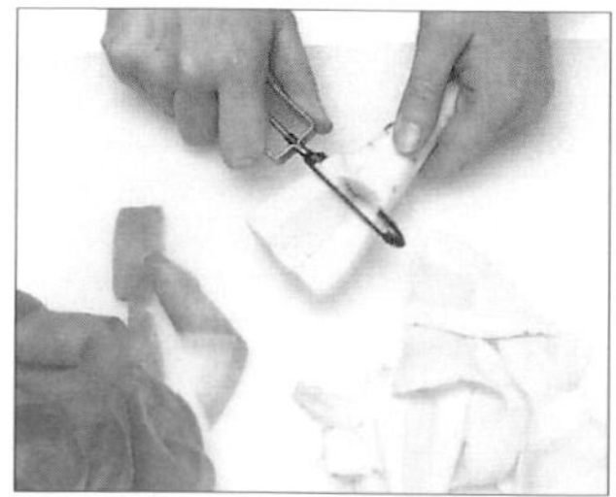

1 Peel all the vegetables, then slice the carrot and parsnips into long, thin ribbons, and the beetroot and sweet potato into thin rounds. Pat dry all the vegetables on kitchen paper.

COOK'S TIP

To save time, you can slice the vegetables using a mandoline, or a blender or food processor with a thin slicing disc attached.

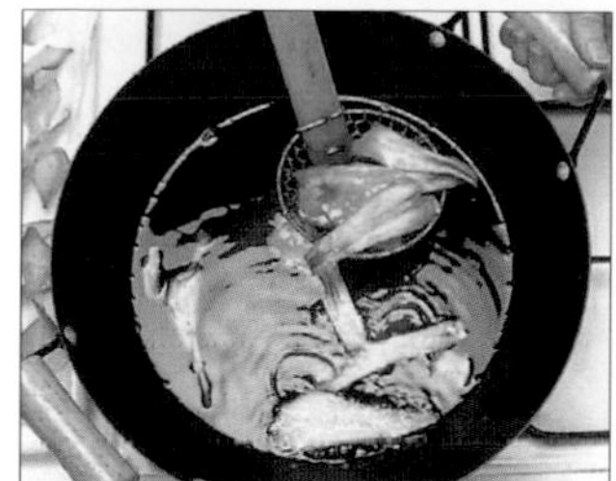

2 Half-fill a wok with oil and heat to 180°C/350°F or until a cube of bread, when added to the oil, browns in 30–45 seconds. Add the vegetable slices in batches. Deep-fry for 2–3 minutes, until golden and crisp. Remove and drain on kitchen paper.

3 Place the cayenne pepper and sea salt in a mortar and grind together to a coarse powder.

4 Pile up the vegetable "chips" on a serving plate and sprinkle over the spiced salt.

Split Pea and Shallot Mash

GREATLY UNDERRATED and under-used, split peas can make a fantastic purée. When this is enlivened with herbs and spices, the purée makes an excellent alternative to mashed potatoes, and is particularly good with winter pies and nut roasts. It can also be served with warmed pitta bread, accompanied by diced tomatoes and a splash of olive oil.

INGREDIENTS

225g/8oz/1 cup yellow split peas
1 bay leaf
8 sage leaves, roughly chopped
15ml/1 tbsp olive oil
3 shallots, finely chopped
8ml/heaped 1 tsp cumin seeds
1 large garlic clove, chopped
50g/2oz/4 tbsp butter, softened
salt and freshly ground black pepper

Serves 4–6

1 Place the split peas in a bowl and cover with cold water. Leave to soak overnight, then rinse and drain.

2 Place the peas in a saucepan, cover with fresh cold water and bring to the boil. Skim off any foam that rises to the surface, then reduce the heat. Add the bay leaf and sage, and simmer for 30–40 minutes until the peas are tender. Add more water during cooking, if necessary.

3 Meanwhile, heat the oil in a frying pan and cook the shallots, cumin seeds and garlic for 3 minutes or until the shallots soften, stirring occasionally. Add the mixture to the split peas while they are still cooking.

4 Drain the split peas, reserving the cooking water. Remove the bay leaf, then place the split peas in a food processor or blender with the butter and season well.

5 Add 105ml/7 tbsp of the reserved cooking water and blend until the mixture forms a coarse purée. Add more water if the mash seems to be too dry. Adjust the seasoning and serve warm.

HEALTH BENEFITS

Split peas, like other pulses, are an excellent source of protein, fibre, minerals and B vitamins. They are particularly good for diabetics as they can help to control blood sugar levels.

Root Vegetable Gratin with Indian Spices

SUBTLY SPICED WITH CURRY powder, turmeric, coriander and mild chilli powder, this rich gratin is substantial enough to serve on its own for lunch or supper. It also makes a good accompaniment to a vegetable or bean curry.

INGREDIENTS

2 large potatoes, total weight about 450g/1lb
2 sweet potatoes, total weight about 275g/10oz
175g/6oz celeriac
15ml/1 tbsp unsalted butter
5ml/1 tsp curry powder
5ml/1 tsp ground turmeric
2.5ml/½ tsp ground coriander
5ml/1 tsp mild chilli powder
3 shallots, chopped
salt and freshly ground black pepper
150ml/¼ pint/⅔ cup single cream
150ml/¼ pint/⅔ cup semi-skimmed milk
chopped fresh flat leaf parsley, to garnish

Serves 4

1 Thinly slice the potatoes, sweet potatoes and celeriac, using a sharp knife or the slicing attachment on a food processor. Immediately place the vegetables in a bowl of cold water to prevent them discolouring.

COOK'S TIP

The cream adds richness to this gratin; use semi-skimmed milk, if you prefer.

2 Preheat the oven to 180°C/350°F/Gas 4. Heat half the butter in a heavy-based saucepan, add the curry powder, turmeric and coriander and half the chilli powder. Cook for 2 minutes, then leave to cool slightly. Drain the vegetables, then pat dry with kitchen paper. Place in a bowl, add the spice mixture and the shallots and mix well.

HEALTH BENEFITS

This gratin contains ground spices, which boost a sluggish digestion and have a beneficial effect on the circulation.

3 Arrange the vegetables in a gratin dish, seasoning between the layers. Mix together the cream and milk, pour the mixture over the vegetables, then sprinkle the remaining chilli powder on top.

4 Cover with greaseproof paper and bake for about 45 minutes. Remove the greaseproof paper, dot with the remaining butter and bake for a further 50 minutes until the top is golden. Serve garnished with chopped fresh parsley.

Vegetables Provençal

THE FLAVOURS of the Mediterranean shine through in this delicious side dish.

INGREDIENTS

1 onion, sliced
2 leeks, sliced
2 garlic cloves, crushed
1 red pepper, seeded and sliced
1 green pepper, seeded and sliced
1 yellow pepper, seeded and sliced
350g/12oz/3 cups courgettes, sliced
225g/8oz/3 cups mushrooms, sliced
400g/14oz can chopped tomatoes
30ml/2 tbsp ruby port
30ml/2 tbsp tomato purée
15ml/1 tbsp tomato ketchup
400g/14oz can chick-peas
115g/4oz/⅔ cup pitted black olives
45ml/3 tbsp chopped fresh mixed herbs
salt and freshly ground black pepper
chopped fresh mixed herbs, to garnish

Serves 6

1 Put the onion, leeks, garlic, peppers, courgettes and mushrooms into a large saucepan.

2 Add the tomatoes, port, tomato purée and tomato ketchup and mix well.

3 Rinse and drain the chick-peas and add to the pan.

4 Cover, bring to the boil and simmer gently for 20–30 minutes, stirring occasionally, until the vegetables are cooked and tender, but not overcooked.

5 Remove the lid and increase the heat slightly for the last 10 minutes of the cooking time, to thicken the sauce, if liked.

6 Stir in the olives and herbs and season with salt and pepper. Serve immediately, garnished with a scattering of chopped mixed herbs.

COOK'S TIP

This dish is also delicious served cold. It can be prepared in advance for a picnic, stored in the refrigerator, and served with plain yogurt or a refreshing tsatziki.

HABITAT
JAPAN

Mixed Vegetables with Aromatic Seeds

A HEALTHY diet should include plenty of vegetables to provide fibre as well as vitamins and minerals. Here, spices transform everyday vegetables into a memorable dish.

INGREDIENTS

675g/1 1/2lb small new potatoes
1 small cauliflower
175g/6oz French beans
115g/4oz/1 cup frozen peas
small piece of fresh root ginger
30ml/2 tbsp sunflower oil
10ml/2 tsp cumin seeds
10ml/2 tsp black mustard seeds
30ml/2 tbsp sesame seeds
juice of 1 lemon
ground black pepper
fresh coriander, to garnish (optional)

Serves 4–6

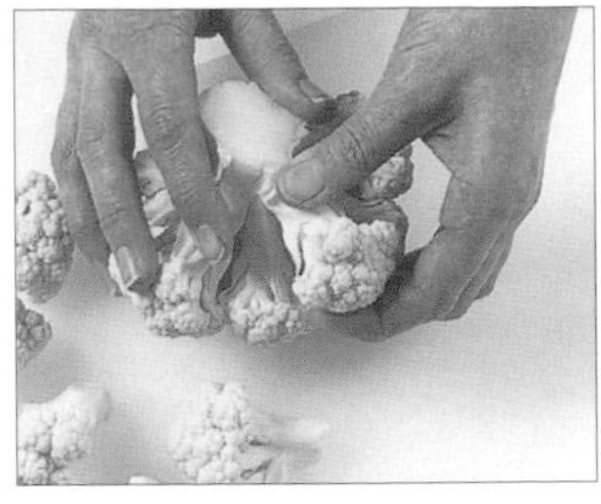

1 Scrub the potatoes, cut the cauliflower into small florets, and trim and halve the French beans.

2 Cook the vegetables in separate pans of lightly salted boiling water until tender, allowing 15–20 minutes for the potatoes, 8–10 minutes for the cauliflower and 4–5 minutes for the beans and peas. Drain thoroughly.

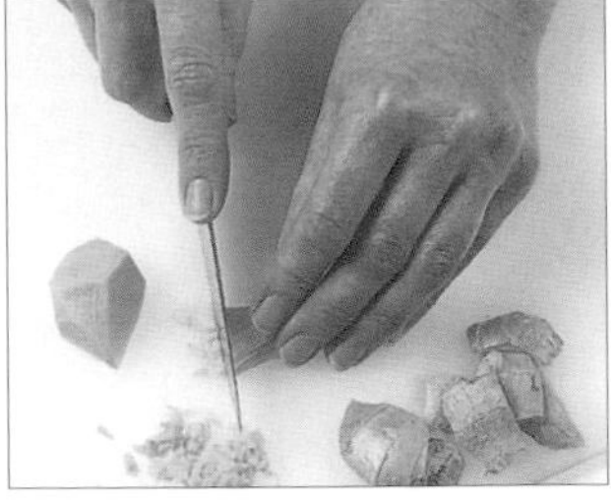

3 Using a small, sharp knife, peel and finely chop the fresh ginger.

4 Heat the oil. Add the ginger and seeds. Fry until they start to pop.

5 Add the vegetables and stir-fry for 2–3 minutes. Sprinkle over the lemon juice and season with pepper. Garnish with coriander, if using.

COOK'S TIP

Other vegetables could be used, such as courgettes, leeks or broccoli. Buy whatever looks freshest and do not store vegetables for long periods as their vitamin content will deteriorate.

Root Vegetable Casserole

POTATOES, CARROTS and parsnips are all complex carbohydrates and make a hearty, sustaining vegetable dish, high in fibre and vitamin C. The carrots are also an excellent source of beta-carotene, which is converted to vitamin A in the body.

INGREDIENTS

225g/8oz carrots
225g/8oz parsnips
15ml/1 tbsp sunflower oil
knob of butter
15ml/1 tbsp demerara sugar
450g/1lb baby new potatoes, scrubbed
225g/8oz small onions, peeled
400ml/14fl oz/1 2/3 cups vegetable stock
15ml/1 tbsp vegetarian Worcestershire sauce
15ml/1 tbsp tomato purée
5ml/1 tsp wholegrain mustard
2 bay leaves
salt and ground black pepper
chopped parsley, to garnish

Serves 4–6

COOK'S TIP

Other vegetables could be added, such as leeks, mushrooms, sweet potato, or celery. Shelled chestnuts make a delicious addition but you could also use canned whole chestnuts or frozen ones.

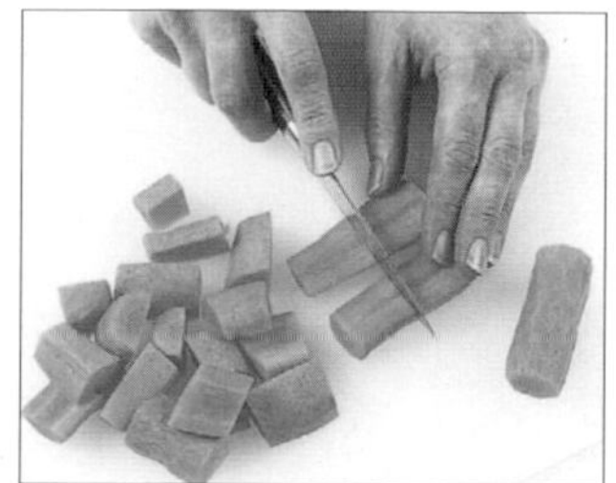

1 Peel the carrots and parsnips and cut into large chunks.

2 Heat the oil, butter and sugar in a pan. Stir until the sugar dissolves.

3 Add the potatoes, onions, carrots and parsnips. Sauté for 10 minutes until the vegetables look glazed.

4 Mix the vegetable stock, vegetarian Worcestershire sauce, tomato purée and mustard in a jug. Stir well, then pour over the vegetables. Add the bay leaves. Bring to the boil, then lower the heat, cover and cook gently for about 30 minutes until the vegetables are tender.

5 Remove the bay leaves, add salt and pepper to taste and serve, sprinkled with the parsley.

Spicy Chick-peas

CHICK-PEAS ARE used and cooked in a variety of ways all over the Indian sub-continent. Tamarind gives this spicy dish a deliciously sharp, tangy flavour.

INGREDIENTS

225g/8oz/1 1/4 cups dried chick-peas
50g/2oz tamarind pulp
120ml/4fl oz/1/2 cup boiling water
45ml/3 tbsp corn oil
2.5ml/1/2 tsp cumin seeds
1 onion, finely chopped
2 garlic cloves, crushed
2.5cm/1in piece of fresh root ginger, peeled and grated
1 fresh green chilli, finely chopped
5ml/1 tsp ground cumin
5ml/1 tsp ground coriander
1.5ml/1/4 tsp ground turmeric
2.5ml/1/2 tsp salt
225g/8oz tomatoes, skinned and finely chopped
2.5ml/1/2 tsp garam masala
chopped fresh chillies and chopped onion, to garnish

Serves 4

1 Put the chick-peas in a large bowl and cover with plenty of cold water. Leave to soak overnight.

2 Drain the chick-peas and place in a large saucepan with double the volume of cold water. Do not add any salt to the water because it has a hardening effect. Bring to the boil and boil vigorously for 10 minutes. Skim off any scum. Cover and simmer for 1 1/2–2 hours, or until the chick-peas are soft.

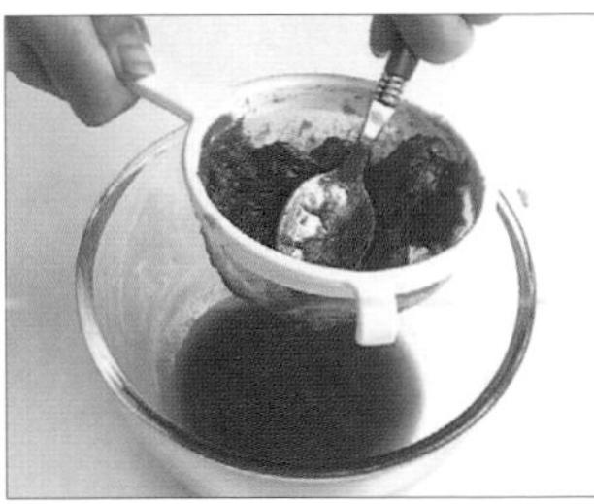

3 Meanwhile, break up the tamarind and soak in the boiling water for about 15 minutes. Rub the tamarind through a sieve into a bowl, discarding any stones and fibre.

COOK'S TIP

To save time, make double the quantity of tamarind pulp and freeze in ice-cube trays. It will keep for up to 2 months.

4 Heat the oil in a large saucepan and fry the cumin seeds for 2 minutes, until they splutter. Add the onion, garlic, ginger and chilli and fry for 5 minutes.

5 Add the cumin, coriander, turmeric and salt and fry for 3–4 minutes. Add the tomatoes and tamarind pulp. Bring to the boil and simmer for 5 minutes.

6 Add the chick-peas and garam masala. Cover and simmer for about 45 minutes. Garnish with chopped chillies and onion.

Frijoles

A TRADITIONAL Mexican bean dish that tastes great with tortillas and vegetable chilli.

INGREDIENTS

350g/12oz/1¾ cups dried red kidney, pinto or black haricot beans, picked over and rinsed
2 onions, finely chopped
2 garlic cloves, chopped
1 bay leaf
1 or more small fresh green chillies
30ml/2 tbsp corn oil
2 tomatoes, peeled, seeded and chopped
salt
sprigs of fresh bay leaves, to garnish

Serves 6–8

1 Put the beans into a pan and add sufficient cold water to cover by 2.5cm/1in.

2 Add half the onion, half the garlic, the bay leaf and the chilli or chillies. Bring to the boil and boil vigorously for about 10 minutes. Cover and cook over low heat for 30 minutes. Add a little boiling water to the pan if the mixture starts to become dry.

3 When the beans begin to wrinkle, add 15ml/1 tbsp of the corn oil and cook for a further 30 minutes, or until the beans are tender. Add salt to taste and cook for 30 minutes more, but try not to add any more water.

4 Remove the beans from the heat. Heat the remaining oil in a small frying pan and sauté the remaining onion and garlic together until the onion is soft. Add the chopped tomato flesh and cook for a few minutes more.

5 Spoon 45ml/3 tbsp of the beans out of the saucepan and add them to the tomato mixture. Mash to a paste. Stir into the beans to thicken the liquid. Cook for just long enough to heat through, if necessary. Serve the beans in small bowls and garnish with fresh bay leaves.

Peas with Baby Onions and Cream

IDEALLY, USE fresh peas and fresh baby onions. Frozen peas are an acceptable substitute if fresh ones aren't available, but frozen onions tend to be insipid and are not worth using. Alternatively, use the white parts of spring onions.

INGREDIENTS

175g/6oz baby onions
15g/½oz/1 tbsp butter
900g/2lb fresh peas (about 350g/12oz shelled or frozen)
150ml/¼ pint/⅔ cup double cream
15g/½oz/2 tbsp plain flour
10ml/2 tsp chopped fresh parsley
15–30ml/1–2 tbsp lemon juice (optional)
salt and freshly ground black pepper
Serves 4

1 Peel the onions and halve them if necessary. Melt the butter in a flameproof casserole and fry the onions for 5–6 minutes over a moderate heat, until they begin to be flecked with brown.

2 Add the peas and stir-fry for a few minutes. Add 120ml/4fl oz/½ cup water and bring to the boil. Partially cover and simmer for about 10 minutes, until the peas and onions are tender. There should be a thin layer of water on the base of the pan. Add a little more water if necessary or, if there is too much liquid, remove the lid and increase the heat to reduce it.

3 Using a small whisk, blend the cream with the flour. Remove the pan from the heat and stir in the combined cream and flour and the parsley. Season with salt and pepper.

4 Cook over a gentle heat for 3–4 minutes, until the sauce is thick. Taste and adjust the seasoning, adding a little lemon juice to sharpen, if desired.

Red Cabbage in Port and Red Wine

A SWEET and sour, spicy red cabbage dish, with the added crunch of pears and walnuts.

INGREDIENTS

15ml/1 tbsp walnut oil
1 onion, sliced
2 whole star anise
5ml/1 tsp ground cinnamon
pinch of ground cloves
450g/1lb/5 cups red cabbage, finely shredded
25g/1oz/2 tbsp dark brown sugar
45ml/3 tbsp red wine vinegar
300ml/½ pint/1¼ cups red wine
150ml/¼ pint/⅔ cup port
2 pears, cut into 1 cm/½ in cubes
115g/4oz/¾ cup raisins
115g/4oz/½ cup walnut halves
salt and freshly ground black pepper

Serves 6

1 Heat the oil in a large pan. Add the onion and cook gently for about 5 minutes, until softened.

COOK'S TIP

You can braise this dish in a low oven for up to 1½ hours.

2 Add the star anise, cinnamon, cloves and cabbage and cook for about 3 minutes more.

3 Stir in the sugar, vinegar, red wine and port. Cover the pan and simmer gently for 10 minutes, stirring occasionally.

4 Stir in the cubed pears and raisins and cook for a further 10 minutes, or until the cabbage is tender. Season with salt and pepper. Mix in the walnut halves and serve.

Beetroot and Celeriac Gratin

BEAUTIFUL RUBY-RED slices of beetroot and celeriac make a stunning light accompaniment to any main course dish.

INGREDIENTS

350g/12oz raw beetroot
350g/12oz raw celeriac
4 sprigs of fresh thyme, chopped
6 juniper berries, crushed
120ml/4fl oz/½ cup fresh orange juice
120ml/4fl oz/½ cup vegetable stock
salt and freshly ground black pepper
Serves 6

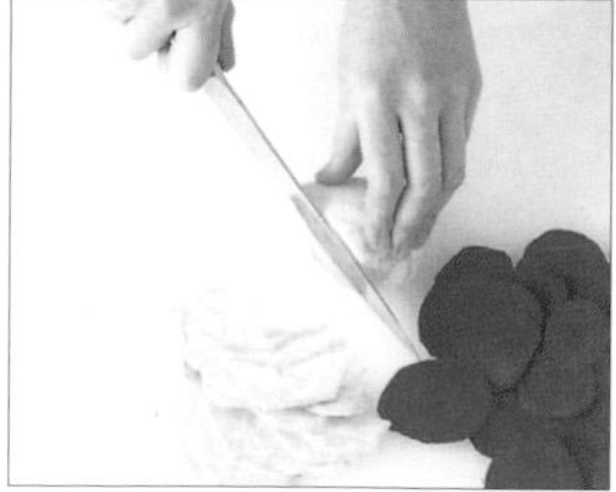

1 Preheat the oven to 190°C/375°F/Gas 5.

2 Peel and slice the beetroot and celeriac very finely.

3 Fill a 25cm/10in diameter, cast iron, ovenproof or flameproof frying pan with alternate layers of beetroot and celeriac slices, sprinkling with thyme, juniper and salt and freshly ground pepper between each layer.

4 Mix the orange juice and stock together and pour over the gratin. Place over a medium heat and bring to the boil. Boil for 2 minutes.

5 Cover with foil and cook in the oven for 15–20 minutes. Remove foil and increase to 200°C/400°F/Gas 6. Cook for a further 10 minutes.

Runner Beans with Garlic

DELICATE AND fresh-tasting flageolet beans and sautéed garlic add a distinctly French flavour to this simple side dish.

INGREDIENTS

225g/8oz/1 1/4 cups flageolet beans
15ml/1 tbsp olive oil
25g/1oz/2 tbsp butter
1 onion, finely chopped
1–2 garlic cloves, crushed
3–4 tomatoes, peeled and chopped
350g/12oz runner beans, prepared and sliced
150ml/1/4 pint/2/3 cup white wine
150ml/1/4 pint/2/3 cup vegetable stock
30ml/2 tbsp chopped fresh parsley
salt and freshly ground black pepper

Serves 4

1 Place the flageolet beans in a large saucepan of water, bring to the boil and simmer for 3/4–1 hour, until tender.

2 Heat the olive oil and butter in a large frying pan and sauté the chopped onion and garlic for 3–4 minutes, until soft.

3 Add the chopped tomatoes to the onions in the pan and continue cooking over a gentle heat, until they are soft.

4 Stir the flageolet beans into the onion and tomato mixture, then add the runner beans, wine, stock and a little salt. Stir. Cover and simmer for 5–10 minutes.

5 Increase the heat to reduce the liquid, then stir in the parsley, more salt, if necessary, and pepper.

Green Lima Beans in Chilli Sauce

TRY THIS fabulous dish of lima beans with a tomato and chilli sauce for warming up on winter evenings.

INGREDIENTS

450g/1lb green lima or broad beans, thawed if frozen
30ml/2 tbsp olive oil
1 onion, finely chopped
2 garlic cloves, chopped
350g/12oz tomatoes, peeled, seeded and chopped
1 or 2 drained canned jalapeño chillies, seeded and chopped
salt
chopped fresh coriander, to garnish
Serves 4

1 Cook the beans in a saucepan of boiling water for 15–20 minutes, until tender. Drain the liquid away and keep the beans hot, to one side, in the covered saucepan.

2 Heat the olive oil in a frying pan and sauté the onion and garlic until the onion is soft but not brown. Add the tomatoes and cook until the mixture thickens.

3 Add the jalapeños and cook for 1–2 minutes. Season with salt.

4 Pour the mixture over the reserved beans and check that they are hot. If not, return everything to the frying pan and cook over low heat for just long enough to heat through. Put into a warmed serving dish, garnish with chopped coriander and serve.

Glazed Carrots with Cider

THIS RECIPE is extremely simple to make. The carrots are cooked in the minimum of liquid to bring out the best of their flavour, and the cider adds a pleasant sharpness.

INGREDIENTS

450g/1lb young carrots
25g/1oz/2 tbsp butter
15ml/1 tbsp brown sugar
120ml/4fl oz/½ cup cider
60ml/4 tbsp vegetable stock or water
1 tsp Dijon mustard
15ml/1 tbsp finely chopped fresh parsley

Serves 4

1 Trim the tops and bottoms of the carrots and then peel or scrape them. Using a sharp knife, cut them into julienne strips.

2 Melt the butter in a frying pan, add the carrots and sauté for 4–5 minutes, stirring frequently. Sprinkle over the sugar and cook, stirring, for 1 minute or until the sugar has dissolved.

3 Add the cider and stock or water, bring to the boil and stir in the Dijon mustard. Partially cover the pan and simmer for 10–12 minutes, until the carrots are just tender. Remove the lid and continue cooking until the liquid has reduced to a thick sauce.

4 Remove the saucepan from the heat, stir in the chopped fresh parsley and then spoon into a warmed serving dish.

COOK'S TIP

If the carrots are cooked before the liquid in the saucepan has reduced, transfer the carrots to a serving dish and rapidly boil the liquid until thick. Pour over the carrots and sprinkle with parsley.

Broccoli and Cauliflower Gratin

BROCCOLI AND cauliflower make an attractive combination, and a yogurt and cheesy sauce gives them extra piquant flavour.

INGREDIENTS

1 small cauliflower (about 250g/9oz)
1 small head broccoli (about 250g/9oz)
150g/5oz/½ cup natural yogurt
75g/3oz/¾ cup grated Cheddar cheese
5ml/1 tsp wholegrain mustard
30ml/2 tbsp wholemeal breadcrumbs
salt and freshly ground black pepper

Serves 4

1 Break the cauliflower and broccoli into florets and cook in lightly salted boiling water for about 8–10 minutes, until just tender. Drain well and transfer to a flameproof dish.

2 Mix together the yogurt, grated cheese and mustard, then season with salt and pepper and spoon over the cauliflower and broccoli.

3 Preheat the grill to moderately hot. Sprinkle the breadcrumbs over the top of the vegetables and grill until golden brown. Serve hot.

COOK'S TIP

When preparing the cauliflower and broccoli, discard the tougher parts of the stalk, then break the florets into same-size pieces so they cook evenly.

Courgettes in Rich Tomato Sauce

THIS RICH-FLAVOURED Mediterranean dish can be served hot or cold, either as a side dish or as part of a tapas meal. Cut the courgettes into fairly thick slices, so that they stay slightly crunchy.

INGREDIENTS

15ml/1 tbsp olive oil
1 onion, chopped
1 garlic clove, chopped
4 courgettes, thickly sliced
400g/14oz/3 cups canned tomatoes, strained
2 tomatoes, peeled, seeded and chopped
5ml/1 tsp vegetable bouillon powder
15ml/1 tbsp tomato purée
salt and freshly ground black pepper

Serves 4

1 Heat the oil in a heavy-based saucepan, add the onion and garlic and sauté for 5 minutes or until the onion is softened, stirring occasionally. Add the courgettes and cook for a further 5 minutes.

2 Add the canned and fresh tomatoes, bouillon powder and tomato purée. Stir well, then simmer for 10–15 minutes until the sauce is thickened and the courgettes are just tender. Season to taste and serve.

VARIATION

Add 1 or 2 sliced and seeded red peppers with the courgettes in step 1.

HEALTH BENEFITS

Like carrots, courgettes are a good source of both beta carotene and vitamin C.

Baked Fennel with a Crumb Crust

THE DELICATE ANISEED FLAVOUR of baked fennel makes it a very good accompaniment to all sorts of pasta dishes and risottos.

INGREDIENTS

3 fennel bulbs, cut lengthways into quarters
30ml/2 tbsp olive oil
1 garlic clove, chopped
50g/2oz/1 cup day-old wholemeal breadcrumbs
30ml/2 tbsp chopped fresh flat leaf parsley
salt and freshly ground black pepper
fennel leaves, to garnish (optional)

Serves 4

VARIATION

To make a cheese-topped version of this dish, add 60ml/4 tbsp finely grated strong-flavoured cheese, such as mature Cheddar, Red Leicester or Parmesan, to the breadcrumb mixture in step 3.

1 Cook the fennel in a saucepan of boiling salted water for 10 minutes or until just tender.

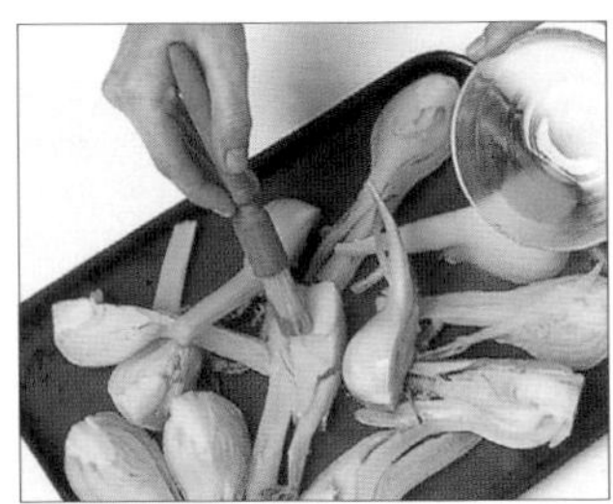

2 Drain the fennel and place in a baking dish or roasting tin, then brush with half of the olive oil. Preheat the oven to 190°C/375°F/Gas 5.

HEALTH BENEFITS

A natural diuretic, fennel is also known for its ability to relieve wind and flatulence.

3 In a small bowl, mix together the garlic, breadcrumbs and parsley with the rest of the oil. Sprinkle the mixture evenly over the fennel, then season well.

4 Bake for 30 minutes or until the fennel is tender and the breadcrumbs are crisp and golden. Serve hot, garnished with a few fennel leaves, if you wish.

DESSERTS, CAKES and BAKES

The delicious aroma of home-baking has an instant appeal, and often it is just too tempting. But desserts and cakes can be indulgent without being fattening as this mouth-watering selection shows.

Raspberry, Fromage Frais and Amaretti Scrunch

THIS PUDDING LOOKS STUNNING, but it is actually very simple to make. The raspberries give a luscious swirl of colour and the amaretti biscuits make a crunchy contrast to the creamy fromage frais or yogurt.

INGREDIENTS

250g/9oz/1 1/2 cups frozen or fresh raspberries
500g/1 1/4lb/2 1/2 cups fromage frais or thick natural live yogurt
30ml/2 tbsp clear honey
finely grated rind of 1 small lemon
75g/3oz/1 1/2 cups amaretti biscuits, broken into pieces
crystallized rose petals, for decoration (optional)

Serves 4–6

1 If using frozen raspberries, allow them to partly defrost. If using fresh ones, partly freeze them.

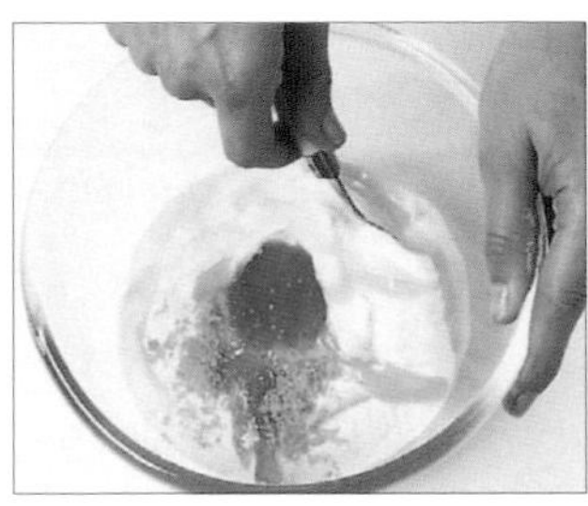

2 Place the fromage frais or yogurt in a bowl and stir in the honey and lemon rind. Add the raspberries and fold in gently, being careful not to over mix. Chill for 1 hour.

3 Stir in the amaretti biscuits just before serving. Decorate with crystallized rose petals, if you wish.

HEALTH BENEFITS

Raspberries are extremely cleansing for the body and can relieve menstrual cramps and cystitis.

Tropical Fruit with Hot Rum and Cinnamon Sauce

DARK RUM AND CINNAMON give this hot fruit dessert a distinctly Caribbean flavour. It is best eaten as soon as it is ready, so prepare the fruit ahead of time, then cook between courses – this will only take a few minutes.

INGREDIENTS

25g/1oz/2 tbsp unsalted butter
1 medium pineapple, peeled, cored and sliced
1 mango, peeled, stoned and cut into 1cm/1/2in cubes
1 papaya, peeled, halved, seeded and sliced
2 bananas, thickly sliced
30ml/2 tbsp clear honey or maple syrup
5ml/1 tsp ground cinnamon
60ml/4 tbsp dark rum
natural live yogurt or yogurt ice, to serve

Serves 4

1 Melt the butter in a large heavy-based frying pan. Add the sliced pineapple and cook for 3 minutes or until it starts to brown, turning it occasionally.

HEALTH BENEFITS

Papaya contains the enzyme, papain, which can help to stimulate the digestion. Like pineapple and mango, papaya is rich in both vitamin C and beta carotene.

2 Add the prepared mango, papaya and bananas to the pan and cook for 1 minute, turning occasionally.

3 Stir in the honey or maple syrup, cinnamon and rum, and cook for a further 2 minutes or until the sauce thickens and the fruit is tender. Serve immediately with yogurt or yogurt ice.

Pan-fried Apple Slices with Walnut Shortbread

SOFT, CARAMELIZED APPLES AND crisp nutty shortbread make a perfect combination. Serve warm with a spoonful of yogurt or fromage frais or a scoop of vanilla ice cream.

INGREDIENTS

25g/1oz/2 tbsp unsalted butter
4 dessert apples, cored and thinly sliced
30ml/2 tbsp soft light brown sugar
10ml/2 tsp ground ginger
5ml/1 tsp ground cinnamon
2.5ml/½ tsp ground nutmeg

For the walnut shortbread
75g/3oz/⅔ cup wholemeal flour
75g/3oz/⅔ cup unbleached plain flour
25g/1oz/¼ cup oatmeal
5ml/1 tsp baking powder
1.5ml/¼ tsp salt
50g/2oz/¼ cup golden caster sugar
115g/4oz/8 tbsp unsalted butter
40g/1½oz/¼ cup walnuts, finely chopped
15ml/1 tbsp milk, plus extra for brushing
demerara sugar, for sprinkling

Serves 4

1 Preheat the oven to 180°C/350°F/Gas 4 and grease one or two baking sheets. To make the walnut shortbread, sift together the flours, adding any bran left in the sieve, and mix with the oatmeal, baking powder, salt and sugar. Rub in the butter with your fingers until the mixture resembles fine breadcrumbs.

2 Add the chopped walnuts, then stir in enough of the milk to form a soft dough.

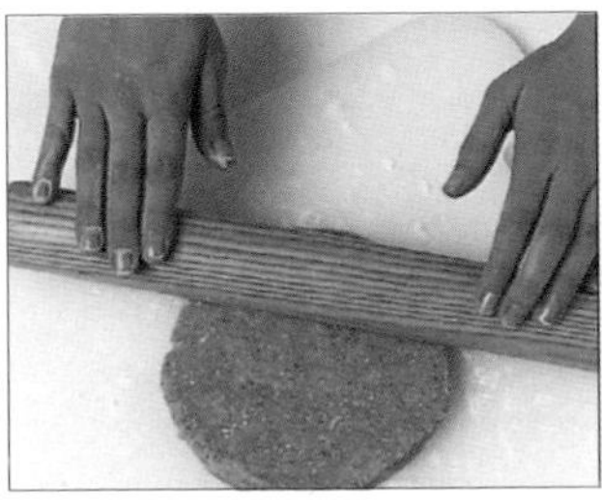

3 Gently knead the dough on a floured work surface. Form into a round, then roll out to a 5mm/¼in thickness. Using a 7.5cm/3in fluted cutter, stamp out eight rounds – you may have some dough left over.

4 Place the shortbread rounds on the prepared baking sheets. Brush the tops with milk and sprinkle with sugar. Bake for 12–15 minutes until golden, then transfer to a wire rack and leave to cool.

5 To prepare the apples, melt the butter in a heavy-based frying pan. Add the apples and cook for 3–4 minutes over a gentle heat until softened. Increase the heat to medium, add the sugar and spices, and stir well. Cook for a few minutes, stirring frequently, until the sauce turns golden brown and caramelizes.

6 Place two shortbread rounds on each of four individual serving plates and spoon over the warm apples and sauce. Serve immediately.

HEALTH BENEFITS

- *Recent studies have shown that eating walnuts regularly can greatly reduce the risk of heart disease and lower the level of blood cholesterol in the body.*
- *There is much truth in the adage: "an apple a day keeps the doctor away." Apples have many health-giving properties. They help cleanse the blood, remove impurities in the liver and inhibit the growth of harmful bacteria in the digestive tract. Apples are also known to treat skin diseases and arthritis.*

COOK'S TIP

To prevent the apples browning after they are sliced, place them in a large bowl of water mixed with about 15ml/1 tbsp lemon juice.

Coconut Rice Puddings with Grilled Oranges

STICKY RICE PUDDING is a speciality of many South-east Asian countries. In these little desserts Thai jasmine rice is cooked with rich and creamy coconut milk.

INGREDIENTS

175g/6oz/scant 1 cup jasmine rice
400ml/14fl oz/1 2/3 cup coconut milk
2.5ml/1/2 tsp grated nutmeg, plus extra for sprinkling
large pinch of salt
60ml/4 tbsp golden caster sugar
oil, for greasing
2 oranges, skin and pith removed and cut into thin rounds
orange peel twists, to decorate

Serves 4

1 Rinse and drain the rice. Place in a saucepan, cover with water, and bring to the boil. Cook for 5 minutes until the grains are just beginning to soften. Drain well.

2 Place the rice in a muslin-lined steamer, then make a few holes in the muslin to allow the steam to get through. Steam the rice for 15 minutes or until tender.

3 Put the steamed rice in a heavy-based saucepan with the coconut milk, nutmeg, salt and sugar, and cook over gentle heat until the mixture begins to simmer. Simmer for about 5 minutes until the mixture is thick and creamy, stirring frequently to prevent the rice sticking.

4 Spoon the rice mixture into four lightly oiled 175ml/6fl oz/3/4 cup moulds or ramekins and leave to cool.

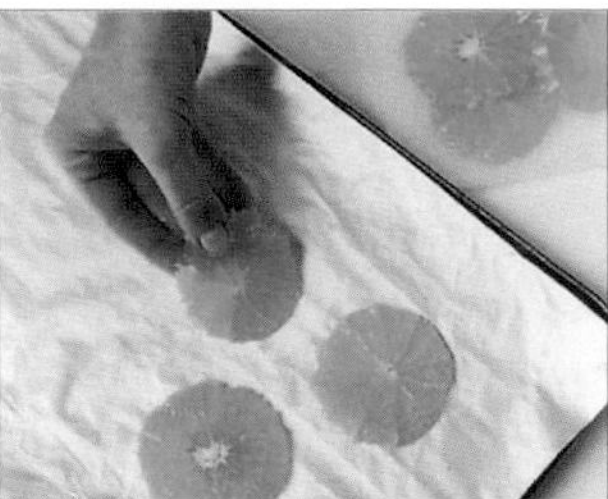

5 When ready to serve, heat the grill to high. Line a baking tray or the grill rack with foil and place the orange slices on top. Sprinkle the oranges with a little grated nutmeg, then grill for 6 minutes until lightly golden, turning the slices halfway through cooking.

6 When the rice mixture is cold, run a knife around the edge of the moulds or ramekins and turn out the rice. Decorate with orange peel twists and serve with the warm orange slices.

HEALTH BENEFITS

• *Rice is gluten-free and therefore can be eaten by coeliacs. Although, more refined than brown rice, jasmine rice is a useful source of energy.*

Date, Fig and Orange Pudding

THIS LIGHT STEAMED PUDDING avoids the use of suet, which is usually made from hydrogenated fat, often animal in origin. The addition of fresh orange juice and rind, and orange liqueur, gives an intense citrus tang.

INGREDIENTS

juice and rind of 2 oranges
115g/4oz/⅔ cup stoned, ready-to-eat dried dates, chopped
115g/4oz/⅔ cup ready-to-eat dried figs, chopped
30ml/2 tbsp orange liqueur (optional)
175g/6oz/¾ cup unsalted butter, plus extra for greasing
175g/6oz/¾ cup soft light brown sugar
3 eggs
75g/3oz/⅔ cup self-raising wholemeal flour
115g/4oz/1 cup unbleached self-raising flour
30ml/2 tbsp golden syrup (optional)

Serves 6

1 Reserve a few strips of orange rind for the decoration and put the rest in a saucepan with the orange juice. Add the chopped dates and figs and orange liqueur, if using. Cook, covered, over a gentle heat for 8–10 minutes, until the fruit is soft.

2 Leave the fruit mixture to cool, then transfer to a food processor or blender and process until smooth. Press through a sieve to remove the fig seeds, if you wish.

3 Cream the butter and sugar until pale and fluffy, then beat in the fig purée. Beat in the eggs, then fold in the flours and mix until combined.

HEALTH BENEFITS

The healing qualities of figs have been recognized for thousands of years and, as a result, the fruit has been used to treat almost every known disease. Widely known as a gentle laxative, figs also contain vitamins B_6 and C, calcium and iron. Dates contain their fair share of vitamin B_6 and iron and feature a useful amount of potassium.

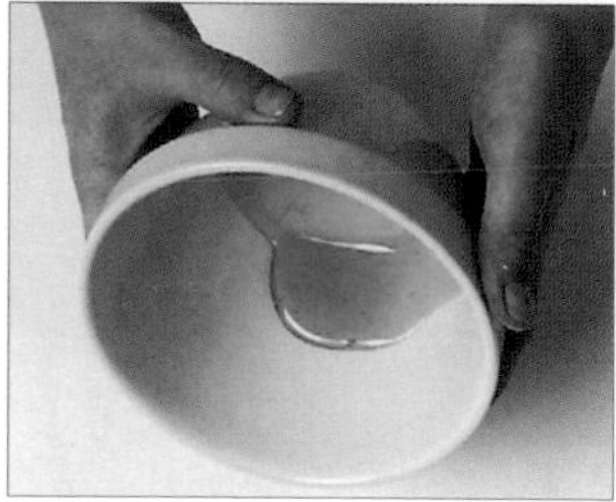

4 Grease a 1.2 litre/2 pint/5 cup pudding basin, and pour in the golden syrup, if using. Tilt the bowl to cover the inside with a layer of syrup. Spoon in the pudding mixture. Cover the top with greaseproof paper, with a pleat down the centre, and then with pleated foil, and tie down with string.

5 Place the bowl in a large saucepan, and pour in enough water to come halfway up the sides of the bowl. Cover with a tight-fitting lid and steam for 2 hours. Check the water occasionally and top up if necessary. Turn out and decorate with the reserved orange rind.

Lemon and Almond Tart

THIS REFRESHING, TANGY TART has a rich, creamy lemon filling set off by a caramelized sugar top. Serve warm or cold with a dollop of crème fraîche or natural yogurt.

INGREDIENTS

2 eggs
50g/2oz/¼ cup golden caster sugar
finely grated rind and juice of 4 unwaxed lemons
2.5ml/½ tsp vanilla essence
50g/2oz/½ cup ground almonds
120ml/4fl oz/½ cup single cream

For the pastry
225g/8oz/2 cups unbleached spelt flour
75g/3oz/¾ cup icing sugar, plus extra for dusting
130g/4½oz/9 tbsp butter
1 egg, beaten
a pinch of salt
Serves 8–10

1 Preheat the oven to 180°C/350°F/Gas 4. To make the pastry, sift together the flour and sugar in a bowl. Rub in the butter with your fingers until the mixture resembles fine breadcrumbs. Add the egg and salt, then mix to a smooth dough.

2 Knead the dough lightly on a floured work surface and form into a smooth flat round. Wrap the dough in clear film and chill for 15 minutes.

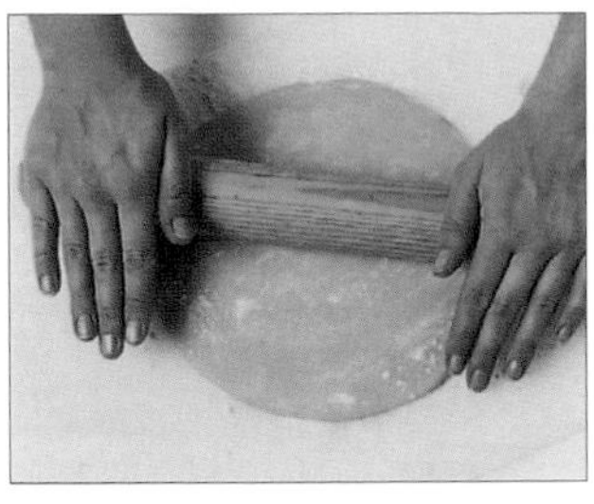

3 Roll out the dough on a lightly floured work surface and use to line a 23cm/9 in loose-bottomed flan tin. Prick the pastry base and chill for a further 15 minutes.

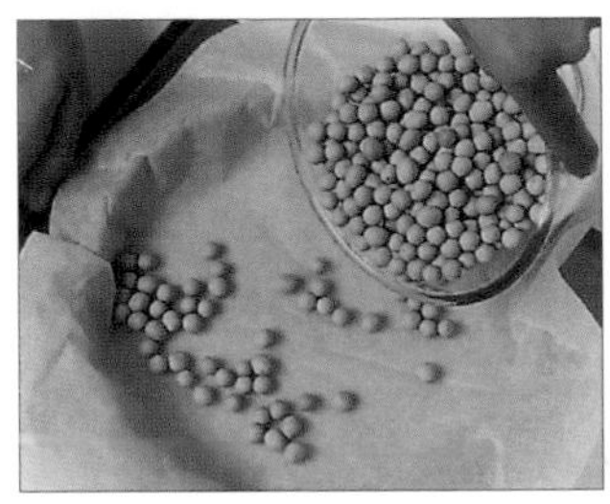

4 Line the pastry case with non-stick baking paper. Tip in some baking beans and bake blind for 10 minutes. Remove the paper and beans and return the pastry case to the oven for a further 10 minutes or until it is light golden.

5 Meanwhile, make the filling. Beat the eggs with the sugar until the mixture leaves a thin ribbon trail. Gently stir in the lemon rind and juice, vanilla essence, almonds and cream.

6 Carefully pour the filling into the pastry case and level the surface. Bake for about 25 minutes or until the filling is set.

7 Heat the grill to high. Sift a thick layer of icing sugar over the tart and grill until the sugar caramelizes. Decorate the tart with a little extra sifted icing sugar before serving warm or cold with crème fraîche.

HEALTH BENEFITS

- *The high level of vitamin C in lemons is widely known but they also contain good amounts of calcium, iron and potassium.*
- *Lemons are a natural antiseptic and have been used for centuries to treat skin problems. They are also used to cleanse the body of toxins.*

COOK'S TIP

- *Spelt flour is a type of wheat flour that is available in some large supermarkets and health food shops. If you can't find it, then use unbleached plain flour instead.*

Baked Ricotta Cakes with Red Sauce

THESE HONEY AND vanilla-flavoured desserts take only minutes to make. The fragrant fruity sauce provides a contrast of both colour and flavour.

INGREDIENTS

250g/9oz/generous 1 cup ricotta cheese
2 egg whites, beaten
60ml/4 tbsp clear honey, plus extra to taste
5ml/1 tsp vanilla essence
450g/1lb/4 cups mixed fresh or frozen fruit, such as strawberries, raspberries, blackberries and cherries
fresh mint leaves, to decorate (optional)

Serves 4

1 Preheat the oven to 180°C/350°F/Gas 4. Place the ricotta cheese in a bowl and break it up with a wooden spoon. Add the beaten egg whites, honey and vanilla essence and mix thoroughly until the mixture is smooth and well combined.

2 Lightly grease four ramekins. Spoon the ricotta mixture into the prepared ramekins and level the tops. Bake for 20 minutes or until the ricotta cakes are risen and golden.

3 Meanwhile, make the fruit sauce. Reserve about a quarter of the fruit for decoration. Place the rest of the fruit in a saucepan, with a little water if the fruit is fresh, and heat gently until softened. Leave to cool slightly, remove any cherry stones, if using cherries.

COOK'S TIP

The red berry sauce can be made a day in advance. Chill until ready to use. Frozen fruit doesn't need extra water, as there are usually plenty of ice crystals clinging to the berries.

4 Press the fruit through a sieve, then taste and sweeten with honey if it is too tart. Serve the sauce, warm or cold, with the ricotta cakes. Decorate with the reserved berries and mint leaves, if using.

HEALTH BENEFITS

- *Ricotta contains about 4 per cent fat, compared with 35 per cent in a hard cheese like Cheddar. It is a good source of vitamin B_{12}, calcium and protein.*
- *All berries are rich in the anti-cancer compound, ellagic acid, which is a powerful antioxidant.*

Apricot Panettone Pudding

PANETTONE makes a rich addition to this traditional pudding.

INGREDIENTS

unsalted butter, for greasing
350g/12oz panettone, sliced into triangles
25g/1oz/¼ cup pecan nuts75g/3oz/⅓ cup ready-to-eat unsulphured dried apricots, chopped
500ml/17fl oz/2¼ cups semi-skimmed milk
5ml/1 tsp vanilla essence
1 large egg, beaten
30ml/2 tbsp maple syrup
grated nutmeg
demerara sugar, for sprinkling
Serves 6

1 Butter a 1 litre/1¾ pint/4 cup baking dish. Arrange half the panettone in the dish, scatter over half the pecan nuts and all the apricots, then add another layer of panettone on top.

2 Heat the milk and vanilla essence in a small saucepan until it just simmers. Put the egg and maple syrup in a large bowl, grate in 2.5ml/½ tsp nutmeg, then whisk in the hot milk.

3 Preheat the oven to 200°C/400°F/ Gas 6. Pour the egg mixture over the panettone slices, lightly pressing down the bread so it is submerged. Leave the pudding to stand for 10 minutes.

4 Scatter over the reserved pecan nuts and sprinkle with the demerara sugar and nutmeg. Bake for 40–45 minutes until risen and golden.

HEALTH BENEFITS

Dried apricots have an even higher concentration of beta carotene than fresh ones. This powerful antioxidant is known to lower the risk of cataracts, heart disease and some forms of cancer.

Indian Rice Pudding

THIS CREAMY PUDDING is scented with saffron, cardamom and freshly grated nutmeg. Shelled pistachio nuts give a subtle contrast in colour and add a delicious crunch to the dessert.

INGREDIENTS

115g/4oz/¾ cup brown short grain rice
350ml/12fl oz/1½ cups boiling water
600ml/1 pint/2½ cups semi-skimmed milk
6 cardamom pods, bruised
2.5ml/½tsp freshly grated nutmeg
pinch of saffron strands
60ml/4 tbsp maize malt syrup
15ml/1 tbsp clear honey
50g/2oz/½ cup pistachio nuts, chopped

Serves 4

1 Wash the rice under cold running water and place in a saucepan with the boiling water. Bring to the boil and boil, uncovered, for 15 minutes.

2 Pour in the milk, then reduce the heat and simmer, partially covered, for 15 minutes.

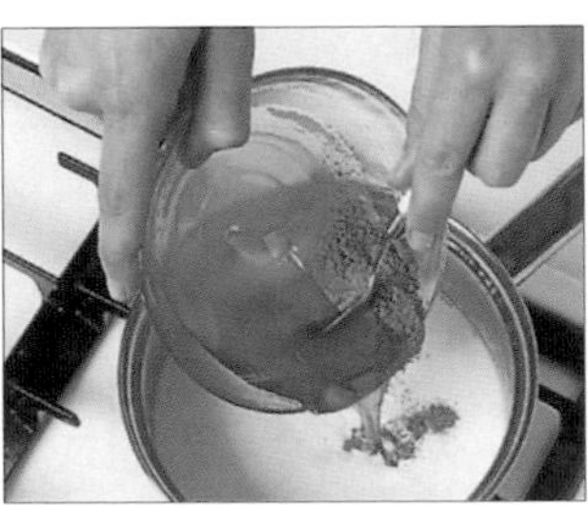

3 Add the cardamom pods, grated nutmeg, saffron, maize malt syrup and honey, and cook for a further 15 minutes, or until the rice is tender, stirring occasionally.

4 Spoon the rice into small serving bowls and sprinkle with pistachio nuts before serving hot or cold.

COOK'S TIP

Maize malt syrup is a natural alternative to refined sugar and can be found in health food shops.

HEALTH BENEFITS

- *Brown rice is unrefined and therefore, unlike white polished rice, retains most of its fibre and nutrients. It is a source of some B complex vitamins and vitamin E.*
- *Pistachio nuts are densely packed with nourishment, being rich in protein, vitamins and minerals. However, because of their high fat content, they go rancid quickly, so buy them in a shop with a high turnover of stock and store them in a cool dry place. Due to their high fat content, pistachio nuts should be eaten in moderation.*

Winter Fruit Poached in Mulled Wine

FRESH APPLES AND PEARS are combined with dried apricots and figs, and cooked in a fragrant, spicy wine until tender and intensely flavoured.

INGREDIENTS

300ml/½ pint/1¼ cups red wine
300ml/½ pint/1¼ cups fresh orange juice
finely grated rind and juice of 1 orange
45ml/3 tbsp clear honey or barley malt syrup
3 small cinnamon sticks
4 cloves
4 cardamom pods, split
2 pears, such as Comice or William, peeled, cored and halved
8 ready-to-eat dried figs
12 ready-to-eat dried unsulphured apricots
2 eating apples, peeled, cored and thickly sliced

Serves 4

1 Put the wine, the fresh and squeezed orange juice and half the orange rind in a saucepan with the honey or syrup and spices. Bring to the boil, then reduce the heat and simmer for 2 minutes, stirring occasionally.

2 Add the pears, figs and apricots to the pan and cook, covered, for 25 minutes, occasionally turning the fruit in the wine mixture. Add the apples and cook for a further 12–15 minutes until the fruit is tender.

3 Remove the fruit from the pan and discard the spices. Cook the wine mixture over a high heat until reduced and syrupy, then pour it over the fruit. Serve decorated with the reserved orange rind, if wished.

HEALTH BENEFITS

- *The combination of fresh and dried fruit ensures a healthy amount of vitamins and minerals, particularly vitamins C, beta carotene, potassium and iron. The fruit is also rich in fibre.*
- *Cardamom and cinnamon soothe indigestion and, along with cloves, can offer relief from colds and coughs.*

Apricot and Almond Tart

Crumbly, rich pastry encases an apricot and almond filling to make this tempting dessert. Serve with Greek yogurt or crème fraîche.

INGREDIENTS

115g/4oz/½ cup soft margarine
115g/4oz/½ cup caster sugar
1 egg, beaten
50g/2oz/⅓ cup ground rice
50g/2oz/½ cup ground almonds
few drops of almond essence
450g/1 lb fresh apricots, halved and stoned
sifted icing sugar, for dusting (optional)
apricot slices and fresh mint sprigs, to decorate (optional)

For the pastry

115g/4oz/1 cup brown rice flour
115g/4oz/1 cup cornmeal
pinch of salt
115g/4oz/½ cup soft margarine
25g/1oz/2 tbsp caster sugar
1 egg yolk

Serves 6

1 To make the pastry, place the rice flour, cornmeal and pinch of salt in a bowl and stir to mix. Lightly rub in the soft margarine until the mixture resembles breadcrumbs.

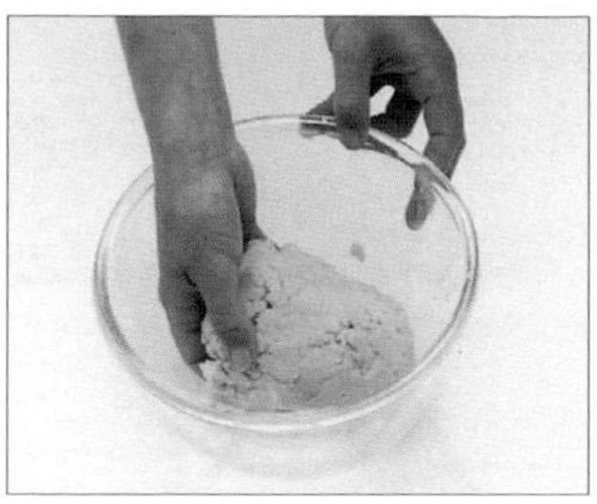

2 Add the sugar, stir in the egg yolk and add enough chilled water to make a smooth, soft but not sticky dough. Wrap the dough and chill for 30 minutes.

3 Preheat the oven to 180°C/350°F/Gas 4. Line a 24cm/9½in loose-bottomed flan tin with the pastry by pressing it gently over the base and up the sides of the tin, making sure there are no holes in the pastry. Trim the edge with a sharp knife.

4 To make the almond filling, place the margarine and sugar in a mixing bowl and cream together, using a wooden spoon, until the mixture is light and fluffy.

5 Gradually add the beaten egg, beating well after each addition. Fold in the ground rice and almonds and the almond essence and mix well to incorporate them.

6 Spoon the almond mixture into the pastry case, spreading it evenly, then arrange the apricot halves cut side down on top.

7 Place on a baking sheet and bake for 40–45 minutes until the filling and pastry are cooked and lightly browned. Serve warm or cold, dusted with icing sugar and decorated with apricots and sprigs of mint, if you like.

Variation

For a change, use ground hazelnuts and vanilla essence in place of the ground almonds and almond essence.

Baked Fruit Compote

INGREDIENTS

115g/4oz/⅔ cup ready-to-eat dried figs
115g/4oz/½ cup ready-to-eat dried apricots
50g/2oz/½ cup ready-to-eat dried apple rings
50g/2oz/¼ cup ready-to-eat prunes
50g/2oz/½ cup ready-to-eat dried pears
50g/2oz/½ cup ready-to-eat dried peaches
300ml/½ pint/1¼ cups unsweetened apple juice
300ml/½ pint/1¼ cups unsweetened orange juice
6 cloves
1 cinnamon stick
toasted flaked almonds, to decorate

Serves 6

1 Preheat the oven to 180°C/350°F/Gas 4. Place the figs, apricots, apple rings, prunes, pears and peaches in a shallow ovenproof dish and stir to mix well.

2 Mix together the apple and orange juices and pour over the fruit. Add the cloves and cinnamon stick and stir gently to blend.

3 Bake for about 30 minutes until the fruit mixture is hot, stirring once or twice during cooking. Set aside and leave to soak for 20 minutes, then remove and discard the cloves and cinnamon stick.

4 Spoon into serving bowls and serve warm or cold, decorated with toasted flaked almonds.

COOK'S TIP

Use other mixtures of unsweetened fruit juices, such as pineapple and orange or grape and apple.

Mango Yogurt Ice

INGREDIENTS

450g/1lb ripe mango flesh, chopped
300ml/½ pint/1¼ cups low-fat peach or apricot yogurt
150ml/¼ pint/⅔ cup Greek yogurt
150ml/¼ pint/⅔ cup low-fat natural yogurt
25–50g/1–2oz/2–4 tbsp caster sugar
fresh mint sprigs, to decorate

Serves 6

1 Place the mango flesh in a blender or food processor and blend until smooth. Transfer to a bowl.

2 Add all three yogurts and blend until thoroughly mixed.

3 Stir in enough of the sugar to sweeten to taste and stir to mix.

4 Pour the mixture into a shallow, plastic container. Cover and chill for 1½–2 hours until it is mushy in consistency. Turn the mixture into a chilled bowl and beat until smooth.

5 Return the mixture to the plastic container, cover and freeze until the ice is firm. Transfer the ice to the fridge about 30 minutes before serving to allow it to soften a little. Serve in scoops decorated with mint sprigs.

COOK'S TIP

The colour of the mango skin will not tell you whether it is ripe or not. However, it should be shiny, unwrinkled and not blemished. It will yield when slightly squeezed in the palm of your hand.

Creamy Lemon Rice

THIS IS a creamy baked rice pudding with a difference, being subtly flavoured with lemon. It is wonderful served warm or cold with fresh strawberries.

INGREDIENTS

50g/2oz/¼ cup short grain white rice
600ml/1 pint/2½ cups semi-skimmed milk
25g/1oz/2 tbsp caster sugar
finely grated rind of 1 lemon
15g/½oz/1 tbsp butter, cut into small pieces
pared orange and lemon rind, to decorate

For serving

225g/8oz prepared fresh fruit, such as strawberries or pineapple
90ml/6 tbsp reduced-fat crème fraîche (optional)

Serves 4

1 Lightly grease a 900ml/1½ pint/3¾ cup ovenproof dish. Add the rice and pour in the milk, then set aside for about 30 minutes, to allow the rice to soften a little. Preheat the oven to 150°C/300°F/Gas 2.

2 Add the caster sugar, grated lemon rind and butter to the rice and milk and stir gently to mix. Bake for 2–2½ hours until the top of the pudding is lightly browned.

3 Decorate with pared orange and lemon rind and serve warm or cold with the fresh fruit.

4 If serving cold, allow the pudding to cool, remove and discard the skin, then chill. Fold in the crème fraîche just before serving, if liked.

COOK'S TIP

Short grain rice (pudding rice) is the only kind to use for this dish. The grains swell and absorb a great deal of liquid as well as clinging together. The consistency will be rich and satisfying.

Peach and Raspberry Crumble

INGREDIENTS

75g/3oz/¾ cup brown rice flour
50g/2oz/4 tbsp soft margarine
25g/1oz/¼ cup buckwheat flakes
25g/1oz/¼ cup millet flakes
25g/1oz/¼ cup hazelnuts, roughly chopped
75g/3oz/scant ⅓ cup soft light brown sugar
5ml/1 tsp ground ginger
3 fresh peaches, stoned and cut into wedges
225g/8oz/1⅓ cups raspberries
60ml/4 tbsp fresh orange juice

Serves 4

1 Preheat the oven to 180°C/350°F/Gas 4. Grease a 1.2 litre/2 pint/5 cup pie dish. Place the rice flour in a bowl and rub in the margarine until the mixture resembles breadcrumbs.

2 Stir in the buckwheat flakes, millet flakes, hazelnuts, 50g/2oz/¼ cup of the sugar and the ginger. Mix well.

3 Mix the peaches, raspberries, orange juice and remaining sugar together and place in the dish. Sprinkle the crumble over the top, pressing it down lightly. Bake for 30–45 minutes, until the crumble is lightly browned; it should not get too dark. Serve warm or cold.

VARIATIONS

Use almonds or walnuts, in place of the hazelnuts and substitute ground cinnamon for the ground ginger.

Firm, ripe nectarines or thinly sliced dessert apples could be used in place of the peaches, if you like.

Fruit Fondue with Hazelnut Dip

INGREDIENTS

selection of fresh fruits for dipping, such as satsumas, kiwi fruit, grapes, physalis and whole strawberries
50g/2oz/¼ cup reduced-fat soft cheese
150ml/¼ pint/⅔ cup low-fat hazelnut yogurt
5ml/1 tsp vanilla essence
5ml/1 tsp caster sugar
3 tbsp chopped hazelnuts

Serves 2

Cook's Tip

If you want to skin the hazeluts, roast them lightly in the oven, preheated to 190°C/375°F/Gas 5, for 10 minutes. Rub off the skins with a clean dish towel.

1 First prepare the fruits. Peel and segment the satsumas. Then peel the kiwi fruit and cut into wedges. Wash the grapes and peel back the papery casing on the physalis.

2 Beat the soft cheese with the yogurt, vanilla essence and sugar in a bowl. Stir in three-quarters of the hazelnuts. Spoon into a glass serving dish set on a platter or small pots on individual plates, and scatter over the remaining hazelnuts. Arrange the prepared fruits around the dip and serve immediately.

Yogurt Sundaes with Passion Fruit Coulis

Here is a sundae you can enjoy every day! The frozen yogurt has less fat and fewer calories than traditional ice cream and the fruits provide vitamins A and C.

INGREDIENTS

350g/12oz/2½ cups strawberries, hulled and halved
2 passion fruits, halved
10ml/2 tsp icing sugar (optional)
2 ripe peaches, stoned and chopped
8 scoops (about 350g/12oz) vanilla or strawberry frozen yogurt

Serves 4

Cook's Tip

Passion fruit when they first ripen have a pale yellow or reddish-purple leathery skin. As they age the skin wrinkles and shrivels – that does not mean they taste any better. To use the pulp rub it through a sieve with a tablespoon of boiling water.

1 Purée half the strawberries. Scoop out the passion fruit pulp and add it to the coulis. Sweeten, if necessary.

2 Spoon half the remaining strawberries and half the chopped peaches into four tall sundae glasses. Top each dessert with a scoop of frozen yogurt. Set aside a few choice pieces of fruit for decoration, and use the rest to make a further layer on the top of each sundae. Top each with a fina scoop of frozen yogurt.

3 Pour over the passion fruit coulis and decorate the sundaes with the reserved strawberries and pieces of peach. Serve immediately.

Mango and Orange Sorbet

FRESH AND TANGY, and gloriously vibrant in colour, this sorbet is the perfect finale to a spicy meal.

INGREDIENTS

115g/4oz/½ cup golden caster sugar
2 large mangoes
juice of 1 orange
1 egg white (optional)
thinly pared strips of fresh unwaxed orange rind, to decorate

Serves 2–4

1 Gently heat the sugar and 300ml/½ pint/1¼ cups water in a pan until the sugar has dissolved. Bring to the boil, then reduce the heat and simmer for 5 minutes. Leave to cool.

2 Cut away the two sides of the mangoes close to the stones. Peel, then cut the flesh from the stones. Dice the fruit and discard the stone.

3 Process the mango flesh and orange juice in a food processor with the sugar syrup until smooth.

4 Pour the mixture into a freezer-proof container and freeze for 2 hours until semi-frozen. Whisk the egg white, if using, until it forms stiff peaks, then stir it into the sorbet. Whisk well to remove any ice crystals and freeze until solid.

5 Transfer the sorbet to the fridge 10 minutes before serving. Serve, decorated with orange rind.

HEALTH BENEFITS

Mangoes and oranges aid the digestion, boost the immune system and are said to cleanse the blood. They are also an excellent source of vitamins A and C.

Rhubarb and Ginger Yogurt Ice

THIS DELICATE PINK YOGURT ice is flavoured with honey and ginger.

INGREDIENTS

300g/11oz/scant 1½ cups set natural live yogurt
200g/7oz/scant 1 cup fromage frais
375g/13oz/3 cups rhubarb, trimmed and chopped
45ml/3 tbsp stem ginger syrup
30ml/2 tbsp clear honey
3 pieces stem ginger, finely chopped

Serves 6

1 In a bowl, whisk together the yogurt and fromage frais.

2 Pour the yogurt mixture into a shallow freezer-proof container and freeze for 1 hour.

3 Meanwhile, put the rhubarb, stem ginger syrup and honey in a large saucepan and cook over a low heat for 15 minutes, or until the rhubarb is soft. Leave to cool, then purée in a food processor or blender.

4 Remove the semi-frozen yogurt mixture from the freezer and fold in the rhubarb and stem ginger purée. Beat well until smooth. Add the chopped stem ginger.

5 Return the yogurt ice to the freezer and freeze for a further 2 hours. Remove from the freezer and beat again, then freeze until solid. Serve scoops of the yogurt ice on individual plates or in bowls.

HEALTH BENEFITS

- *Rhubarb is rich in potassium and is an effective laxative. However, it is also high in oxalic acid, which is reputed to inhibit the absorption of iron and calcium and can exasperate joint problems, such as arthritis. The leaves are poisonous and should never be eaten.*
- *Stem ginger retains many of the health-giving qualities of fresh ginger. It aids digestion and is effective in treating gastrointestinal disorders.*

COOK'S TIP

Take the yogurt ice out of the freezer and transfer it to the fridge 15 minutes before serving to allow it to soften.

Spiced Apple Crumble

ANY FRUIT can be used in this popular dessert, but you can't beat the favourites of blackberry and apple. Hazelnuts and cardamom seeds give the topping extra flavour.

INGREDIENTS

butter, for greasing
450g/1lb Bramley apples
115g/4oz/1 cup blackberries
grated rind and juice of 1 orange
50g/2oz/⅓ cup light muscovado sugar
custard, to serve

For the topping

175g/6oz/1½ cups plain flour
75g/3oz/⅓ cup butter
75g/3oz/⅓ cup caster sugar
25g/1oz/¼ cup chopped hazelnuts
2.5ml/½ tsp crushed cardamom seeds

Serves 4–6

1 Preheat the oven to 200°C/400°F/Gas 6. Generously butter a 1.2 litre/2 pint/5 cup baking dish. Peel and core the apples, then slice them into the prepared baking dish. Level the surface, then scatter the blackberries over. Sprinkle the orange rind and light muscovado sugar evenly over the top, then pour over the orange juice. Set the fruit mixture aside while you make the crumble topping.

2 Make the topping. Sift the flour into a bowl and rub in the butter until the mixture resembles coarse breadcrumbs. Stir in the caster sugar, hazelnuts and cardamom seeds. Scatter the topping over the top of the fruit.

3 Press the topping around the edges of the dish to seal in the juices. Bake for 30–35 minutes or until the crumble is golden. Serve hot, with custard.

Baked Stuffed Apples

THIS TRADITIONAL apple dessert is exceptionally simple and speedy. Bake the apples in the oven on the shelf under the Sunday dinner for a delicious end to a meal.

INGREDIENTS

4 large Bramley apples
75g/3oz/½ cup light muscovado sugar
75g/3oz/⅓ cup butter, softened
grated rind and juice of ½ orange
1.5ml/¼ tsp ground cinnamon
30ml/2 tbsp crushed ratafia biscuits
50g/2oz/½ cup pecan nuts, chopped
50g/2oz/½ cup luxury mixed glacé fruit, chopped

Serves 4

1 Preheat the oven to 180°C/350°F/Gas 4. Wash and dry the apples. Remove the cores with an apple corer, then carefully enlarge each core cavity to twice its size, by shaving off more flesh with the corer. Score each apple around its equator, using a sharp knife. Stand the apples in a baking dish.

2 Mix the sugar, butter, orange rind and juice, cinnamon and ratafia crumbs. Beat well, then stir in the nuts and glacé fruit. Divide the filling among the apples, piling it high. Shield the filling in each apple with a small piece of foil. Bake for 45–60 minutes until each apple is tender.

Lemon Grass Skewers with Lime Cheese

GRILLED FRUITS make a fine finale to a barbecue and the lemon grass skewers give the fruit a subtle tang. You can use almost any soft fruit.

INGREDIENTS

4 long fresh lemon grass stalks
1 mango, peeled, stoned and cut into chunks
1 papaya, peeled, seeded and cut into chunks
1 star fruit, cut into thick slices and halved
8 fresh bay leaves
a nutmeg
60ml/4 tbsp maple syrup
50g/2oz/1/3 cup demerara sugar

For the lime cheese

150g/5oz/2/3 cup curd or low fat soft cheese
120ml/4fl oz/1/2 cup double cream
grated rind and juice of 1/2 lime
30ml/2 tbsp icing sugar
Serves 4

1 Prepare the barbecue or preheat the grill. Cut the top of each lemon grass stalk into a point with a sharp knife. Discard the outer leaves, then use the back of the knife to bruise the length of each stalk to release the aromatic oils. Thread each stalk, skewer-style, with the fruit pieces and bay leaves.

2 Support a piece of foil on a baking sheet and roll up the edges to make a rim. Grease the foil, lay the kebabs on top and grate a little nutmeg over each. Drizzle the maple syrup over and dust liberally with the demerara sugar. Grill for 5 minutes, until lightly charred.

3 Meanwhile, make the lime cheese. Mix together the cheese, cream, grated lime rind and juice, and icing sugar in a bowl. Serve at once with the lightly charred fruit kebabs.

COOK'S TIP

Only fresh lemon grass will work as skewers for this recipe. It is now possible to buy lemon grass stalks in jars. These are handy for curries and similar dishes, but are too soft to use as skewers.

Coconut Jelly with Star Anise Fruits

INGREDIENTS

250ml/8fl oz/1 cup cold water
75g/3oz/1/3 cup caster sugar
15ml/1 tbsp powdered vegetarian gelatine
400ml/14fl oz/1 2/3 cups coconut milk

For the syrup and fruit

250ml/8fl oz/1 cup water
3 star anise
50g/2oz/1/4 cup caster sugar
1 star fruit, sliced
12 lychees, peeled and stoned
115g/4oz/1 cup blackberries
Serves 4

1 Pour the water into a saucepan, add the caster sugar and heat gently to dissolve. Sprinkle over the gelatine and heat gently to dissolve, stirring. Stir in the coconut milk, remove from the heat and set aside to cool.

2 Grease an 18cm/7in square cake tin. Line with clear film. Pour in the coconut milk mixture and chill until set.

3 To make the syrup, combine the water, star anise and sugar in a pan. Bring to the boil, stirring, then lower the heat and simmer for 10–12 minutes until syrupy. Place the assorted fruit in a heatproof bowl and pour over the hot syrup. Cool, then chill.

4 To serve, cut the coconut jelly into diamonds and remove from the tin. Arrange the coconut jelly on individual plates, adding a few of the fruits and their syrup to each portion.

COOK'S TIP

Coconut milk is available in cans or as a powder to which cold water is added.

Tropical Fruit Gratin

THIS OUT-OF-THE-ORDINARY gratin is strictly for grown-ups. A colourful combination of fruit is topped with a simple sabayon before being flashed under the grill.

INGREDIENTS

2 tamarillos
½ sweet pineapple
1 ripe mango
175g/6oz/1½ cups blackberries
120ml/4fl oz/½ cup sparkling white wine
115g/4oz/½ cup caster sugar
6 egg yolks
Serves 4

1 Cut each tamarillo in half lengthways and then into thick slices. Cut the rind and core from the pineapple and take spiral slices off the outside to remove the eyes. Cut the flesh into chunks. Peel the mango, cut it in half and cut the flesh from the stone in slices.

2 Divide all the fruit, including the blackberries, among four 14cm/5½in gratin dishes set on a baking sheet and set aside. Heat the wine and sugar in a saucepan until the sugar has dissolved. Bring to the boil and cook for 5 minutes.

3 Put the egg yolks in a large heatproof bowl. Place the bowl over a pan of simmering water and whisk until pale. Slowly pour on the hot sugar syrup, whisking all the time, until the mixture thickens. Preheat the grill.

4 Spoon the mixture over the fruit. Place the baking sheet holding the dishes on a low shelf under the hot grill until the topping is golden. Serve hot.

Grilled Pineapple with Papaya Sauce

INGREDIENTS

1 sweet pineapple
melted butter, for greasing and brushing
2 pieces drained stem ginger in syrup, cut into fine matchsticks, plus 30ml/2 tbsp of the syrup from the jar
30ml/2 tbsp demerara sugar
pinch of ground cinnamon
fresh mint sprigs, to decorate

For the sauce
1 ripe papaya, peeled and seeded
175ml/6fl oz/¾ cup apple juice
Serves 6

1 Peel the pineapple and take spiral slices off the outside to remove the eyes. Cut it crossways into six slices, each 2.5cm/1in thick. Line a baking sheet with a sheet of foil, rolling up the sides to make a rim. Grease the foil with melted butter. Preheat the grill.

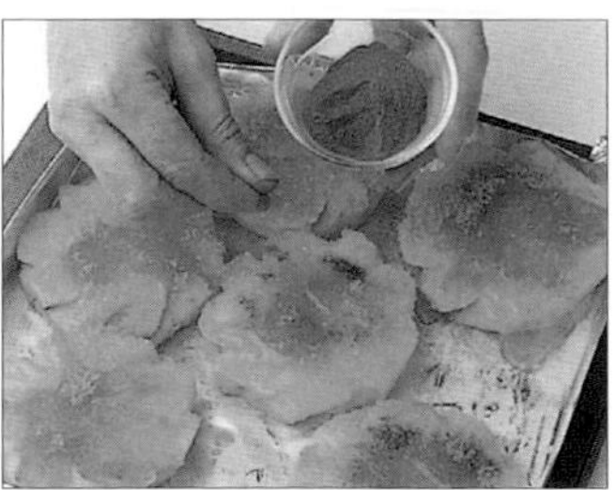

2 Arrange the pineapple slices on the lined baking sheet. Brush with butter, then top with the ginger matchsticks, sugar and cinnamon. Drizzle over the stem ginger syrup. Grill for 5–7 minutes or until the slices are golden and lightly charred on top.

3 Meanwhile, make the sauce. Cut a few slices from the papaya and set aside, then purée the rest with the apple juice in a blender or food processor.

4 Press the purée through a sieve placed over a bowl, then stir in any juices from cooking the pineapple. Serve the pineapple slices with a little of the sauce drizzled around each plate. Decorate with the reserved papaya slices and the mint sprigs.

COOK'S TIP

Try the papaya sauce with savoury dishes, too. It goes well with vegetable kebabs grilled on a barbecue.

Banana and Pecan Bread

BANANAS AND pecans just seem to belong together. This is a really moist and delicious tea bread. Spread it with cream cheese or jam, or serve as a dessert with whipped cream.

INGREDIENTS

115g/4oz/½ cup butter, softened
175g/6oz/1 cup light muscovado sugar
2 large eggs, beaten
3 ripe bananas
75g/3oz/¾ cup pecan nuts, coarsely chopped
225g/8oz/2 cups self-raising flour
2.5ml/½ tsp ground mixed spice
Makes a 900g/2lb loaf

1 Preheat the oven to 180°C/350°F/Gas 4. Generously grease a 900g/2lb loaf tin and line it with non-stick baking paper. Cream the butter and sugar in a large mixing bowl until light and fluffy. Gradually add the eggs, beating after each addition, until well combined.

2 Peel and then mash the bananas with a fork. Add them to the creamed mixture with the chopped pecan nuts. Beat until well combined.

COOK'S TIP

If the mixture shows signs of curdling when you add the eggs, stir in a little of the flour to stabilize it.

3 Sift the flour and mixed spice together and fold into the banana mixture. Spoon into the tin, level the surface and bake for 1–1¼ hours or until a skewer inserted into the middle of the loaf comes out clean. Cool for 10 minutes in the tin, then invert the tin on a wire rack. Lift off the tin, peel off the lining paper and cool completely.

Date and Walnut Brownies

THESE RICH brownies are great for afternoon tea, but they also make a fantastic dessert. Reheat slices briefly in the microwave oven and serve with crème fraîche.

INGREDIENTS

350g/12oz plain chocolate, broken into squares
225g/8oz/1 cup butter, diced
3 large eggs
115g/4oz/½ cup caster sugar
5ml/1 tsp pure vanilla essence
75g/3oz/⅔ cup plain flour, sifted
225g/8oz/1½ cups fresh dates, peeled, stoned and chopped
200g/7oz/1¾ cups walnut pieces
icing sugar, for dusting
Makes 12

1 Preheat the oven to 190°C/375°F/Gas 5. Generously grease a 30 × 20cm/12 × 8in baking tin and line with non-stick baking paper.

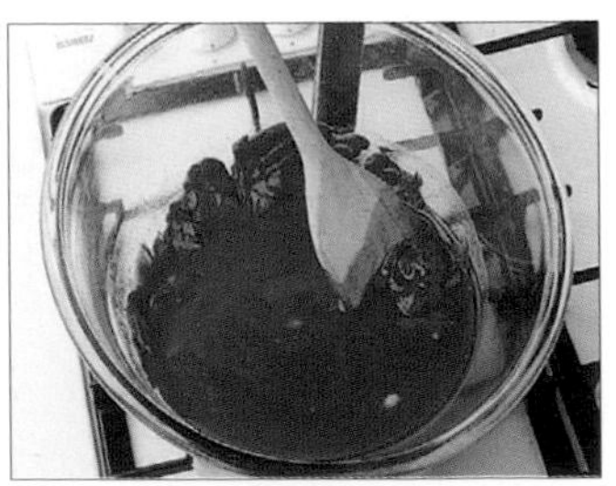

2 Put the chocolate and butter in a large heatproof bowl, over a pan of hot, not boiling, water. Leave until both have melted. Stir until smooth, lift the bowl out and cool slightly.

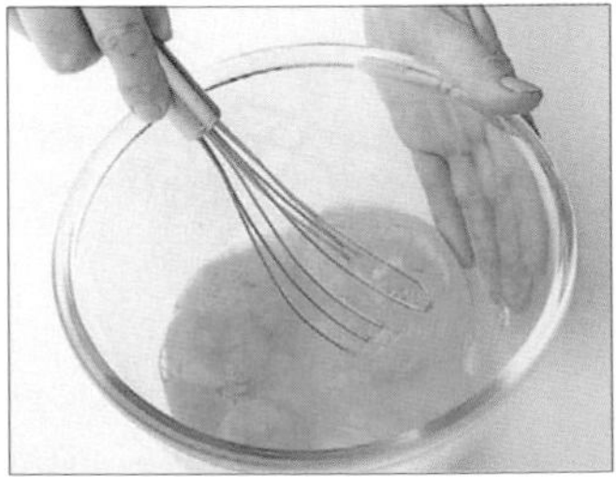

3 In a separate bowl, beat the eggs, sugar and vanilla. Beat into the chocolate mixture, then fold in the flour, dates and nuts. Pour into the tin.

4 Bake for 30–40 minutes, until firm and the mixture comes away from the sides of the tin. Cool in the tin, then turn out, remove the paper and dust with icing sugar.

Dutch Apple Cake

THE APPLE topping makes this cake really moist. It is just as good hot as it is cold.

INGREDIENTS

250g/9oz/2 1/4 cups self-raising flour
10ml/2 tsp baking powder
5ml/1 tsp ground cinnamon
130g/4 1/2oz/generous 1/2 cup caster sugar
50g/2oz/1/4 cup butter, melted
2 eggs, beaten
150ml/1/4 pint/2/3 cup milk

For the topping

2 Cox's Orange Pippin apples
15g/1/2oz/1 tbsp butter, melted
60ml/4 tbsp demerara sugar
1.5ml/1/4 tsp ground cinnamon

Makes 8–10 slices

1 Preheat the oven to 200°C/400°F/ Gas 6. Grease and line a 20cm/8in round cake tin. Sift the flour, baking powder and cinnamon into a large mixing bowl. Stir in the caster sugar. In a separate bowl, whisk the melted butter, eggs and milk together, then stir the mixture into the dry ingredients.

2 Pour the cake mixture into the prepared tin, smooth the surface, then make a shallow hollow in a ring around the edge of the mixture.

3 Make the topping. Peel and core the apples, slice them into wedges and slice the wedges thinly. Arrange the slices around the hollow of the cake mixture. Brush with the melted butter, then scatter the demerara sugar and ground cinnamon over the top.

4 Bake for 45–50 minutes or until the cake has risen well, is golden, and a skewer inserted into the centre comes out clean. Serve immediately as a dessert with cream, or remove from the tin, peel off the lining paper and cool on a wire rack before slicing.

Pear and Polenta Cake

Polenta gives the light sponge that tops the sliced pears a nutty corn flavour, complementing the fruit perfectly. Serve as a dessert with custard or cream.

INGREDIENTS

175g/6oz/3/4 cup golden caster sugar
4 ripe pears
juice of 1/2 lemon
30ml/2 tbsp clear honey
3 eggs
seeds from 1 vanilla pod
120ml/4fl oz/1/2 cup sunflower oil
115g/4oz/1 cup self-raising flour
50g/2oz/1/3 cup instant polenta

Makes 10 slices

1 Preheat the oven to 180°C/350°F/ Gas 4. Generously grease and line a 21cm/8½in round cake tin. Scatter 30ml/2 tbsp of the caster sugar over the base of the prepared tin.

2 Peel and core the pears. Cut them into chunky slices and toss in the lemon juice. Arrange them on the base of the prepared cake tin. Drizzle the honey over the pears and set aside.

3 Mix together the eggs, seeds from the vanilla pod and the remaining golden caster sugar in a bowl.

COOK'S TIP

Use the tip of a small, sharp knife to scrape out the vanilla pod seeds. Or, use 5ml/1 tsp pure vanilla.

4 Beat the egg mixture until thick and creamy, then gradually beat in the oil. Sift together the flour and polenta and fold into the egg mixture.

5 Pour the mixture carefully into the tin over the pears. Bake for about 50 minutes or until a skewer inserted into the centre comes out clean. Cool in the tin for 10 minutes, then turn the cake out on to a plate, peel off the lining paper, invert and slice.

Date and Walnut Spice Cake

THIS DELICIOUSLY MOIST AND richly spiced cake is topped with a sticky honey and orange glaze. Serve it as a dessert with a generous spoonful of natural yogurt or crème fraîche, flavoured with grated orange rind.

INGREDIENTS

115g/4oz/½ cup unsalted butter, plus extra for greasing
175g/6oz/¾ cup soft dark brown sugar
2 eggs
175g/6oz/1½ cups unbleached self-raising flour, plus extra for dusting
5ml/1 tsp bicarbonate of soda
2.5ml/½ tsp freshly grated nutmeg
5ml/1 tsp mixed spice
pinch of salt
175ml/6fl oz/¾ cup buttermilk
50g/2oz/⅓ cup ready-to-eat stoned dates, chopped
25g/1oz/¼ cup walnuts, chopped

For the topping
60ml/4 tbsp clear honey
45ml/3 tbsp fresh orange juice
15ml/1 tbsp coarsely grated orange rind, plus extra to decorate

Serves 8

1 Grease and lightly flour a 23cm/9in spring-form cake tin. Preheat the oven to 180°C/350°F/Gas 4.

HEALTH BENEFITS

• Dried dates offer a more concentrated source of nutrients than fresh ones, including iron, potassium, niacin and magnesium. They also provide soluble fibre, making them a gentle laxative.

• According to a recent American study, a handful of walnuts a day has been found to lower blood cholesterol and therefore helps reduce the risk of heart disease.

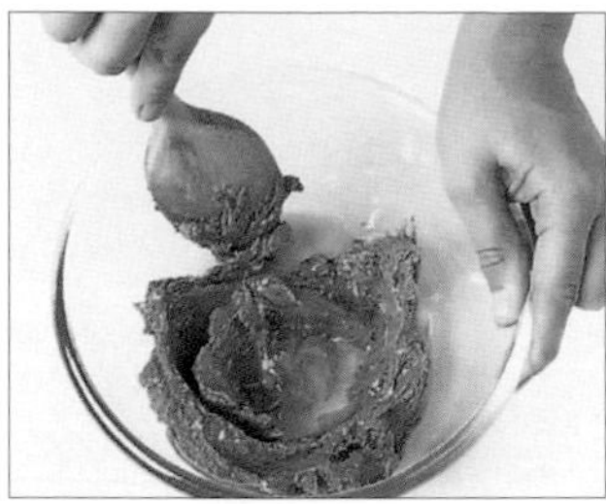

2 Cream together the butter and sugar with a wooden spoon until fluffy and creamy. Add the eggs, one at a time, and beat well to combine.

3 Sift together the flour, bicarbonate of soda, spices and salt. Gradually add this to the creamed mixture, alternating with the buttermilk. Add the dates and walnuts, and stir well.

COOK'S TIP

To make your own buttermilk substitute, mix 15ml/1 tbsp lemon juice with 250ml/8fl oz/1 cup semi-skimmed milk.

4 Spoon the mixture into the prepared cake tin and level the top. Bake for 50 minutes or until a skewer inserted into the centre of the cake comes out clean. Leave to cool for 5 minutes, then turn out on to a cooling rack to cool completely.

5 To make the topping, heat the honey, orange juice and rind in a small heavy-based saucepan. Bring to the boil and boil rapidly for 3 minutes, without stirring, until syrupy. Make small holes, over the top of the warm cake using the skewer, and pour over the hot syrup. Decorate with the orange rind.

Rich Lemon Poppyseed Cake

THE CLASSIC COMBINATION of poppy seeds and lemon is used for this light cake, which has a delicious lemon curd and fromage frais filling.

INGREDIENTS

350g/12oz/1 1/2 cups unsalted butter, plus extra for greasing
350g/12oz/1 3/4 cups golden caster sugar
45ml/3 tbsp poppy seeds
20ml/4 tsp finely grated lemon rind
70ml/4 heaped tbsp luxury lemon curd
6 eggs, separated
120ml/4fl oz/1/2 cup semi-skimmed milk
350g/12oz/3 cups unbleached self-raising flour, plus extra for flouring
icing sugar, to decorate

For the filling
150g/5oz/1/2 cup luxury lemon curd
150ml/5fl oz/2/3 cup double cream, whipped

Serves 8

1 Butter and lightly flour two 23cm/9in spring-form cake tins. Preheat the oven to 180°C/350°F/Gas 4.

VARIATION

Replace the lemon curd and fromage frais filling with a tangy lemon syrup. Boil 45ml/3 tbsp lemon juice, 15ml/1 tbsp lemon rind and 30ml/2 tbsp caster sugar for 3 minutes until the mixture becomes syrupy and glossy. Make a single cake using half the ingredients. Pour the syrup over the warm cake and leave to cool before cutting into wedges to serve.

2 Cream together the butter and sugar with a wooden spoon until light and fluffy. Add the poppy seeds, lemon rind, lemon curd and egg yolks and beat well, then add the milk and mix well. Gently fold in the flour until combined.

3 Whisk the egg whites using a hand-held electric mixer until they form soft peaks. Carefully fold the egg whites into the cake mixture until just combined Divide the cake mixture between the prepared tins.

4 Bake for 40–45 minutes until a skewer inserted into the centre of the cakes comes out clean and the tops are golden.

5 Leave the cakes to cool in the tins for 5 minutes, then remove from the tins and leave to cool completely on wire racks. To finish, spread one cake with the lemon curd and spoon the fromage frais evenly over the lemon curd. Put the second cake on top, press down gently, then dust with icing sugar before serving.

Victoria Sandwich Cake

SERVE THIS light, classic sponge cake sandwiched together with your favourite jam. For special occasions, fill the cake with prepared fresh fruit, such as raspberries or sliced peaches, as well as jam and whipped dairy cream or fromage frais.

INGREDIENTS

175g/6oz/3/4 cup soft margarine
175g/6oz/3/4 cup caster sugar
3 eggs beaten
175g/6oz/1 1/2 cups self-raising flour, sifted
60ml/4 tbsp jam
150ml/1/4pt/2/3 cup whipped cream or framage frais
15–30ml/1–2 tbsp icing sugar, for dusting
Makes one 18cm/7in cake

1 Preheat the oven to 180°C/350°F/Gas 4. Lightly grease and line the bottom of two 18cm/7in sandwich tins.

2 Place the margarine and caster sugar in a bowl and cream together until pale and fluffy.

3 Add the eggs, a little at a time, beating well after each addition. Fold in half the flour, using a metal spoon, then fold in the rest.

4 Divide the mixture between the two sandwich tins and level the surfaces with the back of a spoon.

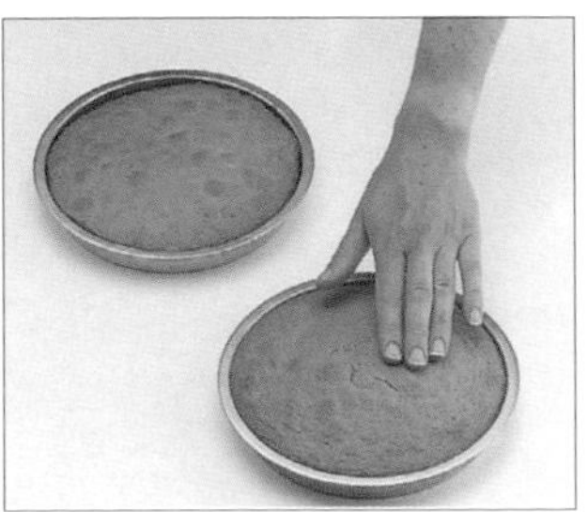

5 Bake for 25–30 minutes, until the cakes have risen, feel just firm to the touch and are golden brown. Turn out and cool on a wire rack.

6 When the cakes are cool, sandwich them with the jam and whipped cream or fromage frais. Dust the top of the cake with sifted icing sugar and serve cut into slices. Store the cake in the refrigerator in an airtight container or wrapped in foil.

VARIATION

Replace 30ml/2 tbsp of the flour with sifted cocoa powder. Sandwich the cakes with chocolate butter icing.

Chunky Chocolate and Banana Muffins

LUXURIOUS BUT NOT overly sweet, these muffins are simple and quick to make. Serve warm while the chocolate is still gooey.

INGREDIENTS

90ml/6 tbsp semi-skimmed milk
2 eggs
150g/5oz/10 tbsp unsalted butter, melted
225g/8oz/2 cups unbleached plain flour
pinch of salt
5ml/1 tsp baking powder
150g/5oz/¾ cup golden caster sugar
150g/5oz plain chocolate, cut into large chunks
2 small bananas, mashed

Makes 12

1 Place 12 paper cases in a deep muffin tin. Preheat the oven to 200°C/400°F/Gas 6. Place the milk, eggs and butter in a bowl and whisk until combined.

2 Sift together the flour, salt and baking powder into a separate bowl. Add the sugar and chocolate to the flour mixture and then stir to combine. Slowly stir in the milk mixture, but do not beat it. Fold in the mashed bananas.

3 Spoon the mixture into the paper cases. Bake for 20 minutes until golden. Cool on a wire rack.

HEALTH BENEFITS

Bananas are rich in potassium, which is vital for muscle and nerve function. They are also a good source of energy.

Apricot and Hazelnut Oat Cookies

THESE COOKIE-CUM-FLAPJACKS have a chewy, crumbly texture. They are sprinkled with apricots and toasted hazelnuts, but any combination of dried fruit and nuts can be used.

INGREDIENTS

115g/4oz/½ cup unsalted butter, plus extra for greasing
75g/3oz/scant ½ cup golden caster sugar
15ml/1 tbsp clear honey
115g/4oz/1 cup self-raising flour, sifted
115g/4oz/1 cup porridge oats
75g/3oz/scant ½ cup ready-to-eat dried unsulphured apricots, chopped

For the topping
25g/1oz/2 tbsp ready-to-eat dried unsulphured apricots, chopped
25g/1oz/¼ cup hazelnuts, toasted and chopped

Makes 9

1 Lightly grease a baking sheet. Preheat the oven to 170°C/325°F/Gas 3. Put the butter, sugar and honey in a small heavy-based saucepan and cook over a gentle heat, until the butter melts and the sugar dissolves, stirring occasionally. Remove the pan from the heat.

2 Put the flour, oats and apricots in a bowl, add the honey mixture and mix with a wooden spoon to form a sticky dough. Divide the dough into nine pieces and place on the baking sheet. Press into 1cm/½in thick rounds. Scatter over the apricots and hazelnuts and press into the dough.

3 Bake for 15 minutes until golden and slightly crisp. Leave to cool on the baking sheet for 5 minutes, then transfer to a wire rack.

HEALTH BENEFITS

Oats provide soluble fibre, which is believed to lower blood cholesterol levels.

Chocolate Chip Cookies

INGREDIENTS

75g/3oz/6 tbsp soft margarine
50g/2oz/ 1/4 cup light soft brown sugar
50g/2oz/ 1/4 cup caster sugar
1 egg, beaten
few drops of vanilla essence
75g/3oz/3/4 cup rice flour
75g/3oz/3/4 cup gluten-free cornmeal
5ml/1 tsp gluten-free baking powder
pinch of salt
115g/4oz/2/3 cup plain chocolate chips, or a mixture of milk and white chocolate chips

Makes 16

1 Preheat the oven to 190°C/375°F/Gas 5. Lightly grease two baking sheets. Place the margarine and sugars in a bowl and cream together until light and fluffy.

2 Beat in the egg and vanilla essence. Fold in the rice flour, cornmeal, baking powder and salt, then fold in the chocolate chips.

3 Place spoonfuls of the mixture on the prepared baking sheets, leaving space for spreading between each one. Bake for 10–15 minutes until the cookies are lightly browned.

4 Remove the cookies from the oven and leave to cool for a few minutes, then transfer to a wire rack using a palette knife and leave to cool completely before serving. Once cold, store the cookies in an airtight container for up to a week, or pack into plastic bags and freeze.

COOK'S TIP

It is well worth having a jar of vanilla sugar for flavouring sweet pastry, cakes and biscuits. Cut a vanilla pod into halves or quarters and store in a jar of caster sugar. It will be strongly scented after a few days.

Cherry Coconut Munchies

YOU'LL FIND it hard to stop at just one of these delicious munchies, which make a wonderful morning or afternoon treat. If liked, drizzle 25–50g/1–2oz melted chocolate over the cold munchies and leave to set before serving.

INGREDIENTS

2 egg whites
115g/4oz/1 cup icing sugar, sifted
115g/4oz/1 cup ground almonds
115g/4oz/generous 1 cup desiccated coconut
few drops of almond essence
75g/3oz/1/3 cup glacé cherries, finely chopped

Makes 20

1 Preheat the oven to 150°C/300°F/Gas 2. Line two baking sheets with non-stick baking paper. Place the egg whites in a bowl and whisk until stiff.

2 Fold in the icing sugar, then fold in the ground almonds, coconut and almond essence to form a sticky dough. Fold in the chopped cherries.

COOK'S TIP

Almond essence is extracted from bitter almonds which are poisonous and cannot be eaten raw. However, they are perfectly safe when cooked and help to enhance the flavour of sweet almonds when cooked together.

3 Place heaped teaspoonfuls of the mixture on the prepared baking sheets. Bake for 25 minutes until pale golden. Cool on the baking sheets for a few minutes, then transfer to a wire rack until cold. Store in an airtight container for up to a week.

VARIATIONS

Use ground hazelnuts in place of the almonds and omit the almond essence.

Sultana and Cinnamon Chewy Bars

THESE SPICY, chewy bars are hard to resist and make a great treat, especially for children.

INGREDIENTS

115g/4oz/½ cup soft margarine
25g/1oz/2 tbsp light soft brown sugar
25g/1oz plain toffees
50g/2oz/¼ cup honey
175g/6oz/1½ cups sultanas
10ml/2tsp ground cinnamon
175g/6oz rice crispies
Makes 16

1 Lightly grease a shallow 23 x 28cm/9 x 11in cake tin. Place the margarine, sugar, toffees and honey in a saucepan and heat gently, stirring, until melted. Bring to the boil, then remove the pan from the heat.

2 Stir in the sultanas, cinnamon and rice crispies and mix well. Transfer the mixture to the prepared tin and spread the mixture evenly, pressing it down firmly.

3 Allow to cool, then chill until firm. Once firm, cut into bars, remove from the pan and serve. Store the bars in an airtight container in the fridge.

VARIATION

For an extra-special treat, melt 75g/3oz plain or milk chocolate and spread or, using a teaspoon or paper piping bag, drizzle it over the cold rice crispie mixture. Allow to set before cutting into bars.

Apricot and Orange Muffins

SERVE THESE fruity muffins freshly baked and warm.

INGREDIENTS

15g/4oz/1 cup cornmeal
75g/3oz/¾ cup rice flour
15ml/1 tbsp baking powder
pinch of salt
50g/2oz/4 tbsp soft margarine, melted
50g/2oz/¼ cup light brown sugar
1 egg, beaten
200ml/7fl oz/scant 1 cup semi-skimmed milk
finely grated rind of 1 orange
115g/4oz/⅔ cup dried apricots, chopped
Makes 8 large or 12 medium muffins

1 Preheat the oven to 200°C/400°F/Gas 6. Lightly grease or line eight or twelve muffin tins or deep bun tins. Place the cornmeal, rice flour, baking powder and salt in a bowl and mix.

2 Stir together the melted margarine, sugar, egg, milk and orange rind, then pour the mixture over the dry ingredients. Fold the ingredients gently together – just enough to combine them. The mixture will look quite lumpy, which is correct, as overmixing will result in heavy muffins.

3 Fold in the chopped dried apricots, then spoon the mixture into the prepared muffin or bun tins, dividing it equally among them.

4 Bake for 15–20 minutes, until the muffins have risen and are golden brown and springy to the touch. Turn them out on to a wire rack to cool.

5 Serve the muffins warm or cold, on their own or cut in half and spread with a little low-fat spread. Store in an airtight container for up to one week or seal in plastic bags and freeze for up to three months.

Cranberry Oat Flapjack

HERE'S A real tea-time treat for everybody to enjoy!

INGREDIENTS

150g/5oz/1 1/2 cups porridge oats
115g/4oz/2/3 cup demerara sugar
75g/3oz/1/2 cup dried cranberries
115g/4oz/1/2 cup polyunsaturated margarine, melted
oil, for greasing
Makes 14

COOK'S TIP

Dried cranberries are a relatively new product, available from larger supermarkets. They have a sweet yet slightly tart flavour and their bright red colour will add visual appeal. They can be used to replace more usual dried fruits, such as sultanas.

1 Preheat the oven to 190°C/375°F/ Gas 5. Grease a shallow 28 x 18cm/ 11 x 7in tin.

2 Stir the oats, sugar and cranberries together in a bowl. Pour in the melted margarine and stir thoroughly until combined.

3 Press the oat and cranberry mixture into the prepared tin. Bake for 15–20 minutes, until golden.

4 Remove the flapjack from the oven and mark into 14 bars, then leave to cool for 5 minutes, in the tin. Remove the bars and place on a wire rack to cool completely. Store for up to 5 days in an airtight container.

Rhubarb and Raspberry Cranachan

INGREDIENTS

350g/12oz rhubarb
30ml/2 tbsp unsweetened orange juice
175g/6oz/1 cup raspberries
30ml/2 tbsp pure fruit raspberry jam
25g/1oz/1/3 cup porridge oats
25g/1oz/1/4 cup mixed chopped nuts
200ml/7fl oz/scant 1 cup light vanilla yogurt
Serves 4

COOK'S TIP

Early rhubarb, which is forced into growth, has thin red and pink stems, and a fresh flavour. Maincrop rhubarb has thick red stems, and a coarser, tart flavour.

1 Cut the rhubarb into chunks. Heat the orange juice in a saucepan and poach the rhubarb gently for 8–10 minutes until just tender. Remove from the heat immediately. Allow to cool, then stir in the raspberries and pure fruit jam.

2 Spread the oats and nuts out on a baking sheet and toast them briefly under a hot grill.

3 Spoon the fruit mixture into four sundae dishes. Top each portion with yogurt, then scatter the toasted oats and nuts over the top.

Wholemeal Apple, Apricot and Walnut Loaf

INGREDIENTS

225g/8oz/2 cups plain wholemeal flour
5ml/1 tsp baking powder
pinch of salt
115g/4oz/½ cup sunflower margarine
175g/6oz/1 cup soft light brown sugar
2 large eggs, lightly beaten
grated rind and juice of 1 orange
50g/2oz/½ cup chopped walnuts
50g/2oz/⅓ cup ready-to-eat dried apricots, chopped
1 large cooking apple
oil, for greasing

Makes 10–12 slices

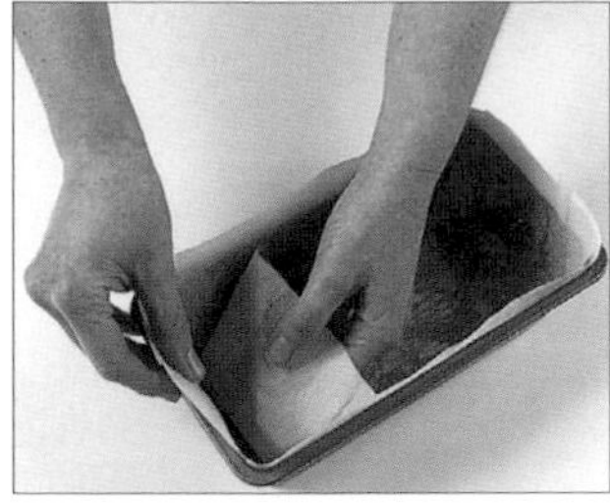

1 Preheat the oven to 180°C/350°F/Gas 4. Line and grease a 900g/2lb loaf tin.

2 Sift the flour, baking powder and salt into a large mixing bowl, then tip the bran remaining in the sieve into the mixture. Add the margarine, sugar, eggs, orange rind and juice. Stir, then beat with a hand-held electric beater until smooth.

3 Stir in the walnuts and apricots. Quarter, peel and core the apple, chop it roughly and add it to the mixture. Stir, then spoon the mixture into the prepared tin and level the top.

4 Bake for 1 hour, or until a skewer inserted into the centre of the loaf comes out clean. Cool in the tin for about 5 minutes, then turn the loaf out on to a wire rack and peel off the lining paper. When cold, wrap in foil and store in an airtight tin.

COOK'S TIP

Unless you are using an organically grown orange, always remember to scrub the skin, wash and dry it. This way you will remove any traces of chemicals used for its growth and preservation.

Spiced Banana Muffins

WHOLEMEAL MUFFINS, with banana for added fibre, make a delicious treat at any time of the day. If liked, slice off the tops and fill with a teaspoon of reduced-sugar jam or marmalade.

INGREDIENTS

75g/3oz/⅔ cup plain wholemeal flour
50g/2oz/½ cup plain white flour
10ml/2 tsp baking powder
pinch of salt
5ml/1 tsp mixed spice
40g/1½oz/soft light brown sugar
50g/2oz/¼ cup polyunsaturated margarine
1 egg, beaten
150ml/¼ pint/⅔ cup semi-skimmed milk
grated rind of 1 orange
1 ripe banana
20g/¾oz/¼ cup porridge oats
20g/¾oz/scant ¼ cup chopped hazelnuts
Makes 12

1 Preheat the oven to 200°C/400°F/Gas 6. Line a muffin tin with 12 large paper cake cases. Sift together both flours, the baking powder, salt and mixed spice into a bowl, then tip the bran remaining in the sieve into the bowl. Stir in the sugar.

2 Melt the margarine and pour it into a mixing bowl. Cool slightly, then beat in the egg, milk and grated orange rind.

3 Gently fold in the dry ingredients. Mash the banana with a fork, then stir it gently into the mixture, being careful not to overmix.

4 Spoon the mixture into the paper cases. Combine the oats and hazelnuts and sprinkle a little of the mixture over each muffin.

5 Bake for 20 minutes until the muffins are well risen and golden, and a skewer inserted in the centre comes out clean. Transfer to a wire rack and serve warm or cold.

Fruit, Nut and Seed Teabread

THIS TEABREAD is delicious with a little low-fat spread, jam or honey.

INGREDIENTS

115g/4oz/2/3 cup dried dates, chopped
115g/4oz/1/2 cup ready-to-eat dried apricots, chopped
115g/4oz/1 cup sultanas
115g/4oz/1/2 cup light soft brown sugar
225g/8oz/2 cups self-raising flour
5ml/1 tsp baking powder
10ml/2 tsp mixed spice
75g/3oz/3/4 cup chopped mixed nuts, such as walnuts and hazelnuts
75g/3oz/3/4 cup mixed seeds, such as millet, sunflower and sesame seeds
2 eggs, beaten
150ml/1/4 pint/2/3 cup semi-skimmed milk

Makes a 900g/2lb loaf

1 Preheat the oven to 180°C/350°F/Gas 4. Lightly grease a 900g/2lb loaf tin. Place the chopped dates and apricots and sultanas in a large mixing bowl and stir in the sugar.

2 Place the flour, baking powder, spice, mixed nuts and seeds in a separate bowl and mix well.

3 Stir the eggs and milk into the fruit, then add the flour mixture and beat together until well mixed.

4 Spoon into the prepared tin and level the surface. Bake for about 1 hour until the teabread is firm to the touch and lightly browned.

5 Allow to cool in the tin for a few minutes, then turn out on to a wire rack to cool completely. Serve warm or cold, cut into slices, either on its own or with low-fat spread and jam. Wrap in foil to store.

VARIATION

Other dried fruit to use in tea breads, which will add an exotic flavour, are dried mangoes, papaya, cranberries and tart cherries. Try making up a jar of dried fruit for tea bread, you can create your own mix which will be always ready for you to use.

Gingerbread

INGREDIENTS

115g/4oz/½ cup light soft brown sugar
75g/3oz/6 tbsp soft margarine
75g/3oz/¼ cup golden syrup
75g/3oz/¼ cup black treacle
105ml/7 tbsp semi-skimmed milk
1 egg, beaten
175g/6oz/1½ cups gluten-free plain flour
50g/2oz/½ cup gram flour
pinch of salt
10ml/2 tsp ground ginger
5ml/1 tsp ground cinnamon
7.5ml/1½ tsp gluten-free baking powder

Makes a 900g/2lb loaf

1 Preheat the oven to 160°C/325°F/Gas 3. Lightly grease and line a 900g/2lb loaf tin. Place the sugar, margarine, syrup and treacle in a saucepan and heat gently until melted and blended, stirring occasionally.

2 Remove the pan from the heat, leave to cool slightly, then mix in the milk and egg.

COOK'S TIP

If you are not able to get gram flour, which is widely used in Indian cookery and ground from legumes, you could substitute gluten-free cornmeal.

3 Mix the flours, salt, spices and baking powder in a large bowl.

4 Make a well in the centre, pour in the liquid mixture and beat well.

5 Pour the mixture into the prepared tin and bake for 1–1½ hours until firm to the touch and lightly browned.

6 Allow to cool in the tin for a few minutes, then turn out on to a wire rack to cool completely. Store it in an airtight container or wrapped in foil.

VARIATION

Fold 50g/2oz finely chopped preserved stem ginger into the raw cake mixture, if liked. Add 5–10ml/1–2 tsp extra ground ginger for a more pronounced flavour.

Cheese and Potato Scones

THE UNUSUAL ADDITION OF creamy mashed potato gives these wholemeal scones a light moist crumb and a crisp crust. A sprinkling of mature Cheddar and sesame seeds adds the finishing touch.

INGREDIENTS

115g/4oz/1 cup wholemeal flour
2.5ml/½ tsp salt
20ml/4 tsp baking powder
40g/1½oz/3 tbsp unsalted butter, plus extra for greasing
2 free-range eggs, beaten
50ml/2fl oz/¼ cup semi-skimmed milk or buttermilk
115g/4oz/1⅓ cups cooked, mashed potato
45ml/3 tbsp chopped fresh sage
50g/2oz/½ cup grated mature vegetarian Cheddar
sesame seeds, for sprinkling

Makes 9

1 Preheat the oven to 220°C/425°F/ Gas 7. Grease a baking sheet.

2 Sift the flour, salt and baking powder into a bowl. Rub in the butter using your fingers until the mixture resembles fine breadcrumbs, then mix in half the beaten eggs and all the milk or buttermilk. Add the mashed potato, sage and half the Cheddar, and mix to a soft dough with your hands.

3 Turn out the dough on to a floured work surface and knead lightly until smooth. Roll out the dough to 2cm/¾in thick, then stamp out nine scones using a 6cm/2½in fluted cutter.

VARIATIONS

- *Use unbleached self-raising flour instead of wholemeal flour and baking powder, if you wish.*
- *Fresh rosemary, basil or thyme can be used in place of the sage.*

4 Place the scones on the prepared baking sheet and brush the tos with the remaining beaten egg. Sprinkle the rest of the cheese and the sesame seeds on top and bake for 15 minutes until golden. Transfer to a wire rack and leave to cool.

HEALTH BENEFITS

Fresh sage is thought to assist the digestion of rich food and also acts as a stimulant to the central nervous system.

Wholemeal Sunflower Bread

SUNFLOWER SEEDS GIVE A nutty crunchiness to this wholemeal loaf. Serve with a chunk of cheese and rich tomato chutney.

INGREDIENTS

450g/1lb/4 cups strong wholemeal flour
2.5ml/½ tsp easy-blend dried yeast
2.5ml/½ tsp salt
50g/2oz/½ cup sunflower seeds, plus extra for sprinkling

Makes 1 loaf

1 Grease and lightly flour a 450g/1lb loaf tin. Mix together the flour, yeast, salt and sunflower seeds in a large bowl. Make a well in the centre and gradually stir in 300ml/½ pint/1¼ cups warm water. Mix vigorously with a wooden spoon to form a soft, sticky dough. The dough should be quite wet and sticky, so don't be tempted to add any extra flour.

2 Cover the bowl with a damp dish towel and leave the dough to rise in a warm place for 45–50 minutes or until doubled in bulk.

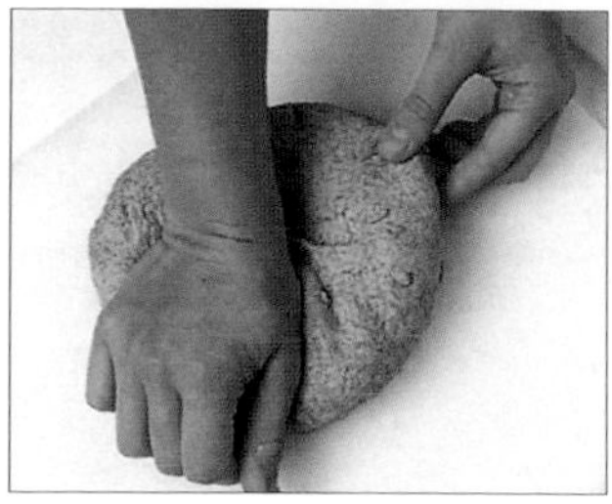

3 Preheat the oven to 200°C/400°F/Gas 6. Turn out the dough on to a floured work surface and knead for 10 minutes – the dough will still be quite sticky.

HEALTH BENEFITS

High in protein, sesame seeds also provide calcium as well as vitamin E and the B complex vitamins.

4 Form the dough into a rectangle and place in the loaf tin. Sprinkle the top with sunflower seeds. Cover with a damp dish towel and leave to rise again for a further 15 minutes.

5 Bake for 40–45 minutes until golden – the loaf should sound hollow when tapped underneath. Leave for 5 minutes, then turn out of the tin and leave to cool on a wire rack.

Spicy Millet Bread

THIS IS A DELICIOUS SPICY BREAD with a golden crust. Cut into wedges, as you would a cake, and serve warm with a thick vegetable soup.

INGREDIENTS

90g/3½oz/½ cup millet
550g/1lb 6oz/5½ cups strong unbleached plain flour
10ml/2 tsp salt
5ml/1 tsp sugar
5ml/1 tsp dried chilli flakes (optional)
7g/¼oz sachet easy-blend dried yeast
25g/1oz/2 tbsp unsalted butter
1 onion, roughly chopped
15ml/1 tbsp cumin seeds
5ml/1 tsp ground turmeric
Makes 1 loaf

1 Bring 200ml/7fl oz/scant 1 cup water to the boil, add the millet, cover and simmer gently for 20 minutes until the grains are soft and the water is absorbed. Remove from the heat and leave to cool until just warm.

2 Mix together the flour, salt, sugar, chilli flakes, if using, and yeast in a large bowl. Stir in the millet, then add 350ml/12fl oz/1½ cups warm water and mix to form a soft dough.

HEALTH BENEFITS

Millet is a versatile – and much underrated – grain. If eaten on a regular basis as part of a varied healthy diet, it can help lower the risk of heart disease and certain cancers.

3 Turn out the dough on to a floured work surface and knead for 10 minutes. If the dough seems a little dry, knead well until the dough is smooth and elastic.

4 Place the dough in an oiled bowl and cover with oiled clear film or a dish towel. Leave to rise in a warm place for 1 hour until doubled in bulk.

5 Meanwhile, melt the butter in a heavy-based frying pan, add the onion and fry for 10 minutes until softened, stirring occasionally. Add the cumin seeds and turmeric, and fry for a further 5–8 minutes, stirring constantly, until the cumin seeds begin to pop. Set aside.

COOK'S TIP

To test if a dough has risen properly, make a small indentation in the top with your index finger. If the indentation does not spring back entirely, then rising is complete; if it springs back at once, the dough is not ready and should be left for another 15 minutes before retesting..

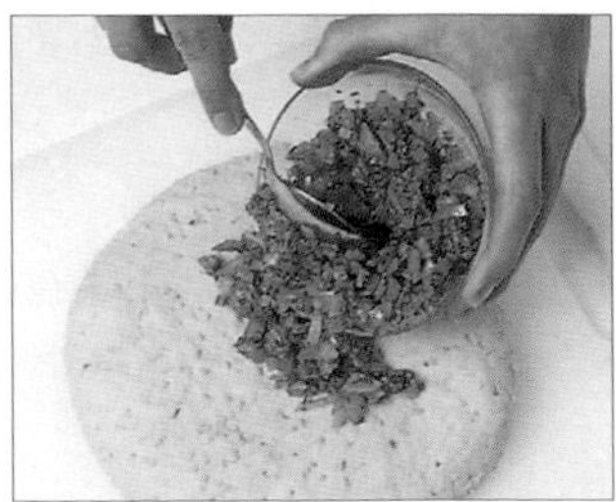

6 Knock back the dough by pressing down with your knuckles to deflate the dough, then shape into a round. Place the onion mixture in the middle of the dough and bring the sides over the filling to make a parcel, then seal well.

7 Place the loaf on an oiled baking sheet, seam-side down, cover with oiled clear film and leave in a warm place for 45 minutes until doubled in bulk. Preheat the oven to 220°C/425°F/Gas 7.

8 Bake the bread for 30 minutes until golden. It should sound hollow when tapped underneath. Leave to cool on a wire rack.

Polenta and Pepper Bread

FULL OF MEDITERRANEAN flavour, this satisfying, sunshine-coloured bread is best eaten while still warm, drizzled with a little olive oi,l and served with soup.

INGREDIENTS

175g/6oz/1 1/2 cups polenta
5ml/1 tsp salt
350g/12oz/3 cups unbleached strong plain flour, plus extra for dusting
5ml/1 tsp sugar
7g/1/4oz sachet easy-blend dried yeast
1 red pepper, roasted, peeled and diced
15ml/1 tbsp olive oil
Makes 2 loaves

1 Mix together the polenta, salt, flour, sugar and yeast in a large bowl. Stir in the diced red pepper until it is evenly distributed, then make a well in the centre of the mixture. Grease two loaf tins.

2 Add 300ml/1/2 pint/1 1/4 cups warm water and the oil and mix to a soft dough. Knead for 10 minutes until smooth and elastic. Place in an oiled bowl, cover with oiled clear film and leave to rise in a warm place for 1 hour until doubled in bulk.

HEALTH BENEFITS

Weight for weight, red peppers contain about three times as much vitamin C as fresh oranges.

COOK'S TIP

Cook the pepper in the oven or under a grill until charred, then place in a plastic bag and leave until cool enough to peel.

3 Knock back the dough, knead lightly, then divide in two. Shape each piece into an oblong and place in the tins. Cover with oiled clear film and leave to rise for 45 minutes. Preheat the oven to 220°C/425°F/Gas 7.

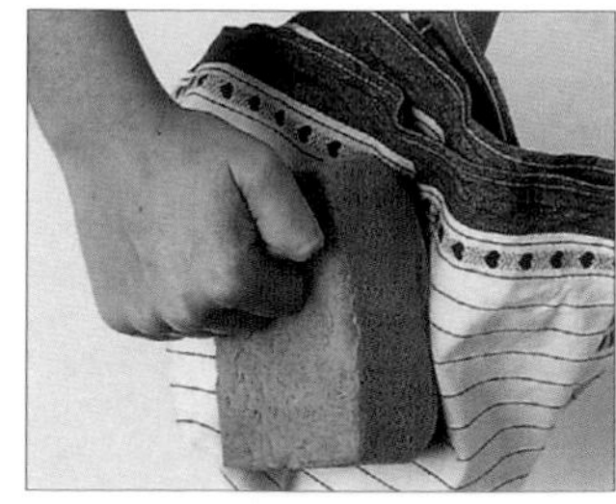

4 Bake for 30 minutes until golden – the loaves should sound hollow when tapped underneath. Leave for 5 minutes, then cool on a wire rack.

Fruit Soda Bread

THIS TRADITIONAL IRISH bread is quick to make as it does not require prolonged kneading or rising. It is best eaten while still warm on the day of baking.

INGREDIENTS

225g/8oz/2 cups unbleached plain flour
225g/8oz/2 cups wholemeal flour
5ml/1 tsp salt
5ml/1 tsp bicarbonate of soda
20ml/heaped 1 tbsp sugar
75g/3oz/¾ cup raisins
50g/2oz/¼ cup ready-to-eat stoned prunes, chopped
1 egg, lightly beaten
300ml/½ pint/1¼ cups buttermilk

Serves 4

1 Preheat the oven to 200°C/400°F/Gas 6. Sift together the plain and wholemeal flours, salt and bicarbonate of soda into a large bowl, adding any bran left in the sieve. Add the sugar and dried fruit, and mix well to combine.

2 Make a well in the centre and add the egg and buttermilk. Mix first with a wooden spoon and then with your hands until it forms a soft, slightly sticky dough. If the dough is too dry, add a little more buttermilk.

HEALTH BENEFITS

Dried fruit is recognized as a good source of fibre as well as minerals, such as potassium and iron.

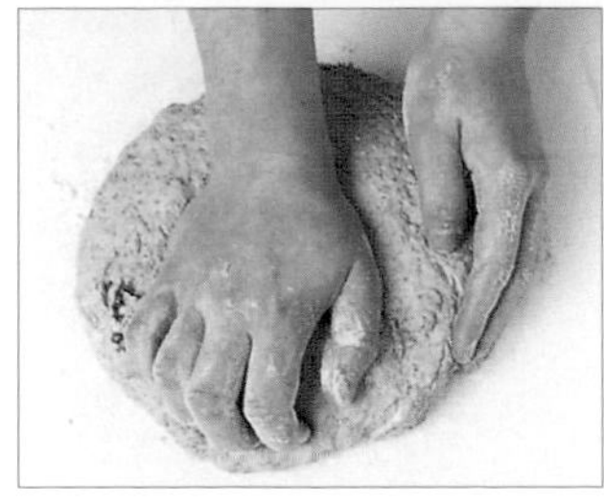

3 Turn out the dough on to a lightly floured work surface and knead lightly until smooth. Form into a flat round, about 4cm/1½in thick.

4 Place on a greased baking sheet and dust the loaf with plain flour.

5 Cut a large deep cross, almost through to the bottom of the dough round. Bake for 30–35 minutes until risen and golden. The bread should sound hollow when tapped underneath. Transfer to a wire rack and leave to cool.

Rosemary and Rock Salt Focaccia

ENRICHED WITH OLIVE oil and flavoured with rosemary, garlic and black olives, this popular Italian bread takes its name from the Italian word for hearth – which is where it was traditionally baked.

INGREDIENTS

225g/8oz/2 cups unbleached plain flour, sifted
2.5ml/½ tsp salt
7g/¼oz sachet easy-blend dried yeast
4 garlic cloves, finely chopped
2 sprigs of rosemary, leaves removed and chopped
10 black olives, stoned and roughly chopped (optional)
15ml/1 tbsp olive oil

For the topping
90ml/6 tbsp olive oil
10ml/2 tsp rock salt
1 sprig of rosemary, leaves removed
Makes 1 loaf

1 Mix together the flour, salt, yeast, garlic, rosemary and olives, if using, in a large bowl. Make a well in the centre and add the olive oil and 150ml/¼ pint/⅔ cup warm water.
Mix thoroughly to form a soft dough.

HEALTH BENEFITS

The oil in olives is monounsaturated and this type of oil is believed to reduce blood cholesterol levels. Olives also provide good amounts of iron and the antioxidant, vitamin E.

2 Turn out the dough on to a floured work surface and knead for 10–15 minutes. Put the dough in an oiled bowl and cover with oiled clear film or a dish towel. Leave to rise in a warm place for 45 minutes, until the dough has doubled in bulk.

3 Turn out the dough and knead lightly again. Roll out to an oval shape, about 1cm/½in thick.

4 Place the dough on a greased baking sheet, cover loosely with oiled clear film or a dish towel and leave in a warm place for 25–30 minutes to rise again.

5 Preheat the oven to 200°C/400°F/Gas 6. Make indentations with your fingertips all over the top of the bread. Drizzle two-thirds of the olive oil over the top, then sprinkle with the rock salt and rosemary.

6 Bake for 25 minutes until golden. The bread should sound hollow when tapped underneath. Transfer to a wire rack and spoon the remaining olive oil over the top.

VARIATIONS

• To make sun-dried tomato focaccia, omit the rosemary leaves and olives, and add 75g/3oz/1½ cups chopped and drained sun-dried tomatoes in oil to the dry ingredients. Add 15ml/1 tbsp sun-dried tomato purée and 15ml/1 tbsp of the oil from the sun-dried tomatoes to the dough when adding the oil and water, then mix well.

• To make saffron focaccia, add a few strands of saffron to the warm water and leave to stand for 5 minutes before adding to the flour. Alternatively, add a pinch of saffron powder to the flour.

Index